The Early
Medieval
Sequence

The Early Medieval Sequence

RICHARD L. CROCKER

University of California Press

BERKELEY · LOS ANGELES · LONDON

University of California Press
Berkeley and Los Angeles, California

University of California Press, Ltd.
London, England

ISBN 0-520-02847-3
Library of Congress Catalog Card Number: 74-84143
Printed in the United States of America

To my Parents

Contents

Preface

This study of the medieval sequence began twenty years ago with my doctoral dissertation, in which I made inventory of the Aquitanian prosaria. Subsequent study, resumed in the mid-1960's, included both exploration of sources beyond the Aquitanian ones, with transcription of a large part of the French repertory before 1100, and an intensive consideration of sample variants with a view to computer-assisted analysis. Supporting researches included an appraisal of our approach to early medieval music (reported in "The Troping Hypothesis"); an investigation into early medieval theory, the hexachord in particular (eventually written up as "Hermann's Major Sixth"); and surveys of contiguous medieval repertories undertaken for the 6th edition of *Groves' Dictionary of Music and Musicians*.

An especially fruitful stimulus was provided by an interdisciplinary course in "The Age of Charlemagne," conceived and guided by Walter Horn (Medieval Architecture), with the participation of Charles Jones (Medieval Latin Literature) and myself. This course, as well as other occasions, offered the opportunity of presenting some of these sequences in public performance. Preliminary publications have included "Some Ninth-Century Sequences" and a survey of the history of the sequence in the *Gedenkschrift Leo Schrade*.

This project has been generously supported by the University of California in the form of continuing research allowances, and especially grants from the Humanities Research Institute first in 1966, then again in 1972, for final preparation of the manuscript. A John Simon Guggenheim Memorial Foundation Fellowship in 1969 provided the opportunity, at last, to see the medieval sources in Oxford, London, Paris, and St. Gall. For all of this support I am profoundly grateful.

The list of those who helped with hands and eyes is, unfortunately, now too long to include here; it includes largely (but by no means exclusively) graduate students at the University of California, some of whom are by this time far advanced in our profession. Without them, of course, the work could not have been done.

Special appreciation is due Dr. Richard Hunt, Keeper of Western Manuscripts at the Bodleian Library, for permission to use the papers of Henry Marriott Bannister, and for his generous help and advice. I am grateful to M. Marcel Thomas, Director of the Department of Manuscripts at the Bibliothèque Nationale for permission to use the Aquitanian prosaria for my transcriptions and to reproduce the plates in this volume. Dr. Johannes Duft, Librarian of the Stiftsbibliothek of St. Gall was also generous in giving permission to publish plates and providing materials.

As an acknowledgment of a different kind, I would like to express here my misgivings about undertaking this particular project. It has long been apparent that the sequence, a combination of words and music, required a combination of expert knowledge in at least music and Latin literature, and probably liturgics as well. Is there such an expert, with leisure to take up the study of the sequence? I myself do not qualify; while I undertake with enthusiasm the essential task of discussing the literary aspects of the sequence, I offer my results with the greatest diffidence, to be considered, *faute de mieux*, only as suggestions, preliminary observations in a rich field yet to be thoroughly cultivated.

RICHARD L. CROCKER

1

Notker and the West-Frankish Sequence

To LIUTWARD, who for his great sanctity has been raised in honor to be a high priest, a most worthy successor to that incomparable man, Eusebius, Bishop of Vercelli; abbot of the monastery of the most holy Columbanus, and defender of the cell of his disciple, the most gentle Gallus; and also the arch-chaplain of the most glorious emperor Charles, from Notker, the least of the monks of St. Gall.

When I was still young, and very long melodies—repeatedly entrusted to memory—escaped from my poor little head, I began to reason with myself how I could bind them fast.

In the meantime it happened that a certain priest from Jumièges (recently laid waste by the Normans) came to us, bringing with him his antiphonary, in which some verses had been set to sequences; but they were in a very corrupt state. Upon closer inspection I was as bitterly disappointed in them as I had been delighted at first glance.

Nevertheless, in imitation of them I began to write LAUDES DEO CONCINAT ORBIS UNIVERSUS, QUI GRATIS EST REDEMPTUS, and further on COLUBER ADAE DECEPTOR. When I took these lines to my teacher Iso, he, commending my industry while taking pity on my lack of experience, praised what was pleasing, and what was not he set about to improve, saying, "The individual motions of the melody should receive separate syllables." Hearing that, I immediately corrected those which fell under *ia*; those under *le* or *lu*, however, I left as too difficult; but later, with practice, I managed it easily—for example in "Dominus in Sina" and "Mater." Instructed in this manner, I soon composed my second piece, PSALLAT ECCLESIA MATER ILLIBATA.

When I showed these little verses to my teacher Marcellus, he, filled with joy, had them copied as a group on a roll; and he gave out different pieces to different boys to be sung. And when he told me that I should collect them in a book and offer them as a gift to some eminent person, I shrank back in shame, thinking I would never be able to do that.

Recently, however, I was asked by my brother Othar to write something in your praise, and I considered myself—with good reason—unequal to the task; but finally I worked up my courage (still with great pain and difficulty) that I might presume to dedicate this worthless little book to your highness. If I were to learn that anything in it had pleased you—as good as you are—to the extent that you might be of assistance to my brother with our Lord the Emperor, I would hasten to send you the metrical life of St. Gall which I am working hard to complete (although I had already promised it to my brother Salomon) for you to examine, to keep, and to comment upon.

With these words Notker Balbulus (ca. 840–912), monk of St. Gall, introduced his "Book of Hymns," *Liber hymnorum*, to his ninth-century readers in the monasteries of Swabia and the East-Frankish regions.[1] The book contained, not what they—and we—might first expect as hymns, but rather a kind of sacred song new to those parts; it had been imported, Notker's Preface tells us, from West Frankishland, sometime around the middle of the ninth century. Notker mentions Jumièges, and the Norman raids he refers to could have been in 851 or 862.[2] It was the structure of these songs that was new: the texts were laid out in none of the traditional structures of Latin sacred verse—not in hexameters or elegaic distichs, or in sapphics, or in the stanza of the Ambrosian hymn. These texts unfolded in a vigorous series of free rhetorical periods, cast, in Notker's case, in the sonorous cadences of classical diction, in the case of his West-Frankish models, in a more exuberant diction rich with assonance. In either case, the texts were in prose—"art-prose," as it has been called,[3] drawing upon the full legacy of elevated Latin discourse available to the Carolingians; and eventually *prosa* became the proper name for this particular kind of text.

The rhetoric was further shaped in accordance with the melodic form, for here text and melody entered into an intricate partnership. As a usual procedure two consecutive lines of text were set to the same phrase of music, forming a prose couplet; the piece as a whole consisted of a series of these couplets (varying in length from one to the next) with occasional single lines. The specific lengths of the lines and the number of lines were the essential ingredients in an overall design that was newly constructed for each piece.

The melodies were striking in their novelty on the Carolingian scene. The melodic phrases, broad-spanned to match the rhetorical prose periods, combined a forceful, direct kind of melodic motion with a graceful lyricism. In its style the new Frankish chant contrasted sharply with the sophisticated "Gregorian" chant that had been brought from Rome to be imposed, as part of the liturgy, by the Carolingian dynasty—Pippin, then Charlemagne—upon the Frankish kingdom since 750.[4] From Notker's Preface we know that this particular type of new Frankish melody bore the categorical name *sequentia*, "sequence." We

1. Text of Notker's Preface from Wolfram von den Steinen, *Notker der Dichter* (Bern 1948), II (Editionsband), pp. 8–10, 160.
2. Johannes Duft, "Wie Notker zu den Sequenzen Kam," *Zeitschirft für Schweizerische Kirchengeschichte* 56 (1962), pp. 201–214; pp. 207–209.
3. Eduard Norden, *Die antike Kunstprosa vom VI Jahrhundert v. Chr. bis in die Zeit der Renaissance* (1898). See also Karl Polheim, *Die lateinische Reimprosa* (1925), especially p. 350.
4. The best account so far is by Bruno Stäblein in *Die Gesänge des altrömischen Graduale* (*Monumenta monodica medii aevi* II) (1970), in the Introduction, especially Chapter VII, "Die Ausbreitung des römischen Chorals ausserhalb Roms." See also the many useful texts quoted in Gerald Ellard, S.J., *Master Alcuin, Liturgist* (Chicago 1956), especially pp. 48–67.

can call such pieces either "prose" or "sequence" depending on whether we have in mind the text or the melody.

We may assume that it was the novelty of this art form that occasioned Notker's Preface, with its intriguing and occasionally puzzling details. And it might be fair to assume that the puzzlement, manifold explanations, and ensuing controversy among modern observers over the sequence and its origins in some way reflects the fact that in the ninth century the sequence was a new, unusual kind of work.[5] At any rate, its origins in the ninth century are not yet clear.

Notker's Preface has been the traditional starting point for inquiries into the early history of the sequence, and rightly so, for it is by far the most substantial, elaborate piece of supporting evidence for this as well as almost any other category of early medieval chant. It appears at the head of the present inquiry, too, indicating its importance for us. Of even greater importance, however, and of far greater real assistance, is the collection of pieces that follows the Preface—Notker's *Liber hymnorum* itself. And just as the Preface has received perhaps more attention than the texts and melodies it prefaces, so Notker's texts have fared better than their melodies: the forty texts have been edited several times, finally and critically by Wolfram von den Steinen in his *Notker der Dichter* (1948), with a comprehensive literary commentary. But the 33 melodies have never been edited critically; most have appeared in one or more of three collections (Drinkwelder, 1914; Moberg, 1927; and de Goede, 1965),[6] each working from relatively late sources and none concerned primarily with Notker. A few appeared only in the remarkable work of Anselm Schubiger, who printed twenty-eight of the thirty-three in his study *Die Sängerschule St. Gallens vom achten bis zwölften jahrhundert* (1858). Perhaps it was Schubiger's melodically unsatisfactory results (unsatisfactory due to problems not yet entirely solved) that have inhibited the making of a comprehensive edition down to the present.

Nor does the present book attempt an edition—not, at least, a critical edition—of the melodies of Notker's *Liber hymnorum*, partly because of the difficulties that still stand in the way of an edition that could be called "critical," partly because of the specific purpose of this book. For this is a study devoted not to Notker, but rather to the early medieval sequence, that is, to the ninth-century repertory of sequences in so far as that repertory can be reached *through* Notker. And here the fundamental, pervasive importance of Notker for this inquiry must be set out as the foundation of everything we are to do.

That a person called Notker actually lived and wrote proses is a basic fact whose importance has not, I think, been sufficiently appreciated, or at any rate, not sufficiently applied to our understanding of early medieval music. In the case of Notker's proses we have art works that were consciously, purposefully composed by a single, identifiable, individual creative agent—an artistic personality—who gave his works definitive artistic

---

5. Von den Steinen, *Notker*, I ("Darstellungsband") pp. 154ff. Heinrich Husmann, "Die St. Galler Sequenzentradition bei Notker und Ekkehard," *Acta Musicologica* 26 (1954), pp. 6–18.

6. Otto Drinkwelder, *Ein deutsches Sequentiar aus dem Ende des 12. Jahrhunderts* (Graz 1914); Carl Moberg, *Über die schwedischen Sequenzen* (Uppsala 1927); N. de Goede, S.C.J., *The Utrecht Prosarium* (*Monumenta musica Neerlandica* VI) (*Amsterdam 1965*); see also Bruno Stäblein, "Notkeriana," *Archiv für Musikwissenschaft* XIX–XX (1962–63), pp. 84–99.

form, a once-for-all form at a particular time and place. It is the principal merit of Von den Steinen's account to show this fact forth in full detail. One does not need to read very far, however, in other modern accounts of early medieval life and art (especially music) to realize how often such personal, purposeful artistic creation is denied in favor of general theories supposing anonymous, corporate modes of creation—or even no creation at all but simply "organic development," automatic reflex to presumed conditions of restriction and control. Notker not only wrote his works, but claimed them for his own, and because of that one obstinate instance we can entertain the possibility that other individuals, too, wrote works intending them to be individual artistic creations with a specific artistic form.

There are, to be sure, certain conditions peculiar to the monastic milieu of the early Middle Ages that suggest very interesting modifications of individual artistic creation; most proses, for example, are not signed or claimed by an individual—nor are Notker's in their usual manuscript ambience. But these conditions must not be given a broader interpretation than they deserve. The student of music history, in particular, needs to know that Carolingian authors of certain kinds of verse, specifically occasional or dedicatory verse, often identified themselves as well as those to whom the verses were intended, and often spoke in first person singular with *ego*.[7] The unsigned, corporate *nos* may well be a condition of liturgical, monastic conventuality, but it is not necessarily one of early medieval artistic creativity in general; Notker is one of the most important demonstrations that the early medieval artist is not necessarily anonymous.

Notker set texts to pre-existing melodies; and because his texts are among the most distinctive of the repertory, they demonstrate that setting texts to pre-existent melodies is not by nature doomed to produce inferior or purposeless results. We need not accept desultory proses as characteristic of the genre but can ascribe their quality to other causes, such as a poor author or a corrupt text state. And while we need not assume Notker's specific qualities to be binding for all prose authors (indeed, they are not), at least they indicate the type of aesthetic criteria that could enter into the making of a good prose. That Notker should have expended his efforts in connection with the melodies he used tells us something of his estimate of their worth, too.

That much in general; perhaps it appears unnecessary, rudimentary, or overly apprehensive to assert such things. Yet by statement or implication, the early sequence has often been placed in conditions that would deny what I have asserted here—what Notker, by his life and work, asserts. Now for the more specific, technical importance of Notker's proses.

From Notker's Preface we learn that he composed his first prose as a young man; the collection, dedicated in 884 to Liutward of Vercelli, was presumably finished by 880. This fixes the composition of the texts within the limits circa 850–880. Since each text is associated intimately with a specific melody, the melodies of Notker's text can be definitely placed in the ninth century—and this is the only sure way of dating any sequence before 900. This is not to disagree categorically with the excellent discussion of other possibly

---

7. Carolingian occasional verse is edited *en masse* in *Poetae latini aevi carolini*, vols. I–IV (1881–) (*Monumenta Germaniae Historica*). See, for example, the *Carmina* of Sedulius in vol. III, especially *Ad Addonem Abbatem* (p. 223), *Sedulius cecinit* (p. 224).

TABLE I
Earliest MS Sources for the Sequence

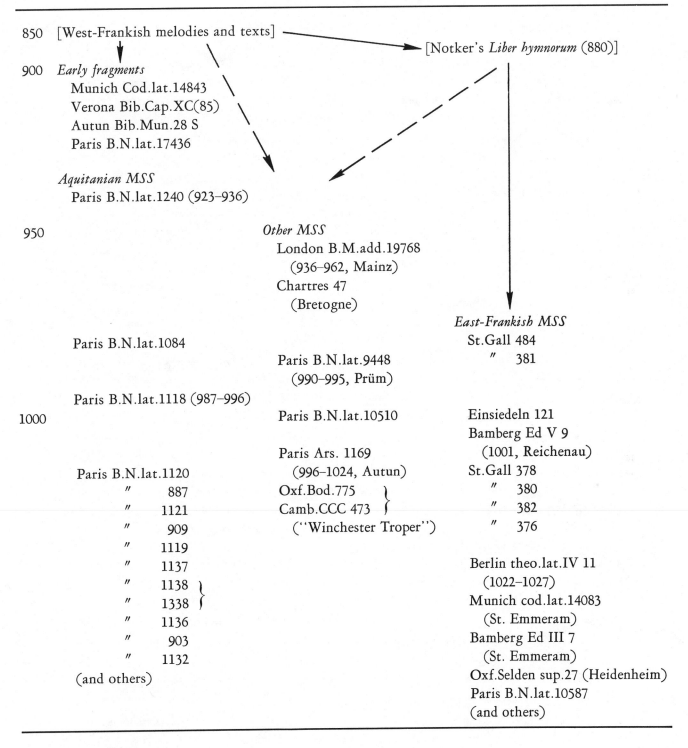

850   [West-Frankish melodies and texts]   [Notker's *Liber hymnorum* (880)]

900   *Early fragments*
      Munich Cod.lat.14843
      Verona Bib.Cap.XC(85)
      Autun Bib.Mun.28 S
      Paris B.N.lat.17436

    Aquitanian MSS
      Paris B.N.lat.1240 (923–936)

950   *Other MSS*
                    London B.M.add.19768
                    (936–962, Mainz)
                    Chartres 47
                    (Bretogne)

                                    East-Frankish MSS
  Paris B.N.lat.1084   St.Gall 484
                    Paris B.N.lat.9448   ″   381
                    (990–995, Prüm)

  Paris B.N.lat.1118 (987–996)

1000   Paris B.N.lat.10510   Einsiedeln 121
                                       Bamberg Ed V 9
                 Paris Ars. 1169   (1001, Reichenau)
  Paris B.N.lat.1120   (996–1024, Autun)   St.Gall 378
      ″   887   Oxf.Bod.775   ⎫   ″   380
      ″   1121   Camb.CCC 473 ⎬   ″   382
      ″   909   ("Winchester Troper")   ″   376
      ″   1119
      ″   1137   Berlin theo.lat.IV 11
      ″   1138 ⎫   (1022–1027)
      ″   1338 ⎬   Munich cod.lat.14083
      ″   1136   (St. Emmeram)
      ″   903   Bamberg Ed III 7
      ″   1132   (St. Emmeram)
  (and others)   Oxf.Selden sup.27 (Heidenheim)
                                       Paris B.N.lat.10587
                                       (and others)

early texts by Von den Steinen (especially NOSTRA TUBA), but only—on this occasion—to approach the problem of chronology with as little dependence as possible on either stylistic factors or dating of manuscripts.[8]

The chronological relationship of the sequences of Notker's *Liber hymnorum* and the early manuscript sources is shown in Table I.[9] The earliest manuscript sources for sequences consist of several fragmentary sources whose dating has been contested; in any case, "circa 900" is the earliest date that can in good conscience be maintained for any of them. More substantial sources commence with Paris B.N. MS lat.1240 (923–936), and continue sporadically throughout the 10th century, then in great numbers after 1000. One prose, STANS A LONGE (whose melody was not used by Notker) is mentioned by Hucbald (ca. 840–930) in his treatise *De institutione harmonica*; the treatise was probably written before 900, but since Hucbald lived well past 900 there is room for doubt.[10]

But there is no doubt about the texts Notker wrote, or the melodies he used; they existed in the ninth century. Through a study of them we can gain a reliable idea of the sequence in the ninth century, and from that idea, in turn, we could decide about other sequences for whose dating no basis other than stylistic comparison is available. For there is no reason to think that the ninth-century repertory is restricted to the melodies used by Notker; but on the other hand, attempts to date sequences on purely stylistic grounds with no recourse to an objective fact—such as use by Notker—have led to arbitrary if not fanciful conclusions. This firm witness of a ninth-century dating is one of the most important aspects of Notker's *Liber hymnorum.*

As a general principle, sequences fit their proses "syllabically," one note per syllable (with exceptions, as we will see). Each sequence has its own unique plan, as expressed in the number of syllables provided for each phrase, the number of phrases in the whole melody; it seems that no two melodies (in the early repertory) are alike in these respects. There may be several different texts to the same melody, and these texts, of course, will have the same or similar syllable count; but only one melody can be found to fit any given text. Therefore, we can obtain the *plan* of a melody from one of its texts, even if we do not have the melody itself. And since the St. Gall manuscript tradition for Notker's texts is exceptionally firm, we possess in his texts precise, reliable witness *from the ninth century* for the plans of the melodies he used. This witness antedates manuscript witness of any kind by several decades, and precedes readable versions of the melodies by a century, since these are first available in Paris B.N. MS lat.1118 (987–996). Melodies cannot be directly recovered from the St. Gall manuscript tradition until two centuries later, as will be discussed below.

Thus the witness of Notker's *texts*, paradoxically, offers a means of restoring West-Frankish versions of the corresponding *melodies* to a ninth-century state. Although this means of restoration was suggested at a number of points in the critical apparatus of the

8. W. von den Steinen, "Die Anfänge der Sequenzen-dichtung," *Zeitschrift für Schweizerische Kirchengeschichte* 40 (1946), pp. 190–212, 241–268; 41 (1947), pp. 19–48, 122–162; for NOSTRA TUBA see vol. 47, pp. 21–22, 46–48.

9. Descriptions of the MSS listed in Table I are referred to in the Appendix.

10. Hucbald's treatise edited by Martin Gerbert, *Scriptores ecclesiastici de musica sacra* (San Blasian 1784) I, pp. 104–121; see Dom Rembert Weakland, O.S.B., "Hucbald as Musician and Theorist," *Musical Quarterly* XLII (1956), pp. 66–84.

Analecta hymnica, especially in volume 53 (1911)[11] edited by Clemens Blume and Henry Marriott Bannister, and devoted to the early sequence repertory, it has been neglected since then in favor of approaches that preserve divergent versions (Notker's and the West-Frankish analogs) side by side as equally authentic representatives of "local custom." The present study will vigorously pursue this means of restoration whenever it is applicable.

The West-Frankish versions are first available in the few isolated sources circa 900–950, then more abundantly in the Aquitanian MSS from the end of the tenth century on. As preserved in these sources, the plans of text and melody show frequent divergence from the plans of Notker's texts to the same melodies. In a few cases the plans of Notker's texts provide for lines not present in the West-Frankish versions; in a much larger number of cases the West-Frankish versions show text for which no provision is made by Notker's plan; for example—to take the most frequent one—a West-Frankish text may show a couplet where Notker's plan has only a single line of text. Reconciling such differences will be one of our principal concerns.

Just as the witness of Notker's *Liber hymnorum* permits us to recover a "text-state" of the West-Frankish versions significantly older than that provided by the earliest manuscripts, so in return these same manuscripts permit us to recover a state of the *melodies* for Notker's texts significantly older than that provided by his own manuscript tradition. This is because the musical manuscripts of Germanic lands became "diastematic," offering more or less precise indication of relative pitch, at a much later date than did the French manuscripts; and—by a happy coincidence—the Aquitanian manuscripts that are among the earliest sources for the West-Frankish texts happen to be the earliest of all European sources to provide consistently diastematic readings for the melodies. Paris B.N. MS lat.1118 in particular, with all its shortcomings both musical and textual, is nonetheless the cornerstone for the establishment of melodic readings for the early West-Frankish repertory.

By way of experiment, the present transcriptions of Notker's melodies (not intended, again, as critical editions) will use the Aquitanian melodic readings where these are compatible with the St. Gall neumatic tradition. This procedure assumes a good deal: it assumes that in any given case there was an original melody with specific readings, that this melody was intended by Notker as well as by the West-Frankish version, and that this single melody was preserved in—and hence recoverable from—the West-Frankish manuscript tradition as well as from the East-Frankish one. The significant difference between the two traditions is that the West-Frankish (or, speaking more precisely of the extant sources, the Aquitanian) tradition takes us roughly two hundred years closer to the source.

It can be argued that, in spite of this time differential, a continuous tradition in one locality is more reliable than another tradition from a locality far removed—particularly from a locality separated in so many important ways as tenth-century Aquitania is from Swabia. The argument is a strong one, and would perhaps prevail, without the imposition of two types of control. The first control is the coordinate comparison of the plans of West-Frankish sequences to the norms provided by Notker's versions, as already described. The second is the comparison of the Aquitanian melodic readings with the adiastematic neumes

11. *Analecta hymnica medii aevi*, ed. G. M. Dreves and C. Blume, 55 vols. (1886–1922); especially vol. 53, *Liturgische Prosen erster Epoche*, ed. Clemens Blume and Henry Bannister (1911).

of the roughly contemporary St. Gall manuscripts, beginning with MS 484. It needs to be explained that even though adiastematic neumes of this type do not permit us to read out an otherwise unknown melody (the neumes simply do not contain the necessary pitch information), they do permit precise and substantial confirmation or negation of a melody already known. That is, the reading of an Aquitanian melody against its presumed neumes in a St. Gall manuscript allows us to confirm that the melody is indeed the same, to provide a melodic reading for the St. Gall version, and even in some cases to make slight modifications in the Aquitanian melody to conform more closely with its use by Notker. The important result of this process is that it seems to provide melodic readings closer to the intent of the St. Gall versions of the tenth century, controlling or eliminating melodic variants that appeared after 1000. For as it works out, the differential in time (between early and late Eastern sources) seems to have produced as many changes in the melody as the differential in place. The results so obtained, which need to be confirmed by close collation of the Eastern manuscript tradition, are offered here not as any kind of critical version, but nonetheless as *possibly* the best readings that can be obtained, under the circumstances, for Notker's *Liber hymnorum*.

The control of the St. Gall neumes has been accomplished in this study with the help of the tables of neumes constructed for Notker's melodies by Henry Marriott Bannister (1854–1919).[12] Bannister, who is best remembered for his help to Blume in the *Analecta hymnica*, and for his *Monumenti Vaticani di Paleografia musicale*, devoted much attention to the sequence and by the time of his death had gathered all the raw material for an edition of the entire early corpus of sequences, which was to have been entitled *Melodiae sequentiarum*. The work may not have progressed as far as has sometimes been thought: it is questionable whether Bannister had in every case arrived at a critical version of the melody based on all his sources. The versions preserved in his papers do not always fulfill the requirements of final critical versions and are probably to be considered working versions. They are based on rich source material, however, and provide an extremely helpful conspectus of the manuscripts. In particular, the tabular transcriptions of the adiastematic sources of Notker's *Liber hymnorum* make possible an overview of the variants in these sources and have furnished the means of achieving the desired control.

The transcriptions of the West-Frankish versions require an explanation, since the procedure followed here differs from the usual one—at least, from that used by Bannister, and by Blume in the *Analecta hymnica*, as well as more generally elsewhere. Instead of seeking as broad a collation as possible, I have restricted the manuscript base to the Aquitanian group. The reasons for seeking a broad collation of all available sources widely separated in date and provenance are strong ones, and they include the hope that some source will

12. Bannister's papers reside in the Bodleian Library (Oxford); the volumes of transcriptions of sequences that concern us are MSS Lat. liturg. c.11–c.15. Consisting as they do of Bannister's working papers, these contain a variety of materials, on different sizes and kinds of paper, assembled and bound only after they came to the library upon his death. For each sequence there is usually a working version of the melody in Bannister's square notation on a staff, with variants added in various ways; and for the East-Frankish sequences, a tabulation of the staffless neumes themselves as found in the earlier, adiastematic sources. A summary and extracts appeared in *Anglo-French Sequelae, edited from the papers of Henry Marriott Bannister by Dom Anselm Hughes* (Nashdom Abbey, Burnham, Bucks, 1934).

preserve an original reading replaced in all other sources by a variant; for no matter how late or remote a source is, it can in principle preserve an original reading otherwise lost, if the source descends from a branch of the stemma of which it is the sole survivor. Of course, all the sources will contain a greater or lesser number of unauthentic readings, and the problem, obviously, is to select the desired readings and leave the others aside. A number of techniques are customarily used for doing this, ranging from highly systematic to deeply intuitive: a source of known value, date or provenance (such as an autograph or corrected proofs) can serve as a standard; or the internal relationships of the manuscripts as determined by the variants themselves, might suggest which variants were posterior and which anterior; or an estimate of the intrinsic value of a source—the overall reliability of the scribe—or external circumstances indicating his access to presumably authentic sources, may give great weight to a source; or finally, the decision may come down to a knowledge of style or conviction of taste.

All such means, however, depend upon considerably more and better information than is now available for early sequences. We have not lived with any readings of particular sequences long enough to have developed convictions about which are good and which are not; lacking even bad or tentative editions of the melodies, we lack the basis for a stylistically informed approach; and we do not have enough information about the sources themselves to rely on one or the other for authentic readings.

In short, the advantages of a broad collation seemed outweighed by the disadvantages. Given this situation, the best thing seemed to be to present versions based on a small number of closely related sources; rather than "the best reading," I have tried to establish "a demonstrably early one." There is a philosophy that values a single source—with all its mistakes—above any collation of sources, arguing that a single source at least presents an historical reality whereas any collation presents a version that exists only when made by the scholar. The argument is a long one and cannot be pursued here; nor do I support it. That the restriction of sources I propose inclines somewhat in the direction of this philosophy has been dictated to some extent by the nature of the sources available. It so happens that some of the earliest West-Frankish sequences are found only in a very small number of Aquitanian manuscripts—sometimes only in Paris B.N. MSS lat.1084 and 1118; for certain important pieces only two or three sources could be used in any case. All the other West-Frankish sequences associated with Notker's *Liber hymnorum* are also represented in the same small group of sources, often with concordances in the larger circle of Aquitanian manuscripts. Therefore it seemed both expedient and justifiable to use this group of manuscripts as the basis for collated transcriptions, with variant readings in an apparatus, to demonstrate the existence of these sequences in at least one branch of the whole manuscript tradition, and to give a fair idea of the actual state of text and melody in these sources. This is what the transcripts and apparatus are designed to do.

Even here compromise and expediency are operative. Certain kinds of variants—spelling, capitalization for the texts, and certain types of slight melodic ornamentation (for example, liquescent neumes) for the music—have not been reported; these kinds of variants would possibly be of great importance in determining the overall behavior of a particular manuscript and the relationship among manuscripts (a task that has some day to be undertaken), but does not substantially affect the texts and melodies as we need to know them here. Variants are given for differences in words (or, where important, case-endings) and in melodic line, and of course for any more substantial differences. The whole problem of what constitutes a melodic variant in staffless notation is a thorny one and will be taken up in Chapter 2.

The versions of texts and melodies given here, then, are to be understood not as critical editions but as collated transcriptions, the selection of manuscripts for collation being in some cases dictated by necessity, but in all cases intended to show the Aquitanian state circa 1000, free from contamination with sources of later date and other locations. The reader must be warned that these Aquitanian sources were accused by Blume of being hopelessly corrupt; he argued further that the extent of corruption was proof of the great age of the sequences involved, since (he said) much time would be needed to bring about such changes in the original text.[13] Both observation and inference have been echoed by others. I ignore the inference as not convincing in itself and not supported by other circumstances; but, more apropos here, I contest the observation. It is true that the Aquitanian versions often fail to conform to received ideas of how sequences should behave, but taken on their own terms they frequently provide consistent, believable readings. It is my conviction that when restored in accordance with Notker's version in the fashion already outlined, the Aquitanian versions are as close to the ninth-century originals as we can now come. I put that forward not as contentious postulation, but as hypothesis, subject to discussion and testing.

In sum, we need much more intensive familiarity with, and discussion of, the materials before we can appropriately address ourselves to the challenge of a *critical* version. The bulk of the present study is devoted to such a discussion. It attempts to seek out the kind of provisional stylistic observation that has to be advanced before questions about critical versions can be answered—or even framed. The discussion of each sequence attempts to grasp the structure of the melody, its relationship to the early texts (Notker's and the West-Frankish ones) and their relationship to each other. The discussion proceeds melody by melody—possibly a tedious procedure, but the only one, in my experience, that can give a sense of reality to the musical style involved. We have so little context for the early sequence, indeed for early medieval music in general; to point out this or that stylistic feature as an instance in just one or two pieces would elicit mild incredulity or at best only provisional belief. One has to experience the typical constructions over and over again throughout the whole early repertory to become convinced of their purposive use in this genre whose name and essence—"prose"—is balanced so precariously between the artistic and the ordinary. One can enter into and understand a discussion of the general issues surrounding the early sequence only after being persuaded by the reality of detailed instances.

Even if it were desirable to precede the account of individual pieces with one of general principles, these principles would be hard to find. It seems to me, at least, that a century of study and speculation on the early sequence has produced no general descriptions that

13. For example, in *Analecta hymnica* 53, p. 75, in connection with the prose ECCE VICIT; the same argument appears elsewhere in this volume.

are not either mistaken or misleading. That may appear to be an overly harsh judgment; at any rate it calls for as much qualification as can briefly be given here. Research into the early sequence has been based on the axiom—always assumed, never proven—that the sequence is a "trope" of the Alleluia of the Mass.[14] In no other area of the history of medieval music has an axiom been accepted so uncritically and with such deleterious results. On one hand, this axiom has taken the place of a basic, systematic inventory of materials such as should be—and elsewhere has been—normally carried out. On the other hand, it has led to unresolvable—at any rate, unresolved—anomalies in conclusions. It is a sad commentary that by far the most fruitful comprehensive approach to the early sequence was made by Von den Steinen, a literary historian, in connection with his study of Notker; he undertook this study of the early sequence simply because it was otherwise lacking.[15] But not being a historian of music, he could not do *all* our work for us, and was forced to rely in many technical aspects on what was available, which in itself severely limited his contribution to a musical understanding of the sequence. While fine isolated observations on the early sequence have been made,[16] they have not been placed within a firm framework of ninth-century materials and repertory, unencumbered by a mythology of origins, and so lack general application or validity. The approach in this study will seem to some to be know-nothing and unnecessarily skeptical, and perhaps it is, in terms of the inconclusive results it achieves. Nonetheless, the weight of what seemed an unproductive tradition was intolerable, and provoked an overriding stimulus to start anew. It also seemed that much of the problem was due to a rarity of published melodies; the remedy, in any case, is to set about deriving valid generalities from the close study of individual cases. Uncertain as the versions of early sequences may be, they constitute the only known, the only given elements. They will be our primary concern.

All the melodies Notker used in his *Liber hymnorum* are listed in Table II in the order in which they will be discussed.[17] They are divided into three groups, A, B, C. Group C contains a smaller type of piece that lacks the couplet structure characteristic of the other two groups and of sequences in general. Although these pieces of group C have usually been considered indiscriminately with the others, I consider them a separate, distinct category, and will not discuss them in this study—except as a group in the final chapters. Group B contains melodies whose incipits quote a known Alleluia melody; group A contains melodies where such a quotation has not been clearly established. All the melodies in groups A and B will be taken up individually, both with Notker's texts and the West-Frankish ones.

14. See my article, "The Troping Hypothesis," *Musical Quarterly* LII (1966), pp. 183–203.

15. "Die Anfänge der Sequenzen-dichtung" (see note 8).

16. For example, Georg Reichert, "Strukturprobleme der älteren Sequenzen," *Deutsche Vierteljahrschrift für Literaturgeschichte* 23 (1949), pp. 227–251. A comprehensive bibliography of literature on the sequence in Bruno Stäblein, "Sequenz," *Die Musik in Geschichte und Gegenwart* ed. F. Blume, 12, col. 522–549, supplemented by my listing under "Sequence" in *Grove's Dictionary of Music and Musicians*, 6th edition. The most important recent studies, those by Stäblein and Husmann, are cited in connection with the discussion in later chapters. The bibliography in this book includes only studies that deal specifically with pieces in the early repertory.

17. Table II appeared originally in my article, "Some Ninth-Century Sequences," *Journal of the American Musicological Society* XX (1967), pp. 367–402. It is given here in revised form, with additions supplied by N. de Goede, *The Utrecht Prosarium*; see my review in *Musical Quarterly*, LII (1966), pp. 521–527. See also B. Stäblein's list of Notker's repertory in "Notkeriana."

TABLE II

Concordances between Early West-Frankish Sequences and
Those of Notker's *Liber hymnorum*

West-Frankish texts	Notker's texts
Group A: lacking a confirmed relationship to an Alleluia	
1. Laudes deo omnis sexus	1. Laudes deo concinat ("Organa")
2. Hæc dies quam excelsus	2. Grates salvatori ("Duo tres")
	Tubam bellicosam
3. Ecce vicit	3. Hanc concordi ("Concordia")
Gaude eja	Petre summe
Epiphaniam	
4. Nunc exultet	4. Laudes salvatori ("Frigdola")
Semper regnans	
Arce superna	
5. Hæc est sancta solemnitas	5. Hæc est sancta solemnitas solem-
	nitatum
	Quid tu virgo ("Virgo plorans")
6. Fortis atque amara	6. Judicem nos ("Deus judex justus")
7. Clara gaudia	7. Johannes Jesu ("Romana")
Dic nobis	Laurenti David
8. Christi hodierna	8. Congaudent angelorum ("Mater")
Rex nostras Christe	
Ecce jam venit	
Pange deo	
9. Rex omnipotens	9. Sancti spiritus assit ("Occidentana")
	10. Agni paschalis ("Graeca")
	11. Carmen suo dilecto ("Pascha")
	12. Summi triumphum regis ("Captiva")
	13. Scalam ad caelos ("Puella turbata")
	14. Concentu parili ("Symphonia")
	15. Natus ante saecula ("Dies sanctifi-
	catus
	16. Benedicto gratias ("Planctus
	sterilis")
Group B: related to an Alleluia	
17. Hæc est vera redemptio	17. Gaude Maria virgo ("Cignea")
Beata tu virgo	
(Alleluia *Pascha nostrum*)	
18. Praecursor Christi	18. Dilecte deo ("Justus ut palma minor")
(Alleluia *Justus ut palma*)	Rex regum

TABLE II (*continued*)

West-Frankish texts	Notker's texts

19. Hæc dies est sancta
    Ecce dies orbis
    Organicis canamus
      (Alleluia *Justus ut palma*)
	19. Sancti Baptistae ("Justus ut palma
	    major")
	    Laus tibi Christe cui sapit

20. Omnipotens deus (Alleluia *Benedictus es*)	20. Festa Christi ("Trinitas")

21. Salus aeterna
    Veniet rex
    (Alleluia *Ostende*)
	21. Clare sanctorum ("Aurea")

22. En virginum agmina
    Jubilemus omnes
    (Alleluia *Veni domine*)
	22. Stirpe Maria ("Adducentur")

23. Regnantem sempiterna
    Pangat laudes
    (Alleluia *Laetatus sum*)
	23. Psallat ecclesia ("Laetatus sum")

	24. Christus hunc diem ("Dominus in Sina")

	25. Agone triumphali ("Vox exultati-
	    onis")
	    Omnes sancti seraphim

Group C: short, aparallel sequences

West-Frankish texts	Notker's texts
26. Qui regis sceptra (Alleluia *Excita domine*)	26. Angelorum ordo ("Laudate deum")
27. Age nunc (Alleluia *Dominus regnavit*)	27. Is qui prius ("Dominus regnavit")
28. In cithara (Alleluia *Exultate deo*)	28. Laeta mente ("Exultate deo")
29. Sancte rex (Alleluia *Omnes gentes*)	29. En regnator ("Qui timent")
30. Jam deprome (Alleluia *In te domine*)	30. Laus tibi sit ("In te domine")
31. (Sequentia) (Alleluia *Confitemini*)	31. O quam mira ("Confitemini")
32. (Sequentia) (Alleluia *Adorabo*)	32. Tu civium ("Adorabo")

33. Veneranda die
    (Alleluia *Dies sanctificatus*)
	33. Christe domine ("Obtulerunt" or
	    "Pretiosa")

The Incipits in quotes are melody titles from the East-Frankish (usually St. Gall) sources. Italics, as in Alleluia *Dies sanctificatus*, refer to Alleluias of the Mass.

Beyond the grouping A, B, C, there is little to guide us, and the order is one of expediency—beginning, however, with the sequence Notker's Preface tells us was his first, LAUDES DEO CONCINAT. Some of the other instances where Notker's text is clearly modeled on a West-Frankish text are taken up early in the series (HÆC EST SANCTA, JUDICEM NOS). The first four melodies considered are those in which more or less substantial restoration of the West-Frankish versions can be carried out. The melodies related to an Alleluia—a relationship filled with complexity then and confusion now—are treated after the others, for only then can the complexity and confusion be dealt with.

11

The Notation of the Aquitanian Sources

THE AQUITANIAN manuscripts provide our earliest access to the sequence melodies. This chapter is devoted to the musical notation of these sources and a brief comparison with St. Gall notation of the same period. Neither a close study nor a comprehensive survey is attempted or intended; rather, the purpose is to introduce the reader to the nature of the documents on which the transcription of the melodies is based, and to share with him some of the problems and uncertainties attendant upon transcription. Indeed, after a first glance at the plates, the reader may well conclude that the sources offer no basis for a reliable transcription of any kind. This, at least, has been the experience of some; but it has also been their experience that after a short exposure to the sources they became convinced that melodies could be read out of the notation with comparative ease and security. In fact, once the initial bewilderment is past, the main difficulty faced by the transcriber may well be overconfidence in the sources and his ability to read them.

The adiastematic notation used in the West in the early Middle Ages was designed to accompany, not replace, an accurate memorization of the melodies. The concept of "oral tradition" is not applicable here, for in the case of the sacred chant after 750—and before that time, too—we are dealing with a "literate" phenomenon, something intended to have a definite, precise form even if the written record does not encode all aspects of that form; "oral tradition," strictly speaking, implies a pre-literate phenomenon and quite different concepts of artistic form.[1] In any event, the adiastematic notation could not be read unless the reader knew how the melody went; but if he did know, then the notation served to confirm and refine his memory.

This still applies in large degree to the earliest group of substantially diastematic sources, the Aquitanian manuscripts.[2] While it is possible—fortunately—to read unknown melodies

1. A summary description of "oral tradition" and what it implies in this precise sense in Alfred B. Lord, "Oral Poetry," *Encyclopedia of Poetry and Poetics*, ed. Alex Preminger (Princeton 1965), pp. 591–593.

2. See the works of Chailley and Husmann cited in the appendix. Aquitanian notation has been described in *Paléographie musicale* 13 (1930): *Le Codex 903 de la Bibliothèque nationale de Paris*, Gradual de Saint Yrieix (XIᵉ

directly from some of these with a fair to good degree of security, that degree is immeasurably increased if the melody is known ahead of time. Almost all of the melodies in Notker's *Liber hymnorum* have at least one later witness in a staff source of some kind; but one melody (BENEDICTO GRATIAS DEO) escapes us, because it is nowhere preserved in a diastematic source.

In studying the notation of the Aquitanian manuscripts in this chapter, the reader will more nearly approximate the intended use of the notation—and be far more persuaded by the discussion—if he first makes himself familiar with the melody to be used as an example, LAUDES DEO, for which Notker wrote his first prose. The melody with Notker's text, LAUDES DEO CONCINAT, is found among the transcriptions, p. 32, and with the early West-Frankish text that is presumably Notker's model, LAUDES DEO OMNIS SEXUS, at p. 30. This version is known in three Aquitanian sources (modified versions that will not be used here appear in two further sources) but in no later staff sources.[3] Notker's LAUDES DEO CONCINAT is known through the adiastematic St. Gall manuscripts and related sources, then in a very few later sources such as the Utrecht Prosarium (University Library MS 417) whence it was published by Fr. de Goede. Thus there is no direct confirmation of the Aquitanian sources by a later staff manuscript of LAUDES DEO OMNIS SEXUS, only the indirect confirmation by the descendants of the St. Gall manuscripts for Notker's version; and it is very reassuring to have the Aquitanian readings confirmed to the extent they are by a manuscript three centuries later from an entirely separate tradition.

The degree of ease and security in transcribing from the diastematic but staffless Aquitanian sources depends, of course, on the sources in question; they vary greatly in their diastematic quality. The three main sources for LAUDES DEO OMNIS SEXUS are the manuscripts Paris B.N. lat.1084, 1118, and 1121. All three were once known as "St. Martial tropers," but many questions about their specific provenance have arisen in the last 75 years. The questions cannot be dealt with here, hence the blanket designation "Aquitanian" used in this discussion; some observations are offered in the Appendix. Dates for the manuscripts can be offered with greater confidence and consensus: MS 1118 has long been dated 987–996 on the basis of the persons named in the *Laudes* (acclamations not related to our sequence). MS 1121 (definitely associated with St. Martial de Limoges) has been dated before 1031 or even before 1020. The least consensus exists for MS 1084, one reason being that it consists of several component parts differing in age and provenance. The part, or parts, in which LAUDES DEO OMNIS SEXUS occurs seem to me to be the oldest; I place them in the last quarter of the tenth century.

In these manuscripts, as in many others of the tenth and eleventh centuries, sequences are written down in two forms—one with the text, one without, the melodies being written as melismas with only the word "Alleluia" under the start of each. The collections of melismatically notated melodies are called *sequentiaria*, the collections that include the texts *prosaria*. MSS 1084 and 1118 contain both sequentiaria and prosaria (as well as several other kinds of chant collections); similarly MS 1121, which, however, lacks a full prosarium. For LAUDES DEO OMNIS SEXUS we have the following entries:

---

siecle), ed. Dom A. Mocquereau; Etude sur la notation aquitaine . . . par Dom P. Ferretti; Gregório María Suñol, *Introduction à la paléographie musicale Grégorienne* (Paris 1935).

3. References for LAUDES DEO in notes, p. 431.

MS 1084: text and melody in the prosarium
          melody in the sequentiarium
MS 1118: text and melody in the prosarium
          melody in the sequentiarium
MS 1121: melody in the sequentiarium

Hence there are five separate entries of the melody and two of the text.

Two of these MSS are for the most part reliably diastematic; but MS 1084 gives the impression—compared to the others—of being whimsically diastematic in its melismatic notation, and unreliable especially in the syllabic notation of the prosarium. Actually its notation is not unreliable if we do not rely on it for information it was not intended to convey: we cannot reliably read unknown melodies out of it, but we can confirm melodies already known, and for that purpose it is a very informative manuscript with many valuable and interesting readings. MS 1121, by contrast, seems far more reliable diastematically, but is apt to provide merely a routine copy, sometimes carelessly.

With that much introduction (and assuming that the reader has spent a few moments with the transcriptions of LAUDES DEO), we are ready to make the acquaintance of the Aquitanian notation. It will be most reassuring, perhaps, to begin with the sequentiaria, in particular the one in MS 1118. A facsimile of fol. 136 and the *verso*, showing the melismatic notation of LAUDES DEO (unlabeled in this source) is given in Plate I. In Example 1 appears the notation of the beginning of the melody copied by hand so that the versions in MSS 1118, 1084 (and St. Gall MS 484) can be aligned for purposes of comparison; in this copy the neumes are spaced right and left differently than in the original but otherwise reproduce the original as closely as was practicable. The groups of neumes have been numbered from 1 to 13 for reference. This much represents phrases 1 and 2 of the melody, as labeled. Neumes for phrase 3 are included, but not numbered individually. The capital D at the end of a phrase represents the same letter indication found in the sources to show a repeat of that phrase for the second line of the prose couplet. The pitch content of the neumes is given by the line of capital letters under the neumes for MS 1118.

Opening phrases of sequences, as we will see many times, are apt to involve ornamental neumes, and for this reason it will be easier to begin with phrase 2, at neume-group "5." In the notation of MS 1118, group 5 shows two dashes, one directly under the other; these represent two pitches, the second lower than the first, for notes in a vertical row are always read from top to bottom in Aquitanian notation. From the spacing on the page it is determined that the pitches represented are a whole tone apart, rather than a third or some larger interval, although the notation does not permit the distinction between whole tones and semitones. Also from the spacing on the page is determined the overall relationship of these pitches to the others; and if it is given from a staff-manuscript—or by hypothesis —that the last note or "final" of the piece is G, appearing here at the end of phrase 1 (neume 4) and of phrase 2 (neume 13), then the two pitches of neume 5 can be determined as D and C, as shown in the letter notation. (This group would be a *clivis* in a more cursive type of neume.) The next group, 6, contains five pitches, E, D, C, B, A.

The determination of pitch in Aquitanian notation is no more complex than that. The principle of the notation is simplicity itself, which helps account for its great importance

Example 1. Notation in the Sequentiaria: LAUDES DEO, beginning

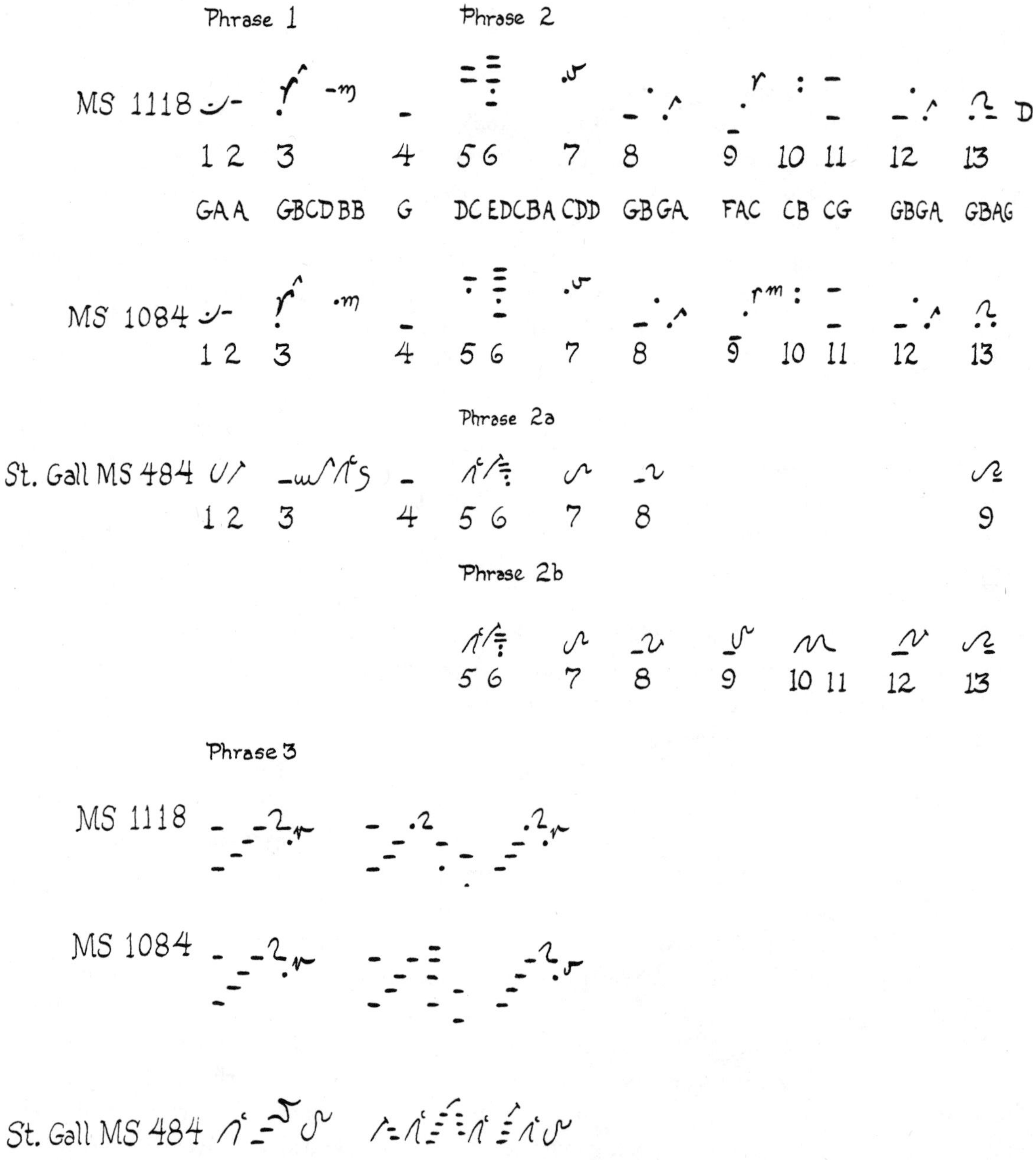

Phrase 1   Phrase 2

MS 1118

1 2   3   4   5 6   7   8   9   10 11   12   13

GA A   GBCD BB   G   DC EDCBA CDD   GB GA   FAC CB CG   GBGA GBAG

MS 1084

1 2   3   4   5 6   7   8   9   10 11   12   13

Phrase 2a

St. Gall MS 484

1 2   3   4   5 6   7   8   9

Phrase 2b

5 6   7   8   9   10 11   12   13

Phrase 3

MS 1118

MS 1084

St. Gall MS 484

in the development of notation during the tenth and eleventh centuries. Clearly, however, everything depends on the spacing of the neumes on the page, and that can vary greatly—in this formative period of diastematic notation—from one scribe to another.

Scribes increasingly used dry-point lines to align the neumes horizontally. At first they used the lines provided by the usual ruling of the page for the text; by writing text on every other line they had a line approximately in the middle of the space left for the notes.

In a sequentiarium, where there was no text, the dry-point lines could be used at the scribe's pleasure. Eventually dry-point lines were inked and labeled in various ways leading directly to the four-line staff of the thirteenth century. In the earlier Aquitanian manuscripts, however, such as 1084 and 1118, the lines seem to be only a convenience for the scribe, not a regular component of the notation, and must be treated accordingly.

The differentiation of dots and dashes in group 6 is without pitch significance—at least, in the state of development represented by MS 1118. It has been thought that the difference has durational significance, the dots representing shorter notes, the dashes longer ones, and that may well be the case; but a systematic interpretation has not yet been worked out.[4] Clear differentiation of dots and dashes is present only in some of the Aquitanian manuscripts, which seem to vary among themselves in the use of these signs. The possible durational significance is not taken into account in the present study.

Group 7 contains a dot, then a more complex sign, bearing a certain resemblance to a radical sign (√), and commonly called a *pes stratus*.[5] It is used regularly in sequentiaria at cadence points, and in combination with the preceding dot represents what we will come to know as the most typical cadence pattern of the sequence repertory—a lower note followed by two more a tone higher, in this case C D D. The syllabic notation of the prosaria may (as required by the text) use only one of the higher notes (C D) or three (C D D D), but the sequentiaria will provide for all of these possibilities simply with this special neume-group.

Continuing in phrase 2, neume-group 8 represents four pitches G B G A, with a dash, two dots, and another sign to be discussed. The dash and the first dot are not vertically aligned: the dot is placed a little to the right of the vertical, and in such placement in Aquitanian notation the lower note is read first, the higher one second. (This group would be a *pes* or *podatus* in a more cursive notation.)

The second dot is placed in a similar relationship to the fourth note, which is a *virga*, a hooked or headed slant-bar representing a single pitch—and in adiastematic notations typically a pitch higher than the preceding or following pitch. In diastematic notation that use, of course, is redundant but nonetheless persists in Aquitanian as well as other types of notation. The virga can have several slightly different shapes seemingly without distinction as to pitch. (The combination here of dot-virga would also be a *pes* or *podatus* in a more cursive notation.)

Group 9 represents three pitches, F A C with a dash, a dot, and a virga (cursive equivalent would be a *scandicus*). Groups 10 and 11 each show two pitches, C B then C G; group 12 duplicates group 8. Group 13, however, represents four pitches with three neumes, for the hook represents two pitches, a higher then a lower one; it is a *clivis*, inherited from the adiastematic cursive notations, where complex marks represented groups of pitches. Neumes such as the clivis tend to be replaced as Aquitanian notation develops by the combinations of discrete signs, each representing a single pitch, that make up most of phrase 2 and indeed most of the notation in the Aquitanian sequentiaria. The discrete signs, ob-

4. See the brief discussion by Jacques Handschin, "Trope, Sequence, and Conductus," *New Oxford History of Music* II: Early Music up to 1300, ed. Dom Anselm Hughes (Oxford 1954), p. 158.
5. See the remarks on *Pes stratus* in the article by Dom Cardine cited in note 9.

viously, portray the diastematic content of the notation much more effectively than do the cursive signs; but in an adiastematic state, it should be noted, just the reverse is true.

Turning back to phrase 1, group 1 represents a lower pitch, then a higher one (GA, or pes) but in a special form called "liquescent," used in this case for the double "l" in *Al-le-lu-ia* (this word is set, *pro forma*, under the first phrase of every melody in a sequentiarium). The liquescent pes, or *epiphonus*, is an inheritance from older notations, as is also the next neume, the *quilisma*. Here, in its Aquitanian form, it includes the dot and the sign following (something like a V), but the little virga at the top is a special addition for this particular melodic configuration. Usually quilismas represent a melodic notation through an ascending interval of a third, presumably with some kind of ornamental significance no longer known. Sometimes, as here, the quilisma can extend over a larger interval. The virga adds another note a whole tone above the quilisma and is followed by a dash, which in turn is followed by a jagged note called *oriscus*. This is typically used for a repeated pitch, as here; and while that meaning is redundant in diastematic notation, it is not so in adiastematic notation whence it comes. Still, it is often considered to have had additionally some ornamental significance, which may account for the fact that its use persists in Aquitanian notation for a surprising length of time.

Phrases 1 and 2 include almost all the basic neume shapes encountered in the Aquitanian sequentiaria; or rather, in Aquitanian notation in general, which tends to proceed by combining simple discrete signs—*neumes à points superposés* in the language of the *Paléographie musicale*. The notation for phrases 1 and 2 as they appear in the sequentiarium of MS 1084 is shown under that for MS 1118 in Example 1 (see also Plate II). Phrases 1 and 2 are identical in the two manuscripts, except that in group 5, MS 1084 uses a dash and dot instead of two dashes, and in group 9, MS 1084 adds an oriscus for the repeated note "C" represented in MS 1118 by a pes stratus. (Casual treatment of repeated notes is common in sequentiaria.) Differences do occur between MSS 1118 and 1084, but this degree of correspondence is by no means unusual, and in many other respects the sequentiaria as well as the prosaria are closely related. Such correspondence clearly indicates that at this stage, at least, we are dealing with the definite intentions and fixity of results characteristic of a composed music in a written tradition, not improvised music in an "oral" one.

There is an important difference between MS 1118 and MS 1084 that does not show up in this particular piece, but does affect readings from MS 1084 elsewhere in the sequentiarium. The diastematic quality occasionally lapses, yielding dubious results in comparison to the almost uniform quality of MS 1118. This difference, however, is far more prevalent between the prosaria of the two manuscripts, with MS 1084 much less consistently diastematic.

There are two weak links in the diastematic representation of any given sequence in these manuscripts. Determination of relative pitch becomes very uncertain at the end of each line on the page. Unless the scribe leaves some specific clue, we can only guess from the spacing what relationship the notes at the start of the next line have to those at the end of the preceding one. The standard scribal solution to this problem is the *custos*, a note appended to the end of a line anticipating the first note on the next. Aquitanian scribes sometimes used a custos (in various forms), but more often not. Some of the manuscripts that concern us use a simple dash for a custos, but written in such a manner as to suggest that the dashes were added subsequently—with all the uncertainties that such addition implies.

The other weak link is far more difficult to deal with because far less obvious. Concordances show that shifts can take place within a line between the end of one phrase and the beginning of the next, that is, after a cadence. These shifts are occasioned by a change in register in the melody; they are equivalent to a change of clef; but with no clefs, the change may be hard to spot. Sometimes the scribes add clues such as *l(evate)*, "raise the pitch," or *e(qualiter)* to show equivalence over the shift. Valuable as they are, these indications cannot be relied on to be present when needed. Real, sometimes permanent, ambiguity is introduced; for later scribes, transcribing from sources such as these onto staff sources, interpreted the shifts in various ways. In this respect as in others, the introduction of the staff did not resolve any uncertainty in melodies preserved up until that time by a combination of written record and aural memory, but merely perpetuated it.

There has been much discussion about the use of two notations—one melismatic in the sequentiaria, the other syllabic in the prosaria. Without in any way suggesting here a definitive answer to the question of why the two notations coexisted, we can observe an important advantage for having both. The melismatic notation we have just examined affords a more precise and perceptible image of the pitch relationships than does the syllabic notation of the prosaria, samples of which appear in Plates III and IV. The reason lies in the fact that, as we saw in the sequentiaria, the diastematic quality of the Aquitanian notation depends completely upon the spacing of the notes relative to each other; and since the notes are much *closer* left and right to each other in the melismatic notation, where they do not have to be spaced out horizontally over their respective syllables, the scribe can (if he wishes) space them vertically with more accuracy, and the reader can perceive the vertical spacing more readily. Actually, the scribe of the prosarium of MS 1118 seems to have maintained the same diastematic quality as found in the sequentiarium; but it is apparent from even a casual inspection of the prosarium of MS 1084 (Plate IV) that its scribe either would not or could not maintain the diastematic quality of the sequentiarium (Plate II) and fell far short of the prosarium in MS 1118 (Plate III).

Since the melismatic and syllabic notations of MS 1118 are approximately equivalent in diastematic value, it is a little hard to see the reason for having or using both. In the case of MS 1084, however, the reason is more apparent; and just as the melismatic notation gives a more informative picture of the pitch relationships of the melody, so the syllabic notation gives a much more informative picture of the relationship between the melody and the text. That assertion may seem gratuitous, but a little experience in attempting to fit a text, given without syllabic notation, to its melody given in melismatic notation would reveal the slight inexactitudes inherent in the melismatic notation that can make the matching of the text frustrating, or indeterminate, or both. Nor is this a purely hypothetical exercise: sequences were published without melodies in the *Analecta hymnica* and without texts in *Anglo-French Sequelae* (edited from the papers of Henry Marriott Bannister by Dom Anselm Hughes),[6] and the two cannot reliably be joined together to produce complete pieces.

The syllabic notation is basic; it alone sets forth the whole form of the piece, of the combination of text and melody. In an adiastematic state, however, and even in a diastematic but staffless state, the syllabic notation suffers from the horizontal spread of signs, and requires as much assistance as a melismatic notation can offer. Even in a "completely adiastematic" state, such as in the tenth- and eleventh-century St. Gall manuscripts, the melismatic notation is still very advantageous, the reason being that such neumes as clivis and podatus, to take the simplest examples, may show melodic direction more clearly than a series of adiastematic dots and dashes. To put it another way (in connection, now, with the early Aquitanian sources), the sequentiarium of Plate II would have to be much less diastematic than it is to be as uncertain as the corresponding prosarium of Plate IV.

Plate III shows the beginning of LAUDES DEO OMNIS SEXUS in MS 1118, under the rubric *Alia*, that is, *Alia prosa de Pascha*, this being the Easter section of the prosarium. In phrase 1 the neumes correspond exactly to those of the sequentiarium, except that the whole group on *de-(o)* includes and ends on a G, followed by a second G for *-o*, whereas only one G was provided in the sequentiarium. (This group of notes on one syllable—a short melisma—is occasional in early sequences, but only on the first phrase, or perhaps the last.) After that, the notation proceeds almost entirely with dots and dashes, as did the melismatic notation. The reader will perhaps appreciate the editorial difficulty of arriving at firm decisions from this notation as to which are dots and which dashes; with the melismatic notation to help us, we could perhaps convince ourselves that *-nis* and *-so-* were dots rather than dashes, but if the melismatic notation did not happen to agree with the syllabic. . .

The cadence neume C D D takes a different form when the pattern is expressed syllabically. Here on *vo-ce*, the syllable *vo-* receives two pitches, C D, and these are represented by one of the distinctive Aquitanian forms for the *pes*. (Usually, however, the cadence pattern is treated syllabically throughout, each of three syllables getting a note for an individual pitch.) Two virgas appear in the continuation of phrase 2, at *(dul)-ces* and at *ut*, on higher pitches but not the same ones that carried virgas in the melismatic notation.

Towards the end of the eighth line on the page, at the new phrase *Nam a primo*, the notator barely squeezed the neumes C G A B into a representation of the actual pitch relationships; at the beginning of the next line he moved the neumes down closer to the text (as if using a higher clef), but even so, at the end of this line, at the words *Ut ipsi*, he did not have room for an accurate representation of the high E and D. In this case he used the indication *l(evate)* at the disjuncture. Two lines further at *Donec auctor*, the low-lying phrase returns, and here he used *e(qualiter)* to show that the pitch for *Do-(nec)* was the same (G) as the pitch for *(dissimi-)li*. But things are not usually that explicit.

The prosarium in MS 1084 is the least encouraging of this set of sources and in many cases can only be used to confirm readings obtained elsewhere. Plate IV begins toward the end of line 2a; *Praecelso regi* starts 2b. It will be observed that the neumes go up or down faithfully in accordance with the reading in MS 1118, but that the distance up or down on

6. *Anglo-French Sequelae*, edited from the Papers of Henry Marriott Bannister, by Dom Anselm Hughes (Nashdom Abbey, Burnham, Bucks, 1934).

the page bears but little relationship to the size of the melodic intervals involved. Even so, it is possible to detect a variant at *hodie surrexit a mortis victor* relative to the prosarium in MS 1118.

```
MS 1118   D E   C    C D E F  G G A   G F  G G
MS 1084   D E   C    C D E G  G A A   G F  G G
          redemptor hodi- e surrexit a mortis victor
```

That the reading of melodies (and consequently, variants) from such sources has a large intuitive factor is not to be denied. Unfortunately, this factor has to be accepted, or no readings at all are possible from these early and very important sources. Accurate physical measurement of the spatial distance between neumes is worse than useless: the scribe spaced by eye and by feel, and we read his intentions best when we rely on these same intuitions. The marks on the page are less than completely meaningful; the communicative circuit is complete only when these marks are being read by a reader who has the melody already in mind. When the circuit is complete, then the results produced *by the reader* have an objective value approaching that of staff notation. This is not to say that I alone can decipher the notation, and that my readings must be trusted; quite the opposite—a consensus among readers who are familiar with the melodies and informed about the notation should yield a very reliable reading. The point is that the raw material is the melody as perceived by the reader, not merely as notated on the page. This is the way the notation was intended, and this is the only way it works.

In the apparatus I have recorded variants only where the variant itself could be made out with some degree of security, tending to accept as agreement those places where no clear disagreement was present. This procedure has the effect of placing more burden on the most diastematic source involved (usually MS 1118); but the opposite procedure would have exactly the same effect, for it would produce a splatter of readings of which the most believable would still be those from the most diastematic source. In short—and this is the purpose of exposing the reader to the sources—there is room for latitude, of certain specific kinds, in the interpretation of the sources and the use of the apparatus.

In reading from the early Aquitanian sources with the help of later staff sources, three situations may arise. First, the later staff sources for a given piece may agree in the general outline of the melody; or, second, they may disagree; or, third, there may be no later staff sources. Each of the three cases requires a brief general comment here.

When the later staff sources agree, there may still be disagreement in detail between them and the Aquitanian manuscripts from circa 1000—that is to say, from two or three hundred years earlier. The problem is whether to prefer the later sources (which may well agree among themselves in certain details in spite of widely different provenance) over the relatively isolated witness of a few uncertain early manuscripts from a localized tradition. I state the problem as harshly as possible so as not to obscure the fact that I have followed the less likely course of action. This course, described briefly in Chapter 1, will be restated here, now that the reader has had a chance to see the nature of the sources involved. My purpose is to establish readings from a small group of closely related sources (in the case of LAUDES DEO OMNIS SEXUS, three sources) as one early witness of the melody—the earliest readable witness, in fact, by more than two hundred years. The nature of the sources allows us (I believe) to establish readings that differ in detail from later staff sources, and where conditions warrent it I have done so, for two specific reasons. First, as already mentioned, there is nothing intrinsically more authentic about the readings contained in a staff source: they are more readable, but not necessarily more reliable—no more so than the staffless versions from which they were made. Corruptions seem to creep into a manuscript tradition at a more or less constant rate, and they are just as prevalent between 1000 and 1200 as at any other time. Using earlier sources circumvents at least these sources of error.

Second, there is every reason to believe that other changes of detail were made deliberately in response to changing ideas of style. Such changes include changes of pitch, introduction or removal of ornamental or auxiliary notes, change in the length of notes by addition or removal of the oriscus. The changes can be made for a simpler or a more complex effect. I think it may be possible someday to show how a given melodic phrase is gradually twisted by a succession of versions that seek to intensify it by shifting one note at a time, a whole or half-step at a time. In all these cases, the earlier sources are of course closer to the original version.

Since my purpose is not the collation of later sources with earlier ones, but rather the collation of the earlier ones alone, I have used the later staff sources—even when they agree with the earlier ones—in what may seem a peculiar fashion. I have regarded them as the equivalent, for me, of the memorized version transmitted orally to the scribe by the singer who knew how the piece went. Thus I have primed myself from the later sources with a general idea of the melody, its outline and final pitch, then have proceeded to transcribe from the diastematic sources such as MS 1118, but without recording variants with respect to the later sources. In these particular circumstances I believe the procedure is justified and produces good results, although I would not recommend its general or indiscriminate use.

What if the later sources disagree in some major point, such as, most typically, the transposition of a phrase, or even the last part of a piece, up a fourth? In this case a more careful weighing of later sources will be necessary; indeed, a real solution will only be possible with a full collation, and must wait for that. The witness of the earlier sources, which are especially susceptible to mistakes in this respect and offer little control over them, must remain provisional.

If, finally, there are no later staff sources, the most severe problem in recovering a version from the earlier ones is deciding on a final pitch. As observed, Aquitanian diastemy does not distinguish between whole tones and semitones, and that is the whole nub of the problem. Struggling with this problem in principle as well as in practice yields many insights into the nature of the diatonic system basic to Western music.

For our purposes, the diatonic system should be regarded as a series of whole tones interrupted at certain points by semitones. In order properly to understand a given melody, it is necessary to know where the semitones come. Medieval development of clefs and the staff has this determination as its primary goal: the clefs finally arrived at—C and F—lie immediately above the two semitones; any other semitones are indicated by flats (or, eventually, sharps) added to the staff. The system of four finals (D, E, F, G) has the semitone in the middle, as does the hexachord (C D E F G A), the foremost medieval tonal construct, developed in the eleventh and twelfth centuries.[7] The system of *species* of fourths, fifths, and octaves developed by Berno of Reichenau (d. 1048) and others likewise revolves around the location of the semitones.[8] Deciding on the final of an Aquitanian sequence is equivalent to deciding where the semitones come in the melody. As far as the early Aquitanian sequentiaria and prosaria are concerned, there is no notational way of determining this.

Since there are seven notes in the diatonic system, it would seem that in deciding on a final pitch for any given sequence, there would be seven possibilities. But one of the earliest, most persistent observations of medieval theorists was that there were only four possibilities, only four finals, in terms of the location of semitones. That is, taking into account the pattern of whole and half steps around the final, three of the diatonic possibilities, A, B, C, are so similar respectively to three of the others, D, E, F, that all together they can be counted as three finals, not six; and G makes the fourth possibility. This seems to be the basic reason (although perhaps not the origin) for the theory of the four finals and hence of the eight modes. The four finals were numbered *protus*, "first," (D or A), *deuterus*, "second," (E or B), *tritus*, "third," (F or C), and *tetrardus*, "fourth," (G). No particular ambitus or range was associated with these finals in this earliest stage of "modal" theory, the association with octave ranges and types being a later refinement.

Within the context of the four finals, B flat has the effect of exchanging one position of, say, *protus*, with the other: *protus* on D can be made exactly like *protus* on A by the addition of B flat. Another, quite distinct effect of B flat is to locate the whole set of finals on still another seat—*protus* G, *deuterus* A, *tritus* B flat, *tetrardus* C.

In actual practice, the choice facing the transcriber of sequences is narrowed even further than the four finals. Judging from staff sources, sequences on F are extremely rare (especially in the early repertory). Sequences on E are infrequent, and can usually be recognized by distinctive cadences and other melodic characteristics. Thus the two most frequent possibilities are *protus* and *tetrardus*, or D and G, their most frequent seats. Since these differ mainly in the major or minor third, they are sometimes not easily distinguished; in some cases, even, the choice remains indeterminate. Occasionally the treatment of the tritone F-B will incline the choice away from *tetrardus*, and toward the *protus*, since the tritone may sit harshly against the final G.

Do sequences conform to the eight modes? The answer is long and complex, because of what we in modern times have made out of the "modal system." In general the early medieval composer seems to have paid it much less heed than we do, or than we think he did. Do sequences use the four finals? Of course, since all diatonic melody must. Do sequences fall into the limits of the eight modes? Often not, because their ranges frequently exceed the allocations that underlie the distinction of eight modes (an "authentic" or higher mode, a "plagal" or lower one for each final). Do sequences use the melodic formulae that characterize the eight modes in Gregorian chant? A much more complex question, not to be answered by theoretical principle but rather by stylistic observation. The answer depends

7. See my article, "Hermann's Major Sixth," *Journal of the American Musicological Society* XXV (1972), pp. 19–37.

8. See Hans Oesch, *Berno und Hermann von Reichenau als Musiktheoretiker*, Publikationen der Schweizerischen Musikforschenden Gesellschaft, Ser. II, vol. IX (Berne 1961), pp. 97–98.

on what the question implies by "melodic formula." If it means, say, F-A-C in tetrardus G, then the answer is yes—but this is hardly a "melodic formula" that shows stylistic similarity between sequences and Gregorian chant; rather, it is simply a set of pitches. If some more sophisticated kind of formula or idiom is meant, then the answer is "no," for sequences are not Gregorian chant and make little use of its idioms, transforming their sense radically when it does.

Turning once more to purely notational matters, we need to see, however briefly, the relationship of St. Gall neumes to the Aquitanian examples already studied.[9] Example 1 includes at the bottom the neumes from St. Gall MS 484, a sequentiarium and the earliest witness of the melodies of the *Liber hymnorum* (see also Plate V). In general the notation of MS 484 can be described as cursive, as opposed to the use of discrete dots and dashes of the Aquitanian system, but in practice this means merely a higher proportion of groups of two pitches, such as clivis and podatus, and of three pitches, such as torculus and porrectus.

Group 1 has a podatus, GA, corresponding to the liquescent pes (epiphonus) of the Aquitanian versions. Neume 2 is a virga. Group 3 has a St. Gall quilisma, followed by clivis DB, and oriscus B. Neume 4 is a dash in all versions. At 5, St. Gall 484 has a clivis, but at 6 a virga followed by a descending series of dashes, analogous to the Aquitanian dots and dashes. At 7, one neume replaces the dot-and-cadential neume. At 8, St. Gall 484 has a dash-and-porrectus instead of a dash, dots, and virga. But what happens after 8 in line 2a? The St. Gall version is too short, and furthermore the next neume after 8 in 2a cannot be made to read the F A C figure in the melody of the Aquitanian sources. A variant can be clearly perceived, even without reference to the transcription. The later staff source for Notker's version shows that his 2a omits groups 9–12, and St. Gall 484 (and the other St. Gall MSS) confirm that this irregularity is present in the earliest sources. The groups 9–12 in 2b, then, conform to the Aquitanian version (groups 10–11 are two clivis) with cursive forms largely replacing dots and dashes. Similarly, in phrase 3 it can be determined that in the St. Gall version the repetition of the first sub-phrase varies from the Aquitanian reading, while the rest conforms.

St. Gall notation is a vast subject in itself, of course, and there are many more problems in just the sequence notation than can be mentioned (let alone treated) here. But pursuing the concordance of late tenth-century Aquitanian and St. Gall versions of LAUDES DEO against the staff source in the Utrecht Prosarium from the thirteenth century does much to reassure one that the melody is determinate, not just in general outline but also in detail, and that it had an identity clearly settled in all details as far back as Notker's time—indeed, before him, for the identity survived intact in the two widely separated traditions. That is the first conclusion to be drawn, not just from this one instance but from a similar study of the entire early repertory. The second conclusion, dependent upon the first, is that many of the *differences* in the two traditions are also determinate, and can be made to yield insight into the formation and structure of the early sequence. We will begin in the next chapter with the difference in line 2a of LAUDES DEO.

9. For a recent study of St. Gall notation, see Dom E. Cardine, "Sémiologie grégorienne," *Etudes grégoriennes* XI (1970), pp. 1–158.

III

LAUDES DEO OMNIS SEXUS
Notker's LAUDES DEO CONCINAT

NOTKER TELLS US in his Preface that he wrote LAUDES DEO CONCINAT as his first attempt in the new genre, in imitation of some *versus ad sequentias* that the monk from Jumièges had in his Antiphonary. Notker's West-Frankish model, not known to Von den Steinen, was first pointed out by Fr. de Goede, who printed LAUDES DEO CONCINAT parallel in text and music to LAUDES DEO OMNIS SEXUS, from the Aquitanian repertory.

The two versions are printed in the transcriptions, pp. 30–33. The West-Frankish version, LAUDES DEO OMNIS SEXUS, is transcribed from three Aquitanian sources (apparatus in the Notes on pp. 431), and Notker's LAUDES DEO CONCINAT is given with a text from Von den Steinen's edition and a melody derived from reading the Aquitanian version against the neumes of the St. Gall sequentiarium MS 484 and the neume-tables of the St. Gall manuscripts in Bannister's transcriptions. A control of the overall melodic outline and pitch level is provided by later staff sources for Notker's version, including the version published by Fr. de Goede in the *Utrecht Prosarium*.

The two versions do not agree exactly in their plans, as can be more easily seen in Example 2. In this diagram the large numbers refer to the musical phrases, which are portrayed by the horizontal lines—two in parallel, if there are two lines of text in a couplet for a melodic phrase, one if there is only one line of text. The small numbers at the ends of the lines indicate the number of syllables in each line of text; the number of syllables is also represented roughly by the length of the lines in the diagram. A break in the line (as in phrase 3) indicates a break in the *melodic phrase*, usually by means of a cadence; breaks in the text, whether by syntax or other means, are not represented. The alignment of the two versions in the diagram shows the correspondence in melodic material: for example, phrases 1, 2, and 3 of the West-Frankish version correspond melodically to 1, 2, and 3 of Notker's version; Notker's phrase 4 has no counterpart in the West-Frankish melody; the West-Frankish phrase 4 has the same melody as Notker's phrase 5.

Example 2. LAUDES DEO OMNIS SEXUS   LAUDES DEO CONCINAT (Notker)

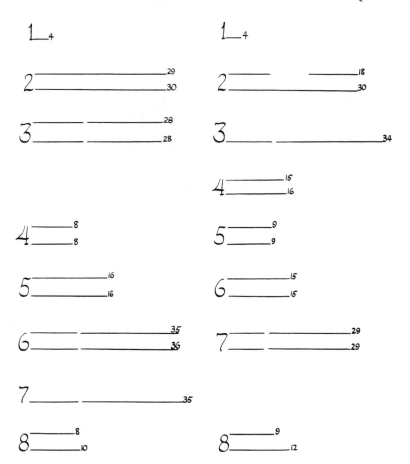

It would be easy to assume that in the formative stage of the sequence, melodies were so fluid that they naturally took on varying shapes when set to different texts. It would be easy to conclude that Notker simply rearranged the basic melody the way he wanted it. But what happens if we actually try to reconcile the differences between the two versions, keeping in mind that Notker said he wrote his text in imitation of a West-Frankish model, and that—of the two versions we have in front of us—Notker's is the one with the older witness? LAUDES DEO OMNIS SEXUS, as it stands, can not have been the exact model. How would it have to be changed in order to make it so, and what would be the effect of these changes on the piece as we have it?

Consider phrase 2, in which Notker's version has lines of unequal length.

(Notker)

1   Laudes deo
2a   concinat orbis ubique totus
2b   Per summi patris indulgentiam: qui miserans, quod genus humanum casu
      (2a)   qui gratis est liberatus
      (2b)   succubuit veterano,

Irregular and unusual as the procedure may at first seem, the result is intrinsically credible: phrase 2a can be construed with a semi-cadence on the higher D (*totus*), dividing the phrase into two sub-phrases of which the first moves around D, while the second gravitates down to G.

> D C E D C B A C DD G BG A GBAG
> 2a   concinat orbis ubique totus, qui gratis est liberatus

The greater length of phrase 2b is due entirely to the material between the two sub-phrases of 2a. This material (*qui miserans quod genus humanum casu*) begins in melody like *qui gratis*, turns aside to a set of pitches not yet in evidence (F A C), then artfully starts the sub-phrase again to end it as before.

> G BAG   F   AC C CB C A G B G A GBAG
> 2b   . . . qui miserans, quod genus humanum casu succubu-it veterano,

Phrase 2b, while repeating 2a, has enlarged upon the musical thought in a logical, intelligible fashion. Once the whole phrase 2a,b is clearly in mind in this convincing form, it may be difficult to imagine it any other way.

And turning to the West-Frankish version, the fully symmetrical form of the same couplet now seems heavy in comparison.

> 1   Laudes deo
> 2a   omnis sexus consona voce *dulces canant melodias crucifixo*
> 2b   Praecelso regi sine fine gratanter hunc paschale mysterium pie
>   (2a)   libantes preces ut decet
>   (2b)   et jubile constipantes.

> (All flesh sings praises to God, sweet songs for the crucified one,
>   with consonant voice, pouring out prayers, as is fitting,
>   to the king ever glorious,
>   thronging together in gratitude on this paschal feast,
>   devoutly and joyfully.)

One would like to omit the words *dulces canant melodias crucifixo* with their notes, and fortunately this can be done, since the words are redundant in the sense of the whole. A verb is necessary to replace *canant*, but—fortunately again—that is provided by MS 1084, which gives *consonat* as a variant for *consona*.

> (restored)
> Laudes deo
> omnis sexus consonat voce, libantes preces ut decet
> praecelso regi sine fine, gratanter hunc paschale mysterium pie
>   et jubile constipantes.

> (All flesh sings praises to God, pouring out prayers,
>   as is fitting, to the king ever glorious, . . .)

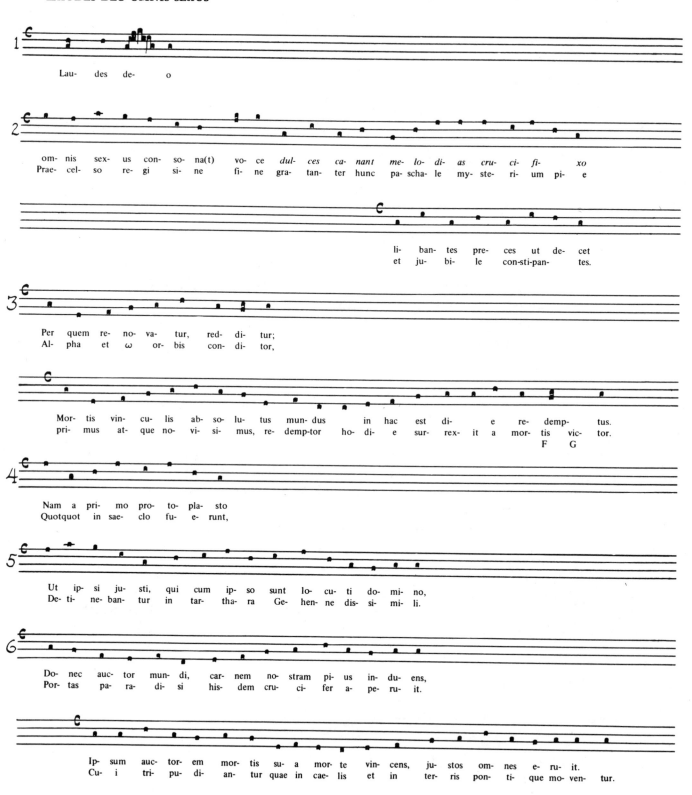

1. Lau- des de- o

2. om- nis sex- us con- so- na(t) vo- ce *dul- ces ca- nant* me- lo- di- as cru- ci- fi- *xo*
   Prae- cel- so re- gi si- ne fi- ne gra- tan- ter hunc pa- scha- le my- ste- ri- um pi- e

li- ban- tes pre- ces ut de- cet
et ju- bi- le con-sti-pan- tes.

3. Per quem re- no- va- tur, red- di- tur;
   Al- pha et ω or- bis con- di- tor,

Mor- tis vin- cu- lis ab- so- lu- tus mun- dus in hac est di- e re- demp- tus.
pri- mus at- que no- vi- si- mus, re- demp- tor ho- di- e sur- rex- it a mor- tis vic- tor.
F G

4. Nam a pri- mo pro- to- pla- sto
   Quot- quot in sae- clo fu- e- runt,

5. Ut ip- si ju- sti, qui cum ip- so sunt lo- cu- ti do- mi- no,
   De- ti- ne- ban- tur in tar- tha- ra Ge- hen- ne dis- si- mi- li.

6. Do- nec auc- tor mun- di, car- nem no- stram pi- us in- du- ens,
   Por- tas pa- ra- di- si his- dem cru- ci- fer a- pe- ru- it.

Ip- sum auc- tor- em mor- tis su- a mor- te vin- cens, ju- stos om- nes e- ru- it.
Cu- i tri- pu- di- an- tur quae in cae- lis et in ter- ris pon- ti- que mo- ven- tur.

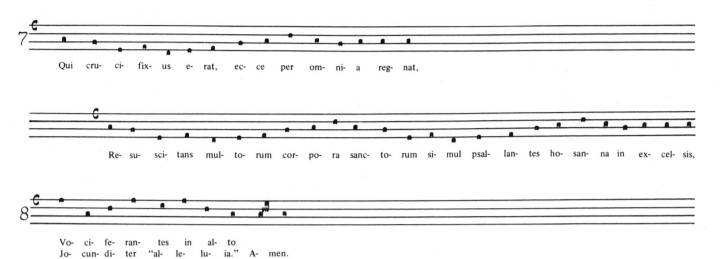

7 Qui cru- ci- fix- us e- rat, ec- ce per om- ni- a reg- nat,

Re- su- sci- tans mul- to- rum cor- po- ra sanc- to- rum si- mul psal- lan- tes ho- san- na in ex- cel- sis,

8 Vo- ci- fe- ran- tes in al- to
Jo- cun- di- ter "al- le- lu- ia." A- men.

It is important to be clear about what we have done. A passage has been taken out of the West-Frankish version because it was not provided for in Notker's plan (whose witness is earlier by at least a hundred years). Once excised, the passage is seen to be redundant and can easily be imagined as an interpolation, made in order to bring about exact parallelism. This process naturally suggests that we could be suspicious of other redundancies, which have often been taken as a trademark—and an objectionable one—of Aquitanian proses. But the prospect of excising redundancy wherever it might appear opens up possibilities too far-reaching to contemplate with calmness. To be anything more than arbitrary, such restoration has to be submitted to the objective criterion of conformity to Notker's version. To put it more strongly, the essential thing is to restore the West-Frankish versions to Notker's plan, if that can be accomplished without doing violence to the West-Frankish version as we have it. If a reduction in wordiness results, that is a fortunate result of the process, not a justification.

Notker's text provides only one line for phrase 3 (*misit huc . . . patriae*), while the West-Frankish version provides two.

3a Per quem renovatur, redditur: mortis vinculis absolutus mundus
   in hæc est die redemptus.
3b Alpha et Ω, orbis conditor, primus atque novissimus, redemptor
   hodie surrexit a mortis victor.

Given the possibility of interpolations such as the one just studied in phrase 2, we can now ask whether one is present in phrase 3. That is, here, too, Notker's version may faithfully represent the plan of the melody as he found it in his model.

As far as the whole sense of the West-Frankish text is concerned, lines 3a and 3b have

Laudes deo concinat (Notker)

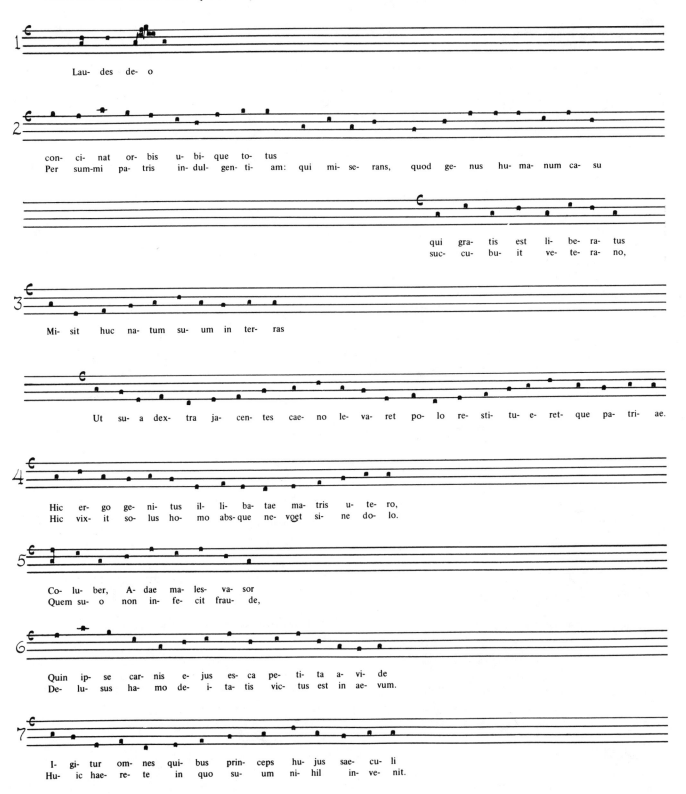

1. Lau- des de- o

con- ci- nat or- bis u- bi- que to- tus
Per sum-mi pa- tris in- dul- gen- ti- am: qui mi- se- rans, quod ge- nus hu- ma- num ca- su

qui gra- tis est li- be- ra- tus
suc- cu- bu- it ve- te- ra- no,

3. Mi- sit huc na- tum su- um in ter- ras

Ut su- a dex- tra ja- cen- tes cae- no le- va- ret po- lo re- sti- tu- e- ret- que pa- tri- ae.

4. Hic er- go ge- ni- tus il- li- ba- tae ma- tris u- te- ro,
Hic vix- it so- lus ho- mo abs- que ne- voet si- ne do- lo.

5. Co- lu- ber, A- dae ma- les- va- sor
Quem su- o non in- fe- cit frau- de,

6. Quin ip- se car- nis e- jus es- ca pe- ti- ta a- vi- de
De- lu- sus ha- mo de- i- ta- tis vic- tus est in ae- vum.

7. I- gi- tur om- nes qui- bus prin- ceps hu- jus sae- cu- li
Hu- ic hae- re- te in quo su- um ni- hil in- ve- nit.

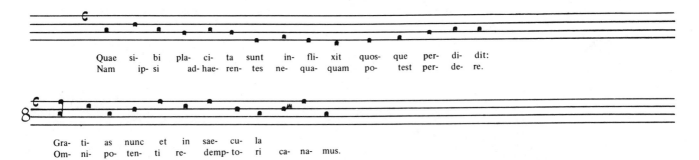

Quae si- bi pla- ci- ta sunt in- fli- xit quos- que per- di- dit:
Nam ip- si ad-hae- ren- tes ne- qua- quam po- test per- de- re.

Gra- ti- as nunc et in sae- cu- la
Om- ni- po- ten- ti re- demp-to- ri ca- na- mus.

about the same meaning and function: they both introduce into the text the theme of re-demption.

3a Through whom [all flesh] is made new, restored. The world, freed from the chains of death, is today redeemed.

3b Alpha and Omega, creator of the world, the first and the last, today the Re-deemer has risen from the dead as victor.

Because of their approximate equivalence, and because each is syntactically independent of the other, either 3a or 3b could be omitted to bring the plan of the text into conformity with Notker's, with immediate reduction of wordiness. This particular kind of wordi-ness, of course, has long been associated with sequence texts: we assume it to be a natural concomitant of the paired melodic phrases—and beyond that it has been compared (if not ascribed) to the *parallelismus membrorum* of the psalms. So perhaps we are not so ready to find an interpolation here. Still, there is Notker's witness. What must be remembered is that if, with Notker's help, we succeed in uncovering his models as he knew them, we have lit-tle reason to expect them to exhibit all the features of the standard sequence, since we may well be looking at sequences that were composed during a formative stage of development.

Which is to be assumed as the interpolation, 3a or 3b? Although the two lines deliver the same message, they have a difference in emphasis: line 3a speaks of the world redeemed, line 3b of the Redeemer and his eternal attributes. Line 3a seems to fit more smoothly into the whole train of thought, which began by speaking of "all flesh," and goes on to men-tion "as many as had been in the world since the first-made [Adam]." The Redeemer and his acts properly enter the scene at line 6a, *Donec auctor mundi*; the tighter construction would be obtained by omitting reference to him in the nominative until that point.

The continuity of 3a with the rest is manifest in the syntactic relationship to 2: *per quem* introduces clauses that continue the thought of the opening lines and are dependent upon them. Notker's text runs on at exactly the same point.

(Notker)
1 Laudes deo
2a concinat orbis ubique totus, qui gratis est liberatus

2b   Per summi patris indulgentiam: qui miserans, quod genus humanum casu
                    succubuit veterano,
3   Misit huc natum suum in terras, ut sua dextra jacentes caeno
              levaret polo restitueretque patriae.

(1   The whole world sings praises to God, (for) it has been freed by grace
2b   through the favor of the Father most high, who, taking pity that mankind had
     fallen prey to the ancient curse,
3   sent his own Son here to earth, that he might raise on high those who lay in
     filth, and restore them to their true home.)

In both versions the continuity of thought from 2 to 3 tends to blur the division of the musi-cal phrases—or to link them together. In addition, the West-Frankish version has a gram-matical stop soon after the start of 3, at *redditur*, with a cadence FG G. The outcome is not as happy as Notker's texting of the sub-phrase structure of 3, *Misit . . . , ut sua . . .* , with a fine placement of the verb *levaret* to support the melodic extension of the phrase, and a final clause in apposition (*restitueretque patriae*) to fit the return of the opening sub-phrase.

```
      G D  E  FG  AG  F  G G
3     Mi-sit huc natum suum in terras
              G FD  E  C D E F  G  A
              ut sua dextra jacentes caeno
              G FD  E C
              levaret polo
        D E FG A  G   FGG
        restitu-eretque patriae.
```

This is happy indeed; was it the lack of such solutions in the West-Frankish version that moved Notker to say in his Preface that he found the Western texts—and he was speaking of this one in particular—*jam vitiate*?

So, in spite of a certain awkwardness of detail, line 3a of the West-Frankish version seems to carry the piece forward better than 3b. And other details speak in its favor against 3b. Compared to Notker's 3, the West-Frankish 3b has an extra C as *hodie*, an extra G at *surrexit*. (All sources agree, incidentally, that the third word of 3b is sung "O" as a single syllable.)

Finally, 3b introduces a slightly different style of text, for the way it heaps up attri-butes in apposition—"Alpha and Omega, Creator of the world, the first and the last, Re-deemer, victor"—contrasts with the direct narrative style that otherwise prevails through-out the text. There is, however, a certain consistency in the language of those interpolations that helps integrate them: the line 3b seems to be more in place coming after 3a (and after the pleonastic interpolation in 2a) than it would be itself in place of 3a.

If we decide that 3b is an interpolation like that in 2a, and if we set these two inter-polations aside, the story being told emerges much more clearly. It is the Harrowing of Hell, the section of the Gospel of Nicodemus commonly called *descensus ad inferos* which circulated in Latin translation from the fifth or sixth centuries.[1] The gist of the story is that between the crucifixion and the resurrection, Christ forced open the gates of hell, set up his cross as a mark of everlasting dominion even in that place of sin and death, and led forth a triumphal procession of patriarchs, prophets, and others who had died before the time of his coming to earth. A reference to the story was imbedded in the Creeds—"he descended into hell." That the story itself (if not the particular texts printed Tischendorf, *Evangelia apocrypha*) was known in the West between the sixth and ninth centuries is shown by a passage from Bede's *Hymnum canamus gloriae*.[2]

> 7. Nam plurimos ab inferi
> Portis reduxit spiritu
> Multos et ipso corpore
> De fauce mortis eruit.

Other such witnesses could easily be supplied.

In the West-Frankish LAUDES DEO OMNIS SEXUS the narrative proper starts in line 4a.

> 4a Nam a primo protoplasto
>   b Quotquot in saeclo fuerunt,
> 5a Ut ipsi justi, qui cum ipso sunt locuti domino,
>   b Detinebantur in tarthara Gehenne dissimili.
> 6a Donec auctor mundi, carnem nostram pius induens,
>   ipsum auctorem mortis sua morte vincens, justos omnes eruit.
>   b Portas paradisi hisdem crucifer aperuit.
>   Cui tripudiantur quae in caelis et in terris pontique moventur.

> (For beginning with the first-fashioned,
> as many as had been in the world,
> such as those righteous ones, who walked with God himself,
> were confined to Hell.
> But the founder of the world, always holy, putting on our flesh,
>   conquering by his death the founder of death itself,
>   raked up all those righteous ones.
> The cross-bearer opened for them the gates of paradise.
>   For him rejoices whatever moves in heaven, on the earth or sea.)

Protoplasto, "first-fashioned," is a special appellation for Adam, the first man; and Adam is particularly mentioned in the apocryphal accounts of the Harrowing of Hell. Perhaps the

1. Texts edited by Constantin von Tischendorf, *Evangelia Apocrypha* (1876), version "A" p. 391, version "B" p. 422; translations and comments by Montague Rhodes James, *The Apocryphal New Testament* (Oxford 1924), pp. 94ff., 117ff. See also Karl Young, "The Harrowing of Hell in Liturgical Drama," *Transactions of the Wisconsin Academy of Sciences, Arts, and Letters*, XVI (1909), Pt. ii, no. 1, pp. 889–947; E. K. Chambers, *The Medieval Stage* (Oxford 1903), II, pp. 73–74; and especially E. K. Rand, "Sermo de Confusione Diaboli," *Modern Philology* II (1904), pp. 266–267.

2. *Anal.hymn.* 50, p. 103; a ninth-century version, in elegant hexameters that contrast strongly with our prose, by Audradus in his *De Fonte Vitae, Poetae latini aevi carolini* III (ed. L. Traube), pp. 81–82.

author also had in mind a stanza of Venantius Fortunatus from the famous song *Pange lingua gloriosi lauream certaminis*.[3] Indeed, he could hardly have kept it out of his mind if he knew anything at all about the European tradition of Christian festival poetry. Stanza 2 (which we will need soon again) goes,

> De parentis protoplasti fraude factor condolens,
> Quando pomi noxialis morte morsu corruit,
> Ipse lignum tunc notavit, damna ligni ut solveret.
>
> (The Creator, having pity on the trick played on the first-made man,
> when he succumbed to death from eating the deadly apple,
> himself set out the Cross, that he might do away the curse of the tree.)

Lines 4b and 5a identify the patriarchs and prophets; line 5b places them in Tartarus. *Gehenne dissimili* is obscure.

Line 6a recounts the deed itself: *ipsum auctorem mortis sua morte vincens*, as much as it recalls the more familiar Pauline texts from Romans 6 or I Corinthians 15, seems rather to spring from II Timothy 1, 10,

> . . . qui destruxit quidem mortem,
> illuminavit autem vitam et incorruptionem . . .

and not directly but through the Easter Preface,[4]

> Qui mortem nostram moriendo
> distruxit et vitam resurgendo . . .
>
> (Who by his death hath destroyed
> death, and by his rising to life again . . .)

Eruit is the key word for the Harrowing—"he raked up" or "ripped out" all the righteous out of hell. Line 6b carries the brief account to its conclusion and prepares the return to the theme of celebration and the singing of praises, so that the prose ends naturally with an *alleluia*.

> 6b . . . Cui tripudiantur quae in caelis et in terris pontique moventur.
>   7 Qui crucifixus erat, ecce per omnia regnat,
>   Resuscitans multorum corpora sanctorum
>   simul psallentes hosanna in excelsis,
> 8a Vociferantes in alto
>   b Jocunditer "alleluia." Amen.
>
>   (For him rejoices whatever moves in heaven, on the earth and sea.
>   He who was crucified, behold, he reigns over all,
>   raising up many bodies of the saints,
>   all singing together "Hosanna in the highest,"
>   Shouting joyfully "Alleluia" on high. Amen.)

3. *Anal.hymn.* 50, p. 71.

4. L. C. Mohlberg, *Liber Sacramentorum Romanae ecclesiae. Rerum ecclesiasticarum documenta* (Series maior, Fontes, IV) 466 (p. 77).

Within this context it seems evident that line 7, which is lacking in Notker's plan, is something of a detour and redundancy. *Multorum corpora sanctorum* refers to the Gospel account (Matthew 27, 52), which certainly is in keeping with the theme, as is the *Hosanna*; but both things have already been said. Line 7 adds fullness and sonorous language, but the story comes to a proper conclusion just as well without it. Actually, line 7 seems to be entirely patched together from other sources: *Qui crucifixus...regnat* is a direct quote from Fortunatus' processional hymn *Salve festa dies*:[5]

Qui crucifixus erat, Deus, ecce per omnia regnat.

And the idea for *multorum corpora sanctorum* seems to have been inspired by its appearance in another hymn, *Gratuletur omnis caro*, where it appears as a consequence of the Harrowing.[6] But this poem (ascribed to Rhabanus by the *Analecta hymnica*) might be no older than the interpolation itself.

As yet another detail, the cadence F G G at the ends of the lines 3a,b 6a,b, 7, varies, and seemingly with consistency. First come the neumes, then the purely syllabic forms, finally with three G's instead of two.

	F FG G	FG G
3a	red-dí-tur	re-démp-tus
b	cón-di-tor	

		F G G
		mór-tis víc-tor

	F́ G G	F G G G
6a	ín-du-ens	é- ru- it
b	a-pé- ru- it	pontí-que mo- vén-tur

	F G G G	F G G G
7	óm-ni- a ré-gnat	in ex-cel-sis

Pontique moventur does not seem a happy way of treating this cadential figure. If an artistic value is to be found at this point, could it perhaps be in the terminal function of these words? That is, if 7 did not follow, then the stumbling or dragging effect of *pontique moventur* could serve the purpose of bringing the melodic repetitions of phrase 6 to a close. It is the reiteration in 7 of the triple G's with their delayed accents that seems to call attention to the awkwardness. Notker tends to shorten the approaches to this cadence so that it is less in evidence at the end of his 7a,b; the triple G he avoids completely.

Line 7, then, is the third item in the West-Frankish version that can be identified as an interpolation. With the setting aside of these three items (part of 2a, 3b, 7) this version of LAUDES DEO is considerably reduced in bulk—though not of melodic material, which all appears elsewhere in the piece—and greatly enhanced in consistency of language, directness of syntax, clarity of purpose and content. In its reduced state, LAUDES DEO OMNIS SEXUS has an identity that otherwise might be obscured: the intent to tell—however briefly—

5. *Anal.hymn.* 50, p. 76 (line 37).
6. *Anal.hymn.* 50, p. 195.

an epic story is not compromised by attributes of praise or other pleonastic features. The evidence does not permit positive assertion that this is the original version, but this is the version we must use for a serious comparison with Notker's LAUDES DEO, for this is the one most likely to have fallen into his hands, whether through the mediation of the monk from Jumièges or in some other way.

Notker does not use the epic theme of the Harrowing of Hell; nonetheless, something about the way the West-Frankish text is laid out seems to guide him. Specifically, the texts in the two versions at phrase 4 (=Notker's 5) seem to be related, even though the texts of the surrounding phrases are not. Notker's text runs briefly through the *Heilsgeschichte*, the story of salvation: how God the Father took pity on man and his fall; how he sent his Son to be born of a virgin, how the Son lived without spot of sin and hence was able to conquer sin and redeem the world. In his line 5a, Notker refers to Adam, at the same point that the West-Frankish version speaks of the *protoplastus*, "first fashioned."

(Notker)

4a	Nam a primo protoplasto	5a	Coluber Adae malesuasor
		b	Quem suo non infecit fraude

Fraude suggests, perhaps, that Notker had caught the echo of Venantius' hymn,

> De parenti protoplasti fraude facta condolens
> Quando primi noxiali morsu mors incubuit,

similar language having already appeared in Notker's 2b, *miserans . . . succubuit*. In any case, Notker seems to have felt that Phrase 4 (= his 5) should have a pivotal function. Previously he has described the godhead, while at this point he introduces the antagonist, who is fooled by the "hook of divinity" (*hamo deitatis*). This expression, not so common, is elucidated by Von den Steinen: Death is fooled into trying to take the divine Christ (which he cannot do, and which results in his defeat) by Christ's human nature, with which the "hook of divinity" is baited. Von den Steinen's texts go back to the fifth century, and the theme, although not the expression, is suggested in the Gospel of Nicodemus. The near source (and for me the most important—not just for Notker's text but also for this and other West-Frankish texts) is an Ambrosian hymn, *Hic est dies versus Dei*.[7]

> Hamum sibi mors devoret
> Suisque se nodis liget
> Moriatur vita omnium
> Resurgat ut vita omnium.
>
> Cum mors per omnes transeat
> Omnes resurgant mortui
> Consumpta mors ictu suo
> Perisse se solam gemat.

7. *Anal.hymn.* 50, p. 16.

Notker felt, apparently, that the account of the godhead should be longer, in particular that he should be described as being alone "without spot of sin." But rather than allow these lines to fall under the melody of the West-Frankish phrase 4, Notker made (or had made) a musical interpolation of his own, so that the melody of the West-Frankish 4 appears in his version as 5. This conclusion, at least, follows from the reconstruction traced so far, unless we wish to imagine that the music of Notker's phrase 5 was once in the West-Frankish melody but was dropped before the time of the extant versions. This is a perfectly possible explanation, but there seems no pressing reason to adopt it; that is, there is no serious gap in the West-Frankish text at the point—indeed, the interpolation of 3b was remarkable precisely because it was redundant. Of course, the presence of irregularity and interpolation at 3 immediately suggests a connection to Notker's 4: perhaps they are structural equivalents, alternate solutions linked by textual or musical transformations that have left no specific trace in the manuscript readings. It seems as likely, however, that they are independent. The West-Frankish interpolation of 3b is most simply understood as a transformation of a single into a double, while Notker's interpolation of his 4 can be regarded as an extension of melodic material of 3.

If Notker had a clear sense of a climax in his phrase 6, he has an equally clear sense of its aftermath in 7, which he begins with a firm *Igitur*, "Therefore . . ." and proceeds to draw the moral.

(Notker)
7a   Igitur omnes quibus princeps huius saeculi
          quae sibi placita sunt inflixit quosque perdidit:
  b   Huic haerete in quo suum nihil invenit.
          Nam ipsi adhaerentes nequaquam potest perdere.

    (Therefore, all ye whom the prince of this world deals with
          as he pleases, and whom he slays;
    Cleave rather to him over whom that prince has no dominion.
          For those clinging to him cannot die.)

One may or may not appreciate the imperative mood of the moral (*haerete*, "Cleave fast!") or its presence in an otherwise festive piece; furthermore, one may find that the language of the whole couplet is over-complex for its hortative, moralising purpose. But Notker was presumably still a young poet; and from a structural, rhetorical point of view phrase 7 has a telling effect.

Language, even more than structure, seems a preoccupation of Notker's in this piece. His choice of words is distinctive right from the start—or rather, from the third word—and is best compared to the West-Frankish version in 2a, where the content of the two versions is still close.

1–2a   Laudes deo omnis sexus consonat voce libantes preces ut decet
(Notker)
1–2a   Laudes deo concinat orbis ubique totus qui gratis est liberatus

2b   Praecelso regi sine fine gratanter hunc paschale mysterium pie
                 et jubile constipantes,

(Notker)

2b   Per summi patris indulgentiam qui miserans quod genus humanum casu
                 succubuit veterano,

Concinat ("sing together") is a more elegant word than *consonat*; at least, it has a more classical usage. *Orbis ubique totus*, or *orbis universus*, Notker's first version as given in his Preface, is far grander than *omnis sexus*, which is similarly not classical in the sense intended here. And *qui gratis est liberatus*, which follows euphoniously to close the line, obviously pleased Notker more than the forceful alternatives strung together somewhat awkwardly in the West-Frankish line 3a. The difference in diction could perhaps be suggested by saying that Notker was concerned to sound "patrician" rather than "patristic". He must have been distressed at the West-Frankish mixture of homely, direct, or awkward syntax with facile or stereotyped expressions such as *sine fine*, *pie et jubile*, *primo protoplasto*, and occasional extravagancies such as *constipantes* ("pressing" or "crowding together"). In any case his own diction is elegant, elevated, refined. His syntax, too, consistently aims at elegance, and is more apt to fall into complexity (as suggested in lines 7a,b) than awkwardness.

Another comparison is provided by 8, where (as in his 5) Notker abruptly moves close to the West-Frankish version as if the particular complex of words and music was at that point important for some formal reason.

                                 (Notker)

8a   Vociferantes in alto   8a   Gratias nunc atque in saecula
  b   Jocunditer Alleluia. Amen.   b   Omnipotenti redemptori canamus.

The West-Frankish text goes directly from *vociferantes* ("crying aloud" or even "screaming" or "bawling" in classical usage), *in alto* ("on high"), *jocunditer* ("cheerfully," "with delight") to the formulas of celebration, *Alleluia, amen*. "Screaming alleluia with delight on high?" Notker has us "sing thanks, now and forever, to the Almighty Redeemer"; no *amen*, instead an elegant placement of the verb, *canamus*, at the melodic flourish that hangs at the end of the couplet.

It would be easy to mistake the lack of classical evenness and refinement in the West-Frankish text for lack of skill and control. A West-Frankish hand also made the melody, and that was good enough for Notker. Perhaps we could take Notker's expression of repugnance in his Preface quite as a matter of artistic preference. The West-Frankish text is certainly non-classical, but what are its positive features? In terms of pure sound—vowels and consonants—the West-Frankish text flows along in a remarkably easy way. In fact, one of the things one might object to is the facility of sound compared to the loftiness of theme; the author manages to rattle through the Harrowing of Hell with almost unseemly ease, which is especially noticeable in singing the piece.

Little or none of the regularity of poetic meter or rhyme being present, it is relatively difficult to point to the sources of the fluidity of sound. One way to start is to notice the lapse into *hiatus* (adjacent vowels at the end of one word and the beginning of the next) in the interpolation 3b.

3b   Alpha / et Ω / orbis conditor

The second hiatus, Ω / *orbis*, is so glaring it must be deliberate. There is only one other case of hiatus in the whole text, at line 2b.

2b   pie / et jubile constipantes.

There the hiatus is not only less obvious, but occurs at a point in the melody where a very slight articulation at the end of the extension is welcome. (There is one other case in the interpolation 7, *hosanna / in excelsis*, but that hardly counts as the work of an author, nor does *alleluia / amen*.)

Avoiding hiatus is a negative factor in euphony; more positive factors are alliteration and assonance. It is at this point that the discussion becomes delicate, for the author's treatment of these factors may be more unconscious than conscious—and so irregular as to be difficult to point out convincingly. Consider line 3a, which in spite of its syntactic awkwardness flows easily in terms of sound; the sounds that seem to me to contribute to the flow are expressed in the letters above the line.

```
                      m                        m
                          u        u u    u  u
     e    e         e        is  i   is
         re-  -tur re-  -tur  -r     l-     l-
3a   Per quem renovatur, redditur; mortis vinculis absolutus mundus
                          u
           e    e  e
                r
        in hac est die redemptus
```

The *-tur* endings at the end of the first sub-phrase are obvious; but beyond that there seems to be a predominance of *e* and *r* in that part of the line, then a shift to *is* and *us* in the middle of the line, finally to *e* again at the end.

These are purely local instances of alliteration and assonance: typically the same sound prevails in several adjacent (or nearly adjacent) words, giving them a continuity; then a shift occurs—sometimes subtle enough to be called a modulation—to another prevailing sound. Arching over these local continuities there may be other repetitions of sound almost well-defined enough to be called rhymes, such as

red- ditur   } *red-* empt- *tus*
              mun-*dus* }

If the assonance *-us . . . -us* can be called an end-rhyme, then *red-* . . . *red-* might perhaps be thought of as a *Stabreim*.

Are these continuities and echoes really a purposive aspect of the text? Similar things could perhaps be picked out of almost any succession of Latin words. And any specific arrangement would be altered by substitution of words or changes in word order, both of which occur in variant readings. But that, it seems to me, is less important than the fact that in any given version the words do appear in the order they do, and have a certain effect, whatever it may be. Some lines are more euphonious than others, some lines make more use of alliteration and assonance. Line 4a, for example, shows more than 4b; (but notice that in a short line such as 4, if 4b contained the sonorities of 4a the result might well have the effect of rhyming, scanning verse.)

Line 5a has a relatively intricate pattern.

5a Ut ipsi justi, qui cum ipso sunt locuti domino

The larger rhythm of the line seems based upon the way *ipso* echoes *ipsi*; thus sounds that are closely linked at the start (*ipsi, justi*) are later spread out over the whole line (. . . *ipso . . . locuti*).

        ipsi

                                ipso
                justi

                                        -cuti

The sound *i* gradually gives way to *o*. But the next line, 5b, makes much less use of such arrangements.

Notker's text has no less than five cases of hiatus.

    4b Hic vixit solus homo / absque naevo / et sine dolo
    6a Quin ipse carnis eius esca petita / avide
    7b Huic haerete / in quo suum nihil invenit
            nam ipsi / adhaerentes nequaquam potest perdere.

Of these only the juxtaposition of a's in 6a, with the second accented, calls attention to itself—and is perhaps attributable to the rough sense of the line.

    But instead he himself [the snake], cheated of the food of
        his flesh, *greedily* sought . . .

In 4b the use of hiatus helps emphasize important words.

    4b Hic vixit solus homo—absque naevo et sine dolo
    (He lived as the only man without spot and without sin)

The first hiatus in 7b corresponds to a comma; only the second is without apparent reason, but is barely noticeable.

One would not expect to find *elision* (or dropping of a final vowel before a following initial vowel) since elision is generally a concern of verse, where it may be required by syllable count or quantity. Ordinarily "prose" would not require elision; but occasionally elision seems to be suggested nonetheless in the case of an extra syllable in one line of a couplet, with no extra note provided by the neumes. Such a case occurs in Notker's 4b; one of the two cases of hiatus—presumably the second—must be elided to preserve the syllable count (*naev' et*). (Cases of unequal count in couplets occur sometimes, and are usually reflected in the pitch count as well, so we should not merely assume that an extra note is to be provided.)

The smoothing, homogenizing effects of alliteration and assonance are not as evident in Notker's text as in the West-Frankish one, due, it seems, to the more elevated diction and more complex syntax. Notker's language here has a more studied effect: it does not at first flow as easily; only upon close examination, perhaps, does the use of alliteration and assonance become evident. In line 2a (the one closest in content to the model) these elements are, to be sure, obvious; but they are less so in lines 2b and 3. That is to say, a line of Notker's typically contains a greater variety of sounds; there is less concentration on any particular sound in any given group of words. There is, however, an awareness of the effects of alliteration and assonance, and a discreet use of them, subject always to the criterion of smooth variety. And following his ciceronian models, Notker uses quasi-rhyming sounds mainly in connection with cadences, but again, discreetly.

<pre>
              um   u
                         en am
2b   Per summi patris indulgentiam
                        u   um um   u u u u
             an   en   an   an
           qui miserans quod genus humanum casu succubuit veterano,
3   Misit huc natum suum in terras
          ut sua dextra jacentes caeno
                            -aret p'   -eret   p'
                         levaret polo restitueretque patriae.
</pre>

The use of *Hic* to pair 4a,b is obvious; but the construction of the couplet 5a,b is more subtle.

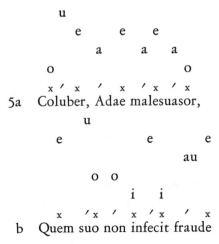

<pre>
           u
        e   e   e
           a   a   a
      o   o
      x ' x   ' x ' x ' x
5a   Coluber, Adae malesuasor,
            u
      e   e   e
                     au
         o o
             i   i
      x   ' x ' x ' x   ' x
  b Quem suo non infecit fraude
</pre>

Here the succession of vowels is arranged in pairs by accents (´) alternating with unaccented (x) syllables. The series

```
x ´ x ´ x ´ x ´ x
o u e, a e, a e, a o
```

seems to generate a certain continuity, which, however, is echoed only indistinctly at the start of 5b, where *non* is a prominent element. At the end of this line, successive accented f's provide a *Stabreim*, while the last word *fraude* is a faint, but distinct, echo of the last two syllables of the preceding line, *suasor*. Such an echo would, of course, not constitute a rhyme in verse, but this is not verse.

A discussion of word accents, and of the rhythms that may emerge from their arrangement, is apt to be even more delicate than the discussion of assonance, for any line of Latin presents a series of alternating accented and unaccented syllables which will have more or less sense of rhythm according to one's taste. The great majority of Latin words in use here seem to have two or three syllables, with relatively few monosyllables or very long words; hence accents occur automatically almost every two or three syllables—and almost any series involving a free mixture of groups of twos and threes can be understood to have a rhythmic flow. But that, I think, is precisely the point: a rhythm is there in the text; the question does not concern its presence but rather how it is used, how the flow of accents is related to other factors such as word placement, syntax, and eventually to musical pitch.

More or less normal procedure for the West-Frankish version can be found in lines 1 and 2.

```
      ´    x   ´x ´   x   ´ x   ´ x x   ´ x   x´   x   ´ x (x)  ´ x
1,2a Laudes deo omnis sexus consonat voce, libantes preces ut decet
       x ´ x   ´ x ´ x ´ x   x´  x  (´)   x  ´ x  x  ´ x x   ´ x
2b   praecelso regi sine fine gratanter hunc paschale mysterium pie
         (x)  ´ x x  x   x ´  x
         et jubile constipantes.
```

The accent of monosyllables (for example, *ut* or *hunc*) is determinate only in context; where an accent is suggested, it is placed in parentheses. From the beginning through the first half of 2a, there is a predominance of groups of two syllables (´ x), with only one group

```
    ´  x x
```
of three (*consonat*); it is nicely placed, and is echoed by another towards the end of the line

```
´ x  x
```
(*preces ut*). The pattern of accents at these two places happens to be the most common of the patterns known as *cursus*—the one called *cursus planus*.[8]

```
   ´   x  x   ´ x        ´ x x  ´ x
   consonat voce . . . preces ut decet
```

although the division of the words is not the most usual one for this cursus (´x / x ´x).

```
                                          ´ x   x
```
The only other group of three in lines 1,2a occurs at the semi-cadence (*voce*, *li-*) and has a different status, since we can assume a slight pause at that point; also, of course, the neume CD on *vo-(ce)* alters the flow of syllables. All things considered, we would better

8. See M. Nicolau, *L'Origine du cursus rhythmique et les débuts de l'accent d'intensité en latin* (Paris 1930).

group *li-* with *-bantes* as a word, observing that it starts the sub-phrase with an unaccented syllable.

Clearly there is little correspondence between 2a and 2b in patterns of accents, except for *vóce* = *fíne* at the half-cadence, *libán* = *et jú-* and *décet* = *-pántes* at the end. The whole last sub-phrase takes the form of another cursus, *cursus velox*,

    ´ x x x   x ´ x
jubile constipantes

which is an argument for not assuming a secondary accent on *con-*. In any case, there is no primary accent on (*jubi-*) *le*, hence 2a and 2b end with different patterns to the same music.

Perhaps more important than comparing 2b to 2a is noticing how one follows the other. *Praecélso* begins with an unstressed syllable, like *libántes*; so does the extension, *gratánter*, then the conclusion, *et jú-*, which contributes to the overall continuity of 1 and 2a,b. The repetition of groups of three during the extension (*paschále mystérium*) leads well into the four unstressed syllables of the cursus velox. Conscious or not, the rhythm of 1,2a,b assumes an effective shape.

In line 3a, the accents also carry out the sub-phrase structure. Similar patterns appear at FG G cadences, and, indeed, going back several syllables before. The beginning (*Per quem*) can be understood to have the same pattern as the second beginning, *mórtis*. But after *mortis*, the pattern varies during *vinculis absolutus mundus*, just as does the melody.

Lines 4a and b have as little correspondence as 2a and b; 4a is all twos, 4b all threes.

4a Nám a prímo pròtoplásto
  b Quótquot in saéclo fuérunt,
5a Ut ípsi jústi qúi cum ípso sŭ̃nt locúti dómino,
  b Detìnebántur in tártara Gehenne dissímili.

Again, it seems they should be read in succession rather than compared; for there is no real cadence at the end of 4, and the unstressed syllable at the start of 5a encourages the continuation. Then the twos in 5a, their consistency set off by the intricate play of vowels, seem to pick up the rhythm of 4a. Lines 5a,b correspond more or less in accent pattern, except for *Gehenne*, which, being a Hebrew word, has an indeterminate accent in medieval Latin. But the cadences correspond, syllabifying with their threes the twos that appeared with neumes at the cadences in line 3.

The last word in a cadence is conveniently designated by the standard terms of classical prosody *paroxytone* and *proparoxytone*; paroxytone if the word ends in ´ x, proparoxytone if ´ x x. Hence in line 5, a proparoxytone cadence replaces the paroxytone of line 3.

Line 6 brings an unusual concentration of twos.

6a Dónec áuctor múndi cárnem nóstram píus índuens
    Ípsum auctórem mórtis súa mórte víncens jústos ómnes éruit

The cadences, *píus índuens* and *ómnes éruit*, continue the proparoxytones of line 5; otherwise all groups are twos, except for *Ipsum auc-* at the start of the second sub-phrase. On the one hand, it seems as though the succession of twos were almost intrinsic to the melody;

that is, it may be possible to imagine the melody grouped differently, but the grouping in twos seems the most obvious, the simplest possible grouping. On the other hand, the group of three at *Ipsum auc-* seems to be just the right means to highlight the slight difference in melodic shape at this point. The result of the rhythmic highlight and the varied melodic repeat acting together is a completely appropriate emphasis on the words *Ipsum auctorem*, which are themselves an emphatic, varied repeat of the start of the line.

6   Donec auctor mundi . . . *ipsum auctorem* mortis . . .

     But then the founder of the world (conquering) the founder of
         death himself . . .

This varied repeat is echoed formally in the play on *mortis sua morte* that follows immediately. Textual and musical materials of this line seem completely integrated.

Line 6b is less regular, more complex—perhaps because the author knew better than to reiterate a good thing. Yet line 6b does not actually contradict the grouping in twos that seems so intrinsic to the melody; by choosing words with one, three, or four syllables, the author weakens or suppresses some of the accents, and also relocates some of the breaks between words. In this way the regularity of

6a   Dónec/áuctor/múndi/cárnem/nóstram/píus/índuens

is replaced by

6b   Pórtas/pàradísi/hísdem/crúcifer/apéruit

The irregular cadence at the end of 6b, noticed before because of its dragging action, may perhaps be better understood in terms of the lesser regularity of the whole line as compared to 6a.

Notker seems to follow similar rhythmic principles, applying them to produce different results. Just as the two lines of a couplet in the West-Frankish version do not usually coincide exactly in their patterns of accents, so the patterns in Notker's text are apt to differ from their West-Frankish model. There are, however, distinct points of similarity, patterns Notker apparently wished to preserve perhaps because he felt they were important for the identity of the melody, or because he admired their effect. The cursus velox, for example, at the end of line 2b (*júbile constipántes*) seems to have stuck in his ear, for he used it in 2a as well.

(Notker)
2a   grátis est liberátus
2b   succúbuit veteráno

He must also have liked the use of initial unstressed syllables in 1 and 2, which he often highlighted with monosyllables.

(Notker)
2a   . . . qui gratis . . .
2b   Per súmmi . . . qui míserans . . . quod génus . . .
                succúbuit . . .

As with the West-Frankish version, the result is an "upbeat" effect at the beginning of each sub-phrase, linking them together the more strongly.

Throughout the first period (which includes lines 1, 2a,b, 3), Notker's rhythms seem to express themselves most readily in the pattern ′ x x ′ x; it appears frequently, (as marked below) and is skillfully modulated into the cadences—both those in cursus velox and the more complex one at the end of the period.

(Notker)

1   Laudes deo
      ′ x x ′ x | ′ x x   ′ x

2   Concinat orbis ubique totus qui gratis est liberatus

b   Per summi patris indulgentiam
                           ′ x   x   ′ x | ′ x
                qui miserans quod genus humanum casu
                      x ′ x x x x ′ x
                    succubuit veterano

   ′ x   x   ′ x | ′ x x   ′ x
3   Misit huc natum suum in terras
         ′   x x ′ x | ′ x x ′ x
    ut suo dextra jacentes caeno levaret
    polo restitueretque patriae

By his repeated use of this pattern, Notker seems to exercise a tighter control—or at any rate a more obvious control—over the details of the rhythmic flow. The result seems more terse than the West-Frankish version; at the same time the West-Frankish version seems to run along a little more casually; it seems to traverse the distance from one cadence to another more easily.

Notker's treatment of the melodic cadence (FGG, or CDD) is less consistent than the West-Frankish model and is at variance with it. In syllabifying the semi-cadence in 2a, he makes it paroxytone.

           B A C D D
  2a   u- bi -que tó-tus
(but: 2b   in-dul-gén-ti- am

The same ambivalence appears in 3,

           A G F G G
  3   sú-um in térras
(but: -etque pá-tri-ae)

and again in 4.

           F G G
  4a   ú- te-ro
   b   dó-lo

This seems as if he were going out of his way to vary the accents at the cadences.

In the latter half of the piece there are strings of twos comparable to those that prevail in the latter half of the West-Frankish version—but not at exactly the same places. In his lines 4b, 5a, 5b, 6a, 6b, Notker's use of groups of two, often in conjunction with two-syllable words, contrasts markedly with the first part of the piece. But in his lines 7a,b (= the West-Frankish 6a,b where the twos were most in evidence) Notker has introduced a group of three at the start of the line with the help of a slight melodic change (E is omitted), changing much of the effect: the group of three, *Igitur*, is thrust forward, the twos are less emphatic; in the second part of the line (where the West-Frankish version had a striking group of three) Notker has only an upbeat, the subsequent group of three then only providing internal variety.

(Notker)
7a Ígitur ómnes quíbus prínceps hújus sáeculi
    Quae síbi plácita súnt infléxit quósque pérdidit

In passing (and for future reference) it is interesting that Notker's text, which we know was made subsequent to the other text, fits the melody very well, in some cases seemingly better than the West-Frankish text we have supposed to be his model. In other words, a close relationship between a given set of words and a melody does not demonstrate that those words were the first to be composed to that melody. It is not too hard to imagine that an author such as Notker would be in a position to make a superior texting of a melody precisely because he could see how a prior texting worked out; he could the better observe the line of the music and judge which kinds of syntax did, or did not, lend themselves to its contours. On the other hand, of course, the later setting is not necessarily the better one, since—here as elsewhere—it all depends on the skill of the author.

There is no particular reason to expect a melody written for a "prose" to exhibit any of the structural symmetries or repetitions so often characteristic of verse, and yet this melody does. In its larger design the melody shows more than one kind of repetition (not counting the repetitions associated with the couplet structure). Referring to LAUDES DEO OMNIS SEXUS, phrase 4 recurs as 8, almost as if it were a refrain. Furthermore, the material of 3 makes an approximate return at 6, as well as at 7 (and Notker's 4). The use of lower and higher registers helps set off the phrases 3 and 6, which always move in the lower register, from the refrain-like phrases 4 and 8, which move between G and the C a fourth above. The remaining melodic material seems to orient itself easily around these higher and lower elements. Phrase 5 can be heard as a simple extension of 4, emphasizing the higher register. Phrase 2 also resembles 4, on the basis of register even if there is no specific similarity.

In terms of these factors, the melody can be understood to have the overall shape

A	B	A	B	A
1,2	3	4,5	6 (7)	8

At least some of the differences between the two versions—Notker's and the West-Frankish—can be understood in terms of this A B A B A plan. If the second and third A's are like a refrain, the two B's are like verses, that is, more or less discursive elements whose quality of leading on may be arrested and bound up into a whole by the return of the refrain. LAUDES DEO is too short to communicate the full force of a verse-refrain construction, but something of that kind seems to be at work. And if that is true, could we not say that variation in the number of "verses," or in their details, could occur without substantially altering the plan of the whole? At any rate, the plan would be far more substantially altered by the absence of 8, say, than by the presence or absence of Notker's 4 or the West-Frankish 7. The essential function of the "refrain," more exactly of 4 (Notker's 5) has struck several observers, and it has more than once been pointed out (but for different reasons) that Notker, in his Preface, identifies this prose as *"Laudes deo . . . et infra Coluber Adae."*

Short as it is, the melody uses three or four distinctly different phrase shapes. The clearest, most compact phrase—or better, sub-phrase—seems to be the one at the start of 3 (*Per quem renovatur, redditur*). It seems to spring from a single melodic impluse, its ending so closely linked to its beginning as to be almost inseparable; yet it is a complete musical thought, not just an open-ended motive. Starting with a leap down from G to D, it spends most of its time moving stepwise back to the G to end there.

```
       G   D  E F G A  G FGG
3a   Per quem renovatur, redditur
       G D   E F G A G F D   E   C
     mortis vinculis absolutus mundus
     D   E  F  GA G  FG  G
     in hac est die redemptus
```

Phrase 3 as a whole is built out of the opening sub-phrase and its extension; it is the manner of making extensions that distinguishes the phrases of LAUDES DEO clearly from one another. In phrase 3, the second sub-phrase (*mortis*) begins like the first, then avoids the cadence by a descent (*absolutus mundus*). This descent effects a melodic elision to a third statement of the sub-phrase (*in hac est die redemptus*) which lacks the initial leap downward from G to D but ends as it did the first time.

Or, phrase 3 can be said to have two parts, of which the second (*mortis . . . redemptus*) begins and ends like the first but is extended in the middle.

```
G D E F G  A G  FG  G
G D E F G A G F  D  E C D E F G  A G  FG  G
```

Or its syntax might be parsed in still other ways, for it is one of those structures whose very simplicity makes possible manifold interpretations. Even though relatively long and compounded of sub-phrases, phrase 3 shows the striking compactness of its opening sub-phrase.

Phrase 6, in many respects similar to phrase 3, begins with a sub-phrase almost as compact; but being slightly longer, it presents itself in two parts, antecedent (descending) *Donec . . . mundi* and consequent (ascending) *carnem . . . induens.*

```
       GF  ED   ECDE   F  G   AG FGG
6a   Donec auctor mundi carnem nostram pius induens
     G G   A G F   G F DE  D C
     Ipsum auctorem mortis sua morte
      D E   F  G   A G F GG
     vincens, justos omnes eruit.
```

Its melodic outline is perceived as a slight extension downward of the range of phrase 3; yet D remains the lower pivot note, as before.

In overall shape, however, phrase 6 is subtly different from phrase 3, for the modifications—even though slight—occur at the very beginning of the second sub-phrase (*Ipsum auctorem*) instead of only later on. The opening sub-phrase is restated only once, not twice as in phrase 3. Put another way, phrase 6 consists of two parts of which the second begins differently, then ends the same.

```
G F E D E C D E F G A G F G G
G G A G F G F D E D C D E F G A G F G G
```

Phrase 4, as observed before, has no real cadence; in a discussion of purely musical sub-phrase structure, phrase 4 is better understood in conjunction with phrase 5, which does have a cadence, and is the melodic extension of phrase 4.

Phrase 4 is shorter—shorter even than the beginning of phrase 3—and like it, may perhaps be included under a single melodic impulse. Even so, phrase 4 consists of two motive-like groups, C G A C and B C A G. Similar groups characterize phrase 5, and it would seem that the relationship between 4 and 5 is to be understood more in terms of motivic groups than in terms of sub-phrases. Phrase 5, moderately long, does not divide readily into sub-phrases. Do we perhaps hear its expansion of 4 as a succession of expansions, as shown here?

```
4  C    G   | A   C   | B C A G
5  CEDBG     | A B C A | B C A G F G G
```

If one statement of phrase 4 were followed immediately by one of 5, the sense of repetition would be subtly different from that in, say, phrase 6. Since 4 and 5 are double, of course, that comparison does not present itself; still, phrases 4 and 5 seem to proceed differently from the surrounding ones.

Phrase 2 is midway between the qualities of 3 and 6 on one hand, 4 and 5 on the other. Phrase 2 has clearly-formed sub-phrases, yet it also has something of the motivic quality of 5, especially in connection with the extension in 2, which furthermore proceeds differently from any of the other extensions. The opening sub-phrase is clearly marked off with its own cadence on D, and its own high realm of pitches; nothing about it returns in the phrase (except in the repetition at 2b), so that a very clear antecedent-consequent structure results. In 2b, the extension shares its opening motivic group (G B G A) with the consequent, and goes on through other motivic groups (F A C C, C B C A G). At a higher level, we should observe that 2a,b has an overall shape not unlike that of phrase 3, that is, two parts (a,b) of which the second begins and ends like the first. The difference here is in the nature of the extension.

In comparison with any of these phrases, the melody of 1 is in a different style altogether. It has no sub-phrase shape other than that of an expressive rise and fall; there is no cadence, no motion toward a cadence to bind it up. Because of this difference in line, phrase 1 easily assumes a special function in the piece as a whole: it stands apart, provides a formal beginning, a frame. The frame is completed by the *Amen* at the end of phrase 8, which similarly stands outside the phrases near it.

It is difficult to know how far to push analysis of works of an unfamiliar type, remote in so many ways from the materials that have formed our musical instincts. In the case of sequences two circumstances come to our aid. Sequences have texts, with sense and syntax to guide and confirm our analytic procedures. And in the cases presently before us there are two different texts to give two different interpretations of the melody. Comparison of closely related versions is one of the most productive means of gaining insight into the unfamiliar. In the two settings of phrase 3, we can see how differences in words and music combine to produce a subtle redistribution of weight in the sub-phrase structure. In the West-Frankish version, the second sub-phrase (*mortis vinculis*) begins exactly like the first (*per quem renovatur*), while in Notker's version the second sub-phrase (*ut sua dextra*) is slightly different from the first—it matches the *third* sub-phrase (*levaret*) which in spite of the syntactic elision now has a clear beginning (it was musically elided in the West-Frankish version). Thinking in terms of three sub-phrases and assigning them letters on the basis of their beginnings, we can represent the West-Frankish phrase 3 as ''a a b,'' Notker's as ''a b b.'' And this melodic difference is faithfully reflected in the syntactic one, for in the West-Frankish version the second and third sub-phrases together give an expansion of the sense of the first.

(a)   Per quem renovatur, redditur;
(a b)   mortis vinculis absolutus, mundus in hac est die redemptus.
        (Through whom it [all flesh] is renewed, restored;
        freed from the chains of earth, the world is this day redeemed.)

That is, at *mortis* the meaning goes back for a fresh start at saying what was said at *per quem*, only at greater length; which is exactly what is achieved in the melody by the repetition of the leap downward from G to D and the sub-phrase structure *a, a b*, with *b* ending exactly like *a*.

In Notker's syntax, on the other hand, the second sub-phrase expresses purpose, and is consequent, rather than apposite, to the first sub-phrase. It is the third sub-phrase (more precisely, its latter half) that is apposite.

(Notker)
(a)   Misit huc natum suum in terras
(b)   ut sua dextra jacentes coeno
(b)   levaret polo restitueretque patriae.

The structure is complicated by the fact that the verbal parallelism, *levaret polo = restitueretque patriae* does not correspond to the melodic one *b = b*, the lack of correspondence being the means of making the syntactic elision. The important point is that the melody for *ut sua* is perceived as belonging with what comes after, not before—with the pitches for *levaret*, not those for *misit*—and it is this that expresses the grammatical construction of purpose.

Notker's phrase 4 has the outward shape of the last sub-phrase of 3, but with changes of detail that add up to a substantial difference.

```
        G F D  E C  D E F G A G   F G G
3    . . . levaret polo restitu-eretque patriae
        G A G  F G F  D E D C   D E  F G G
4    Hic ergo genitus illibatae matris utero
```

We probably hear Notker's phrase 4 as yet another statement of the sub-phrase repeated throughout 3, but now further expanded or varied. On paper it looks as though the first four notes (G A G F) had simply been tacked on, for the fifth note corresponds to the sub-phrase beginning *ut sua*, or *levaret*. But our ear seems to find a new shape in the result, for do we not hear G A G, F G F, D E D . . . and understand it as an ornamented descent G, F, D? Or perhaps the line seems more motivic than it was before, so that 4 is more similar in procedure to 6 than to 3.

At his phrase 7 Notker again uses the sub-phrase beginning that was emphasized in 3 (*ut sua, levaret*), but now with a clear intent of motivic recall.

```
        G F D E  C  D E  F G  A G  F G G
7a   Igitur omnes quibus princeps hujus saeculi
        G  A G  F G F D  E  D C  D  E  F G G
     quae sibi placita sunt inflixit quosque perdidit.
```

And now, when the material of his phrase 4 follows as the second sub-phrase of 7, its relationship as expansion is that much clearer. Here, too, we become aware that the cadence has been shortened by omitting the turn up to A before the final G G, so that in comparison to his first half, Notker's second half seems to end a little abruptly. Was he nervous about over-repetition of this particular approach to the cadence? His endings in 6 are also slightly shortened, as we noticed in connection with his treatment of word accents.

The gap between what we know about Notker's work and what we know of anyone else's seems broader the more one reflects on the early sequence; the more discouraging becomes the ignorance about the circumstances surrounding the sequence, the more reassuring are the facts about Notker—and vice versa. We know not only that LAUDES DEO CONCINAT is Notker's, we know it is a youthful work, a first attempt. About LAUDES DEO OMNIS SEXUS we know nothing, save that it answers to the specifications of Notker's model. Any evaluation of its position in its repertory, or in its author's output, is sheer presumption. And yet we have every right to believe that all the things that could be true of Notker's work could be true for this one—that it had an author, that it was composed earlier or later in his life, that it reflected some phase of his encounter with the new art form.

To choose among the possibilities, then, it seems that the language of LAUDES DEO OMNIS SEXUS (as restored according to Notker's plan) was written with high ambitions tempered by the struggle with an unfamiliar shape. The result could be described not as youthful but rather early—early in the life of the form. While there is no inherent probability that the first sequence (if there was such a thing) would be the one to reach Notker first, still it looks as though LAUDES DEO OMNIS SEXUS might indeed have been one of the first attempts. This is more evident, perhaps, in the melody than in the text; the melody is unusual in its repetitive procedures, even among the early repertory with its many unusual features. It can be argued that the refrain/verse structure reflects uncertainty about how to compose an extended "prose" melody, hence the falling back on techniques more appropriate to verse. It can also be argued that dimensions and proportions are not as they should be, with reference to the melodic material—in a way that suggests uncertainty about more subtle aspects of design. It seems doubtful that LAUDES DEO OMNIS SEXUS would have been written after, and with knowledge of, some of the other pieces to be studied, unless it was written in sheer incompetence; and that was not the case.

Finally, it is of importance for other works, indeed for the whole early repertory, to bear in mind that this, the model for Notker's first prose, enjoyed no great popularity or broad collation, but was preserved only by three Aquitanian manuscripts of the late tenth and early eleventh centuries. We need not be surprised to find other refugees from the early repertory sheltered in the same place.

IV

HAEC DIES QUAM EXCELSUS
Notker's GRATES SALVATORI
and TUBAM BELLICOSAM

THE WEST-FRANKISH counterpart—and presumably model—for Notker's GRATES SALVATORI has been known for some time. Due to important structural differences, however, the two melodies have been treated as related, not identical. As in the case of LAUDES DEO OMNIS SEXUS, the West-Frankish HÆC DIES QUAM EXCELSUS is preserved in only three Aquitanian manuscripts, and nowhere on a staff. As it turns out, however, problems of pitch are the least difficult: the melody seems to be clearly located on G (confirmed by the staff sources for GRATES SALVATORI) and the variants are few. This Aquitanian version is given in the transcriptions, p. 58. Notker's GRATES SALVATORI is given on p. 61 in a transcription based upon the Aquitanian melody and the St. Gall neumes.

The distinguishing feature of this piece—apparent from even casual examination—is the frequent departure from parallelism. The phrases 4, 5, and 6 of HÆC DIES QUAM EXCELSUS could each be understood in a variety of ways, and numbered accordingly. In each case the part of the phrase here labeled "b" begins and (in 4 and 5 at least) ends the same as "a," but departs from it in the middle and is longer. In each case the departure is accomplished differently; the simplest case, phrase 5, involves an almost literal repetition—5b contains two statements of 5a. All three cases bear some resemblance to phrase 3 of LAUDES DEO; that is, to phrase 3 as a single, and it could well be argued that phrases 4, 5, and 6 of HÆC DIES QUAM EXCELSUS should each be considered a single that involved repetition, rather than a modified double. I have numbered according to the latter interpretation only because in this case it seemed more expedient. Much more important than the numbering is the composer's obvious intent to produce a fascinating gem—apparently crystal-clear, yet many-faceted and capable of multiple interpretations.

As it stands in the transcription, then, HÆC DIES QUAM EXCELSUS begins with a melismatic single of 3 syllables set to 14 notes, going on to two regular doubles. But the second of these doubles, phrase 3, already contains the kind of melodic repetition responsible for the ambiguities just touched upon. And by the end of phrase 3 it has become apparent that short groups of notes are being used motivically.

Going back to phrase 2, we can see that it consists of two such motivic groups—the first four notes (C D B G) and the last six (A G G F G G). The first four reappear at the beginning of phrase 3 (*Serenatis*) and again in the middle (*temporibus*), giving the sense of internal repetition at the sub-phrase level, even though only motives, not phrases, are being repeated. The six notes from the end of phrase 2 appear also at the end of phrase 3 (*laeti celebremus*). The rest of phrase 3 consists of two figures that move through an F-A-C realm (A G F / A C A).

In phrase 4 it is probably easier to follow the use of motives than to attempt to construe sub-phrases; that, at any rate, seems to be the experience of hearing the piece. A new motive appears at the beginning of 4 (C C B D B), followed by a new descending group of three (C B G). The rest of 4a, from *sumere*, is identical with phrase 3 from *cordibus*.

Phrase 4b, up through *eruit quos*, begins exactly as phrase 4a; that is, 4b repeats all of 4a except for the six-note cadence. After *quos*, phrase 4b moves through the F-A-C realm (by a new figure) back to begin again (*rapuit* . . .). All goes as it did the first time; but at the end, (*trahens* . . .) the melody either refers to a cadence formula we will encounter in other pieces (C B C A G F G G) or, in an important variant, continues on with the motive C D B G followed by a truncated form of the cadence.

```
        . . . C A  C D  B G  F G G
4b      . . . trahens in antro sulfu-re- o
```

In phrase 5, the motive C D B G reappears a fourth lower as G A D F, beginning the phrase as it did in phrases 2 and 3; then it comes twice more, giving the phrase its sub-phrase repetitions. In spite of the individual inflection contributed by this motive, the phrase as a whole resembles the low-lying phrases in LAUDES DEO.

Phrase 6a has a new opening figure and the motive C D B G. Phrase 6b adds a pair of notes (*trini*—G,F) to extend the opening figure; and, after the last return of the motive C D B G, and the descending group A G F, phrase 6b introduces a new motive, G A B (A) G that is repeated several times in skillful, gracious peroration to bring the piece to an end.

As it stands, the melody seems to present a study—brilliantly conceived and executed—in the gradual dissolution of couplet structure. Phrase 2 is perfectly comprehensible as a couplet of the kind normally encountered. Phrase 3 is still perceptible as a couplet, but the internal repetitions, not part of a clear subphrase structure, tend to blur the parallelism of phrases. Phrase 4a, with its different beginning, might be heard as the first of yet another regular couplet; but that expectation conflicts with the close similarity of phrase 4 to phrase 3 and raises doubts about how the phrase structure will work out: How many more expanded repetitions will occur? In the excessively long phrase 4b, the sense of clear phrase structure is lost, giving way to what seems like a dizzy swirl of motives; actually, the motives come in their usual order within two sub-phrases; but—partly because of skillful alterations of detail, partly because of something about the motives themselves—the larger order is not readily perceived, and a sense of mellifluous prolixity prevails. Clarity is restored by phrase 5, to be disturbed again slightly at the very end of the piece.

The melody seems very well made; there are no obvious weak points in the chain of motives. The words, however, are less well put together. The words are laid out here (p. 56) not strictly according to the melodic phrase structure, but rather in a way designed to show verbal syntax, especially clauses and periods. The periods are numbered with Roman numerals, I–VI, and each begins flush left. Clauses and sometimes phrases are indented, more or less to suggest distance or proximity to the main line of thought; or, two successive units are indented to indicate parallelism (not, however, the parallelism of the musical setting). Such a syntactic display is characteristically ''in counterpoint'' with the phrase structure of the music, as revealed by the type of display used in the transcriptions; the two sometimes coincide only in the period structure of the text—sometimes not even there. Phrases are indicated in the syntactic display by arabic numerals in parentheses.

HÆC DIES QUAM EXCELSUS (syntactic display)

(1) I Hæc dies

$$\acute{/}\ \text{x x x}\ \acute{/}\ \text{x}$$
(2)   quam excelsus ípse fecit Deus,

$$\acute{/}\ \text{x x x}\ \acute{/}\ \text{x}$$
         jucundemur simul et laetemur.

$$\acute{/}\ \text{x x x}\ \acute{/}\ \text{x}$$
(3) II Serenatis cordibus annuis temporibus laeti celebremus.

$$\acute{/}\ \text{x x x}\acute{/}\ \text{x}$$
     III In hac die siquidem creator angelorum,

$$\acute{/}\ \text{x x x}\ \acute{/}\ \text{x}$$
              omnium sanctorum,

(4)   formam servi dignatus est sumere
                   nostri causa salutis

$$\acute{/}\ \text{x x x}\acute{/}\ \text{x}$$
                   nosque liberandum.

$$\acute{/}\ \text{xx x}\ \acute{/}\ \text{x}$$
     IV Rerum creator, de sacro solio descendens,
              eruit
                   quos hostis perfidus rapuit
                        dudum ingerens vitia

$$\acute{/}\ \text{x x x}\acute{/}\text{x}$$
                   et trahens in antro sulfureo.

(5) V Totus mundus exultet,

$$\acute{/}\ \text{x x x}\ \acute{/}\ \text{x}$$
         libans jubila in voce summas laudes, ut decet,
(6)   cum angelis ''Gloria in excelsis deo'' cantantes.
     VI Gloria sit trinitati unicae—patri, filio, paraclito
                        spirito sancto—

$$\acute{/}\ \text{x x x}\ \acute{/}\ \text{x}$$
         nunc et ultra et in aevum.

The first period (I = lines 1, 2a,b) is a paraphrase of Psalm 117 (English, 118), verse 2.

Hæc dies quam fecit Dominus: exultemus et letemur in ea.

From a liturgical point of view, this verse is most familiar as the Gregorian gradual for Easter Sunday (and Easter week) but is also used elsewhere in the Roman liturgy, as well as being a favorite psalm verse in its own right.

The first period, then, focuses attention on "today's" festivity but does not yet specify which day. Even though one might assume Easter, it can in the broadest sense be any day, or certainly any of the major feast days. (The sequel shows that Christmas is intended.) The second period, however, seems tangential: "With happy hearts we joyfully celebrate at the yearly times." The time has become less specific where we would expect it to be more so.

The third period (III = lines 3b, 4a) uses common theological language to specify and explain the occasion.

> III In hac die siquidem creator . . .
> formam servi dignatus est sumere . . .
>
> (For on this day the creator . . . deigned to take on the
> form of a servant . . .)

The fourth period (IV = line 4b) turns abruptly to the Harrowing of Hell, by way of expanding on *liberandum* at the end of the preceding period.

> IV Rerum creator, de sacro solio descendens,
> eruit
>   quos hostis perfidus rapuit
>   dudum ingerens vitia
>   et trahens in antro sulfureo.
>
> (Descending from his holy throne, the creator of all
> things snatched out of those whom the wicked enemy had
> once carried off while hurling crimes and dragging
> [them] into the sulfurous pit.)

The image follows logically on what came before, and adds excitement to what has been up to that point a neutral prose. On the other hand, it shifts the focus decisively from Christmas to Easter—not just by a reference to the Paschal epic, for that could be easily absorbed into a Christmas prose, but rather by the extent and vividness of the reference and by the placement at the point where the musical structures of the beginning, the couplets, have been effaced.

The fifth period (V = lines 5a,b 6a) brings a return to the occasion of Christmas. In fact, it brings a Christmas scene to balance the one of Hell—the angels singing "Glory to God on high!" The whole world should rejoice, "pouring out in a voice the highest praise, as is fitting." This language recalls LAUDES DEO in its reconstructed form.

LAUDES DEO
Laudes deo omnis sexus *consonat voce libantes* preces *ut decet*

HÆC DIES QUAM EXCELSUS
Totus mundus exultet,
libans jubila *in voce* summas *laudes, ut decet*

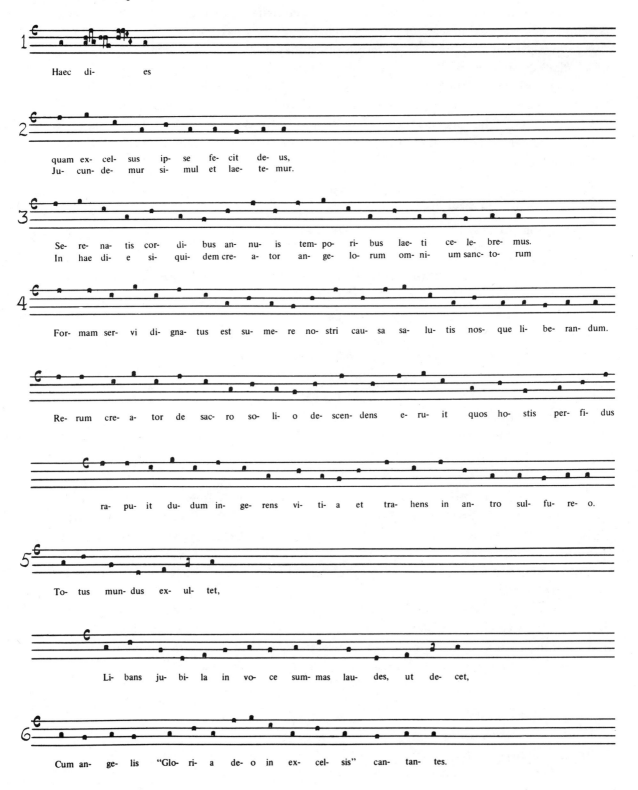

1. Haec di- es

2. quam ex- cel- sus ip- se fe- cit de- us,
Ju- cun- de- mur si- mul et lae- te- mur.

3. Se- re- na- tis cor- di- bus an- nu- is tem- po- ri- bus lae- ti ce- le- bre- mus.
In hae di- e si- qui- dem cre- a- tor an- ge- lo- rum om- ni- um sanc- to- rum

4. For- mam ser- vi di- gna- tus est su- me- re no- stri cau- sa sa- lu- tis nos- que li- be- ran- dum.

5. Re- rum cre- a- tor de sac- ro so- li- o de- scen- dens e- ru- it quos ho- stis per- fi- dus

ra- pu- it du- dum in- ge- rens vi- ti- a et tra- hens in an- tro sul- fu- re- o.

6. To- tus mun- dus ex- ul- tet,

Li- bans ju- bi- la in vo- ce sum- mas lau- des, ut de- cet,

Cum an- ge- lis "Glo- ri- a de- o in ex- cel- sis" can- tan- tes.

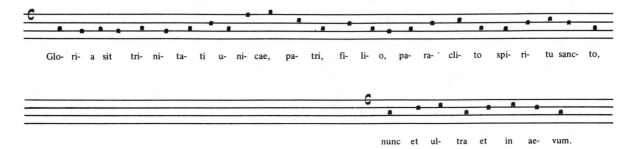

Glo- ri- a sit tri- ni- ta- ti u- ni- cae, pa- tri, fi- li- o, pa- ra- ' cli- to spi- ri- tu sanc- to,

nunc et ul- tra et in ae- vum.

The fifth period runs on from phrase 5b through 6a, where it ends. As a result, phrases 6a and b, parallel enough in music to be a modified double, are split by the syntax, which associates 6a more closely with 5b. The last period (line 6b) is a formal doxology.

The six-note cadence at the end of phrase 2 (A G G F G G) is given a regular accent pattern, most simply expressed as Á G G F Ǵ G. From LAUDES DEO we might expect a proparoxytone for F G G; but while there are slight differences earlier in the pattern, the final paroxytone is maintained throughout. Usually there is a principal accent on the sixth note (A) before the end, followed by three unaccented syllables; but one of these three may be presumed to carry a secondary accent (as when the last word has four syllables). In line 2a, by exception, the fourth syllable from the end carries a primary word accent (*fecit*) which can however be construed in the phrase as secondary to the accent on *ipse* ("which God Himsélf hath made").

This pattern of accents is marked throughout the text on p. 56. In line 3b it appears twice in succession (*creátor angelórum, ómnium sanctórum*), that being the first time the accent pattern appears without the six-note cadence. The other places at which the accent pattern appears without the cadence are in line 4b (*solio descendens*) and at the very end (*ultra et in aevum*). This particular pattern is not one of the traditional cursus (it lacks one unaccented syllable to be a *cursus velox* (′ x x x x ′ x); but given its association with a cadence, it functions like a cursus here. In line 4b, for example, its presence at *solio descendens* has the effect of grouping *eruit* with the following clause. *Eruit* then forms a frame with *rapuit*, instead of acting like an end-rhyme.

4b   . . . eruit quos hostis perfidus rapuit . . .

Similarly, *jubila in voce* suggests a shaping of line 5b slightly different from what we might expect: the cadential accent pattern emphasizes the sense of beginning again at *summas*.

5   Totus mundus exultet, libans jubila in voce
    Summas laudes ut decet.

But since this shape is not supported by the music, it remains only a suggestion.

Except for *temporibus* in line 3a, the four-note motive C D B G never takes an accent on its second note (D). There is usually an accent, most often a primary accent, on its third note (B). There may also be a primary accent on the first note (C).

	C	D	B	G
2a	quam	ex-	cél-	sus
2b	jù-	cun-	dé-	mur
3a	sè-	re-	ná-	tis
	tem-	pó-	ri-	bus (exception)
3b	in	hac	dí-	e
	án-	ge-	ló-	rum
4a	-sa	sa-	lú-	tis
4b	é-	ru-	it	quos
5a	tó-	tus	mún-	dus
5b	lí-	bans	jú-	bi-
	súm-	mas	láu-	des
6a	Dé-	o	in	ex-
6b	-ni-	cae	pá-	tri

Several miscellaneous details of language call for isolated comment, even if they cannot at the moment be given a context. In line 3a, the accents before the concluding pattern are very neatly arranged.

3a Sèrenátis córdibus | ánnuis tempóribus | láeti celebrémus

By giving *se* the weight of a primary accent and by adding pauses at the vertical bars, a hymnlike regularity can be made to appear; it is supported by the internal rhyme *cordibus . . . temporibus.*

The manner in which *laeti* repeats *laetemur* of line 2b immediately preceding is not acceptable in the best prose style. Similarly, *rerum creator* in line 4b (in itself an odd expression) is too similar to *creator angelorum* in 3b; the repetition of the word *creator* calls attention to itself, and would have to be put to some rhetorical use in order to be acceptable. And in line 3b, *creator angelorum omnium sanctorum* seems to lack the enclitic connective (*omniumque?*); at any rate, something about the words does not sit quite right, although the melody flows smoothly enough, with no space left for another note.

To the melody of ʜᴀᴇᴄ ᴅɪᴇꜱ ǫᴜᴀᴍ ᴇxᴄᴇʟꜱᴜꜱ (known in the Swiss-Rhenish MSS as "Duo tres") Notker wrote two proses; of these, ɢʀᴀᴛᴇꜱ ꜱᴀʟᴠᴀᴛᴏʀɪ seems to be the earlier, while ᴛᴜʙᴀᴍ ʙᴇʟʟɪᴄᴏꜱᴀᴍ shows far greater poetic force and control.

The melody for ɢʀᴀᴛᴇꜱ ꜱᴀʟᴠᴀᴛᴏʀɪ is given in the transcription in an inflection that, while corresponding exactly to the neumes of St. Gall MS 484 (and, with very minor variants, to the other St. Gall MSS as well) uses the pitches read out of the Aquitanian MSS for ʜᴀᴇᴄ ᴅɪᴇꜱ ǫᴜᴀᴍ ᴇxᴄᴇʟꜱᴜꜱ. As for ʟᴀᴜᴅᴇꜱ ᴅᴇᴏ, the version so obtained differs slightly from the one found in later German sources.

It is immediately obvious that Notker's melody does not correspond exactly to that of ʜᴀᴇᴄ ᴅɪᴇꜱ ǫᴜᴀᴍ ᴇxᴄᴇʟꜱᴜꜱ. In order to understand the differences, we should begin with Notker's prose, given here in syntactic display.

Grates salvatori (Notker)

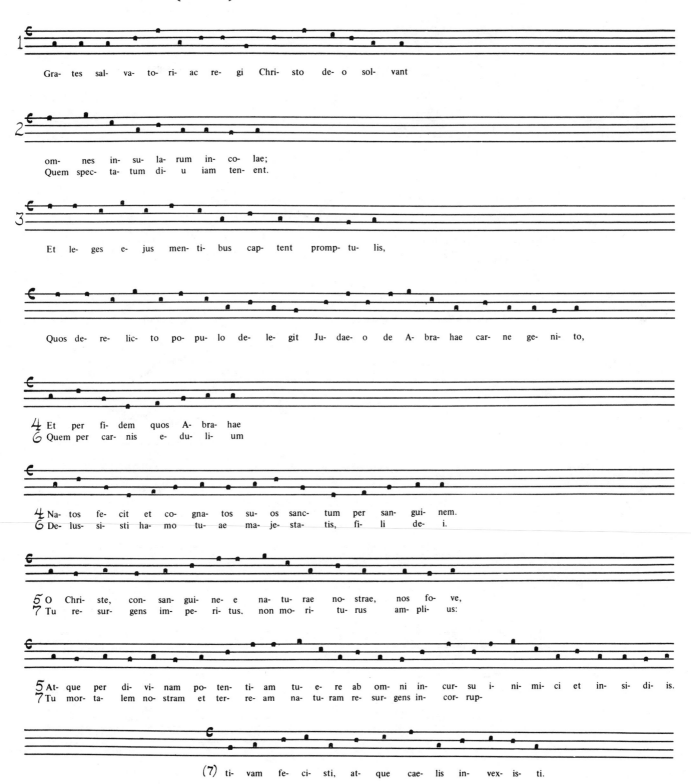

1 Gra- tes sal- va- to- ri- ac re- gi Chri- sto de- o sol- vant

2 om- nes in- su- la- rum in- co- lae;
   Quem spec- ta- tum di- u iam ten- ent.

3 Et le- ges e- jus men- ti- bus cap- tent promp- tu- lis,

   Quos de- re- lic- to po- pu- lo de- le- git Ju- dae- o de A- bra- hae car- ne ge- ni- to,

4 Et per fi- dem quos A- bra- hae
6 Quem per car- nis e- du- li- um

4 Na- tos fe- cit et co- gna- tos su- os sanc- tum per san- gui- nem.
6 De- lus- si- sti ha- mo tu- ae ma- je- sta- tis, fi- li de- i.

5 O Chri- ste, con- san- gui- ne- e na- tu- rae no- strae, nos fo- ve,
7 Tu re- sur- gens im- pe- ri- tus, non mo- ri- tu- rus am- pli- us:

5 At- que per di- vi- nam po- ten- ti- am tu- e- re ab om- ni in- cur- su i- ni- mi- ci et in- si- di- is.
7 Tu mor- ta- lem no- stram et ter- re- am na- tu- ram re- sur- gens in- cor- rup-

(7) ti- vam fe- ci- sti, at- que cae- lis in- vex- is- ti.

Tubam bellicosam (Notker)

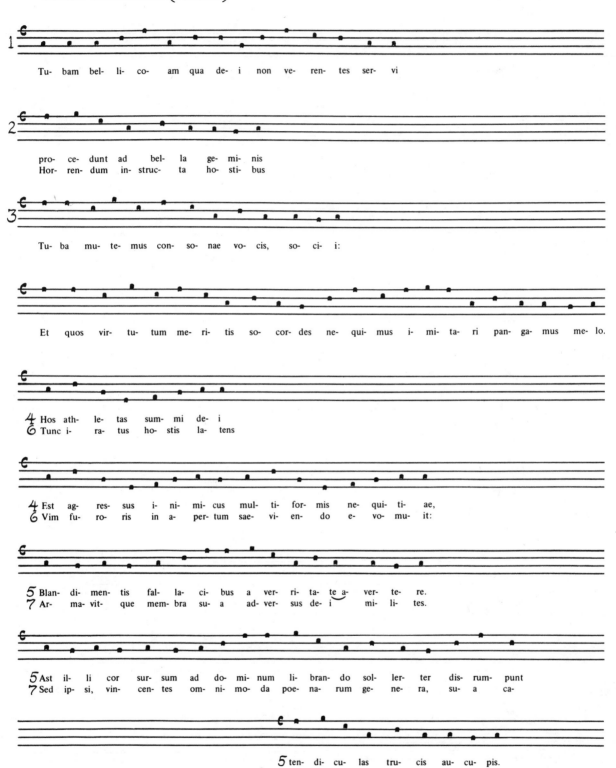

7 pi- ta di- ca- runt Chri- sto re- gi lau- re- an- da.

Notker

GRATES SALVATORI (syntactic display)

(1–2) I Grates salvatori ac regi Christo deo solvant omnes insularum incolae,
             quem spectatum diu jam tenent;

(3)   et leges eius mentibus captent promptulis,
                quos derelicto populo delegit Judaeo de Abrahae carne genito,

(4)   et per fidem quos Abrahae natos fecit
                         et cognatos suos
                            sanctum per sanguinem.

(5) II O Christe, consanguinee naturae nostrae, nos fove,
             atque per divinam potentiam tuere ab omni incursu inimici et insidiis,

(6)   quem per carnis edulium delusisti hamo tuae majestatis, fili dei.

(7) III Tu resurgens imperitas, non moriturus amplius:
         tu mortalem nostram et terream naturam
             resurgens
         incorruptivam fecisti
         atque caelis invexisti.

The first period, inordinately long, extends through phrase 4; the main clause runs on from 1 through 3a, the subordinate clauses occupy 3b, 4a, and b. Phrase 1 is a completely syllabic setting of what was melismatic in HÆC DIES QUAM EXCELSUS—a procedure presumably related to Notker's comment in his Preface, to the effect that in following Iso's instructions to set everything syllabically he found it easy for *le-* and *lu-*, but harder for *-ia* (in the melismatic notation line 1 is underlaid with the word "alleluia"). But the comment is not completely clear in itself, nor does its application here match perfectly the better documented application to LAUDES DEO.

The main clause of the first period is a paraphrase of Psalm 97,1 (Latin 96,1)—a verse used as an Alleluia verse, now assigned to Epiphanytide.[1]

Dominus regnavit, exsultet terra:
    laetentur insulae multae.

(The Lord reigneth; let the earth rejoice;
    let the multitude of the isles be glad thereof.)

1. A verse from Isaiah 42,4, stands even closer: "He shall not fail nor be discouraged, till he have set judgment in the earth: and the isles shall wait for his law."

(Notker)

1–2 Let all the inhabitants of the isles render thanks to God, the King and Saviour, Christ,

Whom they have long awaited.

The coming of the King, and his manifestation to the ends of the earth are, of course, themes of Christmas and Epiphanytide.

The second clause (line 3a) begins syntactically parallel to the first,

3a And let them accept his laws . . .

but the continuation is looser: *quos*, governing the two subordinate clauses that extend through 3b and 4, refers to the "inhabitants," subject of the main clause in line 3a. The ablative absolute in line 3b is long:

3b . . . derelicto populo . . . judaeo de Abrahae carne genito

The syntax in 4 is elaborate: *Et* is not parallel to *Et* in line 3a, as one might at first conclude from its position at the start of the line; and the placing of *per fidem* early in the line, for emphasis, makes it harder to follow the real parallelism.

Quos . . . delegit
Et quos . . . fecit

Finally, this second subordinate clause runs over the sub-phrase structure in phrase 4: *quos Abrahae / natos* bridges the start of the second sub-phrase, *cognatos / suos* the start of the third. This second clause pursues the implication of the opening one that the "inhabitants of the isles" are Gentiles. Referred to here is a difficult doctrine of St. Paul's.

For the promise, that he should be the heir of the world, was not to Abraham or to his seed through the law, but through the righteousness of faith. (Romans 4,13)

The spirit itself beareth witness with our spirit, that we are the children of God; and if children, then heirs; heirs of God, and joint-heirs with Christ. (Romans 8,16–17).

With a little imagination, we can make a seasonal interpretation, for the idea of "sons of God," and "kinship with Christ" is one of genealogy, which is a Christmastide theme, and the adoption of the Gentiles is close to the manifestation to the Gentiles celebrated at Epiphany. Perhaps the rhetorical or linguistic possibilities of the passage attracted Notker's attention; at any rate he makes good use of

natos . . . cognatos

and also, going on to lines 4b–5a,

sanctum per sanguinem . . . consanguinee.

Line 5a starts a new period. It contains a petition ("O Christ . . . support us"), whose second clause, in line 5b, sounds like a reminiscence of a litany:

". . . from all snares and assaults of the enemy . . ."

Line 6a begins a new thought, linked to the preceding only by a *quem* that refers to *inimici*, "the enemy." The new thought is distinctly Paschal, making use of the language of LAUDES DEO CONCINAT.

LAUDES DEO CONCINAT

6a Quin ipse ejus *carnis esca* petita avide
6b *Delusus hamo deitatis* victus est in evum

GRATES SALVATORI

6a Quem per *carnis edulium delusisti hamo* tuae majestatis, fili dei.

Per carnis edulium seems to be intended as part of a succession with *per fidem* (line 4a), *per sanguinem* (line 4b), *per divinam potentiam* (line 5b).

The new thought of Christ the Redeemer is continued in line 9, using this time a construction reminiscent of another youthful work of Notker's, HÆC EST SANCTA SOLEMNITAS SOLEMNITATUM.

HÆC EST SANCTA SOLEMNITAS SOLEMNITATUM

6 *Tu* devictis inferni legibus *resurgens* triumphas:
7 *tu* post crucem per orgem gentibus *imperas*, omnipotens filius dei.

GRATES SALVATORI

7a *Tu resurgens imperitas*, non moriturus amplius:
7b *tu* mortalem nostram et terream naturam *resurgens*,
       incorruptivam fecisti atque caelis invexisti.

While line 7a is simply the Paschal language of victory, line 7b is another reference to Pauline theology.

For this corruption must put on incorruption, and this
mortal must put on immortality (I Cor. 15,53)

As such, its intent seems to be an extension of the thought in lines 3 and 4; but there is no return to the Christmas-Epiphany season, rather a linking forward to Easter. The concluding rhyme *fecisti . . . invexisti*, seems happily placed, used in classical fashion as a solitary, exceptional ornament. But *resurgens* in line 7b is a redictum. It is handled much better than the redicta in HÆC DIES QUAM EXCELSUS (*letemur . . . leti*, lines 2–3; *creator . . . creator*, lines 3–4)—that is to say, Notker does something with the repetition.

Thou, rising, dost rule, never to die again:
       rising, thou hast made incorruptible . . .

In fact, this pair of lines has almost the form of an epanaleptic distich, without its meter.

Notker consistently drops the last note from the six-note cadence used in HÆC DIES QUAM EXCELSUS (A G G F G G), and—except in two cases—makes the last word proparoxytone.

2a	-la-rum	ín-co-lae
2b*	di-u	jam té-nent
3a	cap-tent	prómp-tu-lis
3b	car-ne	gé- ni- to
5a*	no-stra	nos fó- ve
5b	et in-	sí- di- is
7a	-tu- rus	ám-pli- us

*Exceptions

These two cases, both involving a monosyllable followed by a paroxytone (*jam tenent, nos fove*), may be examples of Norberg's thesis that such combinations can be construed as proparoxytone—especially here, where both monosyllables are prominent in their respective phrases, and easily carry a primary accent.[2] Or they may be simple exceptions, such as we have seen before in Notker. As for the five proparoxytones, Notker did not cut the pattern all the way back to the primary accent on the sixth note before the end (which would have made his proparoxytone cadences A G G), but instead seems to have sought out the fourth note from the end (G) as a place on which a cadence *could* fall, and used it regularly.

```
C D B G Á G G F G G
        6 5 4 3 2 1
C D B G A G Ǵ F G
```

The resulting proparoxytone cadence is G F G, which has the effect of including an F, but seems to land heavily on the final G in spite of the unstressed final syllable. It is not clear why he did not simply place the proparoxytone under the cadence as it stood, Ḟ G G (as in LAUDES DEO), unless he felt that the primary accent on the A at the start of the pattern was important (he preserves it in five out of six cases), and that two proparoxytones in succession should be avoided in cadences. But in phrase 4, Notker syllabifies the West-Frankish neumes to produce a proparoxytone F G G in two cases out of four (*sánctum per sánguinem, cárnis eduliúm*), both involving two successive proparoxytones. As for the four-note motive C D B G, Notker carefully maintains at least secondary accents on the first and third notes, or more precisely, he avoids accents of any kind on the second and fourth notes.

The important aspect of the relationship to HÆC DIES QUAM EXCELSUS, however, lies not in details but in the disposition of melodic phrases. Example 3 places side by side the structure of the versions given in the transcriptions.

Phrases 1 and 2 correspond closely. Phrase 3 of HÆC DIES QUAM EXCELSUS seems lacking in Notker's version, and Notker's 3 seems to represent an abbreviation of the West-Frankish 4. The correspondence of Notker's 4 and 5 to the West-Frankish 5 and 6 is again close. From 6 to the end (which corresponds to the Paschal themes of victory and resurrection) Notker repeats his 4 and 5, ending the last in its West-Frankish form.

What happens if we try to reduce the West-Frankish HÆC DIES QUAM EXCELSUS to the form given by Notker's GRATES SALVATORI? Judging from Example 3 it cannot be done, for the West-Frankish 3a,b as a whole cannot be omitted without making nonsense out of

2. Dag Norberg, *Introduction a l'étude de la versification latine médiévale* (Uppsala 1958), p. 22ff.

Example 3. HÆC DIES QUAM EXCELSUS   GRATES SALVATORI (Notker)

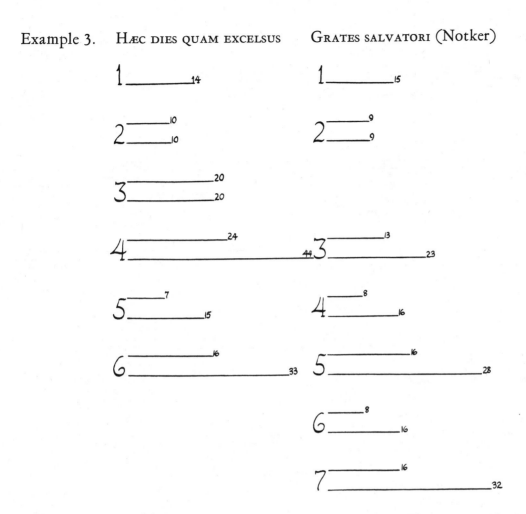

what follows, and even if it could, reducing 4 to Notker's 3 would do violence to the language in a way very different from what we did to LAUDES DEO OMNIS SEXUS.

Line 3a by itself, however, suggests possibilities: it is syntactically complete, its accent patterns point to a different style, and its diction involves a redictum (*laeti*). It can be easily excised, leaving the single *In hac die siquidem* to follow very well after 2b. And *In hac die siquidem* has to stay.

Continuing to probe for soft spots in the verbal construction, we noticed that the end of *In hac die siquidem* seems to be lacking an enclitic; and *creator* is redictum. But it is *creator* that is needed as subject of what follows in line 4. And *angelorum* goes better with *creator* than does *omnium sanctorum*. But if these last words are dropped, the rest of the West-Frankish 3b is about as long as Notker's 3a (*not* his 3b); in fact, exactly as long, if we restore the last G that Notker dropped from the cadence.

(Notker)

3a	Et	le-	ges	e-	jus	men-	ti-	bus	cap-	tent	promp-	tu-	lis,
	C	C	B	D	B	C	B	G	A	G	G	F	G G
	In	hac	di-	e	si-	qui-	dem	cre-	a-	tor	an-	ge-	lo- rum

HÆC DIES QUAM EXCELSUS (restored version)

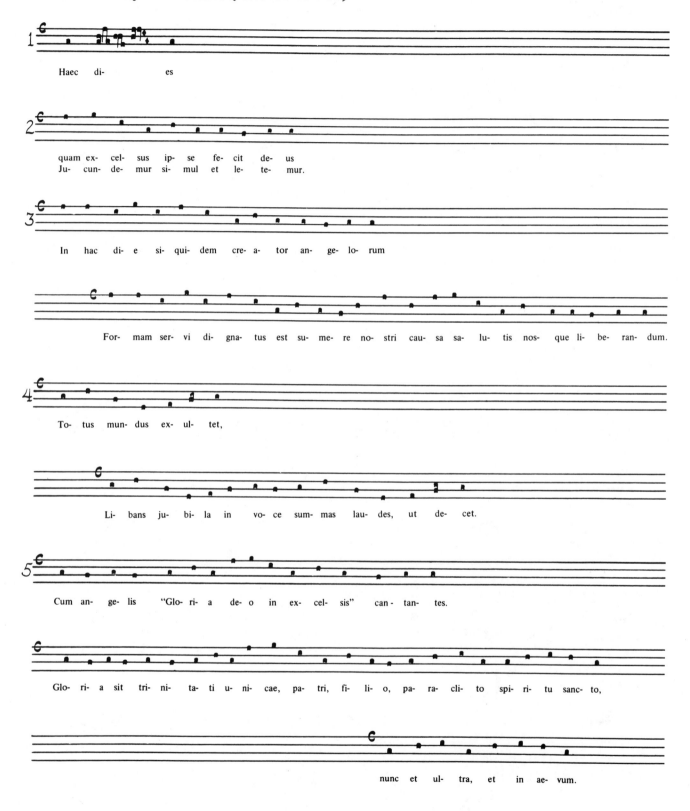

1. Haec di- es

2. quam ex- cel- sus ip- se fe- cit de- us
   Ju- cun- de- mur si- mul et le- te- mur.

3. In hac di- e si- qui- dem cre- a- tor an- ge- lo- rum

   For- mam ser- vi di- gna- tus est su- me- re no- stri cau- sa sa- lu- tis nos- que li- be- ran- dum.

4. To- tus mun- dus ex- ul- tet,

   Li- bans ju- bi- la in vo- ce sum- mas lau- des, ut de- cet.

5. Cum an- ge- lis "Glo- ri- a de- o in ex- cel- sis" can- tan- tes.

   Glo- ri- a sit tri- ni- ta- ti u- ni- cae, pa- tri, fi- li- o, pa- ra- cli- to spi- ri- tu sanc- to,

   nunc et ul- tra, et in ae- vum.

And, of course, the accent pattern is correct for the cadence, for we already noticed it duplicated the pattern of *omnium sanctorum*.

So the alignment indicated in Example 3 was wrong; Notker did not omit 3a,b and his 3a,b then corresponds to the West-Frankish 3b,4a—exactly—not to an abbreviation of 4a,b. The run-on in HÆC DIES QUAM EXCELSUS from 3 to 4 turns out to be merely the conjunction of two lines of a modified double. But we must not shrink from the alarming consequence: the West-Frankish 4b, climax of the piece as we knew it, now has no analog in Notker.

Everything about the language of 4b confirms its nature as an interpolation, once we look at it in that light. *Creator* was redictum and *Rerum creator* suspect; *eruit* was not the normal accentuation of the four-note motive C D B G; at the end we had to choose between a curiously tangential melodic reference to another cadence, or else a serious truncation of the cadence normal to this piece. There is an excessive use of gerundives (*descendens, ingerens, trahens*), giving a loose construction. And, as a whole, line 4b thrust Hell and its Harrowing into the Christmas scene. Only the melody—alas—was perfect.

Perfect, but perhaps not essential to an earlier conception of the whole. In fact, the spectacular nature of 4b was due to the way it dissolved previous expectations about the piece into a haze of motivic repetitions. Without it (and with 3 reconstructed), the effect is less spectacular and more disciplined. It is easy to imagine an effusive musical imagination (if connected to a skilled hand) conceiving just such an interpolation out of the motivic hints provided by lines 2, 3, and 4.

HÆC DIES QUAM EXCELSUS is now fairly short, having neither the expansive 4b in the middle, nor the repetition found at the end of Notker's version. Is a similar repetition lacking in the West-Frankish prose? That is a possibility, of course, although not called for by the prose as it stands, which completes its modest thought with the well-placed quotation "Gloria in excelsis Deo!" But whence came Notker's repetition of 4–5 as 6–7? If it was not in the West-Frankish model, its addition might have left traces in Notker's prose.

As we noticed, Notker's repetition (6 and 7) begins with the turn to themes of victory and resurrection—Paschal themes, such as those introduced into HÆC DIES QUAM EXCELSUS in its line 4b. Yet Notker's piece cannot be cut off at the end of line 5, for the melodic ending in 7 is called for by the West-Frankish 6. Looking more closely at Notker's lines 5,6,7, they are remarkably patchy in their juxtaposition. Line 5b is an abrupt turn from the Pauline doctrine to a relatively ordinary petition. Line 6 has connections to another piece (LAUDES DEO CONCINAT), line 7 to yet another (HÆC EST SANCTA SOLEMNITAS SOLEMNITATUM). Lines 7a,b involve the redictum *resurgens*, and of the two, line 7a is expendable. If lines 5a, 6a,b, and 7a are excised, line 7b places its Pauline doctrine directly after that concluded by *consanguinee* in line 5a, as a relatively discreet foreshadowing of the Paschal implication of the Incarnation.

Did Notker perhaps see and hear both the shorter and longer versions of HÆC DIES QUAM EXCELSUS, one after the other? Stimulated by the idea of a longer piece, but finding the dizzy line 5 not to his liking, he might have expanded his piece in his own way, enlarging on the turn to the Paschal theme already present at the end.

In any case, Notker's other prose to this melody, TUBAM BELLICOSAM, corresponds to the final form of GRATES SALVATORI: and while TUBAM BELLICOSAM takes note of the sectional division at phrase 6 and puts it to rhetorical use, it betrays no sign of discontinuity in conception or technique.

TUBAM BELLICOSAM, a song for martyrs, has as leading image the trump or *tuba*—or rather, two trumps. One is the "war-like trump [with] which the godless servants go forth to the battle with two armies forcefully arrayed." This war-like trump the poet urges the company (*socii*) to exchange for the "trump of blending voice," with which they can celebrate in song "those whose virtuous merits we slothful ones cannot imitate." Is there an echo of the Ash Wednesday antiphon, *Immutemur*?[3]

Let us change our raiment for sackcloth and ashes . . .

The long first period extends through phrases 1, 2, and 3, subsuming not only the simple opening double (2a,b) but also the modified double 3.

Tubam bellicosam
> qua dei non verentes servi procedunt ad bella geminis horrendum instructa
>> hostibus
> tuba mutemus consonae vocis, socii,
et quos virtutum meritis, soccordes, nequimus imitari,
> pangamus melo.

HÆC DIES QUAM EXCELSUS (in restored form) joined 3a and b closely together:

3a   In hac die siquidem creator angelorum (b) formam servi dignatus est sumere. . .

but set them off from 1 and 2; in GRATES SALVATORI 3b contains a relative clause introduced by *quos*. Within its opening period, TUBAM BELLICOSAM uses syntax noticeably more complex than that in the rest of the prose, and seemingly in close relationship with the melody. Phrase 1 receives the leading image (*tubam*) and the beginning of a relative clause (*qua . . .*); its verb (*procedunt*) follows in line 2a, so that that phrase is a direct extension of the first one. But line 2b is also joined closely, for it contains not only the apposite *horrendum instructa*—which by itself could hang as a loose appendage to *bella*—but also *hostibus*, the noun for *geminis*. The end of 2b marks the end of the relative clause; hence it is a half cadence, and the melodic cadence A G G F G is set both times to ′ x ′ x x, as in GRATES SALVATORI 2a (-lárum íncolae); but the four-note motive C D B G is set both times with an accent on its *second* note (*Procédunt, horréndum*), an accentuation found previously only in the interpolated 3a (tempóribus) of HÆC DIES QUAM EXCELSUS.

Phrase 3 continues the main clause of the first period, (1) *Tubam bellicosam . . .* (3) *tuba mutemus consonae vocis, socii*; then the parallel exhortative *Et . . . pangamus* falls neatly under phrase 3b, the melodic parallel to 3a; the subordinate clause *quos . . . nequimus imitari*

3. Gregorian chants of the Mass can be found in the modern publications of the Benedictines of Solesmes, the *Liber usualis*, and the *Graduale romanum* (Desclée, Belgium). Editions, especially of the *Liber usualis*, vary in pagination but are all arranged in liturgical calendar order; this is the best mode of reference and will be used in this book.

leads into the melodic extension through the F-A-C realms, and *pangamus melo* sits firmly on the return to the cadence. I take the variance in accent pattern (*pangámus mélo*) instead of (*vócis sócii*) to be just that—Notker's avoidance of complete regularity in cadences. And I take the coincidence of *imitari* with the return of the C D B G motive, in its first *motivic* return, to be fortuitous, possibly welcomed but not necessarily sought out.

Notker
TUBAM BELLICOSAM (syntactic display)

(1)   I   Tubam bellicosam
(2)   qua dei non verentes servi procedunt ad bella
                                 geminis horrendum instructa hostibus
(3)   tuba mutemus consonae vocis, socii;
         et quos virtutum meritis, soccordes, nequimus imitari,
                 pangamus melo.
(4)   II   Hos athletas summi dei est agressus inimicus multiformis nequitiae,
(5)   blandimentis fallacibus a veritate avertere:
         Ast illi, cor sursum ad dominum librando,
                 sollerter disrumpunt tendiculas trucis aucupis.
(6)   III   Tunc, iratus, hostis latens vim furoris in apertum saeviendo evomuit,
(7)   armavitque membra sua adversus dei militas:
         Sed ipsi,
                      vincentes omnimoda poenarum genera,
                 sua capita dicarunt Christo regi laureanda.

The first period, then, presents us with a poetic motive (as well as a musical one), a description of the forces of evil and of good drawn up for battle, and a ceremonial exhortative to the company assembled both to watch the battle and to concelebrate the victory. As roughly the first third of the piece, the opening period is the exact analog of this section of music, which in Notker's version is the A section of an overall A B B plan.

In the second period (lines 4 and 5), things move more swiftly and directly. "The enemy has attacked these athletes of God most high with all sorts of vileness, to attract them away from the truth with false blandishments. But they, shrewdly inclining their hearts rather towards the Lord, break the little nets of the savage fowler." The hand of the master shows itself in the ease with which elaborate language is incorporated into relatively simple syntax: neither the polysyllables *multiformis nequitiae*, *blandimentis fallacibus*, nor the alliteration of *a veritate avertere*, nor the virtuoso *tendiculas trucis aucupis* impede the flow. (These last words preserve the accent pattern ′ x ′ x x almost in spite of themselves.) I read an elision in *a veritate avertere*, which equalizes the number of syllables and normalizes the cadence; this reading is supported by the neumes placed syllabically over the words in MS London BM add.19768 (Mainz, mid-tenth century), where no note is provided for *a-(vertere)*. In the context of Notker's language, such elision seems to have an effect of brilliance —as if an ornament. The image in *cor sursum ad dominum librando*, if I read it aright, is also virtuoso: the hearts of the faithful are being weighed on the scales, which incline *upwards* to God, the illusion that things intrinsically good have more weight (and would therefore incline the balance *downward*) being one of the "false blandishments." Yet all this, too, fits easily within the second period.

"Then enraged, the hidden foe vomited out the force of his anger furiously into the open, and armed his troops against the soldiers of God. But they, overcoming all manner of torments, present their heads to Christ the King for the laurel wreath." *Dal segno, fortissimo!* The effect of the sectional repeat (6, 7) could easily be orchestrated, and perhaps it was in Notker's time—by change or addition of voice types, if not of mechanical instruments. But the words themselves can be an important means of "orchestration," in music of this kind; and it could easily occur to a 9th-century precentor to encourage his choir to render 4 and 5 softly, 6 and 7 louder. As for the ending, while Notker's classical sources provide him with plenty of violent or war-like language, they seem to offer relatively little in the way of festive description appropriate to Christian victory: the image of athletes receiving the laurel wreath seems severe compared to some of the imagery found in the West-Frankish texts.

Tunc iratus (6a) is only one sign of the larger form; more explicit signs are found in the various details that show parallelism between 4–5 and 6–7.

	4 summi del . . .	-formis nequitiae
5 Ast illi . . .		
	6 hostis latens	-endo evomuit
7 Sed ipsi . . .		

The beginning of lines 5b and 7b, introducing the constancy of response on the part of the faithful, are clearly in parallel. The sub-phrase cadences in lines 4 and 6 are arranged so that the end of 6 can recall only the end of 4 (minimizing the repetition of cadence within the line). Against the similarity of the cadences in 5a and 7a is projected the contrast of *Blandimentis fallacibus* and *Armavitque membra sua*.

The repeat of 6 and 7 is further clarified by the handling of accents within the lines; this factor also helps distinguish the second period (and the third) from the first. In the first period, accentual groups of twos (´x) and threes (´x x) are artfully mixed, as encountered before. There may be only one group of three in a line as in line 1,

Tubam bellicosam quam dei non verentes servi

but it is so placed as to inhibit the effect of a uniform grouping of twos. Not so in line 4 (and 6) however:

Hos athletas summi dei est agressus inimicus multi-

formis nequitiae

Tunc iratus hostis latens vim furoris in apertum saevi-

endo evomuit

Here the persistent grouping in twos, carried out almost to the end of the line, seems to contribute directly both to the increased sense of movement at that point, and to the subtle contrast with the first period. The two fit easily with the melody—indeed the melody, using the same low register (G down to D) as phrase 3 of LAUDES DEO, seems to have the same intrinsic disposition to a grouping in twos. Here in TUBAM BELLICOSAM the melodic grouping is made more explicit by the four-note motive (in phase 4, G A F D), with the intervening notes (E F G G, E F G F) also grouped in fours. In spite of the fact that the arrangement of accents is only slightly different from that in GRATES SALVATORI (and the melody identical), the result seems markedly different.

Line 5 (and 7) re-establishes a balance between groups of twos and of threes. Line 5b inclines toward threes.

```
x ′ x x  ′ x  x  ′  (′)      ′
```
Ast illi cor sursum ad dominum librando

```
  x ′ x  x ′  x   x  ′ x x  ′ x ′  x x
```
sollerter disrumpunt tendiculas trucis aucupis

Here it is the groups of two that provide relief. The predominance of threes has the further effect of making the return in line 6, with its twos, sound fresh. The last line is again balanced, with what seems to be a deliberate repetition of the closing pattern from HÆC DIES QUAM EXCELSUS

HÆC DIES QUAM EXCELSUS

```
                                        ′     ′  x x  x ′ x
```
6b   . . . nunc et ultra et in evum

TUBAM BELLICOSAM

```
                                   ′   ′ x x  x ′ x      ′    ′ x  x  x′  x
```
7b   . . . sua capita dicarunt, Christo regi laureanda.

By supplying secondary accents these words could also be read as a mere series of twos, echoing lines 4 and 6; but since this is the only place in TUBAM BELLICOSAM where the six-syllable pattern ′ x x x ′ x so characteristic of HÆC DIES QUAM EXCELSUS appears at the end of a line, it is perhaps appropriate to hear that echo instead.

TUBAM BELLICOSAM informs and animates the A B B plan of GRATES SALVATORI with remarkable intensity. The repetition of B (= 4,5 repeated as 6,7) is made more distinct, more forceful. Going through the three stages of development represented by HÆC DIES QUAM EXCELSUS, GRATES SALVATORI, and TUBAM BELLICOSAM, one can perceive the transformation from the clear, small, but perfectly proportioned form of the West-Frankish HÆC DIES QUAM EXCELSUS (as restored) to Notker's more prolix GRATES SALVATORI, made half again as long by the repetition of its 4,5, but not particularly clear or forceful in its overall effect. Indeed, in hearing this version one may sense a certain lack of melodic purpose during the latter part of the piece, at least as compared to the West-Frankish version. Then, in Notker's second version, TUBAM BELLICOSAM, purpose is supplied and the form makes sense.

What was changed, however, were the words: the music remained exactly the same in

Notker's second version as in his first. Notker's genius, then, was to shape music with words at the same time that he allowed his words to be given a shape by the music. If we now go on to the West-Frankish expansion of HÆC DIES QUAM EXCELSUS (as in the transcription), perhaps still a 9th-century product, we see what a difference separates this transformation from Notker's; for here the expansion with its brilliant effect is brought about almost entirely with musical means. The additional words (*Rerum creator . . .*), along with the other modification, add a new thought, but not one otherwise formally significant; and the language is barely adequate. It is the melody of *Rerum creator* that transfigures the interior of this version, giving it an effect of brilliance in a small space, unique in the early repertory.

V

ECCE VICIT and GAUDE EJA
Notker's HANC CONCORDI and PETRE SUMME

WITH A VERY BROAD, firm collation and a clear text, the West-Frankish prose EPIPHANIAM for a long time seemed to be the most important representative of its often-texted melody. Bannister selected EPIPHANIAM for a study and sample edition in 1905.[1] The variance of the plan from Notker's two texts, however, remained a basic problem. More recently, Stäblein proposed another text, GAUDE EJA, as the original one; the plan of GAUDE EJA is, in principle, the same as EPIPHANIAM, and Stäblein understood Notker to have shortened this plan for his own use.[2]

Off to one side, throughout the discussion, has stood the prose ECCE VICIT RADIX DAVID, with a small collation in four Aquitanian manuscripts and one from Autun, as well as some Italian sources—and a very difficult text, in which, nevertheless, Von den Steinen saw traits characteristic of the earliest stages of the sequence. But, as we have seen, the small Aquitanian collation need not deter us from thinking of ECCE VICIT as a survivor of the early repertory, especially when one of the sources is MS 1240, the earliest of the Aquitanian, dated 923–36 (the others are MSS 1084, 1118, 1121—the same as for LAUDES DEO). And one reason the text is difficult is its discontinuity and jumbled thought. Could these be due to interpolations that obscure an original text? Let us apply Notker's plan to ECCE VICIT to see if it yields a better text and one that could have been Notker's model; for EPIPHANIAM cannot reasonably be reduced to Notker's plan.

The diagram in Example 4 shows the discrepancies. In the usual West-Frankish form of the melody, represented in the transcription of ECCE VICIT, phrase 3 is identical with phrase 6, and phrase 4 is similar to phrase 7, except that 7 lies a fifth higher. And phrase 5 is the same as phrase 2, except that it has four notes added on to its beginning. As a result, phrases 5, 6, and 7, *en bloc*, more or less repeat 2, 3, and 4, which led Stäblein to understand the

1. H. M. Bannister, "Epiphaniam," *Rassegna Gregoriana* IV (1905). See also J. Handschin, "Trope, Sequence, and Conductus," in *New Oxford History of Music* II (1954), pp. 156–157 (transcription).

2. B. Stäblein, "Die Sequenzmelodie 'Concordia' und ihr geschichtlicher Hintergrund." In *Festschrift Hans Engel* (Kassel, 1962).

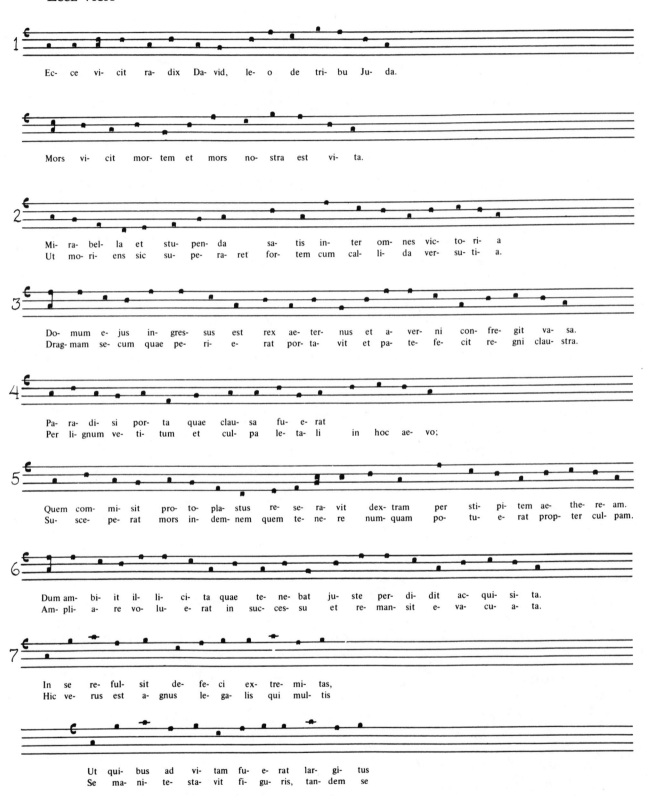

1. Ec- ce vi- cit ra- dix Da- vid, le- o de tri- bu Ju- da.

Mors vi- cit mor- tem et mors no- stra est vi- ta.

2. Mi- ra- bel- la et stu- pen- da sa- tis in- ter om- nes vic- to- ri- a
   Ut mo- ri- ens sic su- pe- ra- ret for- tem cum cal- li- da ver- su- ti- a.

3. Do- mum e- jus in- gres- sus est rex ae- ter- nus et a- ver- ni con- fre- git va- sa.
   Drag- mam se- cum quae pe- ri- e- rat por- ta- vit et pa- te- fe- cit re- gni clau- stra.

4. Pa- ra- di- si por- ta quae clau- sa fu- e- rat
   Per li- gnum ve- ti- tum et cul- pa le- ta- li in hoc ae- vo;

5. Quem com- mi- sit pro- to- pla- stus re- se- ra- vit dex- tram per- sti- pi- tem ae- the- re- am.
   Su- sce- pe- rat mors in- dem- nem quem te- ne- re num- quam po- tu- e- rat prop- ter cul- pam.

6. Dum am- bi- it il- li- ci- ta quae te- ne- bat ju- ste per- di- dit ac- qui- si- ta.
   Am- pli- a- re vo- lu- e- rat in suc- ces- su et re- man- sit e- va- cu- a- ta.

7. In se re- ful- sit de- fe- ci ex- tre- mi- tas,
   Hic ve- rus est a- gnus le- ga- lis qui mul- tis

   Ut qui- bus ad vi- tam fu- e- rat lar- gi- tus
   Se ma- ni- te- sta- vit fi- gu- ris, tan- dem se

Ecce vicit (2)

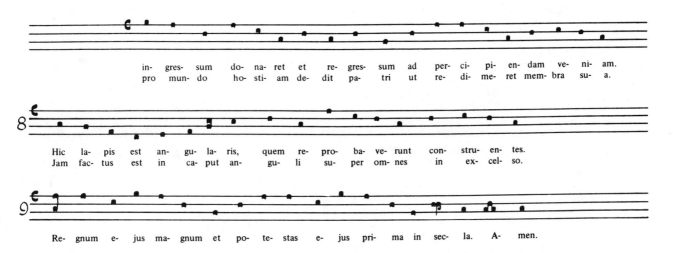

in- gres- sum do- na- ret et re- gres- sum ad per- ci- pi- en- dam ve- ni- am.
pro mun- do ho- sti- am de- dit pa- tri ut re- di- me- ret mem- bra su- a.

Hic la- pis est an- gu- la- ris, quem re- pro- ba- ve- runt con- stru- en- tes.
Jam fac- tus est in ca- put an- gu- li su- per om- nes in ex- cel- so.

Re- gnum e- jus ma- gnum et po- te- stas e- jus pri- ma in sec- la. A- men.

Example 4.

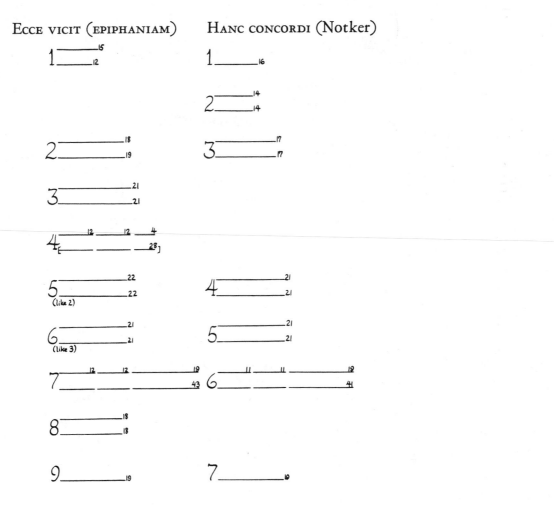

Ecce vicit (epiphaniam)   Hanc concordi (Notker)

Notker's Hanc concordi and petre summe   77

form of the melody as consisting of two strophes framed by introduction (1), a reprise of the beginning of the strophe (8) and a conclusion (9).

1   introduction
2,3,4   strophe 1
5,6,7   strophe 2
8   reprise
9   conclusion

To begin with, phrase 4 of ECCE VICIT (one of those absent from Notker's plan) has two versions: it is a single in MSS 1118 and 1084, but a double in MS 1240.

MSS 1118, 1084

4   Paradisi porta quae clausa fuerat
         per lignum vetitum et culpa letali
             in hoc aevo.

MS 1240 adds:

4b   Quem clauserat Eva tumens conditori
         clauseratque cunctis post modum de stirpe
             sua natis.

This kind of "softness" in the MS-tradition, which is not found in the case of EPIPHANIAM, is what suggests ECCE VICIT as a more likely candidate for restoration.

1a   Ecce vicit radix David, leo de tribu Juda.
 b   Mors vicit mortem et mors nostra est vita.
2a   Mirabella et stupenda satis inter omnes victorias,
 b   Ut moriens sic superaret fortem cum callida versutia.
3a   Domum ejus ingressus est rex aeternus et Averni confregit vasa.
 b   Dragmam secum quae perierat portavit et patefecit regni claustra.
4   Paradisi porta quae clausa fuerat
         per lignum vetitum et culpa letali
             in hoc aevo.
5a   Quem commisit protoplastus reseravit dextram per stipitem aetheream.
 b   Suscepit mors indemnem quem tenere numquam potuerat propter culpam.
6a   Dum ambiit illicita quae tenebat juste perdidit acquisita.
 b   Ampliare voluerat in successu et remansit evacuata.
7a   In se refuscata fecit extremitas,
         ut quibus ad vitam fuerat largitus
             ingressum donaret et regressum ad percipiendam veniam.
 b   Hic verus est agnus legalis qui multis
         se manifestavit figuris, tandem
             se pro mundo hostiam dedit patri ut redimeret membra sua.
8a   Hic lapis est angularis, quem reprobaverunt construentes;
 b   Jam factus est in caput anguli super omnes in excelso.
9   Regnum ejus magnum et potestas ejus prima in saecula. Amen.

We need not, however, concern ourselves at length with the question of whether 4 should be single or double in ECCE VICIT. For if, guided by Notker's HANC CONCORDI, we take phrases 3 and 4 completely out of ECCE VICIT, it can be observed that the result—as far as the sense of the words is concerned—is hardly disastrous and from many points of view is a distinct improvement. Phrase 3a,b is a self-contained syntactic unit.

3a   Domum ejus ingressus est rex eternus et Averni confregit vasa;
 b   Dragmam secum quae perierat portavit et patefecit regni claustra.

These lines bring two separate new images: first, the entrance of the King eternal into the nether regions, breaking the *vasa*, second, the setting up of the standard—the *dragma* or *draco*—and the opening of the gates of heaven. The whole couplet refers to the Harrowing of Hell, but not so cogently as in LAUDES DEO; rather the effect is one of passing allusion crammed into a limited space.

Phrase 4a continues the reference to the gates of heaven (*regnum = paradisus?*). This phrase cannot stand alone: the syntax within these lines is not entirely clear (in itself a fact of importance for their status in the melody), but it does seem that *porta paradisi* depends as object upon *reseravit* in 5a. The subject of *reseravit* then, is the King eternal from 3a; and 4a,b-5a together repeat and elaborate the end of 3b—"he opened the gates of the kingdom."

The construction of 4a,b-5a is immensely complicated by a disturbing number of relative clauses. In 4a, the clause *quae clausa fuerat . . .* describes how the gates had been closed "in this age" through the forbidden tree and the fatal sin. In line 5, this sin is rather qualified: "which the first man committed." Phrase 4b, which is the phrase found only in 1240, goes back to *porta*: "gates . . . which Eve, pregnant with the founder, closed, and closed to all those born afterward of her lineage." *Clauserat* reduplicated looks suspicious, and might be corrupt, but the whole line is so awkwardly placed and so clearly an afterthought that details of its reading seem insignificant.

At the end of 5a, the thought begun in 4a is completed by the balancing of the "second divine tree" against the first "forbidden" one—a common enough thought readily at hand in poetic form in Fortunatus' *Pange lingua*.

Ipse lignum tunc notavit, damna ligni ut solveret.

If this reading construes 4a,b-5a correctly, then the problem is that 3 and 4 cannot be taken out without affecting the status of 5a, and Notker's text as it stands does not call for a single at 5. Possibly 5a could stand by itself without 3 and 4, coming directly after 2, but the effect is not very satisfactory, especially since one of the important benefits that should derive from omitting 3 and 4 is the reduction in this kind of disjoined or fragmentary syntax.

Perhaps 5b is in fact a single—in spite of Notker. The syntax of 5b is irreproachable. It starts a new thought, having no connection with 5a; and most important, this thought follows very logically after 2a,b—so much that lines 3a,b 4a, 5a can all be regarded as unwelcome intruders into a closely reasoned discourse on the relationship of the King of Life to his adversary, Death.

1b Mors vicit mortem et mors nostra est vita.
2a Mirabella et stupenda satis inter omnes victorias,
 b Ut moriens sic superaret fortem cum callida versutia.
5b Susceperat mors indemnem quem tenere numquam potuerat propter culpam.
6a Dum ambiit, illicita quae tenebat juste perdidit acquisita;
 b Ambiere voluerat in successu et remansit evacuata.

> (Death conquered death, and death is our life.
> —a wondrous victory among all others,
> that in dying he should overcome the strong one with expert cunning.
> Death received—as innocent—him whom he never could hold for reason of guilt.
> While casting about, he justly lost those ill-gotten gains he had;
> he had hoped to extend his holdings but in the end he was cleaned out.)

Behind this argument stands, of course, the much used Pauline passages on death, I Corinthians 15, and Romans 6, especially verse 9, which serves as Alleluia verse for the 4th Sunday after Easter.

> Christus resurgens ex mortuis jam non moritur:
>   mors illi ultra non dominabitur.

> (Knowing that) Christ being raised from the dead dieth no more;
> death hath no more dominion over him.

To this basic theme ECCE VICIT adds—in curious language—what seems to be a popular medieval theme, Christ's game-like contest and outwitting of Death (or more often of Satan). The "hook of divinity" in Notker's LAUDES DEO CONCINAT was another aspect of this same theme. Rand's *Sermo de confusione diaboli*, an extensive ninth-century witness of the *descensus ad inferos*, explores other aspects.[3] Here, again, the stanzas quoted on p. 38 from the Ambrosian *Hic est dies verus dei* seem to be immediate sources, even if not in wording.

Notker's version also calls for the elimination of ECCE VICIT phrase 8a,b. Here again, the couplet is syntactically complete and sets forth an image new and largely unrelated to what came before.

> Hic lapis est angularis quem reprobaverunt construentes;
> Jam factus est in caput anguli super omnes in excelso.

> (This is the cornerstone that the builders rejected;
> Now it has been placed on high at the peak of the corner,
> above all the others.)

The source is Psalm 118 (Latin 117), verse 22 (quoted also in Matthew 21,42, Mark 12,10, and the First Epistle of Peter, 2,7), which is used in Easter Week on Thursday as a verse with the Gradual-response *Hæc dies*.

> Lapidem quem reprobaverunt aedificantes
> hic factus est in caput anguli:

3. See note 1, Chapter 3.

In 1084 and 1118, the last phrase (9) is a single, corresponding to Notker's plan.

Regnum ejus magnum et potestas ejus prima in secula. Amen.

In 1240 this phrase is double.

Regnum ejus magnum et potestas ejus *et honor*
Manens in eternum per cuncta semper seculorum

As with line 4b of 1240, the syntax of this double 9 is looser, the effect less focussed, than in the shorter versions. It seems clear in this case that the single is the earlier version, the double being a later conflation.

Notker's HANC CONCORDI provides a line at the beginning for which no parallel appears in the West-Frankish versions. Notker's version can be construed as an opening single, followed by a double whose melody and syllable count differ only slightly from that of the single; or, it might be regarded as a triple with the second and third lines shortened at the start.

(1)   Hanc concordi famulatu colamus solemnitatem,
(2a)   Auctoris illius exemplo docti benigno
(2b)   Pro persecutorum precantis fraude suorum.

(1)   G G G A G A G F A C B D C A A G
(2)   G B A G A F A C B D C A A G

Together, the three lines form a syntactic unit. West-Frankish versions consistently have two lines, not three, corresponding to the first two of Notker's three. Melodically, the first two lines can be understood as an irregular double, in which the first line has a formal intonation, but one so short it cannot be logically separated from the rest of the line; and a second line that avoids this intonation, but instead of omitting it altogether replaces it with other pitches that provide a link with the end of the first line. The basic functions are the same as, say, in HÆC DIES QUAM EXCELSUS, but the implementation is different. The West-Frankish construction, and Notker's treatment of it, find parallels in other cases.

It seems reasonable to imagine Notker supplying the third line of text to form an exact double out of the second phrase of music, and so render the slightly unusual appearance of the West-Frankish version in a form that has a clear opening single followed by a regular double. If this interpretation is correct, we need assume no lacuna in ECCE VICIT after the second line.

This passage excepted, ECCE VICIT can be read much better according to Notker's plan than as it stands in the tenth-century Aquitanian sources; of these, 1240 presents an obviously conflated version, while the conflation in 1084 and 1118—with generally better readings—is less obvious but still demonstrable. In EPIPHANIAM, a popular prose with a very broad MS representation, there is no suggestion of such conflation: the text has the longer form of ECCE VICIT, but is cogent and consequent, with no softness in its own variants at the critical points. It is, however, curious that phrases 3 and 4 are still syntactically complete, and independent in their imagery as well: they *could* come out, with the thought going very smoothly from 2, whose subject is still implied as *Dominus*,

(2b) Quam cuncti prophetae praecinere venturum gentes ad salvandas.
(3a) Cujus maiestas ita est inclinata, ut assumeret servi formam.
(3b) Ante secula qui deus et tempora, homo factus est in Maria.
(4a) Balaam de quo vaticinans, exibit ex Jacob rutilans, inquit stella
(4b) Et confringet ducum agmina regionis Moab maxima potentia.
(5a) Huic magi munera deferunt . . .

directly to 5, *huic* depending on the same subject. Line 5b, however, needs 5a; a single here seems unreasonable. This is not to suggest that EPIPHANIAM was composed in stages, or should in any way be reconstructed to conform to Notker's plan, only that the older form might still leave traces in later texts.

It seems close at hand, then, to assume that the version of ECCE VICIT so restored was Notker's model. If we suppose a single at 5 in ECCE VICIT, we can conclude that Notker himself provided a double at that point. But here, too, there is something to remark.

(Notker)
(3a) O Stephane, signifer regis summe boni, nos exaudi,
(3b) Proficue qui es pro tuis exauditus inimicis!
(4a) Paulus tuis precibus, Stephane, te quondam persecutus Christo credit,
(4b) Et tecum tripudiat in regno, cui nullus persecutor approprinquat.
(5a) Nos proinde, nos supplices ad te clamantes et precibus te pulsantes,
(5b) Oratio sanctissima nos tua semper conciliet deo nostro.

Line 3a continues the thought of line 2:

Oh Stephen, standard-bearer of the King of greatest good, hear us,
thou who hast prayed especially for thine enemies!
Paul—who once persecuted thee, Stephen—by thy prayers believed in Christ.

And in line 5, *nos* directly and emphatically continues the list of those who could benefit from Stephen's intercession.

And especially we, crying to thee as suppliants and hurling prayers at thee,
—may this most holy prayer always reconcile us to our God!

Line 4b, however, has a curious effect in this succession of urgent petitions: it is a decorative modification, shifting the scene and anticipating the joyful conclusion.

And rejoices with thee in the kingdom, where no persecutor draws nigh.

And *tripudiat* is not a frequent word for Notker. Could 3b be a subsequent addition? If so, it is a skillful one; *persecutor* sits very well over against *persecutus* in 4a, and makes a good cadence with *approprinquat*.

In being brought into conformity with Notker's plan, then, ECCE VICIT gains in clarity and logic; the text is still not easy, but the difficulties that remain bear witness to a serious struggle with a high theme, rather than to less responsible patching together of images or sometimes just words. The melody of ECCE VICIT, as it stands in the sources, is not open to that kind of criticism, being basically the same as the melody of EPIPHANIAM. Still, one can agree with Stäblein in seeing in Notker's version of the melody a more compelling progression. Stäblein claims this quality as specifically "Eastern" as opposed to a "play with formal sections, conceived on a harmonious-symmetrical overall design, in the West." But if the West-Frankish ECCE VICIT had the same plan originally, then the difference Stäblein ascribes to place (and tribal traits?) is really one of chronology, of stylistic development.

In any case, in the melody ECCE VICIT, phrase 2 is more logically followed by 5 than by 3. It has been noticed, of course, that the melody of 5, beginning with *protoplastus*, is the same as that of 2, with the preceding syllables *Quem comisit* set to the four pitches G A G F. The more cogent melodic succession furthermore is obtained by reading 5 directly after 2 as a single. Then the whole construction consists of a double (2a,b) followed by the same melody a third time (5), made more emphatic by the four initial notes, as a concluding single. Such a construction, corresponding to phrases 2 and 3 of HÆC DIES QUAM EXCELSUS, would appropriately close off an extended opening period.

ECCE VICIT also recalls LAUDES DEO to some extent, in that it makes use of a lower register towards the beginning (phrase 2); the melody is different from the low-lying phrase of LAUDES DEO, but not so very different: since these melodic progressions in general tend to move directly to their goals, phrases that move into a lower register tend to have a certain similarity.

The low-lying phrases 2 and 5, then, are followed in the reconstructed version by the higher phrase 6, which asserts the change in register at its very beginning (*Dum ambiit*). This upward trend is continued by phrase 7, which brings the high point of the melody. Phrase 9 (*Regnum ejus*), falling back to the original register, provides a relaxation for the close.

The phrase that marks the high point, phrase 7, makes a striking impression and calls for special comment here, as it has in previous studies. First of all, it has a strongly articulated sub-phrase structure, x x y.

7a (x) In se refulsit defici extremitas,
  (x) ut quibus ad vitam fuerat largitur
      (y) ingressum donaret et regressum ad percipiendam veniam

Sub-phrase x leaps up to D, circles around it and cadences there—not with a standard cadence formula but just by bracketing the D with E and C. This much is literally repeated. Sub-phrase y moves back down to G in melodic groups of three (D C A, C B G), then through the F-A-C realm to the cadence pattern used in this melody (A B A G). Considered as a whole, the phrase is very long—43 syllables, far longer than any normal phrase encountered so far. But of course it is not considered as a simple whole, rather as a group of sub-phrases, 12 plus 12 plus 19.

The coordination of the syntax with the sub-phrase structure is not without problems. The reading of the first x is obscure, but *extremitas* marks the end of the main clause; *ut* starts the second x. The relative clause *quibus ad vitam fuerat* is contained in the second x, which at its end continues the purpose clause into y—*ut . . . largitur / ingressum donaret . . . .* In other words, the first melodic articulation is supported, the second is elided. In 7b, both are elided.

7b   (x) Hic verus est agnus legalis qui multis

      (x) se manifestavit figuris, tandem se

      (y) pro mundum hostiam dedit patri ut redimeret membra sua.

If it were not for the first (x) in 7a, one would conclude that the text paid the sub-phrase structure no heed at all; but with the first articulation observed it can be argued, I think, that the subsequent elisions are purposive. It is true that (even without cadence formulas) the sub-phrase structure is strikingly clear. Indeed, the plasticity, the integrity of the sub-phrase x surpasses anything we have seen, and is exceptional, but not unique, in the early repertory as a whole. That, I think, is what provoked the author of ECCE VICIT to do what he did—observe the articulation once, then run over it to keep these exceptionally lyric passages from dominating the whole piece and breaking up the long line at its high point.

The text of 7a is partly obscure, and I am sorry to print, on this one occasion, words in which I see no clear meaning:

7a   In se refulsit defici extremitas

I follow the reading of MS 1240 as *codex antiquior*, finding no better reading among the numerous emendations of later sources. From the second sub-phrase on, things are better (*ut quibus* . . .): here the author seems to refer to ". . . that they might have life, and have it more abundantly." Another text from Ambrose's *Intende qui regis*,[4]

Egressus ejus a patre,

Regressus ejus ad patrem,

helps link the language of ECCE VICIT to the idea—a not uncommon one—of the Word going forth and returning, and of Christian access to life in escape from the world.

The strong arch-form with phrase 7 at its apex is surely the most striking aspect of the melody as a whole. Other, more subtle features are not, perhaps, so immediately apparent. At the motivic level, one such feature is the echo in phrase 9 of phrase 1. It is an echo, not a literal repetition—as, in LAUDES DEO, phrase 8 is a literal repetition of phrase 4. And it is an echo of something heard at the start of the piece but nowhere in between, unlike the use in the last phrase of HÆC DIES QUAM EXCELSUS of the most important motive of the whole piece. Indeed, the echo in ECCE VICIT is fragile enough to be effaced completely by some of the variant melodic readings.

Peculiar to the cadence of phrase 1, as opposed to the cadences of phrases 2 through 6, is the progression D C A G. The D, approached by leap from the B below, and followed eventually by the leap from C to A, is clearly perceptible as the high point of the phrase. All the other phrases (except the last one) have a concluding pattern A B A G, approached through a descent from the C above. Phrase 9, then, without literally repeating phrase 1 in its entirety but simply by moving through the progression A F A C B D C A G embodies a reminiscence of something heard before and perhaps recalled only dimly.

That such a reminiscence can have effect is due first of all to elements of uniformity among the intervening phrases 2,5,6. As mentioned, these end alike, on A B, A G—a cadence pattern we have not encountered before. (The principal pattern has been A G F G G.) In phrases

4. *Anal.hymn.* 50, pp. 13–14 (strophe 6).

2 and 5 the cadence pattern is approached through a descent from C; in phrase 6 this descent is expressed as C C B G, thus repeating a motive used earlier in that phrase.

6   G C C B A C C B G A G A F A C C B G A B A G

Phrase 7 ends the same way as phrase 6. When the motive D C A G reappears near the start of phrase 9 (*ejus magnum*), it recalls something last heard at the cadence in phrase 1. In phrase 9, the motive actually appears twice—once near the beginning of the phrase, then at the end.

G C *C B D C A* F A C *C B D C A* G F A A G

Another echo links phrase 9 with phrase 6. As already mentioned, phrase 9 returns at its start to the pitch-level C, which had been clearly established at phrase 6; the intervening phrase 7 moves up to D. The readings for ECCE VICIT provide a neume GC at the start of both phrases (the neume is usually absent in the more widely known melody for EPIPHANIAM). This is admittedly slight basis for a melodic correspondence, yet the overall control of the line, the cleanness and absence of ornament seem to permit such a correspondence to be heard.

In LAUDES DEO, phrase 8 was a literal repeat of phrase 4, and there the structural implications of the repeat were very clear: this was the refrain-like phrase that returned after intervening "verses." If, in ECCE VICIT, phrase 9 sounds like phrase 1 on the one hand, and phrase 6 on the other, is some subtle reference to a refrain-like structure intended? It is a very faint reference; but it is striking that phrases 2 and 5 recall phrase 3 of LAUDES DEO in more than just low register; and that phrase 7, although the highest part of the piece, has an articulated sub-phrase structure that further recalls the "verses" of LAUDES DEO.

So while ECCE VICIT is most obviously governed by a long melodic curve that rises to a peak in phrase 5, it also embodies a latent refrain-form, different from the curve even though compatible with it. It is this latent suggestion, it seems to me, that may have been responsible for the subsequent West-Frankish form of the melody used for EPIPHANIAM and other proses.

We have to imagine the revisor(s) of ECCE VICIT (or the composer of EPIPHANIAM, if the interpolations in ECCE VICIT were modeled on that) expanding the earlier plan by using some phrases twice. Rather than looking back at Example 4, it may be more convenient to use the diagram in Example 5, which numbers the phrases as in the restored version. Some phrases have been labeled with their register to help recall what the new numbering refers to; the phrases now numbered 4 and 6 are the ones containing a hint of refrain in their incipits.

What the revisor did was to interpolate a statement of 4 after 2 (as shown by "4" in quotes under EPIPHANIAM). This he followed by another interpolation, the phrase that Stäblein identified as 5 placed a fifth lower; but the degree of identity varies with the source used—it is clear in some sources that the two were considered the same, but doubtful in others. In either case, the revisor then doubled 3 (if that had not already been done). The end result was to anticipate the original 3,4,5 with the group 2,4,5, keeping "5" in a lower register so as to maintain 5 at the high point of the piece.

ECCE VICIT (restored version)

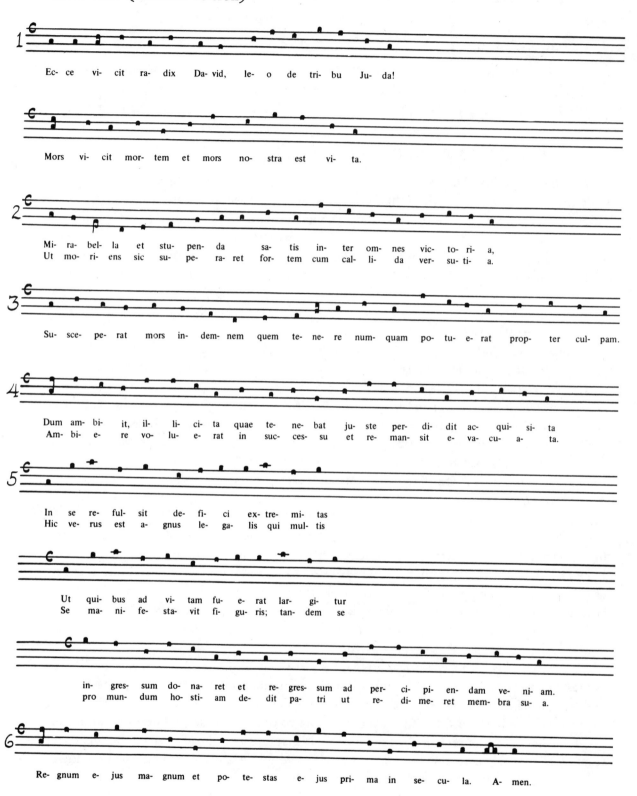

1

Ec- ce vi- cit ra- dix Da- vid, le- o de tri- bu Ju- da!

Mors vi- cit mor- tem et mors no- stra est vi- ta.

2

Mi- ra- bel- la et stu- pen- da sa- tis in- ter om- nes vic- to- ri- a,
Ut mo- ri- ens sic su- pe- ra- ret for- tem cum cal- li- da ver- su- ti- a.

3

Su- sce- pe- rat mors in- dem- nem quem te- ne- re num- quam po- tu- e- rat prop- ter cul- pam.

4

Dum am- bi- it, il- li- ci- ta quae te- ne- bat ju- ste per- di- dit ac- qui- si- ta
Am- bi- e- re vo- lu- e- rat in suc- ces- su et re- man- sit e- va- cu- a- ta.

5

In se re- ful- sit de- fi- ci ex- tre- mi- tas
Hic ve- rus est a- gnus le- ga- lis qui mul- tis

Ut qui- bus ad vi- tam fu- e- rat lar- gi- tur
Se ma- ni- fe- sta- vit fi- gu- ris; tan- dem se

in- gres- sum do- na- ret et re- gres- sum ad per- ci- pi- en- dam ve- ni- am.
pro mun- dum ho- sti- am de- dit pa- tri ut re- di- me- ret mem- bra su- a.

6

Re- gnum e- jus ma- gnum et po- te- stas e- jus pri- ma in se- cu- la. A- men.

Example 5.   ECCE VICIT (restored)   EPIPHANIAM

Phrase "5" assumes a wide variety of forms in the different versions. In ECCE VICIT, as we saw, it is single in MSS 1118 and 1084.

"5"   12+12+4

And in MS 1240 a double.

"5"   12+12+4
        12+12+4

In EPIPHANIAM it is a slightly shorter double.

"5"   9+9+4
        9+9+4

Then in GAUDE EJA, "5" is interlocked with the following 3 in a construction I have elsewhere baptized "overcouplet," more easily shown than explained.

$$\text{``5''}^{12}\ 3^{21}\quad \text{``5''}_{12}\ 3_{21}$$
$$\text{or ``5''a}\ 3a\quad \text{``5''b}\ 3b$$

In this form, found in Paris B.N.lat. MS 13252 (St. Magloire, 12th century) "5" is 12 syllables long. In a still later source, Rheims 695 (13th century), "5" has been expanded to the dimensions of ECCE VICIT.[5]

$$\text{``5''}^{12+12+4}\ 3^{21}\quad \text{``5''}_{12+12+4}\ 3_{21}$$

Here, surely, is to be observed Stäblein's "play with formal sections." But now we need to look more closely at the text of GAUDE EJA, and its claim—or rather, Stäblein's claim—that it goes back to the early repertory. Since in this case some of the sources themselves may go back to the ninth century, they need to be brought into the discussion. The Carolingian Antiphonale from Compiègne, Paris B.N. lat. MS 17436, contains first an Antiphonal of the Mass (fol. 1v–23v), then an Antiphonal for the Office (from fol. 31v); these elements are dated circa 860–880.[6] In between the two antiphonals, on fol. 24–30, are a number of additions, some in the original hand (Alleluia-list, Processional Antiphons), others including a fragment whose text begins *Summa pia* (fol. 24). This fragment is the last half of the prose GAUDE EJA: *Summa pia* is the start of phrase 5b of GAUDE EJA. The earliest sources hitherto known for GAUDE EJA as a complete piece were from the twelfth century; it also appears in the Autun troper, Paris Arsenal MS 1169 (fol. 25) where it lay apparently unnoticed for lack of a clear initial. This new source, however, still does not place GAUDE EJA, with the revised form of the melody, even as far back as MS 1240; the Arsenal troper is dated 996–1024.[7]

Summa pia, as mentioned, is an addition to the ninth-century Compiègne Antiphonal, and cannot benefit from the dating of the Antiphonal itself. It cannot, I think, be safely assigned to the ninth century; rather, it appears to be after 900. The fragment has neumes of the kind associated with Metz.

Summa pia includes a reference to the Norman raids.

(6a) De gente normannica nos libera que nostra vastat deus regna;
(6b) senum jugulat et juvenum ac virginum puerorum quoque catervam

This reference has been taken as conclusive evidence for a ninth-century origin for *Summa pia* —and for GAUDE EJA as well—in spite of the fact that the raids continued undiminished past 900. If anything, they got worse; the pressure increased until it finally resulted in the settlement with Rollo in 911, whereby he received the whole of "Normandy"; and elsewhere the raids continued for longer still.

The relationship of *Summa pia* to ECCE VICIT is made piquant by the fact that *Summa pia* happens to start at the point (5b) where the interpolation into ECCE VICIT could safely be presumed to end; that is, 5b of ECCE VICIT is surely a part of the original text, but 5a may have been added later. Is this merely a coincidence? Probably; but more important, *Summa pia*, as it stands, tells us nothing about the shape of its melody in that portion where inter-

5. Further details in Stäblein, "Die Sequenzmelodie Concordia," and my article, "Some Ninth-Century Sequences."

6. Dom R. J. Hesbert, *Antiphonale missarum sextuplex* (Bruxelles, 1935), especially pp. xix–xx.

7. See Appendix.

polation took place—in that portion where Notker's plan differs from the later West-Frank-ish plan as found in EPIPHANIAM and other versions. Even assuming that *Summa pia* is a ninth-century witness—which is assuming more than either the MS evidence of the refer-ence to the Normans can guarantee—still that does not prove that GAUDE EJA, as it stands in the later sources, represents the ninth-century form of the melody.

It should be added, however, that *Summa pia* repeats the melody of phrase 2 before the last phrase, corresponding in this respect to the conflated version of ECCE VICIT found in MS 1240, and the two sources could well be from about the same time, that is ca. 930. But if *Summa pia* thus supports 1240 in this reading, it contradicts it in having a concluding single. In any case, by that time EPIPHANIAM can certainly be presumed to exist, too; indeed, the interpolations in ECCE VICIT could perfectly well have taken place before 900.

GAUDE EJA

1a   Gaude eja unica columba speciosa
 b   sponsa superno regi consociata.
2a   Beata semper dei genetrix pia virgo Maria,
 b   Precamur alma preces exaudire digneris ut nostras.
        "4"a   Praeclara dies nobis instat qua temporum affert orbita revoluta.
          b   Hæc solemnitas est hodie festivitas nostri merito veneranda.
        "5"a   Celebremus eam lingua vocifera,
           (decantantes laudes debitas domino voce clara.)
        3 a   Gratulemur in ea corde pio dominum laudantes mente pura,
        "5"b   Ut delicta nostra terget manu sua,
           (quibus expediti cantica tollamus in excelsa)
3b   Summa pia gratia nostra conservando corpora et custodita.
4a   De gente fera normannica nos libera quae nostra vastat deus regna:
 b   Senum jugulat et juvenum ac virginum puerorum quoque catervam.
5a   Repelle precamur cuncta nobis mala;
    converte, rogamus domine, supplices
        nos ad te, rex gloriae, es qui vera pax, salus, pia spes et firma.
 b   Dona nobis pacem atque concordiam;
    largire nobis spem integram, fidem simul
        veram caritatem continuam concede nobis et perfectam.
        "2"a   Sanctorum precibus nos adjuvemur ad hæc impetranda
          b   De quorum passione gratulemur modo gloriosa.
        6   Sit laus, [pax] et gloria trinitati quam maxima cuncta per saecula.
                                     [Amen.]

The text of GAUDE EJA is laid out here to show the parts belonging to the interpolated "4" and "5," as well as the two forms of "5," the shorter one from Paris Ars. MS 1169, and the longer, final form in parens. As a whole the text has many confusing aspects, especially when compared to other texts of the early repertory. It begins firmly enough with the ex-hortation *Gaude!* addressed to the Virgin, first in metaphor (1a,b), then in name and epithet

Hanc concordi (Notker)

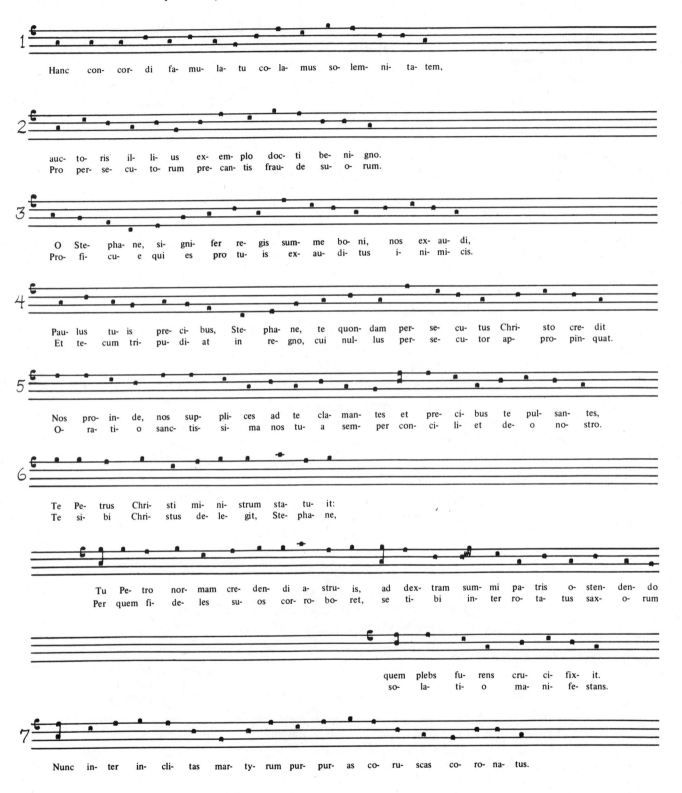

1. Hanc con- cor- di fa- mu- la- tu co- la- mus so- lem- ni- ta- tem,

2. auc- to- ris il- li- us ex- em- plo doc- ti be- ni- gno.
Pro per- se- cu- to- rum pre- can- tis frau- de su- o- rum.

3. O Ste- pha- ne, si- gni- fer re- gis sum- me bo- ni, nos ex- au- di,
Pro- fi- cu- e qui es pro tu- is ex- au- di- tus i- ni- mi- cis.

4. Pau- lus tu- is pre- ci- bus, Ste- pha- ne, te quon- dam per- se- cu- tus Chri- sto cre- dit
Et te- cum tri- pu- di- at in re- gno, cui nul- lus per- se- cu- tor ap- pro- pin- quat.

5. Nos pro- in- de, nos sup- pli- ces ad te cla- man- tes et pre- ci- bus te pul- san- tes,
O- ra- ti- o sanc- tis- si- ma nos tu- a sem- per con- ci- li- et de- o no- stro.

6. Te Pe- trus Chri- sti mi- ni- strum sta- tu- it:
Te si- bi Chri- stus de- le- git, Ste- pha- ne,

Tu Pe- tro nor- mam cre- den- di a- stru- is, ad dex- tram sum- mi pa- tris o- sten- do
Per quem fi- de- les su- os cor- ro- bo- ret, se ti- bi in- ter ro- ta- tus sax- o- rum

quem plebs fu- rens cru- ci- fix- it.
so- la- ti- o ma- ni- fe- stans.

7. Nunc in- ter in- cli- tas mar- ty- rum pur- pur- as co- ru- scas co- ro- na- tus.

PETRE SUMME CHRISTI PASTOR (Notker)

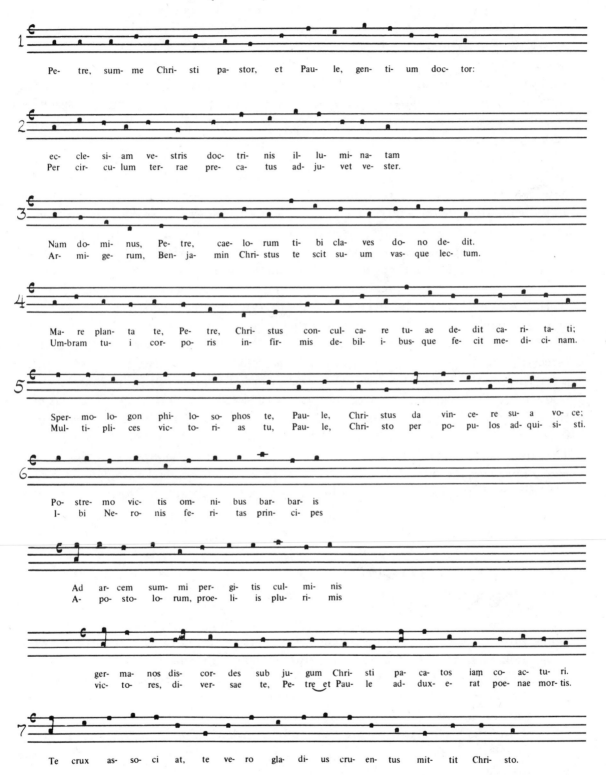

1. Pe- tre, sum- me Chri- sti pa- stor, et Pau- le, gen- ti- um doc- tor:

2. ec- cle- si- am ve- stris doc- tri- nis il- lu- mi- na- tam
   Per cir- cu- lum ter- rae pre- ca- tus ad- ju- vet ve- ster.

3. Nam do- mi- nus, Pe- tre, cae- lo- rum ti- bi cla- ves do- no de- dit.
   Ar- mi- ge- rum, Ben- ja- min Chri- stus te scit su- um vas- que lec- tum.

4. Ma- re plan- ta te, Pe- tre, Chri- stus con- cul- ca- re tu- ae de- dit ca- ri- ta- ti;
   Um- bram tu- i cor- po- ris in- fir- mis de- bil- i- bus- que fe- cit me- di- ci- nam.

5. Sper- mo- lo- gon phi- lo- so- phos te, Pau- le, Chri- stus da vin- ce- re su- a vo- ce;
   Mul- ti- pli- ces vic- to- ri- as tu, Pau- le, Chri- sto per po- pu- los ad- qui- si- sti.

6. Po- stre- mo vic- tis om- ni- bus bar- bar- is
   I- bi Ne- ro- nis fe- ri- tas prin- ci- pes

   Ad ar- cem sum- mi per- gi- tis cul- mi- nis
   A- po- sto- lo- rum, proe- li- is plu- ri- mis

   ger- ma- nos dis- cor- des sub ju- gum Chri- sti pa- ca- tos iam co- ac- tu- ri.
   vic- to- res, di- ver- sae te, Pe- tre et Pau- le ad- dux- e- rat poe- nae mor- tis.

7. Te crux as- so- ci- at, te ve- ro gla- di- us cru- en- tus mit- tit Chri- sto.

(2a). Line 2b is general petition. This is followed directly by—a proclamation of "today's festivity!" Such proclamations, not infrequent, almost always come at the very beginning of a text. Here the language is so general as to be unidentifiable. Not only does it not follow, it is verbose and redundant, strongly reminiscent of line 3a (*Serenatis cordibus . . .*) of HÆC DIES QUAM EXCELSUS.

The next lines continue the out-of-place theme of celebration, now directed toward the Lord (*dominum*), with a further petition in "5"b. But the diction of the whole is suspiciously glib, scarcely more convincing than the expansions of "5"a and b, which contribute little.

Extensive interpolation seems to be present. Notker's plan suggests that we go from 2b to 3b, and that, indeed, straightens out the text considerably. All is not completely clear, however, for *pia* is still redictum, and there is a turn from the Virgin to *deus* in 4a. Presumably the revision left these marks by some dislocation no longer traceable. The fact remains that the text is inconsequent as preserved in the sources, and most of the difficulty is removed by restoring the text in accordance with Notker's plan. GAUDE EJA might be an early text—even Notker's model, but only in this reduced form.

Neither of Notker's two texts gives any clue, or even an impression, of being an early work closely related to the model text. Yet the two are different in conception and technique, and there might be grounds for thinking of HANC CONCORDI as the earlier.

HANC CONCORDI is distinguished from ECCE VICIT by a consistent handling of the cadences, especially the cadence A B A G peculiar to this melody. Notker always sets it ′ x ′ x, and always begins the four-note pattern with a new word. The other cadences—those in 1 and 2 —are handled differently; those in 2a,b receive a cursus planus, *dócti benígno*. The ends of the sub-phrases in 6 are set proparoxytone, usually to one word (*státuit*). This consistent differentiation of cadences is part of an intense overall concern with refined diction in this text. That the concern was fruitful is evident in the fact that while smoothness is almost everywhere apparent, the means of producing it are not. One hesitates to single out words or passages, but perhaps the last line will serve as a credible example of Notker's technique.

```
                                    (uscas)    (atus)
                                    (co      co)
                (te     ta    ty)          (as     as)
            (un  in   in) (a    a) (ru   ur  ur    ru)
    7    Nunc inter inclitas martyrum purpuras coruscas coronatus
```

No one sound is heard as assonant for very long in the line; but between any two adjacent words there is some element of assonance. These are indicated by the parentheses, which link together a specific assonance for the period in which it is effective. At this lowest level, the assonance is remarkably persistent. It may be present at higher levels too, as *inclitas . . . purpuras coruscas*, but that seems less essential to the technique in the piece as a whole. The linking of the last two words is manifold and virtuoso; *-uscas* and *-atus*, in context, have something of the effect of a chiasmus. Next to lines such as this—and most of the lines have something of this smoothness, line 4a (which was suspected of being a later addition) seems just a little lame.

The layout of the text is beautifully matched to the structure of the melody. Yet something (perhaps only the knowledge of what happens in PETRE SUMME, the other text) suggests a reservation. Phrases 1 and 2 proclaim, in Notker's fashion, "today's festivity"—at the beginning, where it belongs. Phrases 3 and 4, lying in the lower register, address Stephen directly, and place Paul in the scene. Phrase 5 matches the C's in the higher register with the insistent *nos proinde, nos* of the petition. Then the sub-phrase structure is coordinated with the *Te . . . tu . . . te . . . (tibi)* containing the paradoxical diptychs.

6a   Thee did Peter ordain as minister of Christ;
          thou gavest Peter a measure of faith
                  by showing him the One whom the raging populace crucified,
                      at the right hand of God on high.
6b   Thee did Christ choose for himself, Stephen;
          through whom he strengthens his faithful,
                  showing himself as comfort to thee amidst the hail of stones.

The ending is formal and very fine.

7   Now amidst the brilliant splendor of martyrs dost thou shine forth, crowned.

Perhaps it was only that the petition came in an odd place, in the middle. But given the structure of the melody, and Notker's typical desire for an overriding image, a petition could hardly come anywhere else.

A different treatment might not be conceivable had not Notker himself provided it. PETRE SUMME seems the result of a concern not so much with diction as with overall concept, and the most brilliant possible exploitation of the musical shape. One can well agree with Stäblein's characterization "grossartig." Diction is hardly slighted: cadences are handled as rigorously as before; the language flows, perhaps a little more forcefully, a little less fastidious about its smooth sonorities. And the textual plan moves, without detour for petition, as straight to its goal as does the melody. This is all the more impressive because of the underlying diptych, Peter-Paul. They are joined in the introduction (1–2), then given separate lines or phrases in alternation—Peter in 3a, Paul in 3b; Peter in 4a and b (which, although syntactically independent, gives no hint here of later addition); Paul in 5a,b. The high point in phrase 6 joins them together, but still under diverse aspects—*diversae poenae mortis*. Only the concluding single joins them together, in Christ.

7   Te crux associat, te vero gladius cruentus mittit Christo.

      (Thee the cross joins—yes, thee the dripping sword sends—to Christ.)

The same qualities that distinguished TUBAM BELLICOSAM from what was surely the earlier setting, GRATES SALVATORI, here seem to attach to PETRE SUMME. In the earlier of two texts, Notker abides by the melody's shape, working within it as best he can, finding out its dimensions and rhythms. When he comes to write the later text, the melody—now firmly fixed in his conception—seems not only to determine the text's layout but also to suggest, through rhetorical shape, some of the key ideas and images.

VI

NUNC EXULTET, ARCE SUPERNA,
and SEMPER REGNANS
Notker's LAUDES SALVATORI

CLOSELY RELATED to LAUDES DEO is the much longer melody to NUNC EXULTET, used by Notker for his LAUDES SALVATORI. The striking dimensions of this melody (one of the longest among early sequences) is expressed by a relatively large number of phrases, eleven, but even more by the length of many of the phrases. These involve a wealth of sub-phrase constructions as well as melodic lines of spectacular thrust and breadth.

The main problem of reconstruction is in the use of certain phrases as singles or doubles. It was long ago observed by Bannister and Blume that another text, ARCE SUPERNA, has single phrases at 3,5,6,9,10. This text comes to us in the Winchester Troper, (Oxf. Bodl. MS 775; Cambridge, Corpus Christi College MS 473) and the corresponding melody appears in the Autun fragment, placed by Stäblein at the end of the 9th century. The text, in honor of St. Benedict, was affirmed by Bannister to be composed at or for Fleury-sur-Loire on the basis of the line "Illius in hac sede tumulata," referring to the relics of St. Benedict generally considered to be preserved at Fleury.[1] Taken as a whole, the text of ARCE SUPERNA does not seem very clear. The overall sense can be made out, and indicates a relatively routine theme and approach for a Saint's day. The obscurity is in syntax and word order: either the author is struggling with sequence form in general (perhaps with this form in particular) or—as seems more likely—he is cultivating an elaborate style of diction, one characteristic of the tenth-century repertory.

The main value of ARCE SUPERNA for us at the moment is in the fact of its numerous singles. These are confirmed by the purely melismatic notation in the Autun fragment—which in any case is an earlier witness than the Winchester Troper.[2] The singles existed, then,

---

1. *Anal.hymn.* 40, p. 150. For the Autun fragment, see Appendix. The *Dictionaire d'archéologie chrétienne et de liturgie* provides at the article "Fleury-sur-Loire" (V, ii, 1709: H. Leclercq) a long and engaging account of how the relics of St. Benedict were thought to come to Fleury from Montecassino.

2. The Winchester neumes, as well as those of Autun, correspond closely to the melody of NUNC EXULTET as

fairly early; our problem is to understand them in terms of the West-Frankish text NUNC
EXULTET, and Notker's LAUDES SALVATORI.

ARCE SUPERNA

1   Arce superna cuncta qui gubernat sidera

2a   Regit arva pariter moderatur mariaque creavit omnia.

 b   Plebs in aula dicata pie Christo precata nunc effunde devota,

3   Patronumque Benedictum exorat
              (ut) cum salute sempiterna veniam capias quo caelestem
              ejus sancta sequens exemplaria;

4a   Ut cujus ovans veneraris festa praeclara quae nitent in orbe annique revixit orbita

 b   Illius in hac sede tumulata dum membra fuere beata coram quae jungaris organa

5   Quem elegit cum excessit ab humo
              atque mundi perlustravit sub solis radio per immensa
              sacra visa deo dante spatia.

6   Polorum regna scandere possis felicia
              ejusdem modo sanctisque jungi qui deo semper adstant tripudiantes,

7a   In patria multiplica quibus doxa

 b   Pro merita micantia dat actea;

8a   Quorum ut queamus unitate

 b   Et consocietate gaudere,

9   Preces supplicum in caelo preferas
              quo nos pietas divina nuper faciat post funus gratulantur.

10   Subveni ulnis almis angelorum
              implorant famulorum sanctae laudes quas celebrat plebs monastica.

11a Nunc ergo pie dies nostros obtentu dona pace et vitam claritate nostra,

 b   Et per saecula regi nostro sit decus et potestas cum sanctis qui donat beata praemia.

The shape of the whole sequence (referring to the transcription of NUNC EXULTET) lends
itself to a schematic expression, for one phrase returns exactly, and others are echoed strongly enough to suggest a return, as indicated here.

1 2 3 4 5 6 7 8 9 10 11
A B C D C D′ E F D″ G D‴

The phrases labeled D are really alike only in their beginning; in other words, the similarity
is motivic. But the appearance of the same opening motive (the pitches G B C D), alternating with the exact return of the melody of 3 at 5, seems to be enough to identify 4 with 6
to at least some degree, and subsequently to suggest a similarity to 9 and 11.

This purely melodic plan is reinforced by the tonal areas in which the phrases move.
Phrase 3, repeated at 5, lies low, centered on the G final and the D a fourth below. This, of
course, is the same low-lying phrase previously met in LAUDES DEO; here in NUNC EXULTET

---

preserved in the Aquitanian sources. ARCE POLORUM is found in Oxford, Bodleian MS 775, fol. 166, and Cambridge
Corpus Christi College MS 473, fol. 108v; text in *Anal. hymn.* 40, p. 150.

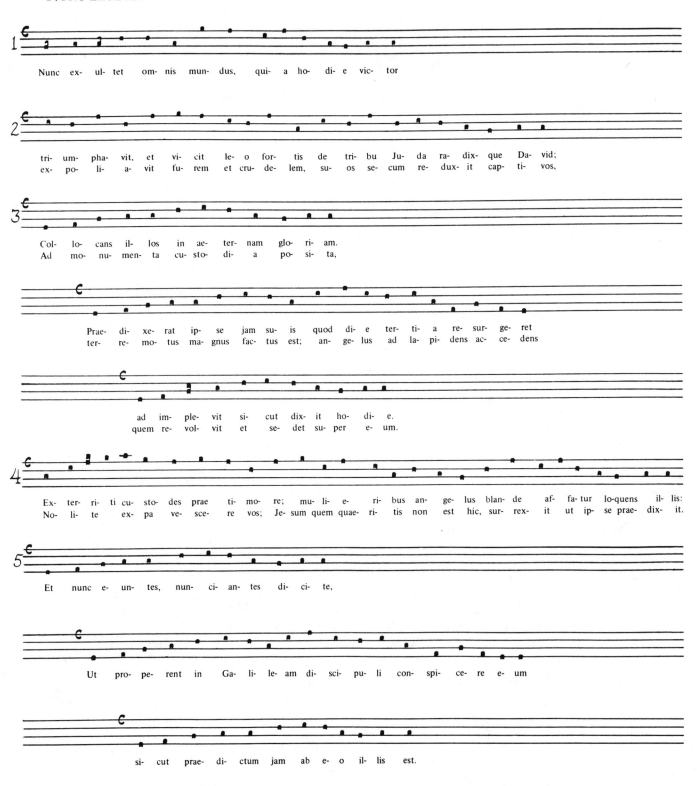

Nunc ex- ul- tet om- nis mun- dus, qui- a ho- di- e vic- tor

tri- um- pha- vit, et vi- cit le- o for- tis de tri- bu Ju- da ra- dix- que Da- vid;
ex- po- li- a- vit fu- rem et cru- de- lem, su- os se- cum re- dux- it cap- ti- vos,

Col- lo- cans il- los in ae- ter- nam glo- ri- am.
Ad mo- nu- men- ta cu- sto- di- a po- si- ta,

Prae- di- xe- rat ip- se jam su- is quod di- e ter- ti- a re- sur- ge- ret
ter- re- mo- tus ma- gnus fac- tus est; an- ge- lus ad la- pi- dens ac- ce- dens

ad im- ple- vit si- cut dix- it ho- di- e.
quem re- vol- vit et se- det su- per e- um.

Ex- ter- ri- ti cu- sto- des prae ti- mo- re; mu- li- e- ri- bus an- ge- lus blan- de af- fa- tur lo- quens il- lis:
No- li- te ex- pa- ve- sce- re vos; Je- sum quem quae- ri- tis non est hic, sur- rex- it ut ip- se prae- dix- it.

Et nunc e- un- tes, nun- ci- an- tes di- ci- te,

Ut pro- pe- rent in Ga- li- le- am di- sci- pu- li con- spi- ce- re e- um

si- cut prae- di- ctum jam ab e- o il- lis est.

96   Nunc exultet, arce superna, and semper regnans

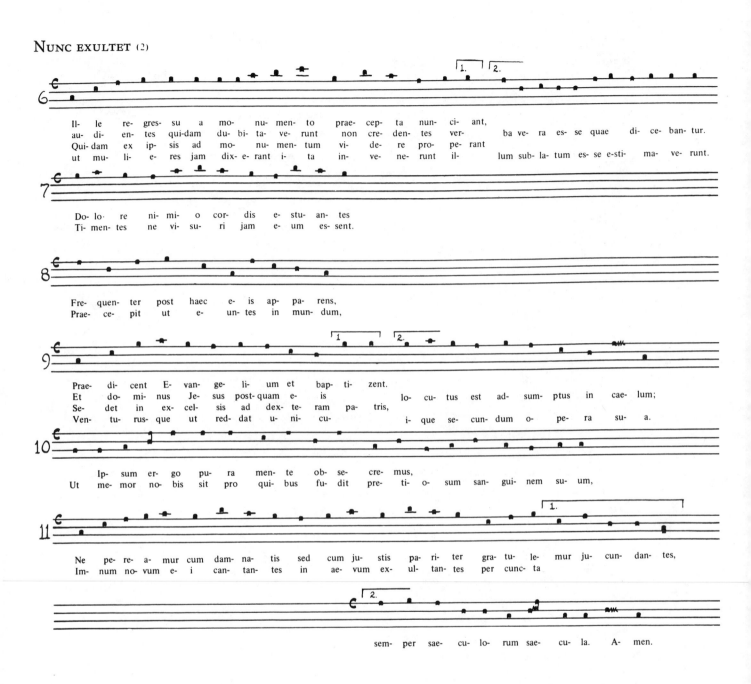

it seems to have much the same function as there, that is, it provides tonal relief, and also gives the impression of a "verse" in between "refrains." Phrases 4 and 6 lie almost completely above the G final, going up to the E above (in phrase 4), then up to the G above in phrase 6. This high G marks the melodic peak of the piece, being followed by a gradual descent through phrases 7 and 8. Phrases 9 and 11 occupy the same tonal area from the G final upwards, without, however, reaching up to the G above or giving the impression of a melodic climax.

Phrase 10 embodies a particularly clear expression of the F-A-C realm identified before as an alternative to the higher and lower realms usually found around a G final. In LAUDES DEO and HÆC DIES QUAM EXCELSUS, the F-A-C realm was touched upon briefly, as here in phrase 4; in phrase 10, however, it is insisted upon for virtually the whole phrase, with the help of a special figure C B C A C G A (F). Coming between two phrases firmly grounded on G (phrases 9 and 11), phrase 10 provides a welcome relief as well as a penultimate departure, against which the G final can be effectively reasserted for the last time.

1-2	3	4	5	6	7	8	9	10	11
				G	F				F
D		D		D	D		D		D
	(C)	C	(C)			C		C	
		A						A	
G	G	G		G	(G)	G	G	(G)	G
		F						F	
	D		D						

Cadence points and patterns also play an important role in the overall shape. A long pattern C B C A G F G G, incorporating shorter ones seen previously, appears at the ends of phrases 1 and 4. In addition, the shorter cadence A G F G G appears at the ends of phrases 2,3,5, and 10. Phrases 6 and 7 end on the D above the G final, suggesting "open" endings as opposed to the "closed" ones associated with the G final. But phrase 8 ends on the G final without the use of a cadence pattern. Phrase 9 has an internal cadence on the D above, then a concluding cadence on the G final, curiously colored by the stress on the C preceding. Phrase 11 ends on the G final in a manner that recalls the ornamented closes of LAUDES DEO and others. The overall plan is very clear, as shown here (italic represents the use of at least the F G G cadence (in phrase 6, C D D).

```
1  2  3  4  5  6  7  8   9   10 11
G  G  G  G  G  D  D  G  D/G  G  G
```

Closely related to cadence plan is the disposition of various phrase shapes. Phrase 1, functioning as intonation, has little of the ornamental character of the opening phrases of LAUDES DEO or HÆC DIES QUAM EXCELSUS; it only has the four-syllable incipit, then the long cadence pattern preceded by a leap up to D. Phrase 2 has two parts, the second beginning like the first, somewhat in the manner of a consequent to an antecedent—as in LAUDES DEO phrase 2, but without any difference between 2a and 2b. There is no obvious cadence marking a sub-phrase structure.

Phrases 3 and 5, being the same, have of course the same shape—a clear, self-contained sub-phrase, repeated in extension, leading directly to another literal repetition (a a' a). Compared to phrase 3 of LAUDES DEO, phrase 3 of NUNC EXULTET lacks the opening G, and rises higher, to B; the extension (a') is more elaborate, with a striking return to the lower register through B G E.

Phrase 4, coming between phrase 3 and its repetition at 5, contrasts with it not only in tonal area but also in shape: it effects a temporary return to the area above G, and it is without a hint of a sub-phrase division.

Phrases 1 through 5, then, already exhibit a variety of shapes, and in an order that is correlated with other melodic factors. In general, the order preserves an alternation between a lower phrase with a sub-phrase articulation, and higher phrases without one.

Phrase 6 brings a kind of phrase new in this piece and in our investigation; it can be represented schematically by a_1a_2b. As a sub-phrase structure it is clearly articulated with a cadence on C D D at the end of a_1; there is very smooth avoidance of that cadence at the end of a_2, and a return to it (but without suggesting a repeat of the sub-phrase itself) at the end of b. The shape as a whole is kept clearly distinct from that of Phrase 5, in spite of the fact that each has three sub-phrases. Also skillfully handled is the relationship between the cadence of a_1 and of b: the first cadence sounds "open" because of being on D after the establishment of a G final. But the second one, also on D, sounds closed—at least, in relation to the first, while at the higher level of the piece as a whole the second one remains open. A subtle differentiation has been made, whether by the approach within sub-phrase b, or simply by making the phrase "come out on the right foot" in the arrangement of weight and accent.

Phrases 7 and 8, besides being very much shorter than the phrases preceding, and lacking any cadence formula, also lack any sub-phrase articulation. In 7 there might be a hint of an ascending sequence (D E D C/E F E D/) but it is expressed completely at a motivic level and does not create a sub-phrase articulation. If there is any sub-phrase present, it is in the grouping of phrases 7 and 8 together—as a a b b—an effect actually quite perceptible, encouraged as it is by the abruptly shorter dimensions of these phrases. Being each roughly a third as long as the preceding phrases, 7 and 8 seem to cluster together to achieve equivalent status.

Phrase 9 is like phrase 6 in structure—a_1a_2b—as well as in initial motive and in register. The open ending of a_1 is unmistakable, the leap up to the fifth being as structurally explicit as it is eloquent. Sub-phrase a_2, at its end, makes clear not just by going on but by omitting the G before the leap up to D, that the composer intended to avoid closure.

Phrase 10 also has an a_1a_2b sub-phrase structure, but somewhat less decisive. Here it sounds as though the composer was primarily interested in finding yet another open ending, this time on A, as a note associated with the F-A-C realm that prevails in the phrase. The pause on A, however, is not handled as for a cadence (compare sub-phrase a_1 in 9), and the effect is closer to that of an arbitrary halt and repeat. We have encountered such halting effects elsewhere near the ends of pieces, used to de-accelerate the piece as it draws to a close.

Real closure takes place in phrase 11: although beginning with the motive from 6 and 9, 11 has little of the sub-phrase articulation found in those phrases. There is, to be sure, a clear sense of repetition, but it operates at the motivic level.

G B / C D E D F E D / C D E D F E D / B C D B . . .

The result is a relatively long line (sustained in a relatively high register) that avoids the clarity found in, say, 9, while at the same time lacking the sweep and expansiveness of 4.

It seems a very good way to end this piece, as a peroration. There is a short second ending for 11b, with a quilisma for a closing ornament, similar to the end of LAUDES DEO. This last phrase is a double (as in LAUDES DEO), not a single, as in HAEC DIES QUAM EXCELSUS and ECCE VICIT (which was given a concluding double in the later interpolations). As has also been the case, the last phrase ends without the F G G cadence, descending instead from above to the G final.

The determination of the early plan of NUNC EXULTET is nowhere as clear as that of LAUDES DEO, simply because Notker's version consistently shows doubles, while it was his use of singles in LAUDES DEO that required the reduction of the West-Frankish text. Instead of Notker's witness, then, we have the Autun fragment, whose dating, being paleographical, has less fixity than that provided by Notker's witness. And we have the witness of the version of NUNC EXULTET given by MS 1240 (ca. 930), which shows singles at 5 and 10, but not at 3, 6, 9. Notker's witness tells us that he, at least, treated these all as doubles—unless there is reason to think that the text preserved as Notker's is not entirely his, which may be the case in one instance.

The main body of the text of NUNC EXULTET was adapted from the Gospel account of the Resurrection. The Gospel story extends from phrase 3 through 9, although in 3 as well as in 9 there is a question of what strictly belongs to the account. Everything in between is concerned with the story: a guard was placed at the sepulchre, there was an earthquake, the angel rolled away the stone; the guards were terrified; the angel spoke to the women, reassuring them and sending them back to the disciples with the message to go to Galilee; they went and reported it, but some did not believe; some of the disciples returned to the sepulchre to see for themselves; they were sorrowful, afraid that they might see him; then after that, he did appear to them many times, telling them to go forth into the world, to preach the Gospel and to baptize; and after he had spoken with them, he was taken up into heaven; he sits on the right hand of the Father, and will come again to render each man his due according to his works.

Except for the end, which becomes more summary (like the *Credo*), the account presents a narrative unlike anything seen so far in terms of amount and concreteness of detail. Lines 3b and 4a are taken from Matthew, lines 4b, 5a, and 5 from Matthew and Mark combined, as shown by a comparison of the wording.

Matthew 27:66
Illi autem abeuntes munierunt sepulcrum signantes lapidem cum custodibus.

28:1
Vespere autem sabbati, quae lucescit in prima sabbati, venit Maria Magdalene et altera Maria videre sepulcrum.
Et ecce terraemotus factus est magnus.
Angelus enim Domini descendit de caelo:
> et accedens revolvit lapidem, et sedebat super eum:
> erat autem aspectus ejus sicut fulgur;
> et vestimentum ejus sicut nix.

Prae timore autem ejus exterriti sunt custodes,
    et facti sunt velut mortui.
Respondens autem angelus dixit mulieribus:

NUNC EXULTET
3b   Ad monumenta custodia posita.
       terremotus magnus factus est; angelus ad lapidem accendens
       quem revolvit et sedet super eum.
4a   Exterriti custodes prae timore; mulieribus angelus blande affatu loquens illis:

Matthew 28:5
Nolite timere vos:
       scio enim, quod Jesum, qui crucifixus est, quaeritis:
       non est hic: surrexit enim, sicut dixit.
       venite, et videte locum, ubi positus erat Dominus.
Et cito euntes, dicite discipulis ejus quia surrexit:
       et ecce praecedit vos in Galileam:
       ibi eum videbitis. Ecce praedixi vobis.

Mark 16:6
Qui dicit illis: Nolite expavescere:
       Jesum quaeritis Nazarenum crucifixum;
       surrexit, non est hic;
       ecce locus ubi posuerunt eum.
       Sed ite, dicite discipilus ejus et Petro quia praecedit vos in Galileam;
       ibi eum videbitis, sicut dixit vobis.

NUNC EXULTET
4b   Nolite expavescere vos;
       Jesum quem quaeritis non est hic, surrexit up ipse praedixit:
5a   Videte locum ubi fuit dominus;
       recordamini quod vivens locutus sit
       quod ipse die tertia resurgeret.
5b   Et nunc euntes, nuntiantes dicite,
       ut properent in Galileam discipuli conspicere eum
       sicut praedictum jam ab eo illis est.

Lines 6a and b are less easily identified; they follow a general story line, but correspond exactly to none of the four Gospels; perhaps they are closest to Luke.

Matthew 28:8
Et exierunt cito de monumento cum timore et gaudio magno, currentes nuntiare discipulis ejus.
. . .
Et videntes eum adoraverunt: quidam autem dubitaverunt.

Luke 24:8
Et recordatae sunt verborum ejus,

  et regressae a monumento nuntiaverunt hæc omnia illis undecim et ceteris
omnibus.
Erat autem Maria Magdalene et Johanna et Maria Jacobi et ceterae, quae cum eis erant,
quae dicebant ad apostolos hæc.
Et visa sunt ante illos sicut deliramentum verba ista, et non crediderunt illis.

NUNC EXULTET

6a Ille regressu a monumento, praecepta nunciant,
      audientesque dubitaverunt non credentes verba vera esse quae dicebantur.
6b Quidam ex ipsis ad monumentum videre properant
      ut mulieres jam dixerant ita invenerunt; illum sublatum esse aestimaverunt.

Lines 7a and b do not seem to be directly represented in the Gospel accounts. Lines 8a,b
and the beginning of 9a return to Matthew and the rest of 9a to Mark.

Matthew 28:18
Et accedens Jesus locutus est eis, dicens:
  Data est mihi omnis potestas in caelo, et in terra.
  Euntes ergo docete omnes gentes,
      baptizantes eos in nomine Patris et Filii, et Spiritus Sancti.

Mark 16:19
Et dominum quidem Jesus postquam locutus est eis,
      assumptus est in caelum, et sedet a dextris Dei.

NUNC EXULTET

8a Frequenter post hæc eis apparens,
8b Praecepit ut euntes in mundum,
9a Praedicent Evangelium et baptizent.
      Et dominus Jesus postquam eis locutus est adsumptus in caelum;
9b Sedet in excelsis ad dexteram patris,

The two Aquitanian MSS from the end of the tenth century, Paris 1084 and 1118, provide this text for 5a.

5a Videte locum ubi fuit dominus;
      recordamini quod vivens locutus sit
      quod ipse die tertia resurgeret.

Line 5a has two ingredients—*Videte locum ubi fuit dominus*, which is part of the angel's
speech as found in both Matthew and Mark; and the rest of line 5a, which is *not* found in
either Matthew or Mark. On the one hand, it is hard to strike out *Videte locum . . .*, an essential link in the story; on the other hand, the rest of the line, *Recordamini . . .*, can very
easily be regarded as an interpolation. Indeed, its reference to the saying of Jesus that he

would rise again after three days shows up in NUNC EXULTET so often as to be immediately suspicious: it appears in 3a, not once but twice (*predixerat . . . sicut dixit*), then in 4b as part of the angel's speech, and in 5a. (Line 5b refers to a separate prediction, one that occurs in Mark as part of the admonition to go to Galilee.) Of these four instances, only the one in 4b is to be trusted as part of the original version.

Reconstruction of a single at 5, then, is suggested, but not entirely clear; it would, however, be possible to imagine a version that read as follows.

Videte locum ubi fuit dominus;
Et nunc euntes nunciantes dicite
Ut properent in Galileam discipuli conspicerent eum.

In this form the syllable count is very nearly appropriate, the articulation into sub-phrases less so; some further rearrangement, for which the basis is not presently apparent, would have to be made. Or, 5a could be omitted completely (as MS 1240 does), imagining its first member to be a subsequent restoration of the end of the angel's speech.

The problem of 5, however, is made more complex by the way the melody is treated—especially in comparison to Notker's version, in which 5 is a double, set to a slightly abbreviated form of 3.

(Notker)	phrase 3	phrase 5
	12 syllables (x)	12 (x)
	19 (x extended)	13 (x modified)
	12 (x)	12 (x)

MS 1084 follows this plan closely.

5a	Videte locum ubi fuit dominus	(12)
	EC	
	recordamini quid vivens locutus sit	(12)
	quod ipse die tertia resurgeret	(12)

5b	Et nunc euntes nuntiantes dicite	(12)
	F C	
	ut properent discipuli in Galileam	(13)
	illum videre sicuti promissum est.	(12)

At the end of the second sub-phrase MS 1084 provides two notes, EC (on *sit*) making the pitch count equal Notker's version even though the syllable count is one syllable short. The wording in 5b, however, differs from MS 1240, leaving out *conspicere eum*, changing word order before that, and rewording what comes after.

MS 1240
5b   Et nunc euntes, nuntiantes dicite,
        ut properent in Galileam discipuli conspicere eum
        sicut praedictum jam ab eo illis est.

MS 1118 seems to be a confluence of the two versions in MSS 1240 and 1084. It has 5a virtually identical with 1084, including the two notes EC on *sit*. Then in 5b, it reads as MS 1240; but over *conspicere eum*, the extension that differentiates Notker's 3 from his 5, no notes appear; the notes resume at the third sub-phrase, *sicut praedictum*.

MS 1118

5b Et nunc euntes nuntiantes dicite	(12)
ut properent in Galileam discipuli *conspicere eum*	(13 6)
sicut praedictum jam ab eo illis est.	(12)

Apparently the scriptor had both texts in front of him and used them, whereas the notator had only the melody from MS 1084.

The choice for 5, then, is between a short double and a long single. As far as the Aquitanian transmission is concerned, 5a gives the distinct impression of an interpolation, with its two-note neume on *sit*; and the instability of the short 5b in MS 1084 and 1118 suggests strongly that the longer version in MS 1240 is the more authentic. Nonetheless, the short double in Notker's version is a firm witness for its existence in the 9th century.

While it is true that lines 6a and b are less closely related to the Gospel than the preceding lines, there is little to differentiate between them on the basis of authenticity. They both seem necessary to the story, and they seem to constitute an original double. Similarly in 9: line 9a actually concludes the clause from Matthew started in 8b (*praecepit ut . . . praedicent*), and 9b is the natural antecedent for the exhortation and petition in 10a.

Phrase 10, like 5, exists in two versions in the Aquitanian MSS, a single in MS 1240, and a long double in MSS 1084–1118. Here again, MS 1118 seems to represent a confluence.

MS 1240

Ipsum ergo puramente obsecramus ut memor nobis sit,
    pro quibus fudit pretiosum sanguinem suum,

MS 1084

(1) Ipsum ergo puramente obsecramus (2) ut memor nobis sit,
(1) Qui pro grege suo mori dignatus fuit
    (1) et hodie a mortuis victor surrexit
        (2) ut nobis pius sit;
(1) Ipse qui hominem perditum reparavit (2) mundet nos a delicto
(1) Qui signum in cruce vexillum nobis dedit
    (1) et sede in excelsis dextri sui
        (2) nobis memor sit,

In MS 1118 the second, longer version contains the full text of MS 1240 as its first three lines (*Ipsum ergo . . . sanguinem suum*). Over this the notator put the melody of MS 1084, until he came to the text *pro quibus fudit pretiosum sanguinem suum*, which appears in MS 1240 but not in MS 1084; this he left without notes. The melody of phrase 10 consists of two parts, the first including the intonation (F G A C) and the sawtooth figure (C B C A C G), the second including the cadence pattern (G A G F G G). These two parts are arrayed as shown by the numbers 1 and 2 in the text just given, revealing an extraordinary amount of repetition in the fully double version of MSS 1084–1118. The melody for MS 1240 has been reconstructed out of the same material in the order 1,1,2. From a textual point of view, the longer version seems badly repetitive, both in itself and in the context of the whole prose. Here a conflation seems obvious, the more so since all the longer version is syntactically suspended between *obsecramus ut memor nobis ist . . . ne pereamus* of 11a. Notker's version, however, corroborates the long double, making it seem likely that it is an alternative version rather than a subsequent conflation; but there are things to be said about Notker's text at this point.

Line 3a of NUNC EXULTET begins with a participle (*collocans*) dependent upon *reduxit* in 2b. Even so, and in spite of the fact that the rest of 3a could be construed as part of the statement of theme, 3a can be still omitted with no real loss either to sense or syntax. And given its redundancy and wordiness, it would seem likely that it was a later interpolation. It is easy to imagine 3a, 5a, and the longer version of 10 being added by the same hand; 3a and 5a stress the Lord's prediction of his rising again, and the long version of 10 provides a pleonastic summary comparable in tone to 3a. Without these lines, the story starts promptly after the thematic statement in 2a,b (recalling the triumphal return from the Harrowing of Hell), proceeds directly to its conclusion, and is followed by straightforward exhortation, petition, and vision of future glory that serves as a doxology.

From the way the adaptor has treated the Gospel account, it seems that he wanted to compress the material into a shorter space—as if he had, in this case, the melody before him. From line 3b to 5b, details from the Gospel are omitted in the prose, with no effort at this point to make the diction more elegant. In general, the syntax is arranged to fit with the melodic phrases; yet in 3b there is a full stop (*factus est. Angelus . . .*) in the middle of a phrase, and both 4a and b include verbal articulations within the melodic unit. The effect is of an accelerated narrative, a succession of verbal units each with an essential detail, all run together in one breath.

The pace does not slacken in 6a,b; but there is a change in diction. These lines, not drawn in their wording directly from the Gospel, have a good deal more sonority and rhythmic swing (note the cursus!) and sit very happily in their melodic frames.

6a   Ílle regrésse a mònuménto precépto núntiant:
      Audiéntes quídam dùbitavérunt, non credéntes vérba véra ésse qui dicebántur.

6b   Quídam ex ípsis ad monuménto vidére próperant:
      Ut muliéres jam dixérant, íta ìnvenérunt: íllum sublátum ésse estimavérunt,

Yet there is syntactic run-on from 6b to 7a, where *estuantes* and *timentes* both depend on the preceding verb, *estimaverunt*.

7a   Dolores nimio cordis estuantes,
 b   Timentes ne visuri jam eum essent.

And from 8b to 9a, following now more closely Matthew's wording.

Laudes salvatori (Notker)

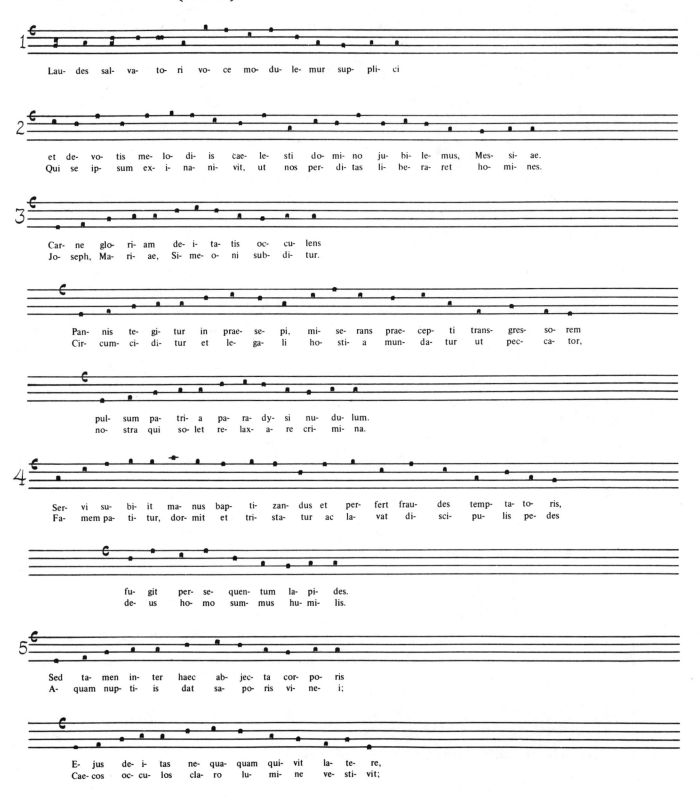

1. Lau- des sal- va- to- ri vo- ce mo- du- le- mur sup- pli- ci

2. et de- vo- tis me- lo- di- is cae- le- sti do- mi- no ju- bi- le- mus, Mes- si- ae.
   Qui se ip- sum ex- i- na- ni- vit, ut nos per- di- tas li- be- ra- ret ho- mi- nes.

3. Car- ne glo- ri- am de- i- ta- tis oc- cu- lens
   Jo- seph, Ma- ri- ae, Si- me- o- ni sub- di- tur.

   Pan- nis te- gi- tur in prae- se- pi, mi- se- rans prae- cep- ti trans- gres- so- rem
   Cir- cum- ci- di- tur et le- ga- li ho- sti- a mun- da- tur ut pec- ca- tor,

   pul- sum pa- tri- a pa- ra- dy- si nu- du- lum.
   no- stra qui so- let re- lax- a- re cri- mi- na.

4. Ser- vi su- bi- it ma- nus bap- ti- zan- dus et per- fert frau- des temp- ta- to- ris,
   Fa- mem pa- ti- tur, dor- mit et tri- sta- tur ac la- vat di- sci- pu- lis pe- des

   fu- git per- se- quen- tum la- pi- des.
   de- us ho- mo sum- mus hu- mi- lis.

5. Sed ta- men in- ter haec ab- jec- ta cor- po- ris
   A- quam nup- ti- is dat sa- po- ris vi- ne- i;

   E- jus de- i- tas ne- qua- quam qui- vit la- te- re,
   Cae- cos oc- cu- los cla- ro lu- mi- ne ve- sti- vit;

LAUDES SALVATORI (Notker) (2)

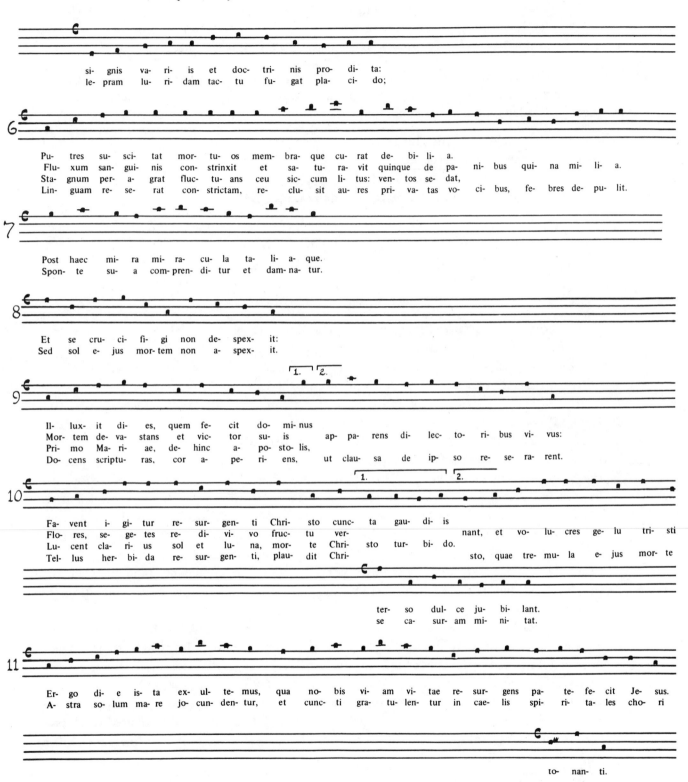

si- gnis va- ri- is et doc- tri- nis pro- di- ta:
le- pram lu- ri- dam tac- tu fu- gat pla- ci- do;

Pu- tres su- sci- tat mor- tu- os mem- bra- que cu- rat de- bi- li- a.
Flu- xum san- gui- nis con- strinxit et sa- tu- ra- vit quinque de pa- ni- bus qui- na mi- li- a.
Sta- gnum per- a- grat fluc- tu- ans ceu sic- cum li- tus: ven- tos se- dat,
Lin- guam re- se- rat con- strictam, re- clu- sit au- res pri- va- tas vo- ci- bus, fe- bres de- pu- lit.

Post haec mi- ra mi- ra- cu- la ta- li- a- que.
Spon- te su- a com- pren- di- tur et dam- na- tur.

Et se cru- ci- fi- gi non de- spex- it:
Sed sol e- jus mor- tem non a- spex- it.

Il- lux- it di- es, quem fe- cit do- mi- nus
Mor- tem de- va- stans et vic- tor su- is ap- pa- rens di- lec- to- ri- bus vi- vus:
Pri- mo Ma- ri- ae, de- hinc a- po- sto- lis,
Do- cens scriptu- ras, cor a- pe- ri- ens, ut clau- sa de ip- so re- se- ra- rent.

Fa- vent i- gi- tur re- sur- gen- ti Chri- sto cunc- ta gau- di- is
Flo- res, se- ge- tes re- di- vi- vo fruc- tu ver- nant, et vo- lu- cres ge- lu tri- sti
Lu- cent cla- ri- us sol et lu- na, mor- te Chri- sto tur- bi- do.
Tel- lus her- bi- da re- sur- gen- ti, plau- dit Chri- sto, quae tre- mu- la e- jus mor- te

ter- so dul- ce ju- bi- lant.
se ca- sur- am mi- ni- tat.

Er- go di- e i- sta ex- ul- te- mus, qua no- bis vi- am vi- tae re- sur- gens pa- te- fe- cit Je- sus.
A- stra so- lum ma- re jo- cun- den- tur, et cunc- ti gra- tu- len- tur in cae- lis spi- ri- ta- les cho- ri

to- nan- ti.

8a   Frequenter post hec eis apparens,

  b   Precepit ut, euntes in mundum,

9a   Predicent evvangelium et baptizent.

      et dominus Jesus, postquam eis locutus, adsumptums est in celum:

The Gospel account in NUNC EXULTET is framed by a liturgical proclamation at the beginning and a petition at the end. The beginning includes an exhortation to rejoice, a statement of "today's" Easter triumph, and epithets close to those of ECCE VICIT.[3]

  (1)   Nunc exultet omnis mundus,

        quia hodie victor

(2a) triumphavit,

        et vicit leo fortis de tribu Juda radixque David;

ECCE VICIT

  (1)   Ecce vicit radix David, leo de tribu Juda!

Line 2b of NUNC EXULTET refers to the Harrowing of Hell.

  2b   Expoliaivt furem et crudelem, suos secum reduxit captivos,

Even in this brief form, the image of Christ leading his own faithful, as his trophies in a *triumphus*, is an impressive one.

Notker's text, LAUDES SALVATORI, shows many signs of his habitual care and resourcefulness of Latinity, as seen in previous pieces; all the more striking, then, is the very same quality of breathless, headlong narration that was observed in NUNC EXULTET. Distinctive among Notker's other proses in this respect, LAUDES SALVATORI seems to suggest that NUNC EXULTET was its model, even though the narrative here is not the Resurrection story *per se*, but rather the *Heilsgeschichte*—the epic of salvation. From 3a through 9b the story goes for the Savior's birth in the manger, his circumcision, baptism, temptation, persecution, his hunger and thirst, and work of humility—all that to show how God had humbled himself to become man. The story continues with the signs of his divinity, which could not be hidden completely beneath the veil of flesh (is there a hint of Docetism here?), the miracles of wine at Cana, of healing the blind, the sick, the dead, the lame, of feeding the five thousand, and the rest. Then, of his own will, he was taken, condemned, and crucified; the sun darkened, but as the Resurrection Day dawned he triumphed over death, and appeared to his disciples.

The overall shape of the text is similar to that of NUNC EXULTET, for this narrative—corresponding in function to phrases 3–9 of NUNC EXULTET—is framed by a thematic statement in lines 1,2a,b, and by an exhortation in lines 10a,b and 11a,b. Petitions are lacking, but the rhetoric is analogous, as shown by the connectives *igitur*(10a) and *ergo*(11a).

The inner structure of LAUDES SALVATORI seems more finely attuned to the overall design of the melody. In particular, the melodic grouping 3 and 4, 5 and 6, created by the return of phrase 3 as phrase 5, and the motivic recall between 4 and 6, is coordinated with the

3. The scriptural source is *Revelation* 5,5.

diptych of God's humility in his human nature and the miraculous powers associated with his divine nature.

3a Carne gloriam deitatis occulens, . . .
                                    . . . deus homo summus humilis.

5a Sed tamen inter hec abjecta corporis
    Ejus deitas nequaquam quivit latere signis variis et doctrinis prodita:

3a (Hiding beneath the flesh the glory of his deity,
        [then follows the description of his humility, from his birth in the manger
        up to the washing of the disciples' feet]
                                    . . . God, man, most lofty, humble.

5a Nevertheless, beneath these lowly things of the body
    His deity could not hide, given away by various signs and teachings:
        [then follows the list of miracles])

The short, high phrases 7 and 8 are joined together by the text, which describes the crucifixion, following the implication of their melodic shapes, which as we saw tend to go together in one larger unit. Then the return of the rising motive in phrase 9 is put to effective use for the Resurrection (*Illuxit dies quem fecit dominus*). This very purposeful alignment of melody and text is not present in NUNC EXULTET, being presumably something that Notker accomplished on his own.

Details of the language also show more consistency than those of NUNC EXULTET. The F G G cadences are proparoxytone throughout, including those at the ends of sub-phrases in 3 and 5 (vínei?). Sub-phrases in 6, 9, and 10 have slightly different melodic form in Notker's version, but he still provides proparoxytones; sédat in 6b, however, is an exception. By contrast—and with consistency—the cadences in 7 and 8 are paroxytone; as observed before, these are not full stops in the melody, and tend to sound like sub-phrases of a large unit, an effect Notker's text supports. The final cadences in 11 do not use the F G G pattern, hence here too paroxytones are used (*Jésus, chóri*). And the special cadence at the end of 9— the "closed" ending that contrasts with the "open" one in the first sub-phrase—is paroxytone (*vívus, reserárent*).

The diction of this particular text seems to show more assonance and near-rhyme than Notker's other proses. In line 3a,

miserans praecepti transgressorem pulsum patria paradysi nudulum

is unusual. In line 5a,

caecos oculos / claro lumine / vestivit
    lepram luridam / tactu fugat placido,

shows a tendency for various kinds of assonance, in conjunction with clausula-like patterns of accent to form units of two words—*caecos oculos, claro lumine, lepram luridam*. In line 7a, assonance becomes more insistent,

Post haec mira miracula taliaque,

culminating in the blatant rhyme in 8a,b

> . . . non despexit
> . . . non aspexit,

which, however, is to be understood as a figure of meaning as much as one of diction: Notker's point here is to accent the effect of the image in 8b.

8a   And he did not disdain to be crucified;
8b   But the sun did not look upon his death.

Apart from these more obvious devices, there is a virtuosity of language seemingly in the service of the style of story-telling. Lines such as 4a,b, and especially 6a,b—the very ones that seemed most effective in NUNC EXULTET—bind up manifold details and episodes of Jesus's life and ministry in a spectacular flow of language.

6a   Putres suscitat mortuos membraque curat debilia
    Fluxum sanguinis constrinxit et saturavit quinque de panis quini milia
 b   Stagnum peragrat fluctuans ceu siccum litus ventos sedat
    linguam reserat constrictam reclusit aures privatas vocibus febres depulit.

All the more impressive because so straightforward, such lines avoid the involute constructions noticed in Notker's earlier texts.

It is difficult to include in this inventory of rhetorical ornament the redicta of 10a,b, or to reconcile the relatively long dwelling within this couplet on its topic with the pace of narration that precedes it.

10a   Favent igitur resurgenti Christo cuncta gaudiis
    Flores segetes redivivo fructu vernant et volucres gelu tristi terso dulce jubilant.
 b   Lucent clarius sol et luna morte Christi turbida
    Tellus herbida resurgenti plaudit Christo quae tremula ejus morte se caesuram minitat.

(Let all things favor with joy the risen Christ:
Let flowers, grasses bloom with re-awakened fruit, and birds sweetly rejoice.
Let sun and moon, darkened by the death of Christ, shine more brightly:
Let the grassy earth, which threatened to break itself open with tremors at his death, applaud the risen Christ.)

Given the fact of a shorter version—a single, without any F G G cadence at the end of the first sub-phrase—in NUNC EXULTET as found in MS 1240, it is tempting to suspect a conflation in Notker's 10b. If it is a conflation, it is not a clumsy one; but the larger rhythm would move on with more sweep directly from 10a to 11a. The wording of 11a, incidentally, coincides in some details with that of NUNC EXULTET; but this may be due to coincidence of theme, of the tendency to close such texts with references to songs of celebration.

Notker

11a Ergo die ista exultemus qua nobis viam vitae resurgens patefecit Jesus
 Astra solum mare jocundentur et cuncti gratulentur in caelis spiritales chori tonanti.

NUNC EXULTET

11a Ne pereamus condempnatis sed cum justis pariter gratulemur jocundantes, seculorum secula. Amen.

The other early text to this melody, SEMPER REGNANS, presents an interesting comparison with the two already studied. SEMPER REGNANS appears unica in the Munich "Toul"
MS, without melody (like the other texts in that MS); it can, however, be matched with
the melody to NUNC EXULTET, with certain adaptations to be discussed in detail.[4]

As shown in the transcription on p. 112 the adaptations in the melody required by the
text SEMPER REGNANS affect phrases 3, 5, 6, and 9—that is, those phrases that appear as singles in ARCE SUPERNA, and have a sub-phrase structure in the versions studied so far. In
SEMPER REGNANS, lines 3a,b seem instead to form a short double, whose melody is just the
first sub-phrase of the longer melody in the other versions. This is admittedly a substantial
adaptation, but one perfectly understandable in terms of the inherent characteristics of the
melody; it does not involve, for example, shortening phrase 2, or taking some arbitrary
portion of phrase 3.

Line 5, then, seems to fall as a single under the *latter* portion (that is, excluding the opening sub-phrase) of the melody for phrase 5 of NUNC EXULTET. Since phrase 5 is the same as
phrase 3, all of the actual melodic material of NUNC EXULTET has been used in SEMPER REG-
NANS; precisely the material omitted from SEMPER REGNANS phrase 3 shows up in phrase 5.

NUNC EXULTET		SEMPER REGNANS	LAUDES SALVATORI		
3	(a a′ a)*	a	a	a′	a
	a a′ a	a	a	a′	a
5	(a a′ a)*	a′ a	a	a″	a
	a a′ a		a	a″	a

*Probably interpolated.

Lines 6 and 9 of SEMPER REGNANS are singles, otherwise conforming to the other versions.
It should be added that line 10 is a double that seems to require a hypothetical version of
the melody somewhat more prolix than that offered for NUNC EXULTET, but less prolix than
the one for LAUDES SALVATORI.

Perhaps the most important aspect of the text is that it, too, is a *Heilsgeschichte*, telling
essentially the same story as LAUDES SALVATORI, but giving somewhat more weight to the
Paschal episode—especially the appearance to the disciples, like NUNC EXULTET. The story
starts with the generation of the *logos*, God's thought to redeem mankind by becoming incarnate. Line 3a places him in the Virgin's womb, line 4a in the manger. The earthly ministry is passed over, and with line 5 we are at the Cross. Line 6 is a remarkable apostrophe to
the Thief—which of the two is not clear: "If you wish to lay hold of righteousness itself,

4. See Von den Steinen, *Anfänge*, vol. 41, pp. 25–29; my article "Some Ninth-Century Sequences," pp. 400–402.

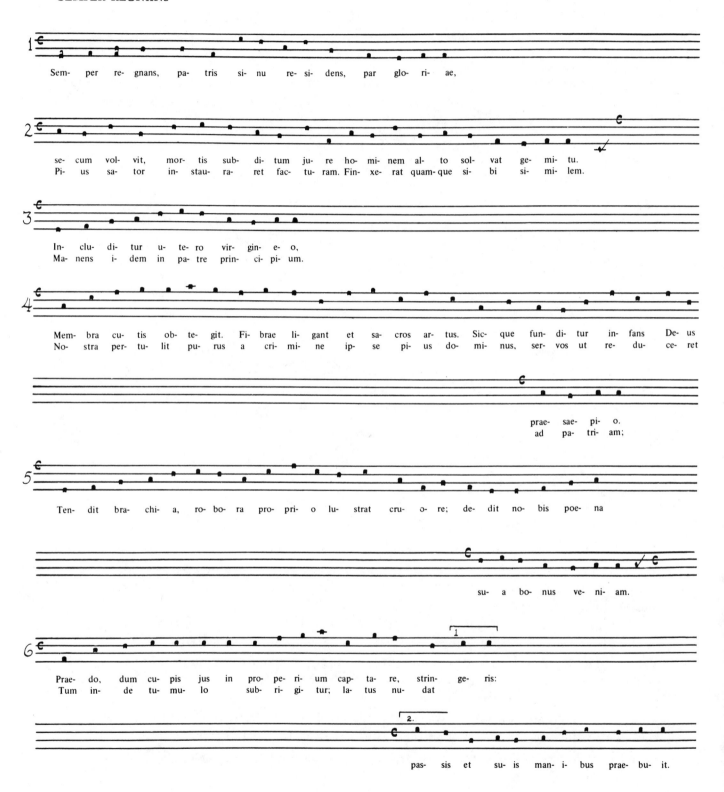

Semper regnans, patris sinu residens, par gloriae,

secum volvit, mortis subditum jure hominem alto solvat gemitu.
Pius sator instauraret facturam. Finxerat quamque sibi similem.

Includitur utero virgineo,
Manens idem in patre principium.

Membra cutis obtegit. Fibrae ligant et sacros artus. Sicque funditur infans Deus
Nostra pertulit purus a crimine ipse pius dominus, servos ut reduceret

prae- sae- pi- o.
ad pa- tri- am;

Tendit brachia, robora proprio lustrat cruore; dedit nobis poena

su- a bonus ven- i- am.

Praedo, dum cupis jus in properium captare, stringeris:
Tum inde tumulo subrigitur; latus nudat

pas- sis et su- is man- i- bus prae- bu- it.

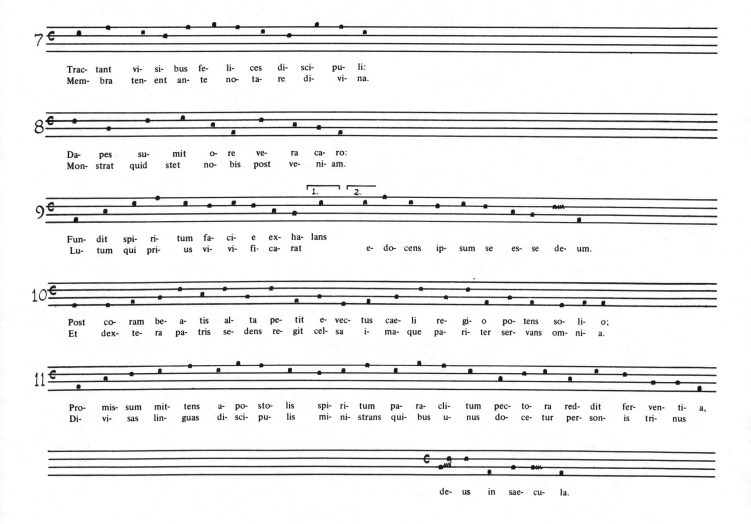

Trac- tant vi- si- bus fe- li- ces di- sci- pu- li:
Mem- bra ten- ent an- te no- ta- re di- vi- na.

Da- pes su- mit o- re ve- ra ca- ro:
Mon- strat quid stet no- bis post ve- ni- am.

Fun- dit spi- ri- tum fa- ci- e ex- ha- lans
Lu- tum qui pri- us vi- vi- fi- ca- rat e- do- cens ip- sum se es- se de- um.

Post co- ram be- a- tis al- ta pe- tit e- vec- tus cae- li re- gi- o po- tens so- li- o;
Et dex- te- ra pa- tris se- dens re- git cel- sa i- ma- que pa- ri- ter ser- vans om- ni- a.

Pro- mis- sum mit- tens a- po- sto- lis spi- ri- tum pa- ra- cli- tum pec- to- ra red- dit fer- ven- ti- a,
Di- vi- sas lin- guas di- sci- pu- lis mi- ni- strans qui- bus u- nus do- ce- tur per- son- is tri- nus

de- us in sae- cu- la.

hold fast to him!'' The rest of line 6 through line 8 concerns the Resurrection and the sojourn with the disciples. Line 9 refers to a platonistic doctrine of the Incarnation:

> He poured forth his spirit, shedding from his form the clay
> just as before he had breathed life into it, showing himself
> to be very God.

One thinks of John the Scot, active as teacher and philosopher at Laon around and after the middle of the ninth century.

Line 10 describes the Ascension, line 11 the coming of the Holy Spirit, moving skillfully into a concluding doxology.

One of the striking differences between this and the other texts is the absence of rhetorical framework. The story starts immediately with no topic sentence, no festal exhortation.

The doxology at the end is scarcely recognizable as a liturgical gesture, so strong are its narrative or doctrinal aspects. Nothing suggests this to be a song of celebration. In place of functional rhetoric there is philosophical or theological comment, as in line 3b.

3a   Includitur utero virgineo,
  b   Manens idem in patre principium.

Similar non-narrative elements appear in lines 8, 9, 10, and 11. In contrast, the purely narrative lines 4a, 5, 6 (the later part), lines 7, 8a, 10a, and 11 recall the rapid-fire narration characteristic of both NUNC EXULTET and LAUDES SALVATORI.

6   Tum inde tumulo subrigitur; latus nudat; panes suis manibus praebuit.

And the story is matched to the melodic structure with skill and sensitivity. The rising from the tomb is placed under the high point of the melody—but under its second appearance, the first being reserved for the apostrophe to the Thief. Before this high point, the low-lying phrases 3 and 5 are associated with the two scenes of humility, the Incarnation and the Crucifixion. After the high point in 6, the gradual drop in melodic line goes with the relatively extended description of his discourse with the disciples; his departure (Ascension) stands off to one side in the F-A-C realm, while the coming of the Holy Ghost (Pentecost) is presented as a triumphal return in conjunction with the motivic recall in phrase 11.

A restoration of the text and melody Notker used as model remains, then, inconclusive, because on one hand the West-Frankish evidence of NUNC EXULTET and ARCE SUPERNA (that is, "Hieronima" of the Autun fragment) as well as of SEMPER REGNANS, points towards a version with singles at 3, 5, and 10, and possibly 6 and 9 as well; while on the other hand Notker's LAUDES SALVATORI, our only 9th-century witness, has doubles at all of these phrases except possibly 10.

In weighing the implications of this situation, several things need to be kept in mind. It seems possible that NUNC EXULTET was the text Notker had before him, because of the rhetorical structure that he followed closely, as well as the narrative concept of the whole, which he apparently imitated and developed further. No other text that we have would suggest the details of these two aspects as clearly.

It seems probable, furthermore, that NUNC EXULTET is closely related in melody to LAUDES DEO; that is, it clearly *is* related, and it seems probable that this is because NUNC EXULTET was conceived as a vastly extended version of LAUDES DEO. In any case, it seems certain that Notker knew LAUDES DEO before he knew NUNC EXULTET, and that his LAUDES SALVATORI was written later than his LAUDES DEO CONCINAT, since he himself tells us that LAUDES DEO CONCINAT was his first attempt; and it is clear on the face of things that LAUDES SALVATORI is a far more masterly piece of work—virtuoso, in fact. Do Notker's incipits (LAUDES DEO, LAUDES SALVATORI) tell us of the kinship between the two pieces? In two other cases, LAUDES DEO and HÆC EST SANCTA, he indicated relationships with West-Frankish texts; and writers of the age—including Notker himself—were fond of acrostics for similar purposes.

In LAUDES DEO, Notker preserved phrase 3 as a single (in the model itself it was later doubled); but Notker probably added, as his phrase 4, another complete double, adapted from the melody of the single. Here, in the case of NUNC EXULTET (Notker's LAUDES SALVA-

TORI), one possible interpretation is that Notker doubled whatever singles he found in his model. Is there risk of contradiction among these various interpretations? I think not; we seem to be dealing with matters of artistic choice, not principle; the instances are separate, presumably occurring over a considerable stretch of time. There seems to be no reason to try to posit one mode of adaptation that would cover all cases.

More complex is the relationship among the other texts—especially if NUNC EXULTET is assumed as the model for the other two; or, at least, if it is assumed that either of the other two was the original. For NUNC EXULTET, even when subjected to a provisional and partly hypothetical reduction, still has doubles at 6 and 9, and these phrases are singles in ARCE SUPERNA. We would have to assume that at the same time that 3, 5, and 10 were expanded to doubles by Notker, 6 and 9 were reduced to singles by other text writers. Now the reduction of a double to a single does not seem, in itself, to be a very likely step in the development of the sequence. If there is a general trend to be observed in this development during the tenth century, it is in the direction of regular doubles; in the sequences studied so far we have seen specific instances of this trend.

The striking thing about the melody in question is that the singles are so persuasive as singles: all of them are complex sub-phrase constructions, with abundant internal repeats comparable to doubles. They occur in such a way that their singleness seems purposeful—they are welcomed as a relief in this very long melody. The fully double version used by Notker is distinctly long-winded in effect. It would be grateful to imagine all these phrases as singles in the original conception of the melody. Assuming that was not the case, however, it is still reasonable to suppose that one or the other writer of text felt that—given singles at 3, 5, and 10—they could also be used at 6 and 9 if desired.

Or more generally: in the case of this melody, with its clear differentiation of phrases, there seems to have been the possibility of using certain of those phrases in different ways. Notker, intent on the Christian epic, can be presumed to have wanted the fullest possible scope for his narrative; at any rate, he uses it. Even with a similar purpose, however, the author of SEMPER REGNANS made consistent use of singles or other shorter adaptations—*of the same phrases*. The doubling in NUNC EXULTET, it should be noticed, is generally not for narrative purposes, but involves other aspects, sometimes simply that of repetition. The best interpretation that can be put upon these doublings is an expansion of the form for the sake of musical consistency.

No other early sequence has such a spectacular variety of phrases; and there, I think, is the key. The melody is put together—brilliantly—out of strongly individual elements. Certain ones, and only certain ones, can be adjusted in various ways without essentially altering the whole; hence the several versions. But this situation need not and should not be taken as characteristic of all early sequences, only of this one.

VII

HAEC EST SANCTA SOLEMNITAS
Notker's HAEC EST SANCTA
SOLEMNITAS SOLEMNITATUM
and QUID TU VIRGO

THE FOUR MELODIES studied up to this point each showed discrepancies between Notker's plan and the West-Frankish plans preserved in the Aquitanian sources; these discrepancies were the means of restoring the West-Frankish versions to their ninth-century state. In three of the four cases it was possible to recover a West-Frankish version that, in corresponding more closely to Notker's plan, was vastly improved in diction, cogency and general credibility. Whether the melody was improved to the same degree is a discussable point. Perhaps the salient conclusion to be drawn from a study of the West-Frankish tenth-century modifications would be that they make much more sense musically than verbally—which in itself might tell us something about tenth-century artistic activity in the Western kingdoms. Even so, it could be argued, I think, that the ninth-century versions of the melodies are in most respects superior. At any rate, they reveal to us the state and ambitions of ninth-century melody.

In the case of LAUDES DEO, Notker left us an acknowledgement of his model. He did the same in the next piece to be studied, HÆC EST SANCTA. And in the one after that, he borrowed the Judgment-Day theme for his JUDICEM NOS from the West-Frankish FORTIS ATQUE AMARA. In no other case do his texts acknowledge a model by such direct correspondence; it is fair to conclude that all three of these texts are early ones for Notker. For the melody of HÆC EST SANCTA he wrote another text, QUID TU VIRGO, just as for GRATES SALVATORI he also wrote TUBAM BELLICOSAM; and in both cases it seems clear that we have to do with an early text and a much later one.

From this point on in our study, the West-Frankish plans correspond much more closely to Notker's; there is no further occasion for such far-reaching restoration as carried out on the first three melodies. Discrepancies in individual phrases will continue to crop up, however, and will be dealt with in a similar fashion.

The West-Frankish prose HÆC EST SANCTA SOLEMNITAS is preserved, like the others studied so far, in the small group of Aquitanian sources—in this case, MSS 1240, 1084, 1118, and 1138. It is curious that the melody seems to be absent from the Sequentiaria in MSS 1084 and 1118; it is not clear what conclusion might be drawn from that absence. HÆC EST SANCTA SOLEMNITAS also appears in a few more sources outside the Aquitanian circle; some are earlier, such as the Toul fragment (Munich MS 14843) and the Verona collection (Verona XC); others later, such as the Beneventan Gradual (Benev. VI 35). I know of no staff source, however. Nor does the Notker tradition seem to yield a completely reliable staff source; but Schubiger edited the melody from Einsiedeln "Fragment I" (now MS 366) with results to be discussed. While it seems clear that the final is G, there are some interesting problems.

Referring to the West-Frankish version in the transcription, p. 118, the opening phrase is best thought of as a long single, even though it has an internal repeat; the construction seems to be one of sub-phrases rather than a full repeat of a complete line. The first note at the point where the repeat starts—be(ati) in the West-Frankish version—is consistently A, not B flat, and the following sub-phrase is shorter. This is like, in miniature, the opening phrase structure of LAUDES DEO, which was counted as a single plus a double, 1, 2a,b; and there is perhaps little reason to do otherwise for HÆC EST SANCTA. Yet if complete consistency were desired, it would be preferable to mark LAUDES DEO like HÆC EST SANCTA, that is, as one long opening single with a sub-phrase repetition. In such cases, incidentally, the MSS regularly lack a capital letter at, say, the beginning of 2a in LAUDES DEO (omnis), although they usually provide one at 2b (Praecelso). The intent, clearly, is to show a close connection of the intonation with what follows.

The difference between Notker's version and the West-Frankish one could perhaps be brought to bear upon the question of the opening structure, and will be taken up in due course. At a higher level, however, what seems to strike the ear is the clarity and concision of the following short doubles, 2 (Ipse namque) and 3 (Christi secutus): in comparison to these, what came before seems indeed to be a long single in spite of its internal repetition.

Phrase 2 is so short, so compact, as to be scarcely a complete phrase. Its repetition seems only natural, and even phrase 3, with its repetition, follows as the logical continuation of a single long melodic impulse—as if 2 and 3 were antecedent and consequent. Phrase 3, of course, is the same as the opening sub-phrase of LAUDES DEO 3, and like it, provides the relief of a lower register; but in HÆC EST SANCTA the lower register comes in consequent position, whereas in LAUDES DEO it provided the contrast for the "verses."

Phrase 4 is high again, recalling the tessitura of 2. Phrase 4 is long, without any pronounced tendency to break into sub-phrases, even though it has a hint of a repetition near the beginning:

C C C A, C D C D C A

As is made clear in phrase 5, the intent is to expand the phrase shapes, making them successively longer and also higher in pitch, while avoiding as much as possible any tendency

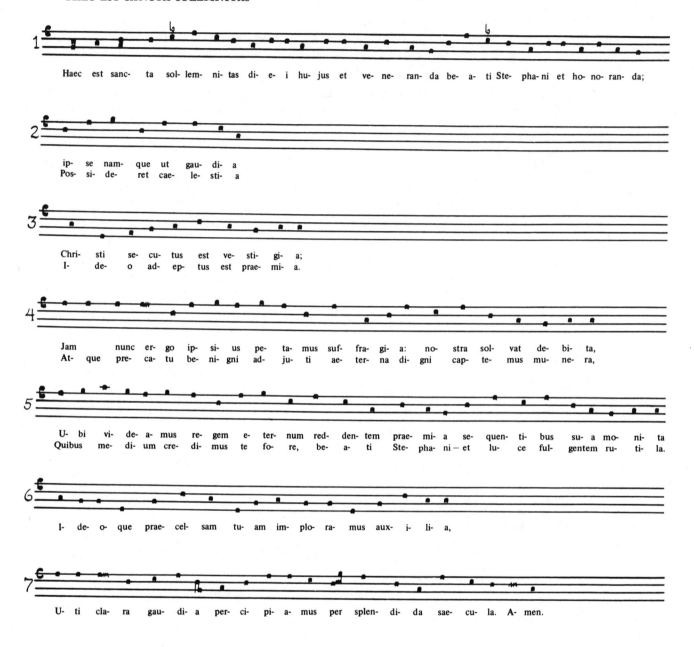

1. Haec est sanc- ta sol- lem- ni- tas di- e- i hu- jus et ve- ne- ran- da be- a- ti Ste- pha- ni et ho- no- ran- da;

2. ip- se nam- que ut gau- di- a
   Pos- si- de- ret cae- le- sti- a

3. Chri- sti se- cu- tus est ve- sti- gi- a;
   I- de- o ad- ep- tus est prae- mi- a.

4. Jam nunc er- go ip- si- us pe- ta- mus suf- fra- gi- a: no- stra sol- vat de- bi- ta,
   At- que pre- ca- tu be- ni- gni ad- ju- ti ae- ter- na di- gni cap- te- mus mu- ne- ra,

5. U- bi vi- de- a- mus re- gem e- ter- num red- den- tem prae- mi- a se- quen- ti- bus su- a mo- ni- ta
   Quibus me- di- um cre- di- mus te fo- re, be- a- ti Ste- pha- ni- et lu- ce ful- gentem ru- ti- la.

6. I- de- o- que prae- cel- sam tu- am im- plo- ra- mus auxi- li- a,

7. U- ti cla- ra gau- di- a per- ci- pi- a- mus per splen- di- da sae- cu- la. A- men.

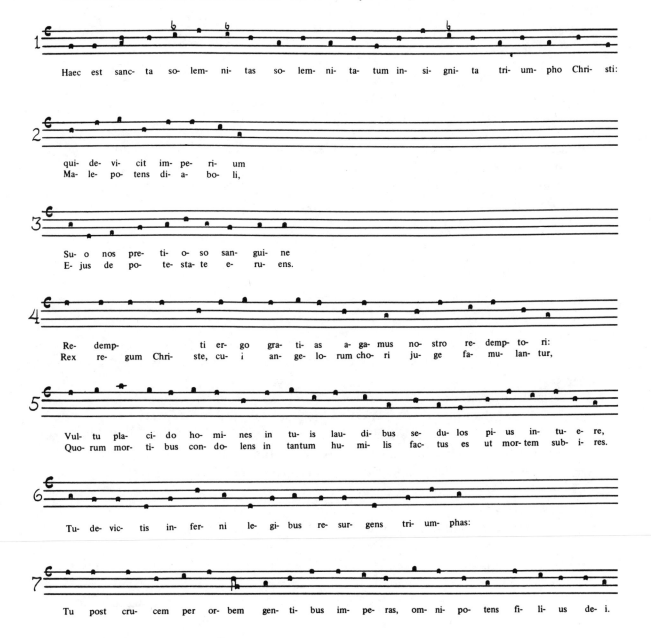

Hæc est sancta solemnitas solemnitatum (Notker)

1. Haec est sanc- ta so- lem- ni- tas so- lem- ni- ta- tum in- si- gni- ta tri- um- pho Chri- sti:

2. qui- de- vi- cit im- pe- ri- um
   Ma- le- po- tens di- a- bo- li,

3. Su- o nos pre- ti- o- so san- gui- ne
   E- jus de po- te- sta- te e- ru- ens.

4. Re- demp- ti er- go gra- ti- as a- ga- mus no- stro re- demp- to- ri:
   Rex re- gum Chri- ste, cu- i an- ge- lo- rum cho- ri ju- ge fa- mu- lan- tur,

5. Vul- tu pla- ci- do ho- mi- nes in tu- is lau- di- bus se- du- los pi- us in- tu- e- re,
   Quo- rum mor- ti- bus con- do- lens in tantum hu- mi- lis fac- tus es ut mor- tem sub- i- res.

6. Tu de- vic- tis in- fer- ni le- gi- bus re- sur- gens tri- um- phas:

7. Tu post cru- cem per or- bem gen- ti- bus im- pe- ras, om- ni- po- tens fi- li- us de- i.

to break down into subdivisions. Phrase 5 rises to E, then makes a long, graceful descent, using melodic "sequences" but no cadences. (The duplication of terms is unfortunate but inescapable; there is, however, relatively little use of "melodic sequence" in ninth-century sequences.)

```
(C D)E D C   D C A
            C D B   C B G
Ubi videamus regem æternum reddentem
```

For a phrase that has no internal cadences, this one is relatively long—26 notes—and very well handled, too. Even more important is its position in the piece as a whole: because of the gradual expansion of the range, and lengthening of the line, phrase 5 is the climax, and in return helps pull together everything that came before.

Phrase 6 is low again, and has an internal repetition.

```
   G FF D   F A G
   Ide-oque præcelsam
D F  G   FF D F  AGG
tuam imploramus auxiliam
```

Something about the conduct of the melody, however, seems to associate this phrase with 1 rather than with 3. It certainly lacks the lyric clarity of 3, seeming to bring the melodic movement to a gradual halt on G, rather than opening the way to further expansion as 3 does. The low register of 6 does, however, provide a moment of relief between 5 and the reaffirmation of the higher register in 7—which clearly recalls 4 in its beginning, so that 6 and 7, to some degree at least, stand in the same relationship as 3 and 4. Phrase 7 then goes on to end in a curiously convoluted melodic style; the difference is admittedly slight, but when emphasized by the ornamental neume on *per* (*splendida*) in the West-Frankish version, phrase 7 is distinctly less fluent than, say, phrase 5, and consequently much more suitable for the conclusion. Since neumes are relatively rare in this piece, those at the end recall those at the beginning, as in LAUDES DEO.

HÆC EST SANCTA seems to have a more artful design than LAUDES DEO. The carefully calculated rise and expansion over the middle of HÆC EST SANCTA (phrases 2 through 5) is at the least a different structural principle than the simple alternation of elements in LAUDES DEO, and possibly a different order of artistry as well. In HÆC EST SANCTA the phrases of a contrasting lower register are relatively brief, instead of accounting as they do in LAUDES DEO for much of the bulk of the piece. This places the emphasis in HÆC EST SANCTA on the flowering of phrase 5, whose simple yet graceful disposition of detail is fully capable of sustaining the importance of the phrase in the larger plan.

There is a certain similarity to LAUDES DEO in the recall of a middle phrase at the end: in HÆC EST SANCTA the beginning of phrase 7 recalls 4, just as in LAUDES DEO phrase 7 recalled 4. In fact, in 4 and 7 of HÆC EST SANCTA can be heard the opening motive of 4 and 8 from LAUDES DEO.

```
          C    G AC  B   C  A  G  FGG
4              suf-  fra-gi-a nostra solvat debita
7         . . . gau-)di-(a) percipi- (amus)
```

LAUDES DEO

```
        C  G  A  C     B  C   A  G
4       Nam a primo  proto-plasto
8       Vo- ci-fe-ran- tes  in  alto
```

Not a convincing similarity when considered merely by itself, but when taken in conjunction with the more obvious correspondence in phrase 3 it shows how the motive C G A C is used in unadorned brevity in LAUDES DEO; ornamented and in company with other material it appears at the same position in the overall plan.

In addition, HÆC EST SANCTA uses the same long cadence as NUNC EXULTET.

```
            C  B C   A   G  F  GG
3                        est ve- sti- gi- a
4                        -a no-stra sol- vat de- bi-ta
5                        -quen- ti-bus su-   a mo- ni-ta
```

We can look upon this cadence, then, as being something of a formula, which—for our purposes here at the moment—means that it can be assumed to have had the force of a cadence quite apart from other factors such as words or placement in the overall plan.

In HÆC EST SANCTA, this cadence closes the phrases throughout the middle of the piece, helping to bind that part even more strongly together. The absence of the cadence at 2, then, has the effect of linking that short phrase with the next into a longer, compound phrase, as already observed. Similarly, the absence of the cadence at 6 suggests a linkage with 7, or at any rate discourages a full stop there. The absence of the cadence at 1 and 7, however, must be rather related to the distinct functions of these phrases as frames—introduction and conclusion—to the whole.

In general, HÆC EST SANCTA seems to move within the same field of pitches as LAUDES DEO. Melodic movement is based mainly around the interval of a fourth between the G final and the C above. The D above the C is a frequent alternate with the C, the E above that being used only for melodic highpoint in phrase 5 (it had a similar function in LAUDES DEO 5). A secondary area of pitch is located between the G final and the D a fourth below—but not, in HÆC EST SANCTA, the C below that.

As an illustration of the problem of determining a final (as discussed in Chapter 2, p. 25), it may be helpful to imagine the cadence C B C A G F G G in all possible locations.

```
C B C A G F G G                       tetrardus
B A B G F E F F                       (tritus)
A G A F E D E E  =  E D E C B A B B    deuterus
G F G E D C D D  =  D C D B A G A A    protus
F E F D C B C C                       tritus
```

As discussed in Chapter 2, there are not seven alternatives (one for each note of the diatonic system) but only four, corresponding to the four finals D, E, F, G. In the case of this particular cadence, an alternative beginning on B natural, being too ugly to be considered, would in practice use a B flat, making it identical with the ending on C. Judging purely from use of this cadence in later sources with staves and clefs, none of the alternatives other than the one beginning on C was used with any significant frequency. Endings on F preceded by E are rare in any case throughout medieval chant. Finals on E or D are more apt to use other cadences; those on D rarely stress the G a fourth above to the extent that this cadence does.

Such general stylistic evidence, however, is by no means conclusive, and we must be especially careful lest it keep us from giving due weight to other indications that may be more decisive, or cause us to neglect an unusual alternative that may actually be the intended one. The first phrase of HÆC EST SANCTA is a case in which an unusual procedure could easily be replaced by a more routine one (as I did in transcribing the melody elsewhere).[1] As given in the transcription, phrase 1 is firmly grounded on F, moving back and forth through the fifth F-C with additional emphasis on A, and approaching the F final stepwise through G. Phrase 2 brings a turn to a G final, which is confirmed in phrase 3— and not until then. The shift from F to G is a striking one—so striking that it seemed at first to be a corruption of the staff-source used by Schubiger (Einsiedeln MS 366); Schubiger read all of 1 and 2 on F, shifting to G on phrase 3. The Aquitanian diastematic sources can be read so as to place phrase 1 on the same G final used for the rest of the piece—a smooth, innocuous solution, but probably the wrong one.

The role of the B seems indeterminate. A flat appears in Schubiger's transcription but is not necessary, for with a little effort the phrase can be sung (starting on F) with a B natural; the B natural in phrase 2 then follows without a hitch. (A very close Gregorian model is given by the most frequent of the Alleluia melodies, known as Alleluia *Ostende* after its use on First Sunday of Advent; with a G final, the melody rises from F to C through B natural.) Or, if a flat is sung in phrase 1, then it can be sung in phrase 2 as well, which postpones the confirmation of the shift to a G final well into phrase 4; indeed, the shift is then scarcely perceptible as such.

The notation of the first four notes of phrase 2 in the diastematic sources is not as firm as it might be; only the location of the whole phrase on C (G) seems certain. This I take to be an indication of scribal uncertainty in the face of an unusual procedure, hence an argument in favor of the beginning on F with a subsequent shift to G. I have followed Schubiger in using a B flat, since that supports and emphasizes the distinctive feature—the location of phrase 1 on F. But I have read phrase 2 as A C D A C C B(natural) G out of the Aquitanian MSS since that seems to provide the best transition to the G final, and places the lift provided by B natural where it does the most good, that is, in the first half of the compound phrase 2 plus 3.

If phrase 1 is indeed intended to be on F, what are the structural implications? The place-

---

1. "The Sequence," *Gattungen der Musik in Einzeldarstellungen: Gedenkschrift Leo Schrade*, ed. W. Arlt et al. (Bern 1973), pp. 269–322.

ment on F seems to emphasize the introductory nature of this opening phrase: so placed it cannot help but stand apart—as if almost alien to the rest of the piece, which might be thought to begin properly with phrase 2. The same effect was observed in LAUDES DEO, there being achieved by an ornamental, quasi-melismatic style. That style is not so much in evidence in HÆC EST SANCTA, yet there will be occasion to refer to it when comparing variants of detail between Notker's version and the West-Frankish one.

The West-Frankish text has three periods, as shown in the syntactic presentation.

(syntactic display)

(1)   I   Hæc est sancta solemnitas diei hujus
           et veneranda beati Stephani et honoranda:
(2)   ipse namque,
          ut gaudia possidere caelestia,
(3)   Christi secutus est vestigia:
      ideo adeptus est praemia.

(4) II Jam nunc ergo ipsius petamus suffragia:
      nostra solvat debita,
      atque precatu benigni adjuti eterna digni captemus munera,
(5)   ubi videamus regem aeternum
           reddentem praemia sequentibus sua monita
    —quibus medium credimus te fore, beati Stephani—
              et luce fulgentem rutila.
(6) III Ideoque praecelsam tuam imploramus auxiliam,
      uti clara gaudia percipiamus splendida per secula. Amen.

According to syntax, the musical phrases are grouped

1, 2, 3; 4, 5; 6, 7

which cuts across to some extent the purely musical grouping,

1; 2, 3, 4, 5; 6, 7

indicated earlier. Perhaps "interlocking" would be a better description than "cutting across": considerable artistry seems to be involved here in the counterpoint of rhetoric and music. The strongly exhortative beginning of the second period, *Jam nunc ergo*, highlights —and is highlighted by—the declamatory, reiterative melody at the start of phrase 4; but when this melodic phrase returns at 7, it is over a subordinate clause of purpose, *uti . . . percipiamus*, important but still grammatically subordinate. In other words, the motivic recall in the music is not hammered home by an exact rhetorical correspondence, but instead allowed to play against the rhythm of the rhetoric. If *Uti Clara gaudia percipiamus* (7) has a rhetorical correspondence, it is to *Ubi videamus* (5), the correspondence being one of alliteration (*Ubi . . . uti*) as well as of content (the celestial vision). Here, of course, is no musical correspondence. And if *Jam nunc ergo . . . petamus* (4) has a rhetorical echo, it is in

Ideoque . . . imploramus (6); both sound and sense are again parallel, without a trace of musical correspondence. If the general level of artistry in the piece were low, then such a lack of correspondence would not be significant. In various other ways, however, artistry is evident (for instance, five out of the six cases of hiatus are carefully placed to enhance articulation, and accent patterns are disposed throughout in smooth variety). It does seem, therefore, as though the disposition of rhetorical and musical correspondence was a careful as well as effective means of integrating the whole, through avoidance of excessive emphasis on any one part. In LAUDES DEO, by comparison, such care is not taken.

Details of verbal construction are strongly dominated by the persistent assonance on ''a.'' Indeed, so strong is this feature that it may be the first or only one that catches the attention. Other instances of alliteration or assonance tend to be effaced by the return of each line, at its end, to a proparoxytone in *-a*, often in *-ia*. Arrangements of accents within the line tend to be absorbed into an overall movement towards the last accent on the proparoxytone. The effect is the more strongly established by the short lines near the beginning (2a, b, 3a,b). From a purely verbal point of view, the lines become exclusively end-accented; this mode of organization, so pervasive in this particular piece, can be represented as follows.[2]

> Hæc est sancta sollemnitas diei hujus et veneranda
> beati Stephani et honoranda;
> Ipse namque, ut gaudia
> Possideret caelestia,
> Christi secutus est vestigia;
> Ideo adeptus est praemia.
> Jam nunc ergo ipsius petamus suffragia:
> nostra solvat debita,
> Atque precatu benigni adjuti aeterna
> digni captemus munera,
> Ubi videamus regem aeternum redentem praemia
> sequentibus sua monita
> Quibus medium credimus te fore beati stephani et luce fulgentem rutila.
> Ideoque praecelsam tuam imploramus auxiliam,
> Ubi clara gaudia
> percipiamus splendida
> per secula.
> Amen.

The end-assonance has an extraordinary effect—the more so because it seems to exist, to a large degree, independently among the other models of organization, both rhetorical and musical. The assonance (one is tempted to say ''rhyme'') usually coincides with some

2. This display has a precedent in London, B.M.add. MS 22,398, fol. 105, where the prose HAC CLARA DIE has been added to a volume of Carolingian capitularies. Each line of the prose starts flush left, but the final ''A'' of each line is written at the right margin. The melody is provided separately in melismatic notation. The *Index to the Catalogue of Additions* (1880) says ''10th century'' (p. 889).

kind of syntactic articulation, and often (but by no means always) with a musical phrase or sub-phrase; but from the point of view of syntax, at least, such coincidence seems to be merely fortunate, for so strong is the assonance it can make its own articulation, as at

regem eternum reddentem *praemia* / sequentibus sua *monita*.

In line 4, *suffragia*, coming at a colon, makes an articulation even though unsupported by the music. Also *aeterna*, in spite of being paroxytone, has something of this effect, but here the strong musical continuity tends to reduce *aeterna* to mere anticipation of *munera*. Towards the end—from phrase 6 on, the assonances come so thick and fast they cause music and rhetoric to fuse and run together.

The assonance in *-a* or *-ia*, with the resulting stress on the end of the line, may be too much of a good thing, for it tends to obscure many other artistic details. The assonances are usually proparoxytone; but in line 1 they are not, and furthermore involve a more elaborate form of assonance that is true rhyme.

et veneranda . . . et honoranda.

(In still another way, then, line 1 is set off from the rest.) These rhymes are coordinated with the melodic shape, whose two parallel phrases are indicated at "ii," but these factors are set in counterpoint to the syntax, which is grouped as shown at "i," for *et . . . et . . .*, to be read "both . . . and . . .," are end-rhymes of parallel units only in sonority, not sense.

FG G GA A B♭ C B♭ A GAA GA A GAG F A CB♭ A G AA G AG F
Haec est sancta solemnitas di-e-i hujus et veneranda beati Stephani et honoranda
                      (i) └───────────────────────────┘
  (ii) └──────────────────────────┘ └───────────┘

Beati Stephani, then, is set out at the beginning of a sub-phrase, at the top of a melodic curve, on a subtly emphatic repetition, and separated by hiatus from the honorific rhyme that frames it.

Another detail that may be overwhelmed by the terminal assonance in *-a* is the correspondence in lines 3a, b, unobtrusive because not aligned exactly in 3b as in 3a.

   1 2 3 4 5 6 7 8 9 10
Christi *secutus est* vestigi- a
1 2 3 4 5 6 7 8 9 10
Ideo *adeptus est* premi-a

In line 4b there are several subtle echoes of the kind found in LAUDES DEO.

              (petamus) -aptemus
Atque precatu benigni adjuti aeterna digni captemus munera

         -u   -u-
             -igni   -igni
                  -erna   -nera
  atque -catu   -apte

These echoes are nicely alternated in a complex rhythm of their own, leading to the terminal assonance. *Captemus* is a faint echo of *petamus* in 4a.

The musical emphasis accumulated at the beginning of line 4 is used to good effect for both 4a and 4b. *Jam nunc ergo . . . petamus* is exhortative ("Let us now ask, therefore"); it starts the syntactic period. *Atque . . . captemus* is a subjunctive of petition, parallel to *nostra solvat debita*, which is tucked in at the end of 4a; but *atque . . . captemus* is the more emphatic member of the parallelism, an emphasis supported by the melodic position at the beginning of 4b. The extra note C might originally have been added out of necessity, but its effect is so appropriate we would not want to do without it. Notker liked the effect so much, apparently, that he made even more of it.

Lines 5a,b are as euphonious as they are mellifluous; here, at least, the internal assonance and alliteration are strong enough to make themselves heard (and also, due to the length of the lines, the terminal assonances are far apart).

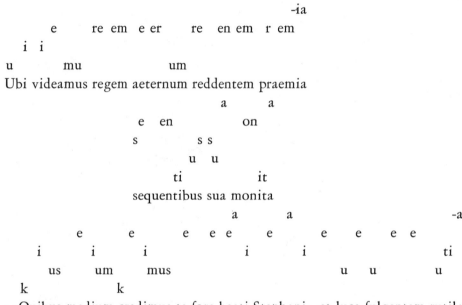

In 5a, the concentration on *-e-*, in conjunction with *-r-* or *-m-*, is unusually insistent, culminating in the accented syllable of the terminal proparoxytone *prae-mi-a*; the same sounds appear in the next word, *sequentibus*, linking that phrase with the preceding.

The procedure in 5b is equally insistent, but different in kind. Descending groups of three pitches in the melody are paralleled by groups of threes in the vowel sounds.

```
C D   E D C   D C A   C D B   C B G   A G F...
i us  [e i um] [e i um] e   e [e a i] [e a i]
```

If it is possible to make a melodic "sequence" in words, the author seems to have done so.

It was clear from its text that LAUDES DEO is a song of public, communal thanksgiving ("Let all flesh sound together the praises of God . . ."); to that extent—and in its ending —it suggests public ceremonial. But HÆC EST SANCTA is more explicit in affirming a festive celebration: "This, today, is the holy festival of blessed Stephen, to be both venerated and honored." The piece is "liturgical" in the sense that it constitutes a particular ceremonial act of praise to be carried out for a purpose specified in the act itself. In addition to honoring St. Stephen, the prose includes—as auxiliary functions of celebration—the briefest statement of his merits ("he followed in the steps of Christ, therefore has gained the prize"), an exhortation, and a petition for grace and favor. There is an exhortation for the company to seek divine favor (*Jam nunc ergo . . .*); and also a petition addressed directly to St. Stephen himself, *Ideoque praecelsam tuam imploramus auxiliam*, the *tuam* echoing *te* in the preceding line.

In addition to these functions of concelebration, the prose includes a luminous image that adds poetic substance. The image is Pauline:

> Know ye not that they which run in a race run all, but one receiveth the prize? So run, that ye may obtain. (I Cor. 24)

and also in the *Epistle of James* (1, 12)

> Blessed is the man that endureth temptation: for when he is tried, he shall receive the crown of life, which the Lord has promised to them that love him.

Behind these passages stands, perhaps, the one from Ps. 19.

> Which is as a bridegroom coming out of his chamber, and rejoiceth as a strong man to run a race.

A popular Christian image, it could certainly be found in many other places as well. In HÆC EST SANCTA it is introduced gradually until it dominates the whole. First, the *gaudia caelestia* are mentioned (2a,b) and in loose apposition the *praemia* (3b); then *aeterna munera*, "gifts," speaking strictly, are mentioned as something that we hope to "carry off" (*captemus*). Then line 5a is explicit: "there [referring to the place implied at the end of 4b] where we hope to see the King eternal giving out the prize." It is surely not accidental that the exhortation is set to the declamatory line of phrase 4, the poetic image to the much more lyric one of phrase 5. But the piece is in honor of St. Stephen, after all, so he is placed in the scene by the brilliant apostrophe of line 5b—"Among whom [i.e., those who follow His commands] we believe *thee* to be, blessed Stephen—" It is not clear whether *fulgentem* refers to St. Stephen or to the King, nor does it seem to matter, for the *gloria* of shining light now envelops the whole image, spilling over into the petition in lines 6 and 7. Perhaps we should not say that the low register of line 6 "expresses" the humility of the plea for aid, but it is at least appropriate to the rhetoric of petition. And in 7, the object of the petition, "that we may perceive those clear joys," is appropriately set to the more assertive melody from 4.

Throughout the prose, the "prize of eternal joy" is the main substance of that series of proparoxytones whose final syllables are linked in a-assonance—*gaudia caelestia, praemia, aeternia . . . munera, praemia, clara gaudia . . . splendida per secula*. A poetic technique and an image, each extended in its own dimension, have been commingled with each other and with a musical shape.

Notker's text, while clearly modeled on ʜᴀᴇᴄ ᴇsᴛ sᴀɴᴄᴛᴀ sᴏʟᴇᴍɴɪᴛᴀs, is not for a saint's day, nor does it refer to the luminous image. Instead, it is for Easter, and picks up the theme of the Harrowing of Hell. The transformation in content seems announced, by way of one-upsmanship, in the opening line: *Hæc est sancta solemnitas solemnitatum*—"this is the festival of festivals."

The Harrowing, however, hardly dominates the scene; indeed, it is mentioned specifically only at the beginning and end, in lines 2–3 and 6.

> (2) qui devicit imperium malipotens diaboli
> (3) suo nos precioso sanguine ejus de potestate eruens.
> . . . (6) tu devictis inferni legibus resurgens triumphas,

> ([Christ] who conquered the devil's evil empire,
> snatching us out of his power by His precious blood.
> . . . the rule of hell overthrown, thou, rising again, dost triumph . . .)

Perhaps the Harrowing is even behind us, for the moment most clearly represented is the *triumphus*—in classical usage, a ceremonial entrance of the victor with his troops and captives into the city of Rome. And the key word, *eruens* (3b) is applied more broadly to *nos* (that is, all men, for all time) rather than specifically to Adam, the patriarchs, and prophets.

More centrally placed are the ceremonial functions of specification, exhortation, and petition—for although Notker's theme is different, he follows closely the rhetorical conception and even some of the details of the West-Frankish version. In line 1, the feast is identified (*insignita triumpho Christo*); in lines 2 and 3 the brief statement of merits (*qui devicit imperium . . .*). Line 4 brings an exhortation closely parallel to the West-Frankish one.

> (West-Frankish)
> 4   Jam nunc *ergo* / ipsius *petamus*

> (Notker)
> 4   Redempti / *ergo* gratias *agamus*

Possibly the haitus (/) is coincidental (although the only other hiatus in Notker's prose appears in line 3, where hiatus appears in the West-Frankish prose as well); Notker uses it in line 4 to emphasize *ergo*.

At line 4b, Notker's rhetorical plan departs significantly from that of his model: line 4b starts a new period, which contains the direct petition to the king of kings *Rex regum Christe vultu placido pius intuere*, and embedded within this petition an image of Christ attended by choirs of angels, *cui angelorum chori juge famulantur*.

> (Notker)
> 4a   Redempti ergo gratias agamus nostro redemptori!
> b   Rex regum Christe, cui angelorum chori juge famulantur,

5a Vultu placido homines in tuis laudibus sedulos pius intuere,

b   Quorum mortibus condolens in tantum humilis factus es ut mortem subires.

The petition thus runs on from 4b to 5a. Line 5b, however, seems again parallel to the West-Frankish model.

(West-Frankish)
5b quibus medium credimus . . .

(Notker)
5b quorum mortibus condolens . . .

Syntax and rhetoric correspond closely, even though here Notker's words refer to the Paschal theme of God taking pity (*condolens*) on man, and overcoming death by death (*mortibus . . . mortem*).

The main point of difference between Notker's prose and its model is the use of 5a, the melodic culmination, primarily for the petition, its image being secondary. Line 5b is clearly intended as a deepening of the image of Christ in glory, through paradox—Christ humbling Himself unto death. But the overall effect has little of the éclat of the West-Frankish piece at that point. Perhaps Notker's image in 5a *is* secondary, and not very vivid. Perhaps the competing paradox in 5b of *mortibus . . . mortem* detracts from the antithesis between 5a and 5b, and is itself not as sharp as it might be. (Compare the far more striking line 4a: *Redempti . . . redemptori.*) Notker probably considered his model too obvious in its procedure; his own procedures, however, seem too complex.

The last pair of lines, too, is complex, but with greater success. From a purely rhetorical point of view, Notker's close seems very fine.

(6)	Tu	devictis inferni	legibus	resurgens	triumphas:	
(7)	tu	post crucem				
		per orbem	gentibus		imperas	
			omnipotens			filius dei:

At the highest level is the parallelism *tu . . . triumphas, tu imperas*, language which could recall either the *laudes* from the Angels' Song (*Carmen angelicum*) *Gloria in excelsis!*

quoniam tu solus sanctus,
tu solus dominus,
tu solus altissimus . . .

or the imperial/pontifical *laudes*

Christus regnat! Christus vincit! Christus imperat!

but different from both of these by virtue of patrician elegance and formality. Line 6 ascends majestically from citation of the deeds (*devictibus . . . legibus*) to the triumph; line 7 portrays its culmination in the stately phrase *post crucem per orbem*—which has the ring of *urbe et orbi*. The deviations from strict parallelism are expertly handled, *imperas* coming earlier than *triumphas* by way of acceleration, and *omnipotens*, the participle, nicely introducing the concluding epithet. *Tu post crucem* goes well with the melody recalled from 4a,b, whose imperial image it echoes. But while the lower register of 6 could be understood to function within the gradual ascent to empire of lines 6 and 7 (or even be considered a sophisticated avoidance of parallelism in the melody as opposed to the text), still the combination of music and rhetoric here seems less than convincing.

In detail, Notker's prose shows some close correspondences with the West-Frankish one, as well as some obvious differences. Accent patterns in lines 2 and 3 are remarkably close and consistent between the two lines of each pair.

(West-Frankish)

2a Ípse námque ut gáudia   3a Chrísti secútus ést vestígia

 b Pòssidéret celéstia

(Notker)

2a Qúi devícti impérium   3a Šuo nos prècióso sánguine

 b Màlepótens diáboli   b Ejus de pòtestáte éruens

In his 3a,b, Notker follows 3a of his model.

In phrases 4 and 5, correspondences to the model are less evident, while those Notker establishes between lines of a pair are more so. His lines 3a,b provided proparoxytones (*sánguine, éruens*) for the F G G cadences; but in 5a,b as well as in 6, the last words are all paroxytones. Since the melodies have been cut short by three notes, it seems clear that Notker, in working on this sequence, felt that the F G G cadence should definitely be proparoxytone, and that if he wanted to use paroxytones (say, for variety) he should cut the melody back to where paroxytones normally occurred in the West-Frankish text.

sólvat (débita)   súa (mónita)

captémus (múnera)   fulgéntem (rútila)

Or conversely, if he wished to avoid the F G G cadence by cutting it short, he should use paroxytones instead of proparoxytones. A paroxytone (*triúmphas*) replaces a proparoxytone also at the end of 6, and the last note is accordingly omitted.

Applying here the general argument of this book, we might conclude that Notker's cadences at the ends of 4 and 5 are the original ones (similar to those in LAUDES DEO at 4 = 5 and 7 = 8). Curiously enough, the West-Frankish HÆC EST SANCTA admits this reconstruction in 5a,b. Endings such as

```
     A  C  B  C  A  G
(5) se-quen-ti- bus su-  is
     et lu- ce  ful-gen-tem
```

could easily be imagined. Comparable endings for 4a,b, however, are less easy to imagine; and of course, the terminal a-assonance characteristic of this prose would be jeopardized.

On the other hand, it is just as easy to imagine Notker making this simple kind of abbreviation of his model; he probably considered it a significant improvement.

It is harder to understand his treatment of accent within lines 4a,b

4a Redémpti érgo grátias agámus nóstro rèdemptóri
4b Rex régum Chríste cúi angelórum chóri júge famulántur

Only the three- and four-syllabled words save these lines from rhythmic monotony or worse. Nothing in the model suggests such an unrelieved regularity of the grouping in two—a primary or secondary accent every other syllable throughout both lines. But in Notker's lines 5a,b, is it not possible to see the results of a careful judgment made on the basis of the model and its choice of rhythms for this phrase? Notker seems to have found the placement of three-syllabled words under the descending melodic groups (as at *médium crédimus*) to his liking; he uses them as much as he can, with carefully chosen patterns in between (following, for example, *te fore*).

$$\overbrace{C\ D}\quad \overbrace{E D C}\quad \overbrace{D C A}\quad C\ \overbrace{D B}\quad \overbrace{C\ B G}\ \overbrace{A G F}\quad \overbrace{A C}\ \overbrace{B C A\ G}$$

5a Vúltu plácido hómines in túis láudibus sédulos píus ìn-tu-é- re
5b Qúorum mórtibus cóndolens in tántum húmilis fáctus ès ut mórtem subíres

The brackets above the letters show the grouping that results from the accents in line 5a. Having found this pattern, he repeated it by repeating the *word structure* (an awkward but useful expression to refer to the number of syllables in each of a succession of words).

5a 2 3 3 1 2 3 3 2 4
5b 2 3 3 1 2 3 2 1 1 2 3

At the end of 5b (*factus es*) he altered the word structure—whether for expediency or variety is not clear.

Notker wrote another prose, QUID TU VIRGO, to the melody of HÆC EST SANCTA. Given the close connection of HÆC EST SANCTA SOLEMNITAS SOLEMNITATUM to its West-Frankish model, QUID TU VIRGO must have been written afterwards; in view of the startling difference in literary style it must have been written a long time afterwards.

While lyric rather than strictly dramatic, QUID TU VIRGO is a dialog between an interlocutor and the sorrowing Rachel. It contains a lament, and in the seventeenth century would have been set *in genere rappresentativo*. And although Rachel laments in relatively Ciceronian phrases, still the language is far more direct and forceful than Notker's earlier prose.

Against this difference in language and conception must be set the fact that QUID TU VIRGO corresponds exactly—but exactly—in syllable count to HÆC EST SANCTA SOLEMNITAS SOLEMNITATUM (word structure and accent patterns often coincide too, but there are several important deviations). Having decided on a topic for the later prose, Notker proceeded to give the topic a verbal shape that corresponded exactly in numbers of lines and syllables to one already existing. As with TUBAM BELLICOSAM, that is a literary tour de force. More interesting from a musical point of view is the heightened response in the second prose to the

Quid tu virgo (Notker)

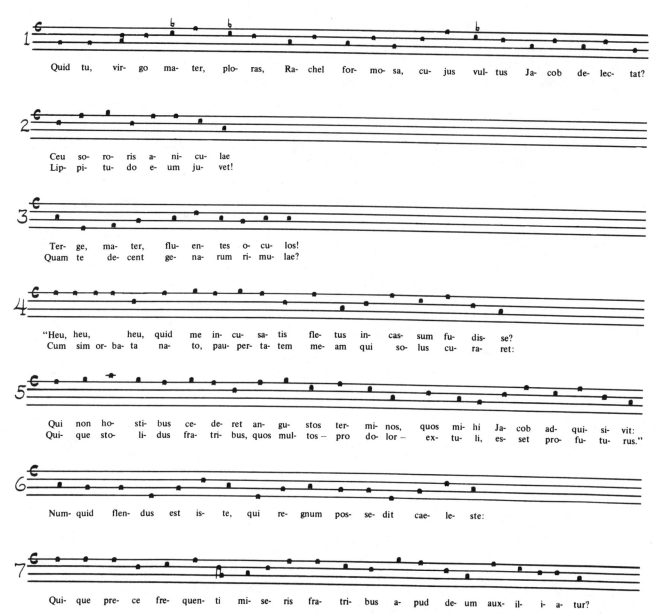

1. Quid tu, vir- go ma- ter, plo- ras, Ra- chel for- mo- sa, cu- jus vul- tus Ja- cob de- lec- tat?

2. Ceu so- ro- ris a- ni- cu- lae
   Lip- pi- tu- do e- um ju- vet!

3. Ter- ge, ma- ter, flu- en- tes o- cu- los!
   Quam te de- cent ge- na- rum ri- mu- lae?

4. "Heu, heu, heu, quid me in- cu- sa- tis fle- tus in- cas- sum fu- di- se?
   Cum sim or- ba- ta na- to, pau- per- ta- tem me- am qui so- lus cu- ra- ret:

5. Qui non ho- sti- bus ce- de- ret an- gu- stos ter- mi- nos, quos mi- hi Ja- cob ad- qui- si- vit:
   Qui- que sto- li- dus fra- tri- bus, quos mul- tos — pro do- lor — ex- tu- li, es- set pro- fu- tu- rus."

6. Num- quid flen- dus est is- te, qui re- gnum pos- se- dit cae- le- ste:

7. Qui- que pre- ce fre- quen- ti mi- se- ris fra- tri- bus a- pud de- um aux- il- i- a- tur?

expressive shape latent in the melody. In the Swiss-Rhenish MSS of the tenth and eleventh centuries, incidentally, this melody was known by the name "Virgo plorans"—a clear indication of the relative impressions made by Notker's two texts.

QUID TU VIRGO has three sections:

1,2,3;   4,5;   6,7

exactly following the period structure of the two previous texts. But an affinity between the melodies of the first and third sections is now revealed by putting these sections in the mouth of the interlocutor, the second section being Rachel's own words. And the interlocutor speaks with Christian insight: he has heard the Sermon on the Mount ("Blessed are they that mourn . . ."), while Rachael knows only Old Testament despair.

Von den Steinen reads the text, convincingly, as an allegory, whereby Rachel represents the Church mourning her martyrs. "Feasts of several martyrs" is the use to which the text was put, and—according to this reading—the use Notker intended. But if that is the case, the text is no ordinary commemoration of martyrs, rather a highly individualistic commentary, one in which the image commands attention in its own right more than it serves as vehicle for liturgical message.

The first section has four periods—all, consequently, much shorter than the first period in HÆC EST SANCTA—which reflects a simpler, more direct syntax. There are two questions, one an imperative, one an expostulation. First comes the topic question, *Quid tu, virgo, mater, ploras . . .?* (line 1). Relatively formal and elaborate, with apposite epithets (*virgo, mater, Rachel formosa*) and a qualifying clause (*cujus . . .*), it fits well with the more intricate melody of phrase 1. Lines 2a,b are compassionate reproof ("As if the red-rimmed eyes of an older sister could do him any good!"). Line 3a, syntactically complete, is the kindly imperative ("Dry thy weeping eyes, mother") and 3b is another question—a rhetorical one ("Do tear-streaked cheeks become thee?"). It seems easy to relate the clear emotional inflections of these lines to the melody—the gently scolding tone of 2a,b to the brief, pert musical quality; the gesture of comfort expressed in 3a,b, in which the interlocutor can be seen bending over the weeping Rachel, then goes perfectly with the gracious downward curve in the melody.

In any case, the placement of the lament itself under phrase 4 is obvious; it would never do, for example, to set *Heu, heu* to the melody of 3. On the other hand, we would probably go too far to think of this as a properly dramatic outcry, for that would suppose expressive forces not available within the limits of the form, which is lyric. Within these limits, the details pre-existing in the musical-rhetorical shape of HÆC EST SANCTA have been exploited with remarkable consistency. The grouping of accents in twos in 4a,b is preserved in QUID TU VIRGO, and seem quite in place following *Heu, heu*; but they are relieved at the end of the line by the pattern of threes Notker had used before at 5b (*ut mórtem subíres*).

4a   Héu héu, héu, quíd me ìncusátis flétus incássum fudísse?

  b   Cum sím orbáta náto pàupertátem méam qui sólus curáret

The unusual successions of two monosyllables (*quid me, cum sim*) are undoubtedly designed to carry out the exclamatory effect of *Heu, heu, heu!* Then, as the lament becomes less exclamatory and more discursive as Rachel elaborates on the causes and conditions of her plight, the melody of phrase 5 shows itself to be the appropriate vehicle. Here the word-structure at the start of each line follows HÆC EST SANCTA SOLEMNITAS SOLEMNITATUM closely, then—as if to maintain a more agitated level, proparoxytones are replaced by more emphatic combinations such as *quos míhi, pro dolor*. The ending patterns for 5a,b (or at least, 5b, since *Jacob* has an uncertain accent) are those previously used at 4a,b (nóstro rèdemptóri) and 5a (pius ìntuére).

In line 6, the interlocutor offers the peculiarly Christian reproof, still in a kindly tone and again with effective, seemingly deliberate use of the lower register. The sub-phrase repetition in phrase 6 is enhanced by a near-rhyme—the first so far encountered in Notker.

Line 7, however, requires a greater effort at understanding, for this is the melodic recall of phrase 4, a recall supported in both previous versions by an affinity of language or image. Such an affinity is here excluded since the recall reaches back to the most characteristic part of Rachel's lament. Can we understand an implied transmutation of hopeless lament into petition for which a benign response is a Christian certainty? Or is the effect of melodic recall merely effaced by the lack of verbal correspondence? But if so, still no essential feature of structure has been lost, the basic three-section plan being perfectly evident —indeed, emphasized—through the alternation of speakers, the functions of central expansion and concluding return clearer than ever.

VIII

FORTIS ATQUE AMARA
Notker's JUDICEM NOS INSPICIENTEM

THE REMARKABLE TEXT, FORTIS ATQUE AMARA, has often caught the attention of those who have come across it. Its melody, while not so striking, is of great interest not only for its intrinsic musical qualities but also for being associated with what is probably one of the earliest proses. Notker's text, seemingly one of his less mature ones, is very close in theme as well as structure to what is obviously its model, suggesting that FORTIS ATQUE AMARA came to him early—perhaps soon after LAUDES DEO.

The text of FORTIS ATQUE AMARA is syntactically straightforward, rhetorically clear and forceful. Lines 1, 2a,b and 3 constitute an opening period that sets forth the theme—the Day of Judgment.

(1,2a) Fortis atque amara   erit tunc dies illa
(2b,3)   in qua perient cuncta quae videntur corporea,
                       tellus et omnia natantia.

> (Mighty and bitter will be that day
>   in which will perish every bodily thing that is seen
>   —the earth and everything that is born.)

Lines 4a and b, joined by an enclitic *-que*, are roughly parallel. Each is complete in itself, with a dependent clause; each speaks of the coming of the Judge.

4a   Judex mitis parebit, ut districte puniat,
 b   Judicabitque saecla, qui creavit omnia.

> (The merciful judge will appear, that he may justly punish,
> And he will judge the world—he who created all things.)

Lines 5a and b are short, independent periods, the second being an exclamation—*O dies illa!*

1. For- tis at- que a- ma- ra

2. e- rit tunc di- es il- la,
   In qua pe- ri- ent cuncta

3. Quae vi- den- tur cor- po- re- a, tel- lus et om- ni- a na- tan- ti- a.

4. Ju- dex mi- tis pa- re- bit, ut di- stri- cte pu- ni- at,
   Ju- di- ca- bit- que se- cla, qui cre- a- vit om- ni- a.

5. Co- lum- na cae- li ad nu- tum il- li- us tre- me- scet al- ta.
   O di- es il- la, in qua ma- ni- fe- sta sic e- runt cuncta!

6. Et quid fa- ci- et vir- gu- la, quid ta- bel- la, si sic pa- ve- scet po- li co- lum- nel- la?
   Et quid sen- ti- et hu- ma- na, quid ter- re- na, si i- ta tre- me- scet po- lo- rum ca- ter- va?

7. O rex sem- pi- ter- ne qui lar- gi- ris no- bis om- ni- a mo- der- na,
   Ne nos si- nas i- re in in- fer- ni tae- tra za- bu- lo- rum lo- ca,

8. Sed duc ad an- ge- lo- rum re- gna. A- men.

5a   Columna caeli ad nutum illius tremescet alta.

  b   O dies illa, in qua manifesta sic erunt cuncta!

      (The lofty pillar of the sky trembles at his nod.
      O that day, in which all things will be revealed!)

Lines 6a and b, the most remarkable of the text, are exactly parallel in thought and wording.

6a   Et quid faciet virgula, quid tabella, si sic pavescet poli columnella?

  b   Et quid sentient humana, quid terrena, si ita tremescet polorum caterva?

      (And what will become of a walking-stick, or a table, if the pillar of the sky
shakes like this?
      And what will humans, and all earthly beings feel, if the host of heaven so trembles?)

One of the two lines is obviously modeled on the other, to go with it in a couplet; as will be shown presently, line 6a probably existed first. Line 6a, furthermore, has internal rhyme—*tabella . . . columnella*; so does 6b, to a lesser degree and in a different place—*humana . . . terrena*. The whole effect is that of a rhyming, scanning couplet interpolated into a prose structure.

With their repetitions and internal rhymes, lines 6a,b approximate those lines articulated into sub-phrases in LAUDES DEO, ECCE VICIT, and NUNC EXULTET. In any case, 6a,b are the longest lines of the text, so that in all respects they function as the most striking event. They are followed by progressively shorter lines. In 7a starts an invocation, *O Rex . . .*, and petition, which runs through to the end.

7a   O Rex sempiterne qui largiris nobis omnia moderna,

  b   Ne nos sinas ire in inferni taetra zabulorum loca,

8   Sed duc ad angelorum regna. Amen.

      (O King eternal, who gives us all things in our daily life,
      Do not let us go into the hateful regions of the devils below,
      But lead us rather to the realms of the angels. Amen.)

The whole construction, from the long complex opening period through pairs of shorter periods to the climactic 6a,b, followed by the longer, less symmetrical closing period, moves with an assurance one might not expect from the sometimes direct, un-stylish Latin. Yet it is wrong to think of an absence of style; merely that the style is not that of classical models—nor of Notker.

In this case of this particular text the stylistic sources are, fortunately, accessible. The ultimate sources for the Judgment-Day theme as it appears here are prophetic: Jerome's Latin version of Zephaniah (i, 14ff.) gives us the language.[1]

Juxta est dies Domini magnus,
juxta est et velox nimis;
vox diei Domini amara,

1. I am grateful to Professor Charles Jones for bringing this passage to my attention.

tribulabitur ibi fortis.
Dies irae dies illa,
dies tribulationis et angustiae,
dies calamitatis et miseriae,
dies tenebrarum et caliginis,
dies nebulae et turbinis,
dies tubae et clangoris
super civitates munitas,
et super angulos excelsos . . .

In passing, we may note that the language of the West-Frankish proses we have studied is considerably less extravagant in its use of rhyme and repetition than this example of so-called "Asian prose," one of the important stylistic alternatives bequeathed to medieval writers by antiquity. In general, it could be said that the West-Frankish proses achieve a compromise between the "Asian" style, especially as preserved by Irish monastic scholars, and the more classical tradition as cultivated by Notker. At the other end of the spectrum could be placed the rendering of the same theme by Bede in quantitative hexameters, in the poem *Inter florigeras* on the topic *De die judicii*.[2]

| _ ∪ ∪ | _ _ | _ ∪ ∪ | _ _ | _ ∪ ∪ | _ _
Terra tremet montesque ruent collesque liquescent,
| _ ∪ ∪ | _ ∪ ∪ | _ _ | _ _ | _ ∪ ∪ | _ _
Et mare terribili confundet murmure mentes.

Even with the heavy alliterations, the hexameters still retain the classic cadence, so different from that of the rhyming prose in the lines now to be taken up.

The incipit of FORTIS ATQUE AMARA is clearly derived from Zephaniah (or some related prophetic source)—*fortis, amara, dies illa*. Line 5a, *Columna caeli*, is a quotation from Job (26:11).

Columna caeli contremiscunt et pavent ad nutum ejus.

The sources for lines 6a,b are more problematic—and interesting. Leopold Delisle, in *Manuscripts patristiques et français ajoutés aux Fonds des Nouvelles Acquisitions* (Partie I, 1891), in commenting upon a bifolium fragment (Nouv. acq. lat. 2243), quoted some lines that especially impressed him.

Quid ergo faciant tabulae si tremunt columnae?
aut quomodo virgulta inmobilia stabunt
    si hujus pavoris turbine etiam caeli quatuntur?

Delisle's commentary to these lines was limited to an exclamation of interest. But he did comment further on the paleography of the fragment, describing it as "minuscule merovin-

2. See also J. Smits van Waesberghe, *Musikerziehung: Lehre und Theorie der Musik im Mittelalter; Musikgeschichte in Bildern*, ed. H. Besseler und W. Bachmann, vol. III, 3 (Leipzig 1969). *Bedae venerabilis opera*, Pars IV (Corpus Christianorum series latina); *Opera rhythmica*, ed. J. Fraipont (Turnhout 1955), p. 439.

gienne tirant sur la cursive,'' and comparing it to MS lat. 9427, which he identified as coming from seventh-century Luxeuil. The fragment itself contains nothing but part (beginning and end are lacking) of a meditation on the human condition in the face of death—in particular, the universal terror in the face of destruction of the self, the reckoning up of the final balance sheet. Eventually the fragment was identified by Dom De Bruynes with an early eighth-century London MS (Add. 11878) of St. Gregory's *Moralia in Job*.[3] E. A. Lowe published a sample from fol. 1v–2 of the fragment in *Codices Latini Antiquiores V*; on the right-hand side of the facsimile can be seen the text quoted by Delisle.[4]

These lines are directly preceded in the fragment by four scriptural citations:

(1) Et tamen David dicit: Ne intres in judicium cum servo tuo:
    quia non justificabitur in conspectu tuo omnis vivens (Psalm 142:2)
(2) Paulus cum diceret: *Nihil mihi conscius sum* caute subjunxit *Sed non in hoc justificatus sum*.
(3) Jacobus dicit: *In multis enim offendimus omnes* (Jac. III,2)
(4) Johannis dicit: *Si dixerimus quia peccatum non habemus, ipsi nos seducimus et veritas in nobis non est*. (I Joan. 1.8)

Items 1, 4, 3, in that order, are cited again by Gregory in his *Homeliae in Evangelium* (lib. II, xxxix). In the bifolium fragment, the four items are followed directly by the lines quoted by Delisle. Is it a fifth quotation? If so, where from? The thought is a familiar prophetic one. Malachi says,

But who may abide the day of his coming?
And who shall stand when he appeareth? (Mal. 3,2)

And Gregory elsewhere writes,[5]

In irae ejus praesentia quae caro subsistet, si ventum movit, et terram subruit, concitavit aera, et tot aedificia stravit?

(In the face of his wrath what flesh shall stand, if the wind moves, and the earth shakes, the heavens and so many buildings leveled?)

The thought is expressed in the *Moralia in Job* a little more directly than in FORTIS ATQUE AMARA.

(Gregory)
What, then, will the tablature do if the columns tremble?
Or how will the saplings stand firm,
        if even the heavens are shaken by the storm of this terror?

3. Dom De Bruynes, in *Revue benedictine* 39 (1927), pp. 186, 194; 43 (1931), p. 7; see also R. J. Dean, *ibid.* 47 (1935), p. 310f.; Gregory, *Moralium libri, sive Exposito in librum B. Job*, Lib. XXIV, cap. XI (J. P. Migne, *Patrologia latini cursus completus* 76, col. 306).
4. E. A. Lowe, *Codices Latini Antiquiores V: France: Paris* (Oxford 1950), p. [49]: "Luxeuil Miniscule saec. VIII in." Further references cited there and at p. [63]; also in *Codices Latini Antiquiores* II (1935), p. [13].
5. Migne, *Patrolgia latini* 76, col. 1081.

The language, clearly in prose, is cast in a loosely parallel double period, *Quid . . . aut quomodo . . .*, but the proportions show no attempt at symmetry, rather a much more discursive handling of dimensions, the second *si* clause running on at much greater length than the first. Gregory's prose is full of rhetorical effects, but still this passage stands out from its context. And in this respect precisely it resembles the "Asian" prose of Zephaniah—rhetorically elaborate, reiterative, colorful, tending to the extravagant.

But now we can observe a precise difference between the bicola of prose, as a purely rhetorical device, and the couplet structure of the sequence. Gregory's prose period is not itself set to a couplet, or even to a sub-phrase structure, a a b—which would have come very close to the syntax as it stands. Rather, the double period from Gregory has been condensed into line 6a, the *virgulta* and the *caeli* being absorbed into the more complex structure of the one line. Line 6b then was apparently made up to provide a more exact parallel to 6a; here the imagery is weaker—or lacking altogether—and 6b merely echoes the form of 6a in the vague generalities *humana, terrena*. It looks very much as though the adaptation was made specifically for the sake of a couplet for this particular melody.

The melody for FORTIS ATQUE AMARA, preserved only in the same few Aquitanian MSS, is extremely clear in its overall design, but—paradoxically—less clear in certain details; there seems to be no staff source. It seems as though all phrases end on A except phrases 1, 2, and 8, which seem to end on G (as transcribed). Cadence patterns such as those found in previous melodies are not used, except in phrase 5 (GA A); the other phrases all fall, by step or by leap, to their finals. The incipit, in particular, is hard to locate on a pitch level; the transcription reflects only a tentative choice among the alternatives suggested by the MSS.

In this melody, however, the final seems not so important—perhaps because of the absence of cadence formulas that would call attention to it. Apart from the final, the melody has a definite locus around C, and a clear sense of motion around, above, or below C.

The melodic outline (even if not the pitch level) of phrase 1 is clear enough, and different from most of the other incipits studied in its downward inflection. Phrase 2, very concise, asserts the C as a principal level, the fall to G at the end coming so abruptly as to give the phrase an "open" feeling—very like the comparable phrase of HÆC EST SANCTA. Here, in FORTIS ATQUE AMARA, phrase 2, with its repetition, serves as the jumping-off point for the much longer, more discursive phrase 3. A single, phrase 3 begins as an extension of 2, then continues (still echoing 2) through two-note neumes and ornamental figures of the kind usually associated with closing phrases. Clearly it *is* the closing phrase of the opening section of the piece.

Phrase 4 makes a fresh start, not dissimilar from 2 in its locus on C and the ensuing drop to G.

(2) C C D B C C G
(4) D C D C B C G   A B C G C C A

Without being obtrusive, and veiled by slight variation, a motivic system runs throughout the melody giving it a remarkable degree of coherence. Here, in phrase 4, the opening seven notes, which represent a modified form of the opening of 2, are repeated more briefly by the next four.

Phrase 5 occupies a distinctly different part of the range, even though the actual difference is slight. The locus is now lower, around G and A. Again there is a motivic repetition: the opening five notes seem to be repeated in a more expansive form. The motive consisting of these five notes receives textual emphasis in wording of 5b.

G A B G A   G A C B C A B G   E G A A
O di- es il- la!

Melodic inflection is carefully controlled so that this phrase appears to be a mirror image of the preceding ones, ascending to the A final from below rather than descending from above. This effect, combined with the different kind of cadence, results in a function analogous to that of the low-lying phrases in HÆC DIES QUAM EXCELSUS or LAUDES DEO, even though the melodic substance is different. But does the graceful figure C B C A B G E recall phrase 3 of NUNC EXULTET?

In phrase 6 the similarity of inflection to another piece is perfectly clear: this phrase, the longest in the piece, with its gradual descent through a varied "sequence," recalls phrase 5 of HÆC EST SANCTA both in shape and function. (And it is HÆC EST SANCTA to which FORTIS ATQUE AMARA seems most closely related in overall conception and design.) Here the melody blossoms out to give the piece melodic point, focus, climax, meaning. And here, paradoxically, melody and text seem so closely related as to serve as each other's inspiration. True, the textual substance of line 6a is drawn from somewhere else, but its form here, with internal rhymes and a sub-phrase structure, is peculiar to this piece. Even so, the wording is so direct, so unencumbered, it is difficult to imagine it as underlay to a pre-existing melody. What would be the chances of getting *virgula*, *tabella*, *pavescet*, and *columnella* to sit so well in sequential descent of a ready-made tune? Through it all the motivic system continues to pull the piece together, with the start echoing the start of 3, and the second half (*si sic*) having an inner affinity to the start of 2 and 4.

(2)   C C D B C C G
(3) C C D E C
(4)   D C D C B C G
(6) C D C D E F D C   C B D C B G

Phrase 7, the invocation and petition, expresses another sequential descent in a more involute way.

C E E D F E   C D B D D C   C B C D CB A

The repeated notes and changes of direction make the phrase insistent instead of flowing; shorter than 6, phrase 7 seems almost to have more to say. Here, too, there is a close relationship of rhetorical function, wording, and melodic inflection. The forward momentum being slowed down by 7, only a single ornamental neume and a drop to F are needed to give the single 8 a closing quality.

It is easy to see that FORTIS ATQUE AMARA is unique in the early repertory on account of its Judgment-Day theme. But it is unusual as well because of the concise relationship of text and melody. Practically all the early sequences show such relationship in greater or lesser degree, each in its own way; but it is hard to find a piece in which the relationship is so clear and specific at so many points. Part of the effect is due to a feature that can, paradoxically, be taken as a defect of prose style—excessive regularity of accent patterns, in particular those in which accents fall every other syllable.

7a   O rex sèmpitérne qùi largíris nóbis ómnià modérna.

The patterns in other lines are usually more varied, but sometimes not very much more. The language often seems to move more like verse than prose. By coincidence, and for different reasons, the same is true of the later work immediately brought to mind by this one, the DIES IRAE. One is apt to think of this as a ninth-century DIES IRAE: logically we should speak of the DIES IRAE as a thirteenth-century FORTIS ATQUE AMARA, in spite of the fact that the composer of the later piece almost certainly was ignorant of the earlier one, which is known only through MSS of the tenth and eleventh centuries—MSS almost surely out of use by the thirteenth century.

Notker's JUDICEM NOS INSPICIENTEM is also about the Judge; it follows the rhetorical and syntactical plan of FORTIS ATQUE AMARA closely, but it fills it with entirely different language and transforms the theme. While very smooth, Notker's text lacks the distinctive quality of FORTIS ATQUE AMARA, and is not particularly outstanding among his own proses.

Lines 1, 2a,b and 3 are combined in one long, complex period, just as in Notker's West-Frankish model.

(1) Judicem nos inspicientem, (2a) cripta cordis rimantem, (2b) in commune precemur
   (3) proprias illi puras conscientias possimus ut exhibere.

This involves an exhortation, *precemur*, which serves to define the conventual act: "Let us pray together . . . ." There is also indirect petition, *ut possimus exhibere*; this, however, is not the principal petition (which comes at the end) but rather seems to be part of the statement of theme. Indeed, Notker's theme is not the Judgment Day itself, which is barely mentioned in line 7b.

Lines 4a,b contain an invocation with a set of attributes, instead of the pair of periods in FORTIS ATQUE AMARA.

4a   Deus patiens, juste clemens atque tremende,
 b   Tu vis parcere magis poenitenti quam plecti.

But here the wording reveals the relationship of the two texts. The West-Frankish text speaks of the *judex mitis*, the clement judge, who punishes strictly. Notker's lines contain the same paradox: *Deus patiens, juste, clemens, atque tremende*; line 4b then goes on to emphasize the forgiving side—"Thou wouldst spare the penitent rather than punish him."

Lines 5a,b are a pair of complete periods, as in FORTIS ATQUE AMARA. Line 5a repeats the form of 4b with its *Tu* introducing an attribute, and line 5b echoes the address to *Deus*. In

JUDICEM NOS INSPICIENTEM (Notker)

1. Ju- di- cem nos in- spi- ci- en- tem

3. crip- ta cor- dis ri- man- tem
   In com- mu- ne pre- ce- mur

3. Pro- pri- as il- li pu- ras con- sci- en- ti- as pos- si- mus ut ex- hi- be- re.

4. De- us pa- ti- ens ju- ste cle- mens at- que tre- men- de,
   Tu vis par- ce- re ma- gis poe- ni- ten- ti quam plec- ti.

5. Tu non pa- sce- ris mor- te mo- ri- en- tum, sed e- os su- sci- tas;
   Nec gau- des, de- us, in per- di- ti- o- ne, qui Sti- gem pro- pe- rant.

6. Tu- is ci- vi- bus an- ge- lis est gau- di- um pra- vo cri- mi- ne su- a pu- ni- en- te.
   Cre- do pe- re- at ut u- nus pu- sil- lu- lus non est pla- ci- tum tu- o in con- spectu.

7. Tu nos ser- va ju- gi- ter om- ni- a ma- lo, de- us ju- ste ju- dex,
   Ut non quan- do ve- ne- ris om- ni- bus di- gna fac- tis red- di- tu- rus

8. Nos- met ha- be- as pu- ni- re, sed mu- ne- ra- ri.

spite of the chiasmus, the effect of a simple series of *Tu* clauses is not really avoided. The effect—in sonority though not in meaning—continues in lines 6a, *Tuis*, and the *Tu* is caught up again in 7a.

> 4b Tu vis parcere magis poenitenti quam plecti.
> 5a Tu non pasceris morte morientum, sed eos suscitas;
> b Nec gaudes, Deus, in perditione, qui Stigem properant.
> 6a Tuis civibus angelis est gaudium pravo crimine sua puniente.
> b Credo pereat ut unus pusillulus non est placitum tuo in conspectu.
> 7a Tu nos serva . . .

In 6 Notker seems to have taken no notice at all of the sequential construction, aside from filling out long, sonorous lines with scriptural thoughts and images of a more discursive kind. The shift to first person, *credo*, in line 6b does seem to be a resourceful means of accenting this point of climax in the melody.

Lines 7a,b and 8, as in FORTIS ATQUE AMARA, are fused together into an invocation and petition. Instead of the West-Frankish *Rex sempiterne*, Notker addresses *Deus juste judex*; but *omnia* in 7a and *ut non* in 7b echo the West-Frankish wording, as does *sed* in 8.

> (Notker)
> 7a Tu nos serva jugiter *omnia* malo, deus juste judex,
> b *Ut non* quando veneris omnibus digna factis redditurus,
> 8 Nosmet habeas punire, *sed* munerari.

> FORTIS ATQUE AMARA
> 7a O Rex sempiterne, qui largiris nobis *omnia* moderna,
> b *Ne* nos sinas ire in inferni taetra zabulorum loca,
> 8 *Sed* duc ad angelorum regna. Amen.

The melody was known in the Swiss-Rhenish books as "Deus judex justus." Since this incipit also corresponds to the text of an Alleluia verse, *Deus judex justus*, it lay close at hand to assume that the sequence was related to the Alleluia. And indeed, later MSS modified the incipit of the sequence to make it resemble the incipit of the Alleluia; but the earlier version of the sequence, as given in the transcriptions, does not correspond to the Alleluia, and indeed the sequence as a whole seems unrelated to the Alleluia. As far as Notker is concerned, *Deus juste judex* is perfectly comprehensible just as a theme, a *topos*. It comes from Psalm 7,11 (Latin, Psalm 7,12), is used for other items in the Gregorian repertory, and was current in the ninth century, for example, in the poem *De Strage Normannorum* ascribed to Sedulius Scottus. [6]

Justus est judex, dominator orbis.

With no cadence formulas to guide him, Notker seems on one hand to have followed FORTIS ATQUE AMARA, on the other hand to have regularized it. He uses a proparoxytone at the end of 3 (exhíbere) following the West-Frankish *natántia*. He also put proparoxytones

6. *Anal. hymn.* 50, p. 232, stanza 13.

under the cadence of 5 (*súscitas*, *próperant*), even though the St. Gall neumes clearly show an F G A cadence instead of the G A A cadence of the Aquitanian MSS. Elsewhere Notker uses paroxytones, which FORTIS ATQUE AMARA does except in 4 (*púniat*, *ómnia*)—a more consistent procedure.

All the more striking, in view of these similarities between the two texts, is the way Notker has transformed the theme. FORTIS ATQUE AMARA is prophetic, apocalyptic, metaphysical, theological; it describes what is to come, briefly but unsparingly. As shown clearly in the climactic lines 6a,b, Man's condition on that Day is incidental, almost inconsequential. With the universe dissolving, what hope does Man have—indeed, of what importance is he? The concluding petition is almost without moral implication: Get us out of there!

Notker, the classicist, is often the moralist, and especially here. Relationship of Man's conscience to God is the whole content of his Judgment scene. He carefully marshals the most important New Testament texts to project a merciful God.

> (6a) . . . Joy shall be in heaven over one sinner that repenteth,
> more than over ninety and nine just persons, which need no
> repentence (Luke 15,9)
> (6b) Are not two sparrows sold for a farthing? and one of them
> shall not fall on the ground without your Father (Matt. 10,29)

Line 5a echoes the Ash Wednesday Collect, "O God, who desirest not the death of a sinner, but rather that he should turn from his ways . . ." (*Deus qui non mortem sed poenitentiam peccatorum*). And the concluding petition asks for reward, not punishment. All this within a human framework; the apocalyptic scene is not invoked, even in the reference to God's coming in Judgment in line 7b.

FORTIS ATQUE AMARA is the most independent artistic effort of the whole early repertory. Without any real liturgical connections—or functions—without formulas of celebration in the text or formulas of intonation or cadence in the melody, its composer set out to give a theme a musical prose shape. In so far as he succeeded, and in spite of idiosyncrasies, FORTIS ATQUE AMARA comes very close to revealing the essence of the sequence.

IX

CLARA GAUDIA and DIC NOBIS
Notker's JOHANNES JESU CHRISTO
and LAURENTI DAVID MAGNI

IN THIS CASE the model used by Notker may be out of our reach. Of the two earliest West-Frankish texts, DIC NOBIS and CLARA GAUDIA, each shows similarities and differences with respect to Notker's version in such a way as to make a decision between them difficult. Indeed, it seems more likely that neither of these extant West-Frankish texts—at least as they stand—is the original text, or the one Notker saw. Notker's two texts to the melody, LAURENTI DAVID and JOHANNES JESU, both show signs of maturity; it is possible that by the time Notker received the melody, more than one version was already in circulation.

The melody seems at first very restricted in range, and lacking in distinctive contours—especially in comparison to those studied; it has little in common with them in terms of melodic idiom. Still, its shape is carefully contrived (even though the detail varies in the different manuscript traditions), and on the shape depend questions of original form. We can best get to know it in Notker's JOHANNES JESU (this short title, like others, is syntactically incomplete; but the sense is complete only at the end of the first phrase, through a suspension entirely characteristic of Notker's earlier style).

As Notker uses it, the melody has eight phrases, the first and eighth being singles, the rest doubles. Phrase 1 is moderately long, phrase 2 abruptly shorter, phrases 3 through 7 longer *and all about the same length*—18, 20, 18, 22, 19 syllables. This equivalence of length throughout the body of the piece is not at all usual in the melodies we have studied. Among other things, it reduces the effect of larger groupings, or of shapes such as a gradual expansion in the length of successive phrases (as in HÆC EST SANCTA). There is overall shape in this melody, brought about by more subtle means; but the impression remains of predominantly isosyllabic—and therefore verse-like—lines.

Grouping is accomplished by melodic inflection. Phrase 1, with its low intonation, stands apart from the subsequent phrases in its melodic materials, except for its cadence, A F A G. Phrase 2 remains within the area F G A, as if on a recitation tone, cadencing on A G. Phrase 3 has the effect of a sequel to 2, expanding the range down to D and up to B flat, then echoing the same cadence. And phrase 4, too, has the A A G cadence, even though the melodic material in the middle of the phrase has moved relatively far from the original modest inflection on F G A. Within the restricted confines of this melody, the descent in phrase 4,

C B♭ A, B♭ A G, A F

constitutes an exuberant roulade. This particular figure—a sequentially descending three-note figure—is frequent in late Gregorian and early Frankish melismas. Here it provides the culmination of the upward melodic motion prevailing in the overall design of the piece.

Phrase 5 exactly echoes the cadence, and the approach to the cadence, of 4, so that on these relatively subtle grounds phrases 4 and 5 are linked together, and set off from phrases 2 and 3 (which are likewise linked by a common approach to the cadence—although this is perceived only in retrospect after the approach has changed in 4 and 5). Phrase 5 begins on G, a new beginning, rises to C and descends but less emphatically than 4.

Phrase 6 also begins on G, being in that respect linked with 5; or, perhaps better, showing a gradual but insistent rise in the tonal level of the piece even within its restricted kind of movement. Phrase 6 has the nearest thing this melody shows to an internal articulation (suggested largely by the original notation, in which a cadence neume appears): the first five notes have the form, but not the substance, of a cadence of the F G G or C D D type; in Notker's settings they always receive two words of the form ′ x / ′ x x.

G F G B♭ B♭   A B♭ C C B♭ D C B♭ A G A A G A F A G

After the opening sub-phrase formed of the first five notes, there follows an ascent to D, the high point of the piece, and a straight-line descent to G. Less expansive, more directed than the descent in 4, this figure stands out as the most notable melodic event. The cadence, too, is distinctive—granting the fact that the range of distinction is here a very narrow one. But the figure F A F G has not exactly appeared since the start; and in some indefinable way this approach to G seems to be more emphatic than the preceding ones.

Phrase 7 is very like phrase 4; the sense of return seems clear at this point, helping to define the melodic climax that has taken place in 6. The more usual form of the cadence, A A G, returns here and in the short concluding phrase 8.

In spite of the apparent simplicity—even monotony—of its recitation character, this melody shows a subtlety of design, a refined control equal to or greater than that of the vastly more exuberant melodies encountered up to now. On the basis of its melodic idiom alone, one would not take this melody to be a member of the same family as the others. It is the first of the melodies studied to use a final on G with a B flat above; that is, a final surmounted by a minor third instead of a major one—it could also have been notated as an A final (with B natural), or as a D final. (Fortis atque amara used an A final for its internal cadences, and the final of the piece as a whole was in doubt; but the melodic formations

JOHANNES JESU CHRISTO (Notker)

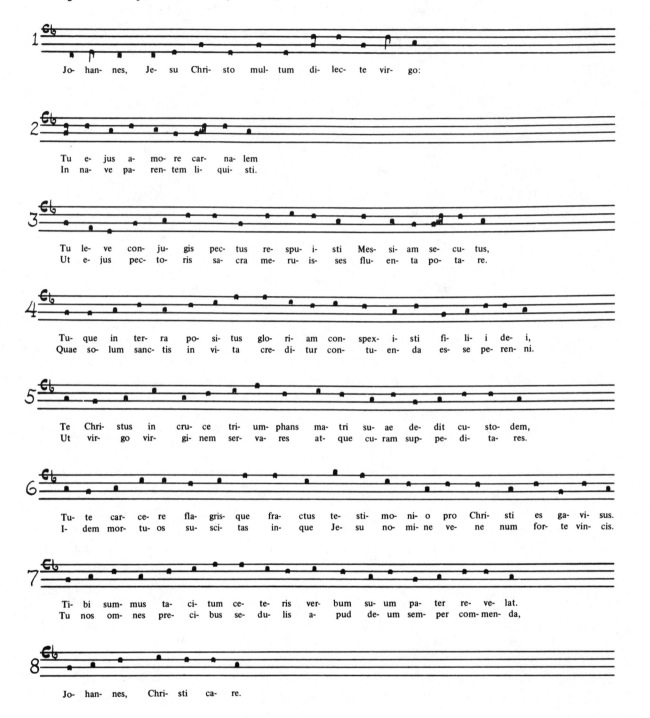

1. Jo- han- nes, Je- su Chri- sto mul- tum di- lec- te vir- go:

2. Tu e- jus a- mo- re car- na- lem
   In na- ve pa- ren- tem li- qui- sti.

3. Tu le- ve con- ju- gis pec- tus re- spu- i- sti Mes- si- am se- cu- tus,
   Ut e- jus pec- to- ris sa- cra me- ru- is- ses flu- en- ta po- ta- re.

4. Tu- que in ter- ra po- si- tus glo- ri- am con- spex- i- sti fi- li- i de- i,
   Quae so- lum sanc- tis in vi- ta cre- di- tur con- tu- en- da es- se pe- ren- ni.

5. Te Chri- stus in cru- ce tri- um- phans ma- tri su- ae de- dit cu- sto- dem,
   Ut vir- go vir- gi- nem ser- va- res at- que cu- ram sup- pe- di- ta- res.

6. Tu te car- ce- re fla- gris- que fra- ctus te- sti- mo- ni- o pro Chri- sti es ga- vi- sus.
   I- dem mor- tu- os su- sci- tas in- que Je- su no- mi- ne ve- ne- num for- te vin- cis.

7. Ti- bi sum- mus ta- ci- tum ce- te- ris ver- bum su- um pa- ter re- ve- lat.
   Tu nos om- nes pre- ci- bus se- du- lis a- pud de- um sem- per com- men- da,

8. Jo- han- nes, Chri- sti ca- re.

Laurenti david magni (Notker)

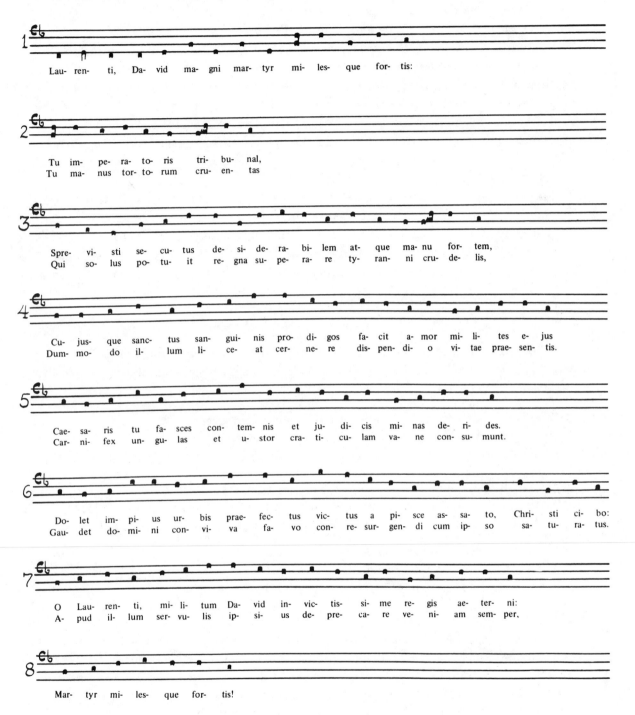

1. Lau- ren- ti, Da- vid ma- gni mar- tyr mi- les- que for- tis:

2. Tu im- pe- ra- to- ris tri- bu- nal,
   Tu ma- nus tor- to- rum cru- en- tas

3. Spre- vi- sti se- cu- tus de- si- de- ra- bi- lem at- que ma- nu for- tem,
   Qui so- lus po- tu- it re- gna su- pe- ra- re ty- ran- ni cru- de- lis,

4. Cu- jus- que sanc- tus san- gui- nis pro- di- gos fa- cit a- mor mi- li- tes e- jus
   Dum- mo- do il- lum li- ce- at cer- ne- re dis- pen- di- o vi- tae prae- sen- tis.

5. Cae- sa- ris tu fa- sces con- tem- nis et ju- di- cis mi- nas de- ri- des.
   Car- ni- fex un- gu- las et u- stor cra- ti- cu- lam va- ne con- su- munt.

6. Do- let im- pi- us ur- bis prae- fec- tus vic- tus a pi- sce as- sa- to, Chri- sti ci- bo:
   Gau- det do- mi- ni con- vi- va fa- vo con- re- sur- gen- di cum ip- so sa- tu- ra- tus.

7. O Lau- ren- ti, mi- li- tum Da- vid in- vic- tis- si- me re- gis ae- ter- ni:
   A- pud il- lum ser- vu- lis ip- si- us de- pre- ca- re ve- ni- am sem- per,

8. Mar- tyr mi- les- que for- tis!

around the A final were quite different from those in the present melody.) This G final occupies an unstable but balanced position between F and the A, equally firm on either side; its color, or quality, is very different from the G final of the other pieces.

There is also, however, the intonation to be considered: it starts on C, rising to D, then F, then A, turning only a little ways down to light on G. In the context of the intonation itself, G is no final; and the piece never again suggests a return to the C at the bottom of the range. Not only in melodic material but in tonal locus the intonation stands apart, never to receive a balancing element at the close, which insists more and more on its G, until the last short phrase seems finally to persuade that the low C had never been. Thus the intonation stands apart; the piece seems properly to begin, and to begin its proper locus, in the concise phrase 2.

JOHANNES JESU, which seems to be the earlier of Notker's two texts for this melody, is the more obvious in its plan. There are no long periods; most often the periods exactly fill out one couplet, with some kind of balanced construction between the two lines. In phrase 6, each line is a complete period. Only the beginning and end involve more complex arrangements. Line 1 presents an acclamatory invocation, syntactically dependent upon 2a,b.

1   Johannes, Jesu Christo multum dilecte virgo:
2a   Tu ejus amore carnalem (2b) in navi parentem liquisti.

The short melodic phrase of 2 is not emphasized nor is its repetition echoed by the text, which runs straight on. And at the end, line 7a is a complete period, and 7b is then linked to the concluding single.

7a   Tibi summus tacitum ceteris verbum suum pater revelat.
7b   Tu nos omnes precibus sedulis apud deum semper commenda,
8   Johannes, Christi care!

The concluding single, *Johannes, Christi care*, is a compact, pointed reprise of the opening invocation, *Johannes, Jesu Christo multum dilecte*; in form it brings to mind the last line of a sapphic stanza—in content, the one by Paulus Diaconus for John the Baptist.[1]

Ut queant laxis / resonare fibris
Mira gestorum / famuli tuorum
Solve polluti / labii reatum
Sancte Johannes!

The main body of the prose proceeds in the series of attributes introduced by *tu*. The prototype, of course, is the *Te deum laudamus*, inspiration for generations of Christian authors in many ways. Notker is especially fond of this figure, often using it for a pair of attributes, as in GRATES SALVATORI or HÆC EST SANCTA SOLEMNITAS SOLEMNITATUM; or more extensively, as in JUDICEM NOS INSPICIENTEM and especially here. The series is varied by changes of pace—one-line units in 3 (and again in 7), two-line units in 4 and 5; or by change of syntax—*te* or *tibi* for *tu*; and by the intensive suffix -*te*, giving *Tute* in 6.

1. *Anal.hymn.* 50, p. 120.

2a Tu . . .
3a Tu . . .
4a Tuque . . .
5a Te
6a Tute . . .
7a Tibi . . .
7b Tu . . .

In general the language seems elaborately worked out without being virtuoso or impressive—comparable to the language of LAUDES DEO CONCINAT or GRATES SALVATORI. Within the straightforward period structure syntactic suspensions and involute word order are common, as in 7a.

Tibi summus tacitum ceteris verbum suum pater revelat.

That is, with less elegance and more directness,

Summus pater tibi revelat verbum suum ceteris tacitum.

Notker seems in some cases to be struggling to control the sonorities of a rich vocabulary. Obvious assonances, however, are relatively few, and a little stiff.

5b Ut virgo virginem servares atque curam suppeditares.

Perhaps the word order is to be linked to a frequent use of cursus planus at line endings, especially these.

4a ésse perhénni
5a dédit custódem
7a páter revélat
7b sémper comménda

Integration with melodic detail seems not very consistently worked out, although certain details—for instance the placement of *testimonio* and *Jesu nomine* on the climactic descent from D in phrase 6—indicate that such integration was in Notker's mind.

Notker's LAURENTI DAVID (another incomplete short title, that is, incomplete for exactly the same reason as JOHANNES JESU) shows a thoughtful disposition of syntax and rhetoric in the melodic shape. It gives the impression of being not merely subsequent to JOHANNES JESU, and thereby benefitting from it, but of being later enough in time to show considerably more mastery of language.

The long opening period, which extends through line 4b, includes a variety of functions.

(1) Laurenti,
    David magni martyr,
        milesque fortis:
(2)   tu imperatoris tribunal,
    tu manus tortorum cruentas sprevisti,

(3)   secutus desiderabilem atque manu fortem
            qui solus potuit regna superare tyranni crudelis,
            cujusque sanctus sanguinis prodigos facit amor milites ejus,
    dummodo illum liceat cernere dispendio vitae praesentis.

Line 1 is an acclamatory invocation much like that in JOHANNES JESU—*Martyr milesque fortis!* It provides the subject of what looks as though it might be another recital of acts and attributes à la *Te deum*. In fact, the construction is more sophisticated than that, for *tu* is merely echoed as the subject of a parallelism: there is only one verb, *sprevisti*, to serve both *tu*'s. The effect is to emphasize repetition of the short phrase 2, and to link it very closely with the melodic sequel in 3. Similarly, the melodic continuity of 3 and 4, as well as the sense of expansion, is mirrored in the accumulation of modifying clauses—*qui solus*, *cujusque*, *dummodo*. And all the time the emphasis is shifting from the martyr to his Lord, so that the text, like the melody, has become something in phrase 4 it was not at the start.

(1) Laurence, martyr and mighty soldier of the great David:
(2) thou spurned the imperial tribunal,
            the bloody hands of the torturer,
(3)   following the strong, much-to-be-desired hand
            that only can overcome the rule of cruel tyrants,
(4)   and whose holy love makes mighty the soldiers of his blood,
            if only they can see him—through loss of present life.

After the opening period, the procedure changes. Lines 5a and b are each complete periods, the shorter syntactical unit accompanying the forward motion of the *acta* and *passio* of the martyr.

5a   Caesaris tu fasces contemnis et judicis minas derides.
 b   Carnifex ungulas et ustor craticulam vane consumunt.

Laurence disdains the official judge and mocks the judgment (5a); he is delivered to the sword and flame (5b). The two lines are linked by an implicit parallelism that evades analysis, and distinguished from each other by a virtuoso assonance—in line 5a on the scornful sibilants, in 5b on the crackling palatals. Notker, then, has been guided by the fact that phrase 5 begins differently from 4, rather than that it ends similarly. Consistently, he groups 6 with 5 on the basis of the same beginning; the text of 6a continues to describe the frustration of the officialdom.

6a   Dolet impius urbis praefectus victus a pisce assato, Christe cibo:
 b   Gaudet domini conviva favo conresurgendi cum ipso saturatus.

(The wicked prefect grieves, beaten by a piece of salted fish—food of Christ:
The Lord's guest rejoices, filled with honey, that he can rise with Christ.)

Line 6b contrasts with that frustration the joyful victory of the martyr, *conresurgendi* standing against the *victus* set to the climactic descent from the high D. The melodic return in phrase 7 receives a reiteration of the opening invocation.

7a O Laurenti, militum David invictissime . . .

And as the melody insists on its G final, the sense of reiteration grows until *martyr milesque fortis*, literally repeated as the short concluding single, has the force of an epigram—or of an inscription. Could Notker imagine a venerable monument in Rome, inscribed with some such epitaph? At any rate, *martyr milesque fortis*, using exactly the same technique as *Johannes Christi care*, seems more deft and effective.

To take up the West-Frankish texts is to turn from an inscribed martyrology of Prudentius to fervent Christian militancy of the Irish. It is also a turn from a Saint's Day to a Holy Day—to the Resurrection and the Paschal feast. Dic NOBIS is an imagined dialog with the Alleluia, banished since Septuagesima and now, on Easter, welcomed back with glad tidings. CLARA GAUDIA is another account of the Harrowing of Hell. Both show significant differences in phrase structure from Notker's plan, but neither yields an entirely satisfactory reconciliation to that plan.

CLARA GAUDIA tells the Harrowing in much more detail than we have seen so far—detail much closer to the Latin texts of the *Descensus ad inferos*. After a festal introduction in phrases 1–2 (which mentions singing the "alleluia"), the story begins in 3a; "Christ through the Cross redeemed the souls in hell." Line 3b is very close to LAUDES DEO.

LAUDES DEO
4a,b Nam a primo protoplasto quotquot in saeclo fuerant,
CLARA GAUDIA
3b A protoplasto quotquot in hoc seculo progenite fuerant

Lines 4a,b enumerate "all those who had gone before," and describe their fate.

4a The Patriarchs, together with all the prophets, kings and high priests
 b Were imprisoned in the hellish confines . . .

In lines 5a,b the Lord enters the gates of hell, and in line 6a he is greeted by the outcry of the demons.

6a Qui es, (demones ululant) crucifer qui nostra ut deus solves vincula cuncta?
 b Fugans tenebras fugerat theatralis horror rutilans lumine perlustrata.

   (Who art thou, Crucifer (the demons wail), who like a god breaks all our chains?
   A spectacular shaking, shining with beams of light, has driven away the shadows.)

Line 7a presents a parallel acclamation from the saints;

7a Clamabant sancti: advenisti O jam domine? regum rex ave!
 b Quem olim vates precinere jam nos ave, redemptor, rex Christe!

   (The saints shouted: have you now come, O Lord? Hail, King of kings!
   Thee whom the prophets foretold we now hail, redeemer, Christ the King!)

Presumably line 7b goes with 7a, but here there are problems, to which we will return. Line 8a concludes the story with the triumphal return of Jesus and his "gloria" of the saints from death to life.

8a Tunc Jesus cum laeta sanctorum gloria processit morte vita(m)

Line 8b provides a not very skillfully worded transition back to the festal frame—the exhortation for the universal singing of the alleluia, as suggested at the end of LAUDES DEO, and also NUNC EXULTET.

As in NUNC EXULTET, the main intent seems to be the telling of the story; niceties of language, or of relationship of words and music, tend to receive less attention. Not that assonance is uncultivated, or that the rhythm sticks; on the contrary, the language rattles along easily and at a good pace. But the writer is more interested in getting the demonic outcry, for example, placed as a whole in phrase 6, than in arranging for just the right words to fall on the descent from the D.

CLARA GAUDIA has one more phrase than Notker's plan—nine phrases in all instead of eight. The problem is, exactly which phrase is the supernumerary one? In terms of the melody, it is CLARA GAUDIA 8 (which is the same as 5). But phrases 7 and 8 provide for the same number of syllables—exactly the same, which is very curious, since this has never happened in any of the pieces we have studied (nor in others of the early repertory, save by rare exception). Blume, in editing the text for *Analecta hymnica*, felt from a textual point of view that the supernumerary lines were 7a,b, since (he said) these alone lacked the terminal assonance in *a*. That is not quite true (see 4: *pontificum*; 5: *sanctorum*) and even though the vowel assonance prevails, it is sometimes clouded by consonances (3: *deditas, fuerant*). Still, the equivalence in syllable count between 7 and 8 should encourage us to consider both in looking for possible additions to the phrase plan.

Line 7a seems very convincing: the demons have asked, in effect, "Who is this king of glory?" The saints have heard from long ago that the Lord is to come; they ask, in 7a, "Have you now come, O Lord?" And seeing that it is indeed he, "Hail, O King of kings!" Line 7b is a relative clause (*Quem*) that introduces a theme familiar from NUNC EXULTET, ". . . whom the prophets foretold." Analogous clauses turned up in ECCE VICIT, NUNC EXULTET, and elsewhere—as interpolations. Line 7b also shows redicta (*jam, ave, Christe*); the use of *ave* as a verb is curious, and the line has an awkward cast. Finally, the sense runs on very well from 7a to 8a.

7a Clamabant sancti: advenisti O jam domine? regum rex, ave!
8a Tunc Jesus cum laeta sanctorum gloria processit morte vita(m)

Line 8b is another relative clause (*Cui*), but a more important one, for it incorporates the reference to the Church universal and thereby the present company, singing this chant in today's liturgy; but it does not do it with great felicity. For the sake of conformity with Notker's plan it, too, could be omitted. The result is weaker liturgically but stronger in every other respect, especially in telling the story, which now runs on smoothly from climax to end.

7a Clamabant sancti: advenisti jam O domine? regum rex ave!
8a Tunc Jesus cum laeta sanctorum gloria processit morte vita (m)
9   Decantans alleluia.

As for melody, lines 7a and 8a, because of the equivalence in syllable count, could have been a couplet to phrase 7 of the melody, making the conformity to Notker's plan exact (save for some variants of detail to be discussed). The interpolation of 7b and 8b, then, would have been accomplished by repeating the melody of phrase 5 (comparable to the interpolation in LAUDES DEO and also in ECCE VICIT), and redistributing the lines of text.

There is, however, another possibility—one that gives somewhat more reason to the interpolation; for what would have been the purpose of filling out the end with just another couplet? The original might have contained 7a to its melody, 8a to its melody. Singles toward the end also appear in HÆC EST SANCTA, and elsewhere, and sometimes occasioned much adaptation. In this case it would follow that Notker regularized the concluding singles into a double. Still, a trace of the singles may remain: in JOHANNES JESU, line 7a is a complete period, a final attribute in the preceding series. Line 7b, in contrast, starts the plea for intercession, which runs on through the end. The syntax would fall elegantly under the reconstruction suggested. (The arrangement in LAURENTI DAVID, while not so suggestive, would at least be compatible with the reconstruction.) Is this possibility reflected in a hesitation—otherwise rare—in the melismatic notation of the melody in St. Gall MS 484?

DIC NOBIS is unusual—unique, even, among early proses, which in general display a high degree of individuality. It is the interlocution of the personified Alleluia, eliminated from the liturgy in a special observance on the First Sunday of Lent (according to a Visigothic custom dating from the early seventh century) transferred to Septuagesima in Carolingian practice; the Alleluia returned at the Easter vigil-mass on Holy Saturday.[2] Phrases 1 and 2 interrogate the Alleluia.

1   Dic nobis quibus e terris nova
2a,b   cuncto mundo nuntians gaudia nostram rursus visitas patriam?

       (Tell us, from what lands do you return again to our country,
       announcing joy to the whole world?)

Line 3a, in narrative style, sets the stage for the Alleluia's response, which runs from 3b through the end of the prose.

3a   Respondens placido vultu dulci voce Alleluia:
 b   "Angelus mihi de Christo indicavit pia miracula . . ."

"An angel told me of the holy miracles of Christ." The Alleluia goes on to tell how he heard of the Resurrection, how he flew back to announce that the old law was replaced by the new Grace. In 5b the Alleluia exhorts the company to join in the joyful acclamation, "Christ today has redeemed us from bitter death!"

5b   Itaque plaudite, famuli, voce clara: Christus hodie redemit nos a morte dira!

---

2. See Michel Robert, "Les adieux à l'alleluia," *Etudes grégoriennes* VII (1967), pp. 41–51; also G. Oury, "Psalmum dicere cum alleluia," *Epheremides liturigcae* LXXIX (1965), pp. 97–108. Whereas the Mozarbic sources indicate the First Sunday in Lent, Heiric of Auxerre (841–876) says Septuagesima.

CLARA GAUDIA

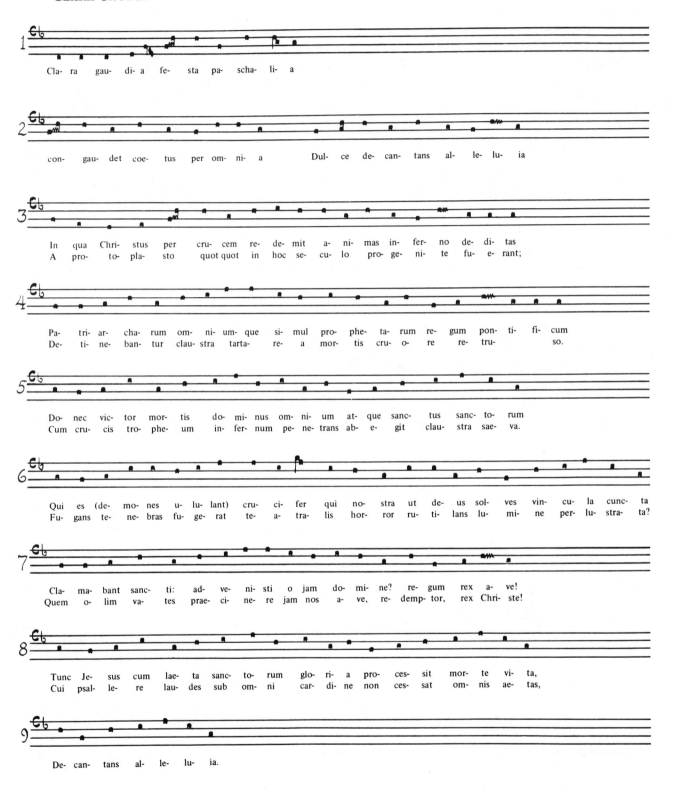

1. Cla- ra gau- di- a fe- sta pa- scha- li- a

2. con- gau- det coe- tus per om- ni- a   Dul- ce de- can- tans al- le- lu- ia

3. In qua Chri- stus per cru- cem re- de- mit a- ni- mas in- fer- no de- di- tas
   A pro- to- pla- sto quot quot in hoc se- cu- lo pro- ge- ni- te fu- e- rant;

4. Pa- tri- ar- cha- rum om- ni- um- que si- mul pro- phe- ta- rum re- gum pon- ti- fi- cum
   De- ti- ne- ban- tur clau- stra tarta- re- a mor- tis cru- o- re re- tru- so.

5. Do- nec vic- tor mor- tis do- mi- nus om- ni- um at- que sanc- tus sanc- to- rum
   Cum cru- cis tro- phe- um in- fer- num pe- ne- trans ab- e- git clau- stra sae- va.

6. Qui es (de- mo- nes u- lu- lant) cru- ci- fer qui no- stra ut de- us sol- ves vin- cu- la cunc- ta
   Fu- gans te- ne- bras fu- ge- rat te- a- tra- lis hor- ror ru- ti- lans lu- mi- ne per- lu- stra- ta?

7. Cla- ma- bant sanc- ti: ad- ve- ni- sti o jam do- mi- ne? re- gum rex a- ve!
   Quem o- lim va- tes prae- ci- ne- re jam nos a- ve, re- demp- tor, rex Chri- ste!

8. Tunc Je- sus cum lae- ta sanc- to- rum glo- ri- a pro- ces- sit mor- te vi- ta,
   Cui psal- le- re lau- des sub om- ni car- di- ne non ces- sat om- nis ae- tas,

9. De- can- tans al- le- lu- ia.

Dic nobis

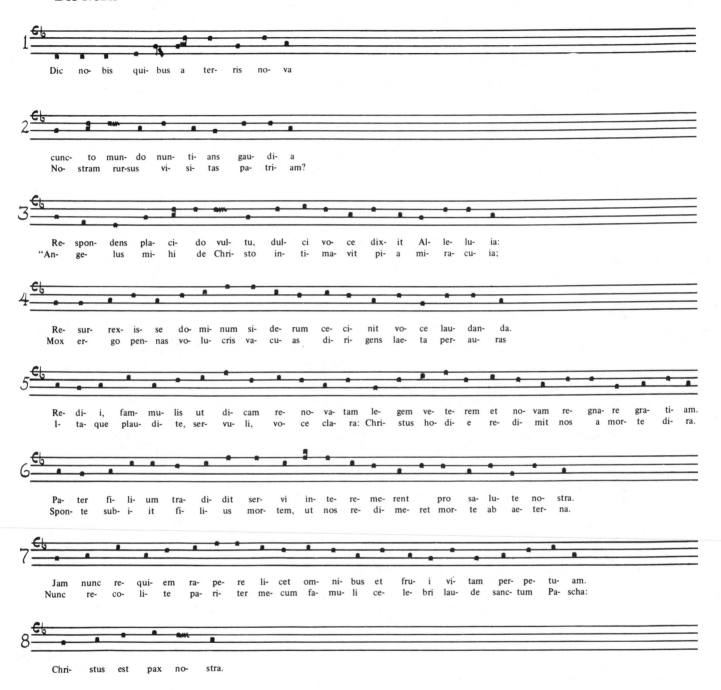

1. Dic no- bis qui- bus a ter- ris no- va

2. cunc- to mun- do nun- ti- ans gau- di- a
   No- stram rur- sus vi- si- tas pa- tri- am?

3. Re- spon- dens pla- ci- do vul- tu, dul- ci vo- ce dix- it Al- le- lu- ia:
   "An- ge- lus mi- hi de Chri- sto in- ti- ma- vit pi- a mi- ra- cu- ia;

4. Re- sur- rex- is- se do- mi- num si- de- rum ce- ci- nit vo- ce lau- dan- da.
   Mox er- go pen- nas vo- lu- cris va- cu- as di- ri- gens lae- ta per- au- ras

5. Re- di- i, fam- u- lis ut di- cam re- no- va- tam le- gem ve- te- rem et no- vam re- gna- re gra- ti- am.
   I- ta- que plau- di- te, ser- vu- li, vo- ce cla- ra: Chri- stus ho- di- e re- di- mit nos a mor- te di- ra.

6. Pa- ter fi- li- um tra- di- dit ser- vi in- te- re- ment pro sa- lu- te no- stra.
   Spon- te sub- i- it fi- li- us mor- tem, ut nos re- di- me- ret mor- te ab ae- ter- na.

7. Jam nunc re- qui- em ra- pe- re li- cet om- ni- bus et fru- i vi- tam per- pe- tu- am.
   Nunc re- co- li- te pa- ri- ter me- cum fa- mu- li ce- le- bri lau- de sanc- tum Pa- scha:

8. Chri- stus est pax no- stra.

The Alleluia elaborates on the details, how the Father gave over his Son, how the Son underwent death for our sake; 6a,b and 7a,b are somewhat repetitious, echoing 5b.

5b Itaque plaudite, famuli, voce clara : Christus hodie redemit nos a morte dira.
6b Sponte subiit filius mortem, *ut nos redimeret morte ab aeterna.*
7b *Nunc colite pariter mecum, famuli* celebri laude sanctum Pascha.

Line 8, *Christus est pax nostra*, is another acclamation, of an epigrammatic type that recalls the concluding lines of Notker's two texts for this melody.

The shape of DIC NOBIS differs from CLARA GAUDIA first by having only 8 phrases in all, thereby resembling Notker's plan in the very respect in which CLARA GAUDIA departs from it; second, by having a longer phrase at 5, which sets it apart from Notker. There seems to be no obvious way in which this long phrase can be reduced to Notker's dimensions. It contains the same melodic substance as Notker's phrase 5, but with an internal repetition that creates a sub-phrase structure, although one without a clear internal cadence.

G F G B♭ G A B♭ C A B♭ A G A,
F A B♭ C A B♭ A G A A F G A G

The melody, of course, could be reduced, but the text permits no easy solution. If a reduction were to be made on purely intrinsic evidence it would be to eliminate 5b, whose *Itaque plaudite* anticipates the exhortation *Nunc colite* in 7b, which seems to be the indigenous one. The acclamation in 5b falls neatly under the melodic repetition (the lower of the two lines of pitches just given), the syntax supporting the sub-phrase construction, but the language is suddenly commonplace in contrast to the distinctive wording elsewhere in the prose. Indeed, one could speculate that line 5b was interpolated in conjunction with an extension of the phrase as it appears in Notker's plan, and that DIC NOBIS originally showed a shorter double in a different wording, no longer recoverable. Line 5a, as it stands, shows little attention to the sub-phrase structure, and incidentally is run on from line 4b

4b   . . . laeta per auras
5a Redii, famulis ut dicam renovatam legem veterem et novam regnare gratiam.

in an unusual fashion. In any case, it is hard to see Notker working from DIC NOBIS in the present version; and it is much more difficult to reconstruct Notker's model from DIC NOBIS than from CLARA GAUDIA—at least as far as the phrase plan is concerned.

The details of the melody present another picture. In several minor respects the melody of DIC NOBIS is closer to Notker's plan than is CLARA GAUDIA. In lines 3, the first part of 5, and 6, 7, and 8, DIC NOBIS resembles Notker's melody in leaving out notes found in CLARA GAUDIA, or in similar melodic details. Aside from 5, only in 7 and 8 is DIC NOBIS further from Notker's syllable count than CLARA GAUDIA—and in 8 it is the inflection of DIC NOBIS that turns up in Notker's melody. CLARA GAUDIA tends towards an excess of syllables, which is sometimes apparent in reduplicated G's at the cadences (phrases 3 and 4; perhaps *regum* should be omitted from line 4, as Blume implies).

Assuming Notker followed his model closely, then, we have to conclude that both DIC NOBIS and CLARA GAUDIA underwent subsequent modifications; neither, as it stands, gives us the model, and it is difficult to choose between them. One possibility is that DIC NOBIS owes its correspondence in detail with Notker's melody to a direct derivation from it (except for the modification of 5): DIC NOBIS has on one hand a concordance in the fairly early MS 9448, from Prüm and another in the mid-tenth century MS BM 19768 from Mainz, and on the other hand is curiously absent from the first prosarium (tenth century) in MS 1084—the second earliest Aquitanian collection—turning up in the supplement section to that prosarium amidst a group of later texts. And even though DIC NOBIS appears in the earliest St. Martial prosarium, MS 1240 (ca. 930), still the principal entry in the sequentiaria (melismatic notation) in MS 1084 as well as MS 1118, is the melody for CLARA GAUDIA, not for DIC NOBIS.

It would be a mistake to think of this melody as representing a primitive stage of development: the restricted range and motion of the melody are rather products of a refined control apparent in the overall shaping, the gradual expansion and rise to the high point, the careful disposition of motivic material in the larger plan. Not all of these things would be visible, perhaps, without an awareness on our part of the more exuberant treatment of ranges, melodic direction, and motives in other sequences. And perhaps the composer, too, benefited from the experience of the other melodies; this melody could just as well be later as earlier. In any case, it stands a little apart from the others studied in its use of different melodic materials.

X

CHRISTI HODIERNA and others
Notker's CONGAUDENT ANGELORUM CHORI

THE MELODY that Notker, in his Preface, refers to as "Mater" comes down to us with more early texts than any other. It is free from major variants, however, except for the ending, whose phrasing takes a variety of forms. These are worth studying in some detail, not just for their own sake but for the insight they give into the melody as a whole. And the ending is an exceptionally clear example of the way major variants, in the early repertory, are not randomly distributed throughout a work, as they might if due entirely to routine mistakes in scribal transmission, but rather tend to cluster around key points in the structure, representing deliberate, purposeful alternatives to that structure. It is true that some of the variants to this ending can be described as mere corruptions; but even these are responses to a specific structural problem in the melody. And other of the variants are not corruptions, but acceptable alternate solutions.

Notker's solution, as always, is the one with the earliest witness, and we need to know it first—if possible to be convinced of its intrinsic acceptability on musical as well as textual grounds. Notker's phrase 8 starts the concluding period, which is to include a (hortatory) statement of adoration leading to a petition.

(8a)　Ecclesia ergo cuncta,
　　　　　　　　te cordibus
　　　　　　　　teque carminibus venerans,
(8b)　　　tibi suam manifestat devotionem,
(9a)　　　　precatu te supplici implorans, Maria,
(9b)　　　　　ut sibi auxilio circa Christum Dominum esse digneris per aevum.

　　(The whole church, therefore,
　　　　　worshipping thee with heart and song,
　　shows forth her devotion to thee,

beseeching thee with suppliant prayer, O Mary,
　　　that thou mightest deign to intercede for her with Christ the Lord for
　　　ever.)

The first participial clause governed by *venerans* falls exactly into 8a, with the parallels *te cordibus . . . teque carminibus* occupying not quite parallel positions in the melodic curve. That can be imagined as deliberate: neither melody nor text considered by itself is exactly parallel, and slight dislocation in their mutual alignment seems appropriate and artful.

(Notker)
```
     F GA GA GA GA G   D  G F  E C
8a   Ec-cle-sia ergo cuncta, te cordibus
                  D F  G  FED  C DD
                  teque carminibus venerans,
     F GA G A   G AG D  G FE C  D
8b   Ti-bi suam manifestat devo-ti-on-em,
      D F E  G A   E DF   E D   C DD
9a   Precatu te sup-pli-ci  implor-ans, Maria,
      D  FE GAE
9b   Ut sibi auxili-
      D F E   EG   A ED  F EC  EG  E E D
     -o circa Christum dominum esse digneris per aevum.
```

From a musical point of view, the main clause *tibi suam manifestat devotionem* breaks off short; that is, the melody in 8b does not continue as far as in 8a. It does stop on the same note, D, but not with the cadence used before (E D C D D). Clearly, a full stop is not intended. Indeed, the syntax as well as the musical sense continues to the second participial clause governed by *implorans*, ending there, at *Maria*, with a full musical close.

The melody, however, for this second participial clause (*precatu . . . Maria*) is new relative to phrase 8, and as the piece continues to the end it becomes clear that this melodic phrase is paired with the concluding one; but 9b contains the purposive clause (*ut . . . digneris*), syntactically more separate from the main verb *manifestat* than are its participles *venerans* and *implorans*. Phrase 9a, therefore, occupies a mean position, linked to what came before by syntactical dependence, musical continuity and cadence, but grouped with what comes after by musical parallelism and the syntax of purpose.

The melody for 9b begins exactly as 9a (*Ut sibi auxili-*), then repeats that phrase with one extra note (*-o circa Christum Dominum*), finally going on to an extension for the close (*esse digneris per aevum*). No particular reference is made in the texting to the melodic repetition, save that *Christum Dominum* gains emphasis from it. The extension is an integral part of the whole line and should be treated as such: there is no reason to set it off by itself as a concluding single numbered "10" (as AH 53 does).

The important moments of 9b—initial parallelism with 9a, repetition at *-o circa Christum Dominum*, and concluding extension—are all essential to the shape of the phrase. The intent is to create a concluding period that extends from *Ecclesia* (8a) to the end, and this in-

Congaudent angelorum chori (Notker)

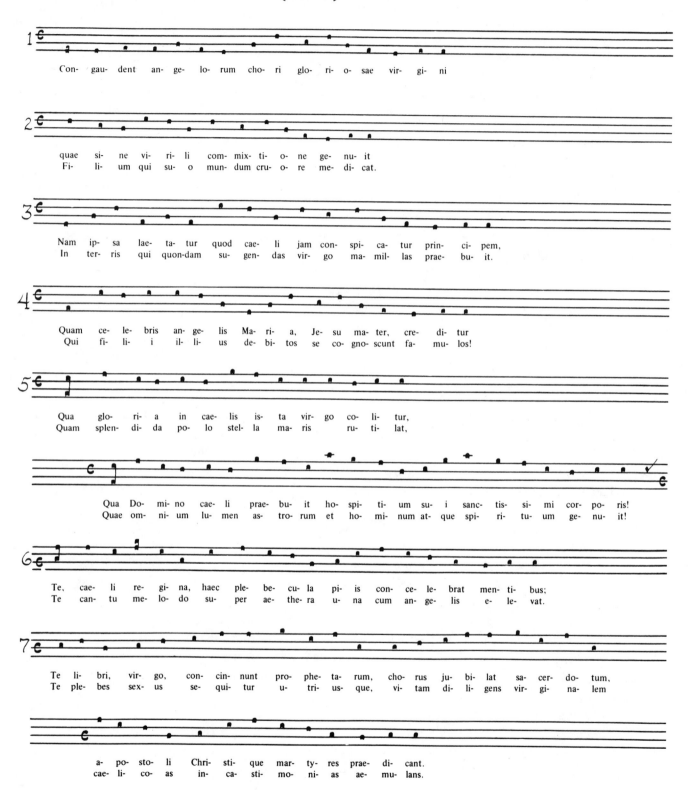

1. Con- gau- dent an- ge- lo- rum cho- ri glo- ri- o- sae vir- gi- ni

2. quae si- ne vi- ri- li com- mix- ti- o- ne ge- nu- it
   Fi- li- um qui su- o mun- dum cru- o- re me- di- cat.

3. Nam ip- sa lae- ta- tur quod cae- li jam con- spi- ca- tur prin- ci- pem,
   In ter- ris qui quon- dam su- gen- das vir- go ma- mil- las prae- bu- it.

4. Quam ce- le- bris an- ge- lis Ma- ri- a, Je- su ma- ter, cre- di- tur
   Qui fi- li- i il- li- us de- bi- tos se co- gno- scunt fa- mu- los!

5. Qua glo- ri- a in cae- lis is- ta vir- go co- li- tur,
   Quam splen- di- da po- lo stel- la ma- ris ru- ti- lat,

   Qua Do- mi- no cae- li prae- bu- it ho- spi- ti- um su- i sanc- tis- si- mi cor- po- ris!
   Quae om- ni- um lu- men as- tro- rum et ho- mi- num at- que spi- ri- tu- um ge- nu- it!

6. Te, cae- li re- gi- na, haec ple- be- cu- la pi- is con- ce- le- brat men- ti- bus;
   Te can- tu me- lo- do su- per ae- the- ra u- na cum an- ge- lis e- le- vat.

7. Te li- bri, vir- go, con- cin- nunt pro- phe- ta- rum, cho- rus ju- bi- lat sa- cer- do- tum,
   Te ple- bes sex- us se- qui- tur u- tri- us- que, vi- tam di- li- gens vir- gi- na- lem

   a- po- sto- li Chri- sti- que mar- ty- res prae- di- cant.
   cae- li- co- as in ca- sti- mo- ni- as ae- mu- lans.

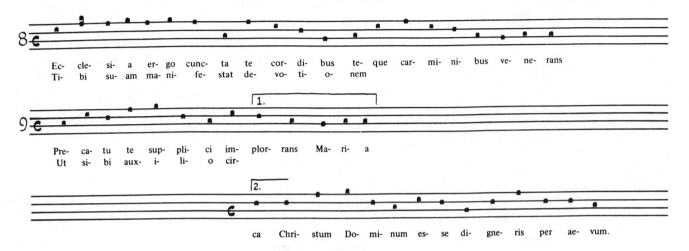

8 Ec- cle- si- a er- go cunc- ta te cor- di- bus te- que car- mi- ni- bus ve- ne- rans

Ti- bi su- am ma- ni- fe- stat de- vo- ti- o- nem

9 [1.] Pre- ca- tu te sup- pli- ci im- plor- rans Ma- ri- a

Ut si- bi aux- i- li- o cir-

[2.] ca Chri- stum Do- mi- num es- se di- gne- ris per ae- vum.

tent seems perfectly realized in both words and melody. Even so, Notker's ending is not easy to grasp; its difficulties may perhaps be appreciated through the attempts of later musicians and copyists to make sense—or some other sense—out of it.

Of the ten proses included in the Toul fragment, no less than four are set to this melody. The Toul fragment (fols. 94v–101v of Munich Cod.lat. 14843) is so called because the version of HÆC EST SANCTA it contains names St. Aper, venerated at Toul, a few miles west of Metz; it is one of the earliest preserved fragmentary sources for the sequence, dated "circa 900." Besides CHRISTI HODIERNA, a broadly represented text for which Toul is the earliest source, there is REX NOSTRAS CHRISTE LAUDES, ECCE JAM VENIT, known only in a few more later sources, and PANGE DEO DEBITUM, unica. No melodies are included for the proses in this fragment.

REX NOSTRAS CHRISTE LAUDES appears in Toul with a long single at 8, and a double at 9.

8   Jesu, tergere curam medicinam vulnera vera adunatae plebis opime.
9a Nunc gloria, laus et honor tibi semper, Christe redemptor, rex saeculorum
9b Cum patre sit, unaque potestas cum sancto spiritu in saecula. Amen.

No melody being provided, the structure of 9 remains indeterminate: 9a and b have identical syllable counts (22), but conceivably these could be adapted to something beside a perfectly regular melodic parallelism—not, however, to Notker's plan. The other source used by the *Analectica hymnica* (Cod. Taurinen. F IV 18, "Graduale from Bobbio, s. XII") provides an 8b,

Pellens nubila tibi supplicantum atque canentum tuos gloriosos triumphos.

Here, too, the situation is indeterminate, since this line, governed by the participle *pellens*, can be omitted without a lapse of syntax. One might argue, however, that the sense requires 8b: the piece as a whole seems to proceed to the doxology somewhat abruptly without it. And a single at 8 is not frequent in the other versions of the melody. Nonetheless, the single is there, in the oldest source.

There is also preserved from later sources a reworking of the whole text, REX LAUDES CHRISTE NOSTRAS, which replaces the whole ending with a short double for 8, and Notker's plan for 9.

8a   Jesu tergere dignare animo mala
8b   Et ut te plebi largire ignea dona
9a   Patri gloria laus et honor permaneat
9b   Cum spiritu una potestas prole quoque beata per cuncta secula.

Looking again at the Toul version, there is no possibility that 8 and 9 should be divided up differently, for 9a has to begin as shown.

Blume called attention to the quotation in 9a of the opening hexameter from Theodulfus of Orleans' famous hymn.[1]

Theodulfus:

   ‒ ᴜᴜ | ‒ ᴜ   ᴜ | ‒   ᴜᴜ | ‒   ‒ | ‒   ᴜ   ᴜ | ‒   ᴜ

Gloria, laus et honor tibi sit rex Christe redemptor!

(All glory, laud, and honor, to thee, Redeemer, King!)

REX NOSTRAS:

Nunc *gloria, laus et honor tibi* semper *Christe redemptor rex* seculorum

Theodulfus (d. 821), active in the court circle from 778, wrote a number of poems; few of them, however, are specifically liturgical. Indeed, *Gloria laus et honor* may originally have been part of an occasional poem for the town of Angers. It is not clear at what point the first half was set to a hymn melody and used in the Palm Sunday procession.

The presence of the hexameter in a version of line 9a that is longer than Notker's plan requires immediately suggests a conflation. Unfortunately, no clear solution presents itself. It is true that the hexameter can be laid very convincingly under the first few notes of the melody.

    D FE G   A   E   D   F   E   D D C D   D
    Glo-ri-a laus et ho-nor ti-bi sit rex Chri-ste re-demp-tor

The rest of the line, however, cannot be accommodated without an unhappy number of repeated pitches, or else some additional turn of phrase not warranted by other versions. Behind this difficulty lies a more basic one: the hexameter is a typical 16 syllables long; Notker's version of 9a is 13 syllables, another short version 14 syllables; the long version runs to 20 or more syllables. An hexameter, in other words, is simply the wrong length line to be used as a unit at this point in this melody. The manner in which it has been adapted

1. *Anal.hymn.* 50, pp. 160–163. *Gloria laus* appears in Paris B. N. lat. MS 1240 (923–36) on fol. 21v, headed VERSUS IN RAMIS PALMARUM (with neumes). See also G. Mesnard, "Vers la restauration du dimanche des rameaux," *Etudes grégoriennes* I (1954), pp. 69–81.

suggests that the version in Munich MS 14843 was conceived originally with a more or less regular double at 9.

Ecce jam venit, another of the texts in the Toul fragment, presents an interesting contrast to rex nostras in the construction of phrases 8–9. Ecce jam venit is provided with a short double that fits under the first half of phrase 8; this is followed by Notker's plan for 9.

```
    F G  A G A G  A   G D   G F E  C D D
8a  Tua, fortissime, supplices misericordia
 b  Petimus ut nobis concedas in hac sollemnia.
9a  Et laudes quas in tui nominis gloria
 b  Ovantes cum caterva sancta, cuncte summe creator, teneamus vita.
```

Even though no melody is provided in Toul, there is no doubt as to how the line fits. (In 8b, *concedas* has to be supplied from a later source.)

Like rex nostras, ecce jam venit shows up in a revised version in later sources; the revisions include primarily a new text at 5a, and a new ending from 8 to the end. This ending includes a long single for 8, and a long regular double for 9.

```
8   Tuam, Christe, recolentes nativitatem suppliciter deposcimus,
9a  Aeterna nobis des praemia quibus sit pura mens ac sincera pectora.
 b  Da digne nobis frequenter natalitia tua, O Jesu redemptor.
```

In this case, the melody for Notker's 9b—used in his version as a concluding extension of 9a—is used for 9a as well, giving the couplet a pleonastic symmetry and eliminating the sense of circling towards the close. In addition, of course, this version eliminates the irregularity of 8b that contributes to the same effect.

If only one of the two cases—rex nostras with its long single at 8, ecce jam venit with its short double—had been preserved in Toul, it would have been possible and perhaps desirable to attempt a morphological progression from one type to the other. But the fact that both forms of the same melody exist in the same early source makes it impossible to proceed to a general description. That still does not mean, however, that both forms coexisted from the beginning, for Toul must stand fifty years at least after the writing of the first sequences. The significant point is that these alternate versions—each believable in itself—come at precisely the most difficult point in Notker's plan. It seems clear that each represents, in its own way, a *lectio facilior*.

Still another text in the Toul fragment is the obscure pange deo. Its ending reads

```
8a  Siccat jam oculos; facescat et pudor taeter, vera sustineas gaudia.
 b  Flecte hinc faciem; imaginem auri primam, dulcem repetito patriam,
9a  Plasmator, durare perennem quam concedas; lux sis nobis meritum.
 b  Tu solus exstas trinus, unus; te voce, te corde, rex laudamus in saecula.
```

The difficult obscurities of this text have long been noted. But these particular lines are greatly clarified by omitting *dulcem repetito patriam*, thereby making 8b correspond to Notker's plan. The sense of the end of 8b continues unmistakably on into 9a:

imaginem auri primam, / plasmator, durare perennem quam concedas.

And 9a properly ends there, in accordance with Notker's plan; *lux sis nobis meritum* is irrelevant. Line 9b, as it stands, provides Notker's long form with its repetition and concluding extension.

Unfortunately there is another soft spot in the language at the end of 8a: *vera sustineas gaudia*, exactly parallel in position to *dulcem repetito patriam*, does not carry on the sense very well. The verbs at the beginning of 8a are third person subjunctive,

Let him dry his eyes; let him confess his shame.

Those at the start of 8b (and continuing in 9a, as reconstructed) are imperatives addressed to God.

Turn thy face hither; let the first golden image, O Maker, last as long as thou will.

Within this discourse, *vera sustineas gaudia* seems syntactically anomalous as well as vague and indecisive in meaning. If, however, it is indeed a conflation, then 8a is turned into the regular short double already encountered in ECCE JAM VENIT.

Before taking up the fourth text in Toul, it may be helpful to glance at a popular later text, CAELICA RESONANT. It is relatively stable in its variants and yet shows practically all the alternatives encountered so far. The most frequent readings for the ending of CAELICA RESONANT are these.

(British Museum, Lansdowne MS 462)
8a Ubi ad dextram patris almam sedet conregnans coeternus per omnia
 b Potenter cuncta disponendo cum eo secla presentia et futura
9a Beata justis donans omnibus premia
 b Praeclara qua lux vere micat que est salus aeterna et nostra gloria.

The plan here for 9a,b is that of Notker's CONGAUDENT ANGELORUM, and this plan appears regularly, with the notable exception of Paris MS 1118, which extends 9a to make the couplet more nearly regular.

9a Beata justis donat cuncta praemia et promissa caelestia
 b Praeclara que lux vera micat que est salus aeterna et cunctorum gloria

The manner of making line 9a longer seems perfectly reasonable: instead of *justis . . . omnibus* (to all the righteous) the text has *cuncta . . . premia* (all . . . rewards,) the *praemia* being further qualified as *promissa caelestia* (promised, heavenly). With the shorter version alongside for comparison, this longer one clearly reveals that extension, involving additional modifiers, has taken place. This does not prove, of course, that the short version of 9a corresponding to Notker's plan is indeed the original one; but it does show that this particular text, CAELICA RESONANT, was first conceived following Notker's plan and then extended in Paris MS 1118 to make 9a more parallel to 9b. There is still the possibility that that was done in accordance with another older—or even original—model in which 9a and 9b were parallel or nearly so.

In phrases 8a,b, a structural ambiguity is present in what seems to be the authentic reading for CAELICA RESONANT. The couplet is made regular by making 8b longer than Notker's 8b. But the words at the end of 8b are additional modifiers, and redundant ones at that: *secla* is already qualified by *cuncta*, and *presentia et futura* is gratuitous ("all ages, present and future"). The line could end at *secla*, at a point in the melody corresponding precisely to Notker's plan.

We can hardly stop there, however. The end of 8a, *coeternus per omnia*, while not precisely redundant, is a little loose. The sense would continue happily,

> sedet conregnans, Potenter cuncta disponendo cum eo secla . . .

(In one MS, Brit.Mus. Add. 30058.A, *presentia* is given a capital "P," with a period just before—the usual indication of the start of a new line.) That is, if desired, line 8a could be made short, and parallel to Notker's 8b. Exactly this short regular double appears in Paris MS 9449, an eleventh-century source (followed by 9a,b according to Notker's plan). As it stands in the more customary long version, then, 8a,b can be read in any one of three ways —long double, irregular double (Notker's), short double—*mutatis mutandis*.

CHRISTI HODIERNA, possibly the oldest text, is also the most problematic. It presents a variety of indications that there might once have been a different form, but no clear indication of exactly what that form was. In its most frequent later form, 8 is a long regular double, and 9 is as regular as the use of a second ending will permit.

> (8a) Monitus in somnis ab angelo ut in Aegypto fugeret cum parvulo,
> (8b) Herodem impium fugeret qui quaerit Christum callide occidere;
> (9a) Nos quoque ipsum adoremus ipsumque deprecemur simul omnes,
> (9b) Nostris ut relaxet delictis perennis donet bonis in aeterna secula.

Already Blume felt that *adoremus ipsumque* should be treated as an interpolation, since it represents the melodic repetition that is lacking in Notker's plan. And indeed, *ipsum adoremus ipsumque deprecemur* is to some degree pleonastic, repeating itself in thought as well as form. Leaving out *ipsumque deprecemur* would raise a problem with the clause *ut relaxet* in 9b: the purposive petition seems to depend on *deprecemur* ("let us pray") more appropriately than on *adoremus* ("let us worship"), although besides its meaning "worship" the word did have a classical meaning "entreat."

It would be possible to achieve the same shortening of 9a by leaving out *adoremus ipsumque* (as Blume suggested):

> Nos quoque ipsum deprecemur simul omnes
> Nostris ut relaxet . . .

Here another problem of sense arises in terms of the connection with 8b preceding.

> He [Joseph] is warned in a dream by the messenger that he should go into Egypt with the young child, [that] he should flee wicked Herod who sought the Christ to slay him cruelly. We also worship him . . .

The account is elliptic: understood are the Gospel's words,

Then Herod . . . said, Go and search diligently for the young child; and when ye have found him, bring me word again, that I may come *and worship him also*. (Matthew 2:8)

Herod sought the child, to slay him; we also [seek the child to] adore him [as Herod said he intended]. The train of thought is clear enough, even though the language is scanty. But to suppress *adoremus* in favor of *deprecemur* would seem to stretch the sense of the *quoque* past the point of credibility—especially in view of further gaps in the discourse of 8b still to be considered.

Both 8a and 8b show soft spots in the large lists of variants amassed by Blume, suggesting a history of revisions at precisely the points picked out in the preceding discussion. *Callide occidere* is one syllable too short, and this, or some other feature of the passage, occasioned a number of variants. If we understand everything in 8b after *Christum* as an interpolation, then the phrase is brought into conformity with Notker's plan. At first glance the excision of *callide occidere* might seem to truncate the sense,

He fled from the wicked Herod, who sought Christ [to kill him ruthlessly]. We, also, worship him . . .

by failing to mention the purpose for which Herod sought the Christ-child. Yet the continuation in 9a can still be understood, if one will, as elipsis in chiasmus.

Herod sought Christ [to slay him]; We also [seek Christ to] worship him.

By now we are dubiously far from the story; yet there is more evidence of the same kind to consider. *Fugeret*, in 8b, is redictum for *fugeret* in 8a, which should be replaced by the variant *pergeret*. But there is no connective for the *fugeret* in 8b. The implication is that the end of 8a is conflation whose removal would leave the short regular double previously encountered. But implementation is not so easy as in other cases, for the discontinuity of discourse becomes harder and harder to swallow, and at the level of detail adjustments have to be made in individual notes to make the excisions work. While revision of some kind can be assumed to have taken place, it is difficult to see exactly what the revision involved, and impossible, I think, to be sure from what original form it began.

The greatest obscurities, then, are in 8a,b, as in the previous cases studied. Lines 9a,b, even though indeterminate as far as original form goes, suggest more believable solutions. For example, by taking advantage of the parallelism in 9b,

ut relaxet delictis
    perennis [-que] donet bonis

which incidentally lacks the connective, lines 9a,b can be reshuffled to conform to Notker's plan while solving the problems of elipsis discussed before.

9a Nos quoque ipsum adoremus simul omnes
  b Ipsumque deprecemur nostris ut relaxet delictis in eterna secula.

This kind of reconstruction is very different from what has been attempted up to this point, for the reshuffling is hypothetical and to some extent arbitrary. It does not simply transfer the objective fact of Notker's plan to another text, accepting deletions as required, but reconstructs the text. Several reconstructions could be imagined to fit the needs of any one situation, and no objective factor would seem present to help decide among them. In the present case we have to be content with seeing that restoration is indicated (and feasible) at a particular point in the plan—at the point of Notker's *lectio difficilior*.

To emphasize an important feature of at least some of the versions studied: there are signs that changes were made deliberately and with the intent of preserving—or effecting —a smooth, cogent result. Not all interpolations involve questionable pleonasm or redundancy. Especially delicate are cases in which a verbal repetition or parallelism is coordinated with a musical one. *Ipsumque deprecemur*, for example, sits very well as verbal echo of *ipsum adoremus* under the melodic repetition that distinguishes that version of line 9a. There are both musical and verbal positive values involved, and they are inextricably intertwined. No obvious flaw serves as starting point for critical revision.

It is both interesting and discouraging, then, to find a similar situation in Notker's text itself. To begin with, two MSS (both Italian) supply words to make 8a,b a long, regular double.[2]

(8a) Ecclesia ergo cuncta te cordibus teque carminibus venerans
(8b) Tibi suam manifestat devotionem *suffragium tuum poscens*

The language, while smooth and correct, is clearly redundant with respect to *precatu te supplici implorans*, which follows (note that one cannot assume the *first* of two mutually redundant expressions to be the authentic one). In this case, literary criteria and manuscript distribution support each other in a generally accepted solution: as Blume said, *suffragium tuum poscens* was added later to achieve exact parallelism.

Much more delicate is the case of line 8a, which as we saw is clearly capable of being shortened in almost all the other texts except CHRISTI HODIERNA, and even there has indications of softness. Notker's line—alas!—involves a verbal repetition:

Ecclesia ergo cuncta te cordibus
                    teque carminibus
                          venerans

The verbal technique is identical to that in CHRISTI HODIERNA:

                    ipsum adoremus
                    ipsumque deprecemur

Although it is not clear exactly how it would be done, *teque carminibus* could in principle come out, leaving a short regular double. But even apart from the stability of Notker's text at this point, we would not, I dare say, consider such a change justified or desirable. Why? The quality of the language, perhaps: the repetition in the form of the words is the vehicle for an important enlargement of sense ("in heart *and* song"). Or perhaps the art-

2. Cited by Blume, *Anal.hymn.* 53, p. 181.

ful way in which this repetition works with the melodic one: the assonance on *-ibus*, which might suggest closure if exactly coordinated with a melodic pattern, is extended by *celebrans* and by the melody of *venerans* to achieve a more subtle effect.

Notker's 8a, then, is eminently believable, making the melody for that line equally so (this melody having been used to end the preceding three phrases, it is a question only of what form it should take in 8a and b). Notker's 8b, on the other hand, might be questioned on musical grounds—not from the point of view of truncating a line to facilitate a movement to the end; the principle seems good, but the particular manner of doing it here is a little abrupt. And while 9a,b is in itself a perfectly believable construction (indeed, a very effective one), still it is striking that 8b, then 9a, should be shorter than expected, *and* that these shortnesses should cause continuing hesitation in the use of the melody for other texts.

Notker had before him, presumably, a West-Frankish set of words, with musical notation either over the words or separately in melismatic form, and a singer who knew how the melody went. Could one or the other have transmuted the end of 8b into the start of 9a? A very simple solution for an archetype would be a long regular double at 8 followed by a single at 9. But again, several such archetypes could be imagined, all having in common the intent to preserve a more nearly regular, more familiar structure. Notker's version is not only the one with earliest witness, it is also the most complex, which is a happy coincidence. For if the most irregular solution were not firmly embedded in Notker's text (which we trust), we might edit it out of consideration as a West-Frankish corruption.

The variants of phrases 8 and 9 are functions not merely of the irregularity in phrase structure, but also of a basic problem in pitch level of the piece as a whole. As often remarked, the melody ends (with reliable MS support) on a note a fifth higher than the note that would have been expected as the final from the opening phrases. As a musical fact, this is so striking as to have overshadowed other features; but I would rather say, the way in which other features are marshaled to support this one makes credible the idea that the peculiar ending was from the beginning a deliberate and essential part of the piece.

Considered at the highest level, the melody falls into two clear sections, the first ending after 4, the second beginning with 5 and going on to the end. Phrases 1 through 4 share a G final, or rather the long cadence formula,

C B C A G F G G

encountered previously in ʜᴀᴇᴄ ᴇsᴛ sᴀɴᴄᴛᴀ and elsewhere. In addition, phrases 2 and 3 precede this formula by D C (C) A; phrases 1 and 4 precede it by F, A, which together with the C of the formula constitute a clear reference to the F-A-C realm also encountered previously. Hence the real differences among phrases 1, 2, 3, 4 are concentrated at their beginnings: phrase 2 begins relatively high, as if in the middle of something—that is, behaving like a continuation of 1; phrase 3 begins with the F-A-C figure; phrase 4 begins on the final, G, being the first to do so since phrase 1. The four phrases are bound tightly together as the first section.

Phrases 5 through 9 all end on D a fifth above the G used as final in 1 through 4. And like the opening group, phrases 5 through 9 share a common approach the final,

G F E C D,   F G F E D C D D

This pattern tends to take up the greater part of phrases 6 and 8. Phrases 5 and 7, on the other hand, are longer, with internal repetitions, so that the ending pattern takes up relatively less of the whole phrase. The regular recurrence of the pattern in phrases 5 through 8 tends to produce the same effect as in phrases 1–4: that is, each phrase is heard to begin with something new, then end with something familiar. By phrase 8 the return to the pattern is well established, and its absence in Notker's 8b (or in 8a in the short version) becomes a salient feature.

The distinctive elements of phrases 5 through 9 need to be considered individually and in the order of their appearance, for each seems to have a role in the formal process of the piece. Phrase 5 accomplished the move to the higher level—although it is not clear at first that the move is going to extend to the end of the piece. The first sub-phrase in 5a, ending on D above, could have been followed by an immediate return to G (as in NUNC EXULTET); or the return could take place in a subsequent phrase (as in ECCE VICIT). Regardless of eventual outcome, however, the detail of 5a is clearly arranged to prepare the move upward. A neume (relatively infrequent) is used for the leap G-D, and followed by insistent circling round the D, with the cadence of the sub-phrase using the formula found in this sequence and others at the ends of principal phrases on the final. The repetition and extension of the sub-phrase then moves up naturally—but with emphasis—to G above and re-approaches the same cadence on D. At this point, of course, neither the pattern from G on nor the D final is established as such; yet the transition has been made.

Phrase 6 presents a strong G at its beginning, touches the A above and falls a fifth to D, before returning to the pattern for the cadence. This seems artfully arranged: the falling fifth A-D has the effect of making the start of the cadence pattern, with its falling fifth G-C, sound as the continuation of a step-wise descent (a "sequence" in the other sense). We are well into the cadence pattern before we are aware of its presence. And yet it is the G, not the A, that remains prominent and stable, the A seemingly tangential to the larger line even while essential to the step downward of the figure.

A G F D,   G F E C

Variants, incidentally, are frequent in the neighborhood of this A; and its function is of course further complicated by being in a neume, GA.

In comparison to the compound sub-phrase structure of phrase 5, phrase 6 is clearly one long melodic impulse; the stepwise descent A-D, G-C, functions very much as the similar construction in the long climactic phrase 5 of HÆC EST SANCTA. Phrase 7 is more like phrase 5 again, for it contains a literal repetition that suggests a sub-phrase structure.

D E C   D E F G A F G D,
         D E F G A F G D   G F E C D F G F E D C D D

There is no real cadence within the line, so that the sub-phrase structure is not nearly so definite as that in phrase 5; nonetheless, the alteration between the plans of 5 and 7 on one hand, and of 6 on the other, can be clearly felt.

Phrase 7 also brings a more pronounced emphasis on the high A, ascending to it stepwise from C, and leaving it by large leaps, then reiterating it in this prominent position. After this reiteration, the G at the start of the cadence pattern is more clearly an established fact—and a relatively stable one compared to what it had been previously.

Phrase 8 tends to fall into two distinct halves (some textings emphasize this more strongly than others), the second half beginning with the approach to the cadence.

F G A G A G A G D,   G F E C D F G F E D C D D

Here, too, there is no real internal cadence, yet still a division. In the first half of the melody reiterates the A much more forcefully than before, with only the use of neumes on GA (in some versions) to soften the effect. At the division the line drops a fourth from G to D, which may or may not be supported by a syntactic division in the text. The effect of two halves seems rather due to the return, now almost refrain-like, to the cadence pattern. And of course the G becomes increasingly stable as the motion up to A is more frequent.

After phrases 5 through 8, phrase 9 has the effect of a change in procedure—and seems clearly intended as such. Its motion, while ascending to A, is definitely bent downward back to D. The long cadence pattern used in 5 through 8 is lacking. The line is less flowing, more tortuous than any of those preceding, being in this respect analogous to the concluding lines of HÆC EST SANCTA and others. All of these things are true regardless of which plan (irregular, short or long double, or single) is considered. And all these things suggest the irregular plan as the most likely concomitant: it, too, would provide an interruption in the formal process of the piece, hence would help to bring it to a close.

It is within this context that the question of the plan of 8b could be profitably pursued. It would appear (from an analytic viewpoint) a matter of option, of musical judgment, whether to start the interruption in 8b as opposed to 9a. At any rate, the omission of the last half of the cadence pattern from 8b would have that specific effect: something very familiar and expected would be broken off in mid-course, to be replaced by something different. The melodic motion is thereby propelled forward with enough momentum to carry past the short phrase 9a, on into 9b, spending its force only with the conclusion of the piece. Phrases 8 and 9 are fused into a musical whole—the exact analog of Notker's syntax. But if one wished a more stable, relaxed effect one could let 8b run on parallel to 8a, providing syntax to match. The effect of the short double at 8, of course, is to interject short, almost breathless phrases into the series of long ones; a long 9 is then almost necessary for a proper conclusion.

With the melodic detail spread out before us we can consider further the question of the D final. The question is, does the piece end properly, does it constitute an artistic whole, in spite of failing to return to the pitch G implied as a final at the start? If the answer were "no", further implications might be, for example, that in spite of its stability the MS tradition was actually corrupt; or that some kind of return to G was understood to be supplied at the ending; or that the written pitch of the last half is only apparent, for the sake of producing a minor third (B flat) instead of a major third (B natural) above the final, still be understood as G (this alternative will be explored more fully in another context). These or other hypotheses could be invoked if there were a need; but if the ending seems satisfactory as it stands, none of these hypotheses is sufficiently compelling in itself to demand an emendation.

There is no doubt that in the version of the piece as it stands the change of tonal locus must be considered both real and deliberate. This version sets out G very clearly as a final in phrases 1–4, and just as clearly D in phrases 5–9. There is no aimless drift, no meandering through indeterminate regions. Like previous pieces studied, this one deals with clear finals—whatever they may be—and in this version there are two such finals, separated by the interval of a fifth, so that they are clearly distinct in terms of register. In addition to this gross difference of tonal level, there is another one: the G final has above it a major third (B), the D final a minor third (F), so that the distinctive patterns of pitches around the two finals are obviously different. It is this kind of difference that underlies the early medieval classification into "modes" or "tones"; the piece begins in *tetrardus* and ends in *protus*.

Without going into questions of theory, is it possible to say in general whether a change of final is conceivable, or is it excluded by some kind of principle? It is true that some statements by some theorists seem to say that a chant should end on the final implied at the start (no theorist would mean, of course, that a chant should always end on the note it began on); and sometimes theorists recommend that emendations be made to make the end conform to the locus of the beginning. But if this can be taken as a norm, it can not be taken as absolute rule: there are chants that—on good MS authority and with musical conviction—end differently, and a theorist who insists that the rule is inviolate is merely being pedantic in the face of artistic exception.[3] We should be prepared to entertain the exception when we meet it; we can, however, think of it as a deliberate exception, and ask that it give a good account of itself in terms of MS tradition as well as intrinsic musical effect.

In these respects the melody presents a much stronger case than HÆC EST SANCTA, whose beginning on an F (as opposed to the eventual final on G) is more conjectural. And the discussion of melodic detail has shown, I hope, that many things about phrases 5 through 9 can be construed as deliberate preparation for the D final—not just as the end of one phrase, or as a subsidiary final for the interior of the piece, but as a conclusive ending for the piece as a whole. It seems to me that the composer wanted his melody to end higher than it began, with a clear sense of rise to a new region, yet with enough finality for completeness—and that in the economy of the piece the balance of detail is just about right to achieve this effect.

Consider, for example, the treatment of the high G as opposed to the still higher A. It is clear that the G, rather than the A, predominates as a stable point of reference in phrases

3. For example, the Introit *Exaudi Domine* for the Sunday after Ascension. Regino of Prüm, ca. 900, classified this and other similar antiphons by their incipits, departing from the usual practice of classifying by final; he comments upon the matter in his *Epistola*. See M. Huglo, *Les Tonaires*, pp. 71–89.

5 through 8. The G occupies a stressed position in the cadence pattern, and together with the C below forms a strong fifth. But if the interval of the fifth is important there, why would it not be even more important based on the final D, which would call for a more stable A above? Is the tonal framework, in other words, as strong as it ought to be for the D final?

The answer lies in the tonal construction of the first half of the piece, phrases 1 through 4. There is a strong fifth, indeed, but it lies between the F below final and C above. This C occupies a stressed position in the cadence formula used in this first half, hence is the exact analog of the G in the second half. In both cases the stable non-final tone is a fourth above the final—not a fifth. In other words, in seeking a way to establish a new final, D, the composer used the same tonal structure in the second half as he had used in the first. We, and perhaps he, recognize the formula of the first half from having met it in other similar pieces; up to now we have not encountered the cadence pattern of the second half.

It does seem that the interval of a fifth is structurally important, but the fifth involved is one not based on the final, rather on the tone below. The final is located within this fifth, and with reference to it as a frame. The end of phrase 9 makes this clear for the D final by suddenly introducing the C E G figure as an additional—perhaps more familiar?—way of confirming the fifth C–G.

In coordination of textural with musical shape, Notker's CONGAUDENT ANGELORUM is technically by far the clearest of the early texts. Aside from a striking enjambement from 2a to 2b (*genuit / Filium*) each individual line of a couplet also has a syntactic close. Beyond that kind of correlation, there is an obvious use of rhetorical forms to highlight the structure of individual phrases and ultimately the structure of the whole.

Notker sets out an image of celebration by the heavenly host in honor of the Virgin Mother of God. Line 1 as topic sentence seems to echo the saint's day Introit—originally St. Agatha's—*Gaudeamus omnes in domino*:

. . '. gaudent Angeli et collaudant Filium Dei . . .

(Notker)
1   Congaudent angelorum chori gloriosae virgini

and also Psalm 148 (*laudate omnes angeli*). The expression became commonplace, of course; here it is given a distinctive adaptation to sequence form.

Lines 2a,b give the specific reason for the celebration; the two relative clauses (*quae . . . qui*) are theologically interdependent in a way that such clauses will not be later on in the piece. Perhaps for that reason they are joined by the enjambement mentioned earlier.

2a   quae sine virili commixtione genuit
  b   Filium qui suo mundum cruore medicat.

    (Who without male intervention bore
    The Son who healed the world with his blood.)

Lines 3a,b present a paradox—the same one stressed in CHRISTI HODIERNA:

3a Nam ipsa laetatur quod caeli jam conspicatur principem,
 b In terris qui quondam sugendas virgo mamillas praebuit.

(For she rejoices that already he is regarded the King of heaven—
he to whom she as virgin once on earth gave her breasts to suck.)

It is easy to imagine Notker with CHRISTI HODIERNA in front of him, stimulated by the paradox, seeking and finding a more elegant expression for it. In lines 3a,b Notker uses the ideals of classical word-order with somewhat greater directness than they are used in REX NOSTRAS.

The assonance *laetatur . . . conspicatur* in 3a adds sonority without being obtrusive, and is placed in the melody so that the greater weight falls on *principem*, both stressing the point of the line and playing down the effect of assonance.

Nam ipsa laetátur . . . conspicatur príncipem

In the main, however, lines 1 through 3 are merely sonorous, not emphatic. Next to verbal subtleties, we should notice that lines 2a,b, belonging to the same period as 1, are joined to it musically by the incipit on C, as noted in dealing with the melody alone. And in line 3a, there seems to be an inner affinity between the expanding, yet still supporting thought introduced by *Nam*, and the musical feeling of the incipit F A C, used so often in the pieces studied as another realm intimately linked with the establishment of the G final.

Lines 4a,b commence a series of exclamations. It is important to note that this starts in phrase 4, not phrase 5: the first exclamation, *Quam celebres*, does not mark off the new section beginning in phrase 5 as it does in PANGE DEO (or as *Ave Maria* does in REX NOSTRAS); instead it points out something about the melody not noticed here before.

4a Quam celebris angelis Maria, Jesu mater, creditur,
 b Qui filii illius debitos se cognoscunt famulos!
5a Qua gloria in caelis ista virgo colitur,
       qua domino caeli praebuit hospitum sui sanctissimi corporis!
 b Quam splendida polo stella maris rutilat,
       quae omnium lumen astrorum et hominum atque spirituum genuit!

The incipit of phrase 4, G D C D, anticipates the rise to D in phrase 5, even though phrase 4 goes on to end on G. Thus, phrase 4 can be considered a mean between 3 and 5—if the text is designed, as Notker's is, to bring out that possibility. And Notker's handling is not a simple one, for by making 4b a relative clause dependent on 4a, rather than a parallel exclamation (as happens in 5a,b) the change in rhetoric is gradual, not abrupt, just as the musical change can be interpreted as a gradual one.

In 5a and b, the combination of exclamation and relative clause (*Qua . . . quae . . .*) is repeated, now falling naturally within the sub-phrase structure. Each exclamation with its relative clause embodies the paradox of God born of woman, so that each time the relative clause expands and deepens the significance of the exclamation, just as the melodic repetition with extension in the second sub-phrase expands the material of the first. The three exclamations 4, 5a, 5b together constitute a *climax* in the strict rhetorical sense, one that coincides with the arrival on the D final as a goal.

Lines 6 and 7 are obviously grouped together by the repeated incipit *Te . . .*, in imitation of the *Te Deum*. But beside this textual model, Notker has before him the musical one of the sequence itself. Phrase 6, a shorter melody, is alloted a single direct thought in each line of the couplet.

6a   Te, caeli regina, hæc plebecula piis concelebrat mentibus;
  b   Te cantu melodo super aethera una cum angelis elevat.
7a   Te libri, virgo, concinnunt prophetarum,
        chorus jubilat sacerdotum, apostoli Christique martyres praedicant.
  b   Te plebes sexus sequitur utriusque,
        vitam diligens virginalem caelicolas in castimonias aemulans.

(Thee, O Queen of heaven, this little congregation honors with devout hearts,
Thee it hymns, singing a song together with the angels.
Of thee, O Virgin, do the books of the prophets sing,
    the chorus of priests rejoices, the apostles and martyrs
    of Christ give witness;
Thee do the people of both sexes follow,
    choosing a life of purity, imitating the angels in chastity.)

Phrase 7, with its melodic repetitions, is given the kind of verbal enumeration found in the *Te Deum*—but there the items enumerated are often set out with each introduced by its own *te*, whereas here Notker preferred to use the *te* only at the start of the line, there being no real sub-phrase structure that would warrant the articulation of a repeated *te* within the line. Some of the enumerations fall appositely on the melodic repetitions.

        A F G D   A F G D
7a   Te . . . prophetarum . . . sacerdotum

Notker's allegiance to Circero, however, seems greater than that to patristic or musical sources: something stays his hand in 7b; together with the *quams* and *quaes* there are now enough repetitions for his taste in Latinity, and 7b, after summing up with an *utriusque* on the same melodic figure A F G D, abandons the parallelism.

If there is an overall division in the text, it comes after 5. The image of the celestial celebration extends from the beginning through 5b; 6a to the end moves to a terrestrial image—this little congregation, the prophets, priests, apostles, martyrs, men and women —the whole church. Line 8a sums up with an emphatic *ergo* that makes clear the rhetorical function of the concluding period and the fact that Notker, regarding 8a,b, 9a,b as a unit, took pains to give it that irregular overlapping structure studied in detail before.

PANGE DEO was discussed at length by Von den Steinen under the heading "Die beiden Weg,—der Weg des Menschen."[4] His specific reasons for grouping PANGE DEO with SEMPER

4. *Anfänge*, vol. 41, pp. 25–29.

REGNANS—the fact that each has 383 syllables (in the versions he was using)—can be set aside; yet in terms of style there is a more important similarity between the two texts: they share a learned, elaborate Latin as well as a highly individual approach (including a latent Platonism) to the Christian epic.

Pange deo

1 Pange deo debitum, lingua, modulando plectrum:
2a Tolle sonos in aera, imple sinus a lacrimis.
 b Sancta manus igitur nos meditata effigiem
3a Pressit nobis suam; flavit et indidit ruri animam;
 b Sursum caput tulit, vultum ut cogitet semper Domini.
4a Tradit amoena loca. Corruit aspidis ingenio;
 b Mox actus in foveam asperis, heu, miser illiditur.
5a O facinus, vitae, proh dolor! memoriam
       quod aspirare non sinis neque fletibus expiare nefas, heu, miserum!
 b Artis ligata serpentis spiris, mens misera,
       umbra volveris ibi nunc horrida cupido quo profudit saeva animi.
6a Dira sorbes venena, sentis vulnera, quae male nutricas, misera,
 b Faces caeco lumine fusa nebulis expers dulcibus, mens misera.
7a Repit virus pectore, sensu captus emoreris, cinis redis ad funera, heu, perstringeris
                                                           in tartara.
 b Tantis potens doluit factor tui calumniis, venit, solvit a vinculis bonos, respires ad
                                                           gratiam.
8a Siccat jam oculos; facescat et pudor taeter, *vera sustineas gaudia.*
 b Flecte hinc faciem; imaginem auri primam, *dulcem repetito patriam,*
9a Plasmator, durare perennem quam concedas; *lux sis nobis meritum.*
 b Tu solus exstas trinus, unus; te voce, te corde, rex, laudamus in saecula.

Pange deo tells the epic of redemption in a peculiar way. Without mentioning Adam or Christ, the author runs through the story as if it happened to one individual—Everyman—concluding with the Christian moral: let Everyman, now redeemed, rejoice instead of mourn. There is little of conventual celebration, of the formulas of public worship, save the first line and a half, and the last.

(1) Pange Deo debitum, lingua, modulando plectrum;
(2a)   tolle sonos in aera;
(9b) Tu solus exstas trinus, unus; te voce, te corde, rex, laudamus in secula.

These expressions (hardly formulas) are quitted and returned to abruptly. The creation of man is described in lines 2 and 3 in Platonic terms, the divine form being impressed as if on clay, and the soul infused. Man is placed in a classical Eden—*loca amoena*; he falls victim to the serpent (4a). Lines 5–7 then describe at greater length the misery of the fall from grace.

The consistent treatment of theme is supported by consistency of language—elevated, literary, clearly modeled on classical usage but just as clearly distinct from the language of REX NOSTRAS. The central section on the fall from Grace is introduced by a formal exclamation—*O facinus!*—and in keeping with that rhetorical mood the insistence on the word *misera* seems an ornament, not a fault; *mens misera* in 5a and again at the end of 6b has the effect of an epanaleptic distich rather than of a redictum.

As in Notker's CONGAUDENT ANGELORUM, the cadences are proparoxytone throughout (with the exception of *pléctrum*, line 1). The text having no melody in its only source, discussion of the musical setting is conjectural but it seems as though the proparoxytones fall under the same pitches as the paroxytones of REX NOSTRAS.

C BCAGFGG
imple sinus a lácrimis

No extra notes, such as those to be supplied for REX NOSTRAS, are needed here.

The exclamation *O facinus!* marks the division into two halves at phrase 5. Some of the articulations of sense, however, are not so clearly placed. The encounter with the serpent —that is, Everyman's catastrophe—occurs in the middle of line 4a. Similarly, the return of Grace comes in the course of 7b. Something of the continuity of 8–9, then, is achieved in the piece as a whole by the overlapping of units of sense with units of melody. At the syntactic level of clauses, text and melody are closely aligned, with the exception of the strong enjambement from 2b to 3a.

(2b) Sancta manus igitur nos meditat effigiem
(3a) Pressit nobis suam;

Thus, even though discussion of detailed relationships between text and music would be conjectural, the larger relationships can be confidently assessed. Up to a point, these larger relationships indicate a careful fitting together of text and music—in treatment of cadences and coordination of syntax with musical phrasing. Beyond that point, text and music seem merely to run concurrent; there is little of the inner affinity of spirit and technique found in, say, HÆC EST SANCTA SOLEMNITAS. The language of PANGE DEO is too occupied with its story on the one hand, its Latinity on the other, to be an analog of the melodic shape.

REX NOSTRAS seems to be a public, convential set of intercessions, cast in formal, elegant language. First comes an intercession addressed to Christus Rex (1–3), then one each to Peter (3–4), Mary (5), and indirectly Michael (6). Line 6b could conceivably be construed as referring to All Saints, although the language is not particularly clear. Christ is invoked again in lines 7 and 8, and is emphasized in the closing doxology, line 9.

REX NOSTRAS

1 Rex nostras Christe laudes vultu nunc sereno sumito,
2a Impius ne nobis, hostis, ut optat, insidietur:
 b Pectora sed casta spiritus almus servet ubique.
3a Tu, princeps populum pastorum hunc, Petre, serva corde benigno,
 b Laxando cui data est nexus caelo terraeque solvere humanos;

4a Obtentus sic pondere ne ruamur iniqui, effice, praesul,

b Gressus qui per caerula valuisti magistri aequora regi.

5a Ave, Maria, virgo virginum valde colenda,

   facta fulgida lucis omnia porta creantis nosque redimentis potenter.

b Et nostri memor esto, poscimus, talia praestans:

   exutis rebus inde corporis carminis novi odas reboantes ovanter.

6a Nam Michaelis sunt suffragia magna nobis requirenda per aevum

b Spiritus atque omnis Christo famulantis in arce polorum beati.

7a Pulsis jam torporibus, Christe sancte, deposcimus, hostem fugacem vincere posse

   dato perituris ab hoste;

b Debellans insidiatoris maligni molimina dira potenter protege clemens tibi famu-

   lantes in aevum.

8a Jesu, tergere curam medicinam vulnera vera ad adunatae plebis opime,

9a Nunc gloria, laus et honor tibi semper, Christe redemptor, rex saeculorum,

b Cum patre sit, unaque potestas cum sancto spiritu in saecula. Amen.

The idea of a series of intercessions addressed to various persons (as opposed to a single person) is most characteristic of litanies and laudes. The content of the initial intercessions, however, does not recall so much the insular tradition of litanies as it does the Roman collect; lines 1–2 especially seem to paraphrase some collect of general intercessory nature —except that Roman collects are not addressed to Christ.

(1)   [Oremus.] Rex nostras Christe laudes vultu nunc sereno sumito,

(2a) impius ne nobis hostis, ut optat, insidietur:

(2b) pectora sed casta spiritus almus servet ubique:
   [Qui vivas et regnas cum Patre . . .]

   ([Let us pray.]
   Receive now with kindly mien our praises, O Christ our King;
   that the wicked enemy have not his way with us,
   but rather that the spirit of love may everywhere keep pure our hearts.
   [Who livest and reignest with the Father . . .])

The intercession to Peter gives him his customary title, *princeps pastorum*, as well as two familiar attributes—the power to bind and loose on earth as in heaven, and the power of walking on water.

3a Tu, princeps populum pastorum hunc, Petre, serva corde benigno,

b Laxando cui data est nexus caelo terraeque solvere humanos;

4a Obtentus sic pondere ne ruamur iniqui, effice, praesul,

b Gressus qui per caerula valuisti magistri aequora regi.

The intercession to Mary is in two parts: first, the angelic greeting, *Ave Maria*, followed by laudatory acclamations; then, in 5b, a short, non-specific petition.

5a Ave, Maria, virgo virginum valde colenda,

   facta fulgida lucis omnia porta creantis nosque redimentis potenter.

b   Et nostri memor esto, poscimus, talia praestans:
    exutis rebus inde corporis carminis novi odas reboantes ovanter.

The remainder of line 5b does not seem to belong to this intercession—which, indeed, has more of the nature of acclamation rather than of intercessory collect. At this point, where the shortness of successive items becomes apparent, we become aware of the litany-like character. Lines 6a,b, for instance, seem much less like paraphrased collects than like paraphrases of *Sancte Michael, ora pro nobis*.

6a   Nam Michaelis sunt suffragia magna nobis requirenda per aevum
  b   Spiritus atque omnis Christo famulantis in arce polorum beati.

In spite of the relatively elaborate wording, line 6a does not seem to have behind it the syntax and rhetoric of a collect; indeed, the elaborate wording could be understood as an attempt to cast the abrupt expression of a litany into more classical form. From 7 on, however, the turn back to Christ coincides with more discursive petition.

7a   Pulsis jam torporibus, Christe sancte, deposcimus, hostem fugacem vincere posse
                      dato perituris ab hoste;
  b   Debellans insidiatoris maligni molimina dira potenter protege clemens tibi famu-
                      lantes in aevum.
8a   Jesu, tergere curam medicinam vulnera vera ad adunatae plebis opime.
9a   Nunc gloria, laus, et honor tibi semper, Christe redemptor, rex saeculorum,
  b Cum patre sit, unaque potestas cum sancto spiritu in saecula. Amen.

The language clearly intends formality through the kind of involute word order associated with classical models, as in the very first line.

(1)   Rex nostras Christe laudes vultu nunc sereno sumito
    (i.e., Nunc sumito, Rex Christe, nostras laudes vultu sereno)

And not without happy results, as in the next line.

(2a)   Impius ne nobis hostis—ut optat—insidietur;

The sense of classical model, of careful ordering of words, is especially strong at the beginning, through line 4b; this far the verbal rhythm seems conceived and controlled by that particular esthetic.

In line 5, while no less careful, the language seems to favor another ideal of sonority and rhythm. The acclamatory expressions already noticed suggest a breaking up of the line into clausula-like units.

(5a)   Áve María / vírgo vírginum / válde colénda /
     Fácta fúlgida / lúcis ómnia / pórta creántis /
     nósque rediméntis poténter /

And while this procedure is not carried out consistently in the lines following, they still seem unusually attentive to sonorous patterns of accent, with frequent correspondence between the two lines of a couplet. Furthermore, from line 5 on, the involute word-order noticed in the opening lines tends to be avoided in favor of more direct discourse.

Line 5a is one of the few instances of Marian acclamations in the early repertory. In GAUDE EJA the Virgin was acclaimed at the start of the text; here she is addressed in the middle of the text. As before, the language of acclamation is relatively discreet and restrained, and its presence does not make the text as a whole "Marian."

While line 5, the start of the second half of the melody, is marked by the turn to the Virgin, still the series of petitions carries right through from the first half to the second. Rather than a division into two halves, sense and syntax of the petitions group the musical phrases 1,2; 3,4; 5; 6; 7,8; 9. In phrase 7, the internal melodic repetitions seem not to be observed in the text. In this as well as in other respects, the text seems merely to place its sonorous rhythms and cadences alongside of those of the music.

The cadences at the ends of the lines are paroxytone (with the exception of *súmito*, line 1, presumably third conjugation future imperative; and Amen at the end, which is indeterminate). Not only do these paroxytone cadences differ from Notker's proparoxytones, but also the syllable count seems to call for an extra note (relative to Notker's version) just before all cadences (except, again, in line 1).

A C B C A(G)GF G G
hostis ut optat insidi- é- tur

(In addition, phrases 2 through 4 have still another supernumerary syllable.) Perhaps both the paroxytones and the extra G required in the cadence are due to the cursus planus, used with remarkable consistency throughout most of this piece.

Von den Steinen observed that ECCE JAM VENIT was, in its diction, "weak Latin." And yet in terms of overall sense, this prose seems to match the melody as well if not better than any of the others—certainly better than REX NOSTRAS, with its elegant but disjointed series of petitions.

At the highest level, ECCE JAM VENIT allots 1–4 to the Nativity scene, 5–7 to God's purpose, the Redemption, and 8–9 to a petition and festal conclusion. The whole is framed with functional references to the celebration of "Today's festivity" by all those gathered together.

Within the first half, the scene itself is described beginning in 2b, so that phrase 2 is split, 2a going with the invocation in 1. Lines 3a,b and 4a,b contain a series of short, compact clauses strung together in narrative fashion; 4a contains two such units, an infrequent procedure in the early repertory; we have observed it only in NUNC EXULTET and related texts.

With 4b the scene is complete: the wise men have seen his star, the kings have brought gifts. Then, with an abrupt shift, 5a.

Let us believe him to be the very Son of God
    and to have come into the world for this—
    that he should redeem us from the pains of hell.

This strong affirmation sits very well on phrase 5 with its rising fifths and articulated sub-phrase structure. Nor is the construction merely one of contrast: the theme of redemption as the purpose of the Incarnation was announced in the first line—*Ecce jam venit nostra redemptio pretiosa*—and the *Credamus* can be understood as a crib-side acclamation by the congregation, wise after the fact and following in order after the adoration of the kings.

Ecce jam venit

1   Ecce jam venit nostra redemptio pretiosa!
2a Gaudeamus in unum cum angelica agmina.
 b Caeli regem in terris arta tenent cunabula
3a Qui mundi patravit cum patre totius mundi fabricam
 b Cum vilis induit vestibus canent sanctorum milia.
4a Lactat mater parvulum. Magi ejus cognoscunt sidera.
 b Qui in praesepe jacet, reges ei offerunt munera.
5a Credamus eum verum esse dei filium,
            atque ad hoc venire in terris
                ut redimat nos de maligni supplicia.
 b Ipse factus est homo qui sine initio
            deus ineffabilis in nulla concluditur
                prisca vel ultima tempora.
6a O mira domini et gratuita quae nobis dedit remedia!
 b Filium unicum misit ut servos revocat in Elysia.
7a Et ostem aetereum condempnaret
            qui proterva contra eum erexerat
                inane quoque superbia,
 b Et claustra mortifera quae repleret
            ex electis forti manu diriperet
                atque reduceret spolia.
8a Tua fortissima supplices misericordia
    Petimus ut nobis concedas in hac sollemnia.
9a Et laudes quas in tui nominis gloria
 b Ovantes cum caterva sancta cuncte summe creator teneamus vita. Amen.

Line 5b is in the style of the Nicene Creed, consequent to *Credamus*. Line 6 continues the theme of redemption, beginning with a glad exclamation *O mira*! for the attack on the high G in the melody. The longer, more elaborate melody for 7, with its sub-phrases, alludes to the overcoming of the forces of evil (the fallen angels), then once again the Harrowing of Hell and the triumphal return.

7   That he might condemn that ghostly foe
            that rose up against him in arrogance bold but vain,
    And from the deathly confines, which that other had filled,
            might snatch out from those elect, with his strong
                right hand, and lead away, his own as trophies.

The concluding phrases 8–9 are set to the functional conclusion in a short regular double, as already studied. Here especially the syntax is not as clear as it might be, but the thought is strong and to the point. Against the difficulties of Latinity, the lack of obvious elegance or ornament, must be set the features that seemed more important to the author—the terminal "a" assonance, the consistent proparoxytones (save the first and last lines), besides the rhetorical layout as described. And the ease with which the piece slips off the tongue! That is a parameter of the text-music relationship that Notker seems not to have understood.

Outside of the early Toul fragment, REX NOSTRAS and ECCE JAM VENIT are known in only a few sources, later, and mostly Italian; they do not appear in the Aquitanian group. The prose that does appear in the Aquitanian group (and in many northern sources), CHRISTI HODIERNA, is puzzling in many respects.

After REX NOSTRAS and PANGE DEO, the unadorned directness of CHRISTI HODIERNA is especially obvious. Both in vocabulary and syntax, the language seems at a different level of sophistication. There is no question of *which* classical model is involved, for model of any kind seems conspicuously absent—except for the Gospel story of the Nativity. The sole intent seems, at first, to tell the story, and that with "unlearned wisdom," leaving aside the traditional literary embellishments. PANGE DEO, too, tells a story, but with rhetorical flourish and moral tone. And ECCE JAM VENIT uses a simple narrative style for the Nativity scene, but then goes on to other things. These four texts, so different from one another, need each other for an informed appreciation. Together they tell us that the ninth-century writer of proses was committed to no one literary style. A series of contrasting, sometimes incompatible, alternatives lay open to him. If he chose the language of CHRISTI HODIERNA it was not because of literary—or musical—necessity. And CHRISTI HODIERNA as well as PANGE DEO tell us not to infer from REX NOSTRAS that this or any sequence was in some necessary way derived from the litanies.

For all its seeming artlessness, however, CHRISTI HODIERNA is not without rhetorical gesture. Introduction and conclusion, as in PANGE DEO, frame the story with ceremonial.

(1)   Christi hodierna pangamini omnes
                          una voce simul consona
            nativitatis magnae.
(9)   Nos quoque ipsum adoremus
                    ipsumque deprecemur
         simul omnes,
              nostris ut relaxet delictis
                    perennis donet bonis in aeterna saecula.

As another non-narrative element, attention is drawn more than once to the paradox of God being born in a manger.

(4b) infantulus a quo regitur omnis mundus . . .
(5b) Dominus quem virgo mater pannis tegit . . .
(6a) Exiguo tegitur diversorio qui arva condidit ac polum . . .

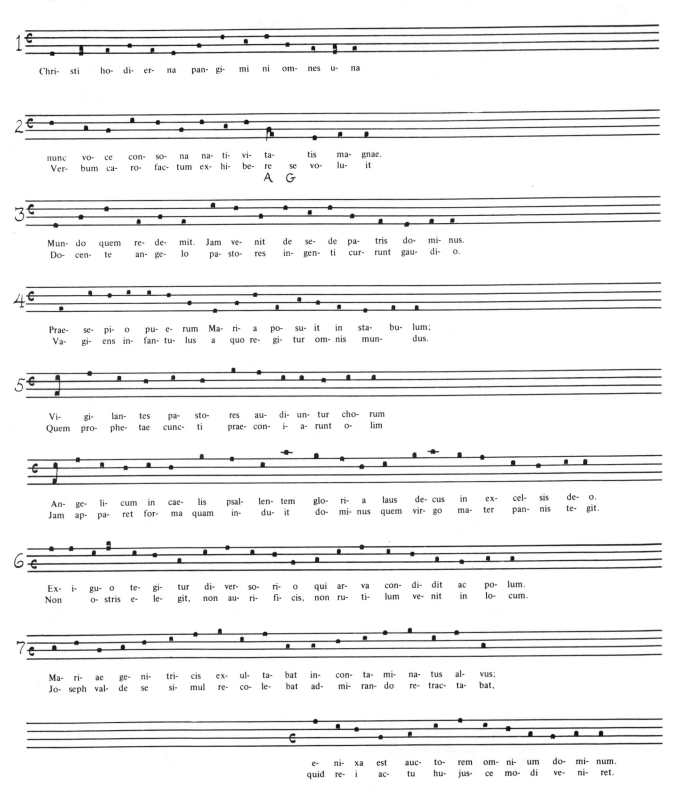

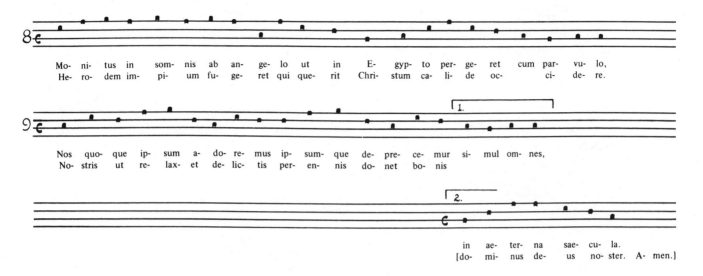

Mo- ni- tus in som- nis ab an- ge- lo ut in E- gyp- to per- ge- ret cum par- vu- lo,
He- ro- dem im- pi- um fu- ge- ret qui que- rit Chri- stum ca- li- de oc- ci- de- re.

Nos quo- que ip- sum a- do- re- mus ip- sum- que de- pre- ce- mur si- mul om- nes,
No- stris ut re- lax- et de- lic- tis per- en- nis do- net bo- nis

in ae- ter- na sae- cu- la.
[do- mi- nus de- us no- ster. A- men.]

And in line 6b there is a relatively elaborate reflection—for this piece—in formal language:

(6b) Non ostris elegit, non aurificum, non rutilum venit in locum.

Ostris, in fact, was sufficiently abstruse to be the occasion for a number of variants.[5] But that was only one of many difficult points in the transmission of the text. On one hand, it moves so directly from one subject to another as to involve awkward connections; on the other hand, when it ventures an elaborate turn of phrase the result is apt to be less than successful. In both cases, copyists seemingly tried to correct or improve; but no one MS tradition is clearly superior, nor is a prototype easily discernible—let alone preferable.

Just as in its text considered alone, so in the relationship of text and melody CHRISTI HODIERNA seems far away from the other three proses studied. The line endings, for example, hesitate between paroxytone and proparoxytone—sometimes with the same couplet (2: mágne/vóluit; 4: stábulum/múndum). While not unusual in other cases, such hesitation is not found in ECCE JAM VENIT (proparoxytone), REX NOSTRAS (proparoxytone), PANGE DEO (paroxytone) or Notker's CONGAUDENT ANGELORUM (paroxytone).

The indeterminate state of the text makes it difficult to discuss the relationship of syntax to musical phrases. In general, couplets seem to be complete in sense and syntax, for example 4a,b, 6a,b, 7a,b, 8a,b, 9a,b (the last two couplets subject to varieties and uncertainties already studied). But there may be a case of run-on from 2b to 3a. The initial period runs on into 2a, which is normal; then, depending on which variants are selected, the period continues on into 2b, and even into 3a, which is not normal. The enjambement to 3a depends on reading

5. See Blume's apparatus, *Anal.hymn.* 53, p. 27.

2b   . . . verbum caro factum exhibere se voluit
3a   mundo quem redemit.

But if instead of *mundo* we read *mundum* (with several MSS), with or without *venit* for *venerat*, a case could be made for 3a as a new, complete sentence.

3a   Mundum quem redemit jam venit de sede patris Dominus.

Nonetheless, the enjambement seems to have been more frequently accepted, with a stop after *redemit*, in the middle of that phrase of music. Another difficult but less serious place occurs between 4a and b. *In stabulum* can be construed with 4a or 4b; *vagiens est* has several variants, not all of which make clear how a clause with *infantulus* as subject is related to 4a.

The repetitions in phrase 7 are handled casually, but with seeming intent:

A F G D   A F G D
exultabat   (-natus alvus)
reco-lebat   retractabat

That is, three out of the four instances are assonant, but it might be difficult to find in their assonance the kind of artistic purposiveness apparent in Notker's treatment of the same music. Still, Joseph's two actions (*recolebat, retractabat*) can be understood as parallel, and the parallelism can be extended to include *exaltabat*.

At a lower level, casual but still purposive treatment can be glimpsed in line 6b—not in relationship to the musical division of incipit and ending pattern, but rather to the descent through three steps, represented abstractly as

(G) A F D, G F E C, F (G) F E D

This alternate understanding of the musical line is supported in 6b by the three-fold articulation:

6b   Non ostris elegit, non aurificis, non rutilum venit in locum.

Whatever the quality of the result, the intent to match formal Latinity with melodic inflection is clear.

The strongly articulated sub-phrase structure of phrase 5 is handled very differently in 5a and 5b. Line 5a (with bothersome variants noted by Blume at *audiunt*) runs on across the start of the second sub-phrase.

(5a) Vigilantes pastores audiuntur chorum/Angelicum in coelis psallentes:

Line 5b, on the other hand, allows not only for a separation but also an antithesis between first and second sub-phrases.

(5b) Quem prophetae cuncti praeconiarunt olim/Jam apparet form quam induit Dominus quem virgo mater pannis tegit.

Line 5a seems awkward in other ways as well—even in the context of this often awkward prose. *Vigilantes pastores audiuntur chorum angelicum* is out of order according to the

Gospel account, in which the shepherds hear the angel (Luke 2:8–12) and the angelic hymn (2:13–14), then hasten to the manger (2:16). In CHRISTI HODIERNA they hear the angel, and hasten "with great joy" in line 3b; to be sure, this is followed in line 4a by the earlier action corresponding to Luke 2:7 ("wrapped him in swaddling clothes and laid him in a manger . . .") but even so the return to the angelic hymn in 5a seems distinctly misplaced. And while the relative *quem* in 5b is correct enough after 5a, it would be smoother and more appropriate after 4b.

> (4b) . . . the babe, by whom the world is ruled.
> (5a) The shepherds keeping watch heard the angelic chorus in heaven, singing: Glory, praise, honor to God on high!
> (5b) He whom all the prophets foretold, now appears in the form which he has put on, as Lord whom the Virgin Mother wrapped in swaddling clothes.

In other words, line 5a seems like an interpolation. The fact that it is a line with subphrases supports the possibility, for doublings of singles was observed in LAUDES DEO in precisely those phrases that had that structure. A single at 5, besides removing the awkwardnesses already pointed out, would provide a clear conclusion to the first half of the melody, and a well-defined pivot point to the second half—just as with the single suggested for phrase 5 of ECCE VICIT.

In this case, however, Notker's plan affords no direct support, and an interpolation presumed here would have a status very different from those cases in which Notker's plan provides clear objective evidence. Still, certain details of Notker's text in line 5a are suggestive. For one thing, *praebuit* is redictum (line 3b), and Notker is usually very careful about such repetitions. Again, *Qua gloria . . . colitur* has one extra syllable—not conclusive, but suggestive. And the expression *sanctissimi corporis* turns up in another Notker text, CONCENTU PARILI, in a line (1c) that was suspected by Blume of being an interpolation. From a stylistic point of view, one could say that while the threefold exclamation in 4, 5a, 5b is believable as Notker's own; still, it is striking in its extremity, and it would be very easy to understand as a later interpolation because of the duplication of syntactical structure with 5b.

Looking back at the other three proses, it would be difficult to speak of an interpolation in the case of PANGE DEO, but easy in REX NOSTRAS, where line 5a—and only 5a—includes the specific address to the Virgin, and where the clausula-like units are most in evidence. Line 5b, as we noticed, is a very general petition: *Et nostri memor esto, talia praestans*, while the rest of the line seemed disjunct from the Marian intercession. But *Et nostri . . .* follows smoothly after 4b, and the rest of the prose then seems less different from the beginning without the distinctive *Ave Maria, virgo virginum* interposed. In ECCE JAM VENIT, 5b adds little except sonorous theological language. Here, too, an interpolation seems possible. Without the positive indication of Notker's plan, however, such interpolation remains only a possibility.

Perhaps the most puzzling aspect of CHRISTI HODIERNA is why it became so popular. As to whether it could be Notker's model, the indeterminacy of some of the detailed readings, as well as the numerous questions surrounding phrases 8 and 9, make that very difficult to decide. The most that can be said is that CHRISTI HODIERNA *could* have been the model, or at any rate could have been old enough for that. It is certainly easier to understand the peculiarities of CHRISTI HODIERNA as an approach *sui generis* among an idiosyncratic first generation of sequences, than to try to imagine it coming after the achievements of that generation.

XI

REX OMNIPOTENS
Notker's SANCTI SPIRITUS ASSIT NOBIS GRATIA

THE POPULAR West-Frankish prose REX OMNIPOTENS and Notker's SANCTI SPIRITUS share a melody that is longer than any studied so far, save that for NUNC EXULTET (Notker's LAUDES SALVATORI). This increase in length seems, in the case of REX OMNIPOTENS, to be in some ways associated with the manner of the prose: it is a relatively long, continuous narrative, following very closely the Gospel language. In this respect as well, REX OMNIPOTENS recalls NUNC EXULTET, which told the Resurrection story more or less in the words of Matthew and Mark. Other proses are narrative, too, especially CHRISTI HODIERNA for Christmas, EPIPHANIAM for Epiphany; but even these do not convey the sense of extended Gospel narration found in NUNC EXULTET and REX OMNIPOTENS.

The grand dimensions of the melody come down in East- and West-Frankish sources with virtually none of the variant problems studied in previous cases. This stability seems associated with a certain restraint in the construction of the melody—evidence, I think, of the composer's search for idioms and a combination of idioms that are in some sense classic among early sequences. At any rate, there is clearly more to the piece than a first reading of its melody might suggest.

REX OMNIPOTENS uses the G final and the long cadence formula frequently associated with that final,

C B C A G F G G

but often only the latter part of that formula,

A G F G G

Either the longer or shorter version of this cadence is found at the ends of phrases 1 through 8, and where the phrases are relatively short (as in 1 through 6) the recurrence of the formula seems insistent if not repetitious. In this connection, the differences among the in-

Rex omnipotens

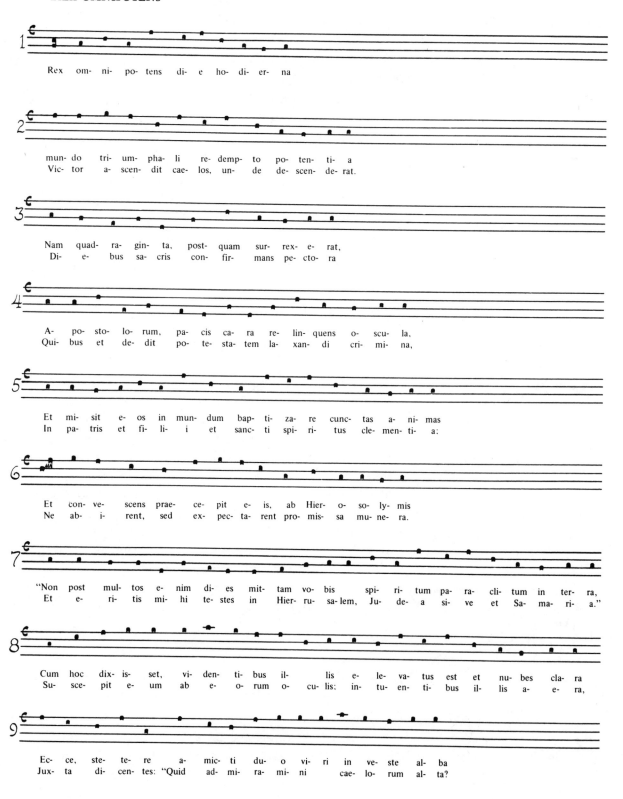

1. Rex om- ni- po- tens di- e ho- di- er- na

2. mun- do tri- um- pha- li re- demp- to po- ten- ti- a
   Vic- tor a- scen- dit cae- los, un- de de- scen- de- rat.

3. Nam quad- ra- gin- ta, post- quam sur- rex- e- rat,
   Di- e- bus sa- cris con- fir- mans pe- cto- ra

4. A- po- sto- lo- rum, pa- cis ca- ra re- lin- quens o- scu- la,
   Qui- bus et de- dit po- te- sta- tem la- xan- di cri- mi- na,

5. Et mi- sit e- os in mun- dum bap- ti- za- re cunc- tas a- ni- mas
   In pa- tris et fi- li- i et sanc- ti spi- ri- tus cle- men- ti- a:

6. Et con- ve- scens prae- ce- pit e- is, ab Hier- o- so- ly- mis
   Ne ab- i- rent, sed ex- pec- ta- rent pro- mis- sa mu- ne- ra.

7. "Non post mul- tos e- nim di- es mit- tam vo- bis spi- ri- tum pa- ra- cli- tum in ter- ra,
   Et e- ri- tis mi- hi te- stes in Hier- ru- sa- lem, Ju- de- a si- ve et Sa- ma- ri- a."

8. Cum hoc dix- is- set, vi- den- ti- bus il- lis e- le- va- tus est et nu- bes cla- ra
   Su- sce- pit e- um ab e- o- rum o- cu- lis; in- tu- en- ti- bus il- lis a- e- ra,

9. Ec- ce, ste- te- re a- mic- ti du- o vi- ri in ve- ste al- ba
   Jux- ta di- cen- tes: "Quid ad- mi- ra- mi- ni cae- lo- rum al- ta?

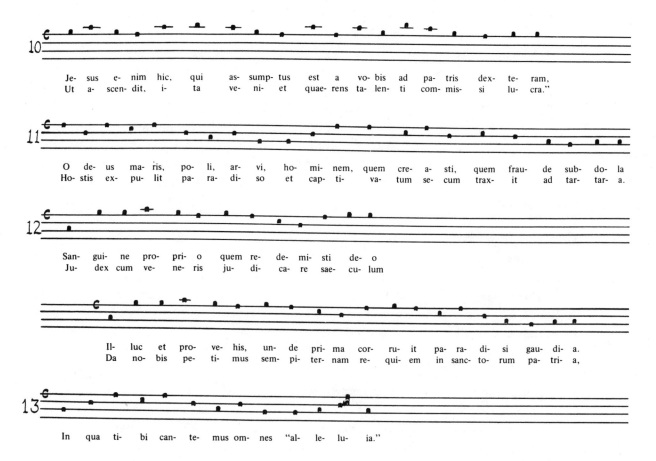

10
Je- sus e- nim hic, qui as- sump- tus est a vo- bis ad pa- tris dex- te- ram,
Ut a- scen- dit, i- ta ve- ni- et quae- rens ta- len- ti com- mis- si lu- cra."

11
O de- us ma- ris, po- li, ar- vi, ho- mi- nem, quem cre- a- sti, quem frau- de sub- do- la
Ho- stis ex- pu- lit pa- ra- di- so et cap- ti- va- tum se- cum trax- it ad tar- tar- a.

12
San- gui- ne pro- pri- o quem re- de- mi- sti de- o
Ju- dex cum ve- ne- ris ju- di- ca- re sae- cu- lum

Il- luc et pro- ve- his, un- de pri- ma cor- ru- it pa- ra- di- si gau- di- a.
Da no- bis pe- ti- mus sem- pi- ter- nam re- qui- em in sanc- to- rum pa- tri- a,

13
In qua ti- bi can- te- mus om- nes "al- le- lu- ia."

cipits of the individual phrases become important as the principal means of variety.

After the intonation in the opening phrase, phrase 2 makes the relatively high attack familiar from NUNC EXULTET and others. By contrast, phrases 3 and 4 lie relatively low, recalling the use of similar low idioms at analogous spots in the plans of LAUDES DEO and NUNC EXULTET. In REX OMNIPOTENS, phrase 4 is clearly designed to function as a sequel to phrase 3 through an expansion of the initial motive. It is not so clear, however, exactly how the expansion takes place, for at this point occurs a minor variant, in which the distinctive turn G A E F loses its distinction by change of E to F. Nor is it just a matter of the relationship of phrases 3 and 4: the variant G A E at the start of phrase 4 recurs at the start of phrase 7, a recurrence that in conjunction with other factors to be discussed heightens the sense of return at that point.

It seems quite possible that such motivic return was, in some cases at least, a later refinement, added to confirm some element of design implicit but not obvious in the original version of a melody. The sequences studied have sometimes exhibited implicit symmetries without the benefit of matching detail to call attention to the symmetry; indeed, the concept of "prose" as opposed to "verse" would favor such irregularity of detail. For example, it is possible to construe phrase 5 of REX OMNIPOTENS as analogous to phrase 1, in spite of a lack of exact motivic correspondence in the incipit. The similarity is to be sought in more general aspects such as the rise from (G) F G to C, as opposed to the attack on C (phrases 2 and 6—some versions lack the A) or the descent to D in phrases 3 and 4. Thus, phrase 7 is heard as a return of—or at least a reference to—phrase 4 simply by virtue of its descent to D. Furthermore, these phrases, 4 and 7, are chiefly responsible for the sense of continuing expansion in the first half of the piece: phrase 4 expands the beginning of 3, phrase 7 fills out the return from D back to G. Something about the way the expansion is handled in these phrases seems to catch up the others in its process—the whole piece seems to grow. An opposition of low phrases to high ones (as was evident in LAUDES DEO and NUNC EXULTET) is lacking here, as is any sense of "verses" in opposition to a "refrain." Less spectacular than NUNC EXULTET, REX OMNIPOTENS is in its first half more finely adjusted for continuity within an overall curve.

The development of larger sequences called for melodic material capable of filling up the interior space. In NUNC EXULTET this material took the form of long surging lines with great thrust and clear direction. In REX OMNIPOTENS we become more aware of another kind of line; we have met it before, but here its function is more apparent. In phrase 6, the ambience around C is accomplished by the figure

D C B A,   D C B G

This figure combines direct scalar descent with a dwelling in a restricted locus; the repeat of the four-note group (D C B A / D C B G) is varied just enough as D C B G to give the figure as a whole a sense of progress rather than of reiteration. (Similar figures are found in ECCE VICIT and in other melodies yet to be studied.) Its function here is to fill out a phrase in the upper register.

The melody as a whole is not divided into large simple sections; instead, the sense of continuity and growth apparent in phrases 1 through 7 continues on to the end. Various elements that tended to produce articulations in other melodies are here balanced off against one another in an artful way. These elements include the rising figure G B C D at the start of phrase 8 (as in NUNC EXULTET phrases 4, 6, 9); the cadences on D in phrases 9 and 10—the only phrases that do not cadence on G; the turn to the F-A-C realm in phrase 11; and the sub-phrase structure of phrase 12.

The rising figure in phrase 8 does, indeed, have the effect of a fresh, exciting start, just as it did in NUNC EXULTET (and this effect is emphatically supported by the text, as we will see); but instead of surging on up to G an octave above, then cadencing on D as in NUNC EXULTET phrase 6, phrase 8 returns to the cadence on G, aligning itself with the previous seven phrases and avoiding a thorough articulation at this point.

If any phrase marks an articulation, it is phrase 9, which begins assertively on C, reiterating its initial motive

C B A C G,   C B A C D

and cadencing on D. If it came directly after phrase 7, this beginning would constitute a clear break; but the presence of phrase 8, especially its initial motive, mediates the contrast and provides continuity.

Phrases 9 and 10 are bound together by their common cadence on D and their high register. Phrase 10 (very like phrase 7 of NUNC EXULTET) seems both like a consequent and an extension of 9, although it is difficult to identify any motivic connections. Rather, the mere reiteration of figure,

D E D C, E F E D C

at the start of 10 seems to echo the reiteration at the start of 9, at the same time filling out the space in the manner of the figure in phrase 6.

More motivic resemblance might be noticed between the latter half of 10

E C E D

and the start of 11

C A C B

The repetition of this motive at the lower pitch, C, is a sign of the downward progress of the whole phrase, whose main function is to interpose the F-A-C realm as momentary relief between the high phrases before and after.

The sub-phrases of 12, introduced by the eloquent leap G D, are the same idiom found in ECCE VICIT phrase 5. Here too, these sub-phrases appear in penultimate position as climax—or better as emphatic confirmation—to the piece; for the D a fifth above the final has been well established, and the melodic high point already achieved in phrase 10. The conclusion in phrase 13 returns to the F-A-C realm using a combination of involute, retarding motion and an ornamental neume to signal the end, as in most of the melodies studied.

The West-Frankish prose REX OMNIPOTENS has a clear, well-ordered rhetorical plan. Even though the main body of the text is narrative, the other rhetorical aspects are presented easily and effectively.

Phrases	1–2	Topic (and liturgical identity)
	3–10	Narrative
	11–12	Invocation and petitions
	13	Functional exhortation

In this case, the topic sentence can perhaps be taken in a sense more specifically liturgical than in some of the other proses studied: Incarnation, Christmas, and Resurrection or Easter are of course liturgical occasions, but are also seasons as well as broad themes, while Ascension, if it is a theme, is a more restricted one, and is associated more than the others with a particular day. In addition to setting forth the topic and identifying "today's" festivity, phrases 1 and 2 manage to include something of a laudatory or triumphal acclamation.

(1) Rex omnipotens die hodierna,
           mundo triumphali redempto potentia,
       victor ascendit caelos unde descenderat.

All these functions are accomplished in a sonorous period that effortlessly encompasses the absolute construction *mundo . . . potentia* with its interlocking word order. The close . . . *ascendit . . . unde descenderat*, while not a standard cursus, has the effect of one, summing up in its verbal resonance the whole cycle of the King's earthly sojourn. Rhetorical skill is apparent in every detail; but besides that, the rhetoric seems to be guided here (more, perhaps, than in previous examples) by a clear sense of what the disposition in musical phrases is going to be—if not in detail, then at least in kind.

The narrative body of the prose (phrases 3–10) calls for a more extended comment to be offered after a briefer consideration of the ending. Phrases 11–12 include two petitions, introduced by an invocation and a compact recital of the preparatory reasons that usually accompany petitions.

O deus maris, poli, arvi,
        hominem
              quem creasti,
          quem fraude subdola hostis expulit paradiso
                  et captivatum secum traxit ad tartara,
          sanguine proprio quem redemisti deo,
      illuc et provehis unde prius corruit paradisi gaudia.
Judex, cum veneris judicare seculum,
      da nobis, petimus, sempiternam requiem in sanctorum patria.

The relative clauses recapitulate the Creation, Fall, and Redemption of man, and the petition (*illuc et provehis*) closes the cycle back to the Ascension—"Take us with you as you return to Paradise," a response to the Lord's promise "I go to prepare a place for you," (John, 14,2). So also here: the second petition addresses the King as Judge, and begs eternal rest. As in the introduction, a great deal is accomplished in a relatively short space, in Latin that is artful and concise.

The last phrase, 13, has no less art, nor is it arbitrary or out of place; it follows naturally in thought and language—" . . . in the homeland of the saints, in which we would all sing *alleluia*."

13   In qua tibi cantemus omnes alleluia.

At the same time, it brings a shift of focus, and deliberately so: it brings an image of the whole company singing praises together and thereby reminds that this very piece is being sung by a company in earthly anticipation of that heavenly event. The phrase has a function, then, analogous to the more straightforward exhortation, "let us sing . . .," in that it self-consciously places the work in its conventual context of performance. It is a frame, which accounts for and justifies the sense of discontinuity with what precedes. Furthermore, the line mentions the alleluia, which might be taken simply as the heavenly song of praise par excellence, or might be a very specific reference to the Alleluia at Mass, sung just before this sequence—if the practice of singing the sequence after the Alleluia was in effect when REX OMNIPOTENS was written. But this kind of reference, encountered also in CLARA GAUDIA (and in ECCE DIES, yet to be studied) does not occur regularly enough to count as a liturgical connection; and cases such as this have to be balanced off against, say, HÆC DIES QUAM EXCELSUS, which instead refers to the *Gloria in excelsis Deo*.

The central narrative, at first glance, is a direct adaptation of the New Testament story of the Ascension; but there is much to be learned from a detailed comparison of the prose with its scriptural sources. Insofar as the text comes directly from the New Testament, it comes from *Acts*, I—that is, from the Epistle for Ascension Day, read at Mass just before the singing of the Alleluia. The Epistle itself extends from the beginning of *Acts* through the account of the Ascension; the portion directly relevant to the prose is the following.

(Acts, 1, 4–11)
Et convescens, praecepit eis ab Jerosolymis ne discederent,
    sed exspectarent promissionem Patris,
        quam audistis (inquit) per os meum;
            quia Joannes quidem baptizavit aqua,
            vos autem baptizabimini Spiritu Sancto non post multos hos dies.
Igitur qui convenerant, interrogabant eum dicentes:
    Domine, si in tempore hoc restitues regnum Israel?
Dixit autem eis:
    Non est vestrum nosse tempora vel momenta,
        quae Pater posuit in sua potestate;
    sed accipietis virtutem supervenientis Spiritus Sancti in vos,
    et eritis mihi testes in Jerusalem, et in omni Judaea, et Samaria, et usque ad ulti-
                                  mum terrae.

Et cum hæc dixisset,
    videntibus illis elevatus est,
    et nubes suscepit eum ab oculis eorum.
Cumque intuerentur in caelum euntem illum,
    ecce duo viri adstiterunt juxta illos in vestibus albis,
    qui et dixerunt:
        Viri Galilaei, quid statis adspicientes in caelum?
        Hic Jesus, qui assumptus est a vobis in caelum,
            sic veniet, quemadmodum vidistis eum euntem in caelum.

It is clear that much is required to turn this text into a prose. Beginning with *Et convescens* (6a) the adaptor followed the scriptural language closely, but had to make many changes. We can follow him, line by line, referring to the text laid out once more as it appears in the prose; roman type shows the wording from *Acts*, italics the major adaptations or additions.

6a Et convescens, praecepit eis, ab Jerosolymis

6b Ne abirent, sed expectarent promissa munera.

7a *"Non post multos enim dies mittam vobis spiritum paraclitum in terra,*

7b Et eritis mihi testes in Jerusalem, Judaea sive Samaria."

8a Cum hoc dixisset, videntibus illis elevatus est, et nubes clara

8b Suscepit eum ab eorum oculis; intuentibus illis aera,

9a Ecce stetere amicti duo viri in veste alba

9b Juxta dicentes: "Quid admiramini caelorum alta?

10a Jesus enim hic, qui assumptus est a nobis ad patris dexteram,

10b Ut ascendit, ita veniet *quaerens talenti commissi lucra.*"

Line 6a remains intact; only one MS (1120) changes *Jerosolymis* to *Jerosolyma* for the sake of a-assonance: assonance probably also explains the changes in line 6b, in conjunction with the need for fewer syllables to match the count in 6a. Line 7a, however, is completely recast. Without knowing how much weight to give it, we should notice that the change from *hos* to *enim* gives 7a an accent every other syllable; since this is one of the low-lying phrases of melody, it recalls a similarly regular accent pattern in LAUDES DEO. Line 7b is then shortened to match 7a.

Between 7b and 8a several lines from *Acts* are passed over. Line 8a shows signs of being cut to fit a pre-existent melodic pattern: one syntactic pause is passed (. . . *elevatus est*), the next not yet reached; *clara* is added—presumably for both syllable count and terminal assonance. Changes in 8b, however, require somewhat different explanations, for *oculis eorum* fits as well that way as inverted; but the inversion is more sonorous and stylish. Similarly, but more tentatively, one can understand the rebuilding of the last half of the line (*intuentibus illis aera*) as an attempt to replace the direct story line of *Acts* with something more elegant—and more appropriate as preparation for the syntactic run-on now required to line 9a.

In phrase 9 it becomes increasingly difficult to distinguish changes in wording made for the sake of Latinity from those that might have been required if the text was being set to an already-composed melody. The choice and placement of *stetere* seem largely due to the clearly defined sub-phrase C B A C G; still, *Écce stetére* is intrinsically preferable as prose to *Écce dúo víri*, because of its clausula-like accent pattern. The choice and placement of *amicti*, separated from *in veste alba*, is clearly due to a desire for more stylish Latin; and *alba* for *albis* to a desire for a-assonance.

Similarly in 9b, *Juxta dicentes* has the same syllable count as *Qui et dixerunt*, hence reflects a choice of wording. On the other hand, it also reflects a condensation of *justa illos* with *qui et dixerunt*, and thereby possibly a need to match syllable count with a melodic model.

The other changes in line 9b call for still another kind of explanation. *Quid admiramini* is not an isolated adaptation of the Gospel, but is found also in the Ascension Introit *Viri Galilei*, which to a musician would have been a strong association. Continuing in line 9b, *aspicientes* seems to be omitted for syllable count, *alta* added for assonance.

In phrase 10, too, the reasons for change are inextricably mixed. But it must be noted that syllable count is not a factor in 10b, for the version from *Acts* has the same count (19) as the version used in the prose. Here, again, the Introit seems to play a role with its more sophisticated word order.

Acts: Sic veniet, quemadmodum vidistis eum euntem in caelum.
Introit: Quemadmodum vidistis eum ascendentem in caelum, ita veniet.
Prose: Ut ascendit, ita veniet *quaerens talenti commissi lucra*.

The prose condenses this idea into a most compact, effective form at the start of the line, then goes on to add a reference to the parable of the faithful steward from *Matthew*, 25.

In a case such as this Ascension narrative, it is clear that the scriptural account is being adapted to conform to certain principles peculiar to the art form. The question is, do these principles include an already composed melody to which the text must fit? Is such a melody the only principle, or are there others? If this general question could be answered on the basis of intrinsic, stylistic evidence, a case in which the source of the text was known, as it is here, would seem one of the most promising.

Close examination of the adaptation of the Ascension narrative has revealed, however, no clear-cut conclusion, but rather the confusing network of overlapping, interlocking demands and results that so often characterizes a truly artistic wrestling with materials: the adaptor was not simply setting words to music, even though he may have had a melody before him; several other desiderata laid heavy demands on him, the most obvious being those engendered by his ideas—or ideals—of Latinity.

Is it even possible to conclude in this case that he did have before him the melody already composed? A few fine distinctions have to be drawn. We need not assume that there was a given melody merely on the basis of adjustments of syllable count in the second lines of couplets, for such adjustments indicate only that the adaptor wished to arrange his text in couplets, and having made one line a certain length, he then wanted to make the next one the same length. Indeed, the most persuasive argument for a pre-existent melody does not involve syllable count directly, but rather the relationship of the length of a line to its syntax, as in 8a, where the end of the line fell in between the syntactic articulations.

The most distinctive structural feature of a given sequence is the relationship among the lengths of its phrases (not the equivalence of the two lines of each phrase). Thus, the strongest argument for a pre-existing melody would seem to be that a text was arranged into phrases whose pattern exactly fitted the melody. Alas, this by itself is no argument at all, for the adaptor could have arranged the text into a pattern, then composed a melody to fit it. There seems, in fact, to be no way of demonstrating the prior existence of a melody on purely stylistic grounds of this type.

That does not prevent us, however, from observing the very close relationship of music and text in REX OMNIPOTENS (as in other cases). Here, this relationship seems to pivot around the beginning of phrase 8. The chief purpose of the text as a whole is to tell the Ascension narrative, and the climax of that narrative is reached at the Ascension itself: "And when he had said these things he was lifted up . . . ." The crux of the text-music relationship was to align this moment of the text with the sense of lift provided by the melodic motive that opens phrase 8. That motive, like the text, had an independent—possibly a prior—existence in NUNC EXULTET. Here, again, it was not necessarily a matter of setting the narrative to an existing melody, but rather of matching up elements that had an inner affinity with each other.

Around this pivot the rest of the materials dispose themselves naturally and effectively. After the acclamatory introduction (phrases 1,2), the phrases 3 through 7 take the story from the Lord's last conversation with the Apostles: he leaves them with a kiss of peace, giving them power to loose from sin (*John* 20:22–23) and sends them into the world to baptize in the Name of the Father, and of the Son, and of the Holy Ghost (*Matthew* 28,19). After this summary and reconstruction, taken not from the Gospel for the day (*Mark* 16) but put together from other New Testament sources, the narrative proper starts in 6; yet the melody recalls earlier phrases (as discussed) so that the continuing story receives a musical continuity. How effective, then, is the rise to the upper register as the story reaches its point! And the fresh melodic figure that starts phrase 9 serves to introduce the angelic interrogation and reassurance, all set in this high D realm. The invocation coincides with the turn downward to the F-A-C realm, and the petitions with the sub-phrases of phrase 12, which here sound especially persuasive in their persistent upward leaps.

Even though it is not the purpose of this study to trace the later development of the repertory, it is perhaps relevant to observe that while many if not most of the earliest pieces did not survive into the eleventh century and beyond, REX OMNIPOTENS did. In terms of its happy combination of text and music it is not hard to see why. NUNC EXULTET, with a comparable text and more spectacular melody, was not known as widely, or for as long. The reason is not merely in the greater competition among Easter pieces (although that is an important factor), but must have something to do with the greater refinement and control of REX OMNIPOTENS.

Notker's text SANCTI SPIRITUS ASSIT NOBIS GRATIA is for the gift of the Holy Spirit. Its liturgical assignation is for the Feast of Pentecost, commemorating the coming of the Spirit to the Apostles gathered together ten days after the Ascension, as told in *Acts* 2,1–13.

In writing a Pentecost text for the melody of REX OMNIPOTENS, did Notker have before him the West-Frankish text as well? A comparison of the rhetorical structure of the two texts produces some suggestive evidence, even though the similarities are sometimes so general that one might prefer to posit a common ancestor rather than a direct relationship. *Contra*, it has been argued that REX OMNIPOTENS was written after SANCTI SPIRITUS.[1] And in any case, Notker does not tell the story of the coming of the Spirit to the Apostles and disciples, which would be the obvious mode of imitating REX OMNIPOTENS; he does not even refer to the two most striking images of the story—the flames of the Spirit and the speaking in tongues. The only reference to that first Christian Pentecost comes in the closing period as part of the liturgical identification. Indeed, so thorough is Notker's avoidance of the story in *Acts* as to make one think it deliberate. Notker devotes his entire attention to the

1. Von den Steinen, *Notker* I, p. 540.

gifts of the Spirit, as those who are far removed from the apostolic occasion might pray for them. The key word is *infunde* (4b), which Von den Steinen traces to Ambrose's hymn *Splendor paternae gloriae*:[2]

> Jubarque sancti spiritus
> Infunde nostris sensibus.

In function, then, SANCTI SPIRITUS is similar to the popular Carolingian hymn *Veni Creator Spiritus* (ascribed, dubiously, to Rhabanus Marus) which achieved a permanent role in the liturgy.[3] The Alleluia verse *Veni sancte Spiritus* is a later piece, found only in sources of the eleventh century and after. (The sequence VENI SANCTE SPIRITUS standard for Pentecost in latter-day chant books is of course a later, twelfth-century product.)

SANCTI SPIRITUS is unusual among Notker's texts in consisting largely of a series of acclamations, straightforward and relatively unvaried in their rhetorical structure. Phrases 1–2 stand outside this series, constituting an opening period analogous to phrases 1–2 of REX OMNIPOTENS, even though the rhetorical function of Notker's text is somewhat less distinct.

> 1   Sancti spiritus assit nobis gratia,
> 2a   quae corda nostra sibi faciat habitaculum,
> b   Expulsis inde cunctis vitiis spiritalibus.

Then, starting from phrase 3, Notker presents a series of attributes and petitions in a clearly defined, though varied, rhythm. Line 3a contains an attribute, *illustrator*, line 3b a petition, *purga*.

> 3a   Spiritus alme, illustrator hominum;
> b   Horridas nostrae mentis purga tenebras.

Line 4a, with its *amator*, and 4b, *infunde*, correspond to 3a and 3b respectively, and constitute another attribute and petition.

> 4a   Amator sancte sensatorum semper cogitatuum:
> b   Infunde unctionem tuam, clemens, nostris sensibus.

Since the melody of phrase 4 is an expanded repetition of phrase 3, these four lines become grouped together into a larger unit.

Line 5a reiterates the structure of attribute and petition (*purificator . . . purifica*), intensifying it by the redictum, and introducing it with the direct address, *tu*.

> 5a   Tu purificator omnium flagitiorum, spiritus,
> b   Purifica nostri oculum interioris hominis,
> 6a   Ut videri supremus genitor possit a nobis,
> b   Mundi cordis quem soli cernere possunt oculi.

2. *Anal.hymn.* 50, p. 11.
3. *Anal.hymn.* 50, p. 193.

SANCTI SPIRITUS ASSIT NOBIS GRATIA (Notker)

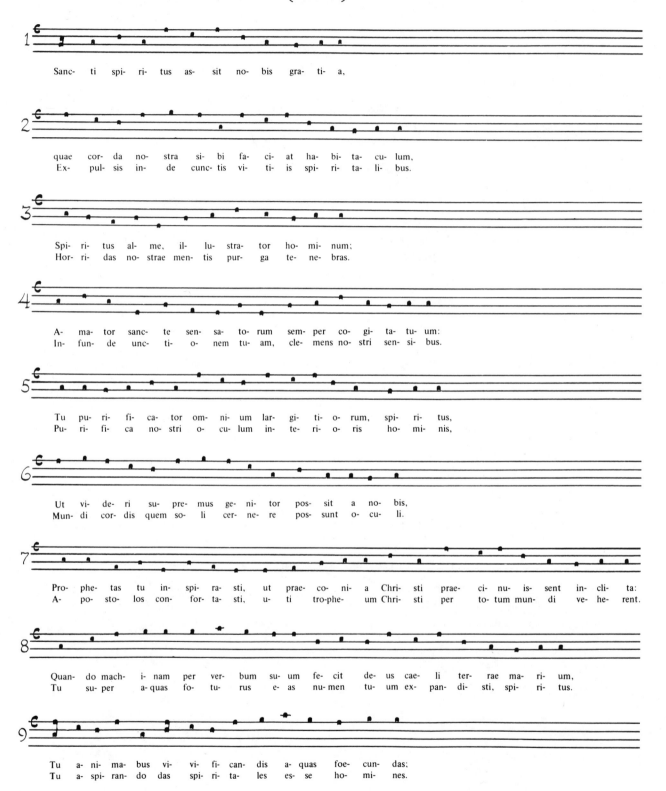

1. Sanc- ti spi- ri- tus as- sit no- bis gra- ti- a,

2. quae cor- da no- stra si- bi fa- ci- at ha- bi- ta- cu- lum,
   Ex- pul- sis in- de cunc- tis vi- ti- is spi- ri- ta- li- bus.

3. Spi- ri- tus al- me, il- lu- stra- tor ho- mi- num;
   Hor- ri- das no- strae men- tis pur- ga te- ne- bras.

4. A- ma- tor sanc- te sen- sa- to- rum sem- per co- gi- ta- tu- um:
   In- fun- de unc- ti- o- nem tu- am, cle- mens no- stri sen- si- bus.

5. Tu pu- ri- fi- ca- tor om- ni- um lar- gi- ti- o- rum, spi- ri- tus,
   Pu- ri- fi- ca no- stri o- cu- lum in- te- ri- o- ris ho- mi- nis,

6. Ut vi- de- ri su- pre- mus ge- ni- tor pos- sit a no- bis,
   Mun- di cor- dis quem so- li cer- ne- re pos- sunt o- cu- li.

7. Pro- phe- tas tu in- spi- ra- sti, ut prae- co- ni- a Chri- sti prae- ci- nu- is- sent in- cli- ta:
   A- po- sto- los con- for- ta- sti, u- ti tro- phe- um Chri- sti per to- tum mun- di ve- he- rent.

8. Quan- do mach- i- nam per ver- bum su- um fe- cit de- us cae- li ter- rae ma- ri- um,
   Tu su- per a- quas fo- tu- rus e- as nu- men tu- um ex- pan- di- sti, spi- ri- tus.

9. Tu a- ni- ma- bus vi- vi- fi- can- dis a- quas foe- cun- das;
   Tu a- spi- ran- do das spi- ri- ta- les es- se ho- mi- nes.

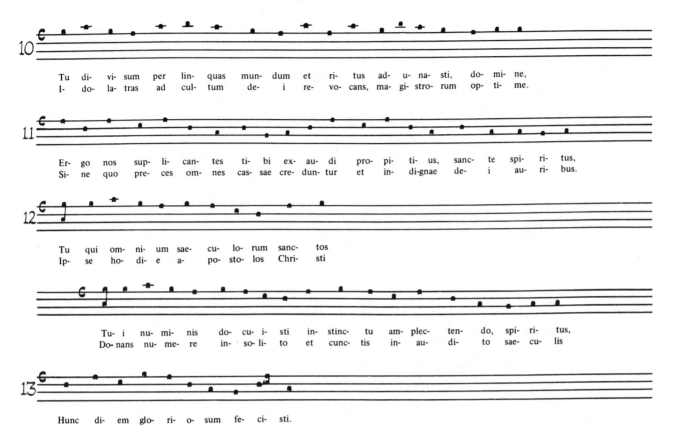

10.
Tu di- vi- sum per lin- quas mun- dum et ri- tus ad- u- na- sti, do- mi- ne,
I- do- la- tras ad cul- tum de- i re- vo- cans, ma- gi- stro- rum op- ti- me.

11.
Er- go nos sup- li- can- tes ti- bi ex- au- di pro- pi- ti- us, sanc- te spi- ri- tus,
Si- ne quo pre- ces om- nes cas- sae cre- dun- tur et in- di-gnae de- i au- ri- bus.

12.
Tu qui om- ni- um sae- cu- lo- rum sanc- tos
Ip- se ho- di- e a- po- sto- los Chri- sti

Tu- i nu- mi- nis do- cu- i- sti in- stinc- tu am- plec- ten- do, spi- ri- tus,
Do- nans nu- me- re in- so- li- to et cunc- tis in- au- di- to sae- cu- lis

13.
Hunc di- em glo- ri- o- sum fe- ci- sti.

Then the rhythm of the petitions is broadened by the insertion of lines 6a,b an explanatory clause of purpose (*ut . . . possit videri*). In this way, 5 and 6 are grouped together with a kind of grouping different from that between 3 and 4: the rhetorical form of this portion including phrases 3, 4, 5, and 6 might be represented as *a, a; a* extended. Musically, phrases 5 and 6 stand in the same relationship as 1 and 2; that is, 6 is an extension of 5 (not an expanded repetition, as 4 is of 3). Notker has mirrored the musical relationship of 3 and 4 on the one hand, 5 and 6 on the other, with a fine touch.

After the petitions come acclamations and attributes—the gifts of the Holy Spirit. In phrase 7 the rhythm of attributes is accelerated: each line, 7a, and 7b, carries an attribute, causing them to pile up—in the manner of a "diminution" in the purely musical sense, or of a "climax" in the strictly rhetorical one. And the close correspondence in wording between the two lines makes the second sound almost like a repetition of the first, adding to the insistence.

7a   Prophetas tu inspirasti, ut praeconia Christi praecinuissent inclita:

7b   Apostolos confortasti, uti tropheum Christi per totum mundum veherent.

Instead of petitions, each attribute is here accompanied by a purpose clause (*inspirasti ut . . ., confortasti uti . . .*). That is, the syntactic element that was introduced in lines 6a,b is continued here, replacing the petitions of 3–5. Structurally, this exchange accomplishes the same kind of developmental continuity as was observed in the overall design of the melody alone.

Notker's treatment of the beginning of phrase 8 has little of the *élan* of REX OMNIPOTENS —an effect generally foreign to Notker's idiom. There is, however, a subtle observance of this important point in the melody. The rhythm of attributes is broken by the insertion of the *Quando* clause (8a)—which takes on the function of a preparatory "wind-up" for the attribute in 8b. And the couplet as a whole enjoys a certain prominence by acclaiming the Spirit's role in Creation itself. Do the words *caeli terrae marium* in 8a recall the *O deus maris poli arvi* of REX OMNIPOTENS 11a, or is it merely a coincidental invocation to the God of Creation?

The fresh melodic start in phrase 9 receives very sensitive treatment: the three subphrases of the melodic line are set to three clausula-like units of text.

```
C B  A  C  G    C B A C   D  E   D  C   D   D
Tú a- ni- má- bus / vì-vi-fi-cán- dis / á- quas foe- cún- das
```

The effect of rhyme lingers just out of reach; all we can identify is the modulating assonance

-mábus   -cándis   -cúndas

yet somehow the effect is stronger than that. Assonance and word pattern continue into the start of 9b with *Tu aspirando*, but there—true to his principle of prose—Notker breaks the patterns, even to the extent of ending with a proparoxytone instead of a matching paroxytone.

9a Tú animábus / vívificándis / áquas foecúndas:
9b Tu aspirándo / das spiritáles / ésse hómines.

Emphasis in phrase 10 is maintained primarily through the melody by itself, and by the text's specific arrival at the theme of liturgy; the rhetoric relaxes into a relatively simple attribute and explanatory participle (*adunasti . . . revocans*) and there seems to be little structural support for the higher register and D cadence.

10a Tu divisum per linguas mundum et ritus adunasti, domine,
   b Idolatras ad cultum dei revocans, magistrorum optime.

Instead, emphasis is reserved for phrase 11, which begins with a strong *Ergo* to introduce the main petition.

11a Ergo nos supplicantes tibi exaudi propitius, sancte spiritus,
   b Sine quo preces omnes cassae creduntur et indignae dei auribus.

At this point, the relationship to REX OMNIPOTENS becomes much more clear, for here, at the beginning of 11, began its petitions. There have been petitions throughout Notker's text, but he obviously took pains to make 11 the decisive one—perhaps because this is where he felt it belonged on the basis of the melody and text he had as a model.

Phrase 12, however, has no petitions; instead it seems at first glance as though the piece would end with more of the kind of attributes already presented, but Notker has something more sophisticated in mind. Lines 12a,b serve as an extended preparation for line 13, which carries the main thought: "This day hast thou made glorious," Furthermore, it is this line that identifies the prose as a whole with "today's" liturgy, fulfilling a function comparable to line 13 of REX OMNIPOTENS, not by a strikingly appropriate postscript but rather by the logical completion of a long, suspended syntactic unit.

> (12a) *Tu*
>> qui omnium saeculorum sanctos tui numinis docuisti instinctu amplectendo,
> *spiritus,*
> (12b) *ipse hodie*
>> apostolos Christi donans munere insolito et cunctis inaudito saeculis
> *hunc diem gloriosum fecisti.*

The period begins with the direct address, *tu*, used frequently in this text, but here followed by a long, complex relative clause, *qui . . . docuisti* (the only other relative clause is in the immediately preceding 11b). Then the subject is reconfirmed: *(tu) . . . spiritus, ipse,* only to be followed by another syntactic digression, governed by *donans*; here the main sense is all but lost in the lengthy qualifications *munere insolito et cunctis inaudito saeclis.* But when it comes, the ending makes everything fall into place.

Notker has matched this most complex period to the sub-phrase articulation of 12, showing us his understanding of the larger musical unit that extends from the beginning of 12 to the end of 13. Indeed, his attention seems to be concentrated at the higher levels; the sub-phrase articulation is not stressed syntactically. As a sophisticated device—almost a trick —the second sub-phrase echoes with its *tu(i)* the opening *tu*, as if we were to hear another series of *tu*-intonations. But this detail is easily subsumed under the lofty syntactic-melodic arc that soars overhead.

What is most striking is the way the sophistication of the final period co-exists with the simple, direct, almost acclamatory style that prevails in the rest of the piece. When he wrote it, Notker obviously had full control of the most elaborate procedures he would ever use, but in this case (unlike some of his earlier works) used such procedures with great economy. There is evident a closer matching of rhetoric and music, a more refined reflection and support of the melody. Was it this that accounted for the popularity of SANCTI SPIRITUS, almost alone among Notker's proses, with the West-Franks? Blume quotes a remark by Ulrich von Zell in *Consuetudines Cluniacenses* (1087) that although the "Galli" did not much like German proses, nonetheless they sang this one.[4] And Blume's collation shows that SANCTI SPIRITUS was well known in France and England. Indeed, one of the Aquitanian sources, MS 887, has a good version of the melody and an excellent one of the text, added as an eleventh-century supplement to the manuscript.[5]

4. *Anal.hymn.* 53, p. 122. See also Von den Steinen, *Notker* I, pp. 539f.
5. Paris B.N.lat. MS 887, fol. 118v.

XII

Six Sequences by Notker

So FAR we have studied some of the Notker texts that have West-Frankish counterparts. Now we need to turn more briefly to some of his that do not, being instead found only with East-Frankish texts, in East-Frankish MSS. Since our concern in this study is not so much with the works of Notker as with the early sequence, we can use these other pieces by Notker primarily to broaden and deepen our knowledge of the ninth-century repertory. In these East-Frankish pieces we will immediately discover certain things (for example, a strong cadence on D) for which we have not yet met a West-Frankish model, but this is because we have not yet exhausted the early West-Frankish repertory. Still to discuss are those melodies that are related to specific Alleluias; we should postpone certain conclusions until we have the whole repertory before us. In principle (by way of anticipation), the East-Frankish practice shows no drastic innovation or departure; what we will find are further examples, sometimes striking ones, of the rhetorical and musical constructions already encountered.

This group of six East-Frankish melodies, with Notker's texts, are conveniently studied in pairs.

AGNI PASCHALIS (MAGNUM TE MICHAELEM)
CARMEN SUO DILECTO

SUMMI TRIUMPHUM REGIS
SCALAM AD CAELOS (CANTEMUS CUNCTI MELODIUM)

CONCENTU PARILI
NATUS ANTE SECULA

No effort will be made to include all the East-Frankish texts composed for these melodies; but MAGNUM TE MICHAELEM and CANTEMUS CUNCTI MELODUM will be mentioned briefly, since they might conceivably have been in existence before Notker wrote his, perhaps even coming to him with the melody.

Each of the first pair of pieces is relatively short. Agni paschalis is distinguished primarily by manifold returns—exact or approximate—of phrases. Phrase 2, not so very different in melodic outline from 1, already suggests a repetition of 1. But then within phrase 2 the melodic pattern, an ascent from F to C and a fall, occurs twice.

2   F G A B♭ C A A G A   F G A B♭ C A G F G G

After phrase 2, which is a double, comes the single 3, still using the same melodic shape (the varying cadences will be discussed soon). Phrases 2 and 3, therefore, present one melodic shape five times.

Phrase 4 brings a not dissimilar shape in the higher register: the melody ascends from C up to F in the upper octave, then falls gradually and at a greater length. The net effect of this phrase is contrast, however, not repetition, because of the change of register; and the similarity in melodic shape is only approximate. Phrase 5 brings a slightly shorter version of 4, so that this shape appears in 4 and 5 four times altogether.

Phrase 6 provides a more clear-cut contrast: the shape descends to the low C, then ascends. One might hear the ascent from C to A as an echo of the ascent in 2 and 3 from F to C; otherwise no detail of inflection links 6 with preceding phrases.

Phrase 7 is a near-literal return of 5, operating as a melodic refrain. Phrase 8 has a different melody, and the retardant motion familiar in concluding singles. The overall design can be understood as a series of "verses," (2,3), a high "refrain" (4,5), a low contrasting phrase (6), the high "refrain" (7), all framed by introduction (1) and conclusion (8).

1	introduction		
2		verse	
3		verse	
4			refrain
5			refrain
6				contrast
7			refrain
8	conclusion		

The cadence at the end of phrase 2 and (also of phrase 6)—at least as far as the last five notes are concerned—is familiar to us from pieces previously studied, except that it is notated here on G with a B flat above. In clara gaudia, that is, Notker's johannes jesu, we found the G final with B flat above, but not this cadence pattern. Like clara gaudia, agni paschalis uses a final that can be described as G-*protus*, as if it was notated on D—which in some sources it is.

Notker sets the cadences at the end of phrase 2 and also phrase 6 with normal proparoxytones:

F G G   F G G
á-ni-mae   Bájulent
pónti- fex rédi-it

AGNI PASCHALIS (Notker)

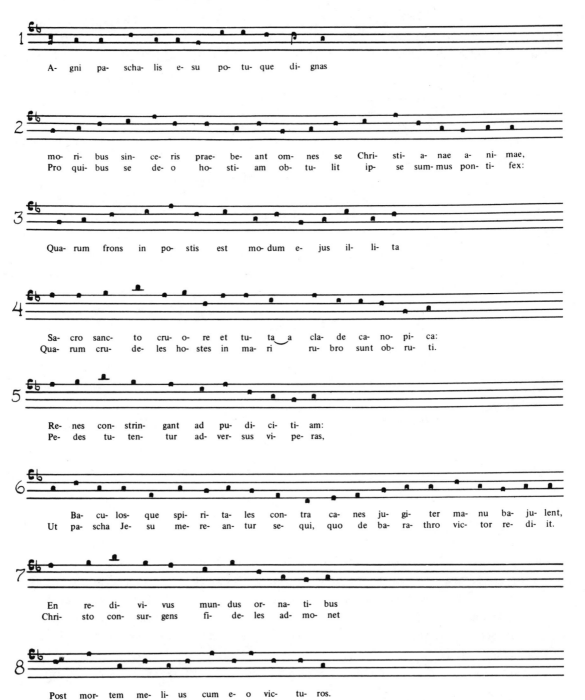

1. A- gni pa- scha- lis e- su po- tu- que di- gnas

2. mo- ri- bus sin- ce- ris prae- be- ant om- nes se Chri- sti- a- nae a- ni- mae,
   Pro qui- bus se de- o ho- sti- am ob- tu- lit ip- se sum- mus pon- ti- fex:

3. Qua- rum frons in po- stis est mo- dum e- jus il- li- ta

4. Sa- cro sanc- to cru- o- re et tu- ta a cla- de ca- no- pi- ca:
   Qua- rum cru- de- les ho- stes in ma- ri ru- bro sunt ob- ru- ti.

5. Re- nes con- strin- gant ad pu- di- ci- ti- am:
   Pe- des tu- ten- tur ad- ver- sus vi- pe- ras,

6. Ut Ba- cu- los- que spi- ri- ta- les con- tra ca- nes ju- gi- ter ma- nu ba- ju- lent,
   Ut pa- scha Je- su me- re- an- tur se- qui, quo de ba- ra- thro vic- tor re- di- it.

7. En re- di- vi- vus mun- dus or- na- ti- bus
   Chri- sto con- sur- gens fi- de- les ad- mo- net

8. Post mor- tem me- li- us cum e- o vic- tu- ros.

In the middle of 2, however, is another cadence, just before the internal repetition occurs.

2   F G A B♭ C A *A G A*   F G A B♭ C A G F G G

This internal cadence has the form A G A, a form Notker occasionally used, as G F G, in alternation with the more usual G F G G in pieces studied earlier (LAUDES DEO CONCINAT, GRATES SALVATORI). He sets this alternative either as paroxytone or proparoxytone; here as proparoxytone.

A   G A
práe- be- ant
hó- sti- am

The same form appears at the ends of phrases 5 and 7 on G, that is, G F G. In phrase 2, the internal cadence, located on A, is surrounded by repeated phrase endings on G, and has the effect of a non-final or "open" cadence. Thus the open cadence on A is nicely differentiated in form (A G A) as well as location from the following closed one on G (G F G G).

Phrase 3 brings a kind of cadence new to our study, indeed, hardly recognizable as a cadence until it has been encountered a few times. In this particular phrase the cadence comes twice, the second time as afterthought.

3   F G A B♭ C A *B♭ G A*   F G *B♭ G A*

The three-note figure B♭ G A is easiest identified as a cadence pattern when it occurs at the end of the phrase; after it is fixed in the ear, it can be heard to operate in the middle of the phrase, as confirmed by the fact that after its occurrence there, the melody echoes the beginning of the phrase with its F G. Both of these cadences—internal and terminal—are located on A, established in phrase 2 as the seat of an open cadence. Clearly, the piece is to move on past the end of 3.

And phrase 4, avoiding an internal cadence, has at the end the new cadence pattern of 3, now placed on G (A F G). It seems as though the intent was to make 4 more final than 3, but less final than 2, or than 5, which returns to a more normal cadence, G F G. By cadence, then, 4 is grouped with 3; by incipit, with 5. The interlocking construction is sophisticated and tends toward a sense of melodic continuity.

Phrase 6 stands outside of this construction, using as it does different melodic material and different register. So effective is the differentiation that here the G final sounds like G-tetrardus; no aura of the prevailing G-protus seems to attach itself to this phrase, which is the low-lying phrase from LAUDES DEO (compare also phrase 4 of GRATES SALVATORI). And, indeed, this phrase seems as though it did not belong in this piece: the contrast seems pushed too far; the carefully constructed continuum seems at this point to break. Phrases 7 and 8 do not remedy the problem, they only effect a return to what was before.

Notker's text is an exhortation to Christians, to the whole church to share in the Paschal victory over sin and death. There is abundant reference to the Easter feast, and even one to Holy Communion (1, *esu potuque dignas*) but none to the alleluia or to the liturgical performance of the piece itself.

The syntactic plan is relatively complex. The opening period extends from 1 through 4b, including three relative clauses (*pro quibus, quarum, quarum*).

(1)   Agni paschalis, esu potuque digna, (2a) moribus sinceris
          praebeant omnes se Christianae animae,
(2b)   pro quibus se deo hostiam obtulit ispe summus pontifex:
(3)   Quarum frons in postis est modum ejus illita (4a) sacro sancto cruore
          et tuta a clade Canopica:
(4b)   quarum crudeles hostes in mari rubro sunt obruti.

Even the opening principal clause is difficult, taking up both 1 and 2a with elaborate word order.

> Let all Christian souls present themselves with thankful hearts, made worthy through the food and drink of the paschal Lamb.

The incipit (1) can stand alone to a certain degree—"made worthy through the food and drink of the Paschal Lamb"— but only in a certain emblematic sense; otherwise 2a is its necessary continuation. Of the three relative clauses, the first (2b) is most closely associated with the main clause in sense. The other two (3-4a, and 4b) belong to each other, bearing as they do the images from the first Passover, the sign of blood on the door posts, the covering cloud, the destruction of the forces of Pharaoh in the Red Sea. There is strong run-on from 3 to 4a, which makes the melodic relationship of these phrases (4a is similar in shape, but at a higher register) even more complex. Notker obviously perceived the manifold melodic relationships in this group of phrases and provided an opening period that would maximize the effect. At the same time, however, his means of doing it----the manifold relative clauses—seem not as advanced as those found in his most mature texts; they have something of the routine procedures of the Credo.

> Et in Spiritum Sanctum, Dominum, et vivificantem;
> qui ex Patre Filioque procedit;
> qui cum Patre et Filio simul adoratur et conglorificatur;
> qui locutus est per Prophetas.

Lines 5a,b, abruptly, proceed in a different manner. These are admonitions.

(5a)   Renes constringant ad pudicitiam;
(5b)   pedes tutentur adversus viperas,
(6a)   baculosque spiritales contra canes jugiter manu bajulent
(6b)   ut pascha Jesu mereantur sequi quo de barathro victor rediit.

> (Let them grid up their loins in chastity,
> let them guard their feet against vipers,
> and brandish walking sticks in their hands against the dogs,
> that they may be worthy at Easter to follow Jesus,
>   when he returns victor from the gates of hell.)

But just as the melody of 5 repeats and accelerates that of 4, so in sense lines 5a,b can be taken as an extension of 3 and 4a,b: the Passover is, by prefiguration, the start of the Christian journey, and the admonitions in 5a,b pertain to the continuation of that journey, through the wilderness to the promised land. The slight irregularity at the start of phrase 6b, which has one more note than 6a, is carefully reflected in the text, which provides an *ut* by way of anacrusis.

6a   Báculosque spiritales
6b Ut páscha Jesus

Exactly the same kind of irregularity, and Notker's treatment of it, was found in his HÆC EST SANCTA SOLEMNITAS SOLEMNITATUM. This kind of irregularity is clearly distinct from the kind in 4a, where an elision is called for—*tuta (a) clade.*

The closing period starts at line 7a; although it has no real inner articulation, still the words are grouped within separate phrases:

(7a)   En redivivus mundus ornatibus,
(7b)   Christo consurgens   fideles admonet
(8)   post mortem melius   cum eo victuros.

And within each phrase one can perhaps detect a clausula-like grouping, as indicated by the separation of the words here. As for larger design, the words here provide the rationale lacking in the music: they speak of "coming to life again," which gives an obvious meaning to the return of the higher register and the melody of 5.

In general, then, the syntactic arrangement is perfectly compatible with the musical one, and in most cases supports the melodic development, without, however, being especially felicitous. Nor is the text itself a striking one. It may be inferred from this as well as from the connections via certain details with LAUDES DEO CONCINAT, that this is one of Notker's earlier texts, and that the melody itself reflects an earlier rather than a later stage of development. The short eleven-syllable lines of phrase 7 stand dangerously closer to verse than to prose, and few of the phrases are really long. A certain incongruity can be felt between the dimensions of the shorter lines and the sometimes difficult language that Notker sets to them. This, too, might reflect some uncertainty about the best procedure for the new art form.

Another text for this melody, MAGNUM TE MICHAELEM, shows up in the early St. Gall sources that suggest it, too, might be a ninth-century text. It is not a very effective text, and not much can be gained from it, save that its syntactical plan is close to Notker's, and also certain details, otherwise inconsequential, show a correspondence to Notker's text.[1]

	AGNI PASCHALIS	MAGNUM TE MICHAELEM
1	. . . dignas	. . . pignus
6b	Ut . . .	Ut . . .
8	Post mortem . . .	Post mortem . . .

1. Also observed by Von den Steinen, *Notker* I, pp. 336–338.

Perhaps one should pay no attention to these coincidences. They do, however, persist in showing up in texts to the same melody and could well be some kind of acknowledgment left by the writer of a text in favor of his predecessor. Here they seem to indicate that the writer of one of these two texts had the other before his eyes.

CARMEN SUO DILECTO

CARMEN SUO DILECTO presents us with another new final—at least, apparently so, for the determination of the final is not absolutely clear. Bannister seems to have followed the transcription by Schubiger, whose transcriptions are in some respects more to be honored than trusted. In any case, this particular transcription hardly makes sense; and the version published by de Goede in the *Utrecht Prosarium* seems not much better. It looks as though anomalies crept into the melody at the point when it was fixed in staff sources. I have ventured a restoration of the pitches in the cadences, following the St. Gall neumes exactly. If the melody is located as Bannister located it, then it would seem from the neumes that the last three notes of phrase 2 through 6 should be C D E. The E final so obtained then presumably comes at the end of the last phrase also, in the cadence F F E. This happens to be an E-cadence familiar from the Gregorian repertory; the cadence C D E can be imagined as an internal, less than final E cadence developed within newer Carolingian chant contexts such as this.

The C D E cadence recurs not in isolation but as part of a longer pattern,

C E G F E F D C D E

which takes up the last half of phrases 2, 3, 4, 6, and all of phrase 5. The whole body of the sequence, then, excluding only the first and last phrases, is dominated by this long cadence pattern. It operates as a refrain; unlike in LAUDES DEO, or AGNI PASCHALIS (where the refrain was a complete phrase that returned once later in the melody) this refrain reappears insistently at the close of every phrase. In this respect it is more like the long cadence pattern

C B C A G F G G

as used in HÆC EST SANCTA, except that here in CARMEN SUO DILECTO the long cadence pattern comes throughout, and occupies a larger share of each phrase, since the phrases are in general short.

Within each phrase, the effect of the long cadence pattern is to break the phrase in two, with a less obvious cadence at the end of each first half. This internal cadence usually has the form D C E. Looking only at the first half of each phrase—the variable half—they all focus more on a D-F-A realm than on the C-E-G realm so clearly stated by the long cadence pattern. Phrase 2 tends to stay around D-F, phrase 3 moves higher to A, phrase 4 leaps boldly from D to A, then descends slowly in groups of threes.

D A B♭ A G   A G E   F E D

Carmen suo dilecto (Notker)

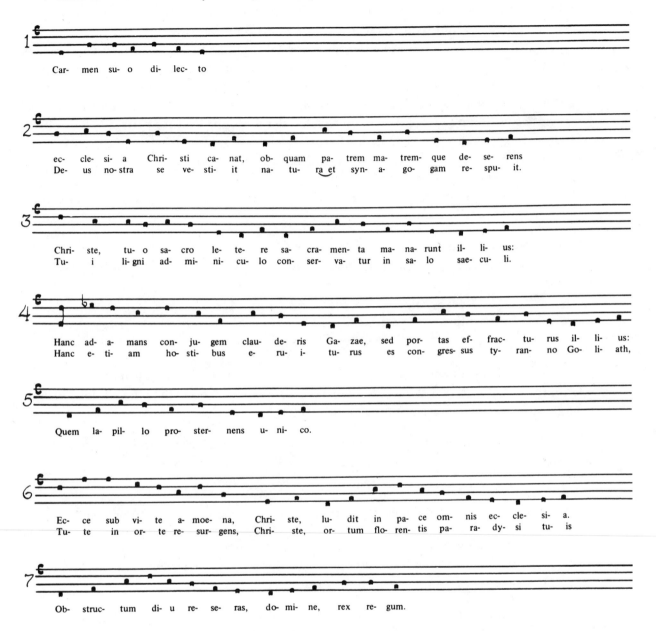

1 Car- men su- o di- lec- to

2 ec- cle- si- a Chri- sti ca- nat, ob- quam pa- trem ma- trem- que de- se- rens
   De- us no- stra se ve- sti- it na- tu- ra et syn- a- go- gam re- spu- it.

3 Chri- ste, tu- o sa- cro le- te- re sa- cra- men- ta ma- na- runt il- li- us:
   Tu- i li- gni ad- mi- ni- cu- lo con- ser- va- tur in sa- lo sae- cu- li.

4 Hanc ad- a- mans con- ju- gem clau- de- ris Ga- zae, sed por- tas ef- frac- tu- rus il- li- us:
   Hanc e- ti- am ho- sti- bus e- ru- i- tu- rus es con- gres- sus ty- ran- no Go- li- ath,

5 Quem la- pil- lo pro- ster- nens u- ni- co.

6 Ec- ce sub vi- te a- moe- na, Chri- ste, lu- dit in pa- ce om- nis ec- cle- si- a.
   Tu- te in or- te re- sur- gens, Chri- ste, or- tum flo- ren- tis pa- ra- dy- si tu- is

7 Ob- struc- tum di- u re- se- ras, do- mi- ne, rex re- gum.

Phrase 6 starts in at the higher level, A-C, so that the steady rise from phrase 2 is maintained almost to the end.

The use of the D-F-A realm around an E final is a familiar one in early medieval chant, and can be found in certain alleluias of the Gregorian repertory—alleluias, however, which seem to be later rather than earlier; Alleluia *Oportebat*, for the 3rd Sunday after Easter, is the best example. And in the *Gloria in excelsis* I,[2] presumably an 8th or 9th-century chant of Frankish origins, occurs, the same upward leap of a fifth, followed by the same kind of a descent, used as a foil to an E cadence (notated on B in the *Gloria*).

In CARMEN SUO DILECTO even the frame, the beginning and end of this remarkably insistent piece, are more or less free of the ornamentation or involute motion often found at these points. Phrase 1 is a brief, incisive intonation. Phrase 7 begins with the C-E-G motive from the long cadence pattern, then proceeds with only a hint of something more elaborate to its own cadence. It will be recalled that the long cadence pattern C B C A G F G G never appeared at the end of a sequence, being replaced in the last phrase by a more traditional stepwise descent to G from A; an analogous procedure occurs here.

Notker's text helps create larger groupings in the melody. In the first half of the piece, the grouping is simple: the opening period runs through 2b; lines 3a and b form two complete, roughly parallel, units.

(1)   Carmen suo dilecto (2a) ecclesia Christi canat,
            ob quam, patrem matremque deserens,
(2b)   deus nostra se vestiit natura
              et synagogam respuit.
(3a) Christe, tuo sacro letere sacramenta manarunt illius:
(3b) Tui ligni adminiculo conservatur in salo saeculi

Lines 4a and b, again are roughly parallel, presenting two Old Testament figures, Gaza and Goliath; but the second is completed by the single 5—"Whom thou layest low with a single stone"—an instance of formal word-painting.

(4a)   Hanc adamans conjugem clauderis Gazae, sed portas effracturus illius:
(4b)   Hanc etiam hostibus eruiturus es congressus tyranno Goliath,
(5)   quem lapillo prosternens unico.

Phrases 4 and 5, then, are linked together; and, in the same pattern, so are 6 and 7.

(6a)   Ecce sub vite amoena, Christe, ludit in pace omnis ecclesia.
(6b)   Tute in orto resurgens, Christe, ortum florentis paradysi tuis
(7)   obstructum diu reseras, domine, rex regum.

Here the linkage depends partly upon sense as well as syntax, for 6a is a complete period; but the image, the Church at peace, extends on into 6b, even though there the Church begs the risen Christ to re-open the gates of Paradise, of which the Church at Mass is an earthly prefiguration.

On the sole basis of lines 6a,b, the text seems destined for the Easter season. A more

2. Melodies for *Gloria in excelsis* (as for *Kyrie, Credo, Sanctus,* and *Agnus Dei*) are found grouped together under "Ordinary Chants of the Mass" in modern chant publications of the Benedictines of Solesmes—the *Liber usualis* and the *Graduale romanum*; for *Gloria* melodies see also D. Bosse, *Untersuchung einstimmiger mittelalterlicher Melodien zum "Gloria in excelsis"* (diss. Erlangen 1954); and K. Rönnau, *Die Tropen zum Gloria in excelsis* (Wiesbaden 1967).

comprehensive topic would be, Christ and his Church. Again, there is no liturgical identification—unless the song (*carmen*) that "the Church sings for her beloved Christ" is imagined to be the Alleluia. The language seems more straightforward and at the same time more effective than AGNI PASCHALIS, suggesting this to be a product of Notker's maturity. On the other hand, 2b requires an elision, *natura et*, to take care of the extra syllable in that line, and the infrequent elisions in Notker's output seem to occur in earlier works rather than later ones.

SUMMI TRIUMPHUM REGIS

SUMMI TRIUMPHUM REGIS and SCALAM AD CAELOS are both large, impressive pieces showing full assurance in both conception and execution. As with the first pair just studied, this pair presents material for which the models are lacking in the West-Frankish melodies studied so far. But works such as these did not spring full-grown in the absence of prior efforts. Later we will see—not the models—but the sources of inspiration for these wide-ranging spacious melodies on D finals; for the moment, however, we can only make their acquaintance.

The most remarkable aspect, at first glance, of SUMMI TRIUMPHUM REGIS is the unusual number of couplets in which the second line is substantially longer than the first. The similarity in technique to HÆC DIES QUAM EXCELSUS (Notker's GRATES SALVATORI) has not gone unnoticed; here, at any rate, a model is evident. In consistency and complexity of application, SUMMI TRIUMPHUM REGIS goes far beyond GRATES SALVATORI. And just as there, the uneven doubles are associated with a carefully worked out motivic system, which must be traced as it develops in context. As a start, however, it is worthwhile representing the overall phrase design with the uneven doubles in a schematic diagram (Example 6).

The gaps in the lines represent passages omitted in the first line of a couplet but included in the second. The "omissions," of course, are not heard as such; it would be more accurate to speak of "additions" in the second lines. The apostrophes in phrases 7 and 8 represent the articulation into sub-phrases. The capital letters at the end of each phrase designate the final: twice the melody ends a fifth higher, on A, which functions as an open ending at the highest level. These open endings are coordinated with the uneven doubles in such a way that together they mark the interior of larger sections. The first section extends through the uneven doubles in 3, 4, and 5, with its open ending on A, and concludes with the regular double 6, ending on D. The second section includes the uneven doubles 7 and 8, of which 7 ends on A, and extends through the rest of the piece.

The motivic system fills out this larger plan, giving it point and definition. The intonation (1) insists on D and F. Phrase 2 starts higher on F and A, then introduces a figure noticeable even on first encounter because of its reiterated leaps, F D, F C, in a predominantly stepwise context—but perhaps we connect this leaping figure to the leaps between D and F in phrase 1, and perhaps that is its source; on the other hand, a similar figure appears in NUNC EXULTET (Notker's LAUDES SALVATORI) phrase 10, with no such derivation.

This saw-tooth figure is followed in 2 by the approach to the cadence through a stepwise descent:

Summi triumphum regis (Notker)

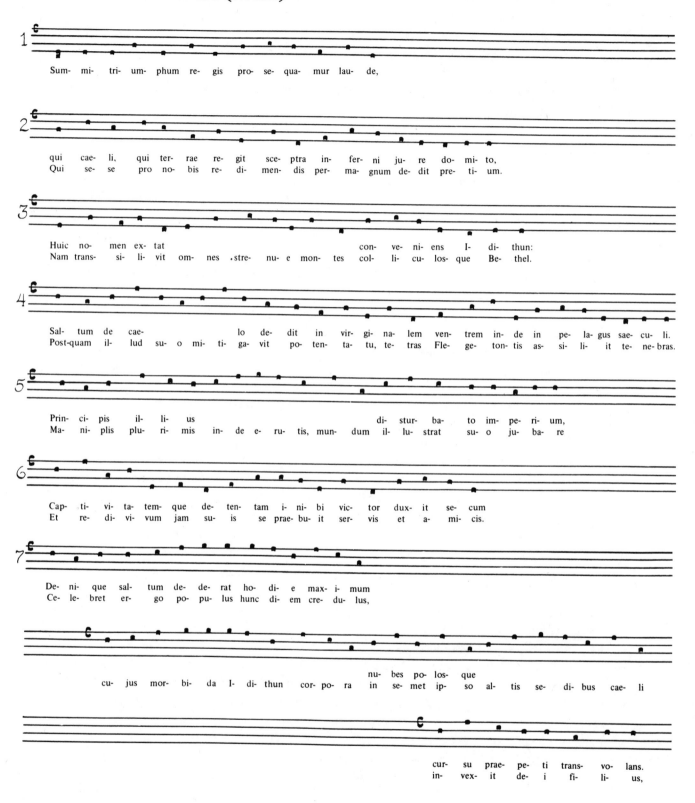

1. Sum- mi tri- um- phum re- gis pro- se- qua- mur lau- de,

2. qui cae- li, qui ter- rae re- git sce- ptra in- fer- ni ju- re do- mi- to,
Qui se- se pro no- bis re- di- men- dis per- ma- gnum de- dit pre- ti- um.

3. Huic no- men ex- tat con- ve- ni- ens I- di- thun:
Nam trans- si- li- vit om- nes .stre- nu- e mon- tes col- li- cu- los- que Be- thel.

4. Sal- tum de cae- lo de- dit in vir- gi- na- lem ven- trem in- de in pe- la- gus sae- cu- li.
Post- quam il- lud su- o mi- ti- ga- vit po- ten- ta- tu, te- tras Fle- ge- ton- tis as- si- li- it te- ne- bras.

5. Prin- ci- pis il- li- us di- stur- ba- to im- pe- ri- um,
Ma- ni- plis plu- ri- mis in- de e- ru- tis, mun- dum il- lu- strat su- o ju- ba- re

6. Cap- ti- vi- ta- tem- que de- ten- tam i- ni- bi vic- tor dux- it se- cum
Et re- di- vi- vum jam su- is se prae- bu- it ser- vis et a- mi- cis.

7. De- ni- que sal- tum de- de- rat ho- di- e max- i- mum
Ce- le- bret er- go po- pu- lus hunc di- em cre- du- lus,

cu- jus mor- bi- da I- di- thun cor- po- ra nu- bes po- los- que in se- met ip- so al- tis se- di- bus cae- li

cur- su prae- pe- ti trans- vo- lans.
in- vex- it de- i fi- li- us,

214   Six Sequences by Notker

Summi triumphum regis (Notker) (2)

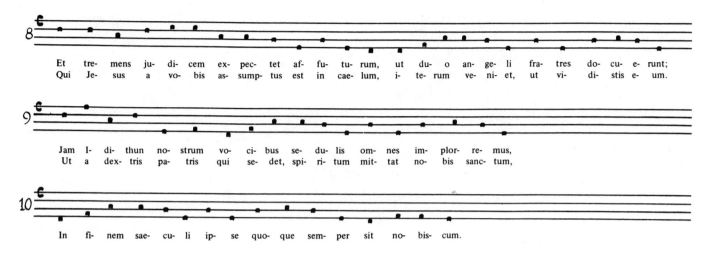

Et tre- mens ju- di- cem ex- pec- tet af- fu- tu- rum, ut du- o an- ge- li fra- tres do- cu- e- runt;
Qui Je- sus a vo- bis as- sump- tus est in cae- lum, i- te- rum ve- ni- et, ut vi- di- stis e- um.

Jam I- di- thun no- strum vo- ci- bus se- du- lis om- nes im- plor- re- mus,
Ut a dex- tris pa- tris qui se- det, spi- ri- tum mit- tat no- bis sanc- tum,

In fi- nem sae- cu- li ip- se quo- que sem- per sit no- bis- cum.

Example 6. Summi triumphum regis (Notker)

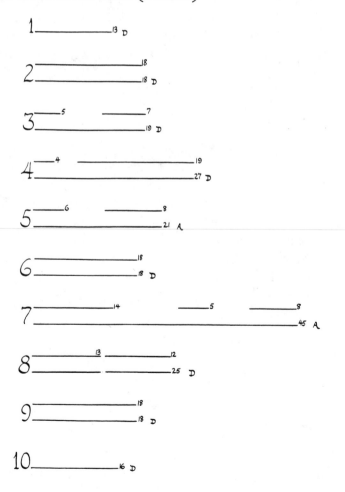

E G F E D C D D

the last three notes representing the normal cadence pattern, which we previously encountered on F G G, now located on D. Within phrase 2, of course, the three elements—beginning, falling figure, and cadence—are not perceived separately but as one melodic impulse.

In phrase 3, the elements are perceived more distinctly. The saw-toothed figure is repeated at the start of 3, immediately attaining a status of motive; in 3a it proceeds directly to the cadence, approached more or less as in 2. In 3b, the opening motive is repeated, this repetition being the cause of the greater length of 3b, which is perceived as a simple expansion of 3a.

3a D *F D F C*   D F E D C D D
3b D *F D F C* D F G *F D F C* D F E D C D D

The relationship of the two can be expressed as

a b, a a′ b.

In phrase 4 the process of motivic expansion becomes ever clearer. Phrase 4a begins with a turning figure on A-C, follows it with the motive F D F C, then a more elaborate approach to the cadence. The elaboration takes the form of the figure E G A D, both noble and expressive, and found elsewhere in early medieval chant (as in *Kyrie Cunctipotens*[3]) with the same effect. Phrase 4b simply repeats the initial turning figure, just as 3b repeated its initial figure.

4a A G A C A   A G F E F D F C
4b A G A C A G A C A G F E F D F C

Phrase 4 as a whole is merely phrase 3 with something higher added on at the beginning.

Phrase 5 is a pivot to the higher register. It begins much like 4, leaves out the motive F D F C, remaining instead at the level of A, and proceeding directly to the cadence—basically the same pattern as 3 moved up a fifth. Phrase 5b then appears to start the same kind of repetition as in 3 and 4, but instead presents the F D F C figure (lacking in 5a for the first time since its introduction) at the new pitch level as C B C G. And the motivic process does not stop there: the mighty leaps at the start of phrase 6 are another, more drastic modification of this figure. To mark the return to the original pitch level, the figure then appears in its original form, F D F C. A shorter, slightly different, and less decisive form of the D cadence ends the phrase and the section.

5a A G A C B A   B C B A A G A A
5b A G A C B A B C D *C B C G* B C B A A G A A
6   A *C G A D* E C E G G *F D F C* F G F D

The expansions in phrase 7 are more complex. Phrase 7 has something of the sub-phrase structure of, say, phrase 5 of ECCE VICIT, or, more closely, phrase 7 of CHRISTI HODIERNA, but

3. Kyrie IV (see note 2, this chapter). On Kyries, see M. Landwehr-Melnicki, *Das einstimmige Kyrie des lateinischen Mittelalters* (Regensburg, 1955). Kyrie IV = Mel. 18. See also *Anal.hymn.* 47, p. 50.

not as fully worked out. There is an opening sub-phrase, ending on the high D's. In 7a this is followed by a descent, using the familiar figure of step and leap (D C A, C B G), then by the motive C A C G, and approach to the cadence on A. In 7b there is a cleverly arranged return to the opening sub-phrase, but without any sense of actually beginning again; the effect is not unlike the endless chains in Irish MS designs.

7a A G A A B C D D D C A C B G
7b A G A A B C D D D C A C B G A B C D D D C A C B G

7a (cont.) A *C A C G*   A C B A A G A A
7b (cont.) A *C A C G* A C D *C B C G* A C B A A G A A

The sub-phrase articulation and the ensuing descent come twice, and when in due course the C A C G motive appears, it is also repeated. Thus, the greater length and inner articulations often associated with the longest, highest phrases occur here in a more veiled, intricate form.

Phrases 8 and 9 are progressively shorter, tapering the piece off toward the end. Phrase 8 starts with the opening sub-phrase of 7, then turns downward—the inverse of phrase 5, which began as 4 then turned upward. The use of material in motivic form makes it increasingly difficult to hear, say, the rest of 8 as similar to any one of the preceding phrases. Instead, the material is now all familiar, and is being used up in different configurations. The bold beginning of phrase 9, however, is unmistakably that of phrase 6. The final cadence is different from all the others, descending stepwise to the D final.

Notker's text is one of his most adventurous: the *Heilsgeschichte* is told with a spirit appropriate to high romance. With its focus on the Ascension and its point of departure the account in *Acts* 1, the text is laid out closely parallel in its rhetoric to REX OMNIPOTENS —festal proclamation in 1–2, a short review of the *Heilsgeschichte* in 3–6, the Ascension scene itself in 7 and 8, ending with the prophecy of the second coming; and a petition in 9 and 10. But Notker tells the story in his own terms, in a way much more distinctive than in LAUDES SALVATORI, his other great telling of the Christian epic. Here, in SUMMI TRIUMPHUM REGIS, the hero becomes *Idithun*. Von den Steinen assembles the texts and reconstructs Notker's development of the image: Idithun, in the English Bible Jeduthun (see the headings of Psalms 39, 62, 77), was a chief musician and prophet; the name was understood to mean "he who leaps over." Notker adapted the name and this meaning to the divine hero.[4]

Line 4a tells how he took a mighty leap (*saltum de caelo*) into the Virgin's womb, thence into the "sea of time" (*pelagus saeculi*). After overcoming the kingdom of evil, he regained heaven by another mighty leap (line 7a). Lines 8a,b, 9a,b, and 10 include subsequent aspects of the epic, intermixed with rhetorical functions of liturgical identity, petition, and exhortation. Already in 7b, the liturgical identification follows hard upon the event of the Ascension: "Let the faithful people, therefore, celebrate this day . . . ." Line 8a announces the eventual coming of the judge, then flashes back to the scene of the two angels at the Ascension itself. Line 9a has the exhortation-petition (*imploremus*) but the substance

4. Von den Steinen, *Notker* I, p. 240.

of the petition includes the sending of the Holy Spirit, the next event (Pentecost) in the epic foretold in the Ascension episode—as well as a plea that he "would be with us until the end of the world," also part of the Ascension episode and a happy way to end, suggesting as it does the *saecula saeculorum* of the lesser doxology.

This combination of story with function is sophisticated, matching in refinement the motivic processes of the melody. In contrast, the syntactic plan is relatively straightforward. First and last phrases are run on with the adjacent double, as is usually the case. Elsewhere, in keeping with the narrative manner, couplets coincide with periods, except that 5b runs on with a conjunction (enclitic *-que*) to 6a. Individual lines, too, are syntactically complete. At the higher level, the sectional plan apparent in the melody is observed in the text: line 7, which starts the second section, arrives at the Ascension, the special theme of "today's" liturgy.

At the lower levels, however, Notker's text has no obvious correspondence with the melody, its motivic repetitions and expansions. One might well expect some reflection of the uneven doubles in either sense of syntax of the text, but none is apparent. And while he generally maintains the same accent pattern on, say, the F D C F motive

F D F C
ré-git scép- tra

even that is subject to modification as in 7:

A C A C G
nú- bes po- lós-que

Still, it can be reasonably argued that all details of musical process need not be reflected in an accompanying text, and that a close relationship of the two can occur when each is controlled separately by processes of special importance—melody by motivic patterns, for example, text by accentual ones. It can hardly be said that Notker is unaware of the low-level melodic processes going on in this piece, for at one point he pays special attention to them. *Captivitatem* is a loaded word in the Ascension liturgy, making its most important occurrence in the second Alleluia, *Dominus in Syna*: "he hath led captivity captive" (*captivam duxit captivitatem*). In Notker's text, the word occurs not just anywhere, but at those striking downward leaps at the start of 6a.

A C G A D E
6a Cap- ti- vi- ta- tem- que

This did not go unnoticed in the tenth century: they called this sequence (that is, the melody) by the name *Captiva*.[5]

Scalam ad caelos

Notker's SCALAM AD CAELOS is set to another spacious D-final melody. In this one, all phrases are regular doubles except the first; even the last phrase is set as a regular double,

5. Von den Steinen, *Notker* I, pp. 552f.

an arrangement not previously encountered except in one of the variants of CHRISTI HODIERNA (Toul). That variant seemed to be a subsequent modification, and it might be possible to conclude that the melody for SCALAM AD CAELOS is a later rather than an earlier melody. Other aspects of the melodic construction would tend to support that conclusion, and Notker's text has signs of maturity.

There is also another, very interesting early text, CANTEMUS CUNCTI MELODUM, often noticed by scholars and actually used as a latter-day hymn in the translation of J. M. Neale.[6] Von den Steinen describes this text as "Alemmanic, early 10th century," but nonetheless it will be mentioned briefly here for comparison.

The melody has a large design not dissimilar to that of SUMMI TRIUMPHUM REGIS but with its own distinctive features. Cadences at the beginning (phrases 1–4) are on D; phrases 5–7 end on A, and in the higher register; phrases 8–11 are on D, tending to lie lower again. All phrases except 1, it should be noted, start on A a fifth above the final, making the transition to the higher register in the middle section very smooth. Phrase 2, beginning on A, has the effect (frequent in the second phrase) of being in some sense consequent to phrase 1 as antecedent; and in this melody, all the rest of the phrases have something of the same effect, because of their beginning on A.

Phrases 4 and 11 are considerably longer than the others and have a sub-phrase structure —but one less clear and obvious than that, say, of ECCE VICIT. Phrase 4 makes an internal cadence on *perviam* (in Notker's text), with a normal cadence pattern, located on B (which is not normal, and perhaps questionable).

> A AC B A G A B^(.) A C B C B A A G A B B,
> 4 Nu- bi-um cur-sus ven-to-rum vo-la- tus ful-gu-rum co-ru-sca-ti-o
> (Notker)
> 4 Hanc ergo sca-lam i- ta Christi a-mor fe-mi-nis fe-cit pervi-am,
>
> G F G FF E D E C E G F E G F E C D D
> et to-ni-tru- um so-ni-tus dul- ce con-son-ent si-mul al -le- lu-ia
> ut draco- ne con- culca-to et Ae-thi- o-pis glad- i- o transi-to

This cadence recognized, a preceding hint of a similar cadence and a corresponding articulation can be perceived at *ventorum* in CANTEMUS CUNCTI MELODUM—but only there, not in Notker's SCALAM AD CAELOS, where only the varied motivic repetition suggests the phrase structure at the lowest level.

Phrase 11 also has an internal cadence, and a hint of another, but in the reverse order. The clear cadence—now on A—comes first, (Notker: *beneficiis*), followed by an incomplete form of the same cadence (*dominum*) elided to a descent and the remainder of the phrase.

CANTEMUS CUNCTI MELODUM

> A C C G F G A A A A C G G F A
> 11 Nunc om-nes ca-ni-te si- mul al- le- lu- ia do-mi-no
> (Notker)

6. *Hymns Ancient and Modern* (London 1909), no. 328.

Scalam ad caelos (Notker)

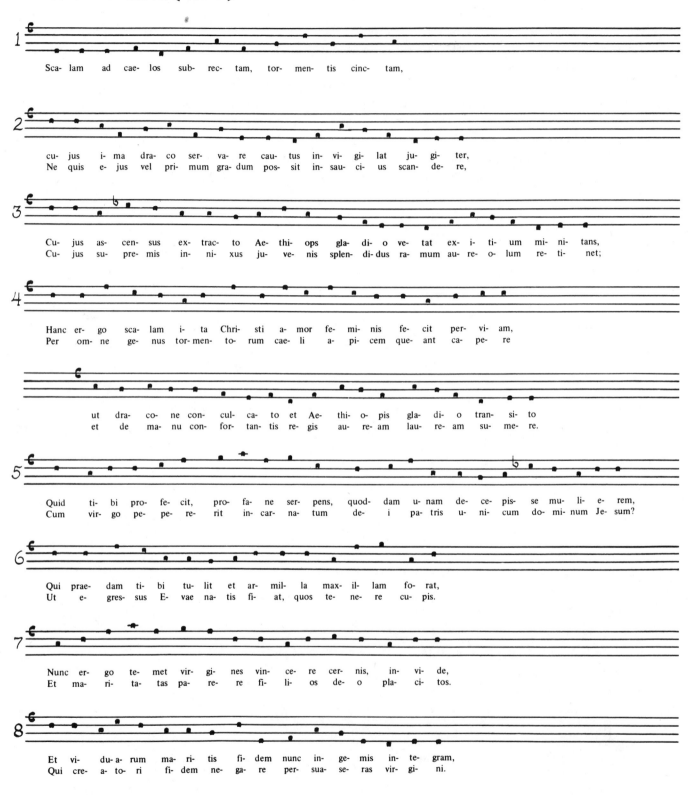

1. Sca- lam ad cae- los sub- rec- tam, tor- men- tis cinc- tam,

2. cu- jus i- ma dra- co ser- va- re cau- tus in- vi- gi- lat ju- gi- ter,
   Ne quis e- jus vel pri- mum gra- dum pos- sit in- sau- ci- us scan- de- re,

3. Cu- jus as- cen- sus ex- trac- to Ae- thi- ops gla- di- o ve- tat ex- i- ti- um mi- ni- tans,
   Cu- jus su- pre- mis in- ni- xus ju- ve- nis splen- di- dus ra- mum au- re- o- lum re- ti- net;

4. Hanc er- go sca- lam i- ta Chri- sti a- mor fe- mi- nis fe- cit per- vi- am,
   Per om- ne ge- nus tor- men- to- rum cae- li a- pi- cem que- ant ca- pe- re

   ut dra- co- ne con- cul- ca- to et Ae- thi- o- pis gla- di- o tran- si- to
   et de ma- nu con- for- tan- tis re- gis au- re- am lau- re- am su- me- re.

5. Quid ti- bi pro- fe- cit, pro- fa- ne ser- pens, quod- dam u- nam de- ce- pis- se mu- li- e- rem,
   Cum vir- go pe- pe- re- rit in- car- na- tum de- i pa- tris u- ni- cum do- mi- num Je- sum?

6. Qui prae- dam ti- bi tu- lit et ar- mil- la maxil- lam fo- rat,
   Ut e- gres- sus E- vae na- tis fi- at, quos te- ne- re cu- pis.

7. Nunc er- go te- met vir- gi- nes vin- ce- re cer- nis, in- vi- de,
   Et ma- ri- ta- tas pa- re- re fi- li- os de- o pla- ci- tos.

8. Et vi- du- a- rum ma- ri- tis fi- dem nunc in- ge- mis in- te- gram,
   Qui cre- a- to- ri fi- dem ne- ga- re per- sua- se- ras vir- gi- ni.

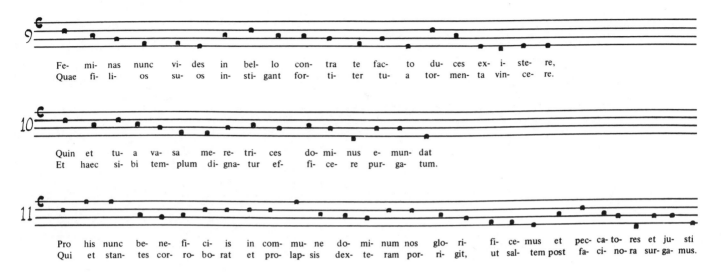

Fe- mi- nas nunc vi- des in bel- lo con- tra te fac- to du- ces ex- i- ste- re,
Quae fi- li- os su- os in- sti- gant for- ti- ter tu- a tor- men- ta vin- ce- re.

Quin et tu- a va- sa me- re- tri- ces do- mi- nus e- mun- dat
Et haec si- bi tem- plum di- gna- tur ef- fi- ce- re pur- ga- tum.

Pro his nunc be- ne- fi- ci- is in com- mu- ne do- mi- num nos glo- ri- fi- ce- mus et pec- ca- to- res et ju- sti
Qui et stan- tes cor- ro- bo- rat et pro- lap- sis dex- te- ram por- ri- git, ut sal- tem post fa- ci- no- ra sur- ga- mus.

11 Pro his nunc be-ne-fi-ci-is   in co-mu-ne do-mi-num
    A   G FE   ED   G A GFCFFD
    al- le-lu-ia Chri- sto pneu-ma- ti-que al-le-lu- ia
    nos glori-fi- ce-mus   et pec-ca-to-res et ju-sti.

All the clear internal cadences are notated in St. Gall MS 484 with the neume usually reserved for final cadences of the normal type—F G G, or C D D, or G A A.

Both these longer phrases (4 and 11) function as climactic conclusions to sections, which (in conjunction with cadence locations) can now be perceived to consist of phrases 1–4, 5–7, 8–11. Even though the continuity provided by the similar beginnings on A, and a good deal of motivic similarity overall, makes the section plan less than obvious, still it does not obliterate it completely. Perhaps the most noticeable feature of the middle section (5–7) is the resemblance of 7 to 5, both rising vigorously to high E. Phrase 6 then appears as an interlude, the three phrases together forming a symmetrical unit.

The most distinctive aspects of the melody are the variations in the cadences or in the approaches to the cadences. At the beginning the approaches are entirely normal, as in 2.

C E G F E D C D D

The framing of the final pitch, D, together with it close relative F, by the group C E G seems to be a characteristic feature of D-cadences; it corresponds to the use of the F-A-C realm around G-cadences, but is used more often and often in closer proximity to the cadence itself, perhaps because it is less of a contrast; the F-A-C realm seems to be more remote from the corresponding pair G-B because of the tritone F/B.

After returning at the end of 3, the same long cadence pattern is delayed in 4 by a reduplication of the notes G F E,

Cantemus cuncti melodum

1. Can- te- mus cunc- ti me- lo- dum nunc, al- le- lu- ia:

2. in lau- di- bus ae- ter- ni re- gis haec plebs re- sul- tet al- le- lu- ia.
   Hoc de- ni- que cae- le- stes cho- ri can- tant in al- tum al- le- lu- ia.

3. Hoc be- a- to- rum per pra- ta pa- ra- di- si- a- ca psal- lat con- cen- tus al- le- lu- ia:
   Quin et a- stro- rum mi- can- ti- a lu- mi- na- ri- a ju- bi- lant al- tum al- le- lu- ia.

4. Nu- bi- um cur- sus, ven- to- rum vo- la- tus ful- gu- rum co- ru- sca- ti- o
   Fluc- tus et un- dae, im- ber et pro- cel- lae, tem- pe- stas et se- re- ni- tas

   et to- ni- tru- um so- ni- tus dul- ce con- so- nent si- mul al- le- lu- ia:
   ca- nae ge- lu nix pru- i- nae sal- tus ne- mo- ra pan- gant al- le- lu- ia.

5. Hinc va- ri- ae vo- lu- cres cre- a- to- rem lau- di- bus con- cin- ni- te cum al- le- lu- ia:
   Ast il- linc re- spon- de- ant vo- ces al- tae di- ver- sa- rum be- sti- a- rum al- le- lu- ia.

6. I- stinc mon- ti- um cel- si ver- ti- ces so- nent al- le- lu- ia:
   Il- linc val- li- um pro- fun- di- ta- tes sal- tent al- le- lu- ia.

7. Tu quo- que ma- ris ju- bi- lans ab- ys- se dic al- le- lu- ia:
   Nec non ter- ra- rum mo- lis im- men- si- ta- tes al- le- lu- ia.

8. Nunc om- ne ge- nus hu- ma- num lau- dans ex- sul- tet al- le- lu- ia:
   Et cre- a- to- ri gra- tes fre- quen- tans con- so- net al- le- lu- ia.

222   Six Sequences by Notker

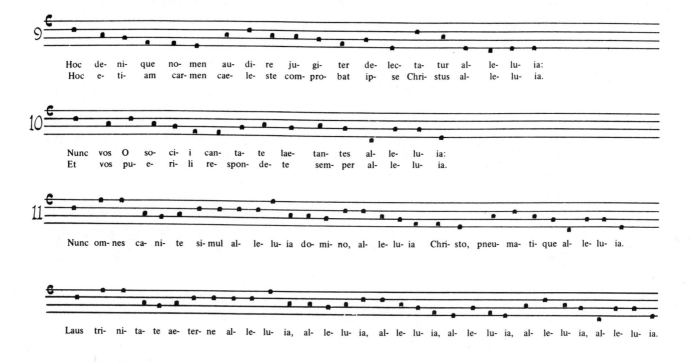

Hoc de- ni- que no- men au- di- re ju- gi- ter de- lec- ta- tur al- le- lu- ia:
Hoc e- ti- am car- men cae- le- ste com- pro- bat ip- se Chri- stus al- le- lu- ia.

Nunc vos O so- ci- i can- ta- te lae- tan- tes al- le- lu- ia:
Et vos pu- e- ri- li re- spon- de- te sem- per al- le- lu- ia.

Nunc om- nes ca- ni- te si- mul al- le- lu- ia do- mi- no, al- le- lu- ia Chri- sto, pneu- ma- ti- que al- le- lu- ia.

Laus tri- ni- ta- te ae- ter- ne al- le- lu- ia, al- le- lu- ia, al- le- lu- ia, al- le- lu- ia, al- le- lu- ia, al- le- lu- ia.

C E G F E *G F E* D C D D

in keeping with the extended sub-phrase structure of the phrase.

In phrase 5, B natural seems called for at the start and B flat at the end, judging from Bannister's concordances. The approach to the cadence is not one of our patterns, but is nonetheless smooth and easy. In phrase 6, on the other hand, the melody terminates with a very distinctive turn, arriving on A convincingly enough but only after an apparent escape up to the D above, and a leap down to G.

G F G A A A G C D G A

Actually, the real cadence seems to be located just before this figure, in a normal form— G A A—and so notated in St. Gall MS 484. The turn, A G C D G A, is then an appendage to the cadence, deriving from it a security of location and at the same time an expressive insistence. Yet the end result is that the normal cadence is obscured, and phrase 6, seemingly without one, is confirmed in its character as interlude between 5 and 7. The detail is finely calculated in that phrase 6 for the most part gives the effect of being lower than 5 or 7 (because of their ascents to E) but does have a high point in this same terminal figure that gives the phrase its identity.

In phrase 8, the descent to the lower register is confirmed by the elegant leap of a fifth, A-D. As in SUMMI TRIUMPHUM REGIS 4, these leaps, in themselves not extraordinary and fully prepared in terms of available pitches and tonal realm, nevertheless seem by some subtle arrangement to posess an inner expressivity, a nobility that escapes definition. Another one, a leap up from D to A, is found in a similar location in the next phrase (9). And comparable effects are achieved by the leaps down to C just before the cadences in 10 and 11; the second instance being nicely intensified by an approach a tone higher.

10 . . . F G *F* *C* F F D
11 . . . GA G *F* *C* F F D

Here the cadences themselves have been varied to the form F F D. In this case the last line (a double, as noted) seems an integral part of the melody: it lacks the ornamental or involute character so often found in concluding singles.

The emphasis on the ends of the phrases achieved by the means just described is strikingly reflected in the anonymous text CANTEMUS CUNCTI MELODIUM, of which every line ends with the word "alleluia." Well-known among hymnologists because of this idiosyncrasy, the text is unique in the early repertory. It recalls the technique of the *Kyrie eleison* in the versions with Latin text popular in the 9th and 10th centuries, where every line ends *eleison*.[7]

> Tibi Christe supplices exoramus cunctipotens, ut nostri digneris *eleison*.
> Tibi laus decet cum tripudio jugiter atque tibi petimus dona et *eleison*.
> O bone rex qui super astra sedes et domine qui cuncta gubernas *eleison*.

As a whole, CANTEMUS CUNCTI MELODUM is modeled on the canticle *Benedicite omnia opera Domini Domino*, the "Canticle of the three children," (*Daniel* 3,57–88,56), sung at Lauds. The main point of the text being the exhortation to each and every part of Creation, the rhetorical structure is basically serial, with less emphasis than usual upon sectional divisions or articulative functions. The only instances of such functions are in lines 8a and 11a. In 8a, an initial *Nunc*, turning to human kind, announces the third melodic section and the return to the D cadence. And line 11a, the conclusion, is given the summary exhortation *Nunc omnes canite simul*.

In any case, it is not the rhetoric that identifies the work, rather the alleluias. At first, their repetition merely reinforces the cadence patterns (2, 3, 4). Then the cadence changes its location to A (5) and also its shape (6), while the alleluia persists. In 8 and 9 a subtle and effective relief occurs by the shift of emphasis to the approach to the cadence, hence away from the alleluia, now appearing as a stable element. Then in 10 and 11 the alleluia gains once more in emphasis—it keeps coming back!—and is associated with the new cadence. The ecstatic, endless string of alleluias at the end is a happy consequence of the long-ranging process.

Notker's text has its own brilliant point. Von den Steinen and also Messenger trace the material from the Vision of Perpetua, mentioned by St. Augustine and recorded in the

7. Kyrie ad. lib. VI. Transcription of text and melody in my book, *A History of Musical Style* (New York 1966), pp. 42–43. See also *Anal.hymn.* 47, p. 45; B. Stäblein, "Kyrie," *Die Musik in Geschichte und Gegenwart* VII, col. 1941.

Passio Ss. Perpetuae et Felicitatis; Messenger also finds echoes of Virgil, Aeneid IV and VI—and, of course, in Jacob's dream of the ladder reaching up to heaven.[8]

1 A ladder upraised to heaven, girt about with tortures,

2 Is continually guarded by a wary dragon,
Lest anyone be able, uninjured, to mount to its highest round.

3 An Ethiopian, with drawn sword, threatening death, forbids its ascent.
A shining youth, resting upon its top, holds a golden bough.

4 Yet the love of Christ causes this ladder to be so easily ascended by holy women, that treading the dragon underfoot, and passing by the sword of the Ethiopian,
Through every kind of torments they are able to achieve the summit and from the hand of the consoling king receive the golden laurel.

5 What did it profit thee, unholy serpent, aforetime to have deceived one woman,
Since a Virgin brought forth the Incarnate Lord Jesus, only begotten of God the Father,

6 Who has carried off thy booty and pierced thy jaw with his spear?
That a way of escape may be made for the sons of Eve whom thou wouldst hold captive.

7 But now, envious beast, thou knowest thyself vanquished by virgins,
And dost lament that wives are nourishing sons pleasing to God,

8 And that the loyalty of widows to their husbands remains unchanged.
Thou who hadst persuaded a virgin to deny her fealty to her creator

9 Now beholdest women leading in the warfare waged against thee,
Women who bravely spur on their sons to conquer thy torments.

10 Nay more, the Lord cleanses even the harlots thy chosen vessels
And makes them worthy to be temples purified for himself.

11 For these mercies let us both sinners and righteous, now glorify the Lord together,
Who strengthens those who stand and stretches out his right hand to the fallen, that we too, after this sinful life, may rise to salvation.

This text, a mature one, involves a subtle relationship between its rhetorical plan and that of the music. Lines 2a,b and 3a,b are all relative constructions dependent upon 4a; the conclusion of the opening period, which coincides with the first musical section, comes only with the purpose clause that ends 4a,b.

(1)   Scalam ad caelos subrectam,
                tormentis cinctam,
(2a)   cujus ima draco servare cautus invigiliat jugiter,
(2b)   ne quis ejus vel primum gradum possit insaucius scandere,
(3a)   cujus ascensus extracto Aethiops gladio vetat exitium minitans,
(3b)   cujus supremis innixus juvenis splendidus ramum aureolum retinet,

8. Von den Steinen, *Notker* I, pp. 408ff. Ruth E. Messenger, "Sources of the Sequence *Scalam ad Caelos*," *Folia* II (1947), pp. 55–63, whence this translation.

(4a) hanc ergo scalam ita Christi amor feminis fecit perviam,
                ut dracone conculcato et Aethiopis gladio transito,
(4b)   per omne genus tormentorum caeli apicem queant capere
                et de manu confortantis regis auream lauream sumere.

His ear attuned to this bold, extended plan, Notker is content to obliterate the articulation near the start of phrase 4; he does, however, mark clearly the mediant cadence of that phrase with *ut* and *et*. And he goes out of his way to set the reduplication in the approach to the last cadence of 4 with a wording that in his canons of prose can only be tolerated as an exception for a special purpose—in this case, a musical one.

        C G G FE   G FE   C DD
. . . regis aure-am laure-am sumere

Line 5a starts an address to the serpent—the dragon that waits at the foot of the ladder. The address takes the form of a rhetorical question that extends through phrases 5 and 6, followed by two elaborate reproaches, each introduced by a *nunc*, each occupying two phrases, 7 and 8, 9 and 10.

(5a)   Quid tibi profecit, profane serpens,
                quondam unam decepisse mulierem,
(5b)   cum virgo peperit incarnatum dei patris unicum dominum Jesus?
(6a)   qui praedam tibi tulit
                et armilla maxillam forat
(6b)   ut egressus Evae natis fiat,
                    quos tenere cupis.
(7a)   Nunc ergo temet virgines vincere cernis, invide,
(7b)   et maritatas parere filios deo placitos.
(8a)   Et viduarum maritis fidem nunc ingemis integram,
(8b)   qui creatori fidem negare persvaseras virgini.
(9a)   Feminas nunc vides in bello contra te facto duces existere,
(9b)   quae filios suos instigant fortiter tua tormenta vincere.
(10a) Quin et tua vasa meretrices dominus emundat
(10b)   et haec sibi templum dignatur efficere purgatum.

This syntactical plan involves a different understanding—less obvious but perfectly reasonable—of the musical plan. Notker takes phrase 6 to be the consequent of 5, then continues the phrase rhythm by taking 8 as the consequent of 7—instead of having 8 start a new section, as CANTEMUS CUNCTI MELODUM did with *Nunc* . . . . Phrases 5 and 7 are similar, hence function easily this way; phrases 6 and 8 are different, the former ending on A, the latter on D. Hence these, in Notker's arrangement, are made to sound open and closed respectively; phrases 5, 6, 7, and 8 together have the effect of X Y, X Z, phrase 8 providing a different consequent, a turn back to the original D area. The motive that begins phrase 9 (A G F E) seems more active than the usual descending motives found at phrase beginnings in this piece; at any rate it is different, and Notker uses this difference to start his third reproach, *Feminas nunc*. Phrase 11 then stands by itself as the exhortation to conventual celebration: . . . *nunc* . . . *nos glorificemus*.

(11a) Pro his nunc beneficiis in commune dominum nos glorificemus,

et peccatores et justi,

(11b) qui et stantes corroborat,

et prolapsis dexteram porrigit,

ut saltem post facinora surgamus.

Notker's language here shows all the mastery one might expect of maturity. Sonorous assonance is used abundantly but never indiscreetly—if one accepts *auream lauream* for the sake of the music. Accent patterns are, for the most part, carefully matched to the melodic inflection; the neglect of the cadence toward the end of 6a is such a glaring exception it must have been deliberate, presumably because Notker did not want to observe the cadence by the melody.

```
     A   A   C   B G   G F G A   A / A   G C   D   G A
6a   Qui prae-dam ti-bi   tu- lit et ar-mil-  la   max-il- lam fo- rat,
6b   Ut   e-gres- sus E-vae na-tis fi-  at, quos te-  ne-re   cu- pis.
```

In general, his cadences are consistent: the normal melodic pattern receives a proparoxytone (2a,b; 3a,b; 4a,b—internal and final; 7a,b; 8a,b; 9a,b); other patterns are construed as paroxytones (1: *cínctam*; 6: *fórat*; *cúpis*; 10: *emúndat, purgátum*; 11: *jústi, surgámus*). Only 5a,b constitute exceptions, and of those only 5b, if we read *mulíerem* in 5a.

Yet it is difficult to imagine this as the original text for this melody—and just as difficult to imagine the melody coming from the same school as the West-Frankish ones. Not that the overall conception is basically different, but the detail is. In particular, the handling of cadences indicates a secondary rather than a primary stage of development and suggests that CANTEMUS CUNCTI MELODUM was the original text, for the insistent terminal alleluias seem the natural complement of the melodic variation.

CONCENTU PARILI

The melodies for SUMMI TRIUMPHUM REGIS and SCALAM AD CAELOS are equal in conception and spirit to any of the West-Frankish melodies; any reservations would concern the occasional angularities of melodic inflection—and that of course is a matter of local style and taste. With the next pair of pieces, however, a different kind of judgment seems possible: CONCENTU PARILI and NATUS ANTE SECULA, both very well known sequences in the East-Frankish repertory, seem to owe their popularity to Notker's texts rather than to their East-Frankish melodies. In any case, these make a curious impression in terms of what we have seen.

CONCENTU PARILI has an important variant at the beginning, as Blume noted. Some versions begin with two lines of text set to the same phrase of melody, others begin with three lines of text set to the same phrase.

Concentu parili (Notker)

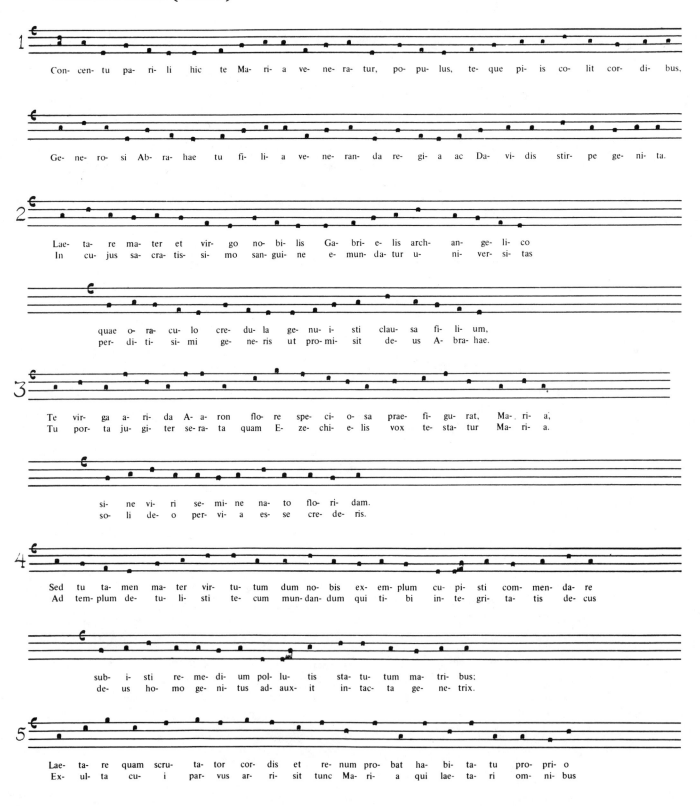

1. Con- cen- tu pa- ri- li hic te Ma- ri- a ve- ne- ra- tur, po- pu- lus, te- que pi- is co- lit cor- di- bus,

Ge- ne- ro- si Ab- ra- hae tu fi- li- a ve- ne- ran- da re- gi- a ac Da- vi- dis stir- pe ge- ni- ta.

2. Lae- ta- re ma- ter et vir- go no- bi- lis Ga- bri- e- lis arch- an- ge- li- co
In cu- jus sa- cra- tis- si- mo san- gui- ne e- mun- da- tur u- ni- ver- si- tas

quae o- ra- cu- lo cre- du- la ge- nu- i- sti clau- sa fi- li- um,
per- di- ti- si- mi ge- ne- ris ut pro- mi- sit de- us A- bra- hae.

3. Te vir- ga a- ri- da A- a- ron flo- re spe- ci- o- sa prae- fi- gu- rat, Ma- ri- a,
Tu por- ta ju- gi- ter se- ra- ta quam E- ze- chi- e- lis vox te- sta- tur Ma- ri- a.

si- ne vi- ri se- mi- ne na- to flo- ri- dam.
so- li de- o per- vi- a es- se cre- de- ris.

4. Sed tu ta- men ma- ter vir- tu- tum dum no- bis ex- em- plum cu- pi- sti com- men- da- re
Ad tem- plum de- tu- li- sti te- cum mun- dan- dum qui ti- bi in- te- gri- ta- tis de- cus

sub- i- sti re- me- di- um pol- lu- tis sta- tu- tum ma- tri- bus;
de- us ho- mo ge- ni- tus ad- aux- it in- tac- ta ge- ne- trix.

5. Lae- ta- re quam scru- ta- tor cor- dis et re- num pro- bat ha- bi- ta- tu pro- pri- o
Ex- ul- ta cu- i par- vus ar- ri- sit tunc Ma- ri- a qui lae- ta- ri om- ni- bus

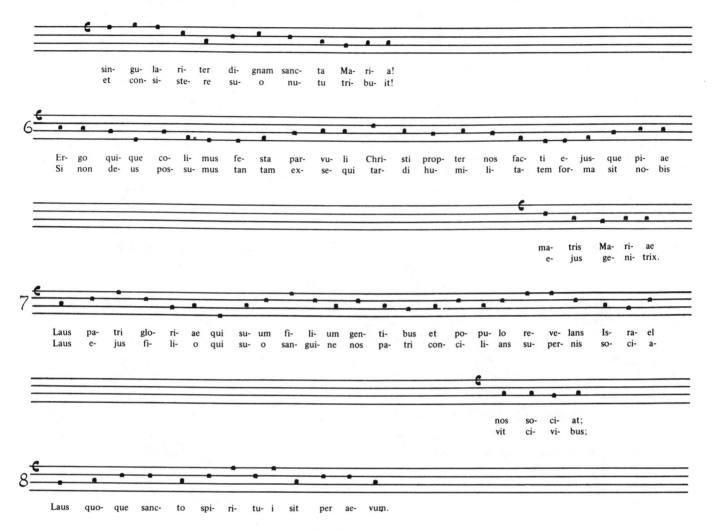

sin- gu- la- ri- ter di- gnam sanc- ta Ma- ri- a!
et con- si- ste- re su- o nu- tu tri- bu- it!

Er- go qui- que co- li- mus fe- sta par- vu- li Chri- sti prop- ter nos fac- ti e- jus- que pi- ae
Si non de- us pos- su- mus tan tam ex- se- qui tar- di hu- mi- li- ta- tem for- ma sit no- bis

ma- tris Ma- ri- ae
e- jus ge- ni- trix.

Laus pa- tri glo- ri- ae qui su- um fi- li- um gen- ti- bus et po- pu- lo re- ve- lans Is- ra- el
Laus e- jus fi- li- o qui su- o san- gui- ne nos pa- tri con- ci- li- ans su- per- nis so- ci- a-

nos so- ci- at;
vit ci- vi- bus;

Laus quo- que sanc- to spi- ri- tu- i sit per ae- vum.

1a Concentu parili hic te Maria veneratur populus, teque piis colit cordibus,
1b Generosi Abrahae tu filia veneranda regia ac Davidis stirpe genita.
1c Sanctissima corpore castissima moribusque omnium pulcherrima virgo virginum

The version with three lines is made to resemble the usual arrangement (phrase 1 single, phrase 2 double) by a minute adjustment in the setting of the first line: two notes are joined in a neume over *Con(centu)*; in compensation an extra D is added over *hic*.

        GA G D FE D D E F G G
1a Con- cen-tu pa-ri-li hic te Ma- ri- a

instead of

```
        G  A  G  D F   E   D  EF GG
1b   Ge- ne- ro- si A- bra- hae tu fi- li- a
```

As shown in the transcription, St. Gall MS 484 preserves a slight difference between phrase 1 and its repetition, and does not provide for the third line of text.

As Blume pointed out, the third line seems in every respect to be an interpolation; presumably what he had in mind was the heaping up of attributes in apposition, the excessive assonance (*sanctissima corpore / castissima mortibus*), and the fact that the line, besides being out of character, does not advance the thought very much.

Leaving out the third line has two interesting implications. The first is that with two nearly identical opening lines, the piece would resemble the incipit of the West-Frankish ECCE VICIT; when setting that melody with his HANC CONCORDI, Notker doubled the second line to give the incipit a regular form—opening single, regular double. The same might have happened in the case of CONCENTU PARILI, except that here it would seem that someone other than Notker added the third line. The other implication, however, is that if the piece was intended to begin with a *couplet* (as opposed to two almost identical lines as in ECCE VICIT), then this form of incipit is unique in Notker's output, and anticipates a form of incipit that eventually—perhaps still within the ninth century—became a normal one. The majority of tenth-century sequences begin with only the word *alleluia* as phrase 1, the text proper starting with a regular double in phrase 2. Notker's CONCENTU PARILI is not provided with such an *alleluia*; and it does exist in tenth-century sources with its third line of text in the traditional arrangement. Thus it stands in an uncertain position between the two types.

It might be significant—or completely coincidental—that phrase 1 is similar to the beginning of the *Kyrie* melody from Mass XIV (of the *Liber usualis*) known as *Jesu redemptor* after one set of "tropes" but appearing in tenth-and eleventh-century sources with several other sets too. This *Kyrie* is most remarkable, however, because as Huglo pointed out it seems to borrow a phrase from a Byzantine polychronon ("Many years!" [for the emperor]) for its incipit.[9]

```
     G    GAGA     FGFG      FE   D EFG   AG
Πολ - λὰ —————— τὰ ἔτη———————τῶν βα  - ϛι - λέ - ων
     GAGAGG DDGFG FEDD  EFGAA GFGG
     Ky- -  -  - ri- e——————— e  - -  -  -  - le-i-son
     G A     G  D     FEDD E       FGG
     Con-    centu   pa-ri-li hic te    Mari- a
```

The rest of the melody proceeds through a simple alternation of lower and higher phrases. Phrase 2 is an expanded version of phrase 1; like it, it occupies the range between the G final and the D below. Phrase 1 used the normal cadence pattern no less than three times —*Maria, -que piis, cordibus* (so notated in the melismatic version in St. Gall MS 484)—although the text observes only the last of these as articulations. Phrase 2 has the cadence

---

9. M. Huglo, in a review of E. Wellesz, *A History of Byzantine Music and Hymnography*, in *Révue grégorienne* 30 (1951), pp. 35–42; see also the second edition (1961) of Wellesz's book, pp. 120f.

only at the end. Towards its middle (*quae oraculo*) phrase 2 starts a modified repetition of its first half, so that the phrase falls into two sub-phrases, but without much melodic articulation, and again without observance in the text. The figure at the start of the phrase,

G A G, F G F

recalls the way the low-lying phrase of Notker's LAUDES DEO CONCINAT was expanded in his phrase 4, added to the West-Frankish model; the same figure appears at the start of HANC CONCORDI (ECCE VICIT) phrase 4, an expansion of phrase 3. The figure on *Gabrielis archangelico*, in phrase 2,

D E F G A G F E D

is like nothing else we have encountered.

Phrases related to 1 and 2 in idiom and construction appear alternately at 4 and 6. In both of these the repetitive aspect of the melody becomes increasingly clear—not only that they repeat the substance of phrases 1 and 2, but that within each phrase there is an uncommon amount of motivic repetition. And in all cases the repetition is not supported by the text, which is designed rather to support a very long line of its own, as we will see.

Phrase 3 has a different melodic substance. Moving mainly within the tonal realm bounded by G and the C above, it shares at least one figure with the "refrain" from LAUDES DEO CONCINAT.

C G A C

Another figure is in a descending scale,

D C B A G

like that on *Gabrielis archangelico* in phrase 2 a fourth lower. The rest of the line is made up of motion through F G A.

Phrases 5 and 7 are, like 3, higher, alternating with 2, 4, and 6, which are lower. But 3, 5, and 7 are more dissimilar among themselves than are 2, 4, and 6. Phrase 4 starts in a G-B-D realm; the following figure, a striking one,

C B C A C G

recalls phrase 10 of Notker's LAUDES SALVATORI, also the "saw-toothed" figure from SUMMI TRIUMPHUM REGIS. The approach to the cadence is through the F-A-C realm. Phrase 7, on the other hand, moves both above the G final up to C, and below the final down to D, recapitulating the tonal movement of the whole piece but giving this phrase a distinctive form. Finally, phrase 7 has Notker's other form for the normal cadence pattern—G F G. Like all the normal ones, this is set proparoxytone, if we except *María* and *Maríae* in 5a and 6a. Phrase 8 is an ordinary single, with a cadence from above but with ornamental neumes.

All in all, not a very distinguished melody, nor a very exciting one. The main difficulty is the extension of the length of the lines past what their melodic substance will permit.

In phrase 3, to take one of the worst examples, the motion through F G A borders on the desultory. The contrast in range seems not enough in view of the extreme length of some of the lines, especially since there is no contrasting final. Indeed, one comes back repeatedly to the length of line as the crucial aspect of the piece. And in this aspect the text is as strong as the melody is weak.

The syntactic plan is very simple and regular. Each regular double is filled out by one or two complete periods; if two (as in phrases 3, 5, 7), then each line is a complete syntactic unit of some kind. Even line 7b and the concluding single, 8, are syntactically independent, even if not rhetorically so.

The rhetorical plan is somewhat more sophisticated—varied and well-coordinated. The functions can be summarized like this:

1a	conventual exhortation (. . . *veneratur populus* . . .)
1b	acclamatory attributes (. . . *tu* . . . !)
2a,b	exhortation to Mary (*Laetare* . . .)
3a,b	prefigurations as attributes (*Te* . . . *Tu* . . .)
4a,b	acts as attributes (. . . *tu* . . .)
5a,b	exhortation to Mary (*Laetare! Exulta!*)
6a,b	conventual exhortation (*Ergo* . . . *colimus* . . .)
7a,b; 8	Doxology (*Laus patri* . . . *filio* . . . *sancto spiritui* . . .)

The first conventual exhortation (1a) is for worship; the second one (6a,b) for imitating the model of humility offered by the Virgin. Together these two exhortations define the shape and content, enclosing the praise of Mary in a frame of celebration. Her praises are sung through acclamation (1b: "Thou daughter of Abraham and born of David's royal stem"); through a paraphrase of the angelic greeting (2a: "Blessed art thou among women," 2b: "And blessed is the fruit of thy womb . . ."), and through the prefiguration of the Rod of Aaron (3a) and the gate of Ezechiel. The forms of address *Tu* and *Te* are used in the fashion of the *Te deum*, but with restraint. Lines 4a,b tell of her acts of humility, lines 5a,b elaborate on her blessed state. The doxology at the end is the most formal we have encountered—a fully trinitarian acclamation of praise.

Beyond the control and refinement usual in Notker's mature style, CONCENTU PARILI contains some of the longest, most sustained lines in his repertory. Lines 4a,b are virtually without articulation into sub phrases, yet are rich in manifold internal relationships of rhythm and assonance.

4a   Sed tu tamen mater virtutum
       dum nobis exemplum cupisti
           commendare subisti remedium pollutis statutum matribus;

The line starts inauspiciously with two monosyllables followed by a juxtaposition of two accented syllables (*tú tá-*), but as the rhythm gathers momentum these are easily subsumed in a grouping in threes, the juxtaposed accents causing just enough hesitation to give invocative emphasis to *tu*.

```
        ´                      ´
 x  ´ ´  x  ´ x x  ´  x
Sed tu ta- men ma- ter vir- tu- tum
       a       a     i
     u             u  u
 e       e     e
```

The resultant grouping in threes (x ´ x x ´ x x ´ x) is remarkably regular for prose; Notker would not have done it carelessly. Here in phrase 4 he seems to want a special rhythm for the sake of the overall plan. At a higher level, *virtútum* provides a strong accent that echoes the invocation (as suggested by the accents in the top row).

Up through *virtutum* seems to form a line of rhythmic verse. It is followed by another of the same.

```
 x   ´ x x  ´   x x  ´ x
dum no- bis ex- emp- lum cu- pi- sti
        i          i  i
  u             u  u
         e  e
     o
```

The -u- and -e- sounds continue to be prominent as the groups of threes roll on unimpeded; but *cupisti* sticks out as a new sound. As it in turn is confirmed by the strongly rhyming *subisti*, accents are momentarily altered to groups of twos (*-pí-sti com- men- da-*),

```
 x    ´ x   x  ´   x x  ´  x
dum no- bis ex- emp- lum cu- pi- sti
       \  x ´   x x  ´ x
        com-men-da   re sub- i- sti
```

then returning to a group of three to support the rhyme (*-dá-re sub-í- sti*). Having made the point, Notker allows the rest of the line to run in prose; the sonorities continue, however, to be carefully controlled. The construction pivots around the assonance

    pol- lú- tis sta- tú- tum

which of course carries out the *tú . . . virtútum* earlier, and the grouping in threes. Around this pivotal assonance are grouped—chiasmus fashion—the words *remedium* and *matribus*, which contain, of course, groups of twos.

```
 x  ´ x  \  x  ´ x x  ´ x  ´  x x
re- me- di- um pol- lu- tis sta- tu- tum ma- tri- bus
```

It is difficult to isolate the factors that make *matribus* end the line so precisely; with that word we know that the intricate structure has run its course, and that the structure is prose not verse. That the same melody is then brilliantly set to a line of quite different structure in 4b is an indication of how much Notker has learned about setting texts to melodies.

Natus ante saecula (Notker)

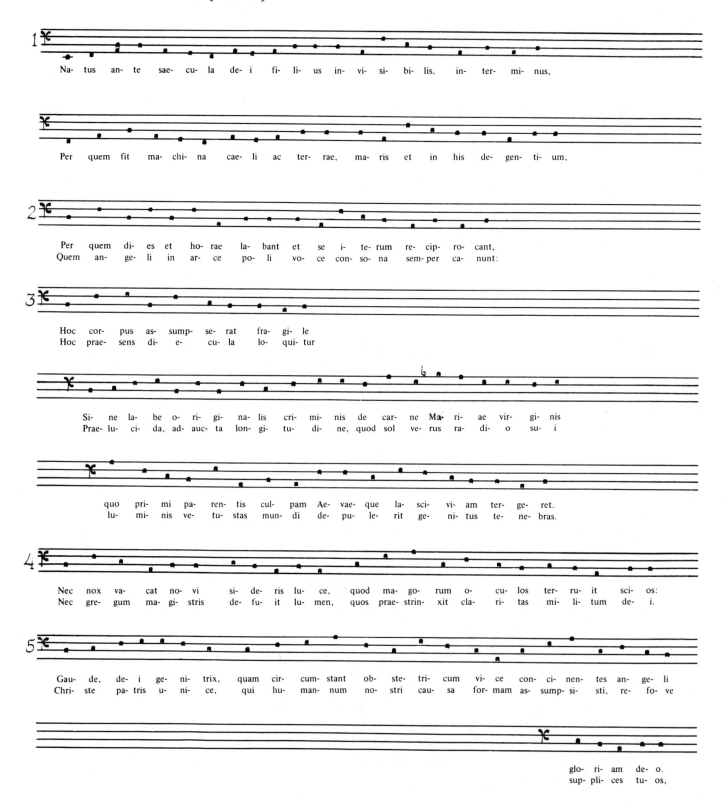

1. Natus ante saecula dei filius invisibilis, interminus,

Per quem fit machina caeli ac terrae, maris et in his degentium,

2. Per quem dies et horae labant et se iterum reciprocant,
   Quem angeli in arce poli voce consona semper canunt:

3. Hoc corpus assumpserat fragile
   Hoc praesens diecula loquitur

   Sine labe originalis criminis de carne Mariae virginis
   Praelucida, adaucta longitudine, quod sol verus radio sui

   quo primi parentis culpam Aevaeque lasciviam tergeret.
   luminis vetustas mundi depulerit genitus tenebras.

4. Nec nox vacat novi sideris luce, quod magorum oculos terruit scios:
   Nec gregum magistris defuit lumen, quos praestrinxit claritas militum dei.

5. Gaude, dei genitrix, quam circumstant obstetricum vice concinentes angeli
   Christe patris unice, qui humanum nostri causa formam assumpsisti, refove

   gloriam deo.
   supplices tuos,

Natus ante saecula (Notker) (2)

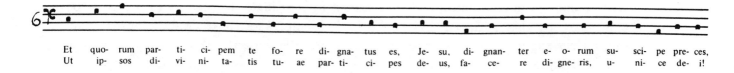

Et	quo-	rum	par-	ti-	ci-	pem	te	fo-	re	di-	gna-	tus	es,	Je-	su,	di-	gnan-	ter	e-	o-	rum	su-	sci-	pe	pre-	ces,
Ut	ip-	sos	di-	vi-	ni-	ta-	tis	tu-	ae	par-	ti-	ci-	pes	de-	us,	fa-	ce-	re	di-	gne-	ris,	u-	ni-	ce	de-	i!

And now it is the text that causes the melody to flow, to keep flowing through its pedestrian, repetitive string of notes.

As often noted, the incipit of CONCENTU PARILI quotes Prudentius, *Inventor rutili dux bone luminis*.[10] Not so often noted, this incipit is in turn cited by the short tenth-century treatise *Instituta patrum*.[11] Schubiger cites the treatise, but without connection to the sequence. The treatise shows, incidentally, that (in the tenth century at least) antiphonal performance was possible but not obligatory; hence the incipit of CONCENTU PARILI—far from indicating that antiphonal performance is normal—may only suggest it for this piece.

NATUS ANTE SAECULA

The melody for Notker's NATUS ANTE SAECULA carries the name "Dies sanctificatus" in the St. Gall MSS, and is on those grounds usually thought to have the incipit of Alleluia *Dies sanctificatus* from the Christmas liturgy (Third Mass). If that were the case, the melody would belong in the group of sequences to be considered later—those that quote Mass Alleluias in their incipits. Because of the minimal nature of the relationship of NATUS ANTE SAECULA to the Alleluia (if indeed that relationship exists at all), and because of variants and details that make the relationship dubious, I have placed the sequence here instead.

Even using the variants that most favor the relationship, it consists entirely in the coincidence of the first five notes.

	C D FG G	(D final)
Alleluia *Dies sanctificatus*	Al- le- lu- ia	
	G A CD D	(D final)
NATUS ANTE SAECULA: variant 1	Na- tus an- te	
	A B C D	(D final)
variant 2	Na- tus an- te	(D final)

The sequence as a whole has a D final, hence the incipit G A CD D is in a different position (a fourth lower) relative to the final than in the Alleluia *Dies sanctificatus*. In the common variant noted as "variant 2" the relationship to the alleluia vanishes.

10. *Anal.hymn.* 50, p. 30.

11. A. Schubiger, *Die Sängerschule St. Gallens*, p. 53: Sequentias si cantamus sive alternatim sive una simul, concentu parili voce consona finiatur. The quotation is from the short treatise *Instituta patrum* (edited by Martin Gerbert, *Scriptores Ecclesiastici de musica sacra*, I) (San Blasian 1784), p. 7.

Much more important, I think, is the fact that NATUS ANTE SAECULA begins, like CONCENTU PARILI, with a regular double. The melodies that are related to alleluias all begin with a single, the relationship being restricted to the single. In the melismatic notation of St. Gall 484, the "variant 1" is used for 1a, "variant 2" for 1b. It would seem that here, too, scribes and perhaps even composer or arranger were uncertain about a relatively new form of incipit, and that "variant 1" could just as well represent their lingering conviction that the very beginning—even in this double—should have some of the distinctive features of an intonation.

In addition to its opening double, NATUS ANTE SAECULA also has a closing double, in a melodic style entirely similar to the preceding phrases. All in all, the plan is unique in the early repertory. With only six phrases, the plan suggests that opening and closing singles are simply missing. An opening single with the text "alleluia" in the newer style could easily be imagined; but the text shows no trace of a lost closing single.

Like CONCENTU PARILI, NATUS ANTE SAECULA gives the impression of a simple, monotonous tune of restricted range—primarily a vehicle for the text. In this case, however, the melody is well made with many subtle features that are musically attractive and interesting. The range around the D final is that of *protus* plagal (or "second tone" in the eight-fold numbering), and the restricted movement might well be ascribed to the somber, reflective mood sometimes associated with Gregorian pieces in this tone (for example—it must be admitted—the Alleluia *Dies sanctificatus*), rather than to mere poverty of invention or to subservience to text. In any case, the idiom of NATUS ANTE SAECULA is different from any of those studied so far, in particular from the other D-final melodies SUMMI TRIUMPHUM REGIS and SCALAM AD CAELOS.

Of the six phrases, 1 is a low intonation and introduction, lying mostly below the final (G or A up to F). Phrase 2, like 1, is short, and in addition relatively simple; it remains with C and F around the final. Phrase 3 is by far the longest of the six, with a subtle sub-phrase structure (to be considered), and rises to the top of the range—A or B flat, depending on variants. It serves as the high point of the piece, in so far as there is one, but is curiously located: the three phrases that follow seem too much to come after a climax. These three phrases (4, 5, 6) are all about the same length and move similarly in the same range.

The last three phrases are also grouped by cadence patterns, which in this piece are distinctive throughout. Phrases 1 and 2 have the peculiar figure C D C D, set three times proparoxytone (*intérminus, degéntium, recíprocant*) and one paroxytone (*sémper cánunt*). Phrase 3 has the normal cadence C D D—the only phrase to do so—set proparoxytone (*tégeret, ténebras*). Phrases 4, 5, 6, then, all have the normal pattern C D D, but treated in a new way as part of a larger pattern,

F E D,   E D C,   D D

That this is the intended grouping is shown by Notker's consistent provision of an accentual cursus for the last five notes (cursus planus, but not with the usual word structure ′ x / x ′ x).

		F	E	D		E	D	C		D	D
4a		ó-	cu-	los		tér-	ru-	it		scí-	os
4b		clá-	ri-	tas		mí-	li-	tum		dé-	i
5a		án-	ge-	li		gló-	ri-	am		dé-	o
5b		re-	fó-	ve		súp-	pli-	ces		tú-	os
6a		e-	ó-	rum		sú-	sci-	pes		pré-	ces
6b		di-	gné-	ris		ú-	ni-	ce		dé-	i

The group F E D is sometimes set as a group of three, sometimes not.

The articulations within individual phrases are as subtle as any yet studied. Many of the internal cadences in the melody are not observed in Notker's text, as in phrase 1: *filius*, C C D, divides the initial lower sub-phrase from the second higher one, without being a syntactic division.

                    C D D
1   Natus ante saecula dei fi- li- us / invisibilis, interminus,

Phrase 2 is without an inner cadence, in spite of the fact that the last part of the melody repeats the last part of 1.

1   A B C D C B A C B C D D   D C F E D C D C D
2   D F D F D F C D D   D C F E D C D C D

Phrase 3 seems to have no less than five sub-phrases—and here in delicate relationship with the text.

       D F G D F   E D D C D
3a   Hic cor- pus as- sump- se- rat frá- gi- le
           D E F GD F D F E F G G
       Si- ne la- be or- i- gi- na- lis crí- mi- nis
       F A G B♭ A G F G G
       de car- ne Ma- ri- ae vír- gi- nis
             A   F E DG C D C
           quo primi parentis cúl- pam
       F F E G F E D C D
       Aevae-que la- sci- vam tér- ge- ret

The first and last sub-phrases use Notker's cadence D C D, proparoxytone (*frágile*, *térgeret*). The second and third sub-phrases use a normal cadence F G G proparoxytone (*críminis*, *vírginis*)—although in this piece, of course, the cadence on G is clearly non-final in effect. The fourth sub-phrase has no proper cadence, but does arrive very persuasively on C, which in the context of first plagal tone is another very important non-final tone.

Expressed in this format, phrase 3 resembles a stanza of a hymn, an effect strengthened by the clausula-like construction of the text, not to mention the rhyme *criminis/virginis*. The phrase as a whole has a most elegant sense of closure; the fall from G to C at the end of the fourth sub-phrase (like other downward leaps in SCALAM AD CAELOS) adds a refined expressiveness. But all the factors that increase the charm of this phrase and of the whole piece tend away from concepts of prose toward those of verse and a verse-like style of melody.

Certain aspects of the text are curious. Some lines show a virtuoso combination of sense and sonority.

> (4a) Néc nóx vácat nóvi síderis lúce
>   quód magórum óculos térruit scíos

Alongside of such unique creations is line 2b, a string of clichés in an undistinguished rhythm.

> (2b) Quem ángeli in árce póli vóce cónsona sémper cánunt

Line 2b is the third in a series of relative clauses (1b: *per quem*, 2a: *Per Quem*, 2b: *Quem*), which in turn follow the three attributes of line 1a—*natus . . . invisibilis, interminus*—a loose construction overworked in the repertory as a whole. The syntax of the whole beginning compares unfavorably with phrase 3 and following. Even there, 3b brings a curious change of subject, and the two invocations in 5a,b (*dei genetrix . . . Christe*) coexist in the same couplet without much connection. Compared, say, to SUMMI TRIUMPHUM REGIS, the continuity of the text is not strong, depending for a central idea to a greater extent on the festal theme of the Nativity.

XIII

Relationship with the Alleluia

THE SEQUENCES now to be discussed all bear some definite musical relationship to an Alleluia of the Mass; those which have been discussed up to this point (with the possible exception of Notker's NATUS ANTE SAECULA) showed no such relationship. Since the relationship to the Alleluia has played such an important role in our traditional understanding of the sequence, it will have to be discussed at some length further on; essential to that discussion, however, is an acquaintance with the facts of the relationship as found in individual cases in the early repertory—and it is the purpose of this part of the book to provide such acquaintance. It may be helpful to preface this part with a brief summary of the manifold ways in which sequences are related to the Alleluia, since these ways have not been sufficiently distinguished in previous research.

First, *all* early sequences are related to "Alleluia" by the fact that the word "Alleluia" appears under phrase 1 of all melodies when they are notated in melismatic form in the sequentiaria. This purely *pro forma* relationship, which has nothing to do either with the prose that goes with the sequence, or with any musical relationship that may exist between phrase 1 and an actual Alleluia from the Proper of the Mass, is a simple fact of the sources; it has never been adequately explained.

Second, the category of sequences is in general related to the Alleluia of the Mass in that at some point in its development—just when has never been determined—sequences came to be sung at Mass immediately after the Alleluia (after the second Alleluia on days when two were sung). This, again, is a general relationship, in this case a purely liturgical one; no specific melodic relationship is necessarily involved.

Third, some proses (although virtually none of the earliest ones except possibly CONCENTU PARILI and NATUS ANTE SECULA, as noted) begin with a regular double, to which is to be prefixed in performance a "phrase 1" with the text "Alleluia." This prefix is regularly provided in the sequentiaria, and is occasionally supplied in the prosaria (sometimes as a marginal addition). This type of relationship is to be regarded as—in principle—textual, rather than musical: the melodic phrase 1 sung to the text "Alleluia" may *or may not* in fact be related to a specific Alleluia of the Mass. Many of the melodies already studied, not in themselves related to a specific Alleluia, were supplied later with new texts that begin with a regular double for phrase 2, leaving phrase 1 to be sung to the text "Alleluia."[1]

1 Christi hodierna pangamini omnes una
2a nunc voce consona nativitatis magnae.
 b Verbum caro factum exhibere se voluit

1 Alleluia
2a Caelica resonant clare camoenas agmina
 b Nunc regis celebrando gratulanter nuptias.

Fourth, in certain melodies phrase 1 shows a demonstrable melodic relationship to a specific Alleluia of the Mass. In many cases this relationship is indicated by the melody's name as provided in one or another of the sources. In the case of the next melody to be studied, the sources provide two names, "Cignea," and "Pascha nostrum." The latter refers to the Alleluia *Pascha nostrum* for Easter Sunday. Yet another name for the same melody is "Paschalis antica"—perhaps a reference to the same Alleluia, and perhaps just an indication of the melody's liturgical function. The first name, "Cignea," has no demonstrable relationship to the Alleluia, nor, indeed, any satisfactory explanation. Apparent references in the melody titles to Mass Alleluias are not completely free of ambiguity. In the majority of cases where a connection is implied, however, it turns out to be clear and beyond question—but only as far as the incipit, phrase 1, is concerned; melodic relationship between subsequent phrases and the alleluia, although sometimes claimed, are often dubious.

Fifth, many melodies—including some of those studied—have incipits that *suggest* a melodic relationship to an alleluia, but a search fails to produce an Alleluia that actually corresponds to the incipit. In some cases elaborate arguments have been devised to substantiate such connections.[2] My own feeling is that these arguments go far beyond responsible demonstration; accordingly I have accepted only those relationships indicated in my Table II (p. 12). But much more important, it seems to me, is the broader question, *why* should certain incipits so strongly suggest a relationship to the Alleluia? This question, too, will be pursued later.

At the moment, then, the task is to investigate those melodies in Notker's repertory that are related to Alleluias in the fourth way—that is, by way of definite melodic quotation. It will be important to observe not merely the relationship via the incipit, but also— and especially—the other features of melody and text in comparison to the works already studied.

The reason so much importance has traditionally been attributed to the relationship with the Alleluia (which for the most part involves merely the incipit of the sequence) is this: the sequence, as represented by the kind of piece we have been studying, has been

1. As I pointed out in my article, "The Repertory of Proses at St. Martial de Limoges in the 10th century," *Journal of the American Musiological Society* XI (1958), pp. 149–164.
2. Especially H. Husmann, "Die Alleluia und Sequenzen der Mater-Gruppe," *Kongress-Bericht Wien* (1956), pp. 276–284.

assumed to be just a larger version of another type, whose relationship to the Alleluia happens to be clear, unequivocal, and decisive for its structure.[3] This other, shorter kind has a text without formal couplets set to a rhapsodic melody lacking the regular cadence patterns we have encountered. Notker set eight such melodies, as listed in group C of Table II. This type can be considered to have been a texting (text-underlay) of a melisma that was used as a replacement for the repetition of the Alleluia and its jubilus after the verse, as sung at Mass.

Alleluia, jubilus
Verse
Alleluia, replacement-melisma

This jubilus-replacement was called "sequentia" in the early ninth century, and this function explains the Alleluia incipit. All is clear in the case of this shorter kind of piece; the problem is whether this function and origin are true also for the larger kind of piece we have studied. Are the pieces in groups A and B of Table II to be explained by the same considerations as those in group C? Those in group A are clearly far from group C in many if not most respects, but those in group B share with group C at least the relationship to the Alleluia, hence might be closer in other respects too. It is in this context that the specific nature of the Alleluia relationship becomes critical.

Hæc est vera redemptio and beata tu virgo
Notker's gaude maria

The first example of a melody related to an Alleluia, hæc est vera redempto (better known as beata tu virgo) is so peculiar in other respects that no conclusions valid for other instances can be derived from it. Furthermore, there are uncertainties about many important aspects of the melody, of its several early texts and their musical relationships. Study of this instance, in other words, is fascinating but inconclusive.

One of the anomalies of this sequence is that on one hand its incipit is clearly related to Alleluia *Pascha nostrum*,[4] a chant with a G-tetrardus final; and on the other hand the sequence ends on a G-protus final, through a change of B natural to B flat. This change is confirmed in later staff sources. One such manuscript accomplishes the same thing by moving the melody up a whole step to end on A, with an explicit B natural;[5] the way in which the change is made (as well as the consistent testimony of the other manuscripts) indi-

---

3. This other kind of piece, and its relationship to the kind studied here, will be taken up in Chapter 22.

4. Alleluia *Pascha nostrum* is for Easter Sunday. Alleluia melodies are listed in Karlheinz Schlager, *Thematischer Katalog der ältesten Alleluia-Melodien* (Erlanger Arbeiten zur Musikwissenschaft Bd. 2, Munich 1965, cited as *Them.Kat.*) and transcribed in K. Schlager, *Alleluia-Melodien* I (*Monumenta monodica medii aevi* VII, 1968).

The melody for Alleluia *Pascha nostrum* in which we are interested is Schlager, *Them.Kat.* 346, transcribed in Schlager *Alleluia-Melodien* I p. 376, notes p. 658. This melody is represented in the earliest musical sources, and the text is firm in Hesbert's *Antiphonale missarum sextuplex*, no. 80.

5. London B.M. Cotton Calig. A XIV, fol. 55–55v. The words (of concinnat orbis) associated with the shift of "key" are *transfixus clavis*. Is this *Augenmusik?*

Hæc est vera redemptio

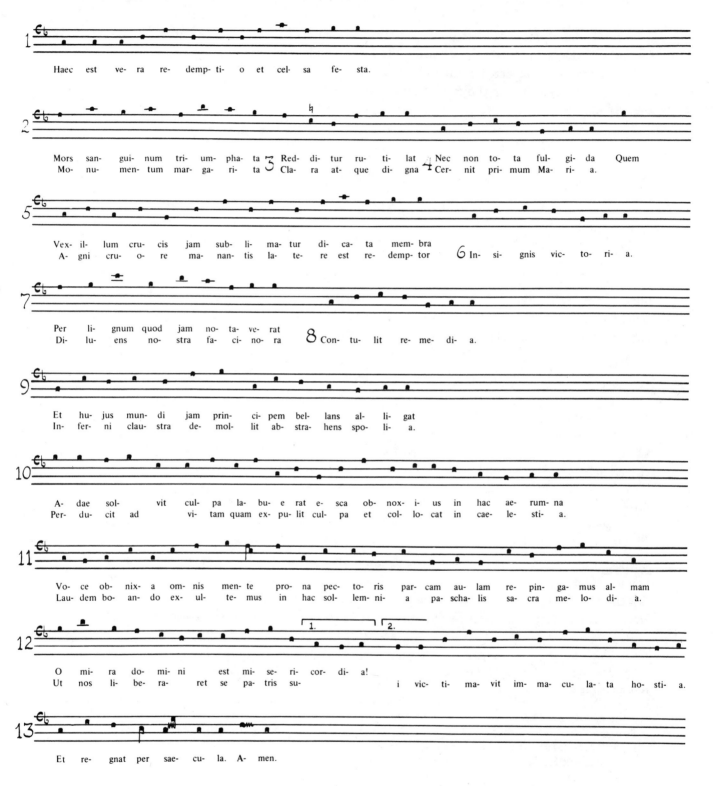

1. Haec est ve- ra re- demp- ti- o et cel- sa fe- sta.

2. Mors san- gui- num tri- um- pha- ta 3 Red- di- tur ru- ti- lat Nec non to- ta ful- gi- da Quem
   Mo- nu- men- tum mar- ga- ri- ta Cla- ra at- que di- gna 4 Cer- nit pri- mum Ma- ri- a.

5. Vex- il- lum cru- cis jam sub- li- ma- tur di- ca- ta mem- bra
   A- gni cru- o- re ma- nan- tis la- te- re est re- demp- tor 6 In- si- gnis vic- to- ri- a.

7. Per li- gnum quod jam no- ta- ve- rat
   Di- lu- ens no- stra fa- ci- no- ra 8 Con- tu- lit re- me- di- a.

9. Et hu- jus mun- di jam prin- ci- pem bel- lans al- li- gat
   In- fer- ni clau- stra de- mol- lit ab- stra- hens spo- li- a.

10. A- dae sol- vit cul- pa la- bu- e- rat e- sca ob- nox- i- us in hac ae- rum- na
    Per- du- cit ad vi- tam quam ex- pu- lit cul- pa et col- lo- cat in cae- le- sti- a.

11. Vo- ce ob- nix- a o- mnis men- te pro- na pec- to- ris par- cam au- lam re- pin- ga- mus al- mam
    Lau- dem bo- an- do ex- ul- te- mus in hac sol- lem- ni- a pa- scha- lis sa- cra me- lo- di- a.

12. O mi- ra do- mi- ni est mi- se- ri- cor- di- a!
    Ut nos li- be- ra- ret se pa- tris su- i vic- ti- ma- vit im- ma- cu- la- ta ho- sti- a.

13. Et re- gnat per sae- cu- la. A- men.

Gaude maria virgo (Notker)

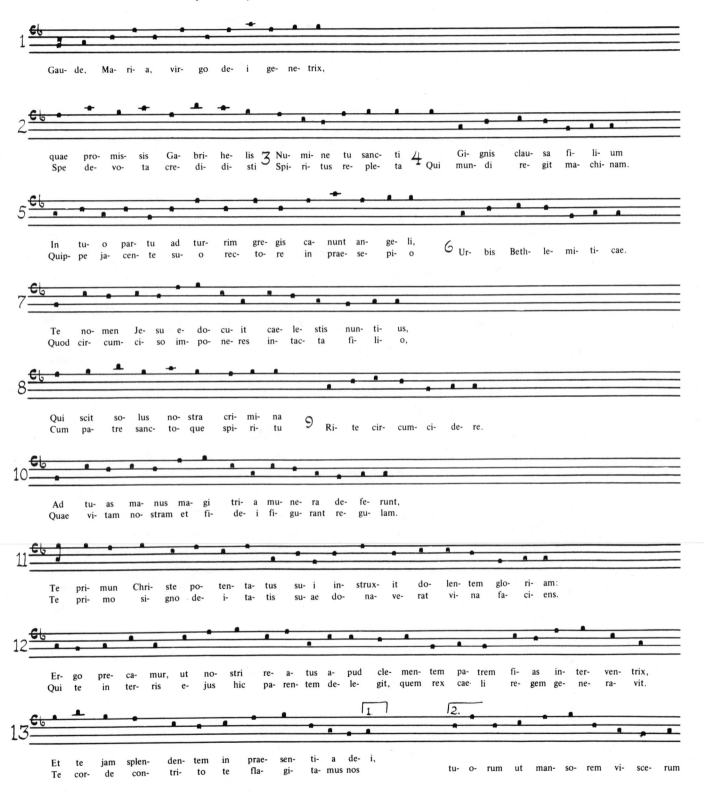

1. Gau- de, Ma- ri- a, virgo de- i ge- ne- trix,

2. quae pro- mis- sis Ga- bri- he- lis 3 Nu- mi- ne tu sanc- ti 4 Gi- gnis clau- sa fi- li- um
   Spe de- vo- ta cre- di- di- sti Spi- ri- tus re- ple- ta Qui mun- di re- git ma- chi- nam.

5. In tu- o par- tu ad tur- rim gre- gis ca- nunt an- ge- li, 6 Ur- bis Beth- le- mi- ti- cae.
   Quip- pe ja- cen- te su- o rec- to- re in prae- se- pi- o

7. Te no- men Je- su e- do- cu- it cae- le- stis nun- ti- us,
   Quod cir- cum- ci- so im- po- ne- res in- tac- ta fi- li- o,

8. Qui scit so- lus no- stra cri- mi- na 9 Ri- te cir- cum- ci- de- re.
   Cum pa- tre sanc- to- que spi- ri- tu

10. Ad tu- as ma- nus ma- gi tri- a mu- ne- ra de- fe- runt,
    Quae vi- tam no- stram et fi- de- i fi- gu- rant re- gu- lam.

11. Te pri- mun Chri- ste po- ten- ta- tus su- i in- strux- it do- len- tem glo- ri- am:
    Te pri- mo si- gno de- i- ta- tis su- ae do- na- ve- rat vi- na fa- ci- ens.

12. Er- go pre- ca- mur, ut no- stri re- a- tus a- pud cle- men- tem pa- trem fi- as in- ter- ven- trix,
    Qui te in ter- ris e- jus hic pa- ren- tem de- le- git, quem rex cae- li re- gem ge- ne- ra- vit.

13. Et te jam splen- den- tem in prae- sen- ti- a de- i,
    Te cor- de con- tri- to te fla- gi- ta- mus nos tu- o- rum ut man- so- rem vi- sce- rum

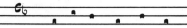

14 tu- e- ri- pre- ce- ris.

cates that no real shift of tonal level is intended, only a notational shift to indicate the use of a minor third above the final (this notational practice has been observed elsewhere in medieval chant).

The point is not just that a change occurs between the final implied at the start of the piece and the actual final established as the piece continues, but rather that the change is away from the final implied by the use of an Alleluia of the Mass, which calls into question the role of the Alleluia in the structure and genesis of the sequence.

Looking for the moment at Notker's version of the melody (each version given in the transcriptions must be qualified by further discussion), and comparing it with the Alleluia *Pascha nostrum*, one can easily see the relationship. Phrase 1 of the sequence is an approximate, though not exact, quotation of the melody over the syllables *Al-le-lu-ia*.

```
G G G   A C A      D      B D D
Alle- lu-  -  -  -  -  --  -  - - ia
F G    G   A C A C A    C E C D D
Gau- de Ma- ri- a virgo   dei genetrix
```

The quotation stops with the first note on *ia*; the following jubilis is not quoted, either in general outline, or, with one exception, in motivic detail. The jubilus turns on E and D, dropping to B, then dwells on C and D, dropping to G through A. This it does twice, then reiterates a single D, and moves through F A C and A B A to its G final. The sequence dwells instead on E and C, making a half-cadence on D, which marks the end of phrase 2. This comes twice, since the phrase is a double; the resulting articulation is absent from the jubilus. Phrase 3, another double, also rests on D, moving to it through C A. This movement is also absent from the jubilus. Leaping down a fifth, phrase 4 makes a firm approach to a normal F G G cadence. The repeat of phrase 4 is prefaced by an isolated D a fifth above, and this is the one point of resemblance to the jubilus—an important one, since the D is prominent.

(3) . . . C D D (4a) G A B♭ A F G G (4b) D G A G A F G G

In that very phrase, however, the shift to B flat (hence to G *protus*) takes place, effectively contradicting the relationship to the Alleluia as it might have been confirmed by the high D. Could the B flat be a mistake, or a modification of the original melody that crept into the MS transmission sometime between the ninth century and the twelfth, when the melody came to be fixed on a staff? This question can be better explored after we have the whole melody before us.

Phrase 5 is clearly intended as a re-intonation: slightly more prolix than phrase 1, phrase 5 resembles it in all important respects, cadencing on the D above. It is followed directly by the cadence pattern on G, as in phrase 4, only now a single—and consequently without the single high D. The effect of the re-intonation is to put everything before it (phrases 1–5) into a single long, complex unit—an opening single and two doubles, all cadencing on D, and a third double cadencing on G. Indeed, phrases 2, 3, and 4 are so short as to be more like the sub-phrases than the phrases we have met in other melodies. And if phrases 1–4 constitute one long phrase, phrases 5 and 6 constitute another, one whose melodic shape appears as a condensation or telescoping of the first unit.

From phrase 7 on, Notker's version shows little or no relationship to the Alleluia—not just because (in the version before us) of the G-*protus* final, but because of the nature of the motivic material. The Alleluia melody, to be sure, moves between D and G, and so does the sequence, but that hardly constitutes a significant point of similarity. The specific ways in which they move are different. The West-Frankish versions to be considered later, however, differ from Notker's after phrase 6, and show more relationship to the Alleluia.

Phrase 7 begins with the alternating figure found at the start of 5, but now placed on B flat/A; this figure culminates in a D and a fall through B flat to G, followed by a simple approach to the cadence. The approach recalls phrases 4 and 6, but is not identical to them, filling in as it does the distinctive skip A-F. Phrase 8, much shorter than 7, lies high and ends on D, like 5, and phrase 9 is a literal repetition of 6, so that phrases 7–9 constitute a third large phrase that departs from the preceding two only to circle back and end the same, with the same kind of "stretto" leading into the cadence pattern.

1 (D) 2a,b (D)   3a,b (D) 4a,b (G)

5a,b (D)   6 (G)

7a,b (G)   8a,b (D) 9 (G)

Notker's phrase 10 repeats his 7, but it is followed by a long new phrase so that the circle is broken, and the melody escapes to a new region. Phrase 11 descends sequentially,

11   (G D) D C D B♭ / C B♭ C G . . .

to an F-A-C figure and the cadence from 7 and 10. Then descending motion is opposed to the strong ascents in 1 and 5, serving to balance them somewhat as consequent to antecedent. Phrase 12, the longest phrase of the piece, works its way up, then down sequentially

```
              D B♭ C G
12        B♭ G B♭ C        B♭ B♭ A B♭ F G F  B♭ A C D B♭ G
   G F G
```

and ends with a figure—hardly a cadence, derived from the fall D B G in the middle of 7 (and 10). Phrase 13, starting higher than any other phrase, approaches the final with a broader sequential motion.

```
13a  D F D C B♭ A
         B♭ C D A G F G
```

The cadence has the G F G form. The repetition of the phrase is extended through an avoidance of this cadence and a short link to a repetition of the first ending.

(13a) . . . B♭ A B♭ C D A G F G
(13b) . . . B♭ A B♭ C D A G F   A G B♭ A B♭ C D A G F G

The phrase structure and specific way of making the link, all skillfully executed, recall CHRISTI HODIERNA in the version of Notker's CONGAUDENT ANGELORUM. A short single with an ornamented neume is very similar to the end of Notker's JOHANNES JESU CHRISTI—and the important point of the comparison is that that melody is unquestionably on a *protus* final, usually notated as G-*protus*.

There are two West-Frankish versions of the melody. One, with the text HÆC EST VERA REDEMPTIO, is close to Notker's version, except that it lacks Notker's phrase 7, so that the third of the three larger phrases (1–4, 5–6, 7–9) is much more telescoped.

The other West-Frankish version, BEATA TU VIRGO, also lacks Notker's phrase 7. Phrases 6 and 8 are both double, so that the single high D appears in each. Then phrase 9 is a uniquely irregular double: 9a begins with a third citation from the Alleluia, running parallel to 1 and 5 up to the C, then turning off to the cadence. Phrase 9b, however, is different—it is the phrase 9 found in HÆC EST VERA REDEMPTIO. This is only one of several peculiar features of BEATA TU VIRGO, but one that increases its relationship to the Alleluia; the others, which concern the text and its relationship to the melody, will be taken up later.

Given this melody in its three versions—GAUDE MARIA VIRGO, HÆC EST VERA REDEMPTIO, BEATA TU VIRGO—is it possible to imagine it on a G-*tetrardus* final, that is, with a B natural instead of a B flat? Could the melody originally have stood closer to Alleluia *Pascha nostrum*, and been subsequently altered? After all, the B flat appears only in twelfth-century sources; the Aquitanian sources of the tenth and eleventh centuries, while diastematic and clear, do not distinguish between tones and semitones, nor do they include any other information that would directly locate the melody on the scale.

If we read the melody (in any of the three versions) as it stands, but with a B natural, we soon become aware of the tritone relationship between the B natural and the F below the final. In phrases 1–6, the tritone appears only at the cadences in 4 and 6.

G A *B* A F G G

Here the tritone is prominent and somewhat awkward—not impossible to sing, however, and by no means to be dismissed as out of the question. (Phrase 1, it should be noted, studiously avoids B natural, although the Alleluia itself does not.)

The cadences on G-*tetrardus* in group A were frequently preceded by the long pattern

A C B C A G F G G

The underlying movement was C A G F G, or more generally, C G; here the B was a mere neighbor-note to the C, and no sense of tritone relationship developed. We could say that the difference between these two forms—one emphasizing the third above the final (B), the other emphasizing the fourth above (C)—could be taken as a point of distinction between *protus* and *tetrardus*, except for one further circumstance. It is known from other studies that earlier, before roughly 1000, B natural was a much more prominent pitch in G-*tetrardus* than it was later, being used, for example, as a reciting note *instead of C* in certain Gregorian pieces or psalm tones.[6] Some time after 900, pressure—whether from taste or performance is not known—was exerted to change the B's that functioned in these ways into C's. As a result, the C emphasized at the top of a stable fourth above the final cannot automatically be assumed to be the normal thing; and the fact that a shift was taking place in the tenth century, at the very time our sequences were being notated in the immediate predecessors of the Aquitanian MSS, makes it at least possible to imagine a state in which the cadence pattern in phrases 4 and 6, with a B natural, would have been acceptable.

Another bit of evidence might point the same way—or in just the opposite way. Hæc DIES QUAM EXCELSUS uses a figure not unlike that towards the end of phrase 7 of Notker's GAUDE MARIA:

GAUDE MARIA 7 . . . C D B G B A   G F G G
HÆC DIES   . . . C D B G   A G G F G G

The figure is perfectly at home in the G-*tetrardus* of HÆC DIES. Why not in GAUDE MARIA? But it could be objected that the two cases are different precisely in the use or avoidance of the B natural.

Two instances of prominent tritones in the melody could be supported by analogous passages from the Gregorian repertory. In GAUDE MARIA phrase 13, the descent

D F D C B A B . . .

is nowhere near as strong an emphasis of the tritone as the Antiphon *Exaudi nos* from the Ash Wednesday office of Imposition of Ashes.

D B D DFFF DC C CED D
Exaudi nos . . . mi- se- ri- cor- di- a tu-   a

Nor is this an isolated instance. And phrase 14 of GAUDE MARIA is no more awkward than the end of Alleluia *Magnus Dominus*.

Alleluia   . . . A   C D A G *F* GG   *B* G F AA G
GAUDE MARIA 13 . . . A B C D A G F G (14) G B G F GAB G

In fact, the whole approach to the ending is so similar one is tempted to look to this Alleluia (in *tetrardus* authentic) as a source for this phrase of the sequence. The only problem here is determining the date of the Alleluia, which is absent from the earliest Mass-books, not only those of Hesbert's *Antiphonale missarum sextuplex*, but also those with notation, St. Gall MS 359, Laon MS 239, Chartres MS 47; the Alleluia appears regularly only in

6. See J. Gajard, "Les recitations modales des 3e et 4e Modes," *Etudes grégoriennes* I (1954), p. 31; D. Ferretti, *Esthétique grégorienne* I (Paris 1938), pp. 136, 303, 307.

sources from around 1000 and after, and shows great variation in its pitch structure.[7] Even assuming the sequence is derived from Alleluia *Magnus dominus*, this hardly clarifies the relationship to Alleluia *Pascha nostrum*, which is an entirely different melody, nor to the Alleluia in general.

There are prominent tritones in GAUDE MARIA, however, for which no support can be mustered. If the original melody were to be read in G-*tetrardus*, then these tritones would have to be emended; and one would have to assume that the readings responsible for the tritones date from the time when the original melody was shifted to G-*protus*. The instances occur at the start of HÆC EST VERA REDEMPTIO 9 (and Notker's 7) and twice in the last half of 11.

HÆC EST VERA REDEMPTIO
9 *F B A B A C D . . .*
11 *. . . B B A B F G F B A C D B G*

More important than such difficulties of detail in asserting an original G-*tetrardus* final are the general difficulties that arise. Granted that the inflections of this melody could be explained by invoking the upward shift from B to C, what about all the other G-*tetrardus* pieces, with their strong C's a fourth above the final in the long cadence pattern? It would have to be further stipulated either that their cadence patterns were all originally different from the way they are preserved in the sources, or that this particular melody alone was affected by the shift because it was significantly older than the rest. Recourse could even be had to the melody title "Paschalis antica" in MS 1084.

To that line of argument, which can be extended indefinitely, overcoming all obstacles, there is no effective direct rebuttal; but such an argument eventually becomes unbelievable simply through its own elaboration and the way it must reinterpret whole categories of evidence to explain relatively limited problems. The need for such arguments did not arise in dealing with the first group of melodies, those not explicitly related to an Alleluia. Only now—in dealing with an Alleluia quotation—do we find ourselves engaged in such far-ranging speculation. The immediate stimulus is the apparent contradiction between the G-*tetrardus* implied by the Alleluia quotation and the G-*protus* indicated by the later sources and by the internal structure of the melody. Actually, there is another, more decisive stimulus, an implicit one; for we could deal with the apparent contradiction more simply than we have. The Alleluia quotation carries with it, for us at least, the implication that the G-*tetrardus* of the Alleluia is the element to be accepted without question, while the G-*protus* of the sequence has to be explained or even edited out of existence. That implication, in turn, rests upon very broad convictions about the role of Gregorian chant in the Frankish musical scene, about the role of authority in the early Middle Ages. Such issues are very important, but the point is, they are issues, subject to eventual substantiation or

---

7. Alleluia *Magnus dominus* was eventually assigned to the 8th Sunday after Pentecost. Schlager *Them.Kat.* 409, *Alleluia-Melodien* I, pp. 298, 680 with varying pitch structure and final (one of the earlier sources is Paris B.N.lat. MS 1084). The MSS referred to are published as follows: St. Gall MS 359 facs. in *Paléographie musicale*, series 2, vol. 2; Laon MS 239 facs. in *Paléographie musicale*, vol. 10; Chartres MS 47 facs. in *Paléographie musicale*, vol. 11.

rejection (no matter how strong our present convictions may be); these issues provide no ready answers such as might serve as axioms with which we could resolve the questions before us. We are not in a position to say that *because* the Alleluia quotation was a given unchangeable element, all other features (such as a G-*protus* final) must be reconciled to it. The major premise is in doubt.

Nor does an objective examination of the art work itself, I think, encourage us to proceed as if the Alleluia quotation were the most stable element. Whether we consider HÆC EST VERA REDEMPTIO or Notker's GAUDE MARIA, the shape of the whole melody is such that the Alleluia quotation is an open-ended element functioning in an introductory capacity (phrases 1, 5; in BEATA TU, also phrase 9a). The cadential element—very consistent in phrases 4, 6, 8, 9, 10—is peculiar to the sequence, not a quotation from the Alleluia. Whatever the final of the piece may be, it owes its finality to these cadences and to their approaches, not to the Alleluia intonation.

Furthermore, the phrases in the latter part of the piece have a closed, song-like shape strongly oriented to the cadence, which gives them a high degree of stability compared to the intonation. In phrase 7 of GAUDE MARIA the first five notes, whose inflection (F B♭ A B♭ A) still recalls the continuing alternation of pitches in phrase 1, are followed by a return and partial closure on G (C D B♭ G); that much of the phrase seems to function as an antecedent, the approach to the cadence then being a consequent.

7　F B♭ A B♭ A C D B♭ G / B♭ A G F G G

The parallel phrase in the West-Frankish HÆC EST VERA REDEMPTIO, phrase 9, is the same except that the fall to G at the end of the "antecedent" is not filled in by B.

10　F B♭ A B♭ A C D G / B♭ A G F G G

Because of the shape of the whole phrase, the fall D G does not sound as much like the single D in phrase 4—nor like the one in the Alleluia jubilus; rather we hear the return to the G.

Phrase 10 of HÆC EST VERA REDEMPTIO, because of its sequential construction, also falls into smaller units, even though these are not bounded by internal cadences nor stand in an antecedent-consequent relationship.

HÆC EST VERA REDEMPTIO
10　D D C D A / B♭ A B♭ G A F / A C A B♭ A G F G G

There is ambiguity about the end of the second group: one could understand it as B♭ A B♭ G /, everything else then belonging to the approach to the cadence. Such a grouping would reflect the sequential, that is, the melodic construction, while the first grouping proposed is based rather on a rhythmic sense. The ambiguity seems deliberate; that is, the intent seems to be to elide the second and third elements to increase continuity and overcome the effect of the melodic sequence. But however the phrase is parsed, its shorter units seem strongly operative.

Similarly, phrase 11 unfolds its long line in a series of smaller units.

	(1)	(2)	(3)	(4)
11	G F G,	B♭ G B♭ C D C B♭ C G,	B♭ B♭ A B♭ F G F,	B♭ A C D B♭ G

Here the sequential repetition a step lower (first ending on G, then on F, groups 2 and 3) is a strong element in the articulation of the phrase, in spite of variations around the element used in the sequence itself.

(2) B♭ G B♭ C D CB♭ C G
      B♭ C A B♭ F G F

Phrase 12 seems to have the strongest approach to its final, even though it is the phrase that swings furthest away.

12   D F D C B♭ A B♭ C D A G F G

Here the antecedent-consequent phrasing is very clear, the A at the end of the antecedent very audible as a half-close a whole-tone above the eventual final. For this reason, the avoidance of the close in 13b, with the extension and reiterated approach to the cadence, is remarkably clear in its operation (precisely this feature is lacking from the similar passage in Alleluia *Magnus dominus*).

All of these shapes work together to produce a remarkably coordinated melodic construction; and assuming a B flat, the construction so firmly revolves around G-*protus* that by the end of the piece any sense of G-*tetrardus* that might have been associated with the Alleluia quotation has been effectively removed. This by itself is not an argument for the B flat, of course, but it does indicate that forces other than the Alleluia are at work shaping the melody, and that the Alleluia quotation could well be understood to have some function other than that of defining the final or tone of the melody. There is no compelling reason—from the internal construction of the melody—for thinking of the conflict between G-*tetrardus* and G-*protus* as a serious one, or as a basis for re-interpreting the structure of the melody (to say nothing of the whole early repertory). And from a broader point of view, other pieces in the early repertory have consistently tended to use a phrase 1 that is distinct in nature and function from the rest of the melody; in ʜᴀᴄ ᴇsᴛ sᴀɴᴄᴛᴀ there was the possibility that phrase 1 was in an F realm distinct from the G final. ᴄʜʀɪsᴛɪ ʜᴏᴅɪᴇʀɴᴀ, of course, provided a much more drastic instance of ending on a tonal locus different from that of the beginning.

Can we even be certain about the Alleluia quotation itself? The quotation is, of course, not literal.

Alleluia	G G G AC AD BD	D
Sequence	G A G AC AC AC E C D D	

The sequence incipit turns thrice on AC, instead of once each on AC, AD, and BD; and concludes after a rise to E with a sequence-cadence on D, where the Alleluia has no cadence. Husmann advanced the theory that connections to the Alleluia were in general closer if the sequence incipit was compared to that point towards the end of the Alleluia verse where the incipit returned (in Alleluias where this occurred), because there the pattern

Example 7.

Hæc est vera redemptio	Gaude maria (Notker)	Beata tu virgo
1^{13}	1^{12}	1^{9}
2^{8}_{8}	2^{8}_{8}	2^{8}_{8}
3^{6}_{6}	3^{6}_{6}	3^{6}_{6}
4^{7}_{8}	4^{7}_{8}	4^{6}_{6}
5^{15}_{15}	5^{15}_{15}	5^{13}_{14}
6^{7}	6^{7}	6^{6}_{6}
	7^{15}_{15}	
7^{9}_{9}	8^{9}	7^{11}_{12}
8^{7}	9^{7}	8^{6}_{6}
9^{14}_{14}	10^{15}_{15}	9^{13}_{17}
10^{21}_{21}	11^{20}_{20}	10^{18}_{19}
11^{24}_{24}	12^{24}_{24}	11^{20}_{16}
12^{13}_{23}	13^{13}_{22}	12^{16}_{24}
13^{9}	14^{6}	13^{7}

of pitches was subject to variation, and (Husmann felt) more apt to correspond to the sequence.[8] He also had recourse to other Alleluias using similar incipits. In practice his procedures seem to have the net effect of searching out the pattern of pitches—wherever it may be found—that will best demonstrate a relationship to a given sequence. On the basis of such procedures, Husmann claimed that the sequence was indeed categorically related to the Alleluia, but to a state of Alleluia development characterized by change and fluidity, before the Alleluia melodies were fixed in form and repertory. This is another instance of a theory that does not hesitate to move heaven and earth to prove a point. But aside from its prodigal means, the theory evacuates the relationship of sequence to Alleluia of much of its traditional significance: by loosening the circumstances of the relationship to the point of a mere sharing of common idioms, the theory denies to the relationship the nature

8. H. Husmann, "Alleluia, Vers, und Sequenz," *Annales musicologiques* IV (1956), pp. 19–53.

of a reference to an official standard of a type that would have a compelling or obligatory effect on the whole structure, or liturgical use, of the sequence.

The discussion of the Alleluia relationship in general will have to be continued in a separate chapter; the point here is that this sequence, as it stands, is not an exact quotation of the Alleluia—in the form in which the Alleluia is recorded in the earliest musical manuscripts of the ninth and tenth centuries. And to compare this sequence incipit with anything except Alleluia *Pascha nostrum* would weaken the presumed relationship rather than strengthen it. Does not the tenth-century name for the sequence, "Pascha nostrum," constitute evidence for the relationship? If one can appeal to that, it would seem equally fair to appeal to the other tenth-century name, "Cignea," which has no perceptible relationship to the Alleluia or to anything else. Which name is right? And if one is right, why is there the other?

Of the two early West-Frankish texts, HÆC EST VERA REDEMPTIO is much closer to the plan of Notker's GAUDE MARIA. BEATA TU in this as in other respects is a work *sui generis*. As the syllable count diagram shows (Example 7), there are persistent similarities in syllable count between GAUDE MARIA and HÆC EST VERA, equally persistent differences with respect to BEATA TU VIRGO.

Another point of difference among the three texts is the number of phrases: Notker's plan has one more (14 instead of 13), the extra one being GAUDE MARIA 7—as already discussed in connection with the melody. A third point of difference is the doubling of phrases 6 and 8 (Notker's 9): these are single in HÆC EST VERA REDEMPTIO and GAUDE MARIA, double in BEATA TU VIRGO.

HÆC EST VERA REDEMPTIO is a difficult text—partly, perhaps, because its author was not yet completely at ease in the techniques peculiar to this art form, but partly because he chose to use relatively elaborate language and images. In either case the occasional awkwardness is not to be ascribed to indifference or expediency; rather, the text seems to have an (admittedly indemonstrable) air of being an early one. It recalls ECCE VICIT, LAUDES DEO, and CLARA GAUDIA in spirit and technique.

HÆC EST VERA REDEMPTIO sings of the Easter triumph, referring to the events of the Resurrection and especially the Redemption in the past tense. The opening period is long and complex: it extends—as does the melodic construction—from 1 through 4; but its syntactical articulations are in counterpoint to the musical ones.

(1)   Hæc est vera redemptio et celsa festa!
(2a)   Mors sanguinum triumphata,
(2b)   monumentum margarita (3a) redditur:
rutilat (3b) clara atque digna (4a) necnon tota fulgida,
         (4b) quem primum cernit Maria.

Line 1 (which does coincide with the musical unit) is an announcement of today's festivity. Line 2a seems to be some kind of nominative absolute; at any rate the construction here seems loose, more acclamatory than discursive in nature. Line 2b runs on into 3a, the short textual units interlocking with the short musical ones. Perhaps the best way to understand the arrangement is to hear the short musical units as relatively weak articulations in a long phrase that encompasses the tumult of acclamation, attribute, image, and report conveyed by the text. Here in particular the author's ambition and intent outran his execution, but the intent was a lofty one.

Lines 5a,b and the single 6 all form one period, consisting of two roughly parallel units both focussed on the image of the body on the Cross. The subject of the second unit, *insignis victoria*, is placed at the end,

(5a) Vexillum crucis jam sublimatur dicata membra:
(5b)   agni cruore manantis latere est redempta (6) insignis victoria.

so that it occupies the single melodic phrase 6, giving it, too, the quality of an acclamation. Otherwise, lines 5a and b sit more neatly in their melodic frames than was the case in phrases 2 to 4: the overall construction clearly sets out an isolated single (1), a complex opening group (2–4), then settles down into a regular double punctuated by a short single (5–6). This section of the piece is concluded by the short double 7 and the single 8.

(7a) Per lignum
            quod jam notaverat,
(7b)   diluens nostra facinora,
(8)   contulit remedia.

These are set to one syntactic period, more complex again and without a parallelism; but *remedia* is placed in 8 to rhyme with, and complement, *victoria* in 6.

That much is centered on the Cross. The next lines refer to the Harrowing of Hell. Lines 9a and b are parallel in chiasmus.

(9a)   Et hujus mundi jam principem *bellans*
          alligat:
(9b)   Inferni claustra *demollit*,
                  abstrahens spolia.

In 9a verb follows participle, in 9b participle follows verb. The defeat of Hell is continued in the more difficult lines 10a,b.

(10a) Ade soluit culpa, labuerat esca obnoxius in hac aerumna:
(10b) Perducit ad vitam quam expulit culpa et collocat in caelestia.

Man is cleansed of guilt and restored to the heavenly kingdom. Pulling the couplet together is the contrast of *aerumna* (desolation) and *celestia* at the ends of the lines.

Lines 11a,b are a pair of exhortations—"let us refurbish" (*repingamus*), "let us rejoice" (*exultemus*). Line 11a is a relatively complex string of dependent elements, put together with more than a passing thought to sonority.

(11a) Voce obnixa omnis mente prona
            pectoris archam aulam repingamus almam:

(11b) laudem boando

exultemus in hac sollempnia paschali sacra melodia.

The opposition of *obnixa* (resolutely) to *obnoxius* (guilty) in 10a makes up for the redictum *culpa* in 10a and 5.

Line 12a is an exclamation—not so frequent in these pieces.

12a   O mira domini est misericordia!
12b   Ut nos liberaret se patris su-

i victimavit immaculata hostia,

13   Et regnat per secula. Amen.

Falling easily under its musical unit, the exclamation is followed by its explanatory clause in 12b—a more complex construction that reaches its main verb (*victimavit*) only on the other side of the point where the melody avoids the cadence of 12a (*su-/i*). With equal care, the sonorities in the extension,

se patris sui victimavit

are chosen to avoid dulling the assonance

misericordia . . . hostia

that marks the cadences, while still offering the preparation

victimavit immaculata.

The cadences in HÆC EST VERA REDEMPTIO show a concern for consistency without a full realization of it. In general the normal pitch patterns on G—that is, at the ends of the larger periods 4, 6, 8, 9, 10, 12—are given proparoxytones, but with some obvious exceptions.

4a	fúlgida	9a	álligat	10b	celéstia
b	María	9b	spólia	12a	misericórdia
6	victória	10a	aerúmna	12b	hóstia
8	remédia				

With even more exception, the other cadences tend to be paroxytone.

1	fésta	3b	dígna	7b	facínora
2a	triumpháta	5a	mémbra	11a	álmam
2b	margaríta	5b	redémpta	11b	melódia (melodía?)
3a	rútilat	7a	notáverat		

These other cadences differ from the normal one either in location (on D—phrases 1, 3, 5, 7) or in form (phrases 2, 11).

In Notker's GAUDE MARIA, on the contrary, the cadences are almost perfectly systematized. With the exception of *repléta* in 3b, all the normal pitch patterns (F G G or C D D) are set proparoxytone; and the other cadences in 2 and 12 (HÆC EST VERA REDEMPTIO 11) are paroxytone. In general, Notker's text shows the control characteristic of his mature work.

GAUDE MARIA VIRGO, "Rejoice, Virgin Mary!" seems to us like just one of a host of such acclamatory greetings. Actually, the host came afterwards; in Notker's time there were relatively few models for his incipit.[9] The most prominent is the text for a responsory used at Matins of Marian feasts (Purification, Annunciation, Assumption, Nativity):

Gaude, Maria Virgo, cunctas haereses sola interemisti in universo mundo.

An alternate reading for *in universo mundo* is *Sancta Dei Genetrix*; and another, much longer, alternate ending is found in one of Hesbert's six sources (Paris B.N. lat. MS 12584, Antiphonale of St. Maur-les-Fossés, 12th century):

interemisti, quae Gabrielis archangeli dictis credidisti,
    dum virgo Deum et hominem genuisti,
    et post partum virgo inviolata permansisti,
                  alleluia.

This version was widespread, appearing for example in the twelfth-century Worcester Antiphonale with the long melisma for *Inviolata* and the prosula (text underlay) *Inviolata integra et casta*.[10] None of that has to do with Notker; but his text with its *Gaude!* joined the original version of the responsory as an early representative of what came to be a very large medieval repertory.[11]

GAUDE MARIA VIRGO is partly a song of praise for the Virgin, partly the Christmas cycle of the *Heilsgeschichte*. Lines 2a,b, 3a,b, and 4a,b lead up to the Incarnation from the Annunciation. Lines 5a,b tell of the Nativity, lines 7a,b, 8a,b, and 9 of the Circumcision, an event commemorated on the Octave of Christmas (1 January), which was observed with special honor for the Virgin. Lines 10a,b tell of the gifts of the Magi, usually associated with Epiphany; line 11a seems to refer to the twelve-year-old Jesus in the Temple, an account read on the Sunday after Epiphany; and 11b refers to the Marriage at Cana, the subject of the Gospel for the Second Sunday after Epiphany.

In rhetorical plan Notker followed his presumed model, HÆC EST VERA REDEMPTIO, closely. Line 1 is the acclamatory exhortation.

(1)   Gaude, Maria, virgo dei genetrix!

As such, it stands alone, although what follows is dependent on it. Phrases 2 and 3 are not bound as closely by syntax as in HÆC EST VERA REDEMPTIO, but the continuity of sense ac-

---

9. R. J. Hesbert, *Corpus Antiphonalium Officii* (*Rerum Ecclesiasticarum Documenta*. Series maior. Fontes VII–IX): I—"Cursus romanus"; II—"Cursus monasticus"; III—Editio critica (Rome 1963–68). See III, 2924, thence the appearances in the MSS used in I and II.

10. *Paléographie musicale*, vol. 12, p. 271.

11. See G. G. Meersseman, O.P., *Der hymnos Akathistos im Abendland* (*Spicilegium Friburgense* 2, 3, 1958–60); I—Akathistos Akoluthie; II—Gruss Psalter, Gaude Andachten. This does not, however, deal with the early sequences.

complishes much the same thing, and Notker clearly intended 1–4 as a larger unit, just as in the model.

(1)   Gaude, Maria, virgo dei genetrix,
(2a)   quae promissis Gabrihelis (2b) spe devota credidisti:
(3a)   Numine tu sancti spiritus repleta,
(4a)   gignis clausa filium
(4b)   qui mundi regit machinam.

Lines 5a,b and 6 also form a unit.

(5a)   In tuo partu ad turrim gregis canunt angeli,
(5b)   quippe jacende suo rectore in praesepio
(6)   urbis Bethlemiticae.

Phrase 7 is the extra one (with respect to HÆC EST VERA REDEMPTIO); it seems from the text that Notker needed the extra music to accommodate the relatively discursive treatment he wished to give the Circumcision. In particular he is concerned—as he often is—to point up a moral; here it is done by way of the paradox that the Judge and Healer, who alone (with the Father and the Holy Spirit) can circumcise our sin, was himself presented for circumcision by his mother.

(7a)   Te nomen Jesu edocuit caelestis nuntius,
(7b)   quod circumciso imponeres intacta filio,
(8a)   qui scit solus nostra crimina (8b) cum patre sanctoque spiritu (9) rite circumcidere.

Also familiar in Notker's style is the series of acts or attributes linked by reiterated *tu* or related forms.

(3a) . . . tu . . .	(10a) . . . tuas . . .	(12b) . . . te . . .
(5a) . . . tua . . .	(11a) Te . . .	(13a) . . . te . . .
(7a) Te . . .	(11b) Te . . .	(13b) Te . . . te . . . tuorum . . .

In 11a, *dolentem gloriam* is a telling expression.

Phrase 12 (HÆC EST VERA REDEMPTIO 11) is the exhortation introduced by *Ergo*, parallel to the exhortations in the presumed model. And even though Notker found it hard to write anything as forthright and luminous as the West-Frankish *O mira domini misericordia!* he still managed to keep 13a reserved for the image of the Virgin in glory, untouched by the humble petition addressed to that image.

(13a) Et te—jam splendentem in praesentia dei—
(13b)   te corde contrito flagitamus nos,
              tuorum ut mansorem viscerum tueri preceris.

BEATA TU VIRGO is most distinguished by its refrain,

O alma Maria, O sancta Maria!

Beata tu virgo

1 Be- a- ta tu, vir- go Ma- ri- a,

2 Ma- ter Chri- sti glo- ri- o- sa 3 Ni- mi- um cre- du- la
De- i- que ple- na gra- ti- a Ga- bri- e- lis ver- ba 4 O al- ma Ma- ri- a, O sanc- ta Ma- ri- a!

5 De te e- nim dix- it E- ze- chi- el pro- phe- ta Qui- a
e- ras clau- sa in do- mo domi- ni por- ta 6 O al- ma Ma- ri- a, O sanc- ta Ma- ri- a!

7 Jam tri- pu- di- as cae- le- sti- a re- gna An- ge-
lo- rum su- per cho- rus ex- al- ta- ta 8 O al- ma Ma- ri- a, O sanc- ta Ma- ri- a!

9 Pe- ti- mus er- go tu- a sanc- ta suf- fra- gi- a: In- ter- ce- de pro no- bis ad e- um qui est sae- cu- li vi- ta.

10 Te e- nim ex- pec- tat sup- plex i- sta et hu- mi- lis ple- bi- cu- la
Ut tu- is ful- ta pre- ci- bus sem- per con- va- le- scat ad me- li- o- ra

11 O be- a- ta De- i ge- ne- trix vir- go Ma- ri- a sem- per glo- ri- o- sa
Quae so- la di- gna fu- i- sti por- ta- re sae- cu- li vi- ta

12 No- stris er- go quae- su- mus me- mo- ra- re pre- ces se- du- la
Ut u- na si- mul te- cum me- re- a- mur gau- de- re per ae- vum in cae- le- sti- a re- gna,

13 o Be- a- ta Ma- ri- a!

(with frequent variants in the several sources). The very fact of a refrain—a textual one—is remarkable for a prose; and the wording of it, too, is unusual, although by no means unique, for HÆC EST VERA REDEMPTIO included an apostrophe in line 12a. Von den Steinen takes this text to be yet another instance of moderate, mild language in early Marian literature—indeed, he considers its tone to be an important index of an early date.[12]

As the most obvious explicit textual means of organization encountered in the pieces studied so far, the refrain of BEATA TU VIRGO might seem naturally to indicate that in this case text was conceived first, then melody constructed to suit. Here, however, we can benefit from acquaintance with other early pieces: the occurrence of musical homeoteleuton has been frequent in the early repertory in the form of cadence patterns and approaches to the cadences; and at the higher levels, too, suggestions of musical refrains have been felt in the absence of textual ones. Granting several differences in the exact way the melodic return occurs in this repertory, still the refrain in 4, 6, and 8 can be understood as a textual highlighting of the return of the cadence pattern. True, it is not a pattern appended to each member of relatively long regular doubles; instead, it comes in a double by itself. In BEATA TU VIRGO this happens each time (4, 6, 8) not just the first (4) as in the other versions, where 6 and 8 are singles. Even so, the fact that a cadence pattern is involved places this refrain within the larger context of the use of cadence patterns in the repertory as a whole.

As for the fact that the refrain returns literally as a double each time, it should be noted that in MS 1871, which frequently presents conflated or revised versions, HÆC EST VERA REDEMPTIO adds text to double the singles at 6 and 8, using apostrophes in apparent imitation of those in BEATA TU VIRGO. In view of this fact, the doubling in BEATA TU VIRGO itself can be understood as a filling-out of a construction that originally included singles at 6 and 8. There would be, in other words, no unobstructed line of argument starting from the refrain as a textual element and leading to the form of the melody, or starting from BEATA TU VIRGO and leading to the other versions.

The rest of the text gives the impression of having been put together out of well-known phrases—an effect we have not encountered elsewhere save in the expanded version of GAUDE EIA, and in REX NOSTRAS, where it was associated with a litany-like construction. Von den Steinen considered the "half-Marian" quality of GAUDE EIA and REX NOSTRAS to be characteristic of early sequences.[13] The interpolations in GAUDE EIA, however, and the possible interpolation in REX NOSTRAS (that is, the Marian acclamation itself) put the "half-Marian" quality in a different light. In any case, it seems that Marian expressions got into the sequence repertory only by fits and starts, and that would apply to BEATA TU VIRGO too, even if no interpolations are involved here. Notker's texts, GAUDE VIRGO MARIA, STIRPE MARIA REGIA, and CONCENTU PARILI are more forthright, seeming to show a second stage of development.

The opening period (1–4) consists of epigrammatic attributes, not entirely dissimilar in subject from Notker's text, nor in technique from the West-Frankish HÆC EST VERA REDEMPTIO.

12. *Anfänge*, vol. 41, pp. 37ff.
13. *Anfänge*, vol. 41, pp. 40–42.

(1)   Beata tu, virgo Maria,
(2a)   mater Christi gloriosa,
(2b)   deique plena gratia,
(3a)   nimium credula Gabrielis verba.
(4a)   O alma Maria!
(4b)   O sancta Maria!

(Notker)

(1)   Gaude, Maria, virgo dei genitrix,
(2a)   quae promissis Gabrihelis (2b) spe devota credidisti;
(3a)   numine tu sancti (3b) spiritus repleta,
(4a)   gignis clausa filium
(4b)   qui mundi regit machinam

Lines 5a,b are devoted to the prefiguration in the prophet Ezechiel.

(5a)   De te enim dixit Ezechiel propheta,
(5b)   quia eras clausa in domo domini porta.
(6a)   O alma Maria!
(6b)   O sancta Maria!

Here the idea of virginity (*clausa*) echoes Notker's text in line 4a. Lines 7a,b juxtapose, abruptly, the image of Mary exalted above the angels, thereby Queen of heaven, even if not yet so named.

(7a)   Jam tripudias caelestia regna,
(7b)   angelorum super chorus exaltata.
(8a)   O alma Maria!
(8b)   O sancta Maria!

Lines 9a,b, introduced by *ergo*, present a remarkably unadorned petition.

(9a)   Petimus ergo tua sancta suffragia:
(9b)   intercede pro nobis ad eum qui est seculi vita.

The language recalls those compact versicles of intercession common in the office. Lines 10a,b contain another petition—and lines 11a,b through 12a,b yet another.

(10a)   Te enim expectat supplex ista et humilis plebicula,
(10b)   ut avis fulta precibus semper convalescat ad meliora.
(11a)   O beata dei genetrix virgo Maria semper gloriosa!
(11b)   quae sola digna fuisti portare seculi vita,
(12a)   nostris ergo quaesumus memorare preces sedula,
(12b)   ut una simul tecum mereamur gaudere per aevum in caelestia regna.
(13)   O beata Maria!

Lines 11a,b are an acclamation and attribute prefatory to the petition, which is introduced in 12a with another *ergo*. Aside from the fact that the specific rhetorical disposition does not coincide with the one found in HÆC EST VERA REDEMPTIO and Notker's GAUDE MARIA, where the analogous construction came in 11 (Notker's 12), the reiteration of petitions and the redictum *ergo* betray a lack of rhetorical coordination unusual in early proses. And the language throughout 11a,b and 12a,b continues to sound centonized,[14] further, *gloriosa* (11a) is redictum to 2a (*mater Christi gloriosa*), *seculi vita* to 9a (*seculi vita*), and *O beata dei genetrix Maria* could be criticized as a casual use of language that elsewhere in the prose is employed more strictly in the refrain structure and in the closing echo of the incipit—*Beata tu virgo Maria . . . O beata Maria!*—a device that is analogous to Notker's *Johannes Jesu . . . Johannes Christi care.*

Indeed, the words of this prose seem to have belonged so strongly together in small pre-existing units that the compiler was loath to alter them by paraphrase to fit the melody exactly. This, at least, seems to be the reason why the piece is neumatic to a degree unique in the early repertory. Several instances of inexact parallelism (5a,b; 7a,b; 9a,b; 10a,b; 11a,b; 12a,b) seem to be due to the same cause. This does not mean that relationships of music and text are defective; on the contrary, the arranger has succeeded in making a sensitive adaptation; but he has done so on a line-by-line, word-by-word basis, without much relationship to the style of other pieces—or of the other versions of this piece.

Another version of BEATA TU VIRGO shows up in the tenth-century manuscript from Mainz (London B.M. Add. 19768), as SANCTA TU VIRGO MARIA. This version was made by someone with Notker's GAUDE MARIA before him; he followed its melody closely, adding Notker's 7, and revising the text of BEATA TU VIRGO to fit. He also eliminated the non-syllabic settings and other irregularities, and reduced 6 and 8 to singles—*alma virgo Maria*. In most cases he simply rearranged the words of BEATA TU VIRGO, going so far as to move lines 11a,b to phrase 10; but for his phrase 12 he added a new couplet.

12a Primo fidelis verbo Gabrielis quae stella maris clara semper nominaris
  b Quae clarum mundo lumen protulisti atque post partum virgo in aevum permansisti.

Could this have been the original version, imitated by Notker in his GAUDE MARIA, and corrupted in the Toul fragment and the Aquitanian sources to BEATA TU VIRGO? The text of SANCTA TU VIRGO is clean and consequent, and the plan corresponds to Notker's in detail as well as design. But the internal rhymes in 12 (the couplet peculiar to this version)—*fidelis, Gabrielis, maris, nominaris; permansisti*—are heavy for the early repertory, and speak rather for the tenth century. And now we can observe a clear connection to the expanded version of the responsory GAUDE MARIA VIRGO quoted on p. 255 (as Blume suggested).[15] These sonorities, incidentally, contrast strongly with the a-assonance shared with BEATA TU VIRGO, and prevailing here except where the text differs.

The position of BEATA TU VIRGO itself is more debatable. Conceivably, some of its features—its irregular melodic construction, its heavy and irregular neumatic (as opposed to syllabic) style, its cento-like text, its proximity to verse through its refrain (unique among

14. Back of 11, *Quae sola digna fuisti portare saeculi,* may stand Venantius' line from *Pange lingua* (*Anal.hymn.* 50, p. 71) stanza 10: *Sola digna tu fuisti ferre pretium saeculi.*
  15. *Anal.hymn.* 53, p. 195.

early proses), and the relationship to the Alleluia—any or all of these features might be used in support of an argument for an early dating or for the distinction of being the original text for this melody. But in most cases, I think, the motivation for using such arguments would be the belief that the sequence was created by underlaying text to a melisma —but that is a belief, not a fact, and its application in this and other cases leads only to circularity. The fact is, BEATA TU VIRGO stands off to one side; even if it were shown to be early, it would still be difficult to show how development led from there to the features that characterize the rest of the early repertory.

XIV

"Justus ut palma minor"

T HE SECOND Alleluia-sequence to be considered raises question at least as complex as those encountered in the study of the first. Because of the difficulty of determining a West-Frankish model, and also the relatively consistent use of the melody title that refers to the Alleluia *Justus ut palma*, we can profitably use that melody title here. We should begin by considering the melody, and we can do that most easily be referring to Notker's setting, DILECTE DEO.

The Alleluia quotation in phrase 1 is, again, only approximate, not exact.[1] There are slight variants among the Eastern and Western sources for the sequence incipit, but in the ending of phrase 1 they always agree on D, not the ending on G a fourth higher that characterizes the incipit of the Alleluia *Justus ut palma* (the final of the Alleluia is D).

Sequence	C	D	F	D	E	F	G	F	E	F	D
Alleluia	C	D	F	D	E	F	G	F	E	F	G	G
	Al-	le-	-	-	-lu-	-	-	-	-	-	-	ia

The melody, as Notker used it, is distinguished by many short phrases of ten to sixteen syllables. Only one phrase, 7, is markedly longer, with 24 syllables. The short phrases are grouped into larger units by a variety of means.

Phrase 1, with its neume and alleluia quotation, stands apart from the following phrases, as usual. Phrase 2 begins with the same kind of alternating figure (G A G A) seen in HÆC EST VERA REDEMPTIO, in phrases that hinted at the Alleluia melody; here, too, phrase 2 stands closer to the Alleluia than most of the others, even if the relationship cannot be made as specific as one might wish. The distinctive figure

2a(b) . . . B♭ A G (B♭ A G) E F E D

---

1. Alleluia *Justus ut palma* is used for feasts of a martyr or confessor, also for John Baptist; Schlager, *Them.Kat.* no. 38; *Alleluia-Melodien* I, pp. 276, 567.

moving through the tritone B♭-E, might have been inspired by the melisma in the Alleluia verse over *sicut cedrus*. The three notes B♭ A G appear twice in 2b, making a slightly irregular double of the type used so persistently in Notker's summi triumphum regis; the phrase itself recalls phrase 4 of scalam ad caelos with its *auream lauream*, set to the three notes G F E. The beginning of phrase 2 on G, followed by its return to D, help give the phrase an appearance of being a consequent to an opening antecedent.

Phrase 3 has quite a different effect: short, strongly focussed, it ends on A with an unmistakable half-cadence. Something about it says "verse" instead of "prose"—perhaps the clearly outlined melodic movement through the notes A-D-C-A, perhaps the regular rhythmic movement

A G A / D A / C B G / A A.

The same epigrammatic quality is found in the next phrase, 4, except that while phrase 3 is a single melodic impulse, phrase 4 falls into two distinct parts, the second being in approximate sequence to the first.

    4   A C A G F G
                F G A E D C D

With its D final, descending sequence, and sub-phrase structure, phrase 4 provides the close to the open ending of 3, and rounds off the opening section that contains phrases 1–4.

Phrases 5 and 6 seem to be grouped together as another antecedent-consequent pair. Phrase 5 begins on A and falls to the final, D; phrase 6 answers it mirror-fashion, starting on C and rising. Phrase 5 is one melodic impulse, while phrase 6 has two distinct parts due to the repetition.

    6   C D F G F D,
         C D F G F,   A F G F D

Both phrases 5 and 6 fall to the final D from the F above, a weaker kind of cadence in comparison to the normal kinds found at the ends of phrases 3 and 4.

Phrase 7 stands by itself—a long, arching phrase, without a clearly articulated subphrase structure. Even here, smaller melodic groupings can be felt, but they are more obvious in the analogous phrases of the other versions of the melody; Notker's seems intended to emphasize the continuity of this longest phrase—rising smoothly to A, falling back to C below the final, then rising and falling again more quickly. A break, if there is one, would come after the low C in mid-phrase approached through the downward motion G-C, D-C.

    7   D C D F E D F G F A F E G C D C,
                F E A G F E E D

Phrase 8 exactly repeats 4; and as 4 stood at the close of the first group, its repetition as 8 has the effect—emphasized by the repetition—of bringing the whole piece to a close.

Dilecto deo galle (Notker)

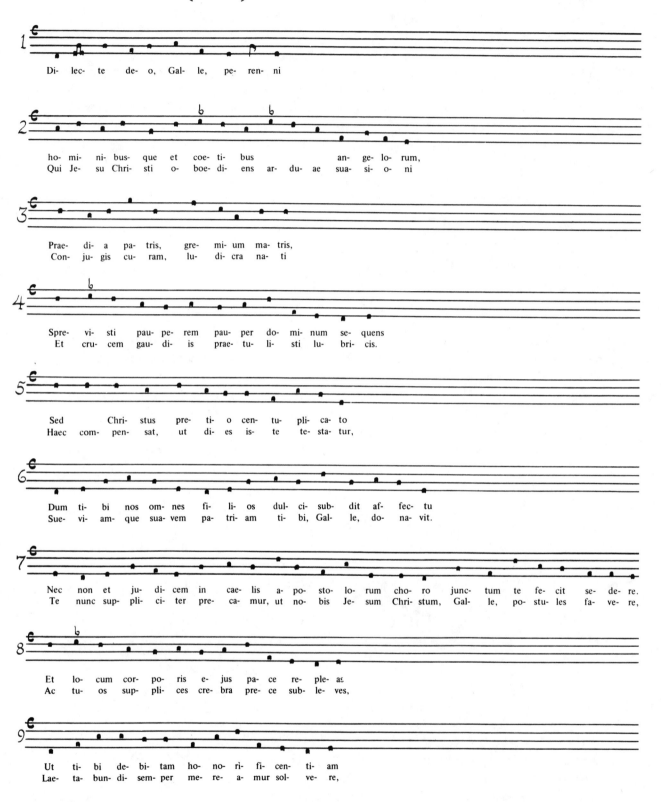

1. Di- lec- te de- o, Gal- le, pe- ren- ni

2. ho- mi- ni- bus- que et coe- ti- bus an- ge- lo- rum,
   Qui Je- su Chri- sti o- boe- di- ens ar- du- ae sua- si- o- ni

3. Prae- di- a pa- tris, gre- mi- um ma- tris,
   Con- ju- gis cu- ram, lu- di- cra na- ti

4. Spre- vi- sti pau- pe- rem pau- per do- mi- num se- quens
   Et cru- cem gau- di- is prae- tu- li- sti lu- bri- cis.

5. Sed Chri- stus pre- ti- o cen- tu- pli- ca- to
   Haec com- pen- sat, ut di- es is- te te- sta- tur,

6. Dum ti- bi nos om- nes fi- li- os dul- ci- sub- dit af- fec- tu
   Sue- vi- am- que sua- vem pa- tri- am ti- bi, Gal- le, do- na- vit.

7. Nec non et ju- di- cem in cae- lis a- po- sto- lo- rum cho- ro junc- tum te fe- cit se- de- re.
   Te nunc sup- pli- ci- ter pre- ca- mur, ut no- bis Je- sum Chri- stum, Gal- le, po- stu- les fa- ve- re,

8. Et lo- cum cor- po- ris e- jus pa- ce re- ple- as.
   Ac tu- os sup- pli- ces cre- bra pre- ce sub- le- ves,

9. Ut ti- bi de- bi- tam ho- no- ri- fi- cen- ti- am
   Lae- ta- bun- di- sem- per me- re- a- mur sol- ve- re,

O Gal- le, De- o di- lec- te!

The clear, cadence-oriented sub-phrases acquire familiarity and warmth through the repetition; the open-closed effect within the phrase becomes increasingly obvious in the measure that the D final is established.

8   A B♭ A *G F G*,   (open)
     F G A E D C D   (closed)

Phrase 9 seems to be an appendage—a brief move through C-E-G comparable to the use of an F-A-C realm near the close of a G-final piece. The end of the phrase reaffirms the ending of phrase 8, so that phrase 9 is really nothing but an echo of 8. The significance of this relationship shows up in a different arrangement of the same melodic material in other versions. Phrase 10 has the epigrammatic force of the short concluding phrases of Notker's JOHANNES JESU and LAURENTI DAVID.

This version of the melody does not have much sweep or expansive power. The general impression is one of shortness and compactness of phrase structure. The only important move away from D occurs early in the piece in phrase 3, and this move, answered immediately by the return in 4, does not open up the interior of the piece to any significant degree. The dwelling on F-D in phrase 6 is a stasis whose effect is felt not just within this phrase but as the center of the piece as a whole. Only phrase 7 gives a sense of swinging movement, and that briefly.

Notker's two texts support the larger grouping of phrases and sometimes reinforce their internal structure to a striking degree. Neither text betrays a very early stage of Notker's development, but perhaps DILECTE DEO GALLE is the less mature. Gallus, disciple and companion of Columbanus, retreated to the wilds west of Lake Constance, and eventually founded the monastery that bore his name. This prose represents Notker's devout and no doubt pleasant homage of his new art to his spiritual patron.

The opening period extends through phrase 4, with strong run-on not just between lines of the same phrase but from one phrase to another, linking these short phrases firmly together.

(1)   Dilecte deo, Galle, perenni (2a) hominibusque et coetibus angelorum
(2b)   qui, Jesu Christi oboediens arduae suasioni,
(3a)   praedia patris, gremium matris, (3b) conjugis curam, ludicra nati,
(4a)   sprevisti, pauperem pauper dominum sequens,
(4b)   et crucem gaudiis praetulisti lubricis.

Rex regum (Notker)

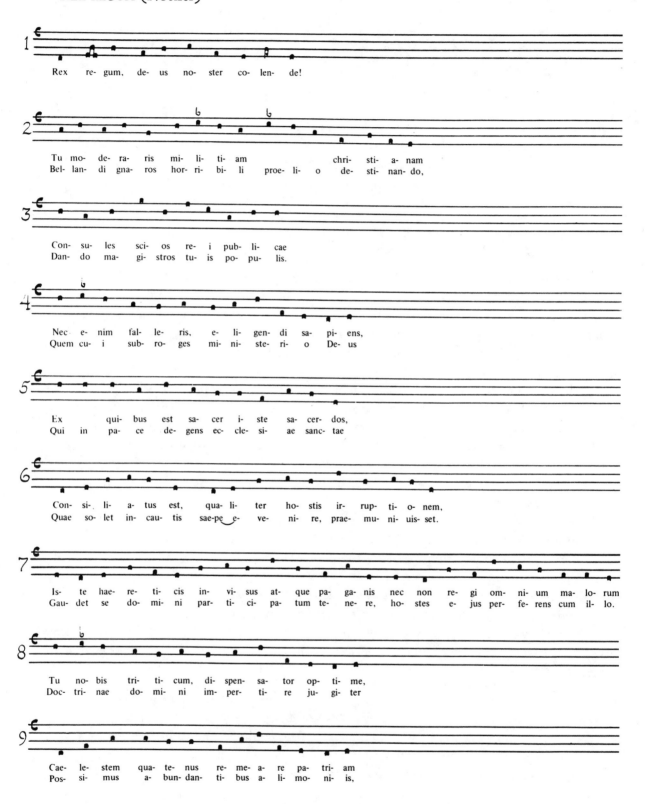

1. Rex re-gum, de-us no-ster co-len-de!

2. Tu mo-de-ra-ris mi-li-ti-am chri-sti-a-nam
   Bel-lan-di gna-ros hor-ri-bi-li proe-li-o de-sti-nan-do,

3. Con-su-les sci-os re-i pub-li-cae
   Dan-do ma-gi-stros tu-is po-pu-lis.

4. Nec e-nim fal-le-ris, e-li-gen-di sa-pi-ens,
   Quem cu-i sub-ro-ges mi-ni-ste-ri-o De-us

5. Ex qui-bus est sa-cer i-ste sa-cer-dos,
   Qui in pa-ce de-gens ec-cle-si-ae sanc-tae

6. Con-si-li-a-tus est, qua-li-ter ho-stis ir-rup-ti-o-nem,
   Quae so-let in-cau-tis sae-pe e-ve-ni-re, prae-mu-ni-uis-set.

7. Is-te hae-re-ti-cis in-vi-sus at-que pa-ga-nis nec non re-gi om-ni-um ma-lo-rum
   Gau-det se do-mi-ni par-ti-ci-pa-tum te-ne-re, ho-stes e-jus per-fe-rens cum il-lo.

8. Tu no-bis tri-ti-cum, di-spen-sa-tor op-ti-me,
   Doc-tri-nae do-mi-ni im-per-ti-re ju-gi-ter

9. Cae-le-stem qua-te-nus re-me-a-re pa-tri-am
   Pos-si-mus a-bun-dan-ti-bus a-li-mo-ni-is,

REX REGUM (Notker) (2)

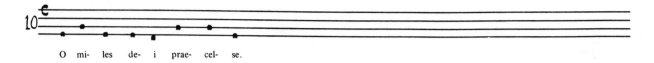

O mi- les de- i prae- cel- se.

The next period runs through 5a,b, 6a,b, and 7a—but not 7b—a procedure we have met occasionally. The first period (1–4) acclaimed Gallus as beloved of God, man, and angels, because, forsaking all others he followed Jesus Christ, embracing poverty. The second period, by contrast, describes Gallus's riches, reward in the flourishing monastery, the land of Swabia itself, and (in phrase 7a) a seat in the heavenly choir of apostles. The run-on of the period into 7a was seemingly undertaken as a special procedure, and a rationale was sought in the sense of the passage. Line 7b starts the invocation and petition to Gallus, now stationed near the throne of Christ; both 7a and 7b, in other words, envisage Gallus in blessedness, so that the image purveyed by the sense overlaps the grouping set out by the syntax, which separates 7a from 7b. The construction recalls that of the West-Frankish HÆC EST SANCTA SOLEMNITAS, in the apostrophe that breaks into phrase 5.

Just as line 4a had carried on the preceding syntax, so its repetition as 8a continues on from 7b. The period goes all the way to the end, 8a,b continuing each a petition, 9a a purpose clause, 10 an apostrophe. Here the similarity to JOHANNES JESU is very close.

Johannes Jesu Christi . . .	Dilecte deo Galle . . .
. . .	. . .
Johannes Christi care!	O Galle deo dilecte!

The inner structure of certain phrases—in particular their tendency to take on carefully chiseled forms of small dimensions—is sometimes supported by a clausula-like construction in the text. Phrase 3, one whose melody has an especially cogent form, is set entirely in short syntactic units, most in a rhythm resembling *cursus planus*; a rhyme is thrown in for good measure.

(3a)	Práedia pátris,	grémium mátris,
(3b)	Conjúgis cúram,	lúdicra náti,

A comparable rhythm appears in phrase 6,

(6a)	Dum tíbi nos ómnes	fílios dúlci	súbdit afféctu,
(6b)	Svéviámque súavem	pátriam tíbi,	Gálle, donávit,

although here the syntax does not conform so closely to the rhythm.

Notker seems to treat all cadences except the normal pattern C D D (F G G), and his frequent alternative D C D (G F G), as paroxytone. So here, paroxytones are found in 1, 2a,b, 5a,b, 6a,b, 7a,b, and 10. It must be admitted that in this text the normal cadences are not so consistently treated. In 3a,b, the repeated accent pattern ′ x x ′ x seems too strong for the expected proparoxytone. And in 4a, *séquens* goes against the D C D pattern as Notker usually treats it. But in LAUDES DEO CONCINAT and GRATES SALVATORI he does occasionally set this alternative form paroxytone; those are earlier texts, and perhaps this one too. The cadences in 8a,b and 9a,b are all regular proparoxytones.

In Notker's other prose to this melody, REX REGUM, the accent patterns in cadences are the same as those in DILECTE DEO GALLE; but the normal cadences in phrase 3 are made regular proparoxytones; and 4a is made proparoxytone, 4b paroxytone.

	DILECTE DEO GALLE	REX REGUM
4a	. . . séquens	. . . sápiens
4b	. . . lúbricis	. . . déus

In REX REGUM the use of clausula-like groups within certain lines—or in general the very careful use of word accent to control the rhythm of the lines—seems even more in evidence than in DILECTE DEO GALLE. In lines 3a,b, sonorities, too, assist the grouping.

3a	Cónsules scíos	réi públicae
3b	Dándo magístros	túis pópulis

Such constructions could easily form the basis for a genre of accentual verse. Similarly lines 4a,b

(4a)	Néc enim fálleris,	eligéndi sápiens
(4b)	Quém cu-i súbroges	ministério déus.

even though irregular in the second cadence, strongly support the sub-phrase structure of the melody. The rhythms engendered by these lines echo through the following ones, but a truly verse-like regularity is avoided by an occasional counter-rhythm.

(5a)	Ex quíbus est sácer	íste sacérdos	
(5b)	*Qui in páce dégens*	ecclésiae sánctae	
(6a)	Consiliátus est	quáliter hóstis	irruptiónem,
(6b)	Quae sólet incáutis sáepe eveníre		praemuniuísset.

As before, even in the presence of counter-rhythms on the level of detail, the grouping of words closely supports the melodic grouping, produced here in phrase 6 by the repetition of figure.

C DFG F   C DF G F
Consili-atus . . . qualiter hostis

(Line 6a seems to include an infrequent case of elision—*saepe evenire*—although this occasioned variants whose syllable count was more regular). The most regular rhythms appear in 8, which sounds as though it came out of a hymn.

(8a)	Tú nobis tríticum	dispensátor óptime,
(8b)	Doctrínae dómini	impertíre júgiter

To this might be compared the hymn for martyrs, attributed to Rhabanus, and in any case probably from the ninth century.[2]

Sanctórum méritis   inclyta gáudia

Pangámus, sócii,   gestáque fórtia:

The period structure of REX REGUM follows that of DILECTE DEO GALLE closely, save that lines 4a,b, being a separate clause, are linked to the opening period by sense rather than syntax. Lines 1 through 4b address God as provider of leaders to the Church; 5, 6 (with strong run-on from 5b to 6a) and 7 describe the bishop as defender of the faith; lines 8 through 10 acclaim him with direct address as dispenser of bread and doctrine—that is, of sustenance for the physical as well as spiritual man. Line 10 is another concluding epigram, *O miles dei praecelse*. As in other instances where Notker has provided two texts to one melody, it seems that once he has decided certain aspects of the relation of text and music, he retains them meticulously in the subsequent setting.

Provided with Notker's very consistent understanding of this piece, we can turn to the relatively confusing and perhaps indeterminate situation in the West-Frankish sources. The problem here is that the early sources furnish two versions, one of which has the text PRAECURSOR CHRISTI (for John the Baptist), while the other—closer in melody and plan to Notker's version—lacks a text. This lack, which is very unusual in the Aquitanian sources, may be due to the fact that the missing text was a version of PRAECURSOR CHRISTI which was superseded by the version actually preserved; or that it was a different text that has not been preserved; or that it has in fact been preserved but, not being provided with a melody in the sources, awaits identification with the preserved melody—which could be accomplished through syllable count (there are a number of such texts, especially in MSS 1084 and 1118).

Neither the version with the text nor the one without coincides exactly with Notker's plan. The text, PRAECURSOR CHRISTI, is not clear or convincing in certain places—which happen to be the very places that differ from Notker's plan. Hence it lies close to hand to conclude that this version could or should be altered to conform to Notker's; but this, alas, can not be done in this case as it was in almost all the other cases where there was a difference. It seems likely that there was another version of PRAECURSOR CHRISTI for the textless melody, and that that version would have more easily permitted a reduction to Notker's plan. That, however, remains conjecture; and a reduction of the melody by itself is likewise mere arbitrary conjecture in the absence of a text to confirm or deny the reduction. All we can do, for the moment, is to study the differences without reconciling them—and to ponder why, for the second time, a sequence with Alleluia connections should present such problems.

In broad outlines, the melodic plan of PRAECURSOR CHRISTI corresponds to Notker's at the beginning and at the end, with the widest divergences in the middle. Phrases 1 and 2 correspond closely. Phrase 3 of PRAECURSOR CHRISTI is a little longer than Notker's 3, and the melody is substantially different, starting on the D final instead of on the fifth above, and cadencing possibly on G, although perhaps A, as in Notker's version, is intended. The

2. *Anal. hymn.* 50, p. 204.

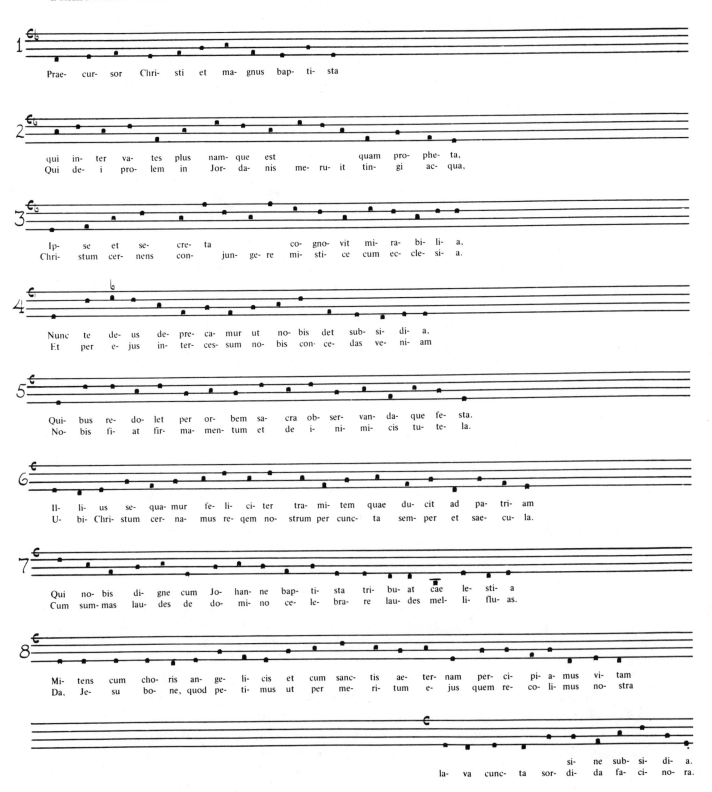

1. Prae- cur- sor Christi et ma- gnus bap- ti- sta

2. qui in- ter va- tes plus nam- que est quam pro- phe- ta,
   Qui de- i pro- lem in Jor- da- nis me- ru- it tin- gi ac- qua,

3. Ip- se et se- cre- ta co- gno- vit mi- ra- bi- li- a,
   Christum cer- nens con- jun- ge- re mi- sti- ce cum ec- cle- si- a.

4. Nunc te de- us de- pre- ca- mur ut no- bis det sub- si- di- a.
   Et per e- jus in- ter- ces- sum no- bis con- ce- das ve- ni- am

5. Qui- bus re- do- let per or- bem sa- cra ob- ser- van- da- que fe- sta.
   No- bis fi- at fir- ma- men- tum et de i- ni- mi- cis tu- te- la.

6. Il- li- us se- qua- mur fe- li- ci- ter tra- mi- tem quae du- cit ad pa- tri- am
   U- bi Chri- stum cer- na- mus re- qem no- strum per cunc- ta sem- per et sae- cu- la.

7. Qui no- bis di- gne cum Jo- han- ne bap- ti- sta tri- bu- at cae- le- sti- a
   Cum sum- mas lau- des de do- mi- no ce- le- bra- re lau- des mel- li- flu- as.

8. Mi- tens cum cho- ris an- ge- li- cis et cum sanc- tis ae- ter- nam per- ci- pi- a- mus vi- tam
   Da. Je- su bo- ne, quod pe- ti- mus ut per me- ri- tum e- jus quem re- co- li- mus no- stra

si- ne sub- si- di- a.
la- va cunc- ta sor- di- da fa- ci- no- ra.

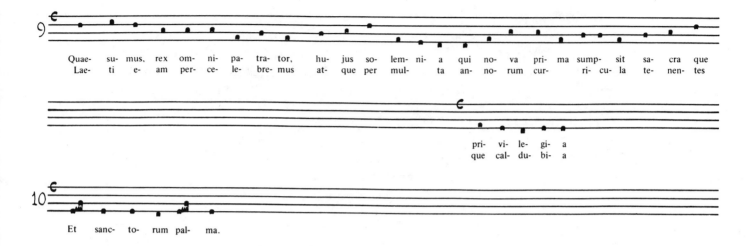

most important aspect of the change is that the short, compact shape with marked shift of register that characterizes Notker's phrase 3 is lacking in PRAECURSOR CHRISTI. Phrase 4 is much closer to Notker's phrase 4: slightly longer, it preserves Notker's shape without the extreme clarity of profile. Phrase 5 of PRAECURSOR CHRISTI can still be related to Notker's 5, even though it is substantially longer. For Notker's 6, however, there is no counterpart in PRAECURSOR CHRISTI, whose phrase 6 seems to be a variant of Notker's 7; but the variation is considerable, and here PRAECURSOR CHRISTI is the shorter, for the first time.

Phrases 7 and 8 seem not to be present in Notker's plan (except to the degree that PRAECURSOR CHRISTI 8 recalls 6, an aspect to be investigated presently). These phrases, especially 8, are long and discursive, unlike anything in Notker's version except his phrase 6. The initial impression is that out of a profusion of material in PRAECURSOR CHRISTI 6, 7, 8, Notker has selected and adapted one, his 6; or, in terms of the procedure we have followed before, that PRAECURSOR in the form we have it includes interpolations somewhere between its phrases 5 and 9.

The relationship of PRAECURSOR CHRISTI 9 with Notker's 8 and 9 is complex. Notker's plan has two short phrases, of the same length (13 syllables), in itself unusual. PRAECURSOR CHRISTI has one very long phrase (30 syllables) that includes the melodic substance of both Notker's 8 and 9, in order. The arrangement of PRAECURSOR CHRISTI, relative to Notker's plan, is another overcouplet.

Notker	PRAECURSOR CHRISTI
8a, b	9a (= 8a, 9a)
9a, b	9b (= 8b, 9b)

The terminology is for convenience, and does not imply that the overcouplet has actually been formed by combining the two shorter couplets, for exactly the reverse may have occurred—an original long couplet might have been broken down into two shorter ones. These alternatives will have to be considered case by case.

The opening period of the text PRAECURSOR CHRISTI extends only as far as 3a,b. The period acclaims (but does not address) the Baptist, including his traditional epithets (1), a reference to the words of Jesus (2a—"Yea, I say unto you, and more than a prophet," Matt. 11, 9), his principal act of baptizing the Lord (2b), and credits him with perceiving how Christ was to be joined mystically to his Church.

(1)   Praecursor Christi et magnus baptista,
(2a)   qui inter vates plus namque est quam propheta,
(2b)   qui dei prolem in Jordanis meruit tingi acqua,
(3a)   ipse et secreta cognovit mirabilia,
(3b)   Christum cernens conjungere mistice cum ecclesia.

Lines 4a,b start a petition to God, *Nunc te* (or *Te nunc*) *deus deprecamur.* The petition is for aid (4a) and grace through John's intercession (4b). Lines 5a,b continue the petition, but in a confusing way: 5a begins with a *quibus* whose antecedent is either *nobis* or *subsidia* in 4a, in which case 5a would follow more easily after 4a. The sense can be construed as being that, with divine aid, the holy feast to be observed may be spread throughout the world. Similarly, even though 5b has no explicit syntactical connection but is merely another item in the petition, it follows more easily after 4b than after 5a.

(4a)   Nunc te, deus, deprecamur   (5a)   quibus redolet per orbem
              ut nobis det subsidia,   sacra observandaque festa;
(4b)   et per ejus intercessum   (5b)   nobis fiat firmamentum
              nobis concedas veniam,   et de inimicis tutela.

Perhaps here, too, an overcouplet is involved, but there is no documentary support for that conclusion, and it seems more likely that there was a transposition occasioned by the closeness in syllable count (16/17) between phrases 4 and 5. Restoration remains conjectural.

Phrase 6 of PRAECURSOR CHRISTI brings another kind of problem. Line 6a starts off reasonably enough—"Joyfully may we follow his path, which leads to the homeland (6b) where we may see Christ our King for ever and ever." But the language is a little loose: it is not clear *whose* path this is—Christ's or John's; the latter would be more germane, but seems hard to justify grammatically. And *Christum cernamus* (6b) is redicta to *Christum cernens* in line 3b, while *per cuncta semper et saecula* is either very elaborate or awkward diction. In general, the couplet seems like a less successful imitation of the climactic couplet in phrase 5 of HÆC EST SANCTA SOLEMNITAS, where we were led logically to a celestial vision of Christ in glory, there to see also Stephen, to whom the text is dedicated.

(6a)   Illius sequamur feliciter tramitem quae ducit ad patriam,
(6b)   ubi Christum cernamus regem nostrum per cuncta semper et saecula;

Lines 7a,b, presumably dependent upon 6a,b (*Qui . . .*), become even looser. The meaning itself of 7a is not clear: the subject of *tribuat* can only be the Lord, which involves an awkwardness with *de domino*, and an infelicitous circularity. *Cum summa laude . . . celebrare laudes mellifluas* is a hopeless redictum, which the alternate reading *preces* for *laudes* was designed to avoid—effectively, but without making as much sense.

(7a) Qui nobis digne cum Johanne baptista tribuat coelestia
(7b) cum summa laude de domino celebrare laudes mellifluas.

These lines are omitted in eleventh-century Italian sources, which adds likelihood to the possibility they were interpolations.

Line 8a adds yet another item to the series of petitions started in 4a.

(4a)	Nunc te, deus, deprecamur	(6a)	sequamur . . .
	ut . . . det . . .	(6b)	cernamus . . .
(4b)	et . . . concedas . . .	(7a)	tribuat . . .
(5b)	fiat . . .	(8a)	percipiamus . . .

In a certain sense, *percipiamus* duplicates *cernamus* of 6b; the thought would be more straightforward without one of them. In any case, this is a large number of petitions, occupying the whole central area of the prose in an unusual fashion. (And we are not yet through.)

(8a) Mitem cum choris angelicis et cum sanctis aeterna percipiamus vita sine suspiria
(8b) Da Jesu bone quod petimus ut per meritum ejus quem recolimus nostra lava cuncta
sordida facinora

Mitem (8a) appears only in the Italian sources, the Aquitanian ones reading *Mitens* or *Mittens*, which seems without sense; *suspiria*, also, is an Italian variant for *subsidia*—an obvious scribal reflex to line 4a. It does seem in this case that the Aquitanian scribes had hold of a bad version as far as these details are concerned, and from that we might argue that their version was far from the original in other, less obvious respects.

Line 8b makes a fresh start—not so frequent in the second line of a couplet, but with an analog in Notker's DILECTE DEO GALLE, whose 7b starts the petition, *Te nunc suppliciter precamur*. In PRAECURSOR CHRISTI, 8b is another petition, but one that makes more of an impression than the others.

(8b) Da, Jesu bone, quod petimus,
        ut per meritum ejus quem recolimus,
        nostra lava cuncta sordida facinora.

The terms of the petition, "that thou mayest wash away our sins," are certainly germane. Line 8b is five syllables longer than 8a, a procedure encountered in phrase 3 (and elsewhere, as in SUMMI TRIUMPHUM REGIS) and perfectly able to stand as it is; still, the words that make the extension are supernumerary modifiers, could be easily removed, and therefore might have been added.

(8a)	. . . vita	sine suspiria
(8b)	. . . nostra lava cuncta sordida facinora	
or:	. . . nostra	lava facinora

Notker's texts have equal lines at this point; yet there are more complex and far-reaching matters to be decided that have a bearing upon this particular detail of reconstruction.

Lines 9a,b continue to provide problems. In line 9a, *Quaesumus* is used with a direct object, "We seek the solemnity . . .," an unusual but perhaps acceptable construction. *Omnipatrator* seems like a good Carolingian divine epithet.

(9a) Quaesumus, rex omnipatrator, hujus solemnia
        qui nova prima sumpsit sacraque privilegia
(9b) laeti ea per celebremus
        atque per multa annorum curricula tenentes que caldubia
(10 et sanctorum palam. Amen.

The enclitic construction *sacraque privilegia* would pass unnoticed if it were not for the similar but less fluent one in 5a,

Quibus redolet per orbem sacra observandaque festa.

And there seems to be still another one in 9b:

atque per multa annorum curricula tenentesque caldubia,

which makes little sense because introduced by *atque*. *Caldubia* (*caltudia*) is *locus desperatus*: it seems likely that this enclitic is a *quae* introducing whatever *caldubia* is a corruption of; or possibly some other expression includes all five syllables after *tenentes*. Except for these five syllables and the *atque*, the line as a whole makes good sense—"Joyfully may we celebrate these solemnities through many circling years, holding fast the . . . . and the palms of the saints."

In general, PRAECURSOR CHRISTI corresponds to Notker's plan reasonably closely through phrase 4, or 5, departs from it in phrases 6 through 8 (corresponding in position to Notker's phrases 6 and 7); then the two versions agree again in the last two phrases (PRAECURSOR CHRISTI 9, 10 = Notker 8, 9, 10) except for the variant disposition of the overcouplet.

PRAECURSOR CHRISTI	Notker: DILECTE DEO GALLE
1	1
2	2
3	3
4	4
5	5
	6
6	7
7	
8	
9	{ 8
	9
10	10

Praecursor christi phrase 7—whose text is problematic and lacking in the Italian sources —is not found in Notker's plan, and can fairly be judged not present in his model. Notker's phrase 6 has no analog in praecursor christi; its status is indeterminate, for it might have been dropped, transmuted, or exchanged in the West-Frankish tradition, or it might have been added by Notker. Its unassuming quality as melodic filler suggests the latter, and equally suggests that the question is not of decisive significance for the shape of the whole.

Before pursuing the restoration further, we need to take into account the textless version of the melody in the Aquitanian sources. This version, labeled "Justus ut palma" in one of the two sources, is different in certain important respects from the melody for prae-cursor. As a further detail of the MS transmission, praecursor christi was entered twice in the supplementary "workbook" section of 1084 (where no liturgical order prevails, the items having been added, presumably, as they became available); the second time it was entirely erased. All this suggests strongly that there were two versions of the text current, or that one version was in process of revision. As a general hypothesis—a first impression—subject to modification or reversal by further collations, it can be hazarded that the sequentiaria (where the textless version is preserved) are more conservative with respect to revision and updating of the repertory than the prosaria. Thus the textless version may well take us closer to Notker's model.

After phrases 1 and 2 in the usual form, "Justus ut palma" presents us with a phrase 3 that has Notker's length and the melody of the East-Frankish tradition. Similarly, phrase 4 has Notker's length. But phrase 5 has the 17 syllables of praecursor christi.

Phrase 6 is much longer (27) than praecursor christi (20), longer even than Notker's phrase 7 (24), the increase being due to a longer approach to the cadence.

E G F E F D E C D

There is, however, another, more complex way of understanding this excess in 6. The following phrase, 7, begins with the descent to low A that is the distinguishing feature of the *end* of phrase 7 in praecursor christi.

"Justus ut palma"

6		(27)	7 low		(37)
6	(20)	7	low	8	

Praecursor christi

This low motive, stated twice, leads in the textless version directly into the melody used for praecursor christi phrase 8, proceeding through it in order but ending like phrase 6, so that the whole phrase is very long—37 notes. It is possible, then, to understand the long cadence in "Justus ut palma" 6 as more or less the beginning of praecursor christi 7, the two versions then proceeding parallel except for cutting up the phrase lengths differently. Or, to put it the other way around, in praecursor christi a new phrase, 7, could have been carved out of the materials of "Justus ut palma."

Phrase 8 of the textless version, in 1118, preserves the overcouplet as in praecursor christi, but with 26 notes (instead of 28/28 or 29/30 in the two sources for praecursor

CHRISTI) corresponding exactly to Notker's count for phrases 8 and 9 together. In MS 1084, phrase 8 appears as a double of 13 notes, corresponding exactly to Notker's phrase 8; phrase 9 of PRAECURSOR CHRISTI is lacking entirely. One way or the other, then, the textless version stands closer to Notker's

Hence the two main problems of restoration concern the central area of PRAECURSOR CHRISTI phrases 6 through 8, and the next to last phrase with the overcouplet. Neither permits a definitive solution. To take the less difficult first, it is possible to rewrite the overcouplet of PRAECURSOR CHRISTI in two regular couplets, as in Notker's plan.

(a) Quesumus, rex omnipatrator hujus solemnia (15)
(b) Qui nova primus sumpsit sacraque privilegia (15)
(a) Laeti ea percelebremus atque per multa (14)
(b) Annorum curricula tenentes que caldubia (15)

The slight discrepancies could easily be absorbed into the emendation that would be required for a believable reading of the text.

The melody of the first of these reconstructed couplets, however, cannot easily be reduced to the 13 syllables of "Justus ut palma" without arbitrary and conjectural emendation; the difference of three notes—one D at the cadence, two extra G's near the beginning—must be regarded as essential to the preserved version of PRAECURSOR CHRISTI. The second reconstructed couplet could be omitted to bring PRAECURSOR CHRISTI in line with the textless version in 1084: the end of the first couplet leads easily to the concluding single.

(a)   Quaesumus, rex omnipatratos hujus solemnia
(b)   Qui nova primus sumpsit sacraque privilegia
(10)   Et sanctorum palma

All the severe textual problems of 9b are thereby finessed.

Of course, from a textual point of view the same is accomplished by considering 9 to be a single, that is, using 9a as it stands and omitting 9b. In this case we would have to imagine Notker splitting the long single and doubling each half; whereas if he had before him a short regular couplet with 13 syllables he would have had to add the whole second couplet.

Perhaps the melodic shape can help us decide between these alternatives. The last half of the melody as it stands in the overcouplet includes a backing-away from the cadence into a C-E-G realm, then a reiteration of the D cadence.

(9) A B A G G G E F E F G A E D C
         C E G G E F E
                 F G A E D C D D

This shape can easily be imagined as a penultimate single of the kind found in CHRISTI HODIERNA—which Notker, alone among all the versions, used as a single. The C-E-G realm seems a very desirable element at this point in the piece, as does the single.

In order to understand the structure of the central portion of PRAECURSOR CHRISTI, we need to compare it to the melody for HÆC EST VERA REDEMPTIO (Notker's GAUDE MARIA).

The latter halves of these two melodies are strikingly similar, but the similarity comes out clearly only when we take all versions of PRAECURSOR CHRISTI and Notker's DILECTE DEO GALLE into account. Phrase 3 of DILECTE DEO (PRAECURSOR CHRISTI), which is high and short, is identical with phrase 7 of HÆC EST VERA REDEMPTIO. Phrase 5 of PRAECURSOR CHRISTI corresponds roughly to HÆC EST VERA REDEMPTIO phrase 10. Phrase 8 of PRAECURSOR CHRISTI corresponds to phrase 11 of HÆC EST VERA REDEMPTIO. And phrase 9, first half, of PRAECURSOR CHRISTI (phrase 8 of Notker's plan), the phrase found also at 4 in all versions, is the same as phrase 12 of HÆC EST VERA REDEMPTIO. Nor are these correspondences simply a matter of similarity among individual phrases; also involved is the overall rise and fall of the melody.

	HÆC EST VERA REDEMPTIO	PRAECURSOR	Notker: DILECTE DEO
high	7	(3)	3
descent		4	4
	9		
descent	10	5	5
ascent	11	(6)8	7
descent	12	9	8=4

The overall line in Notker's DILECTE DEO descends once quickly through 3 and 4 (= 7 and 8), then moves through a longer arc ending similarly in 7 and 8 (= 11 and 12).

In PRAECURSOR CHRISTI, however, there are two phrases that begin with strong ascents —6 and 8. Comparison of these with Notker's 7 and HÆC EST VERA REDEMPTIO 11 shows that it is PRAECURSOR CHRISTI 8, not 6, that corresponds to Notker's 7. This is hard to see at first because of the reduplicated D's at the start of PRAECURSOR CHRISTI 8 (not to speak of the fusion with the preceding phrase in the textless version). But HÆC EST VERA REDEMPTIO makes the functional identity clear.

HÆC EST VERA REDEMPTIO 11 (transposed to D)
D C D F D F G A G F G D   F F E F C D C   F E G A   F D
Notker 7
D C D FED GGF A   FE G D   D C   F E A G F E F D

PRAECURSOR CHRISTI
8a D CD FED F G A G F G D   F F E F C D C   F E G A F D
6 D C D FEF GAGAG   E F G E F   C   F E D

The correspondence between PRAECURSOR CHRISTI and HÆC EST VERA REDEMPTIO is all the more curious because of the Alleluia quotations—one in G-*tetrardus*, one in D-*protus*. There is no question of the D final in the material as it appears in PRAECURSOR CHRISTI. This certainty confirms the discrepancy in HÆC EST VERA REDEMPTIO between the Alleluia quotation and the rest of the piece, and tends to isolate the quotation. It also, by reflex, confirms the version of phrase 3 as found in Notker's version and in "Justus ut palma," as opposed to phrase 3 of PRAECURSOR CHRISTI; and it suggests that phrase 8 of PRAECURSOR CHRISTI might originally have taken a more concise form. Indeed, it would be possible, by omitting the troublesome *Mitem* at the start of 8a, and—arbitrarily—*bone* from 8b, along with *cuncta sordida* as suggested, to bring PRAECURSOR CHRISTI into close correspondence with this phrase in HÆC EST VERA REDEMPTIO, and close to Notker's version.

Adjustments of such an order, however, could have been made by Notker himself; there is no pressing need to assume them in his model. More important is the insight into overall shape afforded by HÆC EST VERA REDEMPTIO. The most direct form of the melody would be one that proceeded from PRAECURSOR CHRISTI 5 directly to 8, as HÆC EST VERA REDEMPTIO goes from 10 to 11.

Hypothetical model	Notker	PRAECURSOR
1	1	1
2	2	2
3	3	3
4	4	4
5	5	5
	6	6
		7
6	7	8
7	8,9	9a,b
8	10	10

Phrase 4 marks the end of the first section, as Notker carefully observes in both his settings. Phrase 5 starts a second section, which is to end exactly like the first, with PRAECURSOR CHRISTI 9 = Notker's 8 (ignoring the problem of the overcouplet for the moment). Notker's 6 is static; PRAECURSOR CHRISTI 6 is an anticipation of 8, progressing not as far and returning via 7. The textual problems of PRAECURSOR CHRISTI are largely solved by omitting 6 as well as 7, along with 9b. Compared to a model reconstructed in that manner, Notker's plan involves merely adding 6, cutting and doubling 9.

XV

"Justus ut palma major"

NOTKER USED another melody that quoted the Alleluia *Justus ut palma*; this other melody was called "Justus ut palma major" in the St. Gall MSS. Since here, again, it is difficult to decide on a West-Frankish model, we can profitably use the melody title "Justus ut palma major." Notker set it twice, to SANCTI BAPTISTAE and LAUS TIBI CHRISTE (CUI SAPIT—these additional words would be necessary to distinguish this text from several others with similar text-incipits in the East-Frankish repertory, but they will not be included in the discussion here). Of these two, LAUS TIBI CHRISTE has been regarded as the second setting, with seeming justification.

There are three early West-Frankish texts to be considered, HÆC DIES EST SANCTA for Christmas, ORGANICIS CANAMUS MODULIS for John the Evangelist, and ECCE DIES for John the Baptist. Still more West-Frankish texts for John Baptist, NATIVITATIS PRAECURSORIS and DA CAMOENA seem clearly to be later. A conspectus may be helpful.

"Justus ut palma major"

	(Notker)
ECCE DIES John the Baptist	SANCTI BAPTISTAE John the Baptist
HÆC DIES EST SANCTA Christmas	LAUS TIBI CHRISTE Holy Innocents
ORGANICIS John the Evangelist	
(NATIVITATIS PRAECURSORIS John the Baptist)	
(DA CAMOENA John the Baptist)	

"Justus ut palma minor"

PRAECURSOR CHRISTI John the Baptist	DILECTE DEO St. Gallus
	REX REGUM Confessors

The melody shared by Notker's texts with HÆC DIES EST SANCTA is remarkably stable, showing no difference essential to the plan. There are, in other words, no problems of restoring the early form of this melody, for it is plainly before us, even though it is hard to tell which of the West-Frankish texts was known to Notker; perhaps this difficulty is a

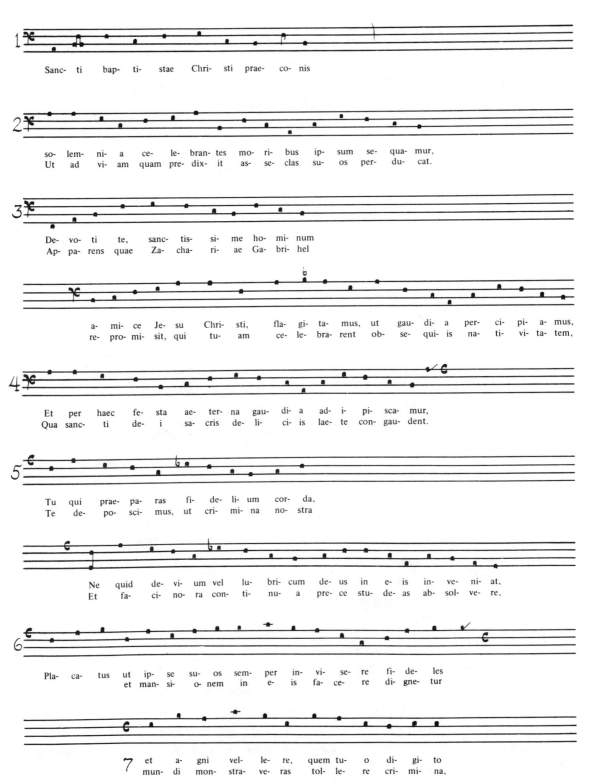

SANCTI BAPTISTAE (Notker)

1. Sanc- ti bap- ti- stae Chri- sti prae- co- nis

2. so- lem- ni- a ce- le- bran- tes mo- ri- bus ip- sum se- qua- mur,
   Ut ad vi- am quam pre- dix- it as- se- clas su- os per- du- cat.

3. De- vo- ti te, sanc- tis- si- me ho- mi- num
   Ap- pa- rens quae Za- cha- ri- ae Ga- bri- hel

   a- mi- ce Je- su Chri- sti, fla- gi- ta- mus, ut gau- di- a per- ci- pi- a- mus,
   re- pro- mi- sit, qui tu- am ce- le- bra- rent ob- se- qui- is na- ti- vi- ta- tem,

4. Et per haec fe- sta ae- ter- na gau- di- a ad- i- pi- sca- mur,
   Qua sanc- ti de- i sa- cris de- li- ci- is lae- te con- gau- dent.

5. Tu qui prae- pa- ras fi- de- li- um cor- da,
   Te de- po- sci- mus, ut cri- mi- na no- stra

   Ne quid de- vi- um vel lu- bri- cum de- us in e- is in- ve- ni- at,
   Et fa- ci- no- ra con- ti- nu- a pre- ce stu- de- as ab- sol- ve- re,

6. Pla- ca- tus ut ip- se su- os sem- per in- vi- se- re fi- de- les
   et man- si- o- nem in e- is fa- ce- re di- gne- tur

7. et a- gni vel- le- re, quem tu- o di- gi- to
   mun- di mon- stra- ve- ras tol- le- re cri- mi- na,

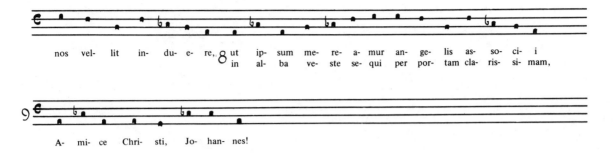

consequence of the stability of the piece. There is, however, a fascinating problem of pitch level in the latter part, this being another piece that (like ᴄʜʀɪsᴛɪ ʜᴏᴅɪᴇʀɴᴀ) may end on a pitch different from the one established as a final at the beginning. As with some of the other cases, the original intention is hard to determine.

Aside from—or partly because of—the problem of pitch level, the melody is one of the most intricately constructed of those studied. We can get to know it in any of the four versions first mentioned, perhaps most conveniently in Notker's sᴀɴᴄᴛᴇ ʙᴀᴘᴛɪsᴛᴀᴇ.

Phrase 1 apparently quotes the Alleluia *Justus ut palma*,[1] with the same reservations as those concerning "Justus ut palma minor": phrase 1 ends closed on D (the final of the Alleluia) instead of open on the G above. In Notker's setting it includes a neume of three notes on the second syllable:

C   DFD F E F   G E   D F D
Sanc- ti   bap- ti- stae Chri-sti- prae- co- nis

Phrase 2 makes a fresh start in a way that the corresponding phrase in "Justus minor" did not do. Perhaps it is because the shape and movement of phrase 2 are so clear, so self-contained: the second four notes respond firmly to the first four; after marking the overall descent from A and G with an F, the line drops quickly to its final, D.

2 *A* A G E, *G* G A D, *F* E C E G F E D

Although neither the rhythmic grouping nor the texting emphasize it, the C E G realm is present as a foil to the D final supported by the A a fifth above.

Compared to the first phrase, 3 is very long, and in spite of short motive-like units comparable to those of 1, attains a remarkable sense of melodic continuity, of long, arching line. A low intonation makes the phrase seem consequent to phrase 2 as antecedent, leading with a sense of arrival to F and D.

2   A A G F, G G A D . . .
3   A C D F G F E D F E D . . .

1. See note 1, Chapter 14.

A straight run, not so frequent in early sequences, from D up to A marks the second half of this phrase (whose inner articulations are not very strong), and after a brief dwelling in the higher register the line turns back to the same pattern that ended phrase 2.

2   . . . F E C E G F E D
3   . . . *D E F G A*
                A F A B♭ A G A F E C E G F E D

Phrase 4 does not exactly repeat 2, yet seems clearly to be a reprise, framing the excursion in 3 with something familiar.

2   A A G F, G G A D . . .
4   A A G F D E F G F E C E G F E D

This is the more remarkable because—while the contour (and with it the neumes in St. Gall 484) differ from 2—the exact pitches vary in the several versions; yet always the same structural point seems to be made. Melodic curve and melodic rhythm seem here to be, in some degree, independent of precise pitch content.

Phrase 5 brings a clearly articulated sub-phrase structure, comparable to phrase 6 of ECCE VICIT or phrase 5 of CHRISTI HODIERNA, except that the melodic substance is different. A short sub-phrase, ending on A a fifth above the final, is repeated, then followed by a fall to the D; the approach to the cadence is still similar to phrases 2–4, and although the internal cadences rise by step to the A, they do not actually use the cadence formula G A A.

5   A C B A G B♭ A G F G A,
       DA C B A G B♭ A G F G A
                   A G E G F E D

The start of the second sub-phrase dips down a fifth to the D, by way of making the reiteration slightly more emphatic. Later versions used this same figure at the start of the first sub-phrase too, by anticipation; but it would seem that Notker's version began the phrase directly on A. In the first and second sub-phrases there are two four-note descents, one from C to G, another from B to F.

       A / C B A G / B♭ A G F

It seems just from inspection that the first B is natural, the second flat, and later staff sources confirm that surmise.[2] No chromaticism seems intended, and none heard; the dominant aspect of melodic organization—as in the preceding phrases—is the grouping into motive-like units, here in descending groups of four notes. These groups themselves, organized into a descending line C, B flat, A, so control the attention that the accidental B flat seems entirely natural, in a manner of speaking.

       A *C* B A G B♭ A G F G *A*

2. For example, Paris B.N. n.a.lat. 495, fol. 51.

That is, the second group of four is heard as a sequential repetition of the first a tone lower, preserving the order of intervals semitone, tone, tone.

After phrase 5, the melody strikes off in a new direction. Indeed, from phrase 6 to the end (phrase 9) can be regarded as one very extended phrase-group made up of a number of much shorter, compact phrases. These shorter phrases are to some extent disguised, and glued together, by careful manipulation at the motivic level. The most important instance is at the very beginning of phrase 6—an instance that caught the attention of those who supplied the early texts, those who later revised them, and those who edited them in modern times.

6   *A C D*   A C B C D   D E D C B G

Phrase 6 as a whole ends open on G—not with a cadence pattern, but simply a fall to a note that cannot possibly be a closed cadence of any kind in this context. Aside from this ending, the phrase moves within the area bounded by A and the E a fifth higher; the melody has moved decisively up to this area from the lower one based on D. The figure consisting of the first three notes (A C D), which is an intonation into the higher area, is repeated in a more extended form (A C B C D), all this forming the first half of the phrase. The second half is the fall to G.

In Notker's texting, the motive A C D is appended to the end of 6a (*fideles*) and also to 6b (*dignetur*), while in other versions the motive starts 6b (as it starts 6a), and appears again as preface to 7.

6a   A C D . . . . G
6b   A C D . . . . G
7a   A C D . . . .

or, in Notker's texting:

6a   A C D . . . . G A C D
                                    fi-de- les
6b   Et mansionem . . . . .G A C D
                                      di-gnetur,
7a   Et agni . . . .

The three notes, in other words, exist as an independent motive whose repetitions surround 6a and 6b.

After this motive, 7 continues with a figure similar to that near the start of 6,

6   *A C D*   A C B C D
7   *A C D*   D F E G F D

except that it climbs still higher into a realm based on the high D, and is recurved in such a way that it indicates closure rather than further expansion. Phrase 7, like 6, falls into two parts, of which this much is the first. The second part is an approach to a cadence, which for the first time in this piece is a normal one, C D D.

7   *A C D*   D E G F D / F E D C D D

Next come two longer motives, used in alternation. The first one, placed in the present numbering at the end of 7, descends from D to G. The second one, at the start of 8, rises from G back to D. It is followed in 8 by the return of the descending motive. Thus the descending motive appears five times in all, framing the ascending motive in the same pattern (x y x y x) as the motive A C D frames the other material in 6.

	(ascending)	(descending)
		D C A C B♭ A G
	G B♭ G A B♭ C D	nos ve-lit in-du- e- re
8a	Ut ipsum me-re- a-mur	an-ge-lis as- so- ci- i
b	In alba veste se-qui	per portam cla-ris-si-mam

The difference in effect is due to the fact that where the motive A C D is short and rises, motive D C A C B A G is longer and falls—to a note that, in interval pattern at least, is the same kind of final as that in the opening phrases (2, 3, 4, 5); that is, it is a *protus* final, even though on G rather than on D. And the approach to it is similar to the approach in 2, 3, and 4, identical to the approach in 5.

```
2,3,4  F E C E G F E D
5          A G E    G F E D
8          D C A    C B♭ A G
```

At these pitch levels (different ones can be read in many of the sources) there are strange twists to the line as it moves toward this G-*protus* final; yet the strong organization at the motivic level and the persistent antecedent-consequent grouping at the phrase level give an extraordinary persuasiveness to the progression.

Another difference between phrase 8 and 6 is the fact that in 6 the motive functions as antecedent, the other material being consequent and including the cadence; but in 8 the descending motive D C A C B♭ A G functions as consequent—at least, when it comes the second and third times. This merely is to express in motivic terms the general aspect of the line: phrase 6 moves basically upwards and remains open, phrase 8 tends downward, as reflex, and toward closure. Then, in phrase 9, the other material in 8 (in itself a rising figure), is transformed into the concluding single, tying up the interplay of motivic patterns in a tight, intricate knot.

```
                    D C A C B♭ A G
8     G B♭ G A B♭ C D D C A C B♭ A G
9     G B♭ G F B♭ A G
```

This concluding single has the epigrammatic force—and very much the same melody—as in JOHANNES JESU CHRISTI.

Persuasive or not, the progression that led to the ending on G-*protus* instead of the expected D-*protus* was counted peculiar in the eleventh and twelfth centuries, and another variant common to many manuscripts preserves an ending on D. The difference usually appears near the start of phrase 7: the motive A C D usually appears just so, then the following figure starts on A instead of on D.

(High version: D F E G F D F E D C D)
7   *A C D* A C B D C A C B A G A A
             A G E G F E D (etc.)

This brings the cadence at the end of 7 out on A, and the descending motive on D—a completely smooth and reasonable result, the more believable because at the crucial point (fourth note of 7) the repetition and extension of the motive A C D occurs at the same pitch level as the motive itself.

The important point, it seems to me, is that the G ending is *lectio difficilior*, not only with regard to the B flat, but also in terms of the high tessitura of phrase 7, and the tonal plan of the whole piece. It takes effort to ascend above the high D in phrase 7, and to understand the G ending as a logical consequent of phrases 1 through 5. If the piece had been originally conceived as ending on D, it would be extremely difficult to explain the consistent readings on G, save as an arbitrary corruption. On the other hand—and for the same reasons—given the original intent to end on G, it is easy to see why the D-ending should occur as a variant: as *lectio facilior* it provides a common-sense solution to a puzzling piece.

Besides the question of intent is that of effect. Ending the piece on G is more problematic; is it convincing? The stress on D at the start is very strong, whether the line approaches it from the C below, rising up to the F and back to D (as in phrases 1 and 3), or from the A a fifth above (as in phrase 2). And the design of the phrase group 2-3-4 is such as to frame the D with these two different approaches: the similarity of 4 to 2 has the effect of reiterating the descent to D from above, while in between phrase 3 first comes at the D from below, then rises from D to A. Another prominent feature of this phrase group is the A, as at the start of 2 and towards the end of 3; the relationship of this A and the D a fifth below is the most obvious foundation of the tonal movement in this part of the piece.

On this foundation is erected the rise to the high D in phrase 6, and in one sense the establishment of D-A-D as the armature of the piece is what makes the ending on G most problematic. The rise to D is prepared in another way, too: phrase 5, while emphasizing A in its internal cadences, also presents a strong C in its attacks; A and C, to be joined together in the rising motive A C D at the start of 6, are thus made essential steps in the longer line that reaches over 5.

Phrase 7, then, confirms the high D with its cadence formulas. At that point there is a sense of arrival, of completion of a tonal plan, robbed of finality mainly by the sense of movement into the higher octave—which is admittedly very strong. The piece clearly cannot end there, for the movement away from the start has gone too far. And yet it has "arrived," posing a problem as to how it is to end after that. In no other piece have we encountered this kind of movement through an octave, with the peculiar paradox of identity in removal that the octave brings.

If the ending on D were to follow after 7 in its high position, it would offer on the one hand a drastic drop in register, on the other so little change (because of octave identity)

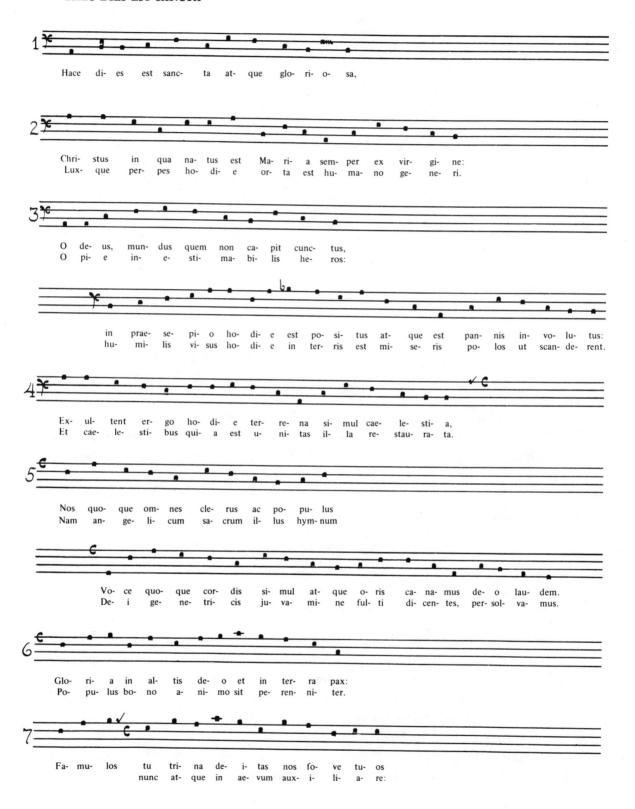

1. Hace di- es est sanc- ta at- que glo- ri- o- sa,

2. Chri- stus in qua na- tus est Ma- ri- a sem- per ex vir- gi- ne:
   Lux- que per- pes ho- di- e or- ta est hu- ma- no ge- ne- ri.

3. O de- us, mun- dus quem non ca- pit cunc- tus,
   O pi- e in- e- sti- ma- bi- lis he- ros:

   in prae- se- pi- o ho- di- e est po- si- tus at- que est pan- nis in- vo- lu- tus:
   hu- mi- lis vi- sus ho- di- e in ter- ris est mi- se- ris po- los ut scan- de- rent.

4. Ex- ul- tent er- go ho- di- e ter- re- na si- mul cae- le- sti- a,
   Et cae- le- sti- bus qui- a est u- ni- tas il- la re- stau- ra- ta.

5. Nos quo- que om- nes cle- rus ac po- pu- lus
   Nam an- ge- li- cum sa- crum il- lus hym- num

   Vo- ce quo- que cor- dis si- mul at- que o- ris ca- na- mus de- o lau- dem.
   De- i ge- ne- tri- cis ju- va- mi- ne ful- ti di- cen- tes, per- sol- va- mus.

6. Glo- ri- a in al- tis de- o et in ter- ra pax:
   Po- pu- lus bo- no a- ni- mo sit pe- ren- ni- ter.

7. Fa- mu- los tu tri- na de- i- tas nos fo- ve tu- os
   nunc at- que in ae- vum aux- i- li- a- re:

laus, ho- nor, im- pe- ri- um,

Po- te- stas at- que vir- tus ti- bi sit re- gi na- to
Qui om- ni- a re- gis si- mul in tri- ni- ta- te

In sae- cu- lo- rum sae- cu- la.

as to be anticlimactic. The effect would be a very weak ending. Indeed, versions that end on D are not arranged this way, but instead always make the change toward the lower register earlier: the high D is not established as a point of arrival, but only touched upon (in 7) as the top of the range. The phrase group 6 through the end stresses A, and the tonal movement makes an overall curve up to this A, then back down to the lower D—a stable, easily understood kind of movement, but not, I think, part of the original conception of this piece.

Of the several texts to this melody in Aquitanian manuscripts, hæc dies est sancta is perhaps the most reasonable candidate as Notker's model. Hæc dies est sancta is a Christmas song, as well as another instance of the proclamation of "today's" liturgy, like hæc est sancta and hæc dies quam excelsus. Far less popular than christi hodierna, it seems to be considerably more cogent in construction and diction. The problem posed by this particular melody is in the last half, and for this hæc dies est sancta has a straightforward, effective solution.

Phrases 1 and 2 are set as the proclamation of the Nativity. Phrase 3 contains a matching pair of apostrophes to God: *O deus . . . O pie . . . .* The grammar seems a little inconsequent. Should we read *es* for *est* throughout 3a,b? Both lines present the paradox of the infinite God become incarnate, and both subdivide syntactically at the place suggested by the melody. Phrase 4, whose melody is a reprise of 2, winds up this opening section with "Let heaven and earth rejoice therefore . . . ."

1   Hæc dies est sancta atque gloriosa,
2a   Christus in qua natus est Maria semper ex virgine:
 b   Luxque perpes hodie orta est humano generi.
3a   O deus, mundus quem non capit cunctus,
        in praesepio hodie est positus atque est pannis involutus:

"Justus ut palma major"   287

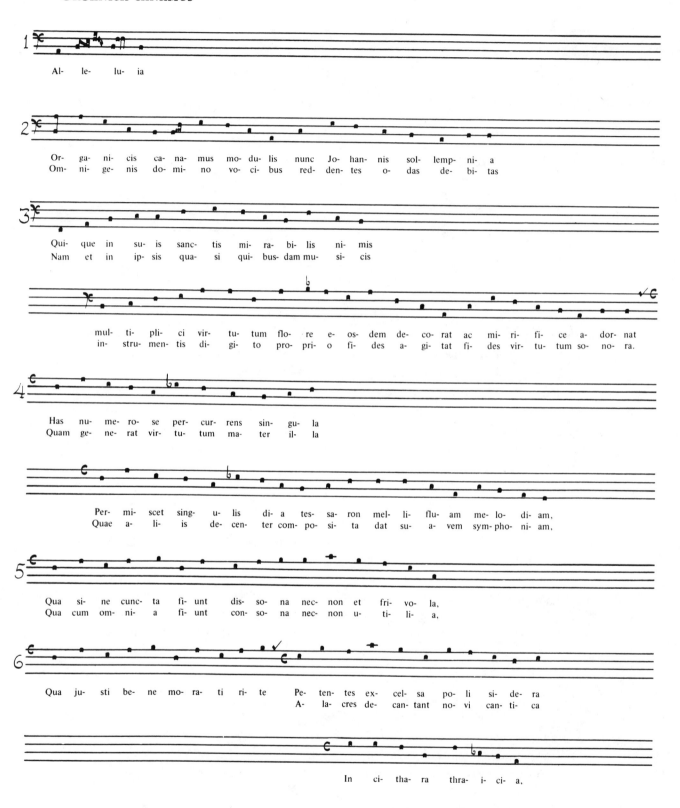

1. Al- le- lu- ia

2. Or- ga- ni- cis ca- na- mus mo- du- lis nunc Jo- han- nis sol- lemp- ni- a
   Om- ni- ge- nis do- mi- no vo- ci- bus red- den- tes o- das de- bi- tas

3. Qui- que in su- is sanc- tis mi- ra- bi- lis ni- mis
   Nam et in ip- sis qua- si qui- bus- dam mu- si- cis

   mul- ti- pli- ci vir- tu- tum flo- re- e- os- dem de- co- rat ac mi- ri- fi- ce a- dor- nat
   in- stru- men- tis di- gi- to pro- pri- o fi- des a- gi- tat fi- des vir- tu- tum so- no- ra.

4. Has nu- me- ro se per- cur- rens sin- gu- la
   Quam ge- ne- rat vir- tu- tum ma- ter il- la

   Per- mi- scet sing- u- lis di- a tes- sa- ron mel- li- flu- am me- lo- di- am,
   Quae a- li- is de- cen- ter com- po- si- ta dat su- a- vem sym- pho- ni- am,

5. Qua si- ne cunc- ta fi- unt dis- so- na nec- non et fri- vo- la,
   Qua cum om- ni- a fi- unt con- so- na nec- non u- ti- li- a,

6. Qua ju- sti be- ne mo- ra- ti ri- te Pe- ten- tes ex- cel- sa po- li si- de- ra
   A- la- cres de- can- tant no- vi can- ti- ca

   In ci- tha- ra thra- i- ci- a,

7. Quo- rum a- gen- tes fe- sta an- nu- a re- co- len- da
Jun- gen- tes lau- dum vo- ta con- sor- ti- um me- re- a- mur

8. In cae- le- sti- pa- tri- a.

b O pie inestimabilis heros:
>   humilis visus hodie in terris est miseris polos ut scanderent.
4a Exultent ergo hodie terrena simul caelestia,
b Et caelestibus quia est unitas illa restaurata.

Line 4b seems at first just an afterthought to 4a: "—and in heaven, because that unity has been restored." *Caelestibus* repeats *caelestia* not by fault but for emphasis, as the first half of a diptych whose second half comes in 5a, *Nos quoque*. Phrases 4 and 5, representing celestial and terrestrial realms, are bracketed together at the lower structural level, producing an elision at the higher level between the first half of the piece, 1-4, and the second half 5-end.

Lines 5a and b both support the sub-phrase structure of the melody; as in some other cases (beginning with ECCE VICIT)—and surely by design—5a supports it more clearly than 5b. In 5a, the second sub-phrase is marked by the redictum *quoque*, and set to the phrase dependent upon *voce*.

5a Nos quoque omnes clerus ac populus
>   voce quoque cordis simul atque oris
>   canamus deo laudem.

In 5b, the second sub-phrase is not marked in any special way. It is set to its own syntactic unit, again an ablative phrase (*juvamine*); but the *dicentes* that follows is so closely associated with that ablative that the second sub-phrase might be considered run on to the approach to the cadence.

5b Nam angelicum sacrum illud hymnum,
>   dei genetricis juvamine fulti / dicentes, persolvamus.

Line 5b, of course, prepares the actual quotation of the angelic hymn in 6; and everything that follows, to the end of the piece, can be construed as part of the hymn that is sung. In this way the extended musical period that starts at 6, working through the network of motives and irregularities to the end, is given a functional analog in the text.

6a   Gloria in altis deo et in terra pax:

b   Populus bono animo sit perenniter.

7   Famulos tu trina deitas nos fove tuos

nunc atque in aevum auxiliare:

laus, honor, imperium,

8a   Potestas atque virtum tibi sit regi nato,

b   Qui omnia regis simul in trinitate,

9   In saeculorum saecula.

The hymn includes a close paraphrase of the beginning of the *Gloria in excelsis deo, et in terra pax hominibus bonae voluntatis* (that is, Luke 2,14). Then follows a petition (*nos fove*), and a concluding doxology (*laus . . . saecula*).

ORGANICIS CANAMUS MODULIS, known in a broad collation of sources, is strikingly different from HÆC DIES EST SANCTA in its persistent terminal a-assonance, and frequent proparoxytones, its dancing accent-rhythms, as well as in several details of melodic construction and in its incipit. All of these features may well indicate a later date of composition, and the inclusion of ORGANICIS CANAMUS here may serve only to throw into relief the early qualities of HÆC DIES EST SANCTA—the lack of terminal assonance, the inconsistent accent patterns at line endings. But ORGANICIS CANAMUS has been thought be to early; and in any case it is dominated by a musical image that is worth knowing for its own sake.

The text of ORGANICIS CANAMUS begins in phrase 2; phrase 1 of the melody is to be sung to the text "Alleluia," laid under the modified quotation from the Alleluia *Justus ut palma*. This procedure (mentioned as the third point in the summary of Alleluia relationships on p. 239) became very frequent in the tenth century, but it is very difficult to tell at what point it actually started. Notker does not use this form of incipit, except possibly for CONCENTU PARILI and NATUS ANTE SAECULA, nor has any of the West-Frankish texts studied so far. The strong trend in the tenth and early eleventh centuries in favor of the Alleluia incipit makes it *likely* that a text such as ORGANICIS CANAMUS is later rather than earlier. This, however, is only a probability; as such, it does not in itself prevent ORGANICIS CANAMUS or any other single instance from being early. It should be added that some have argued that the Alleluia incipit is evidence not only of the earliest text for a given melody, but of the earliest state of the sequence in general, because (the argument runs) it is closest to the Alleluia itself. But that argument can be shown invalid for specific cause. Actually, the search must proceed the other way: sequences with Alleluia incipits must be shown—on other grounds—to be early, in order to establish an early use of the Alleluia incipit.

Lines 2a,b express the functional exhortation to celebrate St. John (Evangelist), in a relatively elaborate way.

2a   Organicis canamus modulis nunc Johannis sollemnia,

b   Omnigenis domino vocibus redentes odas debitas.

The expression *modulis organicis*, "instrumental melodies," is to be taken as verbal ornament or literary image, not performance direction: it is possible that instruments were involved, but it cannot be shown on grounds such as these. Rather, *organicis* is the key word in the dominant image of the piece, spelled out in line 3b.

> 3a   Quique in suis sanctis mirabilis nimis
>   multiplici virtutum flore eosdem decorat ac mirifice adornat.
>   b   Nam et in ipsis quasi quibusdam musicis
>   instrumentis digito proprio fides agitat fides virtutum sonora.

Line 3a is a general statement of God "marvelous in his saints" (*Mirabilis Deus in suis sanctis*, Ps. 67,36). Line 3b then likens him to a cithara player, who awakens faith and virtue in his saints by strumming on their heart-strings. The comparison of the soul to a cithara is an old one, going back at least to Plato's *Timaeus*.

Phrase 2 has been extended (relative to HÆC DIES EST SANCTA and also Notker's version) to include a C D D cadence, proparoxytone (*sollémnia, débitas*). Phrase 3 has a similar cadence, but paroxytone (*adórnat, sonóra*). The reprise of phrase 2 at 4 has been omitted. Phrase 5, now phrase 4, does not have the C D D addition, but ends as in HÆC DIES EST SANCTA. It is difficult to see in these changes any overall pattern.

Phrase 4 fills the lyric sub-phrase structure with assonant, rhythmic extension of the image.

> 4a   Has numerose percurrens singula
>   permiscet singulis diatessaron mellifluam melodiam,
>   b   Quam generat virtutum mater illa
>   quae aliis decenter composita dat suavem symphoniam.

"Running over them rhythmically (*numerose*) he blends one with another in fourths (*diatessaron*), making tuneful melody, which that mother of virtues generates, and which, well fitted together of diverse elements, gives forth sweet harmony (symphoniam)." The syntax lends itself more to sonority than to precise sense; it might be read in more than one way. The meaning, however, is clear: the saints show forth all the beauty of the most exquisite music involving the most elaborate, sophisticated resources of musical art. (*Numerose* is Augustine's translation of the Greek *rhythmike*, in his *De musica*.)

Beginning at 5 (= 6 of HÆC DIES EST SANCTA), ORGANICIS CANAMUS modifies the motivic system in the direction of greater uniformity. The three-note motive disappears; in its place 5 begins with a simple repetition.

> ORGANICIS CANAMUS 5   A C B C D,   A C B C D, . . .
> HÆC DIES EST SANCTA 6   A C D,   A C B C D, . . .

This same repetition also replaces the motive at the start of 6 (= 7 of HÆC DIES EST SANCTA), which lengthens that incipit, giving it the status of a sub-phrase.

Throughout the latter part of the piece the relative clauses (*Qua . . . qua . . . qua . . .*) dependent on the primary image continue, effectively eliminating any rhetorical division into two halves. Just as little attention was paid to the sub-phrase structure of 4 (= 5), so at the higher level the text does little to articulate the overall design of the melody.

Ecce dies

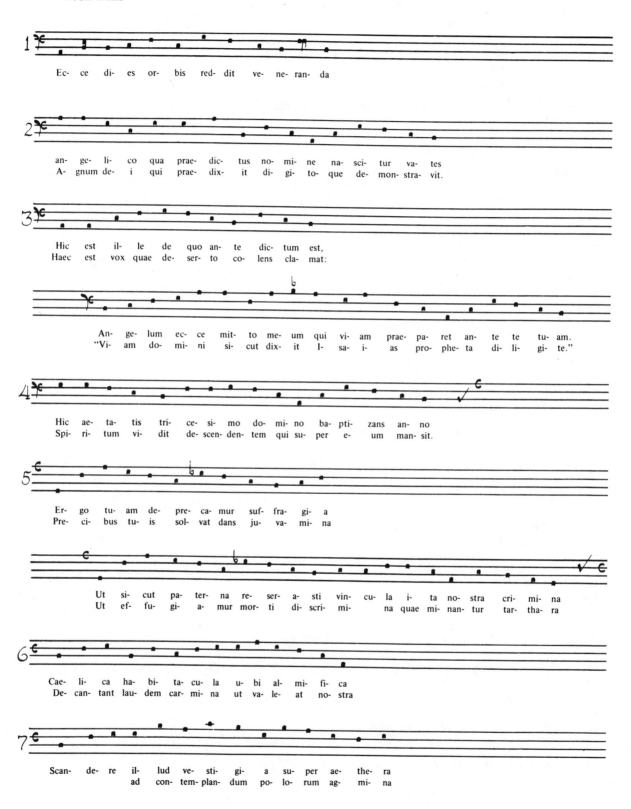

1. Ec- ce di- es or- bis red- dit ve- ne- ran- da

2. an- ge- li- co qua prae- dic- tus no- mi- ne na- sci- tur va- tes
   A- gnum de- i qui prae- dix- it di- gi- to- que de- mon- stra- vit.

3. Hic est il- le de quo an- te dic- tum est,
   Haec est vox quae de- ser- to co- lens cla- mat:

   An- ge- lum ec- ce mit- to me- um qui vi- am prae- pa- ret an- te te tu- am.
   "Vi- am do- mi- ni si- cut dix- it I- sa- i- as pro- phe- ta di- li- gi- te."

4. Hic ae- ta- tis tri- ce- si- mo do- mi- no ba- pti- zans an- no
   Spi- ri- tum vi- dit de- scen- den- tem qui su- per e- um man- sit.

5. Er- go tu- am de- pre- ca- mur suf- fra- gi- a
   Pre- ci- bus tu- is sol- vat dans ju- va- mi- na

   Ut si- cut pa- ter- na re- ser- a- sti vin- cu- la i- ta no- stra cri- mi- na
   Ut ef- fu- gi- a- mur mor- ti di- scri- mi- na quae mi- nan- tur tar- tha- ra

6. Cae- li- ca ha- bi- ta- cu- la u- bi al- mi- fi- ca
   De- can- tant lau- dem car- mi- na ut va- le- at no- stra

7. Scan- de- re il- lud ve- sti- gi- a su- per ae- the- ra
   ad con- tem- plan- dum po- lo- rum ag- mi- na

292   "Justus ut palma major"

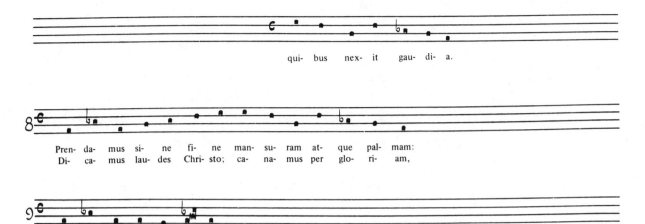

qui- bus nex- it gau- di- a.

Pren- da- mus si- ne fi- ne man- su- ram at- que pal- mam:
Di- ca- mus lau- des Chri- sto; ca- na- mus per glo- ri- am,

Di- cen- tes al- le- lu- ia.

5a   Qua sine cuncta fiunt dissona nec non et frivola;

  b   Qua cum omnia fiunt consona nec non   utilia;

6   Qua justi bene morati rite

                 petentes excelsa poli sidera

                 alacres decantant novi cantica

                         in cithara thraicia

7a   Quorum agentes festa annua recolenda

  b   Jungentes laudum vota consortium mereamur

8   In caelestia patria.

The intent seems rather to permeate the whole piece with the one image by using connected syntax and persistent assonance. Of this, lines 5a,b are the most extreme expression, coming as close to sonorous identity as any in the early repertory.

The use of a strong image that pervades and dominates a whole piece can be characteristic of an early prose; Hæc est sancta is another example. This is perhaps the best argument for an early date for organicis canamus. A strong argument against an early date, however, is the presence of discrepancies relative to Notker's version—the cadence at the end of 2, the omission of Notker's 4, the longer form of the motive at Notker's 6. There is another text in the Aquitanian sources, ecce dies, that follows Notker's plan closely and has several interesting features besides, but the collation may possibly speak against it as an early piece. Ecce dies appears in MSS 1118 and 1084, then also in MS 1338—there, however, in the first of the two long series of proses that constitute the prosarium. At the end of the first series appears the inscription *facta s[unt] prosas novas*, not entirely free of obscurity or barbarism; yet its import seems borne out by concordances, for the proses in this first series are largely unicae, or give other indication of being in fact "new proses."

There are, however, anomalies in some of the concordances, and at least a few of the proses must not be strictly new. So, in the case of ECCE DIES, there is room for doubt.

ECCE DIES is for St. John Baptist—and stands very close to Notker's SANCTI BAPTISTAE. With a little imagination, one can read ECCE DIES as Notker's specific model. The first half of ECCE DIES includes a festal proclamation (1), and liturgical identification (2a,b), making excellent use of the image of John pointing out with his finger the "Lamb of God" (John 1,29). Lines 3a,b and 4a,b continue the account of John and his baptism of Jesus, citing scripture and using a straight-forward kind of diction with no terminal a-assonance.

1   Ecce dies orbis reddit veneranda

2a   angelico qua praedictus nomine nascitur vates;

 b   Agnum dei qui praedixit digitoque demonstravit.

3a   Hic est ille de quo ante dictum est:

         angelum ecce mitto meum qui via praeparet ante te tuam.

3b   Hæc est vox quae deserto colens clamat:

         viam domini sicut dixit Isaias propheta diligite.

4a   Hic aetatis tricesimo domino baptizans anno

 b   Spiritum vidit descendentem qui super eum mansit.

Line 5a then turns to petition with *ergo*, and from here on the a-assonance is prominent not only at line endings but also consistently at the sub-phrase endings of 5 (*suffrágia*, *juvámina*, *víncula*, *discrímina*), and even permeating the whole line, as in 6 and following.

5a   Ergo tuam deprecamur suffragia,

      ut sicut paterna reserasti vincula

            ita nostra crimina.

 b   Precibus tuis solvat dans juvamina,

      ut effugiamur morti discrimina

             quae mirantur tarthara;

6a   Caelica habitacula ubi almifica

 b   Decantant laudem, carmina ut valeat nostra

7   Scandere illud vestigia super aethera

        ad contemplandum polorum agmina,

              quibus nexit gaudia;

8a   Prendamus sine fine mansuram atque palmam;

 b   Dicamus laudes Christo; canamus per gloriam,

9   Dicentes "alleluia."

The syntax in 5a,b is still fairly consequent, but from 6 on both syntax and sense tend to dissolve in the contemplation of celestial glory, whose main vehicles are the sonority and a-assonance—and of course the ecstatic melody, with which the text is intimately associated. Here the musical qualities of language heavily outweigh its other functions, and with such propriety that one hardly stops to question what the last half of the text means or how it is to be parsed. This use of language became, in tenth-century Aquitania, an abuse;

the prosaria are full of examples. Perhaps ECCE DIES should be numbered among them. But the way this language appears only at a certain point, only in the second half, where both sense and melody call for just such an overflow, suggests that ECCE DIES (like HÆC EST SANCTA) might instead be one of the early models of pervasive assonance.

Notker's text for John Baptist, SANCTI BAPTISTAE, is of course in a different kind of language. And perhaps the similarities to ECCE DIES are only coincidental, or occasioned by the common scriptural sources. The angelic visitation of ECCE DIES 2a turns up in Notker's 3b, and Notker's 5 includes a petition, but less obviously introduced than the one in ECCE DIES 5. The "Lamb of God" reference he does not use until 7. And of celestial glory there is little—a fleeting reference in 4a,b, and again in 8a,b. More characteristically, Notker mentions the indwelling of the Lord in his faithful, *et mansionem in eis facere dignetur* (6b). Indeed, the whole encounter with the Baptist is aimed by Notker towards moral edification: *moribus ipsum sequamur* in line 2a turns out to be the dominant message, with *sollemnia celebrantes* from the same line remaining a means toward that end.

Notker's attention was clearly arrested by the melodic construction from phrase 6 to the end. For this construction he provided a single period of remarkable length and complexity.

6a   *Placatus*, ut ipse suos semper invisere
 b   *fideles*, et mansionem in eis facere
 7   *Dignetur*, et agni vellere, quem tuo digito
          Mundi monstraveras tollere crimina,
              Nos velit induere,
8a   Ut ipsum mereamur *angelis associi*
 b   In alba veste sequi *per portam clarissimam*
 9   Amice Christi, Johannes!

This display, based on the melody, shows by italic the short motive that frames 6, and the longer motive, or sub-phrase, that has an analogous function in 8. The motive in 6, as we saw, provides a rising movement, the one in 8 a falling, cadential one, and this is reflected in Notker's texting. But more than that, his text sets an elaborate syntactical counterpoint against the melody, as can be seen by comparing the melodic display just given to this purely syntactic one.

(6) Placatus,
       ut ipse suos semper invisere fideles,
          et mansionem in eis facere dignetur,
(7)   et agni vellere,
            quem tuo digito mundi monstraveras tollere crimina,
          nos velit induere,
(8)   ut ipsum mereamur, angelis associi,
          in alba veste sequi per portam clarissimam,
(9)   —amice Christi, Johannes!

LAUS TIBI CHRISTE CUI SAPIT (Notker)

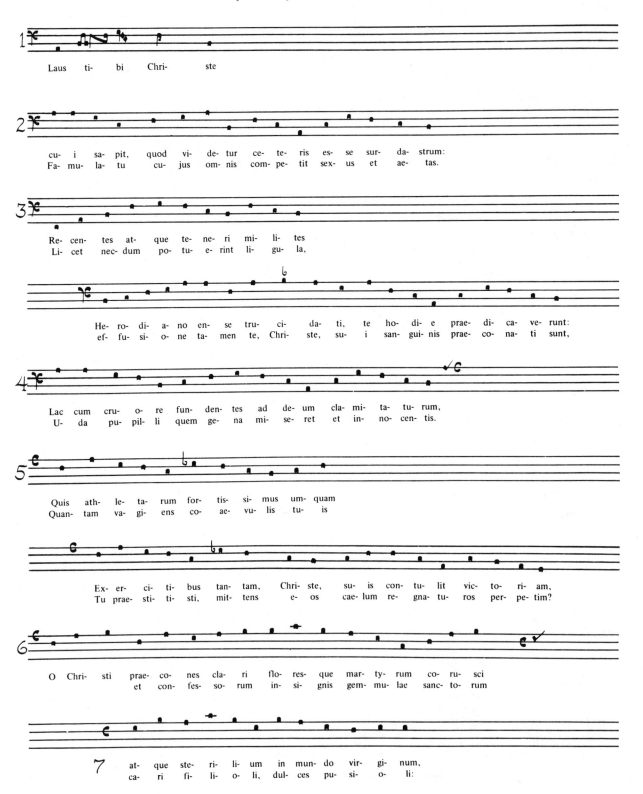

1 Laus ti- bi Chri- ste

2 cu- i sa- pit, quod vi- de- tur ce- te- ris es- se sur- da- strum:
Fa- mu- la- tu cu- jus om- nis com- pe- tit sex- us et ae- tas.

3 Re- cen- tes at- que te- ne- ri mi- li- tes
Li- cet nec- dum po- tu- e- rint li- gu- la,

He- ro- di- a- no en- se tru- ci- da- ti, te ho- di- e prae- di- ca- ve- runt:
ef- fu- si- o- ne ta- men te, Chri- ste, su- i san- gui- nis prae- co- na- ti sunt,

4 Lac cum cru- o- re fun- den- tes ad de- um cla- mi- ta- tu- rum,
U- da pu- pil- li quem ge- na mi- se- ret et in- no- cen- tis.

5 Quis ath- le- ta- rum for- tis- si- mus um- quam
Quan- tam va- gi- ens co- ae- vu- lis tu- is

Ex- er- ci- ti- bus tan- tam, Chri- ste, su- is con- tu- lit vic- to- ri- am,
Tu prae- sti- ti- sti, mit- tens e- os cae- lum re- gna- tu- ros per- pe- tim?

6 O Chri- sti prae- co- nes cla- ri flo- res- que mar- ty- rum co- ru- sci
et con- fes- so- rum in- si- gnis gem- mu- lae sanc- to- rum

7 at- que ste- ri- li- um in mun- do vir- gi- num,
ca- ri fi- li- o- li, dul- ces pu- si- o- li:

LAUS TIBI CHRISTE CUI SAPIT (Notker) (2)

nos ju-va-te pre-ci-bus! ₈quas Chri-stus, in-no-cen-tem mor-tem ve-stram mi-se-rans
pro se-se ma-tu-ra-tam, pla-ci-dus ex-au-di-ens

Nos re-gno su-o di-gne-tur.

All of this (up to 9) is itself a subordinate construction dependent upon the petition *te deposcimus* in line 5b, which is concluded by the vocative in line 9—"we beg thee . . . John, friend of Christ!"

Notker, too, has construed the piece in two halves, 1–4 and 5–9, and in consequence of that, apparently, has provided two different types of cadence for the four-note descending figure in lines 2,3,4,5,6,8. In the first half he sets this consistently paroxytone (*sequámur . . . percipiámus*, etc.), but in the second half always proparoxytone (*invéniat . . . invísere . . . indúere*, etc.). What prompted this? There is no clear suggestion in either HÆC DIES EST SANCTA or ORGANICIS CANAMUS. Could it have been the contrast of the two halves of ECCE DIES with the abrupt turn to a-assonance (which Notker does not ordinarily use) and pervasive proparoxytone rhythms at phrase 5?

LAUS TIBI CHRISTE, Notker's other text to this melody, has the air of authority, independence, of toughness and directness of diction that seems to mark his maturity. The theme is the difficult one of Holy Innocents (December 28th); Von den Steinen explores Notker's solution to the problem, why did God require the murder of all those children.[3]

Assuming that LAUS TIBI CHRISTE is later than SANCTI BAPTISTAE, it may be possible to see in the handling of 6–9 the same full realization of formal possibilities we observed in QUID TU VIRGO or TUBAM BELLICOSAM. The endless, interlocking series of short phrases and motives is here set as a litany—not a very long litany, but enough to summon up the idea as an analog to the melodic structure. Here is the text laid out to show the invocations, which follow the usual order, apostles, martyrs, confessors, virgins.

(6) O Christi praecones clari,
  floresque martyrum corusci,
  et confessorum insignes,
  gemulae sanctorum,
(7) atque sterilium in mundo virginum,
 cari filioli,
 dulces pusioli:

3. Von den Steinen, *Notker* I, pp. 342–347.

(8) —nos juvate precibus!
    quas Christus,
        innocentem mortem vestram miserans pro sese maturatam,
    placidus exaudiens
(9)   nos regno suo dignetur.

The motive A C D is in this text clearly terminal (as *corusci, sanctorum*), in defiance of its rising melody. The resulting tension is not absorbed until *nos juvate precibus* closes the litany on the descending figure that frames 8—or rather, not until 8 itself, functioning as a collect after the litany, has twice repeated that figure. No elegant epigram in the style of *Johannes Christi care*, only the closing petition, *nos regno suo dignetur*, skillfully kept in line with the long-suspended syntax until the very end.

    Cari filioli, dulces pusioli—a striking line and one that recalls the brilliant, poignant little *rhythmus* by Gottschalk of Orbais (d. 868/9).[4]

Ut quid jubes, pusiole,
Quare mandas, filiole,
Carmen dulce me cantare,
Cum sim longe exul valde   intra mare?
O cur jubes canere?

Could Notker have known it?

4. *Poetae latini aevi Carolini* III (ed. L. Traube), p. 731.

XVI

OMNIPOTENS DEUS
Notker's FESTA CHRISTI

A WEST-FRANKISH analog for Notker's FESTA CHRISTI was not noticed until Fr. de Goede pointed out OMNIPOTENS DEUS, found in four Aquitanian manuscripts. Except for slight differences in lengths of lines, and certain melodic details, the two versions correspond well through phrase 7. Phrase 8 of OMNIPOTENS DEUS has no counterpart in Notker's FESTA CHRISTI, and the concluding singles are different. Together, the two versions bear witness to another noble member of the G-*tetrardus* family, but with an interesting use of material shared with PRAECURSOR CHRISTI (D-*protus*) and HÆC EST VERA REDEMPTIO (G-*protus*).

Like these two sequences, OMNIPOTENS DEUS uses an Alleluia quotation, and again one with problematic aspects. The Alleluia referred to is one associated with the verse *Benedictus es*, used for the Mass in honor of the Trinity.[1] This mass was urged for adoption by Alcuin; the prayers (collect, secret, post-communion) and sometimes the preface are credited to his authorship.[2] The origin of the chant propers is not yet clear, but the Alleluia is present in only two of Hesbert's six earliest Mass-books (Senlis, Compiègne), suggesting a late eighth or early ninth-century date.

The West-Frankish text has its own problems, primarily in grammar. Perhaps the text we have is corrupt, but it seems possible the problems go back to the original state of the text. A clear case of corruption appears in 3a,b: the redictum *canit* is firm in the two (closely related) readings MS 1118 and MS 1084, but it can be correct only in 3b; 3a as it stands makes little sense.

---

1. Schlager *Them.Kat.* no. 302; *Alleluia-Melodien* I, pp. 51, 648. It appears in two MSS in Hesbert's *Antiphonale missarum sextuplex*, nos. 172 bis and 199a, and in three of the earliest notated MSS, St. Gall 339, 359, and Chartres 47.

2. See G. Ellard, *Master Alcuin, Liturgist* (Chicago 1956), pp. 147–150, 157–161.

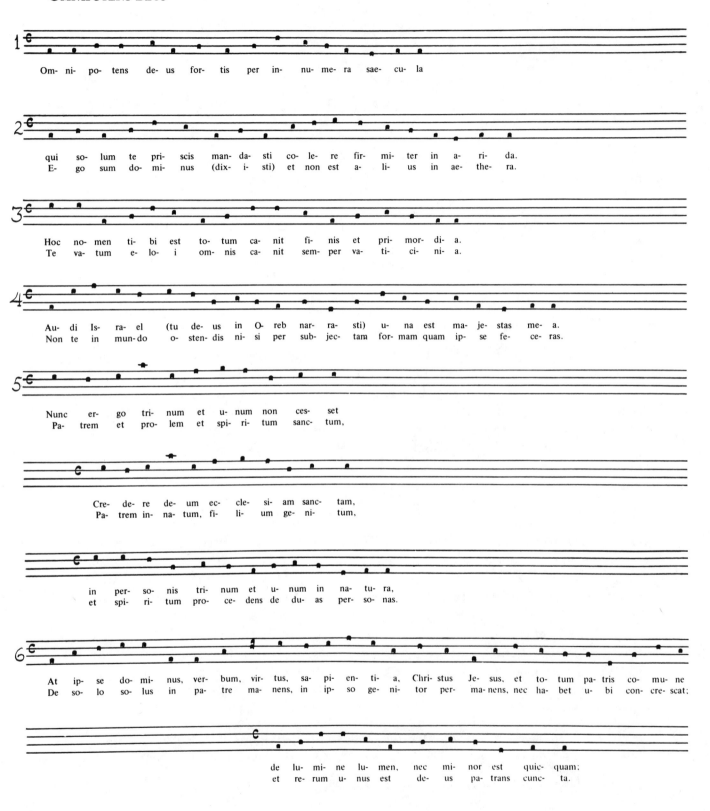

1. Om- ni- po- tens de- us for- tis per in- nu- me- ra sae- cu- la

2. qui so- lum te pri- scis man- da- sti co- le- re fir- mi- ter in a- ri- da.
   E- go sum do- mi- nus (dix- i- sti) et non est a- li- us in ae- the- ra.

3. Hoc no- men ti- bi est to- tum ca- nit fi- nis et pri- mor- di- a.
   Te va- tum e- lo- i om- nis ca- nit sem- per va- ti- ci- ni- a.

4. Au- di Is- ra- el (tu de- us in O- reb nar- ra- sti) u- na est ma- je- stas me- a.
   Non te in mun- do o- sten- dis ni- si per sub- jec- tam for- mam quam ip- se fe- ce- ras.

5. Nunc er- go tri- num et u- num non ces- set
   Pa- trem et pro- lem et spi- ri- tum sanc- tum,

   Cre- de- re de- um ec- cle- si- am sanc- tam,
   Pa- trem in- na- tum, fi- li- um ge- ni- tum,

   in per- so- nis tri- num et u- num in na- tu- ra,
   et spi- ri- tum pro- ce- dens de du- as per- so- nas.

6. At ip- se do- mi- nus, ver- bum, vir- tus, sa- pi- en- ti- a, Chri- stus Je- sus, et to- tum pa- tris co- mu- ne
   De so- lo so- lus in pa- tre ma- nens, in ip- so ge- ni- tor per- ma- nens, nec ha- bet u- bi con- cre- scat;

   de lu- mi- ne lu- men, nec mi- nor est quic- quam;
   et re- rum u- nus est de- us pa- trans cunc- ta.

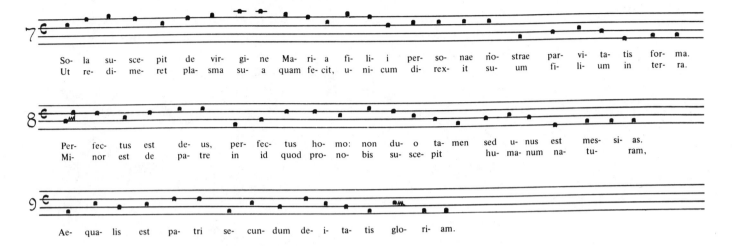

Sol- la su- sce- pit de vir- gi- ne Ma- ri- a fi- li- i per- so- nae no- strae par- vi- ta- tis for- ma.
Ut re- di- me- ret pla- sma su- a quam fe- cit, u- ni- cum di- rex- it su- um fi- li- um in ter- ra.

Per- fec- tus est de- us, per- fec- tus ho- mo: non du- o ta- men sed u- nus est mes- si- as.
Mi- nor est de pa- tre in id quod pro- no- bis su- sce- pit hu- ma- num na- tu- ram,

Ae- qua- lis est pa- tri se- cun- dum de- i- ta- tis glo- ri- am.

3a Hoc nomen tibi est totum canit finis et primordia.

 b Te vatum eloi omnis canit semper vaticinia.

The reading in 3a could be ascribed to scribal anticipation, and perhaps the original word resembled *canit*.

Lines 5a,b present several instances of casual Latin.

(5a) Nunc ergo trinum et unum non cesset credere deum ecclesiam sanctam,

        in personis trinum et unum in naturam,

 (b)   patrem et prolem et spiritum sanctum,

            patrem innatum, filium genitum,

        et spiritum procedens de duas personas.

In 5a, *ecclesiam sanctam* should be nominative; in 5b, *procedens* should be accusative to agree with *spiritum*; and *de duas personas* ("from the two persons") seems truly a Merovingian barbarism even in the sometimes none too meticulous West-Frankish Latin. It could be easily emended to *duabus personis*, omitting the *de* and preserving the syllable count. *Procedens*, however, would have to be *procedentem*, and that would disturb the count—and in a line where *pátrem et prólem et spíritum sánctum* sits so neatly under its melody it would seem inappropriate to disturb the syllable count elsewhere. Perhaps, however, this very neatness of *Patrem . . . sanctum* tells us something about the origin of 5b, for in general such a jingling effect is characteristic of later development in the sequence. An original single at 5 would be entirely in keeping with its sub-phrase structure, and would ascribe these grammatical barbarisms, at least, to the same hand that added the jingle.

Further doubtful details appear in some of the case endings in 6, where masculine and neuter nominatives alternate, either in looseness or irregularity, and in 7a,b where the accusatives *sola[m] forma[m]* and *plasma[m] sua[m]* should apparently be supplied. These, however, can be described as simple mistakes of transmission.

The text as a whole leaves the same general impression as CLARA GAUDIA—an ambitious attempt at a lofty theme that fails to become convincing only because of the technical limitations of the author. He sets out to acclaim the Trinity through the progressive revelation in Old and New Testament. Line 2a,b evokes the God of Moses (Ex. 20); lines 3a,b refer to the prophets. Lines 4a,b quote the text that formed the *Sh'ma'*, the statement of Hebraic faith (Deut. 6,4):

"Hear, O Israel, the Lord our God, the Lord is One . . ."

Lines 1 through 4 begin with the invocation of Almighty God and conclude with the affirmation of Old Testament monotheism; this much stands as a textual unit.

In line 5a, the scene shifts to the Church, *ecclesia sancta*, which steadfastly believes God to be three and yet one; the paradox is expressed here in not quite the orthodox language —*natura* is usually employed for the two natures (human and divine), the unity being expressed as *substantia*. A forceful *nunc ergo* sets 5a off from what came before.

Lines 6a,b and 7a,b go together as an amplification of the doctrine of the persons, the Father and the Son in particular. Lines 6a,b enumerate functions of the Son—Lord, Word, strength, wisdom, . . . light from light; remaining in the Father, one God and Father of all. The elaboration through apposites recalls the second paragraph of the "Nicene" Creed.

> And in one Lord, Jesus Christ, the only begotten Son of God,
> begotten of his Father before all worlds.
> God of god, light of light, very god of very god.
> Begotten, not made, being of one substance with the Father.
> By whom all things were made.

6a At ipse dominus, verbum, virtus, sapientia, Christus Jesus,
    et totum patris commune, de lumine lumen, nec minor est quicquam;
 b De solo solus in patre manens, in ipso genitor permanens,
    nec habet ubi concrescat; et rerum unus est deus patrans cuncta.
7a Sola suscepit de virgine Maria filii persone nostrae parvitatis forma[m].
 b Ut redimeret plasmam suam quem fecit, unicum direxit suum filium in terra.

Lines 7a,b refer to the Incarnation, whereby God took on the form "of the person of the Son"; that is, 7a,b states the duality of natures, against the unity emphasized in 6a,b. Lines 8a,b and 9 then recapitulate the paradox of the two natures, this time using the language of the Athanasian Creed.[3]

Athanasian Creed	OMNIPOTENS DEUS	
Perfectus deus,	8a	Perfectus est deus,
perfectus homo:		perfectus homo:
ex anima rationale		non duo tamen,

3. The Athanasian Creed is traditionally said at Prime on the Feast of the Holy Trinity, and certain other Sundays.

et humana
carne subsistens.

Aequalis patri
secundum divinitatem:
minor patre
secundum humanitatem.

sed unus est messias.

b   Minor est de patre
in id quod pro nobis
suscepit humanum naturam.

9   Aequalis est patris
secundum deitatis gloriae.

The formulation "less than the Father in his humanity" is peculiar to the Athanasian Creed and in OMNIPOTENS DEUS attracts attention by its opposition to 6a, *nec minor est quicquam* ("nor is he in any respect less [than the Father]"). There might be grounds here for thinking that 8a,b–9 was a later addition, a suggestion that will receive support from the comparison with Notker's version.

In its larger design, the text is clearly coordinated with the melody. The Old Testament section is set to a group of phrases (1–4) that remain anchored to the G final. Phrase 5, where the discourse introduces the Trinity, marks a break in the melodic plan in several ways; phrases 5 through 9 constitute a second half in the melody just as clearly as in the text. What might be regarded as the theological point, the statement and purpose of Incarnation in 7a,b, is set to the last insistence on the high G, to be followed only by postclimax in text and melody. Phrases 5 and 6, the longest phrases, lead up to the high point in 7 with the necessary trinitarian qualification and preparation.

After the invocation on the opening single, the Old Testament section 2–4 is set to a group of phrases that move through the fifth above the final, G-D, in an expository fashion. The basic melodic tendency is upwards from the G, as expressed clearly in phrase 2, which can be understood as an extension of the material from the Alleluia quotation in 1. Phrase 3 acts as an answer, in some sense a balancing element, in that it starts higher and descends to the G final. Phrase 4, longer and more elaborate, includes an assertive leap upwards, a descent in groups of threes, a turn to the F-A-C realm, and the cadence pattern to be used for most of the rest of the piece.

4   G D E D C, D C A, B A G A F A C B A B A F G G

This phrase can be understood as the concluding element of the opening section of the melody.

The different functions of the constitutive phrases in this opening section are supported by their differing cadences. Phrases 1 and 2 used the usual pattern

C B A G F   G G
   saé - cu-la
   á - ri-da
   aé-the-ra

The setting hesitates, in typical early West-Frankish fashion, between paroxytones and proparoxytones. Phrase 3 ends with a pattern encountered also in ECCE VICIT, and hardly anywhere else in the early repertory; here it is set proparoxytone.

```
G  A  B   AG
pri-mór-di-a
va-ti-cí-ni-a
```

Phrase 4 brings yet another pattern, distinguished by the skip from A to F, and the relatively strong sense of tritone between B and F.

```
B  A  F  G G
ma-je-stas mé-a
ip-se  fé-ce-ras
```

Here the accent hesitates again between paroxytone and proparoxytone; but in phrases 5, 6, and 7, where the same cadence appears (the pattern now includes the approach as well) the accent is consistently paroxytone.

```
G A B A F G  G
     na-tú-  ram
     per-só-  nas
         quíc-quam
            cúnc-ta
            fór-ma
            tér-ra
```

Furthermore, the same pattern is used in the sub-phrases of 5—there, however, with some variation in accent. In 8a, an extra G is added for *messias*, in a manner that recalls the modification of this cadence pattern in LAUDES DEO, as well as a few other cases; but in 8b, a note has been left out of the approach to the cadence. Here, too, lines 8a,b give the impression of being not indigenous.

The uniformity of cadence from phrase 4 through 8 seems (as in other cases) designed to unify the latter half of the melody; what is distinctive in this case is the variety of pattern up to that point. Phrase 5, beginning on D a fifth above the final, and ascending immediately to G an octave above, clearly marks off a new section of the piece (even while it carries out the upward trend of the melody). The layout of the piece up through 5 recalls CHRISTI HODIERNA as well as ECCE VICIT, for in both those pieces, too, an expository section of four phrases was closed off by a move to a higher register and the appearance of a sub-phrase structure.

Like the sub-phrase structure in ECCE VICIT, this one is extremely pointed in its lyric effect: the first sub-phrase of 5 is immediately noticeable in its high degree of melodic focus, and in its regular rhythms.

```
       D  C  D  GD  E F E   C  DD
5a  Nunc ergo trinum et unum non cesset
       DCD GD  E  FEC D  D
     credere de-um ecclesi-a sancta,
            D  DCA  BA  GAB  A  FGG
            in personis trinum et unum in naturam;
```

Unlike the one in ECCE VICIT, the first sub-phrase has no contact with the G final, hence does not seem like an elaboration of the fifth G-D; instead it sits in the fourth from D up to the high G, giving the sub-phrase an entirely different color.

	ECCE VICIT	OMNIPOTENS DEUS
phrase 5		G
		F
	(E)	E
	D	D
	C	(C)
	B	
	A	
	G	

In OMNIPOTENS DEUS the melodic motion of the sub-phrase fits precisely into its tonal set; its motion seems inevitable, the rhythm locked into threes in some seemingly inalterable way.

/ D C D / G D E / F E C / D D

And, indeed, the accents in three out of the four cases fall at the beginnings of these groups; only *fílium génitum* (5b) is different.

The sub-phrase structure of the melody is not reflected in line 5a at the end of the first sub-phrase (*cesset / credere*), although it is at the end of the second (*sanctam / in personis*) and then obviously in 5b. This instance of blurring a sub-phrase structure is harder to justify than the others we have noticed, but can still, I think, be understood as purposive rather than merely clumsy.

The sub-phrase and its repetition make up most of phrase 5, the rest being simply the approach to the cadence. Phrase 6 produces a different effect, even though it, like 5, has a repetition at the beginning; but the part to be repeated is only a motive, while the rest of the phrase, much longer, moves without clear-cut repetitions to create the sense of a single unbroken phrase.

6 G B C D D, G G B C D C D E D B C B G B . . .

There was some doubt, however, in the minds of the Aquitanian scribes of the sequentiarium of MS 1118 as to whether this phrase began on G (that is, on A, but continuing as transcribed), or on D a fifth higher, which would make the phrase as a whole resemble the tonal realm of phrase 5 rather than 4. This, the reading of the later witness for Notker's version, pays more attention to the motivic relationship between the beginnings of phrases 6 and 7, and interprets 7 as an immediate, emphatic reiteration of the ascent to the high G.

Phrase 7 being shorter, drops sooner to its lower G, and here a special point is made of the drop; the cadence pattern following seems clearly set off from the rest of the phrase. Yet no articulation seems intended: on one hand, the cadence pattern on D is given no recognizable cadential accent pattern, and has an extra D; on the other hand, in both 7a and b a word—and one that might be considered stressed—falls over the drop

```
FDC  DDD D G A BA F  G  G
fi-li-i   personae nostrae parvita-tis  forma
unicum di-rexit su- um  fi-li-um in ter-ra
```

". . . The form of *our* small stature," and ". . . sent *his* only Son to earth"—this placement seems carefully calculated, and to good effect.

The melody for phrase 8 anticipates the effect of a closing single with its quilisma ABC; or perhaps it suggests a penultimate excursion into the F-A-C realm in the fashion of NUNC EXULTET. As the phrase continues, however, its function is seen rather to be an echo of 6, an effect that would be much stronger if 6 were placed in the lower position.

```
alternate reading: 6 G      B C D D, G    B C   D . . .
                   8 ABC C B C D D, G A C C B D . . .
```

In any case, phrase 8 as it stands adds nothing new, but merely substance at the end and symmetry to the whole. The concluding single, 9, while not obviously related to 8, seems to follow naturally enough.

The lyric sub-phrase at the start of 5 is almost the same as phrase 7 of HÆC EST VERA REDEMPTIO, and therefore also similar to phrase 3 of Notker's version of "Justus ut palma minor." In this last case, the passage is at home in a tonal realm on a D final, occupying the upper fourth of the octave segment above the final.

```
        D
A  A     A . . .
  G

(D)
```

The passage clearly revolves around the A, which is heard as non-final relative to the lower D; yet it shares with that D the same kind of tonal color due to the similar arrangement of whole and half steps, that is

```
G   D
F   C
E   B
D   A
C   G
```

In HÆC EST VERA REDEMPTIO, the passage, now based on a G final with a B flat, has a similar location and function—similar, that is, if we ignore the implications of the Alleluia quotation, which is G-*tetrardus*, with B natural.

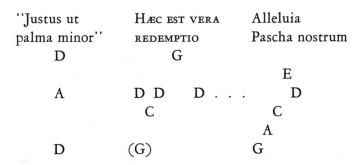

"Justus ut palma minor"	Hæc est vera redemptio	Alleluia Pascha nostrum
D	G	
		E
A	D D D . . .	D
	C	C
		A
D	(G)	G

The passage in question belongs firmly to that part of Hæc est vera redemptio that is based on G-*protus*, rather than the part associated with the Alleluia quotation.

The appearance of the same passage in omnipotens deus, then, is curious, because this melody seems to be clearly on G-*tetrardus*, as shown by the Alleluia quotation, which this time has an explicit B natural. In G-*tetrardus* the passage occupies the same position relative to the final, circling around the fifth above as an important non-final tone; but a difference of tonal color is much more apparent, due to the different arrangement of whole and half steps, that is,

C	G
B	
	F
A	E
G	D
F	C

Christi hodierna again comes to mind as a piece that exploited the contrast between a G-*tetrardus* final and the D a fifth above, where it eventually ended.

Hæc est vera redemptio had a drop of a fifth at the ends of several phrases, just before the cadence pattern

... D / G A B♭ A F G

In beata tu virgo this cadence pattern, set off by the drop of a fifth, was set as a refrain, *O sancta Maria*. This was the first and most characteristic appearance of the B flat. Omnipotens deus has the same drop of a fifth, to the same cadence pattern, at the end of phrase 7. Should B flat be used in omnipotens deus? It would smooth out the tritone in the cadence pattern, if that is felt to be objectionable.

G A B♭ A F G G

The flat could not be introduced at the beginning, for the Alleluia quotation in this case requires the B natural; and there would be no reason to introduce the B flat before the end of phrase 4. It could be done gracefully on *in Oreb* in 4a. No staff sources for omnipotens deus being extant, this problem (like that of the pitch level of phrase 6) remains indeter-

Festa christi (Notker)

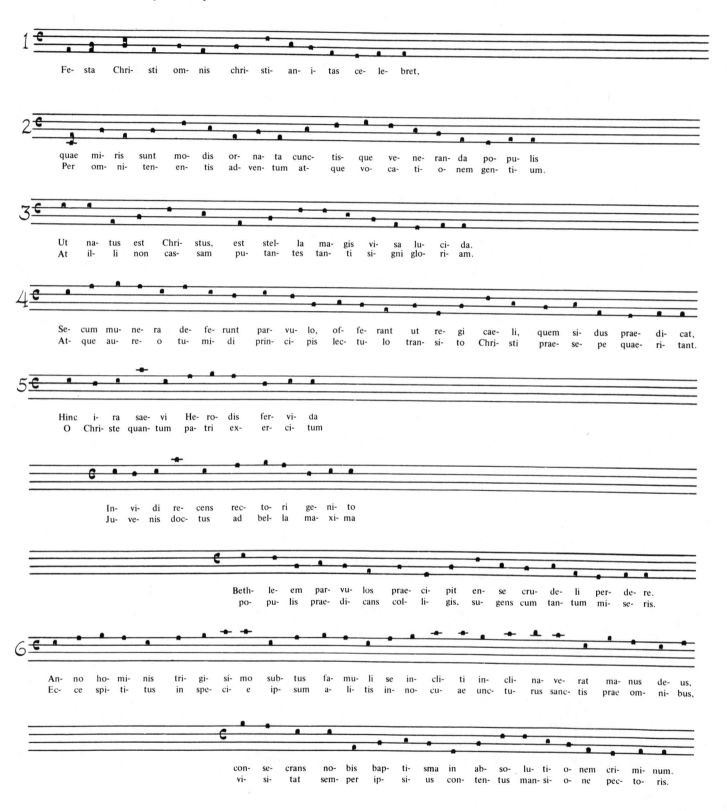

1. Fe- sta Chri- sti om- nis chri- sti- an- i- tas ce- le- bret,

2. quae mi- ris sunt mo- dis or- na- ta cunc- tis- que ve- ne- ran- da po- pu- lis
   Per om- ni- ten- en- tis ad- ven- tum at- que vo- ca- ti- o- nem gen- ti- um.

3. Ut na- tus est Chri- stus, est stel- la ma- gis vi- sa lu- ci- da.
   At il- li non cas- sam pu- tan- tes tan- ti si- gni glo- ri- am.

4. Se- cum mu- ne- ra de- fe- runt par- vu- lo, of- fe- rant ut re- gi cae- li, quem si- dus prae- di- cat,
   At- que au- re- o tu- mi- di prin- ci- pis lec- tu- lo tran- si- to Chri- sti prae- se- pe quae- ri- tant.

5. Hinc i- ra sae- vi He- ro- dis fer- vi- da
   O Chri- ste quan- tum pa- tri ex- er- ci- tum

In- vi- di re- cens rec- to- ri ge- ni- to
Ju- ve- nis doc- tus ad bel- la ma- xi- ma

Beth- le- em par- vu- los prae- ci- pit en- se cru- de- li per- de- re.
po- pu- lis prae- di- cans col- li- gis, su- gens cum tan- tum mi- se- ris.

6. An- no ho- mi- nis tri- gi- si- mo sub- tus fa- mu- li se in- cli- ti in- cli- na- ve- rat ma- nus de- us,
   Ec- ce spi- ri- tus in spe- ci- e ip- sum a- li- tis in- no- cu- ae unc- tu- rus sanc- tis prae om- ni- bus,

con- se- crans no- bis bap- ti- sma in ab- so- lu- ti- o- nem cri- mi- num.
vi- si- tat sem- per ip- si- us con- ten- tus man- si- o- ne pec- to- ris.

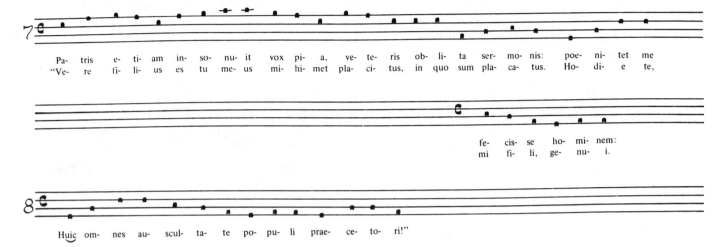

Pa- tris e- ti- am in- so- nu- it vox pi- a, ve- te- ris ob- li- ta ser- mo- nis: poe- ni- tet me
"Ve- re fi- li- us es tu me- us mi- hi- met pla- ci- tus, in quo sum pla- ca- tus. Ho- di- e te,

fe- cis- se ho- mi- nem:
mi fi- li, ge- nu- i.

Huic om- nes au- scul- ta- te po- pu- li prae- ce- to- ri!"

minate. Later sources for Notker's version show both the use of a B flat at 4a and after, as well as occasionally some confusion in pitch levels and general understanding of the melody.

The broader understanding of "degree inflection" in medieval chant requisite for solution of problems such as this, is not yet to be had. CHRISTI HODIERNA is only one witness to the fact that melodies can end differently than they began. Two more examples, much closer to the case at hand, are provided by the two melodies that use the same incipit, the quotation from Alleluia *Benedictus es*. Both texts, BENEDICTA SIT BEATA TRINITAS and BENEDICTA SEMPER SANCTA SIT TRINITAS, are in honor of the Trinity; they circulated in a moderately large number of sources, extending from the Verona MS 85 (ca. 900?), to which BENEDICTA SEMPER is added, to later staff sources, but with curious geographical distributions. One or the other was generally preferred to OMNIPOTENS, which seems unknown outside the Aquitanian manuscripts. The staff sources show that at least some scribes thought that both BENEDICTA SIT and BENEDICTA SEMPER had B flats beginning somewhere in the middle of the melodies (which are different one from the other, especially toward the end)—and this in spite of very clear G-*tetrardus* at the beginning, supported by the use of idioms from other G-*tetrardus* pieces from the early repertory. Just how the B flats are to be applied, and what they might have to do with the original versions, awaits a careful sifting of the variant readings.[4]

Aside from the problem of B flat and degree inflection, the appearance of the lyric subphrase in 5 of OMNIPOTENS DEUS intensifies the problem of the relationship of this material —and of this kind of material—to the sequence. This particular turn of phrase is shared only by sequences related to an Alleluia, but without regard for whether the Alleluia is *protus* or *tetrardus*. The effect of this passage, so sharply drawn and self-contained, is to in-

4. See *Anal.hymn.* 53, pp. 139–144.

trude: it seems in some respects to be applied as a ready-made element—which would be especially curious if we thought of these sequences as in origin an extension, a "spinning-out" of the material of the Alleluia jubilus. In its lyric qualities, as well as its regular rhythms, this passage has points of contact with the sub-phrase structures we have met in sequences not related to Alleluias, structures that more than once evoked the sense of "verse" rather than "prose."

How all these implications fit together is not clear; it is clear, however, that such complex matters cannot be explained by any simple account. But is it possible that when an early composer attempted to write a sequence melody to go with a Gregorian-style Alleluia, he found the usual techniques of melodic extension inadequate to the vast dimensions now used in the new sequence, hence had recourse to lyric phrases as self-contained building blocks?

Notker's FESTA CHRISTI begins with a forthright liturgical exhortation,

(1)   Festa Christi omnis christianitas celebret,

(Let all Christians celebrate the feast of Christ,)

then proceeds to specify and describe, in lines 2–4, the "Theophany," in this case the manifestation to the gentiles. The opening period extends through 2b, straightforward in form and diction.

2a   quae miris sunt modis ornata cunctisque veneranda populis
 b   Per omnitenentis adventum atque vocationem gentium.

Line 2a seems not like Notker's mature style: *miris sunt modis ornata* seems for him too easy a combination of pale words and flowery word order, and *cunctisque veneranda populis* recalls a similar phrase in the West-Frankish HÆC EST SANCTA (in the variant for St. John). Perhaps these are signs of an early piece.

Line 3a tells of the star, line 3b begins the period that describes the coming of the Wise Men; the period runs on past the end of phrase 3 and continues through phrase 4.

3a   Ut natus est Christus, est stella magis visa lucida.
 b   At illi non cassam putantes tanti signi gloriam
4a   Secum munera deferunt parvulo, offerant ut regi caeli, quem sidus praedicat,
 b   Atque aureo tumidi principis lectulo transito Christi praesepe quaeritant.

Thus lines 1 through 4b are closely linked together, just as in OMNIPOTENS DEUS. The melodic difference at the end of 3, here identical with 2, supports this linkage. The difference at the start of 4, however, tends against it. Notker's phrase 4 begins on D and ascends to F (instead of leaping from G to D, then E); and the descent includes one more group of three.

4   D E, F E D, E D C, D C A, B A G, A F A C B A B G F G G

The change in the beginning of 4 has the immediate effect of making it less closely related to the preceding phrases; but more important, the same beginning is used again at the start of phrase 6, and also of 7, which has the ultimate effect of breaking down the entity of the first four phrases.

```
1
2
3
4   D E F E D . . .
5
6   D E F E D . . .
7   D E F E D . . .
8
```

The descending groups of threes in phrase 4, which recall several such idioms within and without the sequence repertory, are set with remarkable consistency to three-syllabled words.

4a   (Secum) munera deferunt parvulo, offerant
 b   (Atque) aureo   tumidi   principis lectulo   transito

Should we fault the West-Frankish author of OMNIPOTENS DEUS for not noticing the groups of threes, or for not being able to set them to three-syllabled words with uniform accents, as Notker did? I think not, for one one hand the West-Frankish author is intent on his theological theme, on the other it would be entirely possible that his avoidance of pat accent patterns and word structures was deliberate. The "state of the art" permits him to do such things whenever he wishes, and in phrase 5 he seizes the opportunity afforded by the threes in the melodic rhythm (*Nunc ergo trínum et únum non césset . . .*). The more obvious opportunity in 4 he foregoes, and I think we should assume he does so by choice. Notker's choice went the other way, and it might be possible to see in his string of three-syllabled words another easy, youthful solution.

Even though, in Notker's version, the melody of phrase 5 is not so different from what came before—phrase 4 having begun in the same register—Notker provides 5 with a new topic, Herod's slaying of the children of Bethlehem, just as OMNIPOTENS DEUS turned at that point to the trinitarian beliefs of the Church. The wrath of Herod, *ira saevi Herodis*, is the motive set at the start of phrase 5 to contrast with the Adoration of the Magi.

5a   Hinc ira saevi Herodis fervida
     invidi recens rectori genito
          Bethleem parvulos praecipit ense crudeli perdere.
 b   O Christe, quantum patri exercitum
     juvenis doctus ad bella maxima
          populis praedicans colligis, sugens cum tantum miseris.

The arrangement is dramatic, and effective. It is also, in a sense, unliturgical, for either Notker is disregarding the calendar order of the feasts of Christmastide, wherein the Feast of the Holy Innocents (December 28th) precedes the coming of the Wise Men associated with Epiphany (January 6th); or Notker is following the Gospel story rather than the liturgical calendar, and writing a seasonal, topical text rather than one strictly for the Feast of Epiphany.

Line 5b is an exclamation, an apostrophe to Christ, a reaction to the slaughter of the Innocents described in 5a, and in its own way as dramatically effective.

> (5b) O Christ, what an army have you collected for the Father, trained for total war while still young, preaching to the people, not yet weaned, dwelling among the poor!

The only reason for scrutinizing it closely is that this is the point at which OMNIPOTENS DEUS might have a line added to double a single, and if that suspicion were justified, then there would be a chance that Notker's original text showed a single, too. Notker's 5b seems so firm that the chance, if there is one, is small; yet 5b is self-contained, as well as standing rhetorically apart from the rest of the piece. It is effective, but so much so that it tends to emphasize the Holy Innocents at the expense of the Epiphany; it also anticipates the climax to some extent. Finally, its word order and diction seem more difficult than the rest of the text, even though some of the language is quite similar to some other Notker texts. By themselves, these are hardly grounds for identifying an interpolation; but in the case of the second line for a sub-phrase structure, where the West-Frankish analog shows any evidence of softness, these grounds acquire more significance. The case is much less strong, however, than the others in which an interpolation in Notker's text was suspected.

Phrase 6, the longest unbroken phrase of the melody, starts the story of John's baptism of Jesus—the third, final, and most extensive episode in Notker's text. The story is liturgically commemorated on the Octave of the Epiphany, confirming the idea that Notker's text is for the season, rather than for the day, of the Epiphany. Notker's long lines roll along well enough in rhythm, but show a striking number of cases of hiatus (*se / incliti / inclinaverat, baptisma / in* in 6a, *specie / ipsum* in 6b.

> 6a Anno hominis trigisimo subtus famuli se incliti inclinaverat manus deus, consecrans nobis baptisma in absolutionem criminum.
> b Ecce spiritus in specie ipsum alitis innocuae uncturus sanctis prae omnibus visitat semper ipsius contentus mansione pectoris.

Notker's use of the baptism story binds lines 7–9 together. As in OMNIPOTENS DEUS, the climax of Notker's piece falls in 7, with the voice of God saying, "This is my beloved Son, in whom I am well pleased." This is the only place in the *Liber hymnorum* where God speaks and one of three occasions when God the Father speaks directly in the four Gospels.[5] The quotation is an integral part of the baptismal story, of course, and once having decided to refer to that story Notker came naturally enough to the quotation. But we have seen him sensitive to the use of literary materials in terms of form and rhetoric, and also inclined to make cross references between different pieces—his own as well as his models. In this connection, the quotation of God's word in OMNIPOTENS DEUS, similarly unique in the early West-Frankish repertory, takes on special relevance.

5. I am indebted to Professor Samuel Garrett, Church Divinity School of the Pacific, for this observation.

(2b)   "I am the Lord (thou hast said), and there is no other."
(4b)   "Hear, O Israel (thou, O God, said in Oreb) my majesty is one."

It would seem entirely characteristic for Notker's imagination, fired by an *Old Testament* quotation in his model, to produce a topic with one from the *New Testament*.

That the cadences of Notker's melody vary from the Aquitanian versions, tending toward the forms found in the other sequences in *G-tetrardus*, seems neither significant nor problematic. More significant, perhaps, is the use of a melodic motive at the start of phrases 4, 6, and 7, as mentioned before. The motive in question appears in OMNIPOTENS DEUS, but only at the start of 7, where it has the effect of lengthening the "wind-up" for the ascent to high G.

OMNIPOTENS DEUS	Notker
6 D E F G G D E F G G . . .	6 *D E F E D E F G G* . . .
7 *D E F E D E F G G* . . .	7 *D E F E D E F G G* . . .

In Notker's version, this preparation (D E F E) for the ascent appears also at 4, as we saw. The effect is to link the first and second halves together, by an obvious motivic system that apparently controls the upward thrust of the entire piece. Why should this feature be lacking in OMNIPOTENS DEUS? The answer, I think, is that such a motivic system need not have been part of the original conception of the melody. The upward thrust is so basic a part of the conception (in this as well as a number of other early sequences) that it stands by itself, supported only by the phrase layout and broad design of the whole. OMNIPOTENS DEUS arrives at the high point with just as much *élan*—possibly more, for the motivic preparation of the last ascent in 7 can be considered to detract as much as add by anticipating the climax. And it seems easier to imagine the motivic preparation being added in the hope of enhancing the upward thrust, than being taken away once it was there. Motivic systems are clearly present and operative in the early sequence, but I do not think we should ascribe to them alone the power to generate these melodies, nor should we assume that when present they are always original.

Notker's version, as noticed, lacks 8a,b of OMNIPOTENS DEUS and has a different concluding single. In this case, 8a,b had a feeling of redundancy, both melodic and verbal, and there seems every reason to suspect that it was a later addition—at a spot where changes and additions were made in various other early pieces, perhaps for some specific musical or textual reason, perhaps simply to gain bulk toward the end. We cannot simply lift out 8a,b, however, for the text of 9 makes sense only after 8a,b; if 8a,b was added, then the text of 9 was changed at the same time; the original text being lost, it cannot be restored. As for the melody of 9, it has a ring of authenticity to it, where the melody of Notker's concluding single is a simple peroration of the cadence pattern used in his version, plus the four notes F A A G, just as in HANC CONCORDI.

As Fr. de Goede pointed out, in this case the St. Gall melody title seems for once to point clearly to the West-Frankish model: the title is "Trinitas," which has little to do with Notker's use of the melody, but is apropos as the name of the melody for OMNIPOTENS DEUS.

XVII

SALUS AETERNA and VENIET REX
Notker's CLARE SANCTORUM SENATUS

THE NEXT THREE melodies to be considered belong together in the sense that, from the eleventh century on, they were assigned to the Sundays of Advent in French prosaria. This common bond may not have much to do with the melodies as we meet them in the early repertory, however, because—even granting that the texts in question are designed for Advent (which is not always clear)—these texts are not necessarily the original texts; and in any case Notker's texts to the same melodies show no liturgical relationship to the West-Frankish ones or to each other. The only basis for the Advent-bond, then, lies in the Alleluia quotations, and these, too, are not free from ambiguity. Indeed, the Alleluia quotations are a mixed lot, including the most frequently-used Gregorian Alleluia (*Ostende*) as well as one of the most unusual ones (*Veni Domine*).

A far more important reason for considering these three melodies as a group can be found in their melodic style. In general they share a quality of melodic continuity, in particular a use of melodic motive, not found in the same way or to the same degree in the other West-Frankish melodies we have studied.

Here is a conspectus of the whole set of melodies and texts to be considered.

Alleluia *Ostende* (1st Sunday of Advent)
    SALUS AETERNA
    VENIET REX
       Notker: CLARE SANCTORUM SENATUS (for the Holy Apostles)
Alleluia *Laetatus sum* (2nd Sunday of Advent)
    REGNANTEM SEMPITERNA
    PANGAT LAUDES
       Notker: PSALLAT ECCLESIA (Dedication of a Church)
Alleluia *Veni Domine* (4th Sunday of Advent)

Jubilemus omnes
Laus beata
En virginum (for Alleluia *Adducentur*)
    Notker: stirpe maria regia

(For the 3rd Sunday in Advent, French prosaria assigned qui regis sceptra, one of the small aparallel texts set to a jubilus-replacement melody.)

The first melody to be considered is clearly related to the Alleluia *Ostende*, for the 1st Sunday of Advent.[1] That is, the sequence incipit quotes the incipit of the Alleluia used with the verse *Ostende* on that Sunday; but that particular Alleluia is used with a great many other verses on other occasions. (Notker, in setting his text for the Holy Apostles, may have had in mind another verse, *Nimis honorati sunt*, used in connection with feasts of Apostles.[2]) With that qualification, the melodic relationship to the Alleluia is clear enough: the sequence quotes the Alleluia through its rising incipit, up to the point where the jubilus begins—in Notker's version, through the words *Clare sanctorum senatus apostolorum*.

Continuing with Notker's version for the moment, the melody has clearly defined sections. Phrases 1 and 2 constitute an elaborate introduction (requiring extensive discussion later). The introduction, beginning with the incipit quoted from the Alleluia, rises from F to C (*Clare . . . apostolorum*). At that point, where the literal quotation from the Alleluia stops, the line descends to its first close on G (*princeps . . . regnorum*). Then follow two more descents to G (2a,b).

Phrases 3 and 4 can be understood as antecedent-consequent, with phrases 5 and 6 forming a complex extension. Phrase 3 rises slowly from G up through E, then falls to a cadence on B—which in context can be understood as a half-cadence. Phrase 4, on the other hand, leaps up immediately to the high E (some versions precede this E with the A a fifth lower to form an initial leap). The line then descends gradually through groups of threes

(A) E, F E D, E D B, C B A

in a figure similar to that in hæc est sancta 5 and carmen suo dilecto 4—but even more reminiscent of the melody *Gloria in excelsis* I (*Domine deus* and others), where the analogous phrase functions as consequent in a similar way. This *Gloria* melody can be presumed current in the ninth century, but can also be presumed to represent a style being actively cultivated at that time; that is, the *Gloria* melody is not necessarily earlier in date of composition than the sequence melody.[3] Also very similar is the melody of the jubilus of Alleluia *Oportebat*, for the 3rd Sunday after Easter. This Alleluia, seemingly not part of the Gregorian repertory, does not appear in the earliest Mass-books (without notation) and only sporadically in the earliest ones, from around 900, with notation.[4] The distinctive feature is

1. Alleluia *Ostende*: Schlager *Them.Kat.* no. 271; *Alleluia-Melodien* I, pp. 368, 639. Hesbert, *Antiphonale missarum sextuplex* no. 1a.

2. As suggested by Peter Wagner, *Einführung in die Gregorianischen Melodien* III: *Gregorianische Formenlehre* (Leipzig 1921), p. 486.

3. See note 2, Chapter 12.

4. Alleluia *Oportebat* in Schlager *Them.Kat.* no. 284; *Alleluia-Melodien* I, pp. 353, 612. It appears in Chartres MS 47.

Clare sanctorum senatus (Notker)

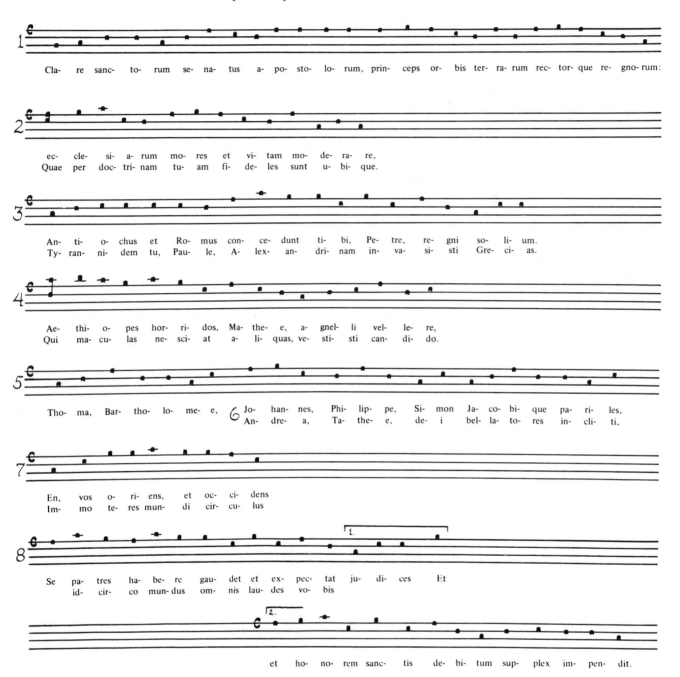

1. Cla- re sanc- to- rum se- na- tus a- po- sto- lo- rum, prin- ceps or- bis ter- ra- rum rec- tor- que re- gno- rum:

2. ec- cle- si- a- rum mo- res et vi- tam mo- de- ra- re,
   Quae per doc- tri- nam tu- am fi- de- les sunt u- bi- que.

3. An- ti- o- chus et Ro- mus con- ce- dunt ti- bi, Pe- tre, re- gni so- li- um.
   Ty- ran- ni- dem tu, Pau- le, A- lex- an- dri- nam in- va- si- sti Gre- ci- as.

4. Ae- thi- o- pes hor- ri- dos, Ma- the- e, a- gnel- li vel- le- re,
   Qui ma- cu- las ne- sci- at a- li- quas, ve- sti- sti can- di- do.

5. Tho- ma, Bar- tho- lo- me- e, 6 Jo- han- nes, Phi- lip- pe, Si- mon Ja- co- bi- que pa- ri- les,
   An- dre- a, Ta- the- e, de- i bel- la- to- res in- cli- ti,

7. En, vos o- ri- ens, et oc- ci- dens
   Im- mo te- res mun- di cir- cu- lus

8. Se pa- tres ha- be- re gau- det et ex- pec- tat ju- di- ces Et
   id- cir- co mun- dus om- nis lau- des vo- bis

et ho- no- rem sanc- tis de- bi- tum sup- plex im- pen- dit.

a phrase built on a fifth (here, A-E, but lacking in some versions) that includes the initial leap up and the slow descent, the whole phrase making a contrast with a previous phrase centered on a major third (here, G-B), with a strong, perhaps cadential emphasis on the top of the third (B).

```
                         F
               E    E    E
                    D    D    D
                         C    C
 B)                                B———————→B
  }                 A
 G)
```

The complex tended to become a formula of Frankish melisma composition. Phrase 4 ends on B, approached this time through C,A instead of A,G. Like the cadence to phrase 3, this one can be understood as a half-cadence.

Phrases 5 and 6 are the most intricate part of the melody; the arrangement of motives is distinctive, basically different from melodic procedures encountered in the previous West-Frankish sequences. Phrases 5 and 6 consist of two motives (x,y) that end the same but begin differently.

(x)   (y)
G A C A A *G* B   C D B A C A *G* B

Phrases 5 and 6 together have the plan x y x y x, and this plan recalls phrases 6–7 of "Justus ut palma major" which Notker set as SANCTI BAPTISTAE and LAUS TIBI CHRISTE. In CLARE SANCTORUM SENATUS the shortness of the phrases, the repetition, the similar endings, all contribute to a remarkable feeling of circularity, which as we will see was noticed by Notker too. The whole complex of 5 and 6 can be understood as an extension of 4, a post-climax to the leap up to the E and ensuing descent. The persistent half-cadences on B, of course, contribute to the feeling of continuity and extension through 6.

Phrase 7, short, high, and with no clear cadence, seems to start something new, providing an articulation in the larger form. This effect of articulation is enhanced by the return, in phrase 8, of material from phrase 2: *se patres* corresponds exactly to *concedunt*.

```
     G   A B   B B   B A C  E D   D B D B   C  A  G B B
  2     An- ti- o- chus et Ro-mus con-ce-dunt ti- bi, Pe-tre,  re-gni  so-li- um
                 C E D   C E D   D B D B   C  A  G B B
  8             se patres ha- be-re    gaudet et ex- pec- tat judi-ces
```

The beginning of phrase 2 has been artfully omitted, so that the return is well under way before we are fully aware of it; but *se patres* provides an anticipatory duplication of the return so that we will be aware of it. In retrospect, phrase 7 appears clearly as preparation for this return.

Phrase 8 has the form of a concluding double with first and second endings, the second ending being relatively long. In this version of the melody, nonetheless, it is linked firmly to the main part of the phrase and cannot be considered a separate concluding single (as it can in other, later versions that make 8a,b end the same without elision to the long second ending). Here, the cadence notes G B B are omitted in 8b, and the melody turns through its figure one more time before making its final approach to the G.

```
        C E D C E D D B D B C A G B B / D
8a   Se patres . . .                          Et
            E D C E D D B D B C A
8b          idcirco
              C D E B D B C A G          A B A A G
            et hono-rem . . .
```

Three passages contribute to the distinctive quality of this melody—the introduction (1 and 2), the extension of the middle group (5 and 6), and the ending (7 and 8). All these passages involve repetition at the motivic level, or insistence on a particular pitch or pitch set. The introduction, by virtue of its third phrase (2b), creates the effect of circling repeatedly back to the G. Phrases 5 and 6 produce the same effect even more strongly, centered on B. The ending in phrases 7 and 8 is not so clearly focused on a single pitch, but is just as insistent in its repeated use of motives. No one of these passages by itself is unique here: the conclusion, for example, is similar to the one in CHRISTI HODIERNA, at least in the version shared by Notker's CONGAUDENT ANGELORUM. Taken together, however, these passages tend to give the melody as a whole a continuity noticeably greater than some of the larger pieces studied previously. Individual phrases seem less clearly articulated than, say. in NUNC EXULTET—and not just because those in CLARE SANCTORUM SENATUS are shorter, but because they tend to be effaced by activity at the motivic level. The effect is closer to such pieces as Notker's AGNI PASCHALIS or CARMEN SUO DILECTO, or especially the latter half of "Justus ut palma major."

To put it another way: here, in the melody for CLARE SANCTORUM SENATUS, we seem closer to a kind of rhapsodic extension that characterizes the replacement-melisma for the repetition of the Alleluia jubilus after the verse. Here, at any rate, a contact between the two kinds of melody—otherwise so different— can be sensed.

Notker's text, in honor of the Holy Apostles, has even more of the mood of imperial ceremonial than, say, GRATES SALVATORI. The Apostles are invoked, collectively and individually, their triumphal attributes sounded forth as if they were heroes at a Roman state occasion. The incipit, of course, makes this reference explicit: "Illustrious senate of the holy apostles . . . ." Phrase 1 is given over entirely to titles; phrase 2 with its double, brings an acclamatory petition, ". . . Rule the life and customs of the churches . . . ." Together, the two phrases form the opening period.

(1)   Clare sanctorum senatus apostolorum,
            princeps orbis terrarum,
            rectorque regnorum:
(2a)   ecclesiarum mores et vitam moderare,
(2b)   quae per doctrinam tuam fideles sunt ubique.

The *ubique* ("everywhere") at the end of phrase 2b opens the door to the enumeration of individual apostles that starts in phrase 3 and continues through 6. The enumeration begins slowly, Peter and Paul each receiving a separate line.

(3a)   Antiochus et Romus concedunt tibi, Petre, regni solium.
(3b)   Tyrannidem tu, Paule, Alexandrinam invasisti Grecias.

Matthew, here curiously prominent, receives both 4a and b, perhaps because the more complex thought required it, perhaps because the longer attribute seemed more appropriate to the climactic nature of the melody in this phrase.

(4a)   Aethiopes horridos, Mathee, agnelli vellere,
(4b)   qui maculas nesciat aliquas, vestisti candido.

The order in which the apostles are named is not that of the Litany of the Saints nor of the Canon of the Mass. The remaining apostles are named in rapid succession, with one epithet—*dei bellatores incliti*—serving for all. The pacing of the names

Thoma,
Bartholomee,
Johannes,
Philippe,
Simon,
Jacobique pariles,
Andrea,
Tathee,
—dei bellatores incliti—

(as opposed to the ordering) is a matter of rhetoric and, compared to the longer units given to Peter, Paul, and Matthew, follows a familiar rhetorical plan of acceleration. What is of the greatest interest is the way the acceleration is timed to coincide with that phrase of melody (5) in which the motivic repetitions are at their most insistent. The passage bears close inspection because of the close connection of melody and rhetoric at more than one structural level.

At the motivic level in phrases 5–6, the text tends to bridge the musical divisions and fuse the motives together.

(x)	G	A	C	AA	GB	
(5) Thoma, Bartholome-e,						

(y)	C D B	AC A G B	(x)G A C	A AGB
(6a)	Johannes, Philippe, Simon / Jacobique pariles			
(y)	C DB A CAGB	(x) G AC A A GB		
(6b)	Andrea, Tathe-e, dei	/ bellatores incliti		

Inherent in the melodic structure is an uncertainty about whether the grouping is xy, xy, x, or x, yx, yx. In 6b, Notker has in effect elided y to the following x by the phrase *dei bella-*

tores incliti—although as soon as we notice that we are struck also by the counter-effect of *Tathée déi,* as if a half-cadence on G B were being supported by sonority while denied by sense. The effect of *dei bellatores incliti,* however, is not felt until the end of the period, and even though *Simon Jacobique pariles* can probably be understood to have a similar effect, it is not as strong; the overall result includes at least some ambiguity in grouping, which contributes to the same fusion of small units into a longer line as the other rhetorical and melodic elements.

At a higher level there is a similar ambiguity of grouping. The musical grouping of phrases, as discussed, is

3, 4, 5, 6 / 7, 8.

Notker's rhetorical grouping is elaborate: in 5 and 6 the names of the apostles are vocatives, hence cannot stand alone; syntactically they go with 7 and 8, which cuts across the musical grouping. But on one hand these vocatives become, in 7a, the object rather than the subject (*vos oriens et occidens . . . gaudet . . .*), and the wrench in syntax coincides with the demonstrative *En* to create a strong sense of articulation at the start of 7. And on the other hand the vocatives in 5 and 6 are indistinguishable from—and surely at first understood as parallel with—the vocatives in 3 and 4, and so expected to be further enumerations. Hence the mere punctuation (the period after 4) does not at all show the rhetorical effect, which is one of overlap and elision from 3 on to the end, analogous to the musical effect even though achieved by different means.

(3a) . . . . . Petre, . . .
(3b) . . . . . Paule, . . . invasisti . . .
(4a) . . . . . Mathee, . . . (4b) . . . . . vestisti candido.
(5)   Thoma, Bartholomee, Johannes, Philippe, Simon Jacobique pariles
(6b) Andrea, Tathee, dei bellatores incliti,
(7)   En, vos oriens et occidens
(8a) Se patres habere gaudet . . .

Notker's text shows that he understood phrase 8 as an extension, or at least a continuation of 7. The two lines of 7 present two parallel subjects of the sentence, the rest follows directly in 8a.

(7a) En, vos oriens et occidens,
(7b) immo teres mundi circulus,
(8a)   se patres habere gaudet
(8b)   et expectat judices.

The accents match up with the melodic inflection to make the continuation smooth; the material from phrase 2 returns at the start of 8 as if this were its natural environment.

           E D E D B C E D D B
(7b) . . . múndi círculus se pátres hábet . . .

The end of 8a includes a verb-and-object construction in parallel,

(8a)   . . . patres habere gaudet,
                    et expectat judices

corresponding to the parallelism in subjects (7a,b) in form—even if in chiasmus—although
not in sense. More important, however, is the further continuity through 8b produced by
the repeated use of *et*: too frequent for ordinary usage, the *et*'s need to be understood as
rhetorical ornament and probably as a musical factor too.

(8a)   . . . *et* expectat judices.
(8b)   *Et* idcirco mundus omnis laudes vobis
                    et honorem sanctis debitum
        supplex impendit.

The second *et* begins the repetition at 8b, so that its insistence is joined to that of the melodic motive now appearing for the fourth time (3a,b, 8a,b). The third *et* begins the second
ending and with it the fifth time for the same material, slightly changed, now as melodic
peroration.

Throughout CLARE SANCTORUM SENATUS the accent patterns and word structures are remarkably consistent. The figure in 3 and 8,

É D, D B, D B, C A

is accented in twos, except for *Alexandrinam* (3b). The groups of three in phrase 4 are set
to three-syllabled words (except *Aethiopes*).

             F E D   E D B   C   B   A
(4a)   Ae- thiopes horridos Ma-the - e . . .
(4b)   Qui maculas nesci-at   a - li-quas . . .

At the ends of lines 1,2 and 8b—all cadences on G—the accentuation is paroxytone. All
the other line endings are proparoxytone, and these all employ the half-cadence on B in
some form or other.

The sonorities of line 1,

(1)   Cláre sanctórum senátus apostolórum, princeps órbis terrárum rectórque regnórum,
(2a)   Ecclesiárum . . .

echo solemnly down the long line. Those of 4b,

    Qui maculas nesciat aliquas

have something of the virtuoso quality heard in LAURENTI DAVID and TUBAM BELLICOSAM.
The redictum in 7–8,

(7b)   . . . mundi circulus . . .
(8b)   . . . mundus omnis . . .

is curious; yet it seems not inappropriate, and can be understood as rhetorical emphasis.

1. Veniet rex in aeternum quem expectant justi ab origine mundi et vita.

2. Rex noster Christus manens sacra invisibilus forma et palma

3. Alme nobilissime gratia deitas.
   Aeternae angelorum voces assiduas

4. Regnant cum Christo per cuncta saecula in sede patria sua,
   Et cantant die noctuque splendidas voces et illorum veras.

5. In coelis quoque in terra universa te laudant
   Volucrumque bestiarum divina mysteria.

6. Gaudent simul et laetantur miracula
   Regi autem saeculorum perpetua.

7. Dominator, princeps pacis, magna lux clara, vera carmina,
   Adjuva, Rex, quoque semper famulos tuos; et dicant gloria
   regna dominator per saecla.

Salus aeterna

1. Al- le- lu- ia

2. Sa- lus ae- ter- na in- de- fi- ci- ens, mun- di vi- ta,
   Lux semp- i- ter- na, et re- demp- ti- o ve- re no- stra,

3. Con- do- lens hu- ma- na per- i- re sae- cla per ten- tan- tis nu- mi- na,
   Non lin- quens ex- cel- sa ad- i- sti i- ma pro- pri- a cle- men- ti- a.

4. Mox tu- a spon- ta- ne- a gra- ti- a as- su- mens hu- ma- na,
   Quae fu- e- rant per- di- ta om- ni- a sal- va- sti ter- re- a.

5. Fe- rens mun- do gau- di- a, Tu a- ni- mas et cor- po- ra
   No- stra Chri- ste ex- pi- a Ut pos- si- de- as lu- ci- da nos- met ha- bi- ta- cu- la.

7. Ad- ven- tu pri- mo ju- sti- fi- ca;
   In se- cun- do nos- que li- be- ra

8. *1.* Ut cum fac- ta lu- ce ma- gna ju- di- ca- bis om- ni- a.
   Comp- ti sto- la in- cor- rup- ta nos- met tu- a

2. sub- se- qua- mur mox ve- sti- gi- a quo- cum- que vi- sa.

There are two West-Frankish texts that might have come to Notker with the melody —VENIET REX and SALUS AETERNA. There are severe problems, however, in seeing either of these as Notker's model, simply because each betrays formal anomalies relative to Notker's plan—anomalies for which there seems to be no ready explanation. They concern principally the structure of the first two phrases.

VENIET REX, found only in three Aquitanian MSS, is a confusing piece, in the details of its diction as well as in other ways. The structure of its introduction is unique among early sequences, although closely related to HÆC EST SANCTA and ECCE VICIT. Line 1 proceeds more or less as Notker's 1, with some differences of detail to be considered soon; the melody moves through the Alleluia quotation (*Veniet rex in aeternum*) then on to the cadence on G (*mundi et vita*).

```
        FGA AG ABCB A  C  C  C      D  C  B  A    C AC DC BA  C  GA  AG
(1)     Veni - et rex    in aeternum quem expectant justi ab origine mundi et vita
```

Line 2, as a whole, is similar enough to line 1 so that the whole could just as well be numbered 1a,b. Line 2, however, begins differently: *Rex noster* is set to a melodic pattern that might be described as a "re-intonation."

```
        G ABC  C
(2)     Rex no- ster
```

It functions in parallel to the Alleluia quotation of line 1 by rising from the G to the C a fourth above, so that the remainder of the phrase may move from C back down to G as it did before.

In HÆC EST SANCTA SOLEMNITAS the introduction had a similar structure, but without the re-intonation: there was a short rising incipit and a continuation that dropped slowly in much the same fashion as here in *quem expectant* . . . . The continuation was then repeated, with its first note different to facilitate the repetition.

> Hæc est sancta solemnitas diei hujus et veneranda
>   beati Stephani et honoranda.

There, too, the introduction could be understood as an irregular double, and numbered 1a,b. In ECCE VICIT the same structure reappeared.

> Ecce vicit radix David   leo de tribu Juda
>   mors vicit mortem et mors nostra est vita

In this case the two lines were more nearly the same length. The melody over *mors vicit mortem* was not the same as the incipit *Ecce . . . David*, being modified to serve—not as "re-intonation"—but rather as a varied link.

In trying to understand Notker's CLARE SANCTORUM SENATUS and the West-Frankish VENIET REX, it is important to note that while Notker left the incipit of HÆC EST SANCTA as he found it, he doubled the second line of ECCE VICIT, making the structure 1, 2a, b.

(1)   Hanc concordi famulatu colamus solemnitatem
(2a)   Auctoris illius exemplo docti benigno
(2b)   Pro persecutorum precantis fraude suorum

(Notker's CONCENTU PARILI has a structure similar to HANC CONCORDI, and since 2b of CON-CENTU PARILI is added, the original version of that melody, too, had an irregular opening.)

What distinguishes VENIET REX from these closely related instances is the quality of re-intonation—the location and direction of the line over *rex noster*, and especially the neume ABC. But among the versions of this melody there are greater complications, for VENIET REX has no phrase that is the analog of Notker's phrase 2, *Ecclesiarum . . . Quae per doctrinam . . . .* What follows in VENIT REX is the analog of Notker's phrase 3.

VENIET REX		(Notker)	
1	Veniet rex . . .	1	Clare sanctorum senatus . . .
2	Rex noster . . .		
		2a	Ecclesiarum mores . . .
		2b	Quae per doctrinam . . .
3a	Alme nobilissime . . .	3a	Antiochus et Romus . . .
3b	Aeterna angelorum . . .	3b	Tyrannidem tu . . .
4a	Regnant cum Christo . . .	4a	Aethiopes horridos . . .
4b	Et cantant . . .	4b	Qui maculas . . .

In terms of detail, however, the end of VENIET REX 1 (and 2) corresponds melodically to Notker's phrase 2 rather than to his phrase 1.

VENIET REX			(Notker)	
	B GA AG			C D C B A G
1	. . . mundi et vita	1	. . . rectorque regnorum	
	B GA A G			B GAG
2	. . . forma et palma	2a	. . . . . . moderare	

The reading of VENIET REX could be aligned with Notker's by omitting "et vita," and "et palma," and the looseness of the verbal construction might support that. But nothing is solved that way, and on the other hand the model of HÆC EST SANCTA SOLEMNITAS with its *. . . et veneranda . . . et honoranda* is strong support for the wording as it stands. Still, the whole of the opening of VENIET REX, as prose, is not reassuring.

(1)   Veniet rex in aeternum
           quem expectant justi ab origine mundi, et vita.
(2)   Rex noster Christus, manens sacra invisibilus forma et palma,
(3a)   Alme, nobilissime, gratia, deitas.
(3b)   Aeterne angelorum voces assiduas
(4a)   Regnant cum Christo per cuncta saecula in sede patria sua,
(4b)   Et cantant die noctuque splendida voces et illorum veras.

The first sentence can be followed:

> May the King eternal come, who the righteous await from the
> beginning of the world; Life, our King, Christ, remaining
> invisible in holy form and loving, noblest, Grace, Deity.

but the diction is not without obscurity, and shows the apposite modifiers we have found to be characteristic of interpolations.

The second sentence is more difficult, or the text is corrupt. The subject is presumably the angels, or their voices: they "reign with Christ . . . and sing . . . ." But *assiduas* is the wrong case; and *voces* is redictum in 4b, in a spot that is not clear either. The period at the end of 3a, with 3b continuing on through 4, can be supported by other instances, but in the context of the other details it can be taken here as a symptom of some prior dislocation in the structure.

If, in some sense, VENIET REX 1,2 is the functional equivalent of Notker's 1, 2a,b and if Notker himself supplied 2b to make a regular double out of an originally single 2, then perhaps VENIET REX 2 is a corruption or modification of that single; or perhaps Notker did more to it than just double it. There is, however, no immediately obvious way to restore VENIET REX 2, even if the textual obscurities all the way through 4b strongly suggest that it should be done. We are left with two alternate introductions for the two versions.

There are other differences between VENIET REX and Notker's CLARE SANCTORUM SENATUS. The most important is the absence, in VENIET REX, of the single 5, leaving a regular double and eliminating all the high-level effects produced by that single. It might be worth noting that the last of the textual obscurities associated with the beginning, *voces et illorum veras*, 4b, immediately precedes the site of the missing single. Another discrepancy, possibly related, is that VENIET REX has a slightly longer form of 4, mostly because the cadence matches the cadence of 5, whereas in Notker's version the two cadences differed slightly.

Other discrepancies, all minor, include a slightly shorter form of 3, an extra D at the end of 7, and a longer first ending of 8a, one that does not correspond to the quotation from 3. Also, first and second endings are virtually the same, the second lacking the quilisma. This quilisma, by the way, suggests the kind of ornamentation found in the Alleluia quotation, and—in some other early melodies—at the end as a closing reference to the opening. It is this kind of detail that indicates that VENIET REX is not to be set aside as a late or local corruption.

As a whole, the diction of VENIET REX is a curious mixture of relatively colorful subject matter and imagery—the eternal praises sung by the apocalyptic host—and relatively skilled sonorous language, set with a general looseness and lack of consequence, in addition to the obscurities already mentioned. The text gives the impression of having been adapted to the melody by a skilled hand in a casual moment, not stopping to solve certain basic problems of design. Or, perhaps here too, a text once clean has been defaced by subsequent modifications.

The other important text to this melody is SALUS AETERNA, a text often noticed by scholars, who tended to take it as a good representative of the early sequence and its presumed close relationship to the alleluia—and through the alleluia to the liturgy. All of that was brought about by the regular appearance of SALUS AETERNA at the beginning of later French prosaria as the prose for the First Sunday of Advent—not in itself sufficient reason for such conclusions.

SALUS AETERNA appears in the same Aquitanian MSS as VENIET REX, then in many other later ones, in a manner that suggests it replaced VENIET REX in the Aquitanian repertory; and finally in a great many other French, English, and Italian sources from the eleventh century on. As a whole, the melody and syllable count is very close to that of Notker's CLARE SANCTORUM SENATUS, so close as to make it seem the obvious model. Yet it differs in one important respect, the structure of the incipit: the text SALUS AETERNA begins with a regular double set to the melody of Notker's phrase 2; phrase 1 has only the text "alleluia," and normally extends only through the rise to the C (that is, the part that corresponds exactly to the quotation from Alleluia *Ostende*).

SALUS AETERNA		(Notker)
1	Alleluia	Clare sanctorum senatus
2a	Salus aeterna indeficiens, mundi vita,	Ecclesiarum . . .
2b	Lux sempiterna, et redemptio vere nostra,	Quae per doctrinam . . .

The second half of the melody of Notker's 1, *princeps orbis terrarum rectorque regnorum*, is normally lacking from SALUS AETERNA, so that this version is, in its way, no more complete in relation to Notker's version than is VENIET REX.

In the details of its diction, SALUS AETERNA is a superior text, relatively free from barbarisms as well as anomalies. There are, to be sure, a large number of epithets in apposition at the beginning,

(2a)   Salus aeterna indeficiens,
        mundi vita,
        lux sempiterna,
        et redemptio vere nostra,

and then a large number of present participles governing the overall structure.

(3a)   Condolens . . .
(3b)   Non linquens . . .
(4a)   . . . assumens . . .
(5)   Ferens . . .

It might be argued that here, as elsewhere, this kind of construction is a mark of expediency. But given the other qualities of the text, I am more inclined to interpret it as an effort to reproduce in the text the continuity of the melody, with its persistent half-cadences on B, and its motivic repetitions.

In its design the text is a skillful analog of the melody. Phrase 2, here the consequent of the Alleluia incipit, is treated completely as invocation; it is therefore grouped with 3, to make an opening period that ends on the half-cadence of 3b (*clementia*).

(1)   Alleluia,
(2a)   Salus aeterna indeficiens, mundi vita, (2b) lux sempiterna,
        et redemptio vere nostra;
(3a)   condolens humana perire saela per temptantis numina,
(3b)   non linquens excelsa,
        adisti ima propria clementia.

Phrase 4 expresses the theology of the Incarnation, as did phrase 3.

(4a)   Mox tua spontanea gratia assumens humana,
(4b)   quae fuerant perdita omnia
        salvasti terrea.

Phrases 5–6, similarly, deal with the Incarnation through a petition.

        Ferens mundo gaudia,
                tu animas et corpora nostra, Christe, expia,
                        ut possideas lucida nosmet habitacula.

Phrase 7, where we noticed an articulation in the larger melodic form, is used as a pivot in the sense: "As you judge us by your first coming, free us by your second," leading to the closing petition, *subsequamur*.

(7a)   Adventu primo justifica;
(7b)   in secundo nosque libera,
(8a)   ut cum facta luce magna judicabis omnia.
(8b)   compti stola incorrupta nosmet tua subsequamur mox vestigia quocumque visa.

Accent and word structure are not as strictly handled as in Notker's CLARE SANCTORUM SENATUS. On the other hand, the author was especially concerned about assonance, not merely at the ends of the lines but throughout; the resonance of "a" is noticeably more intense than in many of the other texts studied.

Neither VENIET REX nor SALUS AETERNA, then, can be identified positively as the probable model of CLARE SANCTORUM SENATUS. The remaining four texts to this melody in the Aquitanian MSS are all almost certainly later, and in any case come no closer to Notker's version. Yet this version of the melody—Notker's version—is present in the Aquitanian MSS, in unusual circumstances. In MS 1084 the sequentiarium that begins on fol.197 verso—an integral collection, liturgically ordered, with marginal labels and a heading INCIPIT CARMINA SEQUENTIARUM— is preceded on the recto by three sequences notated in another hand. The format suggests the appearance of another regular collection; but the items in question have been added between two completed quires (187–196, 197–204). These three items are:

(1)   SEQ [uentia?] DE OSTENDE
        (melody for PRECAMUR?)

(2)   ITEM SALUS AETERNA
      (melody for SALUS AETERNA, found in 1084 not in the
      regular prosarium fol.221–281 verso, but among the
      additions, fol.306)

(3)   ALIA
      (melody corresponding to Notker's CLARE SANCTORUM SENATUS)

The items as a group might be imagined as the beginning of a liturgically ordered sequentiarium, or merely as a series of sequences related to the Alleluia *Ostende*. In either case, it is a group different from the one on the following verso, which actually does begin the sequentiarium in this manuscript, and also from the one that begins the sequentiarium in MS Paris 1118.

What concerns us here is the third item, which corresponds exactly to Notker's CLARE SANCTORUM SENATUS, but for which a search through the Aquitanian manuscripts has produced no text. This is unusual, because texts can be found for almost all the melismatically-notated sequences in the Aquitanian manuscripts. In this particular source (MS 1084), to be sure, there are several shorter melodies, lacking the couplet structure, that seem so far to be textless; but the melody that concerns us has more or less regular couplets, and melodies of that type, as stated, can be identified with texts in all but a vanishingly small number of cases. Another case encountered earlier was "Justus ut palma minor."

It might be argued that SALUS AETERNA, identical to Notker's version in all save the incipit, is identical there too, if the Alleluia incipit is understood to include the descent from C to G as a short jubilus on the *-ia*. Then the Alleluia incipit would correspond to Notker's entire 1 of 26 syllables, rather than just the first half of 13 syllables, and from 2 on the versions would coincide. But the significance of fol. 197 of MS 1084 is that item (2), SALUS AETERNA, does *not* have the descent to G, while item (3) does, making the difference between the two versions unequivocal—as far as this manuscript witness is concerned.

In fact, then, Notker's version is represented in Western sources, but in a manner that allows several interpretations:

(1)   The West-Frankish text for this version (which would have a good chance of being Notker's model) was inadvertently omitted in copying, and lost from the extant repertory. Given the number of items involved (60–70 texts in a normal collection ca. 1000), this could easily have happened, especially in a case such as this one involving several versions with newer texts replacing older ones.

(2)   The text may still be present among a number of texts without melodies, in MS 1084 as well as in other manuscripts (but a search has not revealed it).

(3)   This version never had a West-Frankish text, meaning either

(a) it existed in the West only as a melisma, and was so communicated to Notker, to be texted by him, or

(b) existed in the West only as a transcript from Notker's version, in which case we would have to assume that VENIET REX and SALUS AETERNA were also derived from Notker's version as prototype, or that Notker worked from one or the other of them. CLARE SANCTORUM SENATUS appears in French sources, but not until the twelfth century—except for MS Paris 1087, which is an eleventh-century Cluny manuscript with but few points of contact with the Aquitanian manuscripts.

The form of Notker's incipit seems clearly redundant and not original, with its three-fold cadence on G including the fully cadential opening single and regular double. The evidence of ECCE VICIT would, it seems to me, make it probable that the original form included only 1 and 2a. That this 2a was doubled simultaneously and independently by Notker and the Western version represented by 1084 fol.197 would not be too much to assume in view of the tendency toward doubling we have encountered in the instances studied. VENIET REX could be understood as an alternate derivative modified in some not very satisfactory way, of the form with 1 and 2a only. From a purely morphological point of view, it does seem easiest to understand SALUS AETERNA as a modification of Notker's form, that form being represented in the Aquitanian manuscripts by 1084 fol.197, its phrase 1 provided with an "Alleluia" and shortened melodically to provide a tightened effect.

The verse *Ostende* is from Psalm 85,7 (Latin 84,7).

Ostende nobis, Domine, misericordiam tuam:
 et salutare tuum da nobis.

(Show us thy mercy, O Lord,
 and grant us thy salvation.)

SALUS AETERNA can be understood as a sequel to this verse:

. . . et salutare tuum da nobis, alleluia—salus aeterna,
indeficiens, mundi vita, . . .

(. . . and grant us thy salvation, alleluia—eternal,
never-failing salvation, the Life of the world . . .)

The continuation of the prose can be read as an expansion of this opening apposite construction, through the participles *condolens, non linquens, assumens, ferens*. Thus, the relationship to the alleluia verse would explain this peculiarity of the syntax of the prose. Such is the technique characteristic of texts for the jubilus-replacement, represented in Table 2 in group C. This technique, combined with the nature of the melody as a rhapsodic extension of its Alleluia incipit, would be a strong argument for SALUS AETERNA as the original text. And while (as with ORGANICIS CANAMUS) the use of an Alleluia-incipit makes it more likely that SALUS AETERNA is later, that likelihood would not prevent it from being early.

The text VENIET REX makes a different impression: it has no obvious relationship to the verse *Ostende*, It is, however, an Advent text, by virtue of its topic—the Coming of the King, which is echoed in the antiphons of the Office throughout Advent (*Ecce dominus veniet, Veni Domine, Ecce apparebit dominus*). The apocalyptic imagery, as well as the related acclamations from Isaiah 9,6 (*Dominator, princeps pacis* . . .) are also topical for Advent. This kind of text, as well as this kind of relationship to the liturgical season, seems more characteristic of the proses we have studied than does SALUS AETERNA. If SALUS AETERNA is indeed the original text, then it is of a kind subtly but distinctly different from those seen so far.

XVIII

EN VIRGINUM AGMINA
and JUBILEMUS OMNES
Notker's STIRPE MARIA REGIA

FOR NOTKER'S STIRPE MARIA REGIA there is again a hard choice between two West-Frankish texts, EN VIRGINUM AGMINA, and JUBILEMUS OMNES—with Alleluia-incipit and motivic repetition as important as in SALUS AETERNA. In the present case the melody begins with a quotation from an Alleluia used (in the earliest Mass-books) either at feasts of Virgins—Agnes, Caecilia, Praxedes—and also for feasts of the Virgin, with the verse *Adducentur*; or at the Fourth Sunday of Advent, with the verse *Veni domine et noli tardare*.[1] The quotation extends through phrase 1, including a rise from E to C, and preserving—even in Notker's version—the ornamental neumes characteristic of sequence incipits.

The melody as a whole (as seen in Notker's STRIPE MARIA REGIS) has some features basically different from CLARE SANCTORUM SENATUS: it exhibits an alternation between a recurring, refrain-like element and a more verse-like one. Phrase 5 is an approximate repeat of phrase 3 (the very important irregularities in sub-phrase structure do not affect this function of the phrase). Phrase 4 is a compound phrase, long in comparison with 3 and 5, and has the melodic quality of a reciting tone.

Phrase 3	"refrain"
Phrase 4	"verse"—reciting tone
Phrase 5 (=3)	"refrain"

Analogs of the reciting tone in 4 can be provided, for example, from the verses of the Good

---

1. Alleluia *Adducentur*: Schlager, *Them.Kat.* no. 203; *Alleluia-Melodien* I, pp. 6, 617. Hesbert, *Antiphonale missarum sextuplex* nos. 25, 29b, 127, 140, 165b, 199b, but only in one or two MSS. It also appears, along with Alleluia *Veni domine*, in Chartres MS 47, Laon MS 239, St. Gall MS 359.

STIRPE MARIA REGIA (Notker)

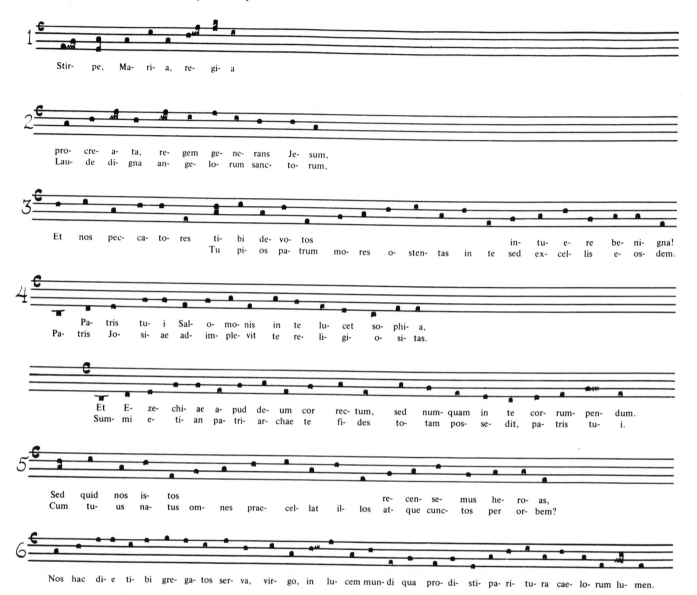

1 Stir- pe, Ma- ri- a, re- gi- a

2 pro- cre- a- ta, re- gem ge- ne- rans Je- sum,
   Lau- de di- gna an- ge- lo- rum sanc- to- rum.

3 Et nos pec- ca- to- res ti- bi de- vo- tos   in- tu- e- re be- ni- gna!
   Tu pi- os pa- trum mo- res o- sten- tas in te sed ex- cel- lis e- os- dem.

4 Pa- tris tu- i Sal- o- mo- nis in te lu- cet so- phi- a,
   Pa- tris Jo- si- ae ad- im- ple- vit te re- li- gi- o- si- tas.

   Et E- ze- chi- ae a- pud de- um cor rec- tum, sed num- quam in te cor- rum- pen- dum.
   Sum- mi e- ti- an pa- tri- ar- chae te fi- des to- tam pos- se- dit, pa- tris tu- i.

5 Sed quid nos is- tos   re- cen- se- mus he- ro- as,
   Cum tu- us na- tus om- nes prae- cel- lat il- los at- que cunc- tos per or- bem?

6 Nos hac di- e ti- bi gre- ga- tos ser- va, vir- go, in lu- cem mun- di qua pro- di- sti pa- ri- tu- ra cae- lo- rum lu- men.

Friday *Improperia*—although no conclusions about age or origin should be drawn from that comparison, beyond the fact that the melody of phrase 4 is a verse formula. Another analog might be the melody for the Greek *Credo* printed by Huglo from Köln, Stadtarchiv MS W.105 (a Processional from the fourteenth century), perhaps representing a melody much older.[2] The formula in phrase 4 begins on C, rises to G, and cadences on E; the second sub-

2. M. Huglo, "Origine de la mélodie du Credo 'authentique' de la Vaticane," *Révue grégorienne* XXX (1951), p. 68.

phrase is slightly extended before the cadence, with the proportions between the two sub-phrases artfully disposed.

Due to the sub-phrase structure of 4, the verse formula appears four times, making the recitation aspect very clear.

(Notker)

    C D FF EF GEG FED CEE

4a   Patris tui Salomonis in te lucet sophia,

    A CD FFEF GE F GE G F E DCD E FFE

    Et Ezechiae apud deum cor rectum, sed numquam in te corrumpendum.

4b   Patris Josiae adimplevit te religiositas.

    Summi eitam patriarchae te fides total possedit, patris tui.

Around this core of verses are grouped, like a frame, phrase 3 and its virtual repetition, 5. Phrase 3 involves motivic repetitions, which together with irregular construction give it the same sense of unphrased continuity that so distinguished SALUS AETERNA phrases 5–6. Here phrase 3 has two motives (x,y); the first, x, takes several forms; the second, y, is terminal.

(3a) x x′   y
           x′ x″   y

The melodic movement is delicately suspended between B and E a fifth below.

    B G, A E

The primary figure consists of two downward leaps that distinguish motive x, and are echoed in motive y as

    A F, G E

The variations among the different forms of x occur at the beginning of the motive: the primary figure is introduced by one note, A in x; by a leap of two notes, D-A, in x′ (this form appears only in some of the Swiss-Rhenish manuscripts, not in the Aquitanian ones); or by a rising scale F G A in x″.

    x :   A B G A E
    x′ :   D A B G A E
    x″:   F G A B G A E

The last form (x″) is reserved for the last appearance of the motive in the phrase, where it adds its subtle insistence to the effect of the reiteration. The phrase as a whole is a double, but the result of the irregularities is rather that of an extended rhapsody whose art recalls—and perhaps depends upon—some kind of pre-Frankish melisma. Indeed, the detail of the motive (the downward skips) recall the jubilus of the Alleluia *Adducentur* (and to a lesser extent the melismas of the verse), so that in this case the relationship to the Alleluia goes beyond the quotation of the incipit. Also in this case, however, the provenance of the Alleluia itself has to be considered: while the Alleluia is well-established in the notated chantbooks around 900 and later, it is not very well represented in the six Mass-books of Hesbert's *Antiphonale missarum sextuplex*, suggesting a date of late eighth or early ninth century—possibly not too far removed from the date of the sequence itself.

Apart from whatever relationship with pre-Frankish melodies can be concluded, the *means* with which the effect in phrase 3 is achieved are so systematically worked out, and at the same time so evident to analysis, as to suggest strongly that the phrase was composed by a Frankish hand in imitation of an older model, rather than being itself old. It is true that this effect of rhapsodic extension is not often found among early sequences; SALUS AETERNA and "Justus ut palma major" are the other important instances. If, however, we construe phrase 3 as a double in which the second line is extended, that construction is familiar from cases such as Notker's SUMMI TRIUMPHUM REGIS and the West-Frankish HÆC DIES QUAM EXCELSUS.

```
(3a)      A B G A A E
          D A B G A   E              F G A F G G E
(3b)  D A B G A   E F G A B G A E F G A F G G E
```

An important factor in the distinctive quality of the melody for STIRPE MARIA REGIA is the pitch-set B-E, which in turn is related to the Alleluia. It should be noted that this is one of 3 sequences in the early repertory with an E-final (the other two, CARMEN SUO DILECTO and CHRISTUS HUNC DIEM, were not known in the West)—as if the reference to this particular Alleluia, similarly distinguished by an E-final, was a way of giving the sequence a distinctive tonal location.

After phrase 3, the verse formula of 4 sits very squarely in its C-G realm (even if it, too, ends on E), contrasting in tonal location as well as in phrase shape and melodic quality. By the same token, the return of 3 at 5 is clear and strong. Here the first x is omitted, so that we are plunged back into the continuation of the swirling melody of 3—an effect not lost upon Notker, as we will see.

It might be argued that phrase 6 begins with a motivic reference to the verse formula in 4, as if the verse were to appear again at a pitch level a fifth higher than before. Such a reference may indeed be intended; but the more important function of phrase 6 is that of concluding single—long, rhapsodic peroration, with ornamental neumes and circuitous approaches to the final, E. Given that function, we can perhaps just as easily hear a reference of 6 to the opening, more precisely to phrase 2, with its similar rise from G to C. At any rate, the overall design shows formal intonation and consequent couplet (1,2); the complex of motivic repetitions (3), that might be taken as an extension of 1–2 (just as in SALUS AETERNA 5 was an extension of 3–4); the central core of verses (4); the reprise of 3 (5); and the concluding single (6).

Notker's text seems responsive to almost all aspects of this design. A prominent feature of the period-structure of his text is the division of 3a,b: 3a is the conclusion of the opening period; 3b, syntactically complete (*Tu . . . eosdem*) is linked in thought and diction with what follows in 4.

(1)   Stirpe, Maria, regia procreata,
(2a)   regem generans Jesum,
(2b)   laude digna angelorum sanctorum,
(3a)   et nos peccatores, tibi devotos, intuere benigna!
(3b)   Tu pios patrum mores ostentas in te,
         sed excellis eosdem.
(4a)   Patris tui Salomonis in te lucet sophia . . .

Lines 1 through 3a contain a petition (*intuere!*) preceded by laudatory epithets, of which the first provides the main theme—"born of royal lineage, O Mary . . . ." Line 3b follows logically enough, "Thou shewest forth the holy ways of the fathers, but excellest them"; but the several clauses in 4, when they come, have the effect of itemizing a general statement in 3b. Perhaps the best way of construing 3b is as a link between the opening period and 4; it is significant, of course, that this linking occurs right in the middle of the complex melodic construction of 3, so that textual and musical continuity are synchronized. Also, phrase 3 is interpreted by Notker's texting as an extension of 2, in much the same way that the enjambement *Stirpe . . . procreata* links 2 to 1.

The verses in 4 are conceived as a unit.

(4a)   *Patris tui* Salomonis in te lucet sophia,
         Et Ezechiae apud deum cor rectum, sed numquam in te corrumpendum.
(4b)   Patris Josiae adimplevit te religiositas.
         Summi etiam patriarchae te fides total possedit,
                         patris tui.

Once again, the accent pattern in the verses shows a predominance of groupings in twos (as we first observed in LAUDES DEO), at least in the first sub-phrase of each line. The "tu" and "te" resonate throughout, as the Old Testament figures are referred to Mary:

Of thy father Solomon the wisdom shines in thee,
        and of Ezechiel the heart set straight with God, in thee never to be deflected;
Of father Isaiah the sanctity fills thee;
        thee possesses even the faith of the greatest patriarch—of thy father.

On top of the carefully worked-out couplet structure is superimposed something of the form of the epanaleptic distich: *patris tui* at beginning and end lock in the couplet.

The reprise at 5 is set to a rhetorical question.

But why do we concern ourselves with those great ones,
when thy son exceeds them all—indeed the whole earth?

(5a)   Sed quid nos istos recensemus heroas,
(5b)   cum tuus natus omnes praecellat illos atque cunctos per orbem?

It is true that there is nothing of reprise in the text; on the contrary, the text here makes a deliberate, striking turn to an aspect previously only touched upon (*generans Jesum*). One might think from that that Notker had ignored the structural implications of the melody. But the effect of the rhetorical question can be taken as a very close analog of the melodic structure, for the sense of abrupt turn (*Sèd quíd nòs ístos . . .*), reinforced by three monosyllables, strongly supports the wrench in the melody as it lifts out of the verse formula back into the motivic flux of phrase 5. And it seems characteristic of Notker to seek out such a rhetorical means rather than a more obvious analog of verbal form or sense.

The concluding single is set to a complex petition-plus-epithet.

(6)   Nos hac die tibi gregatos serva, virgo, in lucem mundi
              qua prodisti paritura caelorum lumen.

        (Keep us, gathered together today before thee, O Virgin, in the light of the world,
              by that birth whereby thou bore forth the light of the heavens.)

Here the circling nature of the melody is supported by the elaborate word order and syntax, as well as the way *lumen* at the end—without seeming to be a redictum—catches up the sense and sonority of *lucem mundi* in the middle.

Notker's theme is the excellence of Mary, and his imagery is her royal lineage. The Alleluia verse *Adducentur* was, to be sure, used for Marian feasts, but its principal use was for feasts of Virgins, that is, it is not specifically Marian. Here we can observe Notker thinking as a poet, not as a liturgist. The text of the Alleluia verse apparently owed its liturgical use to the image of virgins being presented in honor to the king; but one has to bear in mind the associative habits of liturgists—the Epistle for the blessing of the palms on Palm Sunday was chosen solely because it mentions, in passing, seventy palm trees. What the Alleluia verse really says is,

Hearken, O daughter, and consider,
and incline thine ear; forget also thine
own people, and thy father's house;
So shall the king greatly desire thy
beauty: for he is thy Lord; and worship
thou him.
And the daughter of Tyre shall be
there with a gift; even the rich among
the people shall intreat thy favor.
The king's daughter is all glorious
within: her clothing is of wrought
gold.
She shall be brought into the king in
raiment of needle work; *the virgins her*   Adducentur Regi virgines post eam:
companions that follow her shall be brought   proximae ejus afferentur tibi.
unto thee.
With gladness and rejoicing shall they
be brought: they shall enter into the
king's palace. (Ps. 45, 10–15)

Notker, reading it, obviously felt that the appropriate use for the related sequence would be further praise of "her" in some royal context. "She" and the king—her father—are at the center of the stage; the virgins that were the excuse for the liturgical assignment of the Alleluia verse are ignored as "extras."

The West-Frankish EN VIRGINUM AGMINA, on the other hand, is so obviously dependent in theme upon the virgins of the Alleluia verse that the prose can be taken as an extension of the verse in the same way that SALUS AETERNA is an extension of the verse *Ostende*. Beyond that, EN VIRGINUM AGMINA adds a New Testament element—the virgins that go in with the bridegroom in the parable of the five wise and five foolish virgins (*Matthew* 25, 1–13). The parable is summarized, and moralized, in lines 3–5. In this way, the Alleluia for several Virgins is related directly to the Gospel, which is itself the parable from *Matthew*. (Furthermore, the Gospel is the source of the communion antiphon *Quinque prudentes* used in some cases in conjunction with this Alleluia verse.[3])

As it stands in three Aquitanian manuscripts, EN VIRGINUM AGMINA has an incipit structure different from Notker's.

(1)　　　En virginum
(2a)　　　　　　　agmina procellit in gloria.
(2b)　　　　　　　Et inter ceteros ordines fulsit lucidum.
(2c)　　　　　　　Et ovans decurrit in aeva Christo obviam.

Most obvious is the extra line, given here as the third line of a triple; this might be understood as something comparable to the third line Notker added in CLARE SANCTORUM SENATUS. But the melody of 2c, while roughly parallel to 2a,b, is not identical; another interpretation would be to consider *Et ovans . . .* as "3", continuing on into motive x of the following line (which we called 3a in Notker's version).

　　　　　　　　　　　　　　　　　　(x)
(3)　　Et ovans decurrit in aeva Christo obviam cum claro lumine.
　　　　　(x)　　　　　　　　　　(y)
(4a)　　Dignum est enim　　　　　ut in sponsi adventum
　　　　　(x)　　　　　(x″)　　　　(y)
(4b)　　Fidelis turma praestoletur in somnis sum fulgentes lampadas.

From the point of view of phrase structure this interpretation seems preferable, since it preserves a more or less regular double (2a,b), a single (3) in a position we have met before (as in FORTIS ATQUE AMARA), and an expanded double (4a,b) of the type found in SUMMI TRIUMPHUM REGIS. From a motivic point of view, however, this interpretation splits up the first two appearances of motive x in a seemingly illogical way. There are, however, other factors to be taken into account before deciding on the proper interpretation.

Other discrepancies in the incipit of EN VIRGINUM AGMINA concern the E cadence of 2b and 2c, where Notker's version cadenced on G. The West-Frankish incipit feels melodically redundant—the drop to E in 3 has been completely pre-empted by the time it arrives. With

3. See Hesbert, *Antiphonale missarum sextuplex*, no. 25.

En vir- gi- num

ag- mi- na pro- cel- lit in glo- ri- a
Et o- vans de- cur- rit Chri- sto ob- vi- am cum cla- ro lu- mi- ne.

Di- gnum est e- nim ut in spon- si ad- ven- tum
Fi- de- lis tur- ma prae- sto- le- tur in som- nis cum ful- gen- tes lam- pa- das,

Ne re- spu- at nup- ti- a- lis di- gna ha- bi- ta- cu- la
Quid di- gni- us quid- ve no- bis sub- li- mi- us ad vi- tam

E- as con- sor- tes quas in- un- dans re- a- tas in- ve- ne- rit re- qui- e- scen- tes.
Ut il- li sem- per vi- gi- le- mus et fir- mam te- ne- a- mus par- si- mo- ni- am!

Et cum in noc- te so- nu- e- rit me- di- e
Cla- mor ti- men- dus cum o- pe- re per- fec- to in- tre- mus ad nup- ti- as,

Et nec- ta- re- a cunc- tis da- pem re- fau- ci- la- tos Chri- sti fa- ven- tem cum e- lec- tis

si- mul sem- per in- jun- ge lae- ti- ti- a.

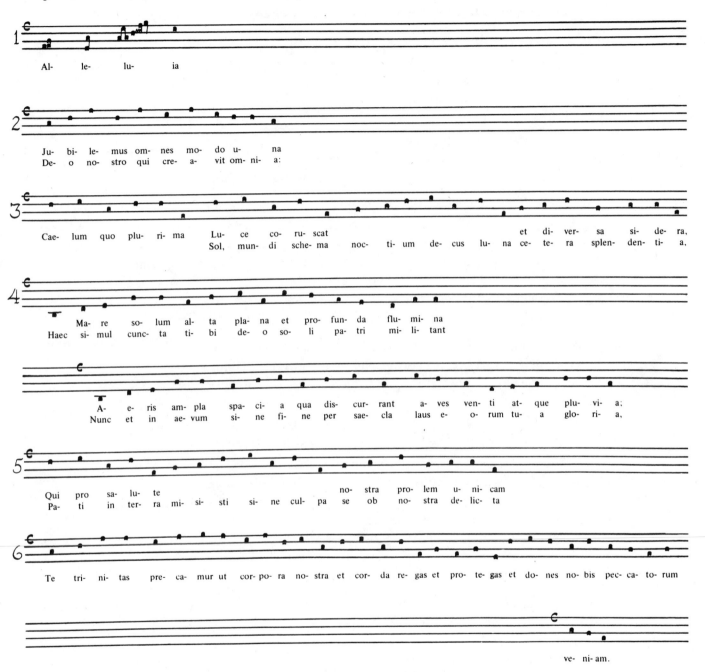

JUBILEMUS OMNES

1. Al- le- lu- ia

2. Ju- bi- le- mus om- nes mo- do u- na
   De- o no- stro qui cre- a- vit om- ni- a:

3. Cae- lum quo plu- ri- ma Lu- ce co- ru- scat et di- ver- sa si- de- ra,
   Sol, mun- di sche- ma noc- ti- um de- cus lu- na ce- te- ra splen- den- ti- a,

4. Ma- re so- lum al- ta pla- na et pro- fun- da flu- mi- na
   Haec si- mul cunc- ta ti- bi de- o so- li pa- tri mi- li- tant

A- e- ris am- pla spa- ci- a qua dis- cur- rant a- ves ven- ti at- que plu- vi- a;
Nunc et in ae- vum si- ne fi- ne per sae- cla laus e- o- rum tu- a glo- ri- a,

5. Qui pro sa- lu- te no- stra pro- lem u- ni- cam
   Pa- ti in ter- ra mi- si- sti si- ne cul- pa se ob no- stra de- lic- ta

6. Te tri- ni- tas pre- ca- mur ut cor- po- ra no- stra et cor- da re- gas et pro- te- gas et do- nes no- bis pec- ca- to- rum

ve- ni- am.

Notker's version before us, we can venture a reconstruction, with very salutory effects on the otherwise discouraging redundancy in the text of 2b,c (*Et . . . Et*).

```
    EEF DG GBGABCD B
1   En  vir-gi-      num
        G   A ABC  ABC C B    C   BA G G
2a      agmina  pro-  cellit  in glori-  a:
                                    A  G G
2b      et  ovans de-  currit Chri- sto obvi- am
                                A   BG A A E
                    (x) cum claro lumine
```

This tighter form of the opening period makes the effect of run-on into motive x (*cum claro lumine*) very strong, with a clear overlap of the syntax, which breaks at *lumine*, and the melodic material, which starts something new with motive x at *cum*. The sense of continuity produced by these irregularities extends through 3a,b, and it is this continuity that we can take as the model for Notker's more sober treatment in STIRPE MARIA REGIA.

Furthermore, EN VIRGINUM AGMINA continues the overlap, at the highest syntactic level, right through 4, since 4b begins a rhetorical question after a full stop.

3a   Dignum est enim   ut in sponsis adventum
3b   Fidelis turma praestoletur insomnis cum fulgentes lampadas,
4a   ne respuat nuptialis digna habitacula eas consortes,
             quas inundans reatas invenerit requiescentes.
4b   Quid dignius quidve nobis sublimius ad vitam
         ut illi semper vigilemus et firmam teneamus parsimoniam!

(For it is a good thing, at the coming of the bridegroom,
    for the faithful to watch, sleepless with shining lamps,
        lest from the chamber worthy of the wedding he reject those brides whom
        he found guilty, sleeping.
What is more worthy, more lofty, for us in life,
    than that we should always keep watch for him,
    and be steadfast in our thrift.)

No effort is made, in EN VIRGINUM AGMINA, to give the verse formula special textual treatment; the author seems more intent on the effect to be achieved at the reprise in phrase 5. The comparison with Notker's procedures at this point in interesting: the West-Frankish text has a rhetorical question at 4b (*Quid dignius . . .*) by way of a moral drawn from the parable; but there is more to the parable—and precisely that effect, of continuing a story broken off in the middle, is the textual analog of the melodic reprise. More obvious, more colorful than Notker's texting, the words, ". . . And when at midnight a fearful noise rings out . . ." sit perfectly on the resumption of the motive in the melody. The petition to be included in the heavenly feast continues through the closing single.

<table>
<tr><td>(3a)</td><td>Dignum est enim ut in sponsi adventum fidelis turma praestoletur in somnis cum
fulgentes lampadas,</td></tr>
<tr><td>(4a)</td><td>ne respuat nuptialis digna habitacula eas consortes quas inundans reatas
invenerit requiescentes.</td></tr>
<tr><td>(4b)</td><td>(Quid dignius
quidve nobis sublimius ad vitam
ut illi semper vigilemus
et firmam teneamus parsimoniam!)</td></tr>
<tr><td>(5a)</td><td>. . . Et cum in nocte sonuerit medie clamor timendus,
cum opere perfecto intremus ad nuptias,</td></tr>
<tr><td>(6)</td><td>et nectarea cunctis dapem refaucilatos Christi faventem
cum electi simul semper injunge laetitia.</td></tr>
</table>

The other early West-Frankish text to this melody, JUBILEMUS OMNES, was far more popular; at any rate it became entrenched in a regular position at the Fourth Sunday of Advent, being connected with the other Alleluia verse, *Veni domine*—although there is no apparent connection in sense between the prose and the verse, and not very much between the prose and Advent. The Mass for the Fourth Sunday of Advent has a curious history, that Sunday originally having no proper Mass—*Dominica vacat*—because of the preceding Ember Saturday,[4] and the text of the verse *Veni domine* is not from the psalter. Furthermore, the melody shows several peculiar features relative to the Gregorian repertory.

The prose can, however, be read as a *Caeli enarrant*, with all parts of creation singing the praises of the Creator, a theme that might have Advent associations. And lines 5a,b refer specifically to the Incarnation.

(5a) Qui pro salute nostra
prolem unicam (5b) pati in terra misisti sine culpa se ob nostra delicta.

(Who, for our salvation, hast sent thine only Son to suffer, without blame, on earth for our sins.)

The incipit of JUBILEMUS OMNES presents interesting variants: there are two main versions, one in which the text *Jubilemus* . . . is set under the melody of phrase 1—that is, under the Alleluia quotation; in the other version the text *Jubilemus* . . . is set under phrase 2, phrase 1 being left with only the text "Alleluia," in the fashion of SALUS AETERNA.

<table>
<tr><td>(1)</td><td>Jubilemus omnes una</td></tr>
<tr><td>(2a)</td><td>deo nostro, qui creavit omnia,</td></tr>
<tr><td>(2b)</td><td>Per quem cuncta condita sunt saecula:</td></tr>
</table>

<table>
<tr><td>(1)</td><td>Alleluia</td></tr>
<tr><td>(2a)</td><td>Jubilemus omnes modo una</td></tr>
<tr><td>(2b)</td><td>Deo nostro qui creavit omnia:</td></tr>
</table>

4. W. Apel, *Gregorian Chant* (Bloomington 1958), p. 57.

The first of these versions (*Jubilemus* = 1) is by far the most frequent in the sources, and became standard in the later ones. The other version (*Jubilemus* = 2) is found only in some Aquitanian manuscripts (1118, and originally in 1084, before *Per quem* . . . was added). The easiest interpretation would be that the prose was conceived first as *Jubilemus* = 1, in the manner of most of the early repertory, then in one or two instances adapted to the form beginning with "Alleluia." Two aspects of the text speak against this interpretation, however, and favor instead the unusual circumstance of a text conceived as Alleluia = 1 being converted into the form *Jubilemus* = 1.

The text of the usual version, considered by itself, reads reasonably well.

(1) Jubilemus omnes una (2a) deo nostro,
   qui creavit omnia,
(2b) per quem cuncta condita sunt saecula:
(3a) caelum, quo plurima luce coruscat,
   et diversa sidera,
(3b) sol, mundi schema;
   noctium decus, luna;
   cetera splendentia;

(Let us all rejoice together for our God,
 who created all things,
 through whom the whole world was founded;
 the heavens, that shine with a great light,
 and the myriad stars;
 the sun, the form of the world,
 the moon, glory of the night,
 and the other shining bodies;)

Yet 2b sticks a little: its diction, *per quem*, refers to the Son, (as in the Credo, *per quem omnia facta sunt*), while the previous line, 2a, referred to the Father, the Creator; and 2b is redundant in its *condita sunt*.

Comparison with the other version supports these impressions of redundancy, and offers an explanation.

(1) Alleluia
(2a) Jubilemus omnes modo (2b) deo nostro,
   qui creavit omnia:
(3a) caelum, quo plurima luce coruscat . . .

In this version, *Jubilemus omnes (modo) una* falls under the melody of 2a, *Deo nostro, qui creavit omnia* under 2b, and *Per quem cuncta condita sunt saecula* is absent. *Caelum* follows directly after *omnia* as the first of the specified items in the Creation. (The presence or absence of *modo* does not seem important.) This shorter version has the same ring of authenticity in its directness that we observed in other West-Frankish versions, when restored to their pre-conflated form. The implication would be that JUBILEMUS was conceived originally as a text with *Alleluia* as line 1.

The items of creation fall easily enough under the repeated motives in phrase 3, but they continue in 4, with no textual response to the verse formulas appearing there in the melody, nor is there much response to the reprise in phrase 5. A petition follows in the concluding single, as in the other texts, with three verbs of purpose as analog of the convolutions of the melody.

(4a)   Mare, solum, alta, plana, et profunda flumina;
             aeris ampla spacia qua discurrunt aeves, venti, atque pluvia;
(4b)   hæc simul cuncta tibi, deo soli patri, militant;
             nunc et in aevum sine fine per saecula laus eorum tua gloria:
(5a)   qui pro salute nostra prolem unicam pati in terra misisti sine culpa se ob
                                                 nostra delicta.

(6)   Te, trinitas, precamur
        ut corpora nostra et corda regas
        et protegas
        et dones nobis peccatorum veniam.

The invocation of the Trinity is more or less unprepared. In some ways it would be easier to relate the splendors of Creation to the Trinity, understanding the whole text as a praise of the Trinity, than it is to justify it as an Advent piece.

All in all, not as distinguished a work as EN VIRGINUM AGMINA. Distinction, of course, is not a necessary condition of historical precedence, and either version of JUBILEMUS could have been Notker's model. The details of syntax, however, suggest that it was EN VIRGINUM AGMINA that Notker saw; that EN VIRGINUM AGMINA was conceived as a pendant to the Alleluia *Adducentur*, possibly for the express purpose of bringing the parable of the virgins into the Mass for Virgins; and that JUBILEMUS was made later to provide an Advent prose, through the use of the Virgins' Alleluia also at the Fourth Sunday of Advent.

If this interpretation were correct, the melody and text of EN VIRGINUM AGMINA would be—of all the sequences studied so far—the one most strongly related to an Alleluia of the Mass in its original conception. It seems to me that the key to making sense out of the confusing and contradictory evidence of the relationship of Alleluia and sequence lies in accepting different degrees of relationship for different pieces—ranging from virtually no relationship for some to a very strong one in the present case.

But if we do accept the close relationship of EN VIRGINUM AGMINA to the Alleluia as having something important to do with the genesis of the piece, then the melodic structure of the sequence must cause us to ponder. One of its phrases (3), to be sure, has all the marks of the kind of melodic extension one would expect of a replacement melisma for an Alleluia jubilus; in this respect phrase 3 stands very close to phrases 5–6 of SALUS AETERNA. Another phrase, however, phrase 4, contains the verse formulas, which are entirely alien to a melismatic jubilus—one could not imagine phrase 4 appearing in textless form in a melisma. Here, in the melody most closely associated with an Alleluia, we find elements that most strongly suggest that a text—or at least provision for a text—was a basic ingredient of the original conception.

To that paradox we can add the fact that the Alleluia itself is not one of the old-line Gregorian items with firm connections to truly Gregorian melodic styles or to universal liturgical practice. Rather, it lies on the interface of Gregorian and Frankish chant, so that a sequence written in the mid-ninth century as a jubilus-replacement for this Alleluia is not far removed from it in time or place.

XIX

REGNANTEM SEMPITERNA
and PANGAT LAUDES
Notker's PSALLAT ECCLESIA

THE THIRD MELODY of this group presents many of the same problems as the other two, and yields the same inconclusive results. In this case the lack of conclusions is even more serious, because Notker's text, PSALLAT ECCLESIA, is by his own account the second one he wrote, hence is an early work (ca. 860?). It seems likely that the melody is early in the West-Frankish repertory as well.

As with the other two cases, Notker's text has two early West-Frankish counterparts: one, REGNANTEM SEMPITERNA, begins with the word *Alleluia*; the other, PANGAT LAUDES, begins with a single in the more usual early fashion. The melody begins with a quotation from Alleluia *Laetatus sum*, used at the Second Sunday of Advent.[1] Here, at least, the Alleluia and its liturgical use seem firmly rooted in the Gregorian repertory. The quotation of the Alleluia extends as far as *Psallat ecclesia* in Notker's version, and *Pangat laudes digna* or *Alleluia* in the other two.

The structure of the whole introduction is complex, and varies substantially among the versions (with many variant readings directly attributable to the difficulty scribes must have had with the complex structure). It does, however, seem possible to reconstruct the underlying development. The Alleluia quotation rises from D to A, and is followed by a leisurely descent in three sub-phrases, to D; the second sub-phrase repeats the first, suggesting a very short couplet. Ignoring for the moment the numbered phrases, we need to keep track of these sub-phrases with letters and subscripts.

---

1. Alleluia *Laetatus sum*: Schlager, *Them.Kat.* no. 113; *Alleluia-Melodien* I, pp. 280, 590; Hesbert, *Antiphonale missarum sextuplex* nos. 2, 182, 199a. Chartres MS 47, Laon MS 239, St. Gall MS 359.

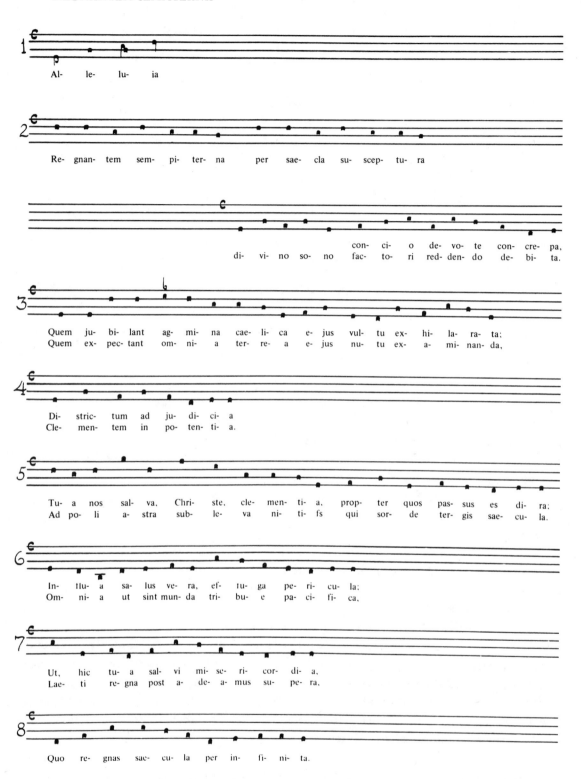

1. Al- le- lu- ia

2. Re- gnan- tem sem- pi- ter- na per sae- cla su- scep- tu- ra

con- ci- o de- vo- te con- cre- pa,
di- vi- no so- no fac- to- ri red- den- do de- bi- ta.

3. Quem ju- bi- lant ag- mi- na cae- li- ca e- jus vul- tu ex- hi- la- ra- ta;
Quem ex- pec- tant om- ni- a ter- re- a e- jus nu- tu ex- a- mi- nan- da,

4. Di- stric- tum ad ju- di- ci- a
Cle- men- tem in po- ten- ti- a.

5. Tu- a nos sal- va, Chri- ste, cle- men- ti- a, prop- ter quos pas- sus es di- ra;
Ad po- li a- stra sub- le- va ni- ti- fs qui sor- de ter- gis sae- cu- la.

6. In- flu- a sa- lus ve- ra, ef- fu- ga pe- ri- cu- la;
Om- ni- a ut sint mun- da tri- bu- e pa- ci- fi- ca,

7. Ut, hic tu- a sal- vi mi- se- ri- cor- di- a,
Lae- ti re- gna post a- de- a- mus su- pe- ra,

8. Quo re- gnas sae- cu- la per in- fi- ni- ta.

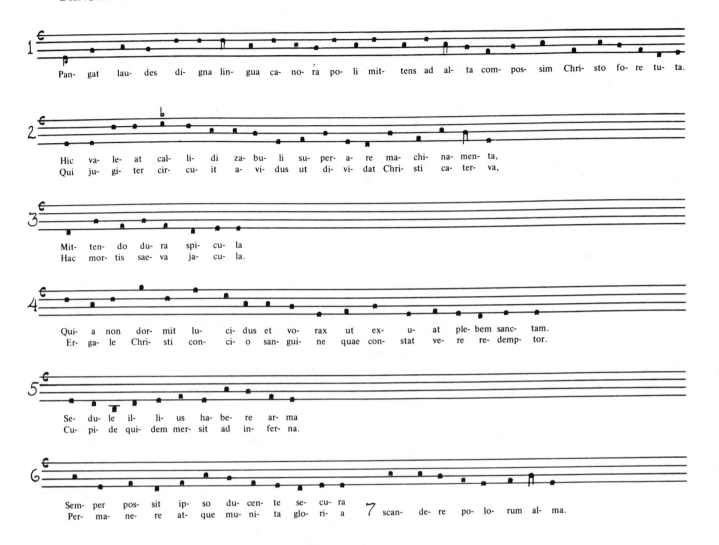

1. Pan- gat lau- des di- gna lin- gua ca- no- ra po- li mit- tens ad al- ta com- pos- sim Chri- sto fo- re tu- ta.

2. Hic va- le- at cal- li- di za- bu- li su- per- a- re ma- chi- na- men- ta,
   Qui ju- gi- ter cir- cu- it a- vi- dus ut di- vi- dat Chri- sti ca- ter- va,

3. Mit- ten- do du- ra spi- cu- la
   Hac mor- tis sae- va ja- cu- la.

4. Qui- a non dor- mit lu- ci- dus et vo- rax ut ex- u- at ple- bem sanc- tam.
   Er- ga- le Chri- sti con- ci- o san- gui- ne quae con- stat ve- re re- demp- tor.

5. Se- du- le il- li- us ha- be- re ar- ma
   Cu- pi- de qui- dem mer- sit ad in- fer- na.

6. Sem- per pos- sit ip- so du- cen- te se- cu- ra 7 scan- de- re po- lo- rum al- ma.
   Per- ma- ne- re at- que mu- ni- ta glo- ri- a 7 scan- de- re po- lo- rum al- ma.

	DC F G F A A		A G A G F
(a)	Pangat laudes digna (b₁)		lingua canora
			AG AG A G F
	(b₂) poli mittens ad alta		
	E F G		E G F E C D
(c)	compossim Christo fore tuta		

This text, *Pangat laudes . . . tuta*, is the opening period. It is not very clear as it stands.

Let the tongue worthily sing praises in sweet melody,
    sending them on high to heaven,
        to be completely safe with Christ.

And while the melody is clear enough in this version, the other versions make it seem likely that this one is corrupt through omission.

REGNANTEM SEMPITERNA adds two more sub-phrases—a new one (d) followed by a repetition of (c).

```
       DC FGFA          A  A  G   A  GG  F
(a)    Allelu- ia   (b₁) Regnantem sempiterna
                        A  A  G A G G F
                    (b₂) per saecla susceptura
                        E F G E G F E   C D
                    (c₁) concio devote concrepa
                                              D F E  F D
                                          (d) divino sono
                        E  F G E  G  F  E C D
                    (c₂) factori reddendo debita.
```

The new sub-phrase, *divino sono*, provides just enough melodic motion to reanimate and extend the phrase that had come to rest on the D. The effect of the whole, including the reaffirmed cadence in (c₂) is not unlike those places involving motivic repetition in SALUS AETERNA and EN VIRGINUM AGMINA. In any case, the phrase seems really to be concluded at *debita* at the end of c₂. The texting in REGNANTEM SEMPITERNA seems consequent and apt for the extension.

> Let the congregation devoutly acclaim the king who reigns forever,
>   in holy song rendering due praise to their Creator.

The sense of the words is perhaps somewhat stretched: *concrepare* means "to clash" or "rattle," as an army rattles its weapons in response to its leader; normally intransitive, it seems here to take "the ruler" as object, as if the army's acclamation was the effective act in confirming his rule (as was the case in imperial Rome). Not as difficult as the text in PANGAT LAUDES, this one seems believable as it stands. Emendations ancient and modern have involved omitting *divino sono* (thereby making a second short regular couplet, a, b₁ b₂, c₁ c₂); conceivably d, c₁ c₂ could all be omitted, making the form identical to PANGAT LAUDES.[2] On purely musical grounds, however, *divino sono* . . . seems not like an interpolation; and the form as given seems easiest accounted for if assumed to be original.

Notker's version, if considered in conjunction with ECCE VICIT and CLARE SANCTORUM, can be satisfactorily derived from REGNANTEM SEMPITERNA: as in the other two cases, Notker here apparently doubled an irregular single. In this case what appeared to him as a single was d, c₂, for that is what he doubled.

(1)   (a) Psallat ecclesia   (b₁) mater illibata,
                                (b₂) et virgo sine ruga,
                                (c₁)   honorem hujus ecclesiae!

2. See also the discussion in *Anal.hymn.* 53, pp. 5–8.

(2a)	(d) Hæc domus aulae	(c₂)	caelestis probatur particeps
(2b)	in laude regis		caelorum et cerimoniis.

In other words, he took the motive (d) to be the start of a new phrase, rather than an extension of a continuing one. This in turn involves a subtly different understanding of (c), which in Notker's interpretation can only be heard as the kind of homeoteleuton frequently encountered. If heard as the functional close, repeated for emphasis, of a single extended phrase (which it seems to be in REGNANTEM SEMPITERNA), then the second repetition in Notker's plan is redundant, and tediously so. It is, by the way, impossible to derive Notker's version from PANGAT LAUDES without crediting him with the addition of an entire couplet, his 2a, b.

In some other details, too, Notker's version corresponds to REGNANTEM SEMPITERNA rather than to PANGAT LAUDES. The two West-Frankish versions differ at the end of 6, where REGNANTEM SEMPITERNA has a cadence C D D added after the descent to D; Notker also has it, but PANGAT LAUDES (5) does not. The last phrase, a single, is shortest in PANGAT LAUDES, longer in REGNANTEM SEMPITERNA, longest in PSALLAT ECCLESIA; again, Notker's can be most easily understood as an expansion of REGNANTEM SEMPITERNA.

PANGAT LAUDES

G GF EDE FE D

7   scandere polorum alma

REGNANTEM SEMPITERNA

C E G G FE C D EED

8   Quo regnas saecula per infinita

PSALLAT ECCLESIA

D E F GFEDG G FEDE G EED

8   Hac domo trinitati laus et glori-a semper resultant

Notker's phrase 7, on the other hand, is two notes shorter than the West-Frankish versions, thereby removing a distinctive figure involving two downward leaps.

REGNANTEM SEMPITERNA

G DEC E G FEDC DD

7   ut hic tua salvi misericordia

PSALLAT ECCLESIA

G G E C E G EE C D D

7   Hic vox (laudis) laeti- ti-ae per-son at

           Hic pax (semper) et gau-dia redundant.

Some manuscripts, to be sure, supply the words in parentheses, thereby giving the phrase the full number of notes, but one of the oldest ones, MS British Museum 19768, does not; and while *semper* is acceptable, *laudis* has no real place in the syntax as it stands.[3]

Considering now the features common to the several versions, the melody shares with the other two of this group (SALUS AETERNA and VIRGINUM AGMINA) an effective use and re-

3. See the apparatus, *Anal.hymn.* 53, pp. 398–399.

use of a motive. The motive (d), which is the means of the phrase extension in 1, is echoed by the very short phrase REGNANTEM SEMPITERNA 4.

REGNANTEM SEMPITERNA

```
    D  F  E  F        D
    di- vi-no  so-     no

    D  F  E  F  EC D D
    Districtum ad judic- i- a
    Clementem in potenti- a
```

The phrase is prominent in its brevity, and the low, modest melody acquires curious significance located between two long, soaring lines.

Completely lacking in this melody is any suggestion of the verse-like formula of EN VIRGINUM AGMINA—or, for that matter, of LAUDES DEO. At the same time, and in spite of the motivic repetition and recall, the melody has little of the unphrased continuity so strong in EN VIRGINUM AGMINA and SALUS AETERNA. Instead, its phrases are clearly shaped and de-limited—once the first one is past. REGNANTEM SEMPITERNA phrase 3, leaping up a fifth at the start, drops smoothly back to the D final in groupings of threes, with a termination F D,

D D A A, *B♭ A G, G F D*, E F D C E F G F D

in a manner that recalls SALUS AETERNA 4, as well as a number of other pieces.

Phrase 4 is the very short one that echoes *divino sono* (motive d); it seems to provide the true cadence (C D D) to phrase 2, but both phrases are sufficiently detached and inde-pendant that little real continuity is felt.

Phrase 5 moves with decision to a higher level—A and the D an octave above the final —in an idiom used for the same purpose in other melodies with Alleluia connections: the incipit

A G A D A C B G

corresponds to HÆC EST VERA REDEMPTIO 7, DILECTE DEO 3, and OMNIPOTENS DEUS 5. The line drops to the D final through groups of threes, as a more intense version of phrase 3.

A G A D A, *C B G, G F D*, E F D E D C D D

Phrases 6, 7, and 8 might, indeed, be considered as elements in a larger grouping, and here might be heard a continuity extending over a longer stretch; still, the phrases them-selves are discrete entities. Phrase 6 lies low, venturing down into a new region below the final, and approaching its cadence from the G a fourth above.

6   D C A C D E G G F E D C D D

Phrase 7 insists on this same G in its opening leaps, and cadences in the same way.

7   *G D E C E G F E D C D D*

And phrase 8, the last one, approaches the cadence once again in the same way, so that the descent G to D becomes a primary event. At the very end, the C D D cadence is replaced by another form with the last step descending, as so often in sequences. The set of pitches C-E-G becomes prominent at the close as a foil to the D.

The design of the whole melody, then, includes an introduction with Alleluia quotation and extension (1,2); two long (but undivided) arching phrases (3,5) articulated by the short, emphatic motive (4); and a conclusion consisting of three phrases (6,7,8) that circle around and close on D approached from G above. For a relatively short sequence, the melodic high point in 5 comes unusually soon; that is, the conclusion (6,7,8) seems long—indeed, almost as long as what comes before the high point. Nonetheless, in its own terms the melody is remarkably well-proportioned; the detail, while often expressive, is carefully disposed in the phrase. As a whole, it gives an impression of greater assurance than LAUDES DEO; and if LAUDES DEO betrays signs of a formative stage in the development of sequence melodies, REGNANTEM SEMPITERNA does not, at least in purely musical terms.

Knowing as we do that Notker's PSALLAT ECCLESIA is an early effort, we may be justified in seeing in it some signs of its genesis. It is not without art: the topic sentence, calling upon the whole Body of Christ to help celebrate the dedication of a particular house of God, sets off "church" against "church" in an effective if not entirely sophisticated way.

(1)   Psallat *ecclesia*, mater illibata, et virgo sine ruga, honorem *hujus ecclesiae*!

Line 2a represents the sometimes awkward diction so successfully avoided by Notker in his mature works.

(2a)   Hæc domus aulae caelestis *probatur particeps*

Although the sources affirm 2b as given, the line is lame, and superfluous; if we wished to see it as a later interpolation, we could read from 2a to 3—in conformity with the West-Frankish REGNANTEM SEMPITERNA—with perfect sense and greater cogency.

(2a)   Hæc domus aulae caelestis probatur particeps
(2b)   (in laude regis caelorum et cerimoniis)
(3a)   et lumine continuo aemulans civitatem sine tenebris,
(3b)   et corpora in gremio confovens animarum quae in caelo vivunt.

    (May this house be found a partner with the celestial halls,
        [in praise and worship of the king of heaven]
    emulating by its perpetual light that city without shadow,
    and sheltering in its bosom the bodies whose souls live in heaven.)

Here, as in several other places in the piece, Notker uses the kind of obvious parallelism found also in LAUDES DEO CONCINAT.

(3a)	Et . . .	(7a)	Hic vox . . .	personat
(3b)	Et . . .	(7b)	Hic pax . . .	redundant
(6a)	Fugiunt . . .	(8)	Hac domo . . .	resultant
(6b)	Pereunt . . .			

Psallat ecclesia (Notker)

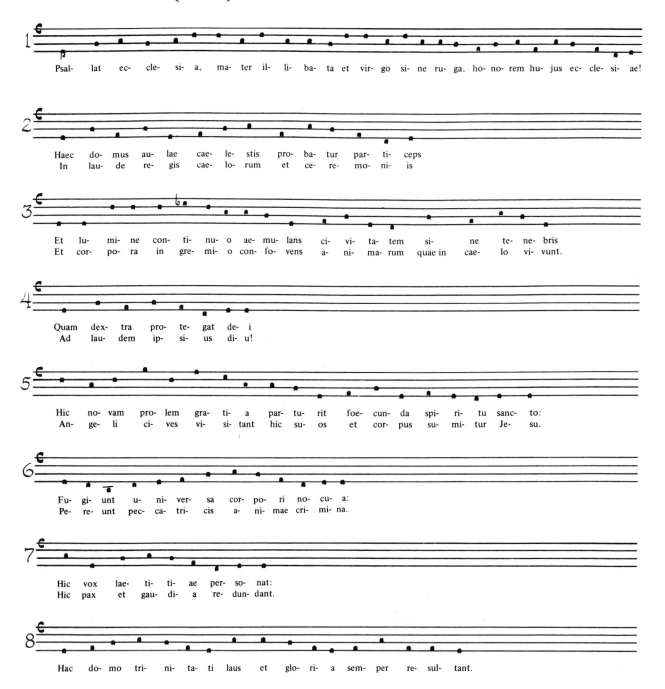

1. Psal- lat ec- cle- si- a, ma- ter il- li- ba- ta et vir- go si- ne ru- ga, ho- no- rem hu- jus ec- cle- si- ae!

2. Haec do- mus au- lae cae- le- stis pro- ba- tur par- ti- ceps
   In lau- de re- gis cae- lo- rum et ce- re- mo- ni- is

3. Et lu- mi- ne con- ti- nu- o ae- mu- lans ci- vi- ta- tem si- ne te- ne- bris
   Et cor- po- ra in gre- mi- o con- fo- vens a- ni- ma- rum quae in cae- lo vi- vunt.

4. Quam dex- tra pro- te- gat de- i
   Ad lau- dem ip- si- us di- u!

5. Hic no- vam pro- lem gra- ti- a par- tu- rit foe- cun- da spi- ri- tu sanc- to:
   An- ge- li ci- ves vi- si- tant hic su- os et cor- pus su- mi- tur Je- su.

6. Fu- gi- unt u- ni- ver- sa cor- po- ri no- cu- a:
   Pe- re- unt pec- ca- tri- cis a- ni- mae cri- mi- na.

7. Hic vox lae- ti- ti- ae per- so- nat:
   Hic pax et gau- di- a re- dun- dant.

8. Hac do- mo tri- ni- ta- ti laus et glo- ri- a sem- per re- sul- tant.

And the ends of 4a,b are a little harsh.

(4a)   Quam dextra protegat dei
(4b)   Ad laudem ipsius diu!

In 4b, incidentally, *laudem* is redictum to *laude* in the suspicious 2b. But on the whole 4a,b sits firmly on its short motivic melody, and shows clearly that Notker heard the force of this phrase and supported it with his fervent exclamation—"May the right hand of God protect her, to his everlasting praise!"

The phrases of the conclusion are set as distinct entities, each a petition in a litany-like series.

(6a)   May all things hurtful to the body flee away!
(6b)   May the wrongs of the sinful soul perish!
(7a)   May the voice of gladness here resound!
(7b)   May peace and joy here abound!
(8)   May the praise and glory of the Trinity always echo in this house!

As an early text, Notker's does not measure up to its West-Frankish counterparts, not being able to match their force and colorful language with the masterful elegance found in Notker's later texts. The contrast with REGNANTEM SEMPITERNA is especially striking in this respect. If Notker's ideal is *ciceronitas*, that of REGNANTEM SEMPITERNA is something else. The parallelisms and alliterations in PSALLAT ECCLESIA are obvious and a little *gauche* because of the prevailing context of elegant variation, yet these parallelisms would appear so mild as to be ineffectual in the language of REGNANTEM SEMPITERNA. Here the context is one of virtual rhyme, with assonance and matching sonorities supporting the accent patterns all the length of the line.

(2)   Regnantem sempiterna, per saecla susceptura,
                    concio devote concrepa,
            divino sono factori reddendo debita.

The two lines of phrase 3 are almost identical, recalling the same phenomenon in FORTIS ATQUE AMARA.

(3a)   Quem jubilant agmina caelica ejus vultu exhilarata;
(3b)   Quem expectant omnia terrea ejus nutu examinanda,

Because of the kind of sonority prevailing from the very beginning of the piece, however, this near-identity of the two lines seems not to be a departure but rather a natural consequence; in Notker's style, of course, it would be a scandal. A similar matching of lines occurs in 4a,b,

(4a)   Districtum ad judicia,
(4b)   Clementem in potentia.

where it serves to intensify the paradox, "Strict in judgment, merciful in power," placed here to excellent effect on the short phrase that echoes the motive of phrase 1.

The sonority of the diction is so pervasive, and so forceful, that it may obscure the rhetorical layout, which responds carefully to the melody. The complex phrase 2 is set to the invocation and exhortation. The first formal couplet, 3, with its long arches, receives a pair of attributes.

> For him rejoices the heavenly host, gladdened by his face;
> For him watches the whole earth, to be judged by his nod.

Then follows—as syntactic conclusion of these attributes—the short paradox in phrase 4; the syntax, then, has the effect of appending the short motive in 4 to the end of 3, just as the *divino sono* (the same motive) in 2 is appended to the opening phrase; Notker treated 4 as a separate period in an exclamation.

Phrase 5 uses the high, assertive melody to project the forthright petition,

> Tua nos salva, Christe, clementia!

> (By your mercy, save us, O Christ!)

the attribute following on the descent to the final.

> propter quos passus es dira

> (for whose sake you have suffered terrible things)

Multiple petitions, litany-like as in Notker's text, follow in phrase 6, with a purpose clause in 7, and a short doxology concluding on 8.

> (6a)   *Influa* salus vera, *effuga* pericula;
> (6b)   omnia ut sint munda *imbue* pacifica,
> (7a)   *ut*, hic tua salvi misericordia,
> (7b)   laeti regna post *adeamus* supera,
> (8)   quo regnas saecula per infinita.

In this case the West-Frankish text is more discursive, more modulated syntactically than Notker's where the grouping together of the phrases was achieved not by anything as consequent as a purpose clause, but rather by piling up petitions at an accelerated rate and marking their reiteration with *Hic . . . Hic . . . Hac*. The West-Frankish solution seems the closer analog of the melody, although each is effective in its own context.

REGNANTEM SEMPITERNA is unusual in its diction even among West-Frankish texts; FORTIS ATQUE AMARA is perhaps the closest among those we have seen—and we have seen all that were set to a melody Notker used, save only the other text to this melody, PANGAT LAUDES. As already discussed, this text is difficult at the beginning, and may suffer from a lacuna. Beyond that, it makes a mixed impression, for on one hand it pursues a high theme, with vivid imagery and elaborate language, while on the other it attains neither Notker's polished urbanity nor the rhythm and suppleness of REGNANTEM SEMPITERNA.

Phrase 2 is nominally an attribute of Christ, *Hic valeat . . . superare*, completing the mention in 1 of his protection. But phrase 2 really describes the devil; the diction of the whole couplet bristles with consonants.

(2a)   Hic valeat callidi zabuli superare machinamenta
(2b)   Qui jugiter circuit avidus ut dividat Christi caterva,

As in REGNANTEM SEMPITERNA, the short phrase following is linked syntactically as an extension.

(3a)   Mittendo dura spicula
(3b)   hac mortis saeva jacula.

The long couplet 4 is split in sense (as occasionally happens), making a transition from the evil one to the effects of Christ's protection of the flock. Phrase 5 has something of the matched effect noticed in REGNANTEM SEMPITERNA.

(4a)   Quia non dormit lucidus et corax ut exuat plebem sanctam.
(4b)   Ergale Christi concio sanguine quae constat vere redemptor.
(5a)   Sedule illius habere arma
(5b)   Cupide quidem mersit ad inferna

And 6 concludes with a strong affirmation of future glory.

(6a)   Semper possit ipso ducente secura
(6b)   permanere atque munita gloria
(7)   scandere polorum alma.

As a whole, the text has higher aspiration than achievement, but this means it does not fall into the slick, automatic formulas frequently found among tenth-century texts in the Aquitanian manuscripts. While it is difficult to see PANGAT LAUDES as the original text for this melody—and as it stands it could not be Notker's model—still, it commands attention as part of the early repertory.

Furthermore, of the two texts, PANGAT LAUDES has the form of incipit more usual for the early repertory. If we take REGNANTEM SEMPITERNA to be Notker's model, we have to assume (as with SALUS AETERNA) that the form with Alleluia incipit existed from the start along with the other form. The argument in this case presses us back even nearer the start of sequence composition, since PSALLAT ECCLESIA is Notker's second work in this genre.

Neither REGNANTEM SEMPITERNA nor PANGAT LAUDES is related to the Alleluia verse *Laetatus* in any obvious way—certainly not as a development or commentary upon a key word. The Alleluia verse is from Psalm 122,1 (Latin 121,1).

Laetatus sum in his quae dicta sunt mihi:
    ibimus in domo domini.

(I was glad when they said unto me:
    Let us go into the house of the Lord.)

How this verse came to be used at the Second Sunday in Advent is not clear, but that is another story. Regnantem sempiterna is clearly an Advent piece, but not by virtue of any textual connection to the Alleluia verse, rather through its topic of Christ the merciful judge. As a passing speculation, it can be pointed out that, from a musical point of view, regnantem sempiterna could begin without the phrase Alleluia = 1; melodically it would then resemble fortis atque amara, although the first (short) phrase would still be double rather than single. That is not to suggest seriously that the Alleluia quotation was added later, only to point out the substantive independence of the sequence from the Alleluia.

The only connection of pangat laudes with the Alleluia verse is the implied one that the *domus domini* mentioned in the verse is safe under the tutelage of Christ. The theme of the evil one can be understood as appropriate to Advent as a time of withstanding temptations. None of these connections, however, can be considered much more than excuses for the author of the prose to link the theme of his choice to a liturgical occasion. The choice itself, as well as the development of the theme, seems subject only to musical and literary conditions, and to imagination.

Notker's choice of theme is related to the text of the Alleluia verse much more closely than the verse itself is related to Advent. As Blume long ago pointed out, Notker's psallat ecclesia for the Dedication of a Church is the most natural application of all for the verse *Laetatus sum*. The implications of his choice seem very important. For since the Alleluia was in no way associated with the Dedication of a Church, and Notker's text in no way with Advent, his choice—insofar as it was conditioned by the verse—was conditioned by its theme, not by its liturgical assignation. And Notker, insofar as he was concerned with liturgical assignations, was making them, not following them. Nor was either of the West-Frankish texts any more "liturgical" in its theme, in spite of the assignation to the Second Sunday of Advent.

One possibility remains to be noted: as in the case of the sequence "De Ostende," the Aquitanian manuscripts include one or more melodies related to this sequence, not immediately identifiable with texts. None of these melodies is close enough to regnantem sempiterna to replace it as Notker's model; yet their existence raises the question, did another version once exist that had all the missing requisites—incipit structure, liturgical theme, identity with Notker's plan. The possibility seems a remote one, and suggested more by our ideas of the medieval artistic process than by theirs. Even if such a version existed, psallat ecclesia shows how Notker treated it.

Three Sequences by Notker

CHRISTUS HUNC DIEM

In addition to SUMMI TRIUMPHUM REGIS, Notker wrote another prose for Ascension Day, CHRISTUS HUNC DIEM, to a melody titled in the Swiss-Rhenish sources "Dominus in Sina." And indeed the melody quotes the incipit of the Alleluia *Dominus in Sina*, which is the second of the two Alleluias used on that day.[1] The whole verse reads (Ps. 67, 18–19; English 68, 17–18):

Alleluia. Dominus in Sina in sancto, ascendens in altum,
 captivam duxit captivitatem.

 (The Lord is in Sinai in his holy place;
 ascending on high, he has led captivity captive.)

The word *captiva(m)* became the melody title for the other prose, SUMMU TRIUMPHUM REGIS, not through any melodic relationship to the Alleluia, but because this key word in the Ascension Day propers was set to a prominent figure in the sequence.

For a Christian reader, this Psalm text is about Christ. The Son, not the Father, is the Lord who this day ascends on high, leading "captivity captive." Notker's text is a logical sequel to the verse in this respect, but fails to have any more specific reference to the verse —as would be provided by repetition of a key word. And Notker's text includes a great deal of new material giving concrete Christian meaning in a procession of vivid images.

After the formal proclamation in 1 of "today's feast" (compare HÆC EST SANCTA SOLEMNITAS), the Lord is given an equally formal acclamation, followed by an epithet describing his visit to earth in terms that recall the Paschal return of the Alleluia in DIC NOBIS:

1. Alleluia *Dominus in Sina*: Schlager, *Them.Kat.* no. 271; *Alleluia-Melodien* I, p. 137 (638-Dominus dixit). Hesbert, *Antiphonale missarum sextuplex*, no. 102A.

CHRISTUS HUNC DIEM (Notker)

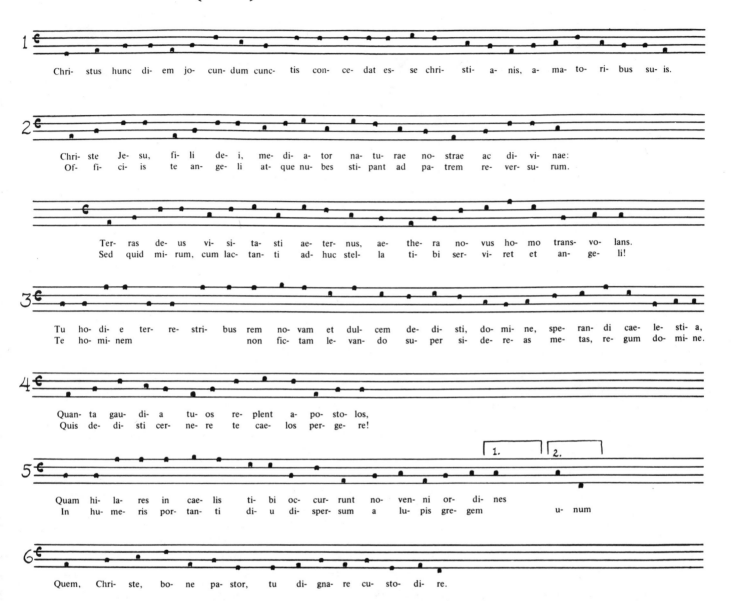

1. Chri- stus hunc di- em jo- cun- dum cunc- tis con- ce- dat es- se chri- sti- a- nis, a- ma- to- ri- bus su- is.

2. Chri- ste Je- su, fi- li de- i, me- di- a- tor na- tu- rae no- strae ac di- vi- nae:
Of- fi- ci- is te an- ge- li at- que nu- bes sti- pant ad pa- trem re- ver- su- rum.

Ter- ras de- us vi- si- ta- sti ae- ter- nus, ae- the- ra no- vus ho- mo trans- vo- lans.
Sed quid mi- rum, cum lac- tan- ti ad- huc stel- la ti- bi ser- vi- ret et an- ge- li!

3. Tu ho- di- e ter- re- stri- bus rem no- vam et dul- cem de- di- sti, do- mi- ne, spe- ran- di cae- le- sti- a,
Te ho- mi- nem non fic- tam le- van- do su- per si- de- re- as me- tas, re- gum do- mi- ne.

4. Quan- ta gau- di- a tu- os re- plent a- po- sto- los,
Quis de- di- sti cer- ne- re te cae- los per- ge- re!

5. Quam hi- la- res in cae- lis ti- bi oc- cur- runt no- ven- ni or- di- nes
In hu- me- ris por- tan- ti di- u di- sper- sum a lu- pis gre- gem u- num

6. Quem, Chri- ste, bo- ne pa- stor, tu di- gna- re cu- sto- di- re.

(1)   Christus hunc diem jocundum cunctis concedat esse christianis, amatoribus suis.
(2a)   Christe Jesu, fili dei, mediator naturea nostrae ac divinae:
       terras deus visitasti aeternus,
            aethera novus homo transvolans.
(2b)   Officiis te angeli atque nubes stipant ad patrem reversurum.
       Sed quid mirum, cum lactanti adhuc stella tibi serviret et angeli!

Line 2b presents the Ascension scene, attended by clouds and angels, and sets beside it the Nativity at Bethlehem—a bold stroke, encompassing Jesus' entire earthly sojourn. These four distinct items represent a great deal of material for the first regular couplet of a prose, yet it seems to be handled with the ease of Notker's maturity. Line 3a begins a direct address, *Tu . . .*, the second line of the couplet matching it with a *te*.

> (3a) Tu hodie terrestribus rem novam et dulcem dedisti, domine, sperandi caelestia,
>
> (3b) Te hominem non fictum levando super sidereas metas, regum domine.

This couplet is less concerned with imagery, more with theological statement. Lines 4a,b contain an exclamation, reverting to the Ascension scene, and lines 5a,b match this image of Christ's departure from earth and the Apostles with an image of his arrival and welcome in heaven by the angelic host; the pair of images has as rhetorical analog the pair of exclamations.

> (4a) *Quanta gaudia* tuos replent apostolos,
>
> (4b)   quis dedisti cernere te caelos pergere!
>
> (5a) *Quam hilares* in caelis tibi occurrunt noveni ordines
>
> (5b)   in humeris portanti diu dispersum a lupis gregem unum,

The heavenly image is identified by Christ's own parable of the shepherd who seeks out the lost sheep and brings it home, rejoicing (*Matthew* 18, 12–13). Notker's use of Gospel material of a moral tone, instead of the apocalyptic language of glory that might be found in a West-Frankish description of such a scene, is characteristic of him.

The melody gives an impression of being very carefully worked out—self-consciously so. While the general procedures are clearly those of the other melodies studied, the specific shape of this melody, as well as the type of motive used, is subtly distinct from the West-Frankish idioms.

Phrase 1 contains the Alleluia quotation—which happens to be the same Alleluia melody as the one used with the verse *Ostende*, being the Alleluia most frequently used in the Gregorian propers. The quotation itself extends halfway through phrase 1 (*Christus . . . concedat*), the rest of the phrase being not dissimilar to the analogous passage in CLARE SANCTORUM SENATUS, with a cadence on G.

An elaborate use of motive begins in phrase 2, with the repeated rise to the C, in groups of fours.

>   G A C C GAC C
>
> (2a) Christe Jesu, fili dei, mediator naturae nostrae ac divinae:
>
>   G A C C
>
> Terras deus visitasti aeternus, aethera novus homo transvolans.

These groupings, supported by the text accent patterns, word structure, and even assonance (*dei . . . deus*), make the motive immediately apparent. The simplicity of the intervening material helps, too: it consists largely of a descending scale figure

D C B A G

replaced in some later variants by a more elaborate figure

D B C A G

and a cadential pause on B. Phrase 2 is articulated into a sub-phrase structure, and just as it is a little unusual to find so much material in the text of the first regular double, so it is unusual to find such a highly developed sub-phrase structure so early in the piece; but an analog does exist in LAUDES DEO. The cadence on B is used for both cadences—internal and final—of the phrase, except that the final is more elaborately and emphatically approached.

Phrase 3 is made a focal point by the coordination of a number of factors. Most obvious is the motivic process: the ascending leap of a fifth is somehow made to sound like a transformation or continuation of the motive at the start of 2. Part of the relationship is due to the ascending leap, now made larger; part to the grouping in fours, although now with an up-beat accent pattern.

	A A EE A A E E
(3a)	Tu hódi-e terréstribus . . .
	A A E E
(3b)	Te hóminem . . .

Part is due to the position at the start of the phrase and to the immediate repetition (in 3a); and part also to the way the motive reappears, at the start of 3b after the cadence on B at the end of 3a. Due to the irregularity at this point, the motive A A E E comes only once, not twice, in 3b, just as the motive G A C C came only once, not twice, at the start of the second sub-phrase in 2a. Thus, there is an analogy between 2a on one hand and 3a,b on the other.

	G A C C GACC G A C C
(2a)	Christe Jesu, fili dei . . . Terras deus
	A A EE A A E E A A EE
(3a)	Tu hodi-e, terrestribus . . . (3b) Te hominem

In effect, 3a,b appears as a single with a sub-phrase structure; and the similarity of material between 2 and 3 makes this single seem to be a third presentation of the melody given twice in 2a,b—now intensified by a higher pitch. The ending of 3, identical to the ending of 2, helps show this relationship of 2 to 3.

The tonal relationship of 3 to 2 involves a move not merely to a higher pitch, but to a well-defined group of pitches whose axis is A-E, replacing the G-B prominent in 2. We encountered this particular relationship before in CLARE SANCTORUM SENATUS, at about the same place in the melody, and we noted that this particular pitch structure could also be found in such pieces as *Gloria in excelsis* I and Alleluia *Oportebat*. In CLARE SANCTORUM SANCTUS as well as here in CHRISTUS HUNC DIEM, this pitch structure follows an Alleluia incipit that belongs to G-*tetrardus*; but the pitch structure is definitely not characteristic of *tetrardus*, rather of *deuterus* (E final), as in Alleluia *Oportebat*. CLARE SANCTORUM SENATUS eventually returned to a G final after persistent internal (half-)cadences on B. CHRISTUS HUNC DIEM, on the other hand, has its final cadence on E, and the end of phrase 5 will make clear that the E final was part of the original plan.

Phrase 3, then, is heard as an intense sequel to 2. The theological point made in the text of 3a,b seems carefully placed to take advantage of this melodic intensity. The climax of the piece seems to be here; what comes before leads up to this; what comes after—the diptych of exclamations in 4 and 5—seems to be post-climax. Yet 4 and 5 seem paired together like 2 and 3; at any rate, 5 recalls the opening motive of 3, using it once, not twice, in each line, and acting almost like a refrain or rounding element in the form a b c b.

```
        G A C C GACC
(2a)    Christe Jesu fili dei . . .
        A  A EE A  A  E E
(3a)    Tu hodi-e terrestribus . . .
               . . .
        A   A E E
(5a)    Quam hilares
```

The cadence of 5a is on B, as all the preceding cadences except 1. Line 5b, however, has as second ending a drop of a fifth down to E.

```
        A B GA BB
(5a)    . . . noveni ordines
        A B G  A B  B E
(5b)    . . . a lupis gregem unum
```

This unique event is set to *unum*, the "one sheep" of the flock, showing (with CARMEN SUO DILECTO) that word-painting was at least in the repertory of things possible for Notker, and that if he made but little use of it he probably had good reasons. (A comparable first and second ending would be known to Notker in the melody for his LAUDES SALVATORI.) The concluding single confirms the E final with downward leaping thirds similar to those used in CLARE SANCTORUM SENATUS at the same spot.

Another *Gloria* melody comes to mind, *Gloria* XIV, which begins much like *Gloria* I, indicating a G final; then later, using motivic material from a melody circulated in the ninth century with a Greek text (*Doxa in ipsistis*) finds its way to an ending on E.[2] Other cases are *Kyrie lux et origo*, and *Kyrie tibi Christe supplices*, both with strong G's at the beginning and E finals.[3] That is not to cite precedents, necessarily, for all these pieces may well rather be cognates. What is important in the sequence, however, is that here in CHRISTUS HUNC DIEM, an incipit that involves an Alleluia quotation is once again disassociated from the rest of the melody.

This melody not only seems carefully worked out, it gives clear signs of having been

2. See M. Huglo, "La mélodie grecque du 'Gloria in excelsis,' et son utilisation dans le Gloria XIV." *Révue grégorienne* XXIV (1950), pp. 30–40.

3. Kyrie *lux et origo*: Kyrie I, Melnicki Mel. 18; Kyrie *tibi Christe supplices*: see note 7, Chapter 12.

worked on. It does not give the impression of exuberance, of melodic inspiration, that flows so freely in the West-Frankish melodies. This is not to belittle the melody of CHRISTUS HUNC DIEM, but simply to confirm its origin in a place that did not take a lead in developing the sequence, but rather studiously assimilated the techniques observed in melodies that came from somewhere further West.

AGONE TRIUMPHALI and OMNES SANCTI SERAPHIM

Notker wrote two proses for a melody called "Vox exultationis," which quotes the Alleluia with verse *Vox exultationis* used for feasts of martyrs, but also for All Saints and Dedication of a Church.[4] The Alleluia appears in the earliest notated chant books, but not in the Mass-books of Hesbert's *Antiphonale missarum sextuplex*, indicating that it entered the repertory during the ninth century. This is the only instance in which Notker wrote two texts for a melody not found in West-Frankish sources. The two texts are very different in technique, one of them, OMNES SANCTI SERAPHIM, being unique in his output. For Wolfram von den Steinen, the fact that the melody quotes an Alleluia for martyrs is sufficient indication that AGONE TRIUMPHALI was the first of the two texts; but, while that may be the case, the Alleluia itself is not a sure indication. For one thing, the other text, OMNES SANCTI SERAPHIM, *was* written, and for some other occasion; and if it could be written *after* the more "proper" text for martyrs, why not before? That the melody was known by the incipit of the verse, "Vox exultationis," proves nothing about precedence, for HÆC EST SANCTA was known by the title "Virgo plorans," referring to the second prose Notker wrote to that melody. In general, the relationship to the Alleluia is subject to too many uncertainties to make it the main point of evidence in deciding which text came first.

The melody itself bears a general resemblance in melodic idiom to AGNI PASCHALIS, but makes a similarly repetitive use of material; and one very specific resemblance to HÆC EST SANCTA. The phrases are usually short, and the piece as a whole has modest proportions. The last phrase ends on D, which can be taken as the expected final, (except that the Alleluia ends on F—about which more later). All other phrases end on A, usually with the cadence pattern.

B♭ G A

which can be taken as a half-cadence. This cadence, in conjunction with the motivic system to be described, gives the melody the sense of continuity heard in parts of CLARE SANCTORUM SENATUS and STIRPE MARIA REGIA.

The Alleluia quotation takes up about a third of phrase 1 (*Agone . . . summi*). It is followed by a motive leading to another form of half-cadence (*Dies iste celebris*), which after four notes (*est populis*) is repeated (*ipsi regi credulis*):

4. Alleluia *Vox exultationis*: Schlager, *Them.Kat.* no. 223; *Alleluia-Melodien* I, pp. 552, 626, usually for feasts of martyrs but also for All Saints or Dedication. Not in Hesbert, *Antiphonale missarum sextuplex*, but in St. Gall 359, Laon 239, Chartres 47.

Agone triumphali (Notker)

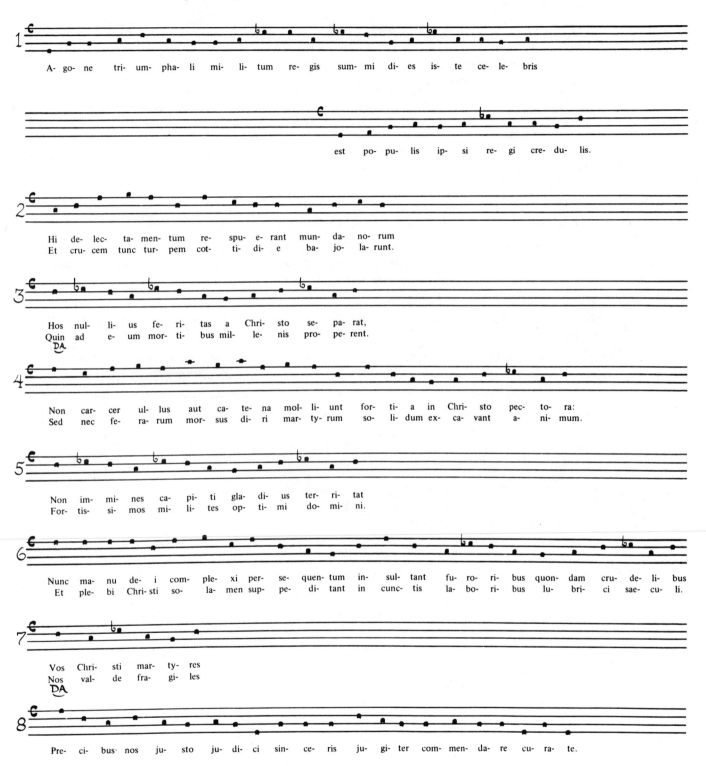

1. A- go- ne tri- um- pha- li mi- li- tum re- gis sum- mi di- es is- te ce- le- bris

est po- pu- lis ip- si re- gi cre- du- lis.

2. Hi de- lec- ta- men- tum re- spu- e- rant mun- da- no- rum
Et cru- cem tunc tur- pem cot- ti- di- e ba- jo- la- runt.

3. Hos nul- li- us fe- ri- tas a Chri- sto se- pa- rat,
Quin ad e- um mor- ti- bus mil- le- nis pro- pe- rent.
DA

4. Non car- cer ul- lus aut ca- te- na mol- li- unt for- ti- a in Chri- sto pec- to- ra:
Sed nec fe- ra- rum mor- sus di- ri mar- ty- rum so- li- dum ex- ca- vant a- ni- mum.

5. Non im- mi- nes ca- pi- ti gla- di- us ter- ri- tat
For- tis- si- mos mi- li- tes op- ti- mi do- mi- ni.

6. Nunc ma- nu de- i com- ple- xi per- se- quen- tum in- sul- tant fu- ro- ri- bus quon- dam cru- de- li- bus
Et ple- bi Chri- sti so- la- men sup- pe- di- tant in cunc- tis la- bo- ri- bus lu- bri- ci sae- cu- li.

7. Vos Chri- sti mar- ty- res
Nos val- de fra- gi- les
DA

8. Pre- ci- bus nos ju- sto ju- di- ci sin- ce- ris ju- gi- ter com- men- da- re cu- ra- te.

```
          (Alle--------------------lu---------------ia------)
          D  F F G Bᵇ   GF  FGBᵇ   BᵇG  A   A
(1)       A-gone triumphali militum regis summi
              (cadence x)                (cadence x)
          F G Bᵇ G GF  A,D   E FG F G BᵇG  G FA
          Dies iste celebris est populis ipsi regi credulis.
```

Phrase 2, the first regular double, moves higher, ascending to the high D. Phrase 3 dwells on the A that ends every phrase except the last, concluding with another cadence pattern (y).

```
F G A Bᵇ G A
    (cadence y)
```

This cadence, stronger than the end of phrase 2, helps group phrases 2 and 3 together into a larger unit.

Phrase 4 ascends again, this time up to E, and seeming in its first half to dwell on the high C. This phrase is the longest since phrase 1, and is clearly felt as more important than the short phrases 2 and 3. Yet it, too, ends with the cadence y, rhyming with phrase 3. Phrase 5 repeats phrase 3 exactly, framing the high phrase 4 and confirming the recurrent cadence pattern y.

Phrase 6 begins with a strong repeated C, very reminiscent of HÆC EST SANCTA—that is, Notker's HÆC EST SANCTA SOLEMNITAS SOLEMNITATUM, but the last half of this long phrase is identical with phrase 3 (= 5) as a whole. If we call phrase 3 "R," then the plan of phrases 2 through 6 (including both lines of the doubles) can be represented like this.

```
A A R R B R' B R' R R C R C R
2 2 3 3 4   4   5 5 6   6
```

The material represented by A, B, C all lies high, generally above the pitch A. R moves around the pitch A, approaching it from the F below, so that the tonal contrast between R and the other material is clear.

Phrase 7 recalls cadence x from phrase 1—and here we need to have the whole scheme of cadences before us.

```
1  . . .              cadence x . . . cadence x
2  . . .
3  . . . cadence y
4  . . . . . . . cadence y
5 (=3) . . . cadency y
6  . . . . . . cadence y
7  cadence x
```

At this point, however, a curious thing happens; after the reiterations of cadence y in phrases 2–6, the memory of cadence x is dimmed, and phrase 7 seems more like a transformation of cadence y than a distinctive recall of something from phrase 1. And yet the relationship to phrase 1 is not lost completely, and phrase 7 has important higher-level functions because of it. On one hand, phrase 7 tends to close off the large, complex grouping built up from 2 through 6; on the other hand, it seems to prepare and lead directly into the following phrase. This, the concluding single, is completely unrelated to the motivic system of cadences x and y; it descends in groups of threes, dwells on F, then finds its way to the D final with a conclusion that recalls the Gregorian idiom.

Phrase 3 (=5) has a slight but important difference in the second line of the couplet: the first time begins A, the second time D A, with a leap up a fifth on the first syllable. The same happens in phrase 7, which has the immediate effect of emphasizing the similarity of cadences x and y. A similar differentiation occurred in SANCTI BAPTISTAE 5. The more remote similarity is to *Gloria in excelsis* XIV again—in those very phrases that most resemble the Greek *Doxa en ipsistis*. The distinguishing features of this phrase are recitation on or around B, with a leap of a fifth up to the B when the figure is repeated.

G B B B A G A C A B, *E B B B A G* . . .

The difference in pitch-location—a tone higher in the *Gloria* than in the sequence—is scarcely noticeable since both melodies use a virtually gapped scale. The *Gloria* lacks F until the very end and the sequence lacks the corresponding (or rather, the anomalous) tone E except once in phrase 1 and once in phrase 8, just before the end.

This similarity to a *Gloria* melody need not be taken too seriously; or at any rate, it is difficult to see exactly what it might imply. The one important conclusion, for our purposes, is that the relationship shows how melodic material from the body of a sequence can be practically the same as idioms that are used elsewhere not for melismatic passages but for neumatic or syllabic ones.

The relationship to the Alleluia *Vox exultationis* includes, besides the incipit (*Agone . . . summi*), possibly also a short fragment out of the melisma on (*taber*)*na*-(*culis*) in the verse, which is similar to the beginning of phrase 2 of the sequence (*Hi delectamentum*); and shortly afterwards, still on *-na-*, cadence y. The Alleluia verse, like the body of the sequence, cadences only on A; but the Alleluia itself ends on F, not D; and furthermore ends with a formula more characteristic of *tetrardus* (G final) plagal rather than *tritus* (F final) plagal (a Beneventan source gives the Alleluia on G instead of F).[5] Of course, the sequence could stand on E instead of on D, and because of the gapped scale this would make no great difference. On E, the sequence would be similar to CHRISTUS HUNC DIEM in beginning with a strong G and ending on E; it would also resemble the *Gloria* XIV that much more. In any case, the Alleluia quotation is once again isolated from the tonal structure of the sequence as a whole.

To this melody, a relatively spare one by West-Frankish standards, Notker wrote the text in honor of martyrs, AGONE TRIUMPHALI. Exhibiting no unusual characteristics, it seems fairly representative of his maturity. The syntax follows the couplet structure very regularly; the only run-on occurs at the end, where the short phrase 7 is firmly linked to the concluding single.

5. See Schlager, *Alleluia-Melodien* I, pp. 552, 626.

(7a)   Vos Christi martyres

(7b)   nos valde fragiles

                                                        precibus nos justo judici sinceris

(8)   jugiter commendare curate.

Here, too, the only strong matching of lines of a couplet—the opposition of *Vos* to *nos*, which is the pivot on which the text turns to the concluding petition.

> Ye martyrs of Christ,
> take care to commend us—feeble as we are—with fervent prayer to fair judgment.

The two cadential motives x and y are always given proparoxytones (*célebris*, *séparat*, etc.), emphasizing their similarity, as well as setting them off from the end of phrase 2, set with paroxytones (*mundanórum*, *bajolárant*).

Line 5b, with its acclamatory effect,

(5b)   Fortissimos milites optimi domini.

helps articulate the larger form at that point, phrases 2, 3, 4, 5 containing the attributes of the martyrs. Line 6a, whose melody contains the reference to HÆC EST SANCTA, contains in its text a reference to the rhetoric as well.

AGONE TRIUMPHALI
(6a)   *Nunc* manu dei . . .
HÆC EST SANCTA SOLEMNITAS SOLEMNITATUM
4a   Redempti *ergo* gratias agamus . . .

The reference to the West-Frankish model is even stronger.

HÆC EST SANCTA SOLEMNITAS
4a   *Jam nunc ergo* . . .

Here the rhetoric serves to set off 6a,b as a conclusion, followed only by the petition in 7 and 8. Whether such a reference implies that AGONE TRIUMPHALI is an early piece, to be grouped chronologically with HÆC EST SANCTA SOLEMNITAS SOLEMNITATUM, is hard to say; certainly AGONE TRIUMPHALI was written after the other, which is one of Notker's earliest, imitating as it does the West-Frankish model closely.

Such questions are much more difficult in the case of Notker's other prose to this melody, OMNES SANCTI SERAPHIM. This seriatim invocation of all the members of the Church Triumphant, the celestial congregation of the blessed, is cast in a kind of diction that seems a one-time exercise by Notker in West-Frankish Latinity.

(1)   Omnes sancti seraphim,
            cherubim,
            throni quoque dominationesque,
            principatus,
            potestates,
            virtutes,

(2a)   archangeli,
                         angeli,
          vos decet laus et honores.

It is true, of course, that such a listing is peculiarly appropriate to the celestial vision, and perhaps Notker's diction here can be just as well accounted for on those grounds. Still, the text has other peculiar features. There is a slight irregularity in phrase 2: 2b is one syllable and one note shorter, and unlike cases such as HÆC EST SANCTA SOLEMNITAS SOLEMNI-TATUM there seems to be no musical or rhetorical reason for it here. The matching of 3a and b is unusually close (for Notker) and a trifle forced.

(3a)   Quos in dei laudibus   firmavit   caritas
(3b)   Nos fragiles homines   firmate   precibus

In 3b, *Nos fragiles homines* recalls *Nos valde fragiles* of AGONE TRIUMPHALI 7b—which was matched with *Vos Christi martyres* of 7a. This kind of echo is not surprising between two proses by Notker, of course; but it can also occur between a prose by Notker and another prose to the same tune by someone else, as in the case of AGNI PASCHALIS and MAGNUM TE MICHAELEM.

In 4a, *spiritales pravitates* stands out in a couplet not otherwise striking in its sonori-ties; the effect seems not characteristic of Notker's maturity. Also, the accent patterns in the cadences do not match (*fórtiter . . . sácris*), whereas in AGONE TRIUMPHALI Notker handled the cadences very consistently. In 5, too, the cadences are paroxytone instead of proparoxy-tone.

All of those details seem not characteristic of Notker's mature style. In its larger design, however, the text shows a kind of organization we might well expect from Notker. It falls into two main sections, parallel in intent, and in rhetorical detail as well.

I		II	
(1)	Omnes . . . (seriatim list)	(5a)	Vos quos . . .
(2a)	. . . vos decet . . .	(6a)	Vos . . . (seriatim list)
(3a)	Quos . . .	(7a)	Nos adjutorium
(3b)	Nos . . .	(7b)	Nunc et perenniter . . .
(4a)	Ut . . .	(8)	. . . ut . . .
(4b)	Nunc et in aevum . . .		

Each large section invokes a portion of the celestial host in the distinctive seriatim list-ing—although the first list (1–2a) heads its section, while the second list (6a,b) is preceded in its section by phrase 5. Each section has a *quos* clause for epithets, and a *nos* clause for petitions, expressed through *ut* and including the parallel phrases *nunc et in aevum* or *nunc et perenniter*. The clear intent, on the one hand, to make the sections parallel, with the equal-ly clear intent, on the other, to vary the syntactic order of the elements, seems especially characteristic of the kind of Latin style Notker cultivated. The large-scale parallelism, furthermore, makes explicable the persistence of the sonorities *vos/quos/nos*, which would be quite uncharacteristic of Notker's Latin if considered only in terms of sonority.

Omnes sancti seraphim (Notker)

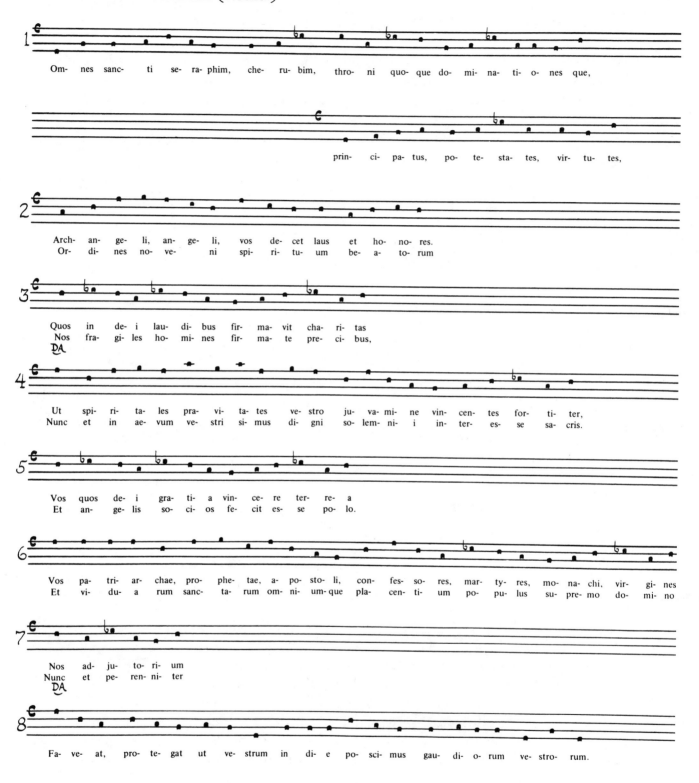

1 Om- nes sanc- ti se- ra- phim, che- ru- bim, thro- ni quo- que do- mi- na- ti- o- nes que,

prin- ci- pa- tus, po- te- sta- tes, vir- tu- tes,

2 Arch- an- ge- li, an- ge- li, vos de- cet laus et ho- no- res.
Or- di- nes no- ve- ni spi- ri- tu- um be- a- to- rum

3 Quos in de- i lau- di- bus fir- ma- vit cha- ri- tas
Nos fra- gi- les ho- mi- nes fir- ma- te pre- ci- bus,
DA

4 Ut spi- ri- ta- les pra- vi- ta- tes ve- stro ju- va- mi- ne vin- cen- tes for- ti- ter,
Nunc et in ae- vum ve- stri si- mus di- gni so- lem- ni- i in- ter- es- se sa- cris.

5 Vos quos de- i gra- ti- a vin- ce- re ter- re- a
Et an- ge- lis so- ci- os fe- cit es- se po- lo.

6 Vos pa- tri- ar- chae, pro- phe- tae, a- po- sto- li, con- fes- so- res, mar- ty- res, mo- na- chi, vir- gi- nes
Et vi- du- a- rum sanc- ta- rum om- ni- um- que pla- cen- ti- um po- pu- lus su- pre- mo do- mi- no

7 Nos ad- ju- to- ri- um
Nunc et pe- ren- ni- ter
DA

8 Fa- ve- at, pro- te- gat ut ve- strum in di- e po- sci- mus gau- di- o- rum ve- stro- rum.

The large sectional structure is not clearly coordinated with the melody; but perhaps it could not be, given the nature of the melody and its motivic repetitions. The second section begins at phrase 5, a short phrase that literally repeats 3 and sounds like a refrain. Here, too, there seems to be artful intent, for it is at this point in the text that Notker inverts the order of events with respect to the first section. Phrase 5, in beginning section II with *Vos quos*, refers musically as well as textually to phrase 3 of section I. Then section II continues with its seriatim listing, now set to the long, proclamatory phrase 6.

One could well imagine, then, that Notker first made the reasonable but much less imaginative setting AGONE TRIUMPHALI, then later made OMNES SANCTI SERAPHIM, taking advantage of his prior experience with the melody to relate the text to it in the sophisticated manner described—just as in TUBAM BELLICOSAM he took advantage of the melodic structure in a way he had not done in GRATES SALVATORI. In the present case, however, the order of priority seems indeterminate, for the technical lapses in OMNES SANCTI SERAPHIM are hard to explain as products of Notker's maturity.

The reference to the Alleluia verse *Vox exultationis* would not be a decisive factor, given Notker's treatment of such references. The decisive factor in the theme of PSALLAT ECCLESIA was the intrinsic meaning (not the liturgical destination) of the verse *Laetatus sum*. According to the same factor, OMNES SANCTI SERAPHIM might be considered more closely related to the verse *Vox exultationis* than is AGONE TRIUMPHALI. "The voice of rejoicing and salvation is in the tabernacles of the righteous" (Ps. 118,15). The feast of All Saints was just becoming established during the first half of the ninth century: insular in origin, its adoption on the continent was urged by Alcuin.[6] Here again we can imagine Notker helping to create liturgy out of images and verbal associations.

6. See Ellard, *Master Alcuin, Liturgist*, pp. 91–92. E. Münding, *Die Kalendarien von St. Gallen . . . Texte und Arbeiten der Erzabtei Beuron* 36 (1948), pp. 18–20 (cited in Huglo, *Les Tonaires*, p. 236) places the introduction of All Saints at St. Gall circa 850.

XXI

Structural Aspects of the Early Sequence

THE PRECEDING CHAPTERS have surveyed all the sequences that can with certainty—on the basis of Notker's witness—be dated from the ninth century. This is the primary significance of Notker's *Liber hymnorum* for the study of the early sequence: these melodies, at least, existed before 900, or more precisely before 880. It is probably the case (if not certainly so) that other sequence melodies also existed in the ninth century; but *which ones* can be decided only on stylistic or repertorial grounds, whose inherent uncertainty can be reduced to an acceptable minimum only by means of Notker's repertory.

Having examined the items of this repertory one by one, we need to consider them all together, in order to sharpen as much as possible our idea of the ninth-century sequence. In this chapter will be considered some of the purely structural and stylistic features of the repertory. The following chapter will take up some of the issues (in part imposed by modern research) relating to the repertory—especially those of liturgy and the Alleluia.

Before attempting to make observations of general validity for the early repertory, it must be stated that the items of this repertory are so marked by individual traits as to render many generalities invalid. This is perhaps the single most important conclusion to emerge from a consideration of the early sequence: we have become accustomed to thinking of medieval music as governed by absolute restriction and prescription, and as consisting of invariable forms and categories; we need always to be reminded that throughout the Middle Ages individual composers labored and rejoiced to produce new works in new forms, or individual variations of old ones. Once known, the individual items of the ninth-century repertory of sequences retain their individual identities in spite of any attempt to subsume them under general characteristics or laws of behavior. Getting acquainted with these individual identities has been the purpose of this study up to this point, as the indispensable antecedent to meaningful generalities. The long suspended arcs of NUNC EX-ULTET, the lyric sub-phrases of ECCE VICIT, the insistence, through everchanging melodic inflection, on the upper fifth in CHRISTI HODIERNA, the leaps in Notker's SUMMI TRIUMPHUM REGIS—such things are unique properties of individual pieces, at least in the ninth-century repertory, nor is the uniqueness really threatened by later imitations in the rapidly multiplying repertories of the tenth and eleventh centuries.

Having taken due note of that uniqueness, we can go on to consider what these melodies have in common. And perhaps it is not too much out of order at this point to exclaim over the quality of melodic exuberance everywhere apparent in this repertory. How bright they sound, how gratefully they sing! They combine forceful direction in melodic profile with gracefully animated detail, restrained in quantity, discretely proportioned and positioned. They combine a clear sense of tonal locus with an easy kind of motion capable of spanning great distances. The early sequence is an extraordinary adventure in lyricism, not exactly unprepared, since no style of melody that came after the Gregorian could be called unprepared; but nonetheless fresh, and different, *sui generis*, a major accomplishment in the history of music.

The most distinctive structural feature of the sequence, for the medieval musician as well as for the modern observer, has always been the use of couplets, of "doubles," and this remains valid for the early repertory. The flexibility of the early use, however, can lead us to a far more fruitful understanding than has prevailed in the past. Two things, it seems to me, have impeded our understanding of couplet structure in the sequence. First, a tendency to regard couplet structure as some kind of categorical, obligatory rule that the composer had to follow. Second, a tendency to provide a categorical explanation in terms only of the text, or only of the music.

The shape of Notker's texts—and of the early West-Frankish texts as restored with the help of Notker's—show us that while doubles were a regular aspect of early sequences, they were not an invariable one. Singles were frequent, and not just as first and last phrases but in between as well. The significance of the use of the single, especially in the interior of the sequence, is that it shows the use of the double to be a matter of artistic choice, not obligation; and this immediately places the whole question of origins in quite a different light. If the use of doubles were obligatory, then it would be essential to know the provenance of the technique and the reason for the obligation. But in the presence of artistic choice, origins are not binding: as soon as a composer may or may not use doubles, according to his choice, then it is no longer essential to know the origin of the technique, even though it may still be of great interest. It does become essential, however, to understand his artistic choices, as we perceive them in and through individual works. The important thing becomes not the origins of doubles (and of singles) but rather the effects of their use.

The effect must ultimately be studied in terms of text and music together. The couplet, as used in the sequence, is not just a textual phenomenon that happens to have been set to music; nor is it just a musical phenomenon that acquired textural underlay. Wilhelm Meyer, in what was probably the most valuable approach to the antecedents of the sequence, understood the couplets as manifestations of "art prose" (*Kunstprosa*), as *bicola* or clauses paired through similar structure, sense, and sonority.[1] But as valuable—and as true—as

1. Wilhelm Meyer, "Anfang und Ursprung der lateinischen und griechischen rhythmischen Dichtung," and

this insight was, it did not take into account the essential difference between a sequence and a passage of prose with bicola: in a sequence the members of a couplet are set to the same melody, and the musical force of this technique is such as not only to produce "bicola" where they may not be found in the prose, but also to integrate the bicola into a realm— a musical realm—of structure otherwise alien to them in their purely textual state.

The antecedents of doubles have been sought by others in melodic repetitions in melismas, especially in the replacement melismas for the Alleluia *jubilus*.[2] That, too, is an extremely valuable contribution, but on purely musical grounds it does not show (because of the differing dimensions) how the repetitions in sequences operate or how they came about. Furthermore, it is hard to find examples of repeated phrases (as opposed to shorter motivic groups) in melismas that can be firmly dated before 850. Beyond that, the melismatic technique cannot by its nature take into account the rhetorical structure of the text and its interaction with the melody. The essence of the couplet structure lies in text and music at once, together, in their relationship; only as we succeed in grasping that elusive relationship do we appreciate the effect of the couplet structure, and so come to an understanding of why the composer used it.

Wolfram von den Steinen sought to illuminate couplet structure by comparing it to psalmody, specifically to antiphonal performance of psalmody between boys and men. "Antiphony led to *Antistrofik*—out of the alternation between two half-choirs came the basic poetic principle of the sequence."[3] Antiphony is of course most closely allied with the psalmody of the Office. There may well be profit in comparing the sequence to psalmody, if the result is to show the Franks at work creating a new psalmody—a "Frankish psalmody," to set alongside the old Hebrew psalmody in the same sense that Charlemagne was understood (at court) to be a new David. And of course the new psalmody, the sequence repertory, soon outstripped the old in numbers, if not in permanent value. The comparison, incidentally, is more appropriate between psalmody and the metrical kind of hymn known in the Middle Ages as "Ambrosian" and in modern times as Common Meter (eight syllables in a line, four lines in a strophe) especially if we note that it was out of the medieval metrical hymn that the Reformation developed the real "new psalmody," the metrical psalter (for which actual precedents already existed in the Latin metrical psalm paraphrases of the rhymed offices). From Carolingian times on, the Ambrosian hymn was cultivated with an intensity that left an immense repertory (10,000 or more items?) and a permanent mark on the Office.

The comparison between psalm and sequence, however, does not result in a similitude: there are decisive technical differences. In psalmody one melodic formula (the "tone") is repeated throughout the psalm, once for each verse, while in a sequence each double (or single) is in principle set to a new melody, immediate repetition from one couplet to the

"Die rhythmische lateinische Prosa," in *Gesammelte Abhandlungen zur Mittellateinischen Rhythmik*, II (1905). See also Eduard Norden, *Die Antike Kunstprosa vom VI. Jh. v. Chr. bis in die Zeit der Renaissance* (1898), and Karl Polheim, *Die lateinische Reimprosa* (1925), especially p. 350.

2. See Stäblein, "Sequenz," col. 529–531; also J. Handschin, "Trope, Sequence and Conductus," *New Oxford History of Music* II (1954), pp. 130–148; and Husmann, "Alleluia, Vers und Sequenz," p. 25 and passim.

3. *Notker* I, p. 134.

next being nonexistent and repetitions later in the piece being special events. Again, in psalmody the tone has two halves that function as antecedent and consequent; they usually share the same reciting tone, but have different cadences so that the first half is never confused with the second. In this way the verse structure of the Latin psalmody is made clear, the two halves of the verse falling under the two halves of the tone. If the couplet of a sequence were compared to a psalm verse sung to a psalm tone, the comparison would show that in a sequence the same melody is exactly repeated, with an effect quite different from the antecedent-consequent structure of the psalm tone.

> One verse of a psalm: antecedent / consequent
> One couplet of a sequence: melody / melody repeated

The element of psalmody most frequently invoked as similar to the sequence is the *parallelismus membrorum*, the parallelism between the first half of the verse and the second.

> (Psalm 2,9)
> Thou shalt break them with a rod of iron:
> thou shalt dash them in pieces like a potter's vessel.

This is likened to the couplet structure of the sequence. But the similarity is purely nominal: the parallelism of psalmody is entirely one of sense, not of syllable count (at least, in the Latin psalter). Indeed the two parallel members often differ greatly in length. The parallelism of the sequence couplet, on the other hand, is primarily one of syllable count; it may also be one of sense, but it can be so in a wide variety of rhetorical ways only one of which is the parallelism characteristic of the psalter. If the texts of the sequence repertory had been preserved purely as texts with no trace of any melody and no clue to the melodic couplet structure, it would be hard to connect them—on this point—to psalmody.

The relationship of couplet structure to antiphonal performance would properly require a full discussion of the modes of performance of early medieval chant, a subject for which actual evidence is very scarce and, for early sequence, almost non-existent.[4] The point seems to be, in view of the factor of artistic choice in the use of doubles, that antiphonal performance could hardly have given the rule to the new musical form. At best, it would have been a standard technique much used in other kinds of chant (especially psalmody), that would lend itself to sequences—sometimes happily, other times only with a certain amount of adjustment. The point of genuine, traditional antiphony is that it can be used automatically, without rehearsal, by an untrained congregation. Bishop Ambrose could have, apparently did, use it that long night in Milan, when he kept vigil with his faithful, besieged by the armed guard of the Arian Justina; for that was the occasion, Augustine tells us, when Ambrose introduced metrical hymnody as a form of antiphonal singing to the West.[5] And monastic congregations throughout the first millenium could sing their daily psalmody (and hymnody) in antiphonal fashion without the special train-

---

4. Much of the evidence that has been adduced is contained in the proses themselves (especially CANTEMUS CUNCTI MELODOM, lines 10a,b); I find none of it conclusive. See also note 11, Chapter 12.

5. *Confessions*, Book IX, vii.

ing and practice required of the *scola* for the more elaborate forms of chant. Such automatic performance would not be possible for the sequence—at least, not in its early ninth-century form, with all its singles and irregularities. And if something more elaborate was involved, then it was because the sequence itself was of a far more elaborate structure, not guided or controlled in any decisive way by antiphony as a principle.

Given the factor of artistic choice, we can consider the use of doubles from the point of view of effects rather than of origins: wherever the idea might have come from, why would a composer—a whole generation of composers—want to use it in this particular fashion? What did it accomplish? The answers are nonetheless important for being obvious. The first effect of using doubles on a regular basis is to increase substantially the length of the melody, to double the length, if all phrases are double. This factor becomes significant when we consider that sequences are among the longest pieces of music in the early Frankish repertory, that they rival the Graduals and Tracts of the Gregorian repertory, and that their bulk can be taken as one piece of evidence among several that the sequence was an ambitious kind of chant with a "will to greatness." That is, its composers clearly intended greater things thereby than they did with an antiphon or a hymn melody. A metrical hymn, of course, achieves great length through a number of stanzas, but since it is perfectly evident that the melody itself is not long, the length does not really count in artistic terms. The repetition in a sequence, however, has a rather more sophisticated effect: it is not responsible all by itself for the great length, it only doubles the length of an already substantial amount of melodic material. No subterfuge is involved, any more than in the case of a sectional repeat, or a recapitulation, in a Beethoven symphony or a Bach aria; merely a careful balance between new material and material already presented, to the benefit of both and for the sake of a convincing large-scale design. Repetition, with its twin forces of projection and organization, must have suggested itself almost automatically to the orderly-minded Frankish artist. How this particular kind of repetition became established in the sequence is certainly due to a complex train of artistic decisions, but in any case the expansive power of the sequence, as well as its efficient use of melodic resources, can be seen as direct results of the couplet structure.

Other more specifically musical factors are involved, too. If a man wants to write a long piece of chant, he must write a lot of melody—melody, not some other kind of musical event. Granted that continuous, endless melody is the goal (and often the achievement) of most great composers of opera, symphony, and concerto; but there are many passages of such works that are not *obviously* melodious and that depend upon intricate manipulations of factors such as rhythm, harmony, texture, or timbre for their duration. The great lengths attained by such pieces can be attributed in part to the increased resources of instrumentation on the one hand, and to polyphony (as opposed to monophony) on the other. Repetition, then, can be understood as a resource for expansion valued by the chant composer (and by the symphony composer too!) to ease the burden of continuous melodic invention.

It must be admitted that the Gregorian Graduals achieve significant length either with no repetition or no easily perceptible repetition. The full performance of a Gregorian Gradual involves a literal repeat—Response, Verse, Response—but the dimensions of each section are broad enough, and filled with such diverse melodic detail, that it takes a sharp ear to identify the repeat as a literal one. The effect tends to be one of continuous melodic invention. Perhaps the secret of that art was lost to the Frankish composer, although he could make passable imitations of the outward technique. What is striking is the Frankish development of different techniques (such as repetition in doubles) to achieve different but comparable results.

Doubles have a decisive effect upon the phrase structure of a sequence—another elementary but important circumstance. The immediate, perceptible repetition of a phrase helps make evident the fact that a phrase has occurred. Even the absence of other obvious indications such as cadence patterns (as in FORTIS ATQUE AMARA, for example) the repetitions clearly reveal the phrase structure by showing how much is to be regarded as a melodic unit, how much belongs together in one phrase as a single melodic impulse.

The couplet structure has the power, then, to define the phrase structure of the piece, but only if it exercises that power wisely and in accordance with the underlying melodic reality of the piece. It is possible to imagine a sequence divided up arbitrarily into sections without regard for cadence patterns or other aspects of melodic shape, and performed with each section repeated; such repetition, unrelated to melodic shape, would have no power to create *convincing* shapes, but would still have tremendous power to create shapes whose force could be gauged by their very disturbing effect. The short pieces (in group C of Table II, p. 13) that lack couplet structure sometimes suggest that their phrase divisions are a product of the text rather than the melody; such divisions seem to sit uncomfortably on the rhapsodic, quasi-Gregorian style of the melodies. If such "phrases" were repeated in a couplet structure the effect would be something like that just imagined. But these short sequences do not have couplet structure, and this may be one reason why. In any case, it is a point of substantial difference between the two kinds of sequence.

Beyond helping to define the phrase structure, the use of doubles bestows tremendous emphasis upon each phrase as a whole as well as on its parts and attributes. The most immediate, most pervasive consequence of such emphasis is the degree to which a sequence melody becomes perceptible, comprehensible, even familiar, already on first hearing— something best understood in comparison to the experience of hearing a Gregorian Gradual. Even if a phrase of a sequence is similar to an idiom of the Gregorian repertory (which is seldom the case) its effect is different in its Gregorian setting, where it slips by as one event in an endless chain of ever new and varied melodic ornaments, gone before it is fully perceived; we scarcely grasp it, let alone remember it. In the sequences, on the other hand, the passage is clearly articulated before and after, and repeated for emphasis. Saying something twice is a time-tested way of making it understood. We know a sequence better than a gradual because listening to it once we have heard most of it twice. Like most other factors of the sequence, this one cannot be considered in isolation, but it can be singled out nonetheless as one of the factors most responsible for giving a sequence melody its identity, a circumstance that surely must have entered into the calculations of the early composers.

By giving emphasis, the repetition makes evident and operative a number of melodic attributes whose operation in the Gregorian style can be doubted—specifically, melodic motives, register, and the tonal structures described by later theorists as "species." These will be taken up later in this chapter. The point here is that any aspect of the melody will be made more prominent and usually more effective by the repetition in the couplet structure.

All of that pertains to the purely melodic effects of the doubles. This repetition, of course, does not occur in the text; in fact, verbal repetition of any kind is avoided in the best proses (the refrain *O sancta Maria, O alma Maria* in BEATA TU VIRGO, and the *alleluia* in CANTEMUS CUNCTI MELODUM are rare and special exceptions). Verbal repetition in conjunction with melodic repetition is frequent in certain other forms, for example, in processional *versus*; Fortunatus' *Salve festa dies* was used this way, with the first line (or first and second lines in alternation) returning as refrain after verses.[6] Immediate repetition of text and melody is not so frequent, but one would not want to assert that it did not occur in the form-rich spectrum of early medieval chant. This is to show that immediate repetition is not simply out of the question, rather it could be imagined as a point of comparison to the sequence, which has immediate melodic repetition without verbal repetition. For as soon as we try to imagine the possibility of immediate verbal repetition in the sequence, we see how alien to the form it would be. The sequence as we know it depends as much on the continuation in the text as it does on the repetition in the melody. And the changing text gives the repetition of the melody a sense quite different from that of simple repetition: difficult to describe, this sense involves such things as forward motion, continuity, development, formal sophistication, as opposed to naïveté.

In spite of the fact that the text does go on to ever new content and construction, it falls into formal units—clauses and periods—and these seem to be related to the units of the melody. For another important effect of the couplet structure is to articulate the piece as a whole into so many couplets. The couplet, rather than the phrase, becomes the primary unit of articulation, for a phrase and its immediate repetition could hardly be placed in separate formal units without the most elaborate manipulations by the composer. And this effect of the doubles seems more closely coordinated with the text than are the other effects. The early proses tend to show significantly less run-on from one couplet to the next than from one line to the next of the same couplet. Hence, in the text—as in the melody—the couplet tends to be the decisive unit.

It is true that the effect in the case of the text is less pronounced. That is, the purely formal effect of the music (the couplets) seems stronger relative to the melodic "sense," than is the purely formal effect of the text relative to the textual sense. Still, in principle it seems fair to conclude that the early sequence was conceived as a coordinate system of musical and rhetorical couplets. In other words, we can take Wilhelm Meyer's *bicola* as effective units of the text, synchronized with the melodic units produced by the repetitions —with the nice division of labor that the structure of the text, being more flexible, contributes more to continuity and larger grouping, while the structure of the melody (in so far as couplets are involved) being carried out more rigorously, contributes more to the articulation.

6. See *Anal.hymn.* 50, pp. 76–84.

For even after all irregularities of detail have been considered, the fact that the repetitions are literal remains paramount, and striking. Many forms, even Gregorian ones, can be construed to have approximate repetition in adjacent melodic members, isolated or in a series; the repetitions in a sequence, however, have always stood out as something special, because so literal and persistent. It is these qualities that make the combination of the melodic repetitions with a prose text so intriguing. Indeed, the persistence of repetition is such as to make the purely melismatic existence of the sequence artistically not believable. Only when relieved by the continuity of a text do the repetitive couplets show the same level of artistry that is apparent in other aspects of melody.

Singles appear most often in first and last lines. Singles appear in all first lines of the early repertory, except perhaps for the special case ECCE VICIT (Notker compensated for this by doubling the second phrase) and Notker's similar cases CONCENTU PARILI and NATUS ANTE SAECULA. And in the case of certain items such as SALUS AETERNA we have to take the Alleluia as phrase 1. Sometimes the opening single is very short.

1   Laudes deo
2a   omnis sexus consonat . . .

1   Hæc dies
2a   quam excelsus . . .

Others are much longer.

1   Nunc exultet omnis mundus, quia hodie victor

1   Rex omnipotens die hodierna

Some, again, are relatively ornamented: both LAUDES DEO and HÆC DIES carry decorative groups of several notes over a single syllable. Other incipits frequently carry ornamental neumes of some kind. Some incipits, however, are relatively straightforward and syllabic, such as REX OMNIPOTENS, and FORTIS ATQUE AMARA. Combined with the ornamental quality is a tendency for the melodic motion of the first line to move in a convolute manner and in its own orbit; the piece sometimes seems to begin properly at phrase 2, after an introduction, as in HÆC EST SANCTA. And yet many incipits—especially shorter ones—are run on in textual sense to the following couplet (2a), counteracting the force of the musical break.

Singles appear at last lines, but with at least as much variety. The concluding single may be nothing but *Amen*, as in LAUDES DEO OMNIS SEXUS. Or it may be a long, independent, ornamented phrase, as in HÆC EST SANCTA. The most complex cases involve first and second endings for the last couplet, the second ending being sometimes extended like a coda. The most striking example, CHRISTI HODIERNA, involved radical variants to the conclusion, many of which tended to replace this complex structure with a straight double; but Notker's version indicated that the most complex version was the earliest. The fact of a concluding single is usually coordinated with some rhetorical feature; special emphasis is shown by Notker's texting for JOHANNES JESU CHRISTI and LAURENTI DAVID MAGNI, where the concluding single has epigrammatic force,

—Johannes Jesu care!
—Martyr, milesque fortis!

suggesting that Notker heard in the melody a formal emphasis calling for textual support.

The melodic style of the opening and closing singles, together with other considerations—in particular, the fact that when a relationship to a Gregorian alleluia is present, it is almost always manifested in the opening single—has suggested that it was these portions of a sequence that were most closely associated with the Alleluia-and-melisma as antecedent of the sequence. Insofar as the Alleluia-and-melisma was an antecedent, the association seems valid, but with qualifications that will require careful consideration in the next chapter. In principle, it seems that the relationship of sequence to Alleluia-and-melisma is one of stylized paraphrase, as an artistic option, rather than mere derivation as a morphologic necessity. That is, it seems likely that opening and closing singles were given an ornate character deliberately to suggest the style of the Gregorian alleluia, even if no relationship to a specific alleluia was present.

It is the appearance of singles in the interior of sequences that calls for special comment, for these more than the opening and closing singles seem to be significant exceptions to the practice of doubles. The occurrence of singles must be taken up in the broader context of all kinds of interruptions to the regular series of doubles. Within that context (but leaving out of account the opening and closing singles), the frequency of such interruptions in the early repertory may be considered to be high: of the sixteen melodies shared by Notker with West-Frankish versions, every one except REX OMNIPOTENS and OMNIPOTENS DEUS shows some kind of irregularity. If we were to include as an irregularity the use of a sub-phrase structure, then all these sixteen melodies would be involved. There is no pressing reason, however, to think of sub-phrase structure as an irregularity, and it would be better to say that in making regular use of doubles the early sequence composer usually felt the need to vary it with some more elaborate device. The 9 melodies used by Notker without West-Frankish analogs are, statistically speaking, less irregular: 4 of them (SCALAM AD COELOS, CONCENTU PARILI, NATUS ANTE SAECULA, AGONE TRIUMPHALI) show no true irregularity, nor even a clearly articulated sub-phrase structure, but proceed regularly in doubles; but the lines in the first three of these are sometimes unusually long and complex.

While the total number of exceptions to regularity makes an easily perceptible and striking impression, the different ways in which the exceptions occur do not—which is simply to say that they are exceptions. Singles can be used in several ways, and among the sixteen West-Frankish melodies there are only two or three examples of any one way. Singles are used to close off extended periods, as in FORTIS ATQUE AMARA (phrase 3). A single is also used in penultimate position, just before the closing single, and as part of the same closing function, in HÆC EST SANCTA SOLEMNITAS (perhaps also in CLARA GAUDIA). And still with a closing function, singles are used in HÆC EST VERA REDEMPTIO as a refrain.

On the other hand, a single appears in LAUDES DEO OMNIS SEXUS as a "verse" (phrase 3); and the same phrase, with a similar function, appears as a single in NUNC EXULTET. This single, as well as the others in NUNC EXULTET, embodies a sub-phrase structure—in this case a a′ a, in other cases a a b—and it is difficult to decide whether we are dealing with a single that involves an internal repeat or with a modified double of some kind. The important aspect, of course, is that this kind of phrase is an interruption of the regular doubles. The extreme case is HÆC DIES QUAM EXCELSUS, which in its restored West-Frankish form has only one regular double, phrase 2.

There are also modified or irregular doubles that do not involve singles. The second line of a double may be longer by several syllables, usually by an interpolation in the interior of the line, as in LAUDES DEO OMNIS SEXUS, "Justus ut palma minor," and especially Notker's SUMMI TRIUMPHUM REGIS. The most complex of all irregularities involves a group of notes too short for a phrase and sometimes too long to be a motive, interpolated as a single in and around short doubles that use related materials. The instances in "Justus ut palma major" (phrase 6 to the end), "Ostende" (phrases 5–6), "Veni Domine" (phrases 3 and 5), and REGNANTEM SEMPITERNA (phrase 2) all create the effect—if only momentarily —of a swirl of melody that obliterates the phrase structure produced by regular repetitions while preserving the sense of repetition itself.

In the West-Frankish tradition, irregularities of all kinds were normalized during the tenth and eleventh centuries; the documentation can be abundantly supplied from the transmission in the Aquitanian sources as well as others. Many of the cases of singles or irregular doubles among the sixteen West-Frankish melodies were normalized by the end of the tenth century—the time of the Aquitanian sources MSS 1118 and 1084—some of them earlier in the century, as shown by readings in MS 1240. The irregularities have been restored in this study with the help of Notker's texts, which preserved many of them intact. Other cases of irregularities survived into the eleventh century, usually engendering alternate forms of a given melody, one regular the other not. The regularization can often be observed in process. The complier of MS Paris B.N. n.a.lat.1871 took it as his special task to normalize everything possible: this prosarium is full of unica versions of standard items, with text added at all internal singles or modified doubles. For this reason, the source has to be used with the greatest caution. Blume thought that it alone among the Aquitanian sources preserved uncorrupted versions of certain pieces;[7] but while it is true that the manuscript is a convenient source, having a broad, standard repertory and very clear diastematic display, and seems in other respects to have good readings apparently derived from a reliable tradition, still the most distinctive aspect of the readings is the pervasive interpolation or revision of text in favor of regular doubles.

If the trend is toward regular doubles, away from the singles and irregular doubles attested by Notker's ninth-century versions, does it not lie near at hand to imagine an even earlier state in which sequences (not these, necessarily, but others now lost—or not yet identified as such) consisted primarily of singles, with occasional and informal repetitions? One of the most confusing things about the history of the sequence has been the absence of examples that would clearly represent a stage morphologically just prior to the ninth-century repertory—whether this stage is to be called the "original" one or some kind of antecedent, not yet a true sequence. The examples of sequences we can all recognize as such

---

7. See, for example, the apparatus in *Anal.hymn.* 53, pp. 81–82. This MS, and Blume's use of it, has been noted several times by others.

seem to appear abruptly on the scene, emerging fully formed like Venus from the rucksack of the Monk from Jumièges. There is, of course, group C of Table II, with its aparallel sequences—8 in Notker's *Liber hymnorum*—and these have been taken to be the prototype that uses no repetition or only informal repetition. These pieces, however, have no clearly defined phrase structure, marked by cadences, in the manner of the sequences we have studied from groups A and B. They do not just lack doubles, they might even be said to lack singles, in the sense that their structure proceeds according to other principles. The difference in phrase structure is so great as to make these two different types of melody, one of which cannot possibly be the immediate, or only, prototype of the other.

Clear phrases, along with cadence formulas, appear in the company of doubles—and only there. It would be easy enough to recognize a piece that had this type of clear phrase, but as singles; yet so far one has not shown up, neither in the vast repertory sources of the late tenth century and after (where identification would be purely stylistic) nor in some special, earlier source. It seems as though the singles and other irregularities surveyed here, far from being antecedents or prototypes that were eventually subjected to doubling, actually owe their existence to the doubles. They are, then, what they seem to be, exceptions to a practice of regular doubles. As such, they take us no nearer to the antecedents of the sequence as we know it. If the argument in favor of singles as antecedents were correct, then HÆC DIES QUAM EXCELSUS (in restored form) would have a claim as a prototype; here, if anywhere, we could see the free unfolding of clear shapes with irregular repetition that points towards nascent doubles. But what HÆC DIES QUAM EXCELSUS really shows is an unusually sophisticated study in *modified* doubles—modifications that depend for their effect upon the expectation of regular doubles, like the one in phrase 2.

Sub-phrase structure can not be described as an irregularity, but it does provide one of the most welcome kinds of relief to the succession of regular doubles. And it is the occasion for the most lyric moments in the early repertory.

Sub-phrase structure may appear with a greater or less degree of articulation. The clearest cases, such as in ECCE VICIT phrase 6 (restored version), REX OMNIPOTENS phrase 12, NUNC EXULTET phrases 3 and 5, involve cadence formulas at the ends of at least the first sub-phrase. Ordinarily these are supported by textual articulations; these may in some cases be overrun, but usually in such a way as to suggest deliberate clouding of the sub-phrase structure, as in ECCE VICIT. This particular melody, one of the most charming of the early repertory, has a curiously nostalgic aura about it; it swings about the D in an unbroken succession of groups of two, giving the impression of a completely familiar tune. It does, in fact, happen to be very similar to a French popular melody *En passant par la Lorraine avec mes sabots*. There is no reason, however, to think about a "folksong" origin in the ninth century; on the contrary, it would seem that in this and other cases we are witnessing the generation of what is to be folksong idiom out of early monastic sacred music—"The birth of folksong from the spirit of chant."

Such idioms bring special problems for the sequence: their very lyricism is anomalous in the context of prose, and the anomaly becomes apparent in the way the lyric sub-phrase dominates the whole piece. Its effect is closed, rounded, perfect, static; its short span can be easily grasped, far more easily than the longer phrases surrounding, and it tends not only to attract attention away from them but even to make them seem unwieldly and inarticulate in comparison. The lyric sub-phrase is, in a word, verse, and as verse endangers the prose context in which it is set. The long prose couplets are at best difficult to project as believable entities; shorter, jingling verse is much easier to make and hear. Thus the most striking moment in ECCE VICIT is also from some points of view the weakest, even if the weakness is not obvious until later on, in the eleventh century, when lyric sub-phrases permeate the whole of the later sequence repertory, bringing with them regular accent patterns and rhymes, and the end of the prose. I take the instances of textual run-on in ECCE VICIT phrase 6 as an immediate, perhaps purely instinctive, precaution against the dangerous effects of the intrusion of verse. A more blatant texting of an almost identical melodic idiom can be studied in ECCE PULCRA phrase 7, a West-Frankish prose from the early tenth century or perhaps the late ninth century.[8]

Sub-phrase structures and similar idioms are found in REX OMNIPOTENS phrase 12 and CHRISTI HODIERNA phrase 5; both cases involve a move from G up to D, the tonal function of the sub-phrase being to insist on the D. The shape is the same as in ECCE VICIT—*a, a* extended, with C D D cadences at the end of the first sub-phrase. The idiom is less lyric, however, and blends better with the surrounding melody. A comparable instance, but on D-A rather than G-D appears in "Justus ut palma major" phrase 5; there the shape is more clearly *a a b*.

Alongside this group of sub-phrases, related among themselves in melodic profile, appears another group that share the low-lying phrase first found in LAUDES DEO phrases 3 and 6. This type appears several times as a single, rather than as a double. Instances appear in HÆC DIES QUAM EXCELSUS phrase 5 (restored version), and NUNC EXULTET phrases 3 and 5. This structure tends to have the shape *a a′ a*, and while it shares with the other the tendency to proceed in rhythmic groups of two, it has a different melodic quality, being nowhere near as lyric. A distinct but comparable instance appears in "Veni domine" phrase 4. NUNC EXULTET, treasure house of phrase shapes, has another sub-phrase structure *a a b* in phrases 6, 9, and 10; this was occasionally used elsewhere in the repertory but not often as strong as in NUNC EXULTET phrases 6 or 9, rather in the manner of phrase 10, and as a penultimate or closing phrase with extended second ending.

These are the clear examples of sub-phrase structure. Less clear—that is, less clearly articulated—instances can be found in a number of other sequences. Long phrases in general tend to break into sub-phrases at the encouragement of an internal cadence or a melodic repetition, even if only suggested. On the other hand, very short phrases can be grouped together (as in HÆC EST SANCTA) in such a way as to sound like sub-phrases within a larger phrase. Groupings and larger groupings are inherent in the nature of the early sequence; the sub-phrase structures surveyed here are only those special cases that result from clear articulations within numbered phrases.

The types of sub-phrase structure studied are intimately related to length of line: in-

8. See my *History of Musical Style*, pp. 36–37.

deed, sub-phrase structure seems to be a way of extending the length past its usual limits —as if the span of a bridge was extended by using several arches rather than one. Length of line is one of the most critical, and interesting, factors of the sequence; and here must be emphasized again the importance of dealing with the real length of line, as shown in the transcriptions in this book, but generally neglected in other studies and editions. Only the *Analecta liturgica*, an abortive anthology started by E. Misset and A. Weale (1888–1892), printed sequences in a form that showed the long lines, and for this as well as other aspects the editors were roundly criticized by Blume (who could be bumptious on such occasions) for ignoring the shorter divisions—sub-phrases that Blume saw or tried to see in *every* line of every sequence; for Blume could understand the sequence (or perhaps was commited in the *Analecta hymnica* to understanding it) only as a hymn, that is, with verses comparable in length to the eight-syllabled lines of the Ambrosian meter. Even that is a point to carp about: it may be wrong to think of the Ambrosian stanza as four eight-syllabled lines; at any rate syntax, sense, and especially medieval hymn tunes favor a construction of two lines each of sixteen syllables (admittedly with subdivision into eights) —a length of line closer to the norm of proses on one hand and hexameters on the other.

The point about sequence lines, of course, is that, being prose, they have no "normal" length, but vary over a wide range—much wider than the range used in verse. Although prose lines are no shorter than verse (for verse can be very short), they are longer, reaching lengths of thirty or forty syllables, even without subdivisions, whereas verse hardly ever goes beyond the sixteen syllables of an hexameter.

Even more distinctive than the range of variation is the fact that variation over a wide range can and does occur in a single prose, from one phrase to the next. The *change* in length from one couplet to the next is as distinctive of the early sequence as is the literal repetition within the couplet. So basic a principle is this one of changing length that exceptions to it are cause for suspicions of a bad text (and exceptions are extremely rare). A piece in which all or many lines were the same length would be scarcely recognizable as a sequence —that is, as an *early* sequence—even in the presence of couplets and prose rhythm. But prose rhythm, strictly speaking, could not be present if the lines were the same length; for that equality is a mark of verse, and a basic distinction from prose. This is one important reason why REX CAELI, usually described as a "sequence with double cursus" (i.e. large-scale repeat) is not a sequence, but something closer to a versus (the piece is probably from the ninth century, being cited in examples that accompany the treatise *Musica enchiriadis*).[9]

And still further, it is characteristic of the early sequence that the exact pattern of line lengths is unique to a given piece. The profile formed by the number of phrases, and the number of syllables in each phrase, seems to be as individual a matter as a fingerprint; if we can match the syllable count of a text preserved without melody to a melody, we can positively identify the two (SEMPER REGNANS and PANGE DEO were identified with their melodies in this way).

9. Transcription in J. Handschin, "Über Estampie und Sequenz," *Zeitschrift für Musikwissenschaft* XII (1929), pp. 19–20; see also XIII (1930), pp. 113ff. Stäblein, "Sequenz," *Die Musik in Geschichte und Gegenwart*, 12 (1965), between col. 528–529.

Example 8.

FORTIS ATQUE AMARA

1————7

2——7 / 7

3————————18

4————14 / 14

5————16 / 16

6————23 / 24

7————18 / 18

8————11

Example 9.

HÆC EST SANCTA SOLEMNITAS

1————————————29

2——8 / 8

3————10 / 10

4————————21 / 22

5————————————26 / 26

6————17

7————————21

Example 10.

CLARA GAUDIA

1————11

2——9 / 9

3————————19 / 19

4————————21 / 19

5————————19 / 19

6————————24 / 24

7————————19 / (19)

8————————19 / (19)

9——7

The fact that the profiles are unique to each piece seems to be a matter not of random distribution, but of intent; the phrase lengths do not vary randomly but, first, with discernible artistic purpose in any given sequence and, second, in occasional conformity with some principles of form that can be inferred from a study of the profiles in the whole early repertory. In some cases there actually seems to be at work a conception of a basic form, a shape common to several sequences—inconsistent as this may seem with the uniqueness of the profile. What happens is that the common shape is approximated by a number of sequences each with slightly different syllable counts. In other sequences, only the procedures, not the resulting shape, seem to be held in common.

In attempting to discern these shapes and procedures, it is necessary to take into account other factors at the same time, especially register, location and kind of cadence, nature of the melodic inflection, and nature of the phrase (whether it has sub-phrases). As we observed in studying individual examples, these factors are usually integrated in any one piece in a purposeful manner. In FORTIS ATQUE AMARA, for example, after the opening period that terminates in a long single (phrases 1–3), there is a carefully paced movement through

Structural Aspects of the Early Sequence   383

a high double (4), a low, slightly longer double (5), to the longest and highest double that includes the descending sequential motion (not yet sub-phrases, but clearly articulated nonetheless) and internal rhymes in the text. The next couplet (7) is shorter, and almost as high, and the concluding single is shorter and lower. The result is a very clear arch, subsuming lengths of line, height of register, and complexity of phrase structure (see Example 8).

Hæc est sancta shows exactly the same plan, with a gradual heightening and lengthening of phrase from 2 through 5 (see Example 9). The other examples from the sixteen West-Frankish melodies include ecce vicit (in its restored version), which ascends gradually to the lyric sub-phrase structure at the climax, but with only the concluding single as "post-climax." Nunc exultet sets out the basic plan on a grandiose scale: the approach to the high point in 6 includes the repetition of the low-lying phrase (3,5) while the descent from the high point includes a resurgence in phrase 9, and a very effective post-climax in the F-A-C realm in phrase 10, as well as the elaborate concluding couplet 11. Clara gaudia presents the plan in muted tones; here the phrases are remarkably similar in count (see Example 10) and in two cases identical 3,5; 7,8)—but one case involved interpolations and a question as to what the original form was. Like the syllable count, the register varies gently throughout the piece; but with the plan in mind, the lengthening and ascent through phrase 5 (which in dic nobis breaks into sub-phrases in the text) can be discerned. Rex omnipotens, being a long piece, called for some kind of expansion of the plan, but a kind different from that of nunc exultet. In rex omnipotens the approach to the high point is delayed, phrases 1–4 remaining low and relatively static. Phrase 8 begins as if for a climax, but does not carry through. With phrase 9 we can feel a sense of increased animation and urgency, as the melody now presses on to fulfill the plan. The high point is reached in the sub-phrase structure of 12, placed—as in ecce vicit—in penultimate position.

"Laetatus" has a very clear climax in phrase 5, high, long, and full of momentum, like phrase 5 of hæc est sancta. In "Laetatus," however, this central phrase is not prepared by growth and development in phrases 1–4, and the post-climax seems long in comparison, making phrase 5 seem either less effective or slightly out of place.

"Justus ut palma major" has one of the most carefully worked-out realizations of all. A sub-phrase structure in 5 lifts the piece out of the preparation (which included a repetition, 2/4, as in nunc exultet), but the high point comes after the sub-phrase structure, in the intricately motivic passage in which the doubles are fused together to form one long phrase.

"Justus ut palma major," however, is one of the melodies that does not end on its expected final, but higher (on G instead of D), and this constitutes a change in plan. It could be taken as an indication that the upward expansive movement was more essential to the basic plan than the relaxation at the close, and that in "Justus ut palma major" this upward expansion carried the piece as a whole into a higher tonal realm. The same thing happens in christi hodierna, and here the higher realm is nailed down by a second sub-phrase structure that forms a second climax in phrase 7.

Even such a preliminary discussion of the plan has involved us immediately in the idiosyncrasies of individual pieces, showing that the plan is really only a matter of procedures and aspirations. Discussion of the other West-Frankish sequences that do not exhibit the plan would lead us even more into individualities. But since the primary fact of the early repertory, again, is individuality, and only twelve out of the sixteen West-Frankish melodies can be related to the plan, it is not the exceptions that need explanation but rather the plan itself. What artistic impulse does it represent?

To speak further of effects rather than origins, the effect of organizing an extended, articulated melody around a clearly prepared high point that brings several parameters to a climax is to create a melody strikingly different from Gregorian art—at least, from the art of the Gregorian Gradual. Graduals regularly have an extended range; but the melody moves freely through the range at any point in the piece, and little use is made of locus within the range to project an overall plan, let alone a clear design. In the Easter Gradual *Hæc dies*, for example, an exquisite excursion to a high G, the highest note of the piece, occurs shortly after the start of the verse; and while this could be described as roughly the middle of the piece, it could not be located in any integrated, clearly articulated formal process; rather, it seems to be an intensely expressive moment.

Against such an art, one of surpassing sophistication, the Frankish composer set his sequence, articulated into clear phrases, hammered home with abundant, literal repetition, moving with perceptible logic towards a high point of tone and rhythm that draws the whole piece into an ordered unity. The effect in this case seems to me so explicit as to permit unhesitating identification with the composer's purpose—deliberate, conscious purpose. The sequences that exhibit the simple plan, being the most prominent of the early repertory, can fairly be taken as representing the highest aspirations of the early medieval composer in his desire to set a new Frankish chant next to the old Gregorian one.

Such a plan, even if it holds for only some of the early sequences, can help us understand a curious development within the "second generation" of sequences, around 900; although not properly a subject of this study, the development in question has often been involved in discussions of the origin of the sequence.[10] The Aquitanian sequentiaria include nine melodies that are partially underlaid with text—short lines of text, located at certain points in the melody, specifically at phrases 5 and 8; or 5 and 9; or 5, 9, and 11; or 5, 9, and 13, depending on the total number of phrases. These same text phrases reappear in the full texts provided in the prosaria, sometimes integral in sense and syntax, sometimes to be understood in the context of the prose only with difficulty. Generally these "partial texts" of the sequentiaria appear unchanged in each of the several different complete proses provided for a given melody.

These partial texts are further distinguished by unusually lyric construction, tending toward short verses, regular accent patterns, and rhyme, as in this most famous instance.

Ecce puerpera / genuit Emanuel / regem in saecula,

Deum oraculis / prophetarum promissum / magnum in saecula,

Nobis det ut omnia / quae sunt patris et sua / praemia aeterna.

Salus et victoria / illi sit et gratia / omnia per saecla.

10. See *Anal.hymn.* 53, pp. xxiiiff. The two principal discussions are by Stäblein, "Zur Frühgeschichte der Sequenz," *Archiv für Musikwissenschaft* XVIII (1961), pp. 8–33; and Husmann, "Sequenz und Prosa," *Annales musicologiques* II (1954), pp. 77–91.

The melody for this and other partial proses is similarly distinct in style from its surroundings, containing occasional two-note neumes and exhibiting an acclamatory manner that protrudes from the typically long arching lines before and after.

All these aspects, long observed, have resulted in several different explanations, polarized around two extremes. On one hand, it has been claimed that the partial texts, with their melodies, were a first stage of sequence composition, the rest of the sequence being composed around these compact lyric phrases. On the other hand, it is argued that these partial texts with their melodies are posterior additions to existing proses.

Obviously, if the explanation requires an absolute principle, then one of these two explanations is wrong. Against the first it can be argued that none of the sequences involved seems to be a very early one: none of them is used by Notker, stylistic comparisons with the early repertory as defined by his use are not encouraging, and repertory formation, too, suggests a later date—but not much later than 900. Also, there are intrinsic difficulties in trying to show that each partial text preceded its complete prose. Husmann showed that one case, *Gloria victoria*, was clearly an interpolation; the whole melody, and other texts, have a solid manuscript witness without the partial text and its melody. But if that demonstration holds in that case, it does not in others.

The striking aspect has always been the location of the partial texts in phrases 5 and 8 (or 9, 11, or 13, as mentioned). Under either explanation, this remains unexplained. But if we know that at least some early sequences were constructed according to a plan that embodied careful thought about the nature and location of phrases—especially of phrases with sub-phrase structure; if we know from a study of structural variants that much revision was devoted to getting the right length phrase at a certain critical point in a given piece; if we have even one example, such as CHRISTI HODIERNA, or "Justus ut palma major," or ECCE VICIT, or OMNIPOTENS DEUS, in which a sub-phrase structure has been purposefully located at phrase 5; then we can begin to understand the location of a "partial text" at the same point. This is not to appeal either to "number symbolism" or to "numerical composition" (which are two different things), not to number as such, but to the observable properties of a series of musical events; nor do we need involve any theoretical principle (although such principles might well be available), but merely observe that sequence composers did sometimes pay special attention to phrase 5 as a point where some more complex or higher-level event would be in order. A forceful acclamation in short, highly integrated verse-like lines would be such an event. That kind of contrast might well come twice, so as not to seem a mistake; it should return, not too soon but not at the very end—say, after two or three intervening phrases, and if the piece were very long, after two more. This, it seems to me, could well represent the train of thought of the sequence composer, seeking to emphasize or highlight the shapes presented by the early repertory. I believe the "partial texts" of the three most important and stable items—CELEBRANDA (Christmas), CELSA POLORUM (St. Stephen), and FULGENS PRAECLARA (Easter) to have been composed integrally with the complete text and melody.[11] Some of the others may well involve subsequent interpolation or modification in the manner of *Gloria victoria* in EXULTENT ELEGANTIS.

11. *Anal.hymn.* 53, pp. 37, 62; transcription in Stäblein (see note 10).

What seems most misleading about the other two explanations is that neither is willing to consider such rational calculation of musical effects (calculation attributed without question to composers of modern times) as factors in the generation of medieval forms. Both explanations assume an almost automatic, growth-like process with little intervention of a thinking composer save for the most timid, unimaginative steps—and those involved with text, not music. Something more is required to explain the early sequence.

The discussion of an ideal shape, or at least procedures, that existed over and above individual pieces raises the question of the composition of texts in relationship to such ideal shape and procedures. Even if we reject the notion that all early sequence melodies were ancient melismas underlaid with text, still the artistic problem of text underlay recurs persistently in the history of the sequence.

It is certainly true that text underlay played an important role in the sequence repertory, a role that requires our close attention and precise understanding. This role, however, tended to become more prominent in later stages than in the initial stage, as has been commonly assumed. Where several texts (sometimes twenty or more in the eleventh century) exist for one melody, then obviously all but one were laid under a pre-existing melody; of that there can be no question. Every text Notker wrote for a West-Frankish melody was likewise underlaid. It is not clear how many this includes, but certainly a large part of the 16 melodies that have West-Frankish counterparts. Furthermore, whenever Notker wrote two texts to the same melody, one of them was underlaid to a pre-existing melody. In some cases we are reasonably sure which text was first, and we can observe that the earlier one is not necessarily the more skilled or imaginative of the two; in fact, the reverse seems to be true. From this it follows that underlay does not, by itself, imply lower artistic standards, for according to some tastes Notker's texts are far better than his West-Frankish models, and his second attempts better than his first. Now in fact the repertory of texts did not generally get better and better as more and more texts were supplied to existing melodies, but the point is that there was nothing inherent in the process of text underlay that precluded artistic merit.

That, however, is only the first point. The process of text underlay is more subtle than might appear. It is useful to consider the different, but related, case of hymn texts and melodies—Ambrosian hymns. Any text in this form fits any melody, as if every text had been underlaid to every melody. What really happened, of course, is that text and melody were each composed in accordance with a scheme of four lines each of eight syllables. Once this scheme existed (and it had to be created) a text could be composed that would fit a melody not yet written. Or a melody could be composed that, similarly, would fit a text not yet written. Just because a given melody was composed with no particular text in mind would not mean that that melody had no aptitude for a text, or was intended to be melismatic, or perhaps performed by an instrument.

It is obvious that sequences are different from Ambrosian hymns precisely in the fact that they do not use such a scheme. Insofar, however, as sequences use a common shape, or common principles, they may lend themselves to the same analysis. Given such principles, it would be possible to compose a good text, arranged in couplets of such sense and length as would lead towards a climax; a melody could then be composed that would both fit the text and still have the purely melodic features of other sequence melodies. On the other hand—and this is the most important part—a melody could be composed first, in phrases of varying lengths (with an idea of which were to be double and which single), provided with cadence patterns, arranged so as to lead to a climax, all in a way that would fit appropriately with a text composed to go with it. In other words, the fact that a sequence melody was composed before its text (or texts) would not preclude the influence of text upon it; the intention that a text was to be set would have a decisive effect upon the construction and inflection of the melody.

All of this assumes that the common shape or common principles were in existence, and it is obvious that these principles would be of a more sophisticated order than those involved in the Ambrosian scheme. How the principles themselves came into existence remains, for the time being, out of our reach. But we would not need to imagine more than three or four models, and we would not—could not—imagine them to be exclusively melodic (that is, melismas) or exclusively derived from melodic components. The early sequence as we know it is so intricate a combination of text and melody that rhetorical considerations were necessarily a part of its original conception.

A close relationship of music and text does not mean subservience of music to text. It is sometimes thought that the closest union of music and text is achieved when the music reflects every nuance of textual meaning, or every inflection of verbal accent and sonority. But that is mere madrigalism on one hand, or recitative on the other; and there is more to music than that. The problem is to compose music that makes purely musical sense by itself *and* fits its text. In early sequences there is a close relationship between a text that tells its story (when restored) and a melody that for the most part has a high degree of independence (which does not mean antagonism) vis-à-vis text. That is, the melodies do not resemble psalm tones, in that they have sufficient inflection to stand by themselves as melodies. But this does not mean that the melodies came into being before, or independently of, the texts.

Considered purely as melodies, early sequences display several characteristics that have attracted attention but no consistent interpretation. It has become clear to those who have studied the melodies seriously that they are basically different from the Gregorian, primarily because of a greater directness in the conduct of the melodic line.[12] This quality has led some to speak of "folk" origin or influence, without, however, making clear what this might mean either in terms of Frankish culture of the eighth and ninth centuries or of the exclusively monastic, bookish environment in which the sequence was cultivated, used, and transmitted. Any such far-reaching conclusion must await a broader consideration than can be attempted here. In any case, a necessary first step would be a more precise understanding of the role of the early sequence within the forms and styles of composed chant as preserved in written sources.

It has been apparent from the preliminary study in this book that the melodies used by Notker—especially those shared with West-Frankish texts—make use of common idioms,

12. See, for example, Stäblein, "Sequenz," col. 538f., also col. 531f. See also Ewald Jammers, *Der Mittelalterliche Choral* (Mainz 1954).

and that these common idioms usually but not always appear in melodies having the same final. It is of course no surprise that several melodies use the same final: there are only four finals (in this classification), so that of any five or more melodies more than one will necessarily use the same final. And it is no real surprise to find melodies with the same final sharing common idioms; still, the kind and degree of similarity among the early sequences on G-*tetrardus* is striking, and has called forth comment.

The important point is what this similarity might imply about the techniques and circumstances of composition. Husmann has imagined a state of cantorial improvisation, in which specific melodies were put together out of a stock of formulas; he tends to find solutions to problems of confused text-states of early sequences, and their manifold interrelations, in the improvisatorial flux he postulates as the formative phrase of sequence composition.[13]

The situation seems to me very different. The kinds of variants encountered in the manuscript tradition of any given sequence do not suggest to me a prior state of improvisational flux; the smaller variants seem often to be routine scribal variants characteristic of *manuscript* transmission, while the larger variants—some of them discussed in the studies of individual sequences—usually seem to reflect the kind of revision a composer or performer applies to a piece that has reached him in written form. The various elements of the piece are not juggled or modified in an improvisational way, rather some are preserved intact with a high degree of faithfulness, while a few are revised in ways that indicate a careful overview of the structure of the whole piece.

Nor does the use of similar idioms in a group of pieces seem to me to be done in a way that suggests improvisation: one of the most striking of the common idioms, for example, the lyric sub-phrase of ECCE VICIT, is most distinguished by its placement within whatever melody uses it. In general, the early sequence seems to be a thoroughly "composed" piece, not an improvised one, in the sense that its components are carefully located with respect to one another, in ways that indicate more than improvisational calculation and reflection.

There is a more basic issue involved, however, in the idea that shared idioms indicate, *ipso facto*, improvisational use of familiar formulas—more specifically, of ancient, traditional formulas, as the theory has it. Shared idioms crop up in numerous other historical circumstances, and without examining all of them systematically it can be asserted that shared idioms do not always imply ancient materials, or improvisation as opposed to composition. The idioms shared by Haydn and Mozart, for example, were mostly recent ones, scarcely more than a few decades old, if that much. In other words, it is possible for there to be what appears at a distance a highly idiomatic repertory that does not preserve ancient formulas in virtually unchanged form. It does no good to argue that the case of Haydn and Mozart is not parallel to the sequence, that "conditions were different in the early Middle Ages," for we have no valid general principles to tell us what the conditions of musical composition were at that time; we can only reconstruct them as we come to know the music itself in more concrete terms. The fact is that the two cases are roughly similar in their use of shared idioms. Without arguing from analogy, we can use the more familiar case as a source of hypotheses: what is true of one *might* be true of the other.

13. "Alleluia, Vers, und Sequenz," *Annales musicologiques* IV (1956), 19–53; pp. 26, 42.

In this context, the use of shared idioms by itself in no way sets sequence composition apart from composition in other periods (even from the mid-twentieth century). From the case of Haydn and Mozart we might learn that shared idioms *can* imply merely a school (or less), not a tradition. We might also learn that while an art based on shared idioms may include some kind of improvisational combination, the masterworks of the art can be products of the most thoughtful kind of composition. And we might learn that the highest values of such an art reside not in the idioms themselves, but rather in the specific way they are combined in a given work, with subtlety and refinement of timing, proportion, and imagination making the difference between a routine work and a great one.

In the case of the sequence, we have no way of knowing whether the idioms are old or not, simply because we have no written record of any musical idioms for the period in question (the centuries before the ninth), and no liturgical matrix for the sequence such as exists for Gregorian chant and to a much lesser degree other chant repertories. But at least there is nothing on those grounds to contradict the idea that the shared idioms of the early sequence repertory belonged to the rapid efflorescence of a *novum canctium*, a new school of melodic composition, in which new turns of phrase that were felt to be happy inspirations were used exuberantly in more than one work.

It is possible, on purely structural grounds, to find a meaning for certain re-uses of material, and for the prevailing quality of melodic directness, that has nothing to do with improvisation or tradition on one hand, or with folksong on the other. In many cases where a sharing of idioms is felt, it is not possible to identify a specific idiom, but only to sense a certain similarity; this is often the case among the G-*tetrardus* melodies. The similarity can usually be attributed to melodic motion that remains within the same interval of a fourth or a fifth: two phrases (in two different pieces) that move through the fourth G down to D, for example, are apt to sound alike. Perhaps the similarity is an incidental by-product; perhaps the more important question is, why should a composer restrict his melodic inflection at the same time that he limits his range (within a given phrase) so as to bring about this similarity?

The answer seems to be that he wishes to clarify the large design so that its contours will be more effective. He deliberately restricts and simplifies the melodic motion of a phrase to show more clearly its locus, so that the contrast with—and eventual movement to—another locus, higher or lower, will be stronger. A phrase that moves within the locus G up to C will form a strong contrast with the one that stayed below G. Richness of melodic movement at the higher level is maximized by foregoing intricate inflection at the lower level. The same principle can be applied in a more complex way to obtain movement between two overlapping areas: the clearest, most functional case is the movement from an area dominated by G-B (or D-F) to F-A-C (or C-E-G); the melodic motion may use the same range and the same pitches, but simplicity and directness of motion permit the composer to make the shift very clear, and to use it for the establishment of a contrasting area for relief just before a cadence.

Such dwelling within restricted ranges later (in the tenth century) received theoretical rationalization in the doctrine of the *species*—the enumeration of the several species of fourths, fifths, and octaves as basic tonal constructs. One possible application of the doctrine of species is to provide the musician with a clear concept of whatever fourth or fifth he happens to be singing in. Berno of Reichenau, writing in the first half of the eleventh century, provided the following scheme of the species:[14]

Fourths

1st species	*2nd species*	*3rd species*
G	A	C
tone	tone	semitone
F	G	B
semitone	tone	tone
E	F	A
tone	semitone	tone
D	E	G

Fifths

1st species	*2nd species*	*3rd species*	*4th species*
A	B	C	D
tone	tone	semitone	tone
G	A	B	C
tone	tone	tone	semitone
F	G	A	B
semitone	tone	tone	tone
E	F	G	A
tone	semitone	tone	tone
D	E	F	G

There are purely abstract reasons for this kind of enumeration; but there is also the practical application for it in the kind of melody, beginning with the sequence, cultivated from the ninth century on. The point of theory as well as practice is to be sought not within one phrase or species, rather in the sense of tonal movement in going from one to another. In this movement, the melodic style of directness plays an essential role: clarity and lucidity of melodic design liberate the vigor of large-scale movement, whereas a wealth of expressive detail would obscure or even hinder it. The single most important feature of early sequence melodies seems to be the clarity of overall design, and this by itself is sufficient to account for the melodic style. There is indeed reason to search out why the Frankish melody should sound so different from the Gregorian; but the answer, it seems to me, lies close at hand in the very nature and destiny of the composed artwork.

14. See H. Oesch, *Berno und Hermann von Reichenau als Musiktheoretiker* (Bern 1961), pp. 97–98.

XXII

Sequence, Alleluia, and Liturgy

Versus alleluia tangit cantorem interius, ut cogitet in quo debeat laudare Dominum aut in quo laetari. Hæc jubilatio, quam cantores sequentiam vocant, illum statum ad mentem nostram ducit, quando non erit necessaria locutio verborum, sed sola cogitatione mens menti monstrabit quod retinet in se. Finitur hic secunda periocha praedicationis; usque ad memoratum statum currit sermo praedicationis; quae ultra sunt, velata sunt aliis seraphim.

AMALARIUS, *Liber officialis* (ca. 830)[1]

AFTER A STUDY of the early sequence repertory as defined by Notker's *Liber hymnorum*, the relationship to the Alleluia, once thought to be the most firmly established aspect of the sequence, now seems one of the least firm and most problematic. That some relationship existed is clear; the problem is, how much, and of what kind? On the resolution of this problem depend our assessments of aspects such as artistic originality and freedom in conception and design.

What the relationship of the sequence to the Alleluia implies—or seems to imply—is that the sequence is in essence a jubilus-replacement provided with a text; and that, as a consequence, the sequence existed first as a melisma, the text being laid under it; and as a further consequence, that the couplet structure as well as other formal features were to be derived exclusively from the melody and its antecedents. Still further consequences, all stemming believably if not quite necessarily from the Alleluia relationship, are that the melodies, as jubilus-replacement melismas, are "very old," and that the ninth-century contribution was limited to laying text under these melodies.

At the beginning of Chapter 13 were summarized the facts about the Alleluia relationship as it prevails in the repertory and sources circa 1000. Now we can add the few facts that can be dated in or near the ninth century, hence pertain more directly to the early

---

1. Ed. J. M. Hanssens, *Amalarii Episcopi opera liturgica omnia* II (1948): *Liber officialis*, book III, De officio missae, xiii–xiiii.

repertory. The fact with the earliest firm date is the statement by Amalarius, quoted at the head of this chapter. This statement, made before 830, establishes the existence at that time of the type of melody sung as an ad libitum replacement for the repetition of the Alleluia jubilus *after* the verse (note that many Alleluias include the melody of the jubilus as the conclusion of the verse, but this is not what is replaced).

Alleluia, jubilus
Verse (in some pieces ending with the melody of the jubilus)
Alleluia, replacement melisma

Amalarius calls this jubilus-replacement a *sequentia*, or rather, he says that singers call it a *sequentia*—*Hæc jubilatio, quam cantores sequentiam vocant*—and it is convenient to retain this term, in its Latin form, for this precise meaning, while continuing to use the English translation "sequence" for the type of piece we have been studying.

The Antiphonary of Mont-Blandin (Bruxelles, Bibl.royale cod. lat. 10127–10144), dated by Hesbert "8th–9th century,"[2] includes at the end a list of Alleluias for the Mass, six of which include the rubic *cum sequentia* (the end of this list, including the last three with this rubric, appears on the last recto in Hesbert's hand C). These six Alleluias are listed in the left-hand column of Table III cited exactly as in Hesbert's edition in the *Antiphonale missarum sextuplex*.

As Stäblein showed, all six of these Alleluias have either sequences or *sequentiae* connected with them in later manuscripts;[3] Stäblein's references are incorporated in the middle and right-hand columns of Table III. Further references to the Aquitanian sources MSS 1084 and 1118 have been added. The effect of Stäblein's demonstration was to show that the specific items intended by the Mont Blandin rubrics may indeed be present among the melodies that we can recover from the sequentiaria. We cannot be sure, however, precisely which they are. For our purposes we can and should differentiate between sequences and *sequentiae*, and to do this Stablein's data has been distributed between the middle and right-hand columns.

For five out of the six cases, *sequentiae*—jubilus replacements—can be found in later sources, as indicated in the middle column of Table III. Four out of these five also have texts, but from there on, generalities are hard to make and cases must be treated separately. For no. 2, Alleluia *Dominus regnavit*, there is a West-Frankish text and one by Notker. For no. 3, Alleluia *Beatus vir*, there are no texts of that kind preserved, only a jubilus-replacement, appearing as a melisma in MSS 1084 and 1118. For no. 4, West-Frankish sources preserve the text ARVI POLIQUE. For no. 5, Alleluia *Cantate domino* (and another verse, *Notum fecit*), there is a text by Notker, intended to follow another verse; a *sequentia* in MS 1084; and a West-Frankish text for still another verse. For no. 6, Alleluia *Confitemini* (and its two additional verses), there is a sequentia in MS 1084, and a text by Notker.

Only two of the six Alleluias, no. 1, *Jubilate Deo*, and no. 3, *Beatus vir*, are connected to sequences (in a third case claimed by Stäblein, NOSTRA TUBA, the Alleluia relationship

2. *Antiphonale missarum sextuplex*, pp. xv–xviii.
3. "Zur Frühgeschichte der Sequenz," pp. 4–7.

TABLE III

Alleluias "Cum sequentia" of the Mont-Blandin Antiphonale

	Sequentia	Sequence
1. Alleluia Jubilate Deo omnis terra. Cum sequentia.		(a) = All. Adducentur EN VIRGINUM AGMINA STIRPE MARIA (Notker) (b) = All. Veni domine VENIET REX
2. Alleluia Dominus regnavit decore. Cum sequentia.	IS QUI PRIUS (Notker) AGE NUNC	
3. Alleluia Beatus vir. Cum sequentia.	MS 1084, fol. 214 MS 1118, fol. 133v	GLORIOSA DIES
4. Alleluia Te decet ymnus Deus in Sion. Cum sequentia.	ARVI POLIQUE	
5. Alleluia Cantate Domino canticum novum. V. Notum fecit Dominus. Cum sequentia.	(a) = All. Qui timent EN REGNATOR (Notker) (b) MS 1084 fol. 213 (c) = All. Omnes gentes SANCTE REX	
6. Alleluia Confitemini Domino & invocate nomen. V. Cantate ei & psallite ei. V. Laudamini in nomine. Cum sequentia.	O QUAM MIRA (Notker) MS 1084, fol. 213v	

of the sequence in my opinion is the result of a later modification of its incipit, not an original feature of the piece). But in the case of no. 1, Alleluia *Jubilate deo*, the sequence is connected only indirectly; the Alleluia is the same as that used for the verse *Adducentur*, in which case the sequences are EN VIRGINUM AGMINA, and Notker's STIRPE MARIA; and for the verse *Veni Domine*, hence VENIET REX. None of these texts, then, is related to *Jubilate deo*, and we could assume a relationship of the sequence *melody* to Alleluia *Jubilate deo* only if we also assumed that the sequence melody existed as a melisma long before it was texted. That assumption, unlikely in general, is especially unlikely in the case of this particular melody, as discussed on p. 343. It is dubious, then, that the rubric really refers to the sequence melody we have studied. In the case of no. 3, Alleluia *Beatus vir*, GLORIOSA DIES is present in the Toul fragment and is in all probability from the early repertory.[4] The Mont-Blandin rubric could, however, just as well refer to the true *sequentia* in MSS 1084 and 1118; as in the case of Alleluia *Cantate domino* and Alleluia *Confitemini* this sequentia is transmitted only as a melisma, without a text.

4. Munich clm 14843 fol. 95v. Transcribed in my article, "The Troping Hypothesis," pp. 200–201, with the *sequentia* from MS 1084.

We can, therefore, take the Mont-Blandin rubrics to refer consistently to the kind of jubilus-replacement described by Amalarius, the one for Alleluia *Jubilate* being counted as lost; we need not conclude any necessary connection to the kind of sequence we have been studying—even though, given the curious features of EN VIRGINUM AGMINA, it is intriguing to find it indirectly involved here, and even though GLORIOSA DIES (as well as NOSTRA TUBA) can both be dated early on other grounds. We can also conclude that at least for Mont-Blandin the repertory of *sequentiae* was not very large by 800.

Further knowledge of the early relationship of Alleluia and sequence can only be gained by comparing this evidence with Notker's *Liber hymnorum*. The identification of Amalarius's *sequentia* with the type of piece—better, types—represented in Notker's collection and in the corresponding West-Frankish repertory is exceedingly delicate; and it is difficult to keep the evidence in strictly chronological order. Between 850 and 880 Notker wrote texts for two distinct types of pieces, the type with frequent couplets (groups A and B of Table II), and the smaller type without couplets (group C). The existence of these melodies, in the form in which we now have them, is therefore attested only by the fact, and from the moment, that he wrote the texts. Of the type with couplets, nine melodies (those in group B of Table II) are definitely related to an Alleluia of the Mass. If we consider only those with West-Frankish counterparts, and take groups A and B together, only seven out of sixteen melodies are definitely related to an Alleluia. On the other hand, of the eight melodies in group C (all represented in the West-Frankish repertory one way or another), *all* are definitely related to an Alleluia.

We can distinguish between the Alleluia relationships of groups B and C in a more refined way: the relationships in group C are clear and verifiable (in spite of the variations between the West-Frankish designations and Notker's—as has been shown more than once), while those in group B pose certain problems, as we have seen. The use of the Easter Alleluia *Pascha nostrum* (G final) for a sequence with a D final and a Marian text assigned to the Octave of Christmas is not in itself clear. There is the slight but persistent discrepancy between the incipit of "Justus ut palma minor" and also "Major" and the Alleluia *Justus ut palma*. And there is Notker's own curious disregard of the use of certain Alleluias: he sets the melody "Laetatus" (Alleluia *Laetatus sum* for Second Sunday of Advent) to PSALLAT ECCLESIA for the Dedication of a Church; the melody "Trinitas" (Alleluia *Benedictus es* for the Mass for the Holy Trinity) to FESTA CHRISTI for Epiphany; and the melody related to Alleluia *Adducentur* (for Virgins) to the Marian text STIRPE MARIA. These anomalies are part of a more pervasive looseness in liturgical associations that will be taken up later; but the cases cited here concern specific Alleluia relationships.

Notker's Preface is not as helpful in this connection as it might be. Notker calls his book a "book of hymns," which holds in some ways but not in all; for a hymn is a song of praise to God (Ambrose), and as Von den Steinen points out (but not in this connection) the Martyr sequences are not explicitly in praise of God. Notker describes the item shown him by the monk from Jumièges as *aliqui versus ad sequentias*, thus identifying the melody of LAUDES DEO, at least, as a *sequentia*, but also identifying the text as *versus*, which is not proper, and Notker knew better, even though in the Preface he consistently refers to the texts (his own as well) in this way. Notker also refers to the Alleluia, apparently to the process of laying text under a melody previously set to the syllables Al-le-lu-ia. It is true that the original readings Notker quotes in his Preface, *universus* (for *ubique totus* in the final version) and *redemptus* (for *liberatus*), result in neumatic readings, while those in the final version result in syllabic readings in accordance with Iso's advice. From that it has been concluded—it seems rightly—that Notker's discussion of setting text to a melody associated with the word *Alleluia* has some basis in fact.[5] Unfortunately, neither LAUDES DEO nor "Mater," that is CONGAUDENT ANGELORUM (two of the three melodies he cites in this connection) is positively related to an Alleluia. The third "Dominus in Syna," or CHRISTUS HUNC DIEM, has an E final for a G-final Alleluia. The net effect of these references in Notker's Preface, then, is to indicate a relationship to the word *Alleluia* but to leave unclarified the more precise relationship to the Alleluia of the Mass.

We have to imagine Notker writing his Preface some time after his first encounter with the new art form (just how long after is not clear). He had good reasons of a purely literary nature for telling the story the way he did, for his Preface had to introduce his work and the new art form to the Swiss-Rhenish monastic audience. For this purpose the story had to have verisimilitude, but not necessarily historical accuracy. In any case his terminology is at least loose, and possibly faulty, and the most that can be concluded *from the Preface* is that the texts he wrote were related in some general way to *sequentia* on one hand and to *alleluia* on the other. The relationship to the Alleluia he had in mind might have been nothing more than the use of a melody written down as a melisma with the syllables Al-le-lu-ia laid under the beginning. Such became the normal form of notating all sequence melodies, whether or not related to an Alleluia of the Mass, in the tenth century (first in the Autun fragment and in the Compiègne Antiphonale Paris B.N. lat. 17436). Whether this was the practice in Notker's time cannot be shown. That Notker's own texts are set to "very long melodies" is as plain as day; but he nowhere says that the "very long melodies" that gave him trouble as a youth were the same ones—or even the same kind—he later set.

The contents of the *Liber hymnorum*, however, tell us of the two distinct kinds of piece; one kind with, the other without, couplets. Only one of these kinds fits the description provided by Amalarius: only the small aparallel melodies of group C could be imagined as replacement-melismas for the repetition of the Alleluia after the verse, for only these have the appropriate dimensions and the consistent relationship to a known Gregorian Alleluia. The *type* of melody represented by the items in group C can be identified as the *sequentia* referred to by Amalarius and the Mont-Blandin gradual. Of the melodies set by Notker, three can be identified with the Mont-Blandin rubrics.

And yet these three seem to tell us little about the kind of piece that makes up the *Liber hymnorum*; for the texts to these little *sequentiae* could be omitted from consideration without seriously altering our conception of Notker's achievement. He himself, it will be noticed, does not mention any of them in his Preface. The other kind, the big kind—are they, too, *sequentiae* in some sense? That is the nub of the problem. Later, beginning in the latter half of the tenth century, they were called *sequentiae* in the anthologies. Notker refers

5. See especially Husmann, "Die St. Galler Sequenz tradition bei Notker und Ekkehard," pp. 6–13.

loosely to their melodies as *sequentias*. But from the *sequentia* as described by Amalarius to LAUDES SALVATORI or even to LAUDES DEO is a long way; the gap is not easily filled in.

That Amalarius did not in fact have in mind the kind of piece represented in groups A and B of Table II is strongly suggested by a revision in a later source of the *Liber officialis*. The words describing the *sequentia* quoted at the head of this chapter were placed in a *capitulum* of their own, with a separate heading, *De sequentia*.[6] That at least takes proper account of the size and independence of the kind of piece in question—a recognition that seems to have been forced upon the editor by the actual state of the repertory by that time —the tenth century. And (to add an argument that is both *ad hominem* and *ex silentio*) Amalarius himself can hardly be described as a man of few words; if there is something to comment upon, he comments, some say with *garrulitas*. It seems inconceivable that he would have so little to say about *sequentia* if by that was meant a piece such as LAUDES DEO.

The fact that has to be absorbed, then, is that the early repertory of what we call "sequences" is largely made up of pieces that are different from Amalarius' *sequentia* in their size, their use of couplet structure, and their lack of clear relationship to an Alleluia of the Mass. A comparison of the pieces in group C with those in groups A and B shows that much more was involved in the making of the latter than can be explained by the *sequentia*. The musical ambitions and abilities involved could be neither derived from nor contained in the jubilus-replacement; as far as musical form goes, the jubilus-replacement seems almost incidental to the creative forces streaming past it. And yet the larger pieces came to be called *sequentiae*, even while they maintained their differences with respect to the smaller aparallel ones. What we need is a way to understand the connection of the big *sequentia* to the small one without burdening the big *sequentia* with the artistic and functional limitations of the jubilus-replacement; we need an understanding of the big *sequentia* that will correspond realistically to the powerful musical and literary conceptions that created it.

There is no intrinsic difficulty in the appearance, in mid-ninth century, of pieces in prose, with couplet structure, of para-liturgical nature and content, set syllabically to melodies in a new, non-Gregorian style. Considered on their own terms (as they were in the preceding chapter), such pieces can be described as novel, but not problematic. The only problematic aspect is the persistent but conflicting relationship to the Alleluia—the fact that these melodies come to be called *sequentiae*, and that when notated melismatically (a development in itself not entirely clear) they carry the word "Alleluia" under their incipits.

It is, however, far easier and more appropriate to deal with these problems when expressed this way rather than the other—and this, it seems to me, is the most important point of the whole discussion. That is, if only the terms *sequentia* and *Alleluia* are at issue, an explanation is possible, even though it is only hypothetical. But the task of beginning with the axiom that the sequence (of whatever kind) was by nature a derivation from the Alleluia—that was too much for rational processes of investigation, simply because it was at variance with reality at so many points.

6. J. Hanssens, *Amalarii opera* I (1948), p. 170.

As for the explanation, it can be imagined that at an early stage of its development (perhaps around mid-ninth century) this new kind of piece with prose couplets became identified with Amalarius' *sequentia*: it adopted the name, *sequentia*; it took up an analogous position at Mass, not strictly as a jubilus-replacement, but simply following the Gregorian Alleluia; and it imitated the incipit of an Alleluia. Now the jubilus-replacement as such did not have its own Alleluia-incipit; it was preceded, intoned, by the incipit of the Allelulia into which it was inserted. In imitating the jubilus-replacement, the new kind of piece showed a persistent ambivalence. On one hand, the melody of its first phrase (phrase "1"), corresponding to the Alleluia, remained distinct in several ways from the rest of the new piece, as we have often seen. On the other hand, the new kind of piece imitated the whole form as it appeared in an Alleluia; that is, just as the jubilus-replacement *in situ* began with the word "Alleluia," so did the new kind of piece (when notated melismatically), but with no attention paid to the fact that the Alleluia-incipit of the jubilus-replacement was the incipit of an Alleluia of the Mass. As far as the imitator was concerned, it was simply the word "Alleluia" under the beginning of a melisma.

An example may help make this seemingly byzantine process believable. There is one sequence we have not studied that can probably be dated in the ninth century, STANS A LONGE (cited by Hucbald) but not set by Notker.[7] The distinctive aspect of this sequence is that it takes its incipit—text *and* melody—from an antiphon now assigned to Lauds on the Tenth Sunday after Pentecost. The antiphon refers to the story of the Pharisee and the Publican, the Gospel for that day, and the sequence tells the same story. Thus, the incipit is preempted: it can have no relationship to an Alleluia. Yet in all other respects it is a good —even classic—representative of the kind of piece we have studied; and when notated melismatically, its incipit bears the text *alleluia*.

STANS A LONGE presents a peculiarly nice combination of what have so often appeared as baffling contradictions in the early sequence. Because of its text—it is a "Gospel-song" —it has as strong a claim as any sequence to be sung before the Gospel, hence after the Alleluia, on a particular Sunday. Yet it has no connection with the Alleluia liturgically assigned to that day (even taking into account ninth-century variation in such assignments) or with any Alleluia. It is not a *sequentia*. Should it be attached like a trope to "its" antiphon, and sung before or after, or instead of, a psalm at Lauds? Hardly. It ungraciously refuses to live by any of the laws, liturgical or morphological, that have for so long been thought to be binding on early medieval music. I take this to indicate that these laws are in fact inoperative; not that one case can disprove them, but that one case can reveal how that age did not live by rigid law any more than does our own; the rigidity is one we have imposed on them.

Allow the ninth-century composer the conditions taken for granted in other ages, and the baffling contradictions disappear. Attracted by a Gospel text, he writes a paraphrase, sets it to a melody in the new style; for a beginning he selects an appropriate incipit from a piece he knows—it happens to be an antiphon from the Office. What does he do with

7. Text in *Anal. hymn.* 53, pp. 158–160. Von den Steinen, *Anfänge* 41, pp. 136ff. Melody in de Goede, *Utrecht Prosarium*, p. 115. See my article, "The Repertory of Proses at St. Martial de Limoges," pp. 158–159.

his piece? It finds favor with the cantor, with the brethren, with the abbot; they learn it and sing it at some convenient moment, perhaps on the day of the Gospel, perhaps at Mass, but perhaps at some other time. Eventually it is recognized as part of a repertory of such pieces evolving in this monastery and others, and as a member of a repertory it finds an "official" place in the liturgy. In that process there are no systematic or morphological problems.

This is not to neglect the wealth of liturgical associations revealed by scholarship, but rather to use them as wealth, rather than to the impoverishment of artistic impulse and achievement. Indeed, if we can imagine a sufficiently unencumbered state of artistic production, supported by adaptation and association with the rich heritage of literature, music and ceremonial available to the ninth-century Frankish composer, we can even see how he could have gotten from Amalarius' *sequentia* straight to the new sequence. For this purpose, however, it is necessary to understand something about the *sequentia* that has sometimes been obscured. It is true that Amalarius speaks in another connection of a triple melisma (*neuma triplex*) that the Roman singers sang to the Responsory *In medio* for St. John Evangelist, but that Frankish singers transferred to the Responsory *Descendit* for Christmas.[8] This text, however, should not be taken to imply that all such movable melismas were old, or that there was a reservoir of such melismas dating from time immemorial, and that any such melisma (including the jubilus-replacement) necessarily came from that reservoir; that is to imagine far more than Amalarius' reference—or any other—warrants. It seems much more reasonable to assume that, on the model of the *Descendit* melisma (itself presumably an eighth-century Roman product) and a few others like it, the Frankish cantors developed their own repertory of replacement melismas. These latter, then, would represent new composition, even if the style of composition was controlled by a close imitation of the manner of the Roman model. Stäblein shows how one, or perhaps two, of the six Mont-Blandin *sequentiae* might have been melodies from the Old-Roman repertory (preserved, to be sure, only in MS Vatican latin 5319, an eleventh-century source).[9] But at least some (probably most) jubilus-replacements can be seen as new Frankish contributions. And for the sake of gaining insight into Frankish artistry we should recognize the jubilus-replacement for what it was—a melody that *replaced* a Gregorian melody because it was considered more splendid, more elaborate, in some sense more desirable. Replacement melismas were not composed because they were mere servile imitations of the original, but because they went beyond the original in some way, expressing the ambitions of someone for whom the Gregorian was not enough. It is possible to feel the force of these ambitions in going through the melodies of group C in Table II; and at the same time it is possible to feel that the ambitions are not being fully realized, either because the nature of the chosen form, or the ability of the composer, does not permit.

Imagine, then, a monastic composer in 840 contemplating the possibility of creating new text and music for worship. The desire for a substantial text would involve the various considerations discussed in the previous chapter concerning couplets. In considering

---

8. J. Hanssens *Amalarii opera*, III (1950), pp. 54–56. The passage has been often cited and discussed.
9. See note 3, this chapter.

appropriate melodies the composer could eventually come to the *sequentia*—too small in itself, but a convenient starting point, if only because it was performed at Mass, right after the most important Gregorian music, the Gradual and Alleluia. The composer seizes upon the *sequentia* as an opportunity: he writes his text and melody, putting together its elements out of a rich supply of materials at hand, according to laws known only to an artist in the process of creation. He may, of course, use techniques or ideas from the *sequentia* or even the Alleluia—turns of phrase, the idea of motivic repetition, a particularly impressive arch form of a recently composed Alleluia melody. In some cases, as we saw, he uses an Alleluia incipit; and in our present imaginative context we can remark the number of times he does this, instead of worrying about the number of times he does not. It is just as easy to imagine him using only the *style* of a Gregorian incipit. Those sequence incipits that sound so tantalizingly like Alleluias that *should* be familiar (but cannot be found) were probably intended to create the impression, and to fulfill the function, of an Alleluia intonation in the Gregorian manner. And governing the whole process would be the concept of a new artistic form, realized in a measure limited only by the composer's imagination and skill.

Such a process of composition could bridge the gap between Amalarius' *sequentia* of 830 and, say, LAUDES DEO in 850—if, and only if, the process is allowed to include a large admixture of artistic fancy and originality, unrestricted by ideas of what might be possible or permissible. Such a process would account easily for those sequences in group B— "Justus ut palma major," SALUS AETERNA, EN VIRGINUM AGMINA—that seemed in melody or text to be extensions of their Alleluias in some degree. And only such a process could make sense out of EN VIRGINUM AGMINA, which includes side by side a phrase that seems to reproduce the rhapsodic effect of a *sequentia* and one that has an uncompromising recitation character and verse formula. The appearance of rhapsodic extension, it should be noted, is achieved here by manipulation of motives, in a way that certainly recalls the structure of the later Gregorian Alleluias of the eighth century (while going beyond them in constructivism), but is quite dissimilar to the earlier Gregorian repertory. The particular kind of motivic construction in the sequence can, I think, be taken as Frankish, specifically as a Frankish means of understanding and reproducing melodic spans supported in Gregorian art by a less definable technique.

In any case, we have to do not with unthinking habit or reflex but with conscious rapprochment: the effect of the *sequentia* is being reproduced for a purpose in a context other than its normal one, or at least in a context with dimensions far exceeding those of a *sequentia*, dimensions that can include other, sharply contrasting elements. As a corollary, it can be said that the closeness to the *sequentia* is one of style, not necessarily one of chronology or development; for if the rapprochement is by choice rather than reflex, then we need not think of, say, SALUS AETERNA as earlier than the larger pieces of group A. At any moment within the development of the sequence—later as well as earlier—a composer could have elected to write a melody that resembled an Alleluia in some way, whether by quoting an incipit or by imitating rhapsodic extension. Indeed, only the factor of choice makes sense out of the apparently strong tendency for Alleluia quotations, as well as Alleluia-incipits (phrase 1 = "Alleluia") to *increase* in the tenth century as compared to the ninth.

So while it is possible, granting the proper conditions, for some sequences to have been composed with the *sequentia* in mind, it seems clear that the composers of the sequences in group A had their minds fixed on other things. Indeed, while the composers of group A can be imagined to proceed directly to their goals in the construction of text and music, those of group B seem to hesitate among alternative associations with Alleluias and other aspects of liturgy and music, producing alternate or even conflicting relationships and versions—as if their allegiance were somehow split between the *sequentia* and the kind of piece represented by group A.

The manifold features of the early repertory require manifold explanations; a single, straightline theory of development from a single starting point, especially the Alleluia, will not do. And any explanation that accounts for the development taking place within the limits circa 830–850, as assumed, must include the fact of a creative leap. That assumption may or may not be justified, but we should not let our own inadequate information of the conditions of musical composition blind us to the possibility that it could have happened. It is we who would lose by requiring the excitement of new artistic creation to be spread over the preceding two or three centuries, in timid adaptation and adjustment of handed-down materials.

Primarily because of the Alleluia relationship, the sequence has been involved in questions of liturgy, not infrequently with the effect that restrictions are imagined to have been operative upon the artistic conception of the sequence. The sequence is sometimes thought to be "liturgical" in the sense that it is circumscribed in its use of musical and literary materials by its function at Mass. It is also called "para-liturgical," sometimes with the implication that it did not satisfy "official" requirements of liturgy. Recent ideas of liturgical reform, not to mention the merits of the case itself, invite and encourage a less bureaucratic approach to the position of the sequence in Carolingian liturgy.

One customary meaning of "liturgical" is "conventual." That is, a "liturgical" text should properly express the intention of the whole congregation gathered together; it should not be merely personal in the sense of being idiosyncratic; not contentious or divisive. It follows that liturgical texts are properly cast in first person plural—"we"—not first person singular. In this sense, proses are universally "liturgical" (a *credo* in Notker's JUDICEM NOS is the only exception that comes to mind).

This is surely a reasonable conclusion, but perhaps the ease and reasonableness with which we arrive at it makes us overlook some of the historical anomalies. The model of "objective conventual" poetry is usually taken to be the psalms as used in the Gregorian Propers; from the sixth century on, these psalmodic Propers were the bulwark of good liturgical taste against the *psalmi idiotici*, texts newly composed by individuals.[10] But the psalmist himself frequently speaks in first person singular, and it is a far cry from his im-

10. P. Wagner, *Einführung in die Gregorianischen Melodien. I: Ursprung und Entwicklung der liturgischen Gesangsformen* (Leipzig 1911), p. 43.

passioned Hebraic expressivity to the language of the West-Frankish prose (to say nothing of Notker). The psalms appear "objective" in their Gregorian settings due to chronological and cultural distance, which must have been as important a factor in sixth-century Rome as in twentieth-century America. Perhaps, too, the music has something to do with it, even though the same confusion may obtain there too. In any case, the "we/I" distinction may be too broad to reveal by itself the truly liturgical quality of ninth-century texts.

Another common application of "liturgical" is that a liturgical piece has a recognized position in the "official" order of service—at Mass or in the Office. Thus we could say that the sequence was not liturgical because no provision was made for it, either by rubric or repertory, in the earliest chant books representing the Gregorian rite brought north from Rome. Or we could say that the *sequentia* was liturgical because it was attached to the Alleluia (which did have an official position) by Amalarius, who was an "official" of the Church. But Amalarius was discredited, on other grounds, in the Council of Quierzy in 838.[11] Other, later officials, however, gave the sequence a recognized place in the Mass. But we could also say that only five sequences are liturgical because only five appear in modern official chant books—appea*red*, that is, before the Council of Rome 1964, called "Vatican II." And when we take into consideration that the Introit (among other items) could be called unliturgical because apparently not provided for in the order of service before the fourth century, it becomes clear that this criterion of "liturgical" is difficult to apply in any universal sense, being largely an historical matter: liturgy is what the Church says it is at any given moment. Even that is indeterminate to some degree, for ad hoc appeals to the diocesan liturgical authority or to the Sacred Congregation of Rites, as to their ninth-century counterparts, are difficult to make and not assured of conclusive results. The sequence was not a liturgical chant before it was invented; the Franks invented it, and then, for good measure, made it official; but these things take time. The critical point would be, to what degree, and in what manner, did the intention to make the sequence an official part of the service affect the design of early sequences?

The most common scholarly application of "liturgical" is in the sense of "calendric": a sequence is liturgical if clearly intended for a specific feast of the church year. We should note that this meaning is fundamentally alien to the first three Christian centuries, before the Church entered into and sanctified the secular calendar. Speaking of the fourth century, Dom Gregory Dix writes:

> [The eucharist] ceased to be regarded primarily as a rite which manifested and secured the *eternal consequences* of redemption, a rite which by manifesting their true being as eternally 'redeemed' momentarily transported those who took part in it beyond the alien and hostile world of time into the Kingdom of God and the World to come. Instead, the eucharist came to be thought of primarily as the representation, the enactment before God, of the *historical process* of redemption, of the historical events of the crucifixion and resurrection of Jesus by which redemption had been achieved.[12]

11. C. J. Hefele, *Historie des Conciles* (trans. and ed. M. Leclercq), vol. IV, pp. 102–103.
12. *The Shape of the Liturgy* (Glasgow 1945), p. 305.

As is well known, the Eastern Church never experienced, at Mass, the degree of calendric "properizing" found in the Latin West. So the calendric application is appropriate only to the Latin West, and—like the "official" application—subject to historical changes not merely in the addition of new feasts but in the degree of strictness with which the idea of a fixed, specific calendar of feasts was observed. Arbitrary applications of this calendric meaning, depending far too much on post-Tridentine ideas of liturgical propriety, have it seems to me been serious obstruction to an understanding of the early sequence.

The whole matter of relationship to the Alleluia, as already discussed, falls under this heading, for one of the clearest ways of making the sequence calendric is through association with an officially assigned Alleluia; and if it is assumed that the sequence, as a liturgical or paraliturgical chant, must be specific to a day in the liturgical calendar, then it lies close at hand to assume or construct a relationship to an Alleluia in every case. Beyond that, there has been on one hand a tendency to require every text to have been intended for a specific feast, on the other hand to criticize a text for not properly implementing the specific festal association forced upon it. It may well be that specificity is a virtue; but it is a literary, more precisely, a poetic virtue, pertaining to image and intent, not a liturgical one. In what calendric way is the *Te deum* or the *Gloria in excelsis* specific?

At this point must be recalled the well-known facts about the calendric assignments of the Alleluia itself in the ninth century. In the earliest manuscripts with Gregorian propers (texts only, no musical notation), only some Alleluias are assigned to regular positions in the liturgical calendar; the others are placed in a list to be used as needed—especially for Sundays after Pentecost. Local usage assigned Alleluias in various ways, to the extent that the assignments have been developed by modern scholars into a means of determining manuscript provenance.[13]

This optional aspect of the ninth-century Alleluia seems to have little direct bearing on the use of Alleluias in sequences. However, it surely provided the atmosphere in which Notker could interpret Alleluia relationships as he pleased, as in the case of "Laetatus sum." And in general, the existence of the option in the Alleluia should indicate to us that insofar as sequence is related to Alleluia, it is related to something not fixed but in a state of becoming. In going over the Alleluias involved in group B to see what their status in the calendar was, one can observe that on one hand there seems to have been no one principle of selection operative in this group, while on the other hand many of these Alleluias can be imagined to have some special—and different—property responsible for use in a sequence.

Alleluia Pascha nostrum
Alleluia Justus ut palma
Alleluia Benedictus es
Alleluia Ostende
Alleluia Adducentur (Veni domine)

13. See M. Huglo, "Les listes alléluiatiques dans les témoins du Gradual gregorien," *Speculum musicae artis. Festgabe für Heinrich Husmann zum 60. Geburtstag* (Munich 1970), pp. 219–227.

TABLE IV

Calendric Assignment of Early Sequences

West-Frankish		Notker	
Advent			
1	SALUS AETERNA		
(1)	VENIET REX		
2	REGNANTEM SEMPITERNA		
(2)	PANGAT LAUDES		
3	JUBILEMUS OMNES		
Christmas			
4	CHRISTI HODIERNA		
(4)	REX NOSTRAS		
(4)	ECCE JAM		
5	HÆC DIES QUAM EXCELSUS		
6	HÆC DIES EST SANCTA		
			[NATUS ANTE SAECULA
St. Stephen			
7	HÆC EST SANCTA	8	HANC CONCORDI
St. John Ev.			
(6)	ORGANICIS	10	JOHANNES JESU
Holy Innocents			
		(6)	LAUS TIBI CHRISTE
Epiphany			
8	EPIPHANIAM	15	FESTA CHRISTI
Easter			
9	NUNC EXULTET	9	LAUDES SALVATORI.
(8)	ECCE VICIT		
10	CLARA GAUDIA		
(10)	DIC NOBIS		
11	HÆC EST VERA REDEMPTIO		
			[AGNI PASCHALIS
12	LAUDES DEO	5	GRATES SALVATORI
		12	LAUDES DEO CONCINAT
			[CARMEN SUO
		7	HÆC EST SANCTA
		16	JUDICEM NOS
Ascension			
13	REX OMNIPOTENS		
			[SUMMI TRIUMPHUM
			[CHRISTUS HUNC DIEM

TABLE IV (*continued*)

West-Frankish texts		Notker's texts	
	Pentecost		
		13	SANCTI SPIRITUS
			[BENEDICTO GRATIAS
	St. John Bapt.		
14 PRAECURSOR			
(6) ECCE DIES		6	SANCTI BAPTISTAE
	Ss. Peter & Paul		
		(9)	PETRE SUMME
	St. Laurence		
		(10)	LAURENTI DAVID
	St. Gall		
		14	DILECTE DEO
	St. Benedict		
(9) ARCE SUPERNA			
	B.V.M.		
(8) GAUDE EJA			
(11) BEATA TU VIRGO			
		11	GAUDE MARIA (Circumcision)
			[CONCENTU PARILI
		4	CONGAUDENT (Assumption)
		3	STIRPE MARIA (Nativity)
	Common of Saints		
		1	CLARE SANCTORUM (Apostles)
			[AGONE TRIUMPHALI
		(5)	TUBAM BELLICOSAM (Martyrs)
		(7)	QUID TU VIRGO (Martyrs)
		(14)	REX REGUM (Confessors)
(3) EN VIRGINUM (Virgins)			
			[SCALAM AD CAELOS
		2	PSALLAT ECCLESIA (Dedication)
			[OMNES SANCTI SERAPHIM
	Holy Trinity		
15 OMNIPOTENS DEUS			
	General and topical		
16 FORTIS ATQUE AMARA			
(4) PANGE DEO			
(8) SEMPER REGNANS			

Sequence, Alleluia, and Liturgy   405

Alleluia Laetatus sum
Alleluia Dominus in Sina
Alleluia Vox exultationis

Justus ut palma is one of the favorite texts for saints and martyrs, and its melody is one of the most distinguished representatives of a group in *protus* (D) that must have been prominent in the eighth-century repertory. Alleluia *Benedictus es*, on the other hand, is a late piece and not a particularly distinguished one, but it had the advantage of being unequivocally associated with the Trinity-Mass, which was valuable for anyone wishing to write a Trinity sequence.

Comparable reasons cannot be suggested in every case; but it does seem that some such *ad hoc* association, including but hardly limited to calendric assignment, must have been at work. The important moment, it seems to me, is that *when* a sequence was connected to an Alleluia, it was because something in a particular Alleluia either fired a composer's imagination, or served to illustrate and support an idea already formed. The Alleluia represented—not restrictions—but opportunities, of which the excuse to have a sequence sung at Mass on a particular day was only one.

Calendric propriety is largely a matter of texts: we can tell by reading a text whether it is proper to a specific feast, and if so, which one. Melodies are not proper in the same way, for their propriety is through association, either with an Alleluia or with some other already existing chant. In the early repertory, this kind of association seems to have had very limited effect. In any case, the associations, if present in the West-Frankish use, were not conveyed to Notker.

Table IV is designed to compare the West-Frankish calendric assignment of the early repertory with Notker's use of the same melodies. Both columns are arranged to the liturgical calendar, as labeled. The West-Frankish pieces are numbered consecutively; these numbers appear in Notker's column attached to the same melodies. The numerical order in Notker's column, then, indicates the amount of shuffling that took place in the calendric assignment of melodies.

Only in two cases, Notker's LAUDES DEO CONCINAT and LAUDES SALVATORI, is his calendric assignment the same as the West-Frankish one. It is extremely interesting, if inscrutable, that these cases involve two closely related melodies, one of which (LAUDES DEO) was the first Notker used; and that the feast is Easter.

Aside from those cases, and the correspondence of SANCTI BAPTISTAE and ECCE DIES for John Baptist, the calendric assignments absolutely fail to correspond—and this must be taken as the primary fact of the Table. Nor is there as much coincidence as there might be when two of Notker's texts, or two West-Frankish texts, are set to the same melody.

HANC CONCORDI St. Stephen, Martyr
PETRE SUMME Peter and Paul, Apostles

JOHANNES JESU St. John, Apostle and Evangelist
LAURENTI DAVID St. Laurence, Martyr

LAUS TIBI CHRISTE Holy Innocents (Martyrs)

Sᴀɴᴄᴛᴇ ᴊᴏʜᴀɴɴᴇꜱ ʙᴀᴘᴛɪꜱᴛᴇ St. John Baptist (Martyr)

Hᴀ̃ᴄ ᴇꜱᴛ ꜱᴀɴᴄᴛᴀ Octave of Easter
Qᴜɪᴅ ᴛᴜ ᴠɪʀɢᴏ Martyrs

Dɪʟᴇᴄᴛᴇ ᴅᴇᴏ St. Gall, Confessor
Rᴇx ʀᴇɢᴜᴍ Confessors

Gʀᴀᴛᴇꜱ ꜱᴀʟᴠᴀᴛᴏʀɪ Easter
Tᴜʙᴀᴍ ʙᴇʟʟɪᴄᴏꜱᴀᴍ Martyrs

What agreement can be found here depends on the classifications within the "Common of Saints," which as a ninth-century liturgical category seems to be a matter of considerable difficulty and little stability. For the West-Frankish duplicate texts, considering only those taken up in this study, some cases show a clear calendric identity, such as ᴄʟᴀʀᴀ ɢᴀᴜᴅɪᴀ / ᴅɪᴄ ɴᴏʙɪꜱ, but this identity is ignored by Notker. One West-Frankish sequence was used at Easter (ᴇᴄᴄᴇ ᴠɪᴄɪᴛ), Epiphany (ᴇᴘɪᴘʜᴀɴɪᴀᴍ), and as a half-Marian, general intercession (ɢᴀᴜᴅᴇ ᴇɪᴀ).

Against all of this it might be argued (among other things) that Notker's repertory is strictly calendric, and that this fact outweighs all other uncertainties. I think it has quite the opposite effect. But first, it is permissible to call to mind some of the uncertainties in Notker's own assignments. Von den Steinen describes the propriety of the finished *Liber hymnorum* very persuasively, but without quarreling with the conclusion one can note some interesting facts about the ingredients—as does Von den Steinen himself. Sᴀɴᴄᴛɪ ꜱᴘɪʀɪᴛᴜꜱ is primarily about the gifts of the Holy Spirit, rather than the Feast of Pentecost; the piece is made calendric by the last half of the last couplet, *Ipse hodie . . . hunc diem gloriosum fecisti.* Qᴜɪᴅ ᴛᴜ ᴠɪʀɢᴏ may indeed have been conceived for a martyr's feast, but the poetic conceit is carried so far that the calendric function does not sit happily on the piece as it is. Similarly, in ᴛᴜʙᴀᴍ ʙᴇʟʟɪᴄᴏꜱᴀᴍ and ꜱᴄᴀʟᴀᴍ ᴀᴅ ᴄᴀᴇʟᴏꜱ Notker builds such an intensive image as to draw attention away from, rather than toward, the calendric association. Jᴜᴅɪᴄᴇᴍ ɴᴏꜱ, like its model ꜰᴏʀᴛɪꜱ ᴀᴛ\ᴏ̨ᴜ\ᴇ ᴀᴍᴀʀᴀ, is another "topical" piece; its association—if there is one —to an Alleluia is through the topic ("Deus juste judex"), and even the assignment of the Alleluia to its calendric position in the *Liber hymnorum* (Second Sunday after Easter) is a matter of Notker's personal choice. Cʟᴀʀᴇ ꜱᴀɴᴄᴛᴏʀᴜᴍ is on the *theme* of "All the apostles," there being no such feast. Gᴀᴜᴅᴇ ᴍᴀʀɪᴀ is in honor of Maria, rather than being proper to a feast. Whether or not one agrees with Von den Steinen's description of how Notker "recognized" ʟᴀᴜᴅᴇꜱ ᴅᴇᴏ to be his "Friday hymn" after the rest of the Easter-week cycle was finished, the fact remains that ʟᴀᴜᴅᴇꜱ ᴅᴇᴏ must have been originally conceived merely as an Easter piece.[14] And ʜᴀ̃ᴄ ᴇꜱᴛ ꜱᴀɴᴄᴛᴀ, while clearly appropriate to some day after Easter Sunday, makes no reference to themes one might expect on the Octave of Easter. What these cases show is borne out in the other, more clearly calendric sequences of the *Liber hymnorum*: theme and image run so strongly through all the texts as to obliterate the sense of *mere* calendric association, and—on occasion—pre-empt or override it as the governing conception.

14. *Notker* I, pp. 237–238.

To return to the implication of Notker's calendric cycle for the West-Frankish analogs, Notker forged his cycle (Table IV tells us) by original, individual adaptation. Yes, he made a cycle, but it was of his own making, and that shows how little sense of calendar there was in his sources, either in individual melodies or in the repertory as a whole. Notker's treatment of second texts (HANC CONCORDI—PETRE SUMME, for instance) is symptomatic: there seem, indeed, to be "hidden connections," as Von den Steinen says, between such pairs, even in spite of some superficial calendric impropriety; and if these connections are "hidden," in Notker's own work, what are we to say about such connections between texts of two different West-Frankish authors, or between two different melodies? There is nothing there on which to build a case for strong calendric determinants.

The negative conclusion, then, is that the calendar of liturgical occasions does not impose significant limitations or requirements on the composer; it only offers him opportunities, of which he may or may not avail himself. And then, given texts that are not strictly calendric, we should further conclude that texts we might in other circumstances ascribe to strictly calendric impulse owe their existence to something slightly different. For example, the relatively large number of Easter texts might, in strictly calendric context, indicate a demand for special texts for the days of Easter week, or for the Sundays of Paschaltide. Von den Steinen argues that this was the case, at least for Easter week, in the *Liber hymnorum*. But it was clearly not the case in the West-Frankish repertory: the calendric casualness of the repertory as a whole encourages us to understand the multitude of Easter pieces rather in terms of the richness of the Easter theme—especially the Harrowing of Hell. And if it was liturgical propriety that encouraged the sequence in Paschaltide but discouraged it in Lent (as in the case of the Alleluia), that did not keep the author of FORTIS ATQUE AMARA from his somber theme. In any case, Lent versus Paschaltide is a very broad "liturgical" distinction. In fact, the calendric distribution in the West-Frankish column of Table IV is "liturgical" to about the degree one would find in an American Protestant hymnal of a thousand years later, a type of source that would not generally be considered "liturgical" —least of all by its customary users. Such a source would contain hymns for Christmas and Easter, perhaps a few saints' days (depending on the denomination) and the rest topical or "general" items.

We should not imagine, then, for the early repertory, that the composer begins by consulting the prosarium to see which Holy Day or Saints Day needed a sequence, then the cantatorium to find the proper Alleluia, then the sequentiarium to see if there existed an (official?) *sequentia* for that Alleluia, then proceeded to underlay the *sequentia* with a gloss or commentary of the Alleluia verse. Precisely this process *can* be imagined for the short aparallel texts of group C (except that they were not systematically selected for the calendar), but it is in this respect that the early sequence differs so much from the *sequentia*. In the later development of the repertory (the late tenth century), the sources do indeed suggest that a filling out of the calendar became a stronger factor than before, but this factor operated more on the compilers than on the composers. And while proses for individual saints' days multiplied rapidly, so did proses for Christmas and Easter. The early repertory seems to owe its genesis largely to artistic impulse; what calendric distribution there is can best be ascribed to a tendency of a creative spirit to seize upon themes and topics not yet attempted by others.

The Franks encountered Roman liturgy at a point that seems to have had little relationship to their own inner artistic state. What they encountered—what Charlemagne imposed on them—was a highly refined system of sung ritual and ceremonial with specific daily prescription throughout the year. This was the end product of several centuries of development in and around Rome. Frankish creative energies, however, were hardly at a terminal stage of development, and as a result Frankish approaches as well as results in the liturgical arts were very different. Frankish energies could not be simply "plugged in" to the Roman liturgical calendar; nor did they merely ooze timidly out around the edges, as has been suggested. The creative spirit blew as it pleased. For the Franks, liturgy was in many respects something they themselves made, not merely something they did according to the book. The best proof of that is the difference (if it can be subsumed under that mild term) between the liturgy the Franks inherited from the ancient world in the eighth century and the one they bequeathed to the modern world in the sixteenth.

Is the early sequence non-liturgical for being not strictly calendric? Of course not. It *is* liturgical, because designed as an appropriate conventual response in melody and word to divine worship. Whether through the formulas (noticed especially by Von den Steinen) proclaiming "today's festivity"—HÆC EST SANCTA, ECCE DIES, HÆC DIES QUAM EXCELSUS, HÆC EST VERA REDEMPTIO—all derived ultimately from verse 23 of Psalm 117 (English Psalm 118,24), *Hæc dies quam fecit Dominus*, used in Gregorian chant for Easter; whether through all the other rhetorical means of exhortation to concelebration; as expressions of Christian response to the epic of salvation, spelled out by the Church in daily worship—in these ways is the sequence truly liturgical.

In the sequence, the Franks were initiating a new line of music for worship, in effect, a new genre of liturgy. That it failed to correspond to the imported Roman rite is a sign only of its originality. That it failed to survive the Roman rite, that it ceased to be a living art form by the end of the Middle Ages, is a sign only that—unlike the Gregorian chant—its substance became an integral part of the mainstream of European music.

XXIII

The Sequence in Ninth-Century
Life and Letters

Perhaps the most discouraging difficulty of research into the early sequence has been the lack of identity, of relationship to other aspects of Carolingian culture. No name of place or person—Notker always excepted—is attached to an early sequence in such a way as to provide a clear, informative identity.

The lack of names is part of a broader gap that exists between music, that is, actual chant repertories, and Carolingian life and letters in general. In terms of raw material, the music historian is apt to find the ninth century sparsely furnished with historical fact. To a large extent he lacks, for music, the catalogs of persons and places available in other historical disciplines. General historians are accustomed to using such standard tools as *Jahrbücher des fränkischen Reiches unter Karl dem Grossen* by S. Abel and B. Simpson (1889), which accounts for the emperor's movements, not just year-by-year or month-by-month, but often day-by-day throughout a large part of the century, by the capitularies dated and signed by the emperor on his perpetual administrative circuit. On a less formal basis, much is known about the movements of other persons of the court, their characters, activities and escapades, especially in the self-conscious and verbal days of Charlemagne, but also under his successors Louis the Pious (814–840) and Charles the Bald (king, 838–, emperor 875–877).

Church affairs are scarcely less well documented. Comprehensive lists of bishops and archbishops, extending back to late antiquity, provide hundreds of names in Carolingian times alone.[1] The numerous councils of the ninth century are voluminously reported in volumes 3 and 4 of the standard work of C. J. Hefele, translated and edited by Dom H. Leclercq as *Histoire des Conciles* (11 vols. 1907–1952). Just as it has been possible to write numerous detailed biographical sketches of prominent persons, both ecclesiastics and laymen,[2] so it has been possible to write continuous histories of towns and localities. Charlemagne him-

---

1. *Dictionaire d'archeologie chrétienne et de liturgie*, vol. 9, 1, "Listes Episcopales."
2. E. L. Duckett, *Carolingian Portraits, A Study of the Ninth Century* (Ann Arbor 1962); Ellard, *Master Alcuin*.

self, of course, is a favorite topic; but there is also a formidable literature on, say, Hincmar of Rheims.

Accounts in the form of chronicles are numerous in the ninth century, and often very detailed for the years in which they were written. The Annals of St. Bertin, the Annals of Fulda are representative of monastic chronicles (the inexhaustible *Monumenta Germaniae Historica* prints many of them); there are also such works as Flodard's *Historia Ecclesiae Remensis* for Reims, and Nithard's fascinating account of mid-century politics and military adventure.[3] The most famous monasteries—Jumièges, St. Riquier, Corbie, St. Bertin, St. Amand, Prüm, Fulda, Lorsch, Gorze, Luxeuil, St. Gall, Reichenau (to make an arbitrary and purely illustrative selection)—coexisted with a very large number of monastic establishments (as shown by the listing in L. H. Cottineau, *Répertoire topobibliographique des abbayes et prieurés*, 1935–37), ranging from solitaries in the wilderness to vast complexes of up to four hundred monks, supported and attended by hundreds of lay servants. Merovingian times had produced an army of local saints, listed in A. Molinier's *Les sources de l'histoire de France*, and their cult in turn focused monastic inclinations into places of observance all over Europe.

Although a great deal of monastic life is unrecorded, precious documents remain to give some idea of the scale and manner in which they were conducted. The continuing series *Corpus consuetudinum monasticorum* edited by K. Hallinger (1964—) is very informative. Two especially revealing documents, edited long ago, show the material basis upon which monasteries stood. In 1853 M. B. Guérard published *Polyptyque de l'abbaye de Saint-Remi de Reims*, and in 1895 A. Lognon published a similar document, *Polyptyque de l'Abbaye de Saint-Germain des Prés au temps de l'abbé Irminon*. These documents list all the land holdings of the monastery, manse by manse, with the names of the tenants, and their rents in the form of livestock, produce, building materials, and gold. (For the tax collector, no one is anonymous; but it is very reassuring—for me at least—to know that on a certain manse in Villeneuve-Saint-George there lived a *colonus* named Ansgaudus and his wife Radoildus, *homines sancti Germani*, with their five sons Ansgarius, Eligaudus, Radoardus, Radulfus, Radoinus.) The rents, when added together, indicate the income of the monastery, which was obviously far above a mere subsistence level. It is abundantly clear from these and other sources that the wealthier monasteries had the wherewithal to support whatever arts they fancied. The famous "Plan of St. Gall" shows in exquisite detail the physical plant that was considered necessary for a well-appointed monastery.[4]

One of the most fascinating monastic chronicles is the *Gesta abbatum Fontanellensium*, for St. Wandrille or Fontanelle.[5] The account lists among other things the possessions of Bishop Ansegisus as he willed them at his death. The amount of gold, silver, and other precious items, suggests the rate at which wealth could accumulate even under monastic conditions.

3. *Annales Bertiniani, Monumenta Germaniae Historica*, Series 26: *Scriptores rerum germanicarum in usum scholarum separatim editi*, vol. 5; *Annales Fuldenses*, vol. 7. Flodoard, *Historia Remensis ecclesiae: Les annales de Flodoard*, ed. P. Lauer (Paris 1905). Nithard, *Historiarum libri quatuor: Histoire des fils de Louis le Pieux*, ed. P. Lauer (Paris 1926).
4. Walter Horn and Ernest Born, *The Plan of St. Gall* (University of California, 1975).
5. *Gesta abbatum Fontanellensium, Monumenta Germaniae Historica, Scriptores*, vol. 28 (1886), pp. 47–59.
See also E. Lesne, *Histoire de la propriété ecclésiastique en France: IV—Les Livres, "Scriptoria' et Bibliotheques du commencement du VIIIe a la fin du XIe siècle*, pp. 199–200.

The number of persons and places to which he bequeathed these items indicates the far-flung nature of monastic connections (it was not unusual for an influential house to have dependencies in all corners of Western Europe), a fact that gives support to the other evidences of widespread travel and communication. One modern description of Trier in the second half of the tenth century says,

> To get some idea of the fluid state of the church as a whole, we might look at Trier in the second half of the tenth century. We find there an abbot from England, monks from all over France, monks from Flanders, monks from Holland, not to mention monks from parts of Germany like Fulda and Aachen. Where the outward radiation of Trier influences is concerned, we find the archbishop's own representative in Normandy and England, a Trier priest in Wiltshire, Trier monks in France, Trier monks propably in Italy and Trier monks scattered through large areas of Germany—in Magdeburg, Cologne, Regensburg, Tegernsee, St. Gallen, Worms and Hildesheim. Trier, of course, was a particularly important centre but it does no more than mirror the active circulation within the Church as a whole.[6]

We can remember that—according to Notker's story—it was a monk from Jumièges that brought LAUDES DEO to St. Gall.

The account of Fontanelle also includes several lists of books, reflecting relatively rich holdings at the abbey in the eighth and early ninth centuries. A monastic library was designed to contain one particular field—scriptural and pastoral studies, patristics. Within that field a typical small collection could include enough material to occupy a diligent student for a number of years. It would be an erudite man—and, given inclination and grace, an edified one—who had digested all the books given by Ansegisus to the monastery at Flavigny. The list includes works of Jerome, Augustine, Ambrose, John Chrysostom, Origen, Isidor, Hilary, Gregory, Bede, Prosper, Cyprian, Alcuin, the Rules of St. Basil as well as St. Benedict, and Histories of Eusebius, Sozomenus, Theodoretus, and Socrates.

One detail of these and other such lists manifests the gap between musical and other kinds of sources in the ninth century. The contents of almost all the books listed at Fontanelle can be identified (and have been edited in modern times). Not so with liturgical books (and chant books)—unless they happened to be sufficiently precious in their format or binding to warrant precise description. A typical entry appears in the list of books copied by Harduin, a monk in a nearby cell: on the one hand he is credited with volumes containing the Four Gospels, Epistles of Paul, Homilies of Gregory, Augustine's City of God (books 11–18), Bede—all quite identifiable; on the other hand, with "three volumes of sacramentaries, one lectionary, one gospel book, . . ." and, for us, "one antiphonale of the Roman Church." We can guess what sort of a book this was, but we cannot know.

And so it is with the situation as a whole. The gap between the scarcity of musical facts and sources, and the relative abundance in other fields, cannot be filled, at least at present. We cannot yet produce, from this wealth of material, the names and addresses of the men who

6. C. R. Dodwell and D. H. Turner, *Reichenau Reconsidered: A Reassessment of the Place of Reichenau in Ottonian art* (Warburg Institute Surveys II, 1965), p. 30.

created the sequence; so far we do not have even any hard clues. Such an interesting and informative study as that by Bruno Stäblein on the melody for ECCE VICIT, linking it by its St. Gall melody-title "Concordia" to social and political events and circumstances of the middle of the century, remains circumstantial in nature.[7]

So the gap remains, but the problem it represents needs to be understood precisely. Knowing by name the locale and personnel associated with the early sequence would not increase the reality of its existence. The sequence is there, in itself a hard, obstinate fact of history. It is the circumstances that need to be related to the sequence, rather than the other way around. The importance of this understanding becomes clear when we consider the powerful reasons that could be adduced against the very existence of such an art form during the last half of the ninth century.

The Normans! . . . beginning in 814, they appeared at Noirmoutier, then in 820 along the north coast of the Frankish realm; at that time they were scared off, but from 834 on, for a hundred years, they struck repeatedly, and with terrifying success, at the Frankish realms.[8] By the end of the century they had, it would seem, devastated a large portion of Europe, reduced the Frankish rulers to impotence, and generally disrupted social and economic life to such an extent that culture of any kind could not be maintained. And yet these were the years in which the sequence came to fulfillment. The music historian must find a way to read the record so as to allow the actual to become possible.

That the sequence could and did exist under the scourge of the Normans is documented by the text SUMMA PIA, the fragment of GAUDE EJA (melody of ECCE VICIT) that preserves the invocation for aid against the Normans. Whatever the Normans did, their coming did not prevent the writing of this text, but rather stimulated it. Beyond that, the overall picture of desolation that appears unrelieved in modern summaries on the one hand, and in contemporary deplorations on the other, is altered to some degree by certain interstices that show up in the actual historical record. For example, the Normans struck Dorstad in 834, and apparently laid it waste. The extent of the actual damage must be assessed, however, against the fact that they struck three more times, then *occupied the town in 840*. Clearly the first four raids had left something worth occupying.

To point this out is not to deny the raids or their terrible effects upon the victims, but merely to find some room for the sequence in the overall picture drawn by historians. The raids were at certain places, at certain times; they were not constant military pressure exerted against the whole realm, or even the whole north coast, throughout the half-century or even a large portion of that time. For twenty years there were so few raids in Flanders that when the Normans returned after 870 they found a rich, thriving community to plunder anew. Reims saw no Normans before 882; and even before 900 Archbishop Foulques was rebuilding his cathedral as if he did not expect to see them again.[9]

Other details permit latitude, too. For how long a period did a raid disrupt a monastery? Noirmoutier eventually had to be abandoned; but at St. Riquier, on one occasion, the monks

7. "Die Sequenzmelodie Concordia und ihr geschichtlicher Hintergrund."
8. One of the best accounts in T. D. Kendrick, *A History of the Vikings* (London 1930), Chap. VII.
9. Flodoard, *Historia Remensis ecclesiae*, IV, viii; see also IV, xiii.

fled into the hills, then after three weeks returned to the monastery. Monastic buildings were usually made of wood; that, of course, is the reason why they were so easily put to the torch. But by the same token they could be quickly rebuilt. The *Gesta abbatum Fontanellensium* brings this out clearly in bewailing what was felt to be a much more grievous fate—the lay abbot. Woe to the monastery, says the account, if it falls unto the hands of a lay abbot, for then its lands are given away and can never be recovered. Far better that it should be burned to the ground, *for then it can be rebuilt*.[10] And the wealth of a monastery lay largely in the soil. Modern experience has shown that even a far more sophisticated campaign of terror by fire may not succeed in reducing an economy based largely on rural agriculture.

One of the reasons the raids were as devastating as they were is that there was often no defense at all. Imperial forces could not be mustered quickly enough to meet the hit-and-run attacks. Under the empire, apparently, local landowners were not willing to take the responsibility for protection; perhaps it seemed cheaper to accept the losses—sporadic and unpredictable—than to take on the expense of preventing them. At least one agonized first-hand account in a monastic chronicle includes the exclamation *nullo resistente*—as if in echo of the psalmist's *et non est qui adiuvet*![11] That, seemingly, was an accusation directed at the higher powers whose duty was protection. A well-prepared and motivated Frankish force could rout the Normans in a pitched battle, and even the inhabitants of a beseiged town, on occasion, sallied forth and put them to flight. But Charles the Bald often found it cheaper to buy them off, and Louis the Stammerer finally let Rollo settle in what was to be Normandy, for the same reason. The overall picture in this respect is one of a wealthy, complacent society, injured and even more insulted by the raids precisely because they were so unused to violent disruption. Society-at-large seemed concerned to cut its losses and escape from the situation with as little inconvenience as possible.

Like all disasters, these were infinitely painful for the victims; yet between and around the disasters cultural life not only went on but—in the case of music—flourished. The career of Hucbald of St. Amand shows this clearly.[12] Born around 840, he was trained at St. Amand under his uncle Milo. He came into contact with Heiric of Auxerre (who was not, however, Hucbald's teacher, for as Van de Vyver pointed out Heiric was born about the same time, 841), and also with Remi of Auxerre. Hucbald was charged with organizing schools at Reims and St. Bertin; in 872, after his uncle's death, he seems to have returned to St. Amand, where he functioned as cantor and teacher until his death in 931. He wrote a musical treatise, as well as a set of *Gloria* tropes and some offices; but he could just as well have written sequences. How many Hucbalds would be necessary to account for the ninth-century sequence? A dozen trained, gifted cantors circulating around the West-Frankish monasteries could surely provide the base for the repertory as we know it. The cruel Norman raids can not be imagined so pervasive as to interdict the activities of such a group.

10. *Gesta abbatum Fontanellensium*, p. 32.
11. *Annales Bertiniani*, pp. 32(845), 35(847), 36(848), 37(849).
12. See Dom Rembert Weakland, "Hucbald as Musician and Theorist," *Musical Quarterly* XLII (1956), pp. 66–84; "The Compositions of Hucbald," *Etudes Grégoriennes*, III (1959), pp. 153–162. A. Van der Vyver, "Hucbald de Saint-Armand, écolâtre, et l'invention du Nombre d'Or," *Université de Louvain: Recuiel de travaux d'histoire et de philologie*, 3ᵐᵉ série, 26ᵐᵉ fasc., pp. 61–79 (Louvain 1947).

But was not the general cultural decline, the inner decadence of the empire (quite apart from the Normans), so severe in the last half of the ninth century as to make the appearance of a group of trained, gifted cantors unthinkable? The sons and grandsons of Charlemagne quarreled and warred continually among themselves; the empire was partitioned a dozen times in a dozen different ways; lines of authority and communication, the political machinery, the roads—all fell into decay; all the lofty values of education, letters, morals, religion, so emphasized by Charlemagne, the very idea of empire, all were disregarded; order itself gave way at the end to anarchy. Such is the picture painted by historians of the end of the Age of Charlemagne. Again, it is not for the music historian to take upon himself the revision of a general historical picture, but only to find a little elbow room for the sequence. We can note, however, that the historians who drew the picture may well have held the values of the Age of Queen Victoria, or of Bismarck, among which centralized power was one of the foremost, virtually identified with Order; and many twentieth-century historians might hold the same conviction. At any rate, the decay they trace is the decay of the *empire*, the uppermost layer of administrative order, recent in origin and superimposed on the sturdy individualism of the Frankish tribes (not to mention all the other peoples involved) only by Charlemagne himself. It can be argued that what really happened throughout the ninth century was the return of power to where it had always been—but for the genius and strength of Charlemagne—in the hands of the land-lords; these powerful faceless ones can be seen at every council of Charles the Bald, letting him know by their silent assent or lack of it what he could or could not do. And there are those who argue that local or regional administration by landed interests is not just the only real political power, but the best. However that may be, the political process in the ninth century can be construed as a change, rather than a withering away. That the empire *decayed* is unarguable; but the fact that the *empire* decayed does not in itself demonstrate that life and culture decayed. Nor should we listen only to those who favored empire, either out of devout memories, or real conviction, or expediency, to the exclusion of all other evidence. Some monasteries and towns flourished in the way of localism; culture requires only some, not universal, order.

But it was not monasticism itself so corrupt, so disordered in the second half of the ninth century that it could produce no art? There are indeed documentary evidences of corruption, and in particularly severe instances one would have to discount the establishments involved as purveyors of culture and art. There are documentary evidences of disorder, too, but these need to be treated with much greater care in interpretation. First, however, as a matter of internal consistency, it seems not entirely fair to find no evidence of good in late ninth-century monasticism. For if reform is good, if specifically the reforms of the tenth century were good, their origin has been traced to Berno, who can be regarded as a product of the ninth century.[13] And the interesting aspect is that his dreams of reform were given fulfillment with the aid—not of an Emperor Louis the Pious, who in 817 backed Benedict of Aniane in a reform from the top that never reached down—but of William of Aquitaine, one of those "anarchical" landholders so despised by the advocates of imperial power.

13. E. Sackur, *Die Cluniacenser* (Halle 1892–1894); J. H. Pignot, *Histoire de l'ordre de Cluny* (Paris 1868); Guy de Valour, *Le monachisme clunisien des origins an XVe siècle: II—L'ordre de Cluny* (Paris 1970).

The question, as phrased here, reveals the contradiction inherent in medieval Western monasticism. The purest purpose of a monastery is not the cultivation of art but of men's souls; art is a means, and a dangerous one. The history of Western monasticism could be viewed as a continual struggle between a tendency toward the production and accumulation of art forms, and the puritanical demands of reformers. Even Cluny, apparently favorable to some manifestations of artistry, seems to have treated music with rigidity and distrust, the sequence in particular.[14] In response to the question as put, a reformer might well say that only a disordered monastery would abandon itself and its calling to the production of art, which of itself could hardly be a mark of order.

The principles involved, then, are complex, and we should not conclude from the complaint of disorder that a monastery was incapable of artistic activity, for much would depend upon the intent and meaning of the complaint, much upon the actual condition of the monastery. Just as we must be circumspect in interpreting a description of dire desolation in a monastic account of a Norman raid, or a description of cultural decadence in the reminiscences of an old court scholar, so with deprecations on monastic disorder; for in this case the opposite of disorder (and antidote to it) is Benedictine order and the rule of reform, and while history shows that the genius of St. Benedict left a Rule that permitted art a happy place in the monastic life, much still depended on the temper of the reformers applying the Rule. In general it could be assumed, I think, that evidence of worldly opulence would be a better index of artistic activity than would evidence of spiritual purity. Of such opulence there was plenty in the ninth century. And if we were to interpret disorder in the sense of lack of conformity to a single kind of order, there would be evidence of a lively individuality among monasteries; that, too, would seem conducive to the generation of new musical forms.

It seems to me, then, that the image of a declining West in the second half of the ninth century permits enough exceptions and qualifications to accommodate the historical reality of the sequence. It may, of course, be profoundly indicative that Notker's sequences and all they imply were written relatively far from the Norman raids, in a monastery free for the moment of charges of corruption or disorder, an outpost of all that had been hoped for monasticism by Charles and his court two generations earlier—that, in other words, the sequence came to fulfillment only where none of the inimical conditions of the late ninth century prevailed. Still, the sequence was not created at St. Gall, nor did its subsequent development take place there; and Notker's achievement, while brilliant and abiding, was not the most indigenous to the style of melody, or the most distinctive of it. Main-line development ran through the West-Frankish monasteries; it did so whatever may be the prevailing image of that time—did so in spite of the falling-off of interest and achievement that apparently did affect the other arts. And could it not be that our image of general decay has taken shape in part to account for this decay in the other arts? Perhaps the image should be revised to account for music. Or perhaps, through cosmic recompense, music alone flourished.

14. The famous MS Paris B.N.lat. 1087 represents the eleventh-century Sequence repertory—a very limited one—at Cluny; Husmann, *Tropen-und Sequenzen Handschriften*, p. 123.

Even more delicate problems of interpretation arise when we consider the relationship of the sequence to the specific values of the Carolingian reforms. During the personal reign of Charlemagne, the salient development in literature was the attempt to restore classical letters. This attempt was expressed at the highest level by Charlemagne's grouping together at his court the best-lettered scholars of the West—Alcuin, Peter of Pisa, Theodulfus of Spain, Paul of Aquileia, Paul the Deacon.[15] At the lowest level the restoration of letters meant improving the general literacy, especially of the clergy, as promulgated in Charlemagne's famous capitulary of 789. The immediate effect of this edict is of course hard to gauge; but the results of the court literary circle are well documented and have been often studied. Classical skills and techniques were indeed restored: quantitative dactylic hexameters were composed with varying degrees of success but with great facility, judging from the vast quantity preserved. Other classical forms, especially elegaic distichs and sapphics, were copiously imitated. Classical manner and imagery were absorbed and reproduced in numerous works in prose and verse destined for court occasions, formal and informal. The assessment has been that artistic quality and originality, where present, make themselves felt in spite of the classical manner, not because of it.

The salient development in music, forming a diptych with the restoration of classical letters, was Charlemagne's promulgation of the Roman rite, including Gregorian chant. This development, also frequently studied,[16] occupied the Carolingian dynasty for a century, from 750 to 850 but most intensively under Charlemagne's personal initiative during the last quarter of the eighth century. As a result of the reform, the Frankish realm henceforth worshipped according to a modified "Gregorian" rite, relatively uniform throughout the realm, as distinct from whatever "Gallican" or "Gelasian" versions, varying widely among themselves, had been in use up to that time. It is not clear what kind of chant, or how much chant, was in use in the Frankish realm prior to the introduction of the Gregorian. The earliest chant sources present a core of Gregorian arranged according to its liturgical matrix, surrounded by non-Gregorian items that seem to be primarily new additions; but any one of these might, of course, be a survival from an older repertory, now officially superseded. Picking out presumed survivals is at best a delicate matter.

In any case, the newly imposed liturgy and chant can be identified as that used in the personal chapel of the Pope (as distinct from other versions used in Rome). It was an extremely refined repertory: in music, as in letters, Charlemagne sought the best available sources. The position of this chant in liturgy in the Frankish scene requires our careful understanding. It can hardly be imagined—nor does the evidence suggest—that the "new liturgy" was received with spontaneous enthusiasm in all quarters. History and practical experience teach us that people in general are not receptive to liturgical change; and insofar as they notice the liturgies they use, they notice the minute deviations from received custom, not the broad similarities between the new and the old. Nor would it be a persuasive argument to point out that the "new liturgy" might in fact be older than the one they had been using. What-

15. Among numerous accounts, see J. de Ghellinck, *Litterature latine au moyen age* (1939).
16. See note 4, Chapter 1.

ever the reaction of the people, the fact was that the "new liturgy" had to be pushed long and hard by the reformers, and although in the end they succeeded, the documents show that the end result was in many details so changed by adaptation that it might well have been no longer acceptable at the Gregorian source. Tradition and innovation, restoration and reform, are so inextricably and peculiarly intermixed in the imposition of the Gregorian chant on the Frankish realm that only a prolonged, discriminating discussion will ever be able to sort out the matter clearly. It is clear, however, that for the Franks the Gregorian, however "traditional" it might be, was not *their* tradition; functionally, it was an innovation. If it was a restoration, it restored something that had never been, and felt more like a reform. It is even possible that what look to us like Frankish departures or innovations from the "official, traditional" chant (meaning the Gregorian) might well be in fact continuations of well-established local traditions. This possibility has more than once been adduced to explain the sequence, among other things.

It is not, however, the only possibility. The imposition of the Gregorian chant could well have had the effect of stimulating a whole range of new developments. If so much can be changed, renewed, reformed, why not even more? As a matter of historical record, such was the actual long-range Frankish reaction, as manifested in the tropes for the Gregorian propers, especially for the Introit. Such tropes, appearing sporadically in sources throughout the tenth century and collected in great anthologies (in the same sources as the sequences) by 1000, were presumably composed from the middle of the ninth century on, but perhaps lagging behind the sequence rather than preceding it. Many of these tropes show in their wording that they were designed for a particular Gregorian piece.[17]

I Adaeterne salutis gaudia et nos salvandi gratia
   PUER NATUS EST NOBIS,
II Rex, lumen de lumine regnat in justitia,
   CUJUS IMPERIUM SUPER HUMERUM EIUS:
III Qui celestia simul et terrestria fundavit patris sapientia,
   ET VOCABITUR NOMEN EJUS
IV Altissimi filius et MAGNI CONSILII ANGELUS.

Here the text in capitals is the Gregorian introit for Christmas (Third Mass, antiphon only); the text is from Isaiah 9,6. The text in lower case is a ninth- or early tenth-century set of tropes, interpolated before and between the musical phrases of the Gregorian introit. It is clear from syntax that the trope is not a pre-Gregorian survival but rather a post-Gregorian innovation, for it cannot stand without the Introit. It is subtly distinct from the Gregorian in form and style (both musically as well as verbally) but comparable to it in bulk; it co-exists with the Gregorian like an interlaced diptych (if there were such a thing), a Frankish innovation to match the Gregorian one.

Many tropes are in hexameters, as for example this one to the Easter Introit.

17. The first example from Gunther Weiss, *Introitus-Tropen* (*Monumenta monodica medii aevi*, Bd. 3, 1970), Trope no. 275; the second example is Trope no. 219; both are edited from the Aquitanian tropers.

I   Ecce pater cunctis, ut jusserat ordo, peractis

     RESURREXI, ET ADHUC TECUM SUM, ALLELUIA:

II   Victor ut ad celos calcata morte redirem,

     POSUISTI SUPER ME MANUM TUAM, ALLELUIA:

III   Quo genus humanum pulsis erroribus altum scanderet ad caelum

     MIRABILIS FACTA EST SCIENTIA TUA, ALLELUIA, ALLELUIA.

The hexameter form makes the trope distinct from the scriptural text of the Gregorian introit; but more than that, the use of the hexameter evokes the world of classical antiquity. Thus two antiquities—one Roman, the other Hebrew-Christian—stand side by side in the diptych. We do not go far wrong, I think, if we imagine that the Carolingian scholar or composer looked upon these two antiquities in more or less the same way: that is, we cannot assume that he necessarily felt closer to one than to the other.

Although some tropes (as in the first example) are closely linked to specific Gregorian items by their wording, and sometimes (though far less often and less specifically than once thought) by their melodic inflection, other tropes, as in the second example, are not so linked; or the linkage is only topical, to the feast rather than to a specific Introit text. In the case of the second example, the hexameter verse form enhances the independence of the three verses over against the psalmodic prose of the Introit itself, and the interdependence of the three hexameters among themselves. Sometimes the three hexameters of a set of tropes clearly follow a single line of thought that skips over the intervening phrases of the Introit. The melody of the tropes often supports their independence, for it frequently is in a neutral style without specific motivic relationship to the melody of the Introit.

Such tropes, considered in themselves, are indistinguishable from the kind of formal epigram Carolingians composed for numerous public occasions. They closely resemble, for example, some epigrammatic verses printed in the *Patrologia latina* under the title "De singulis festivitatibus anni" ascribed to Walafrid Strabo.[18] As a logical possibility it might be imagined that some Carolingian writers and composers intended, on occasion, to *replace* the Gregorian item, not merely add to it. Was not one antique restoration as good as another?

This radical suggestion cannot be pursued seriously here, for lack of space. The point is simply that this idea of replacement would not have been so unthinkable to a Frankish composer as it might seem. And there are several texts of other kinds that may point in the same direction. From before and during Carolingian times there come a number of psalm paraphrases, cast in classical verse forms; Carolingian examples are provided especially by Florus of Lyons, contemporary and contender with Amalarius.[19] Florus is also credited with a metrical paraphrase of the Song of the Three Children (a liturgical canticle),[20] and also with what

18. *Patrologia latina* 114, cols. 1083–1086.
19. *Anal.hymn.* 50, pp. 213–215.
20. *Anal.hymn.* 50, p. 215.

seems to be a paraphrase or analog of the Paschal *Exultet*.[21] Another "Song of the Three Children," *Omnipotentem semper adoret*,[22] is ascribed to Walafrid, along with a *Pater noster* in hexameters, *Omnipotens auctor, caeli regnator in aula*;[23] further, a Christmas hymn beginning *Gloriam nato cecinere Christo*,[24] whose incipit recalls the liturgical *Gloria in excelsis*, although not as clearly as the *Gloria Deo in excelsis hodie* of Paulinus of Aquileia.[25] A metrical Litany of the Saints is ascribed to Rhabanus Maurus,[26] and to Hincmar of Reims a metrical communion piece, beginning *Agnus lux mundi*,[27] that seems to be an analog of the *Agnus dei*.

For what purpose, or purposes, could these texts have been written? Simply to be read silently, for individual edification? Or at meal time in the monastery? Or were they actually to be performed *viva voce*—and if so, as part of the liturgy? None of them can adequately be described as a trope of any kind. Some items, such as the *versus more litaniae* ascribed to Rhabanus, could only replace, not coexist with the Litany. Others, such as the Christmas hymn of Paulinus, use only the incipit of the liturgical hymn *Gloria in excelsis* (that is to say, it uses only the Angel's Hymn as found in *Luke* 2). Paulinus's hymn could not replace the *Gloria in excelsis*, but still is not a trope of it. In fact, the concept of troping is strikingly unable to account for this range of phenomena, partly because its range is so broad, partly because the impulses involved seem sometimes so little bound by the "official" or "traditional" concepts of liturgy as we think of it.

We can imagine, then, that the imposition of the new liturgy and chant—both the fact that it was imposed and that it introduced the Frankish observer to a musical repertory of the highest quality—provoked a whole series of artistic reactions, including new forms of musical composition. It would be natural, however, that such new forms would appear subsequently, not concomitantly, with the stimulus. It would take time for the new material (the Gregorian) to be absorbed and digested, in order for it to have the effect of stimulating novel ideas. For we are not considering mere adaptation or imitation (although time would be required for that too), but rather the generation of forms such as trope and sequence as well as others for which we have no handy label, forms that are so distinct from the Gregorian as to stand to some degree in opposition to it. The rhythm of stimulus and creative reaction might well involve two or three generations of composers. If this were the case, it would explain why the development of new musical forms seems to take place from the middle of the ninth century on, not during the reign of Charlemagne himself.

That timetable of musical events runs parallel with one of literary development, and since the sequence is text and music, we need to keep in mind the development of both simultaneously. The foremost result of Charlemagne's emphasis on education was a first generation of monastic scholars who could write more or less correct Latin in the classical forms that were used as schoolroom materials. These scholars learned their lessons diligently, absorbing

21. *Anal.hymn.* 50, p. 217.
22. *Anal.hymn.* 50, p. 169.
23. *Anal.hymn.* 50, p. 175.
24. *Anal.hymn.* 50, p. 167.
25. *Anal.hymn.* 50, p. 127.
26. *Anal.hymn.* 50, p. 183.
27. *Poetae latini aevi carolini* III, p. 414.

and digesting the stimulus of an elevated language and literature; that, however, seems to have taken almost the full measure of their energies. A strong, free, fully creative spirit did not appear until two generations later, in the person of Gottschalk of Orbais (died 868/69), whose novel rhythms and poetic individuality set him off sharply even from the genial Walafrid or Sedulius.[28] They, too, belong to the subsequent generation rather than to the first fruits of the Carolingian reform.

As much as the sequence may owe to this reform, it is not an immediate product of it. That much is clear from the comparison of the West-Frankish texts with Notker's; for the Latinity of Notker's texts can indeed be ascribed to Charlemagne's insistence on education, through the person, say, of Rhabanus Maurus, "schoolmaster of Germany." There is more to Notker than correct classical Latin, of course; but that is what distinguishes his proses from his West-Frankish models.

On the other hand, even though the West-Frankish texts stand apart from the restoration of classical forms and styles in the schoolroom, they appear to be subsequent to these reforms. It is difficult to imagine them springing directly from an eighth-century pre-Carolingian base, even an Irish or Anglo-Saxon one. That insular ingredient is very strong, and we have seen it contributing in large part to the difference between Notker and the West. Still, there is a big difference between a ninth-century West-Frankish prose and an Irish hymn, and even though channels and contacts of Irish and insular influence on the Franks are abundant, the sequence is clearly a Frankish product, not an insular one.[29] Indeed, the comparison with Irish hymnody is instructive precisely in that it suggests the degree to which that colorful rhythmic and rhyming diction was disciplined to a more sober, comprehensible state. It is this discipline that makes the prose subsequent to, dependent upon, the Carolingian reform. The synthesis of diction, along with its integration into the new form, could only have been possible with a lapse of time; the dating of the sequence from "circa 840," a date derived from the circumstances of Notker's story, seems to be supported by the course of literary as well as musical events.

If the sequence is subsequent to, and dependent upon, the Carolingian restoration of classical studies, it is nonetheless a big step beyond. Hexameter tropes could—as far as the texts go—be considered an immediate product of such restoration; it would be no surprise to find them very early in the century, emanating from the original court circle (although that in itself is not sufficient grounds to date them so far back). Something about the sequence, on the other hand, prevents us from imagining it in the same circumstances. The sequence, the prose, is no classical form; it is hard to conceive of anyone in the court circle developing the form, or finding it congenial if it were presented to him. It is true that the technique of the bicola can be derived from precepts of classical rhetoric going back to Quintilian, but— if we can distinguish between antecedents and precedents—we can say that there was no precedent (certainly not a classical one) for the particular shape of the ninth-century sequence, and the way the bicola were integrated into the musical couplet-structure. It seems reasonable, then, that the sequence should not appear as an immediate product of the revival

28. *Poetae latini aevi carolini* III, pp. 705–738.
29. Irish hymnody in *Anal.hymn.* 51, pp. 257ff.

of letters in Charlemagne's time, but only later, when instead of imitation there could be a new synthesis.

In more than one way, then, the sequence turns out to be disassociated from specifically Carolingian values—from the court, from the revival of classical letters, from the installation of Gregorian chant, and also from the kind of monastic reform envisaged by Benedict of Aniane and Louis the Pious. If we were to look for possible names and addresses of sequence composers we should probably not look among the court circle, for those men seem too close to—and too committed to—the processes of literary revival and musical restoration. The things being restored had innovative thrust, as we have seen, but they also made clear artistic demands that left little room for originality. There was nothing to do with Gregorian chant but sing it, or imitate it, and the imitation made sense in the measure that it resembled the original. No, we would better look where Notker told us, in the monasteries, around mid-century. He could have said St. Riquier, which would have pointed closer to the court, for St. Riquier was built for Angilbert by Charlemagne. But instead he said Jumièges, which tells us little; perhaps that was the point. And perhaps that was one reason the sequence could flourish during the last half of the century, when the empire, its programs, values, and ideals, fell into disrepair and disrespect.

For the empire was Carolingian—specifically Carolingian—while the sequence can now be regarded as less Carolingian and more Frankish. It is obvious that Charles was a brilliantly successful administrator, and also, in his passion for organization, one of the best representatives of the Frankish people. It has been argued, however, that his empire was ephemeral, of little account in the overall development of Western Europe. Even if that judgment is too harsh, it is clear that Charles' empire was but part of the much more momentous process of the acculturation of the Franks. Located right on the interface of the pre-literate tribal culture crowding down from the north and east, and of the highly literate Roman civilization—rather, the memory of it—the Franks with their peculiar gifts were able to select and organize the elements of a whole new society, not just an empire. That, of course, is a story in itself; what concerns the sequence is the mode of acculturation, the rhythm of appropriation and creation. First came the attempt to imitate a Roman custom or artifact, then afterwards the attempt to create something analogous, but sometimes so original that the model can only be guessed at. Underlying this process was the fact that the Frank was not a Roman: he stood at a distance, he had no traditional associations with the things he imitated (at least, no typically Roman association). He perceived, selected, and organized without necessarily referring to what things had been, respecting only what they might become for him. Within this framework of naiveté and pragmatism, the imitation could be embarrassingly literal, while paradoxically the creation could be startlingly original, as single elements of style were exaggerated far beyond their traditional limit, or combined with other elements in some hopelessly untraditional way. In all cases, however, there was unusual opportunity for organization to be manifest in the art work—Frankish modes of organization. These modes involved syllable count, close duplication in the two lines of a couplet, uniform cadences, direct melodic progressions emphasizing a restricted tonal locus, clear layout of phrases in progressions from shorter to longer, lower to higher, motivic systems that bind a piece together by judicious repetition of short melodic patterns. All of these means made order clearly apparent in the finished product, when considered in itself. Perhaps the ninth-century Frankish composer did think of his sequence as a *sequentia*, after all; but if that were the case we would be bound to exclaim the more over the exuberant fantasy on the one hand, the resourceful, original means of control on the other, that brought the new song to pass.

Appendix: List of Manuscripts, with some Observations on Provenance

Descriptions of the manuscripts listed in Table I (p. 5) can be found as follows, with special reference to these two works.

Husmann TS=H. Husmann, *Tropen- und Sequenzen-Handschriften* (Répertoire International des Sources Musicales B V¹, (1964).

Chailley=Jacques Chailley, "Les anciens tropaires et sequentiaires de l'école de Saint-Martial de Limoges (Xᵉ–XIᵉS.)," *Etudes Grégoriennes*, II (1957), pp. 163–188.

Early Fragments

Munich Cod. lat. 14843: Husmann TS, p. 78; Von den Steinen, *Anfänge*, vol. 40, pp. 256–263.

Verona Bib. Cap. XC(85): Von den Steinen, *Anfänge*, vol. 40, pp. 253–56; Hans Spanke, *Deutsche und französische Dichtung des Mittelalters* (Stuttgart 1943), pp. 33f.

Autun, Bib. Mun. 28 S (fol. 64): B. Stäblein, "Zur Frühgeschichte der Sequenz," *Archiv fur Musikwissenschaft* XVIII (1961), Facs. 1.

Paris B. N. lat. 17436 (fols. 24–30): Dom R. J. Hesbert, *Antiphonale missarum sextuplex* (Bruxelles 1935), pp. xix–xx.

Other Manuscripts

London B. M. add. 19768: Husmann TS, p. 152; Von den Steinen, *Notker* II, pp. 208–9.

Chartres Bibl. 47: *Paléographie musicale* XI (1921); G. Benoit-Castelli and M. Huglo, "L'Origine bretonne du gradual Nº 47 de la Bibliothèque de Chartres," *Etudes grégoriennes* I (1954), 173–178.

Paris B. N. lat. 9448: Leon Gautier, *Histoire de la poésie liturgique au moyen age: Les tropes* (Paris 1886), p. 123; Von den Steinen, *Notker* II.

Paris B. N. lat. 10510: L. Gautier, *Les tropes*, p. 124.

Paris Arsenal 1169: Husmann TS, p. 110.

"Winchester Troper" (Oxford Bodleian 775, Cambridge Corpus Christi College 473): Husmann TS, pp. 150, 158; Andreas Holschneider, *Die Organa von Winchester* (Hildesheim 1968), pp. 14–27.

Aquitanian Manuscripts

Paris B. N. lat. 1240: Husmann TS, p. 137; Chailley, p. 165; H. M. Bannister, "The Earliest French Troper and its date," *Journal of Theological Studies* II (1901), pp. 420–29.

Paris B. N. lat. 1084: Husmann TS, p. 120; Chailley, p. 171

Paris B. N. lat. 1118: Husmann TS, p. 124; Chailley, p. 177

Paris B. N. lat. 1120: Husmann TS, p. 128: Chailley, p. 167

Paris B. N. lat. 887: Husmann TS, p. 117; Chailley, p. 180

Paris B. N. lat. 1121: Husmann TS, p. 130; Chailley, p. 169; Paul Evans, *The Early Trope Repertory of Saint Martial de Limoges* (Princeton, 1970) pp. 48, 121 ff.

Paris B. N. lat.   909: Husmann TS, p. 118; Chailley, p. 174

Paris B. N. lat. 1119: Husmann TS, p. 126; Chailley, p. 181

Paris B. N. lat. 1137: Husmann TS, p. 135; Chailley, p. 186

Paris B. N. lat. 1138: Husmann TS, p. 136; Chailley, p. 179

Paris B. N. lat. 1338: Husmann TS, p. 136; Chailley, p. 179

Paris B. N. lat. 1136: Husmann TS, p. 134; Chailley, p. 186

Paris B. N. lat.   903:   Chailley, p. 172; *Paléographie musicale* XIII (1930)

Paris B. N. lat. 1132:   Chailley, p. 184

East-Frankish Manuscripts

St. Gall 484: Husmann TS, p. 47; Von den Steinen, *Notker* II, pp. 198–9

St. Gall 381: Husmann TS, p. 42; Von den Steinen, *Notker* II, pp. 199–200

Einsiedeln 121:   Von den Steinen, *Notker* II, pp. 204–6; *Paléographie musicale* IV (1894)

Bamberg Lit 5 (Ed V 9): Husmann TS, p. 58; Von den Steinen, *Notker* II, pp. 206–7

St. Gall 378: Husmann TS, p. 35; Von den Steinen, *Notker* II, pp. 201–2

St. Gall 380: Husmann TS, p. 39; Von den Steinen, *Notker* II, pp. 200–1

St. Gall 382: Husmann TS, p. 44; Von den Steinen, *Notker* II, pp. 202

St. Gall 376:   Von den Steinen, *Notker* II, pp. 200

Berlin theol. lat. 4° 11: Husmann TS, p. 62; Von den Steinen, *Notker* II, pp. 203–4

Munich cod. lat. 14083: Husmann TS, p. 74; Von den Steinen, *Notker* II, p. 211 f.

Bamberg Ed III 7: Von den Steinen, *Notker* II, p. 210 f.

Oxford Selden sup. 27: Husmann TS, p. 163; Von den Steinen, *Notker* II, p. 212 f.

Paris B. N. lat. 10587: Von den Steinen, *Notker* II, p. 204

Ever since Dreves published sequences from the Aquitanian prosers in 1889 (*Analecta hymnica* vol. 7), under the title "Prosen der Abtei St. Martial zu Limoges," the provenance of these MSS has been the subject of lively dispute. The various problems are not yet resolved, nor are they likely to be in the near future. There has been no thorough, systematic study of the problem—at least, none published; and indeed it seems as though the questions of provenance would have to wait upon detailed studies of the contents of the MSS. It will apparently be necessary, for example, to analyze the transmission of each sequence individually before an accurate idea of the relationship of MSS can be formed; and similarly for the other categories of chant involved.

To recapitulate all the discussion about provenance would require more space than is available here. A recent state of investigation can be observed in Husmann's *Tropen- und Sequenzen Handschriften*, in connection with the two most important—and most difficult—cases, MSS 1084 and 1118. In dealing with MS 1084, one must follow Husmann's argument through from his discussion of MS Paris B. N. lat. 887 (p. 117): he says that MS 887 comes from St. Géraud d'Aurillac (near Limoges) because of evidence in the Sanctorale (on p. 118 he concludes from the Sanctorale that MS 887 corresponds closely with MSS 1084 and 1871), and because of comparison of repertory with MSS 1084 and 1871. On p. 120 he says the main part of MS 1084 may come from St. Géraud d'Aurillac even though it does not emphasize St. Géraud (while subsidiary parts of the manuscript do), since this main part corresponds to MSS 887 and 1871 (the rest of the argument on p. 120 seems gratuitous). In discussing the Sanctorale of MS 1084, Husmann says no firm conclusions can be drawn, and only repertory and variants show it to be from St. Géraud. Then in discussing MS 1871 (p. 147) he argues that the Sanctorale, repertory, and variants all point to St. Géraud. The circularity of much of this argument is clear: only MS 1871 offers any firm ground at all in favor of St. Géraud d'Aurillac. The rest of the burden falls on comparison of repertory and variants, and concerning this two observations—one specific, the other general—need to be made.

First, no positive conclusion can be drawn from a comparison of repertory or variants with either MS 887 or MS 1871: each is unique in its own way, and cannot be grouped closely with any other manuscript known to me. It is incorrect to say that MS 1871 corresponds closely with MS 1084 (or with MS 1118, for that matter). Thus MS 1871 offers no witness for provenance of either MS 887 or 1084 (see also Evans, *The Early Trope Repertory*, pp. 50–53). The most that could be said would be that the repertory of MS 1871 (or of MS 887) was derived from some standard prototype before being subjected to individual treatment.

Second, the discussions by Husmann and others have injected increasingly refined and sophisticated distinctions into the question of provenance—which is all to the good. After previous over-hasty conclusions about provenance based on witness from the Sanctorale, it is now recognized that such evidence is often conflicting or indeterminate (see Husmann's discussion of MS 1118, pp. 125–6); and furthermore, that it may be irrelevant since these manuscripts, like others, may well have been prepared in one place, on order and for the use of some other place. Most important, however, is the reliance on repertory and variants in establishing provenance. One reason we are interested in provenance is to help sort out the variant tradition: provenance, independently established, gives us a handle on that tradition; but provenance established *from* variants and repertory is obviously useless for that purpose. It is tautological, merely saying the same thing in another way. And if we imagine repertories being passed freely around the countryside through exemplars—as we now do—then the question of manuscript provenance becomes irrelevant there too. This is not to deny the importance of provenance when it can be established independently, but only to interject even more caution into the investigation.

MS 1118 offers similar problems. It has become customary to speak, with caution, of an origin in Toulouse (see M. Huglo, *Les Tonaires*, Paris 1971, pp. 132–37 and passim), but firm witness seems lacking. Huglo's discussion reveals many interesting details that point in a variety of directions.

As far as the prosaria are concerned, the central fact about MSS 1084 and 1118 is their very close relationship, hardly matched by any other manuscripts in the Aquitanian group: either the prosarium and sequentiarium of MS 1118 was copied from MS 1084 (first layer, fol. 197v–212v, 221—222–223 is interpolated—to 281v), or—more likely—they had a common source. And this would be true even if their respective "provenance" were from opposite ends of Europe. It seems wise to concentrate first on the relationship of readings (as do Gunther Weiss, "Zum Problem der Gruppierung südfranzosischer Tropare," in *Archive für Musikwissenschaft* XXI, 1964, pp. 163–171, and David Hughes, "Further Notes of the Grouping of the Aquitanian Tropers," in *Journal of the American Musicological Society*, XIX, 1966, pp. 3–12), leaving the explanation of how these relationships came about, through the physical whereabouts of the manuscripts, to be pieced together subsequently.

Notes to Transcriptions

The sequences transcribed here include all those listed in Table II, groups A and B (p. 12), except GAUDE EJA, EPIPHANIAM, ARCE SUPERNA, REX NOSTRAS CHRISTE, ECCE JAM VENIT, PANGE DEO, and Notker's BENEDICTO GRATIAS—the last because no melody has been preserved on a staff source. Thus, the transcriptions include all but one of Notker's sequences (excluding the small, aparallel *sequentiae*), and the earliest representatives of all of these melodies known to have been in use in the West-Frankish kingdom.

The melodies are transcribed here on a four-line staff with C or F clef, in the so-called "square notation," a form of chant notation developed during the 12th and 13th centuries, then commonly used for chant books down to the present time. This type of notation has several advantages, one being the ease with which tonal movement can be perceived on a four-line staff as opposed to the five-line staff traditionally used for polyphonic music. Furthermore, traditional polyphonic note shapes all have durational significance, so that their use for chant necessarily imputes that significance to chant (unless the shapes be modified in some way); but the square notation, as it was used in the later Middle Ages, has no such significance, hence avoids suggesting more about the rhythm of the chant than we actually know. (See, however, the remarks on duration in Aquitanian notation on p. 19.)

An extensive introduction to the way square notation is used in modern chant books can be found in the *Liber usualis*. Sequences usually use only a small variety of the note shapes found in Gregorian chant—mostly just the square punctum. Other shapes and ornamental neumes appear infrequently; the special significance of the ornamental neumes—quilisma and oriscus—and of the liquescent notes is not of decisive importance for our purposes. In these transcriptions, the sign for B flat may be used as a signature, at the start of each staff and holding throughout the piece; in that case it indicates, in effect, that the "modal" finals usually found on D, E, F, G appear instead at G, A, B flat, and C. When the sign for B flat occurs only as an accidental, just before the note it affects, it indicates that the accidental is supported by some aspect of the MS tradition. The B flat holds only for that note, or a repetition of the note, either immediately or in the same word. The sign for B flat can also be placed *over* the note it affects, in which case it represents an editorial suggestion.

In general, each syllable has only one note, usually written as a square; and each syllable receives only the square note placed directly above it. Occasionally there is one more syllable in one line of a couplet than in the other. The note for this supernumerary syllable is supplied on the staff, but is used *only* for the line of text that has the supernumerary syllable; when the other line is sung, the note is omitted. Other melodic discrepancies between the two lines of a couplet are shown by letters (indicating pitches) below the second line. Modern signs for "first ending" and "second ending" have been added in certain cases.

The layout of the transcriptions is intended to make the phrase structure of the melodies as clear and self-evident as possible. Where space permits, each phrase is on its own line. Very long phrases either fall naturally into subphrases, which are placed on a new line and slightly indented, beginning with capital letters, or are broken at some arbitrary point with the run-on indented further and with no capital. In every couplet, the first line of text is to be sung through to the end of the couplet before beginning the second line of text—even though this may mean running on through two or three lines of music.

Each melodic phrase or subphrase (except 2a) begins with a capital in the text, as in the MS tradition. Punctuation, however, is completely a function of the syntax of the text, and has been supplied throughout by the editor, the MSS having none. In singing, there is presumably a pause of some kind at the end of each phrase or subphrase, but this is not indicated in the musical notation, either in the MS sources or in these transcriptions.

As discussed in Chapter 1, the versions of the sequences in this book are presented as collated transcriptions, and the purpose of these notes is to give an idea of how each piece appears in the early sources. Neither critical versions nor complete reports of variants have been attempted here. Only those variants are reported that (1) show a substantially different intent, or (2) reflect a state of doubt or hesitation on the part of the scribe that suggests a prior disturbance in the transmission, which might have implications for the structure of the piece.

Types of variants reported under (1) include alternate wordings, anything that affects syllable count, and differences (such as those of grammatical inflections) that seem to intend a different sense; not reported are the frequent variants in spelling and the seemingly purposeless or careless differences in inflections or wording. The transcriptions attempt to follow the norms of the scholastic tradition in spelling, these being just as frequently represented—in these sources, at least—as are the various reductions or overcompensations ascribed to "medieval practice."

With all reservation due the type of staffless notation involved, I have attempted to report all melodic variants that affect the conduct of the line. To this procedure there are two major kinds of exceptions. The first concerns the diastematic quality of the Aquitanian staffless notation: the quality varies from MS to MS, and sometimes from piece to piece; sometimes the intent is just not clear. Frequently I have had to exercise personal judgment as to whether a particular MS intended a melodic variant. In general, when a MS could be taken to support a melodic reading already established, I have so taken it. As part of the same problem, a melody that is generally clear in a given MS may show an inexplicable vagary at a certain point, so that the phrase ends up in a senseless location. These instances, not so frequent, I have identified by the note "disjuncture."

The second exception concerns the ornamental neumes quilisma and oriscus, and the liquescent signs. Much remains to be explained about these signs, even in Gregorian notation; I regret that I have not been able to follow a clear, consistent practice in transcription. The means exist to solve at least some of the problems, through extensive comparison of first and second lines of couplets in syllabic and melismatic notation, but I have not had the opportunity to pursue this to a conclusion. MS variants on these neumes are not reported in the Notes.

As a general principle, the melismatic notation of the melodies in the sequentiaria is less careful with respect to syllable count than is the notation in the prosaria. Inexactitudes occur primarily in the case of repeated pitches for adjacent syllables (see *Ipsum auctoris*, 6a and b of LAUDES DEO OMNIS SEXUS in MS Paris B. N. lat 1118, fol. 136v). Such variants have not been reported when the intent is clear.

The foregoing qualifications apply to the West-Frankish versions; Notker's have been treated differently. Notker's texts are taken from Von den Steinen's edition. The purpose of including Notker's pieces here is not to edit his *Liber hymnorum* (although all but one of his sequences—not counting the small, aparallel *sequentiae*—are included) but rather to provide materials for comparison with the West-Frankish repertory. The melodies for Notker's texts have been derived from Bannister's transcriptions, as read against the St. Gall neumatic tradition on one hand and the contemporary Aquitanian tradition on the other; they do not represent the eventual critical versions that will have to be established on the basis of the whole German MS tradition.

Notes for each transcription will include (1) the references to the manuscripts used for the transcription of the West-Frankish version; (2) the variants for text and melody (see below); (3) reference to other manuscripts consulted but not collated; (4) other editions of text and melody. Then, for Notker's version, will follow (1) references to Von den Steinen's edition of the text and his commentary; (2) reference to Bannister's transcription and collation of the melody in the St. Gall manuscripts, with comments concerning the version given in this book; (3) other editions of the melody.

In the variants, manuscripts are cited by their shelf number alone; the full reference is given at the head of each set of notes. "P" refers to the version in the prosarium (syllabic notation), "S" to the sequentiarium (melismatic notation). If the reference to the transcription is clear, the variant reading is given by itself, for instance, "2 canat 1118-P," which means, in phrase 2, the version in the prosarium of MS 1118 reads *canat* for *canant* as given in the transcription. Where the reference is not obvious, the variant will read, for instance, "in *for* hunc." Melodic variants are given by letter, with the text in parens beneath, for example

B D C A
(Ut ip- si ju-)

This procedure is used to refer either to readings in the prosaria that involve only melody not text, or to readings in the sequentiaria, (using the text as a means of locating the variant). If the text given below the pitch letters is not in parentheses, then it, too, is a variant reading.

The citation of other sources is intended to be merely representative and is not complete; in some cases there are a great many other MS sources. The listing in *Analecta hymnica* is a useful guide to the distribution in the sources.

For Notker's texts, the notes give references to Von den Steinen's critical text and apparatus (*Notker* II) and to his interpretation and commentary (*Notker* I). Then come references to Bannister's transcription and tabulation of the St. Gall neumes, as found in one of the five volumes Oxford, Bodleian lat.lit. MSS c. 11 through c. 15. In the case of two of Notker's texts to the same melody, Bannister transcribes these one under another on the same page. His tabulations are in principle made without reference to specific texts (being usually taken from the melismatic notation, although neumes from syllabic versions are sometimes included), hence are identified by Bannister by the melody title, placed here in quotes. Neither Bannister nor Von den Steinen include page references to the St. Gall MSS, so I have included paginations for the five earliest MSS, 484, 378, 380, 381, 382; Bannister usually includes MSS 376 and sometimes 379 in the tabulation, and occasionally others. Often he made another tabulation of MSS from outside St. Gall, but I have not referred to these. Further references include the *Analecta hymnica* vol. 53, even though it is superseded by Von den Steinen, for the sake of the comprehensive MS citations; but note than Von den Steinen complains that its apparatus is up to one third wrong. Versions of the melody are often available in the following editions, cited in the notes by the short titles shown here in quotes.

"Schubiger"—A. Schubiger, *Die Sängerschule St. Gallens vom VIII bis XII Jahrhundert* (1858); the transcriptions are paginated separately at the end.

"Drinkwelder"—O. Drinkwelder, *Ein deutsches Sequentiar aus dem Ende des 12. Jahrhunderts* (Graz 1914)

"Moberg"—C. A. Moberg, *Uber die schwedischen Sequenzen* (Uppsala 1927)

"de Goede"—N. de Goede, *The Utrecht Prosarium* (Amsterdam 1965)

"Aix-la-Chapelle"—R. J. Hesbert, *Prosaire d'Aix-la-Chapelle* (*Monumenta musicae sacrae* III, Rouen 1961); a facsimile of a 13th-century staff source containing a large part of Notker's repertory.

LAUDES DEO OMNIS SEXUS

Manuscripts

Paris B.N.lat.1118, fol. 174: Prose
Paris B.N.lat.1118, fol. 136: Sequence
Paris B.N.lat.1084, fol. 248v: Prose
Paris B.N.lat.1084, fol. 203: Sequence
Paris B.N.lat.1121, fol. 71: Sequence

Variants

2a consona 1118-P; consonat 1084-P
    canat 1084-P
    crucifixa 1118-P
       A F G
    (dulces canant) *and 2b* 1118-P
       B
    (preces) 1121-S
2b in *for* hunc 1084-P
    jubilet 1084-P
3a renovantur 1118-P
    G A
3b (surrexit) 1084-P
    B D C A
5a (Ut ip-si ju-) 1121-S
    FG
6b (ter-ris) & (*no note*) 1084-P
7 (Resuscitans . . . excelsis) *om.* 1121-S
8 8a,b *exchanged* 1084-P

Other Versions

A later version, LAUDUM LAETA, appears in Paris B.N.lat.1338, fol. 44v, and Paris B.N.n.a.lat.1871, fol. 81v, 130; and an expanded version, LAUS DEO NOSTRO, in MS 1871, fol. 130v.

Published versions

Anal.hymn. 53, p. 81 (LAUS DEO NOSTRO); Fr. de Geode, who first connected LAUDES DEO OMNIS SEXUS with Notker's LAUDES DEO CONCINAT, printed text and music from MSS 1084 and 1121 (*Utrecht Prosarium*, pp. xxxiii–xxxiv); Crocker, "The Sequence," p. 292.

Notker: LAUDES DEO CONCINAT

Text

Von den Steinen, *Notker* II, pp. 38, 165; I, pp. 163ff., 534–36; see also *Anfänge*, vol. 40, p. 199.

Melody

Bannister, melody A-55, Bodleian lat.lit.c. 14, fol. 78 (transcription); fol. 79–80v (tabulation), which collates St. Gall MSS 484 (p. 274), 381 (p. 405), 378, 380(p. 75), 382(p. 34), 376 (as well as other sources). Bannister's transcription agrees with the one given here from the Aquitanian version, apart from a few slight variants. The tabulation of St. Gall neumes shows no discrepancy.

Published versions

Anal.hymn. 53, p. 93; De Goede, *Utrecht Prosarium*, pp. xxxiii–xxxvi, 30; Schubiger, p. 16.

HÆC DIES QUAM EXCELSUS

Manuscripts

Paris B.N.lat.1118, fol. 163, fol. 186v: Prose (twice)
Paris B.N.lat.1118, fol. 136v: Sequence
Paris B.N.lat.1084, fol. 251v: Prose
Paris B.N.lat.1084, fol. 204v: Sequence
Paris, B.N.lat.1121, fol. 71v: Sequence

Variants

    GABG . . .
1 (di-) 1121-S
      C D C
3a (temporibus) 1084-P
4a ad (liberandum) *canceled* 1118–163,
    erased 1118–186v.
      C A
4b (dudum) 1118–163, 186v
      C A B AG
    (dudum ingerens) 1121-S
    ACAC D B G
    (vitia et trahens in) 1084-S, 1118-S
    G A B
    & traens 1084-P
    G A G F
6b (paraclito); (sanc-) A *om.* 1084-S, 1118-S
    A B C A A B C B A A B C A B C B A
    (paraclito . . .)   1121-S
Amen *no notes* 1118–163, 186v

Published versions

Anal.hymn. 7, p. 37; H. Husmann, "Die Sequenz Duo tres. Zur Geschichte der Sequenzen in St. Gallen und in St. Martial," *In memoriam Jacques Handschin* (Strasbourg 1962), pp. 66–72: transcription of melody from MS 1121. R. L. Crocker, "Some Ninth-Century Sequences," *Journal of the American Musicological Society*, XX (1967), 380–385: transcription from MSS 1118, 1084.

Notker: GRATES SALVATORI

Text

Von den Steinen, *Notker* II, pp. 36, 165; I, pp. 229ff., 544f. (see especially the parallel display with LAUDES DEO CONCINAT).

Melody

Bannister, melody A 43: Bodleian lat.lit. c. 13: transcription fol. 82–82v, 84–84v, 89–89v, 94–94v; tabulation ("Duo tres") fol. 85–87v, collating St. Gall MSS 484, p. 273; 378, p. 208; 380, p. 173; 381, p. 403; 382, p. 132 (and others).

Published versions

Anal.hymn. 53, p. 92; Schubiger, p. 16; de Goede, p. 29.

Notker: TUBAM BELLICOSAM

Text
Von den Steinen, *Notker* II, pp. 84, 173; I, pp. 397f., 592f.

Melody
Bannister, see GRATES SALVATORI: St. Gall MSS 380, p. 239; 381, p. 403.

Published versions
Anal.hymn. 53, p. 371.

ECCE VICIT

Manuscripts
Paris B.N.lat.1240, fol. 48: Prose (text only)
Paris B.N.lat.1118, fol. 178: Prose
Paris B.N.lat.1118, fol. 136: Sequence
Paris B.N.lat.1084, fol. 247v: Prose
Paris B.N.lat.1084, fol. 216: Sequence
Paris B.N.lat.1121, fol. 71: Sequence

Variants
    G
1a (vicit) 1084-P
      B
1b (Mors) 1084-P, S, 1121-S
    sui ut *for* vicit 1118-P
    ED
2a (-bel-) 1118-P,S
     E
    (stu-) *om.* 1118-S, 1084-S
    A G
    (satis) *om.* 1121-S
3a Bonum 1118-P
     C   A
    (Do-) 1084-S; (Do–) 1121-S
    vasa *canceled*, claustra 1084-P
     AFG
4a (fuerat) *om.* 1121-S
4b Quem clauserat eva tumens conditori clauseratque cunctis post modum de stirpe sua natis 1240-P
    E G
5a (-sera-) *om.* 1084-S, 1121-S
    AB AGG
     ethere-am 1084-P
    materiam 1169-P
5b poterat 1240-P
    C
6a (Dum) 1084-S
    abiit 1084-P
    inlicitam quem . . . aquisitam 1118-P, 1084-P
    justam 1118-P
    quem 1240-P
6b Ambiere 1240-P
    D
7a (re-) *etc.* 1084-S, 1121-S
    refusa deficit 1118-P, 1084-P

refulsit defici 1240-P
a *for* ut 1118-P
  G   D
(ut qui) *om.* 1121-S
largitur 1240-P
ingressus . . . regressus 1118-P, 1084-P
  AB AGG
(-dam veni-am) 1084-P
7b (qui) in 1084-P
    G C B A B CAGG
8a probarunt edi-fican-tes 1118-P
    G C B A G ABA G
    reprobarunt edificantes 1084-P
     E G
    (-gu-la-) *om.* 1084-S
    AG
8b (cel-) 1118-P
    in alto 1240-P
    C
9a (Re-) 1084-S
    AC
    (Re-) 1121-P
    A G FG   G
    (prima in se-) cu- (la) 1084-P
     A
    (se-) cu- (la) amen (*no notes*) 1118-P
    Regnum ejus magnum et potestas ejus et honor
    Manens in aeternum per cuncta semper seculorum
    secla. Amen 1240-P

Other manuscripts
Rome, Casanat.1741, fol. 76v (facs. ed. J. Vecchi *Troparium Sequentiarium Nonantulanum* (*Monumenta Lyrica Medii Aevi Italica* I, 1955).
Paris, Arsenal 1169, fol. 37v
Paris, B.N.n.a.lat.1235, fol. 213
London, B.M. Royal 8.C.XIII, fol. 17v (text only)
Benevento, Bib.cap. VI 34, fol. 145 (facs. ed. *Paléographie musicale* XV)
Vercelli, Bib.cap. CLXII, fol. 184
Verona, Bib.cap. CVII, fol. 89v

Published versions
Anal.hymn. 53, p. 73; B. Stäblein, "Die Sequenzmelodie 'Concordia' und ihr geschichtliche Hintergrund," *Festschrift Hans Engel* (Kassel 1964), pp. 364–392, especially pp. 371–2 and 386–92. R. L. Crocker, "Some Ninth-Century Sequences," *Journal of the American Musicological Society* XX (1967), 390–95.

GAUDE EJA

Text is essentially that given by Stäblein, "Die Sequenzmelodie Concordia," pp. 386–392, collated with the two earliest sources. Paris B.N.lat. MS 17436, fol. 24: Prose (*Summa pia*) (as transcribed). Paris, Arsenal MS 1169, fol. 25: Prose: variants follow.

2b nostra

"5"a ea: decantantes . . . clara *om.*

3a domini

"5"b tergat; quibus . . . excelsa *om.*

3b sua *for* summa; conserventur

4a fera nos libera paganica; regnat

b hac *for* et; caterva

5a supplices domine; est *for* es; adfirma

b ad perfectam

6 Laus sit et; amen *om.*

Published versions

Anal.hymn. 9, p. 54; Stäblein, *Die Sequenzmelodie Concordia*, pp. 364–368; Von den Steinen, *Anfänge*, pp. 39f.; R. L. Crocker, "Some Ninth-Century Sequences," pp. 390–395.

Notker: HANC CONCORDI

Text

Von den Steinen, *Notker* II, pp. 14, 161; I, pp. 365ff., 582ff.

Melody

Bannister, melody A 34; Bodleian lat.lit. c. 12: transcription fol. 152–152v, 154–155v; tabulation ("Concordia"); fol. 185–188, collating St. Gall MSS 484, p. 259; 378, p. 161; 380, p. 130; 381, p. 342; 382, p. 98 (and others).

Published versions

Anal.hymn. 53, p. 345; Drinkwelder, p. 21; Moberg no. 15a; de Goede, p. 8; Aix-la-chapelle, p. 75.

Notker: PETRE SUMME

Text

Von den Steinen, *Notker* II, pp. 62, 169; I, pp. 359ff., 579ff.

Melody

Bannister: see HANC CONCORDI; St. Gall MSS 378, p. 239; 381, p. 435; 382, p. 152.

Published versions

Anal.hymn. 53, p. 336; Schubiger, p. 26; Drinkwelder, p. 41; de Goede, p. 51; Aix-la-chapelle, p. 81.

NUNC EXULTET

Manuscripts

Paris B.N.lat.1240, fol. 50v: Prose (text only)

Paris B.N.lat.1084, fol. 245v: Prose

Paris B.N.lat.1084, fol. 203: Sequence

Paris B.N.lat.1118, fol. 172: Prose

Paris B.N.lat.1118, fol. 137v: Sequence

Paris B.N.lat.1120, fol. 149v: Prose (text only)

Variants

       G F

1 (hodi)e rex 1118-P, 1084-P

       C B

2a (tri-um) 1084-S

2b furem qui crudeles 1084-P

furemque 1118-P

fortem 1120-P

5a Videte locum ubi fuit dominus

       G   A   BA   G F D EC

Recordamini quid vivens locutus sit

quod ipse die tercia resurgeret 1118-P, 1084-P

5b (conspicerent eum) *notes lacking* 1118-P,S, 1084-S

   G   ABAG   F DEC

in Gali-le-am discipuli 1118-P,S, 1084-S

    G A BAG   FEFC

discipuli in Galile-am

    D E EFGG ABA G F G G

  illum videre sicuti promissum est 1084-P

6b a monumento 1240-P

illum *om.* 1240-P

8a eis post et 1240-P

Phrase 8 is a tone too high 1118-S; *disjunct from 7* 1084-S

9b adsumptus est 1118-P, 1084-P, 1120-P

10 *1118-P, 1084-P, and S read as follows:*

    F   G   A   C   C   C   B   C   A   C   G   A

10a Ip- sum er-   go pu- ra men-te ob- se- cra-

Ip- sum qui ho-mi-nem per-di- tum re- pa- ra-

    F   G   A   G G F G   G

mus ut me- mor   no- bis sit   F   G G

vit mun-det nos a de- lic-to   (ad no-xa 1084)

(Pro quibus fudit pretiosum sanguinem suum 1118-P *no notes*)

    F G   A C C C   B C A   C G A F

10b Qui pro gre-ge su- o mo- ri di- gna- tus fu- it

Qui si-gnum in cru-ce ve-xillum no- bis de- dit

    F G A C C   B C A   C G A F

et ho- di- e a mor-tu- is vic-tor sur-rex-it

et se- det in ex-cel-sis dextri su   i

      G A G F G G

ut no- bis pi- us sit

no- bis me-mor sit

Of this version, 1118-S has only 10a, Ipsum ergo . . . nobis sit.

11b cantitantes *for* ei cantantes 1240-P

    C   C

(cum . . . -stis) 1084-S

    C

(-stis) 1118-S

ei *om.* 1118-S, 1084-P,S, 1120-P

    C D C

(-mur ju-cund-) 1118-S, 1084-S

Amen *om.* 1118-S, 1084-P,S, 1120-P

Other manuscripts

Oxford, Bodleian Douce MS 222, fol. 99v

(The subphrases of 6 are interchanged; phrase 10 is a short double.)

Paris, B.N.n.a.lat.495, fol. 76

(The subphrases of 6 are interchanged still differently; phrase 10 is a short double.)

Published versions
Anal.hymn. 53, p. 126; R. L. Crocker, "Some Ninth-
Century Sequences," pp. 396–402.

SEMPER REGNANS

Manuscripts
Munich, Cod.lat.14843, fol. 98v: Prose (text only)

Variants
6 passis et (suis)
7a nisibus
9 vivificarit
10a caeli *om.*

Published versions
Anal.hymn. 42, p. 49. Von den Steinen, *Anfänge*, vol.
41, pp. 25ff. R. L. Crocker, "Some Ninth-Century
Sequences," pp. 400ff., identified the melody.

Notker: LAUDES SALVATORI

Text
Von den Steinen, *Notker* II, pp. 28, 164; I, pp. 206ff.,
542f.

Melody
Bannister, melody A 57: Bodleian lat.lit. c. 14: transcription fol. 94–99v; tabulation ("Frigdola") fol.
100–103v, which collates St. Gall MSS 484, p. 269;
378, p. 195; 380, p. 163; 381, p. 392; 382, p. 124 (and
others). Bannister's transcription of this piece, among
others, illustrates the persistent use of C for B that
characterizes the *later* German tradition. This of
course is not represented in the adiastematic MSS,
which correspond just as well to the Aquitanian
version.

Published versions
Anal.hymn. 53, p. 65; Schubiger, p. 13; Drinkwelder,
p. 29; de Goede, p. 23; Aix-la-chapelle, p. 77.

HÆC EST SANCTA SOLEMNITAS

Manuscripts
Paris B.N.lat.1240, fol. 48: Prose (text only)
Paris B.N.lat.1084, fol. 304v: Prose
Paris B.N.lat.1118, fol. 156v: Prose (St. Stephen)
Paris B.N.lat.1118, fol. 158v: Prose (St. John)
Paris B.N.lat.1138, fol. 60: Prose
Munich, Staatsbibl. Cod.lat.14843, fol. 96v: Prose
(text only)
Paris B.N.lat.n.a.1871 (not collated)

Variants
    G A
1 cunctis *for* diei hujus et 1240-P, 1118 fol. 158v,
    1084-P, 1138-P, 14843-P
    Johannis 1118-fol.158v, 1084-P, 1138-P
    Apri 14843-P

2b celestia *om.* 1240-P
3b Idcirco 1240-P, 14843-P, 1138-P, 1118-fol. 158v,
    1084-P
4a solvantur 1240-P
    (nostra solvat) nostra, *no notes* 1118-P fol. 156v
    Phrases 4a,b exchanged 1118 fol. 156v
5 Johannes 1118 fol. 158v, 1084-P, 1138-P
    Apri 14843-P
    Phrases 5a,b exchanged 14843-P

Between 5 and 6, a long interpolation in 1118 fol. 158v,
1084-P, 1138-P;
    Atque domini sequens vestigia cum innumera
    populi milia
    Et dulcis canora odas resonabis candidissima cum
    turba maxima.
    Et voce decantabis angelica
    Cum quatuor celi animalia ter:
        Agius, agius, agius kirrius:
        Hoc est sanctus, sanctus, sanctus dominus.
    Et domino decantabis munera:
    Et maxima videberis in gloria. (1118 fol. 158v)
6 clemencia *for* auxilia 1118 fol.158v, 1084-P
    precamus *for* praecelsam 14843-P
7 (per splendida) per 1084-P
    splendida per secula 1118-156
    CBA AAG A A G
      in secula   1138-P, Amen *om.*

Other manuscripts
Verona, Bibl.cap.XC (olim 85)
Verona, Bibl.cap.CVII, fol. 99v

Published versions
Anal.hymn. 53, p. 381. See also Von den Steinen,
Anfänge, vol. 41, pp. 22ff.; Crocker, "The Sequence,"
p. 291.

Notker: HÆC EST SANCTA SOLEMNITAS SOLEMNITATUM

Text
Von den Steinen, *Notker* II, pp. 42, 166; I, pp. 232f.,
546f., with parallel display with HÆC EST SANCTA
SOLEMNITAS.

Melody
Bannister, melody A 45: Bodleian lat.lit. c. 13; transcription fol. 146–148v; tabulation ("Virgo plorans"), fol. 138–139v, collating St. Gall MSS 484,
p. 276; 378, p. 214; 380, p. 178; 381, p. 408; 382, p. 137
(and others).

Published versions
Anal.hymn. 53, p. 98; Schubiger, p. 17.

Notker: QUID TU VIRGO

Text
Von den Steinen, *Notker* II, pp. 86, 174; I, pp. 399ff.,
593f.

Melody

Bannister: see HÆC EST SANCTA SOLEMNITAS SOLEMNITA-
TUM: St. Gall MSS 378, p. 294; 380, p. 241; 381, p. 483; 382, p. 206.

Published versions

Anal.hymn. 53, p. 379.

FORTIS ATQUE AMARA

Manuscripts

Paris B.N.lat.1240, fol. 52v: Prose (text only)
Paris B.N.lat.1084, fol. 277v: Prose
Paris B.N.lat.1084, fol. 212: Sequence
Paris B.N.lat.1118, fol. 240v: Prose
Paris B.N.lat.1118, fol. 143: Sequence
Paris B.N.lat.1121, fol. 198: Prose
Paris B.N.lat.1121, fol. 68: Sequence
Paris B.N.lat.1338, fol. 82: Prose
Paris B.N.lat.909, fol. 123v: Sequence

Variants

```
      A A  B A A G
1   (Fortis atque amara) 1084-P,S; 1338-P
      B
    (atque) 1121-P
3   (quae) disjuncture 1121-P
      C  BA
    (omnia) 1084-S
      C  AG
    (omnia) 1118-S
      C  BG
    (omnia) 1338-P
      CB A
    (-ti- a) 1118-P
    (que . . . natantia) a tone lower 1121-P
    (que . . . corporea) a tone lower 1121-S
      C om.
4a  (pare-) 1084-P
      C B
6a  ita for sic 1084-P,S; 1121-P,S
    virgulta 1084-P
      B BA       B G
6b  (polo- rum caterva) 1338-P
              G
    (columnella) 1338-P
      E  ? E D B
7   (sempiterna qui) 1118-S
      E  DE D C
    (sempiterna qui) 1084-S
      F  DF E
    (sempiterne) 1121-P,S
      E C ED
    (sinas ire) 1121-P
              A
    (moderna) 1338-P
```

              B
    (moderna) 1121-S
8   loca for regna 1121-P
    Amen om. 1118-S, 1121-S, 1084-S, 1240-S

Published versions

Anal.hymn. 53, p. 160; see also Von den Steinen, Anfänge, vol. 41, p. 141; Crocker, "The Sequence," p. 285.

Notker: JUDICEM NOS

Text

Von den Steinen, Notker II, pp. 44, 166; I, pp. 217f., 548ff.

Melody

Bannister, melody A 51: Bodleian lat.lit. c. 14: transcription fol. 48–48v; 51–51v; tabulation ("Deus judex justus"): fol. 50v, 50, 49v, 49, collating St. Gall MSS 484, p. 276; 378, p. 215; 380, p. 179; 381, p. 410; 382, p. 138 (and others).

Published versions

Anal.hymn. 53, p. 100; Schubiger, p. 18.

CLARA GAUDIA

Manuscripts

Paris B.N.lat. 1118, fol. 177v: Prose
Paris B.N.lat. 1118, fol. 136: Sequence
Paris B.N.lat. 1084, fol. 244v: Prose
Paris B.N.lat. 1084, fol. 205: Sequence
Paris B.N.lat. 1138, fol. 78v: Prose

Variants

```
      FE  AAG
1   (paschali-a) 1118-P
       F   AAG
    (paschali-a) 1118-S
       F   AAF
    (paschali-a) 1084-S
         AG              F
2   (omni-a) 1138-P  (congaudet) and 2b 1118-S
      GA G  F AAG
    (decantans alleluia) 1138-P
              F
3a  (Chri-stus) and 3b 1084-P
      —  FE D E FGA
3b  (A protoplasto quot) 1138-P
      A  G
5b  (saeva) 1118-P
6a  Quid & 1084-P
    Quis de (demones) 1138-P
          A A
    (demones) and 6b 1118-P, 1138-P
       GA A
    (tenebras) 1118-P
            B
9   (decantans) 1138-P
```

G   A C B G ?
(decantans)   1084-S

Other manuscripts
Paris, B.N.lat.903, fol. 186v
Paris, B.N.n.a.lat.1871, fol. 119
Paris, B.N.n.a.lat.495, fol. 70
Paris, B.N.lat.778, fol. 77
Verona, Bibl. cap. 107, fol. 88v
Vercelli, Bibl. cap. 146, fol. 103v
Rome, Casanatense 1741 (facs. ed. Vecchi), fol. 80
Benevento, Bibl. cap. VI 34 (facs. ed. Pal. Mus. XV) fol. 135v
Oxford, Bodleian Douce 222, fol. 95v

Published versions
Anal.hymn. 53, p. 71

DIC NOBIS

Manuscripts
Paris B.N.lat.1240, fol. 54: Prose (text only)
Paris B.N.lat.1084, fol. 322v: Prose (neumes to 6b)
Paris B.N.lat.1118, fol. 171: Prose
Paris B.N.lat.1138, fol. 138v: Prose (added)
Paris B.N.lat.1120, fol. 118v: Prose
Paris B.N.lat.887, fol. 107v: Prose (not collated)
Paris B.N.lat.887, fol. 90: Sequence (not collated)
Paris B.N.lat.1121, fol. 61v: Sequence
Paris B.N.lat.909, fol. 114v: Sequence
Paris B.N.lat.1119, fol. 168v: Prose & Sequence
Paris B.N.lat.1137, fol. 67: Prose
Paris B.N.lat.1137, fol. 43: Sequence
Paris B.N.lat.1136, fol. 21: Prose
Paris B.N.lat.1136, fol. 94: Sequence
Paris B.N.lat.1132, fol. 134v: Prose

Variants
C C CDFED F G A   A F A   A G
1 Dic nobis   quibus aethenebris nova 1084-P
   aeterris 1120-P
   e terris 1138-P, 1119-P, 1240-P
   aetheris 1137-P
   aeteris 1136-P
   etheris 1132-P
   F G   A A(?) GAG F AG
2a (cuncto mundo nuntians gaudi-a) 1084-P
   F G   A A GAG F AG
2b (Nostram rursus visitas patri-am) 1084-P
   A A G A G F A G
3 (voce dixit alleluia) 1084-P
   B   B
4a (resurrexisse dominum) 1084-P
   A G F A G
   (voce laudanda) and 4b 1084-P
   A F G A G
   (voce laudanda) and 4b 1119-P & S, 1137-P

B
(pennas) 1084-P
G
4b (leta per) 1118-P, 1132-P
B
(dicam) 1136-S, 1121-S
B
(veterem) 1121-S, 909-S, 1136-S
A G F
5a (regnare) 1084-P
A
(gratiam) 1132-P
A
6a (filium) 1121-S, 909-S, 1119-S, 1137-S, 1136-S
A
6b (aeterna) 1138-P
6a,b *pitches dubious* 1084-P
FG
7a (Jam) 1132-P
A
(requiem) 1121-S, 909-S, 1119-P,S, 1137-S, 1136-P, S
G F
(vitam per-) 1132-P
A
perpetuam 1138-P, 1137-P *and* 7b
CA
7b (pariter) 1132-P

Other manuscripts
Paris, B.N.lat.9448, fol. 36v
Paris, Arsenal, 1169, fol. 24v
Paris, Arsenal 135, fol. 244
Paris, B.N.n.a.lat.1235, fol. 211
Paris, B.N.n.a.lat.495, fol. 85
Rome, Casanatense 1741 (facs.ed Vecchi), fol. 81v
Verona, Bibl.cap. CVII, fol. 90v
Benevento, Bibl. cap. VI 34 (facs.ed. *Paléographie musicale* XV), fol. 131
Oxford, Bodleian 775, fol. 185
London, B.M. Royal 8.C.XIII, fol. 14v

Published versions
Anal.hymn. 53, p. 69; Crocker, "The Sequence," p. 288.

Notker: JOHANNES JESU

Text
Von den Steinen, *Notker* II, pp. 17, 161; I, 361ff., 581f.

Melody
Bannister, melody A 48: Bodleian lat.lit. c. 13: transcription fol. 186–188v; tabulation ("Romana"), fol. 183–183v; 185–185v; collating St. Gall MSS 484, p. 261; 378, p. 166; 380, p. 137; 381, p. 350; 382, p. 102 (and others).

Published versions
Anal.hymn. 53, p. 276; Schubiger, p. 1; Moberg, no. 26; de Goede, p. 11; Aix-la-chapelle, p. 75.

Laurenti david

Text

Von den Steinen, *Notker* II, pp. 64, 170; I, 374ff., 584ff.

Melody

Bannister: see johannes jesu; St. Gall MSS 378, p. 247; 381, p. 439; 382, p. 157.

Published versions

Anal.hymn. 53, p. 283; Drinkwelder, p. 46; de Goede, p. 61; Aix-la-chapelle, p. 84.

Christi Hodierna

Manuscripts

Munich Clm 14843, fol. 97v: Prose (text only)
Paris B.N.lat.1240, fol. 46: Prose (text only)
Paris B.N.lat.1084, fol. 231: Prose
Paris B.N.lat.1084, fol. 199v: Sequence
Paris B.N.lat.1118, fol. 148v: Prose
Paris B.N.lat.1118, fol. 132v: Sequence
Paris B.N.lat.1120, fol. 108: Prose (text only)
Paris B.N.lat.887, fol. 150v: Prose (not collated)
Paris B.N.lat.887, fol. 88: Sequence (not collated)
Paris B.N.lat.1119, fol. 145: Prose & sequence
Paris B.N.lat.1121, fol. 59: Sequence
Paris B.N.lat.909, fol. 112: Sequence

Variants

    G G A
1 (Christi) 1118-P, 1084-P,S, 1119-P&S, 1121-S, 909-S
    hodierne 1118-P
    C B A D C A C
2a Voce simul consona 1084-P
    C B A D C A C   B C A G F G G
    Voce simul consonant nativitatis magnae 1118-P
    Voce simul consonat 14843
    nativitatem magnam 1240-P, 1120-P, 1119-P
    A
2b Quod (verbum) 1084-P
    C   B A D C C A
    Quod (verbum caro factum) 1118-P, (14843)
    C B C A G
    (exhi-be-re), se *om.* 1084-P
    se *added* 1119-P (*but no clivis*)
3a Mundo/m 1084-P
    Mundum 1118-P, 1120-P, 1119-P
    redimi 1240-P
    redemi/t 1084-P
    redimere 1120-P, 1119-P
    venerat 14843
    C AC
    venerat 1084-P

    C C A
    venerat 1118-P
3b Nuntiat angelus pastoribus 14843-P
        D C A C
    Nuntiat angelus pastoribus 1084-P
        D C C A
    Nuntiat angelus pastoribus 1118-P
4a (posuit *and* 4b) *confusion in* 1118-S
    G D D C
4b Vagi-ensque 1084-P
    C G B A C F G G
    (reg-i-tur omnis mundus) 1084-P,S, 1119-P&S
5a audiunt nam 1120-P, 1119-P
    audiuntque 1084-P, 1118-P
    G G F G A F D
6a (Exiguo tegitur *and* 6b) 1084-P,S, 1119-P&S, 1121-S, 909-S
    A E D
    (tegitur) 1118-S
    E
    (qui) 1118-P
6b rostris 1240-P, 1084-P, 1119-P, 14843-P, 887-P
    nostris 1118-P, 1120-P
        F G
7a (genetricis *and* 7b) 1118-P, 1084-P, 1119-P&S, 1121-S, 909-S
    D E F G G A F
    incontaminatus *and* 7b 1084-P, 1119-P&S, 1121-S, 909-S
7b actu *om.* 1118-P
    E D C D D
    accider-et 1118-P
8a in *om.* 1120-P
    ut egypto in 1120-P
    egiptum 14843-P
    fugeret 14843-P, 1118-P
    A G A G A G D G F E C D F G F E C
    (in somnis ab angelo ut in egypto pergeret cum
    C D D
    parvu-lo) 1084-P
            G A G A G D G F E C D F G F
    in *om.*; (somnis ab angelo ut in egypto pergeret
    E D
    cum) 1119-P&S
    C D D
8b dominum *for* Christum 1084-P
    E D
    (occidere) 1084-P, *neume incorrectly written* 1118-P
    callide occidere *om.* 14843-P
    D F E G A F D F E F G A F D
9a (Nos quoque . . .   1084-P, 1119-P&S, 1121-S, 909-S
    ergo *for* quoque 1084-P
9b donet *om.* 14843-P

E E D D
(aeterna secu-la) 1118-P
dominus deus noster 1240-P, 1120-P
C E G G F E D
dominus deus noster 1119-P, 1121-S, 909-S
E D
amen 1084-P, *no notes* 1240-P, 1118-P

Other manuscripts
Verona, Bibl.cap. CVII, fol. 73
Benevento, Bibl.cap. VI 34 (facs.ed *Paléographie musicale* XV), fol. 18v
Oxford, Bodleian Douce 222, fol. 83
Paris, B.N.lat.778, fol. 47
Paris, B.N.lat.903, fol. 181v
Paris, B.N.n.a.lat.495, fol. 52v
Paris, Arsenal 1169, fol. 5v

Published versions
Anal.hymn. 53, p. 25; Crocker, "The Sequence," p. 296.

REX NOSTRAS CHRISTE LAUDES

Manuscripts
Munich, Cod.lat.14843, fol. 96: Prose (text only)

Variants
3a Aper *for* Petre; benignum
4b que; adquire
7a poscimus
7b *omitted*

Published versions
Anal.hymn. 37, pp. 61–62; Von den Steinen, *Anfänge* vol. 41, pp. 31f., 45f. The absence of 7b does not have quite the same effect as the absence of 8b, since it does not concern the alternate forms of the ending. It is, however, conceivable that 7 was a single in this version.

The other version, apparently later, is REX LAUDES CHRISTE NOSTRAS, *Anal.hymn.* 37, pp. 60–61, edited from Paris B.N.lat.9449 (Nevers, 11th century), and Paris B.N.n.a.lat.1235 (Nevers, 12th century). See Von den Steinen, loc.cit.

ECCE JAM VENIT

Manuscripts
Munich, Cod.lat.14843, fol. 100v: Prose (text only)

Variants
3a fabrica
4a lactet
4b praesepio lacet
6a O: *virga above?*
   lesidia
7a aerea; inanem
7b mortiferam; quam
8a concedas *om.*

Published versions
Anal.hymn. 37, pp. 15–16, edited from two 12th century MSS. Another version, with the same incipit, is given on pp. 16–17, from Verona, Bibl. cap. 107 (11th century). See Von den Steinen, *Anfänge*, vol. 41, pp. 31, 45. Lines 9a,b, while certainly rough, are to me not so "*unverständlich*" as they are to Von den Steinen.

PANGE DEO

Manuscripts
Munich, Cod.lat.14843, fol. 99v: Prose (text only)

Published versions
Anal.hymn. 42, p. 47; Von den Steinen, *Anfänge*, vol. 41, pp. 25ff. R. L. Crocker, "Some Ninth-Century Sequences," p. 385f., identified the melody.

CONGAUDENT ANGELORUM

Text
Von den Steinen, *Notker* II, pp. 66, 170; I, pp. 299ff., 566ff.

Melody
Bannister, melody A 19: Bodleian lat.lit. c. 11: transcription fol. 215–215v; 218–220v; tabulation ("Mater"): fol. 269–272v, collating with St. Gall MSS 484, p. 270; 378, p. 249; 380, p. 205; 381 (?); 382, p. 159.

Published versions
Anal.hymn. p. 179; Schubiger, p. 26; Drinkwelder, p. 47; de Goede, p. 3; Aix-la-chapelle, p. 85.

REX OMNIPOTENS

Manuscripts
Paris B.N.lat.1240, fol. 51v: Prose (text only)
Paris B.N.lat.1118, fol. 187: Prose
Paris B.N.lat. 1118, fol. 137v: Sequence
Paris B.N.lat.1084, fol. 255v: Prose
Paris B.N.lat.1084, fol. 205v: Sequence
Paris B.N.lat.1138, fol. 92v: Prose
Paris B.N.lat.1120, fol. 120: Prose
Paris B.N.lat.1119, fol. 173: Prose & sequence
Paris B.N.lat.1137, fol. 70v: Prose
Paris B.N.lat.1137, fol. 43v: Sequence
Paris B.N.lat.1136, fol. 22: Prose
Paris B.N.lat.1136, fol. 94: Sequence
Paris B.N.lat.1132, fol. 118v: Prose
Paris B.N.lat.1121, fol. 61v: Sequence
Paris B.N.lat.909, fol. 115: Sequence
Paris B.N.lat.903, fol. 187v: Prose

Variants
  G
1 (Rex) 1119-P&S, 1137-P, 1136-P, 1132-P
  B
2a (tri-um-) 1118-S, 1084-P,S

4a (-lo-) *and* 4b 1119-P&S, 1136-P, 1121-S (?)
    B A

5a (mundum bap-) *and* 5b 1119-P&S, 1137-P,S, 1136-P,S, 1121-S, 903-P, 1132-P; *erased, notes om.* 1118-S
    F G G

6b (promissa) munera *om.* 1137-P
    A F

7a (post mul-) *and* 7b 1137-P
    A   F E
(post multos) *and* 7b 1132-P
    FG
(vo-bis) 1118-P, 1138-P

7b (sive) et *om.* 1240-P, 1137-P, 1136-P, 1132-P, *added* 1118-P
    AG
(Samaria) 1137-P, 1136-P
    FG
(Samaria) 1120-P, 1119-P
    A F GG
Samari-a 1132-P

8a (illis elevatus est in nubes clara)
    C C CC A C B C AGF G G 1137-P
    C A CC A C B C AGF G G 1132-P
    C A CC A C B C A GFG G 1136-P, 1119-P
    C A BB A C 1120-P

    B
8b ab oculis eorum 1138-P
    C C
(-lis in-) 1137-P,S, 1136-P,S, 1121-S, 909-S, 1119-P, 1132-P
    A

9a (stetere) *and* 9b 1137-P, 1136-P, 1132-P
in *om.* praeclara *for* alba 1240-P
    E D C DD
(viri)veste praeclara 1118-P, 1132-P
    DD E D C DD
viri in veste praeclara; in *elided* 1084-P
    DE D C DD
viri veste clara 1120-P, 1119-P
    DCE DC DD
viri in veste clara 1137-P
clara 1138-P, 1136-P, 903-P
    C E D CD D
9b caelorum alta 1137-P
    F D F
10a (est a vo-) *and* 10b 1137-P,S, 1132-P, 1136-P,S, 1121-S, 909-S
    F C F
(est a vo-) 1119-P
    E C F
(est a vo-) 1119-S

    F D F
10b (quaerens ta-) 1119-P
(quaerens) a vobis 1240-P
    A B
11a (maris po-) 1132-P
(quem) formasti fraude subdola 1240-P, 1120-P, 1119-P, 1132-P, 1136-P (S *confused*), 1121-S, 909-S; quem *added* 1118-P
    G
(formasti fraude) 1137-P,S, 1132-P
    A
(maris *and* 11b) 1137-P
    C A C AC B GAGF
11b (Hostis expulit paradi-so) 1132-P
ad *om.* 1240-P, 1119-P, 1137-P, 1132-P, *added* 1118-P
    G A G
(secum traxit) 1119-P, 1137-P, 1136-P, 1132-P
retraxit tartara 1084-P
12a ad (gaudia) 1240-P
12b quaesumus *for* petimus 1240-P, 1118-P, 1120-P, 1119-P, 1136-P, 1137-P, 1132-P
sempiterna gaudia 1136-P, 1137-P
13 omnes *added* 1084-P, 1120-P
    A C G A G
cantemus omnes 1137-P

Other manuscripts
Paris, Arsenal 1169, fol. 40v
Paris, B.N.lat.n.a.1871, fol. 136
Paris, B.N.lat.n.a.1177, fol. 62v
Paris, B.N.lat.9449, fol. 47v
Paris, B.N.lat.10508, fol. 67
Oxford, Bodleian 775, fol. 145
Cambridge, Corpus Christi Coll. 473, fol. 99v
London, B.M. Royal 8.C.XIII, fol. 20 (incomplete)
London, B.M. Reg.2 B IV, fol. 97v (incomplete)
London, B.M. Cotton Caligula A XIV, fol. 61
Paris, Arsenal 135, fol. 246
Paris, B.N.n.a.lat.1235, fol. 217v
Rome, Casantense 1741 (facs.ed. Vecchi), fol. 159
Verona, Bibl.cap. CVII, fol. 92v
Oxford, Bodleian Douce 222, fol. 101 (incomplete)
Vercelli, Bibl.cap. 146, fol. 104v
Vercelli, Bibl.cap. 161, fol. 124
Paris, B.N.lat.n.a.495, fol. 90
Published versions
Anal.hymn. 53, p. 111.

Notker: SANCTI SPIRITUS
Text
Von den Steinen, *Notker* II, pp. 54, 168; I, 181ff., 538ff.
Melody
Bannister, melody A 88: Bodleian lat.lit c. 15: transcription fol. 87–90v; tabulation ("Occidentana"):

fol. 74–77v, collating St. Gall MSS 484, p. 281; 378, p. 233; 380, p. 192; 381, p. 428; 382, p. 147.

Published versions
Anal.hymn. 53, p. 119; Schubiger, p. 22; Drinkwelder, p. 35; Moberg, no. 14b; de Goede, p. 40; Aix-la-chapelle, p. 27.

Notker: AGNI PASCHALIS
Text
Von den Steinen, *Notker* II, pp. 34, 165; I, 227ff., 544.
Melody
Bannister, melody A 2: Bodleian lat.lit. c. 11: transcription fol. 14–14v; 17–17v; tabulation ("Greca") fol. 15–16v, collating St. Gall MSS 484, p. 273; 378, p. 206; 380, p. 172; 381, p. 401; 382, p. 131, and others. Bannister's "Norma" is from London B.M.add.18032.

Variants

	B	
1	(potuque digna)	
	C C C	
4a	(et tuta)	
	CB	
8	(mortem)	

Published versions
Anal.hymn. 53, p. 89; Schubiger, p. 15; de Goede, p. 28; Aix-la-chapelle, p. 79.

Notker: MAGNUM TE MICHAELEM
Text
Von den Steinen, *Notker* II, pp. 122, 183.
Melody
Bannister: see AGNI PASCHALIS; St. Gall MSS 378, p. 265; 381, p. 451; 382, p. 168.
Published versions
Anal.hymn. 53, p. 310; Aix-la-chapelle, p. 87.

Notker: CARMEN SUO DILECTO
Text
Von den Steinen, *Notker* II, pp. 40, 166; I, pp. 232, 545f.
Melody
Bannister, melody A 18: Bodleian lat.lit. c. 11: transcription fol. 207–207v; tabulation ("Amoena") fol. 208–209v, collating St. Gall MSS 484 (?); 378, p. 212; 380, p. 176; 381, p. 407; 382, p. 135. Bannister's transcription includes a version from Schubiger, and another from pitch letters added to MS 380 (for this piece only). Schubiger's version, in turn, is from Einsiedeln MS 366. Against all of these, I have read the cadences in phrases 2–6 as C,D,E (and in phrase 7 as F,F,E) to reflect the salicus in the St. Gall MSS, for which the reading B,C,D seems intrinsically not believable. If the salicus, however, was a "salicus at the unison," (see Cardine, "Semiologie grégorienne,"

p. 108ff.) then it could be read C,D,D (and the final cadence F,F,D); but it is hard to see why a pes stratus was not used if that was the intent. Einsiedeln MS 366, apparently the earliest diastematic source, is not decisive.

Published versions
Anal.hymn. 53, p. 96; Schubiger, p. 4; de Goede, p. 32.

Notker: SUMMI TRIUMPHUM REGIS
Text
Von den Steinen, *Notker* II, pp. 50, 167; I, 239ff., 552ff.
Melody
Bannister, melody A 97; Bodleian lat.lit. c. 15: transcription fol. 270–270v, 273–274v; tabulation ("Captiva") fol. 265–267v, collating St. Gall MSS 484, p. 278; 378, p. 220; 380, p. 183; 381, p. 414; 382, p. 141 (and others).

Variants

	A		F F G E F
2	(qui caeli, terrae, inferni jure)		
		F E D	F
4	(in virginalem ven-)		
		C	
5	(illius)		
		F F EF	D
6	(duxit secum)		
		CC	F
8	(judicem, docerunt)		
		G	F
9	(Jam, imploremus)		
			F E E
10	(quoque semper)		

Published versions
Anal.hymn. 53, p. 114; Schubiger, p. 20; de Goede, p. 38; Aix-la-chapelle, p. 79.

Notker: SCALAM AD COELOS
Text
Von den Steinen, *Notker* II, pp. 90, 174; I, 408ff., 596ff.
Melody
Bannister, melody A 17; Bodleian lat.lit. c. 11: transcription fol. 180–180v, 201–203v; tabulation ("Puella turbata") fol. 197–200v, collating St. Gall MSS 484, p. 290; 378, p. 181 (CANTEMUS); 380, p. 244; 381, p. 486.

Variants

	F	
2	(cujus)	
	G C	C C D F
4	(Hanc, scalam, perviam, et Aethiopis)	
	B	
6	(armilla)	

F
9 (vides)
   A   BB F G B B   F E F
11 (his beneficiis, dominum nos, glorificemus, justi)

Published versions
Anal.hymn. 53, p. 393.

CANTEMUS CUNCTI MELODUM

Text
Von den Steinen, *Notker* II, pp. 132, 186.

Melody
Bannister: see SCALAM AD COELOS; St. Gall MSS 308,
p. 247; 381, p. 490.

Published versions
Anal.hymn. 53, p. 60; Schubiger, p. 10; de Goede, p.
128.

Notker: CONCENTU PARILI

Text
Von den Steinen, *Notker* II, pp. 24, 163; I, pp. 315ff.,
571ff.

Melody
Bannister, melody A 25; Bodleian lat.lit. c. 12: transcription fol. 2–5v; 19–19v; tabulation ("Sympho-
nia") fol. 6–7v, collating St. Gall MSS 484, p. 266;
378, p. 185; 380, p. 155; 381, p. 379; 382, p. 117, and
others.

Variants
   D E F
1a (teque piis)
   D E F D E F
1b (tu filia, ac Davidis)
   G A
3 (praefigurat)
       F   F
4 (cupisti, pollutis)
       F E
6 (Ergo quique)

Published versions
Anal.hymn. 53, p. 171; Schubiger, p. 12; Drinkwelder,
p. 27; de Goede, p. 20; Aix-la-chapelle, p. 77.

Notker: NATUS ANTE SAECULA

Text
Von den Steinen, *Notker* II, pp. 12, 160; I, pp. 266ff.,
559f.

Melody
Bannister, melody A 68: Bodleian lat.lit. c. 14: tran-
scription fol. 237–237v; 246v, 247v, 247; tabulation
("Dies sanctificatus") fol. 240–241v, collating St.
Gall, MSS 484, p. 258; 378, p. 155; 380, p. 125; 381,
p. 333; 382, p. 94, and others.

Variants
   A B C D
1a (Natus ante)
   C DD
3 (tergeret)
   G
5 (circumstant)

Published versions
Anal.hymn. 53, p. 20; Schubiger, p. 6; Drinkwelder,
p. 18; de Goede, p. 6; Aix-la-chapelle, p. 74.

HÆC EST VERA REDEMPTIO

Manuscripts
Paris B.N.lat.1118, fol. 185: Prose
Paris B.N.lat.1118, fol. 134v: Sequence
Paris B.N.lat.1084, fol. 312v: Prose (text only)
Paris B.N.lat.1138, fol. 84: Prose
Paris B.N.lat.n.a.1871, fol. 127v: Prose (not collated)

Variants
1 A A A C A C A C E CD D 1118-S
    D E
7a (Per li-) 1138-P
    G
9a Ut 1138-P
    G AG A F
   (Et hujus mundi) 1118-P
10a culpa labuerat
    A B A B *and* 10b 1118-P
    B C A B ? 1138-P
11a (repingamus) aulam 1084-P
   archam aula . . . alma 1138-P
       D F D C BB
12a O *om.* (Mira domini est) 1138-P
    A C A B A C D AG F GG
12b (victimavit immaculata hostia) 1118-P, 1138-P
   victi/mavit *disjuncture* 1118-S
    G B G F G A BG
13 Et regnat nunc per tempora 1138-P, 1118-S
   Amen *om.* 1138-P, 1118-S

Other versions
Paris B.N.lat.1118, fol. 248v
Paris B.N.lat.1084, fol. 215: "Paschalis antica"
Paris B.N.lat.1121, fol. 61: "Hæc est vera"
This version has variants at the start of phrases 3 and
11, and substantial differences from phrases 7 through
10.

Published versions
Anal.hymn. 7, p. 77; 53, p. 77 (this is the later version
from Paris B.N.n.a.lat.1871).

BEATA TU VIRGO

Manuscripts
Paris B.N.lat.1118, fol. 154v: Prose

Paris B.N.lat.1138, fol. 72: Prose
Munich Clm 14843, fol. 101: Prose (text only)

Variants

1   tu *added* 1138-P
4   O alma virgo maria O beata maria 14843-P
    G G
5a (De te) 1138-P
5b erat et (clausa) 14843-P
            DG ABA
6   O alma virgo semper Maria 1138-P
    as 4 14843
7a (Jam) enim tripudia 14843
            C D C C
7b (coros) sublimata 1138-P
    sublimata 14843-P
8a *as 4* 14843-P
8b *om.* 1138-P
10b avis *for* tuis 1118-P
    D D C   D   A
    (Ut tuis) suffulta 1138-P
    B   A FGG
    (ad meliora) 1138-P
11b laxare *for* portare 14843-P
    hujus (seculi) 14843-P
    CD BA
    vi- ta 1138-P
12a Nostri 14843-P
     B A B
    (quaesumus) 1138-P
12b tecum simul 14843-P
    A B CDAG A BCABA B C DAG
    (tecum mereamur gaudere per aevum in caeles-tia
    FG F
    regna) *pitch disjuncture somewhere in the middle*
    1138-P

Other versions

Paris B.N.lat.n.a.1871, fol. 151v: Prose (fol. 81:
Sequence). Heavily reworked, much text erased.
Verona Bibl.cap. XC (olim 85)

Published versions

Anal.hymn. 53, pp. 191–193; Von den Steinen, *An-fänge* vol. 41, p. 36.

SANCTA TU VIRGO

Manuscripts
London B.M.Add.19768, fol. 5v

Published versions
Anal.hymn. 53, p. 194.

Notker: GAUDE MARIA VIRGO

Text
Von den Steinen, *Notker* II, pp. 20, 162; I, pp. 310ff.,
569ff.

Melody
Bannister, melody A 40: Bodleian lat.lit. c. 13: transcription fol. 60–63v; tabulation ("Cignea") fol.
66–67v, collating St. Gall MSS 484, p. 263; 378, p.
176; 380, p. 145; 381, p. 365; 382, p. 109 (and others).

Published versions
Anal.hymn. 53, p. 45; Schubiger, p. 8.

PRAECURSOR CHRISTI

Manuscripts
Paris B.N.lat.1118, fol. 206: Prose
Paris B.N.lat.1118, fol. 138v: Sequence
Paris B.N.lat.1084, fol. 258v: Prose
Paris B.N.lat.1084, fol. 206: Sequence
Paris B.N.lat.1138, fol. 96v: Prose
Paris B.N.lat.887,   fol. 152v: Prose (text only)
Paris B.N.lat.1121, fol. 72v: Sequence

Variants

1   C D E DE 1118-S, 1084-S
    C D F DF 1121-S
3   *There is a pitch disjuncture somewhere* 1118-P,S,
    1084-S
        AG
    (mi-ra-) 1118-P
        D CB A CB A ?
3b (conjungere mystice cum) 1084-P
4a Te nunc 1084-P, 1138-P
        — F
5a (-vanda) 1118-S, 1084-S
5b dei inimicus 1138-P
        F F
6a (ducit) *and 6b* 1084-P
6b in aeterna *for* saecula 887-P
7b preces *for* laudes 1084-P
    summa laude 887-P
8a Mittens 1118-P, 887-P
    Mitt/t/ens 1084-P
    Mitens 1138-P
8b lauda *for* lava 1118-P
    cuncta *om.* 887-P
9a sacra *added*, qui 1118-P
    G EFE
9b (curricula) 1138-P
    celebremus 887-P
    caltudia 1084-P, 887-P (*locus obscurior*)
10 alma 1084-P, 1138-P
    EE D
    Amen *added* 1138-P (*no notes* 1118-P)

Other manuscripts
Benevento, Bibl.cap. VI 34, fol. 199

Published versions
Anal.hymn. 53, p. 273; Husmann, "Justus ut palma,"
Revue belge de musicologie X (1956), pp. 121–128.

Notker: DILECTE DEO GALLE

Text

Von den Steinen, *Notker* II, pp. 72, 171; I, pp. 379ff., 586ff.

Melody

Bannister, melody A 71: Bodleian lat.lit. c. 14: transcription fol. 262–264v; tabulation ("Justus ut palma minor") fol. 272–273v, collating St. Gall MSS 484, p. 282; 378, p. 269; 380, p. 223; 381, p. 455; 382, p. 171.

Published versions

Anal.hymn. 53, p. 246; Schubiger, p. 30.

Notker: REX REGUM

Text

Von den Steinen, *Notker* II, pp. 88, 174; I pp. 405ff., 594f.

Melody

Bannister: see DILECTE DEO GALLE; St. Gall MSS 378, p. 245; 380, p. 242; 381, p. 441; 382, p. 186.

Published versions

Anal.hymn. 53, p. 390; de Geode, p. 123.

HÆC DIES EST SANCTA

Manuscripts

Paris B.N.lat.1118, fol. 154: Prose
Paris B.N.lat.1118, fol. 133: Sequence
Paris B.N.lat.1084, fol. 233: Prose
Paris B.N.lat.1084, fol. 198v: Sequence

Variants

1   gloria *for* gloriosa 1118-P
        F
2a   (qua) 1118-S
        E
     (Ma-) 1118-S
        F
     (ex) 1118-P
        E D
4a   (ergo) 1118-S
        A C   B A G B A G F G A A
5a   voce simul *corrected to* celsa cordis simul atque oris
     and 5b, 1084-P
5b   fulti/dicentes *disjuncture* 1084-P
        A B D G B A   B D ?
6a   (Glori-a in altis de-o)   *and 6b* 1118-P
        A C E
     (Glori-a) 1118-S
        A B D
     (Glori-a) 1084-S *and 6b*
        B A
     (terra pax) 1084-S
        A B C ?
7   (Famulos) 1118-S
        D C D
8a   (auxiliare) 1084-P

                B G A B C C
8b   (omnia regis si-) *and continuing a tone too low* 1118-P

Other manuscripts

Paris, B.N.n.a.lat.495, fol. 51

Published versions

Anal.hymn. 53, p. 38; Husmann, "Justus ut palma." Crocker, "The Sequence," p. 301.

ORGANICIS CANAMUS

Manuscripts

Paris B.N.lat.1118, fol 159: Prose
Paris B.N.lat.1118, fol. 134: Sequence
Paris B.N.lat.1084, fol. 237: Prose
Paris B.N.lat.1084, fol. 201: Sequence
Paris B.N.lat.1138, fol. 61: Prose
Paris B.N.lat.1120, fol. 113: Prose
Paris B.N.lat.1119, fol. 154v: Prose & Sequence
Paris B.N.lat.1137, fol. 60: Prose
Paris B.N.lat.1137, fol. 41v: Sequence
Paris B.N.lat.1136, fol. 18v: Prose
Paris B.N.lat.1132, fol. 132: Prose
Paris B.N.lat.903, fol. 184v: Prose
Paris B.N.lat.909, fol. 113: Sequence

Variants

1   Al- le-   lu-   ia
     C   D E D E F G F E D F F D 1118-S
     "   D E FED 1084-S
     C   D F D E F G F E D F F D 1137-S
        D E G
2a   Canamus *and 2b* 1118-P, 1084-P, 1138-P
        F
     (Nunc) 1084-S
        D A A G F E F G A G F D *disjuncture* 1118-S
     D A A G F E F G
     Organicis canamus 1137-P
3a   A C C E E 1118-P,S, 1084-P,S, 1136-P,S, 1132-P,
     1119-P&S
     A C C D D 1137-P
     suis, et *om.* 1132-P
        F
     (ac) 1118-S
3b   A B C D D 1137-S
     (agitat) fides *om.* 1132-P
4a   perstringens 1084-P, 1138-P, *corrected to* currens
     1136-P
     permiscens 1084-P, 1138-P
        A B
4b   (Quam) 1132-P
     4b om. 1137-P
5   *om.* 1118-S
5b   *om.* 1084-P
6   E G F G A, E G F G A, A C B D C A *continuing to*
     a D-final 1118-S

C DD

sidera *and 6b* 1119-P&S, 1118-P, 1084-P, 1132-P, 1137-P *but varies in 1137-S*

rite/petentes *disjuncture in* 903-P

Alacres *om.* 1132-P

7a   annua . . . vota *om.* 1084-P, *is interpolation?*

     B B G

7b   (patria) 1138-P, (1120-P), 1118-S, 1084-P,S

     A AG

     (patri-a) 1118-P, 1119-P&S, 1137-P,S, 1136-P, 1132-P

Other manuscripts

Paris, Arsenal 1169, fol. 9v

Paris, Arsenal 135, fol. 262

Paris, B.N.lat.778, fol. 58v, 59v

Paris, B.N.n.a.lat.1235, fol. 225v

Paris, B.N.n.a.lat.495, fol. 58v

Verona, Bibl.cap.CVII, fol. 109v

London, B.M. Cotton Caligula A XIV, fol. 71

Oxford, Bodleian 775, fol. 138

Published versions

Anal.hymn. 53, p. 385; Husmann, "Justus ut palma."

ECCE DIES ORBIS

Manuscripts

Paris B.N.lat.1118, fol. 204v: Prose

Paris B.N.lat.1084, fol. 320: Prose (text only)

Paris B.N.lat.1338, fol. 58v: Prose

Variants

     A AG   E   G A D

2a   Angeli-co (*canceled*) quod praedictus 1118-P

     G G F D *and 2b* 1338-P

3b   (domini) diligite sicut Isaias propheta 1084-P

4a   -mo / do- *disjuncture* 1338-P

     anno baptizans 1084-P

4b   A A G F D F F A F (*and 4a?*) 1338-P, (1118-P?)

     A C B A   G B A G F

5a   Ergo tuam deprecamur de *similarly* ut sicut . . . *and 5b* 1338-P

     clemenciam *for* suffragia 1338-P

5b   effugiamus marti dum 1338-P

     morticinum 1084-P

     (morti)cinum *canceled* 1118-P

7   gloria *for* gaudia 1084-P, 1338-P

8b   (per) secula 1338-P

           D C D E F D

9   (dicentes) amen (alleluia) 1338-P

Published versions

Anal.hymn. 7, p. 160.

NOTKER: SANCTI BAPTISTAE

Text

Von den Steinen, *Notker* II, pp. 60, 169; I, pp. 351ff., 576ff.

Melody

Bannister, melody A 95, Bodleian lat.lit. c. 15: transcription fol. 184–187v; tabulation, collating St. Gall MSS 484, p. 262; 378, p. 236; 380, p. 197; 381, p. 433; 382, p. 150.

Published versions

Anal.hymn. 53, p. 267; Schubiger, p. 25; Drinkwelder, p. 40; Moberg, no. 17; de Goede, p. 49; Aix-la-chapelle, p. 81.

NOTKER: LAUS TIBI CHRISTE CUI SAPIT

Text

Von den Steinen, *Notker* II, pp. 18, 162; I, pp. 342ff. 574f.

Melody

Bannister: see SANCTI BAPTISTAE; St. Gall MSS 378, p. 171; 380, p. 138; 381, p. 439; 382, p. 106.

Published versions

Anal.hymn. 53, p. 256; de Goede, p. 12; Aix-la-chapelle, p. 76.

OMNIPOTENS DEUS

Manuscripts

Paris B.N.lat.1118, fol. 194v: Prose

Paris B.N.lat.1118, fol. 142: Sequence

Paris B.N.lat.1084, fol. 287v: Prose

Paris B.N.lat.1138, fol. 129v: Prose

Paris B.N.lat.1121, fol. 72: Sequence

Variants

     G G G GA AB

1   Omnipotens de- 1138-P

3a   (totum) canit 1118-P, 1084-P, 1138-P

     F G G *added at end* 1118-S

     FG

5a   natura *and 5b* 1118-P

     ecclesia sancta 1138-P

     (ecclesia)m *added* 1084-P

5b   in *for* de 1138-P

     A

6a   (At) 1118-S, *starts as though D*

     CD

     (virtus) 1118-P, 1084-P, 1138-P

     G A

8a   (-men sed) *om.* 1118-S *disjuncture*

     G

     (-men) *om. and disjuncture* 1121-S

8b   (de patre) est 1138-P

Published versions

Anal.hymn. 7, p. 258; de Goede, p. CI, pointed out the connection to Notker's FESTA CHRISTI.

NOTKER: FESTA CHRISTI

Text

Von den Steinen, *Notker* II, pp. 22, 162; I, pp. 280ff., 563f.

Melody
Bannister, melody A 38; Bodleian lat.lit. c. 12: transcription fol. 221–221v; 230–231v; 234–238v; tabulation ("Trinitas") fol. 224–227v, collating St. Gall MSS 484, p. 264; 378, p. 178; 380, p. 147; 381, p. 367; 382, p. 111 (and others).

Published versions
Anal.hymn. 53, p. 50; Schubiger, p. 9; Drinkwelder, p. 25; Moberg, no. 16b; de Goede, p. 15; Aix-la-chapelle, p. 76.

SALUS AETERNA

Manuscripts
Paris B.N.lat.1118, fol. 144v: Prose
Paris B.N.lat.1084, fol. 306: Prose
Paris B.N.lat.1084, fol. 197: Sequence
Paris B.N.lat.1138, fol. 39: Prose
Paris B.N.lat.887, fol. 96: Prose
Paris B.N.lat.887, fol. 87: Sequence
Paris B.N.lat.1120, fol. 106v: Prose
Paris B.N.lat.1119, fol. 140v: Prose & Sequence
Paris B.N.lat.1137, fol. 51v: Prose
Paris B.N.lat.1137, fol. 39v: Sequence
Paris B.N.lat.1136, fol. 17: Prose
Paris B.N.lat.1136, fol. 92v: Sequence
Paris B.N.lat.909, fol. 110v: Sequence
Paris B.N.lat.1132, fol. 113v: Prose

Variants

    FGA AG ABCB ACCC C
1 Al- le-   lu-   ia 1084-S, 887-S
         "   CDCAG BACDCBAAG
                  909-S, 1137-S, 1119-P&S
        "   "
    AFAG 1132-P
2 C D E B A 1138-P *and 2b*
    C D E B G A C B A G B G A G *and 2b*, 887-P,
                    1137-P,S, 1136-P?
    C D E C G A C B A G B G A G 909-S, 1119-P&S
    C D E D A B D C B A B G A G (?) 1132-P *and*
                          2b
    G
3a (Condolens) *and 3b* 1120-P, 1119-P&S, 1137-P,S,
    1132-P, 909-S, 1084-P, 1136-P
    C
    (saecla) 1137-S
3b Re(linquens) 1120-P, 887-P, 1119-P (no note), 1136-P
4a Vox 1132-P, 1119-P
      E D C
    (spontanea) 1137-S, 1119-P&S, 1132-P, 909-S
5a G A C A A G B *and 5b* 1120-P, 1119-P&S, 1137-P,
    S, 1132-P, 909-S, 887-S, 1084-P, 1136-P
      B
    (et) *and 5b* 887-P

    C B
(animas et) *and 5b* 1120-P, 1119-P&S, 1137-P,S, 1132-P, 909-S (*second halves of 5a,b seem added in* 1119-P&S
    C
(animas) 1136-P
    GA B
6 (Nosmet) 1118-P, 1138-P
7a G B D D D D E D C *and 7b* 1084-P
    G B D D E D E D C *and 7b* 887-P,S
    B D D D E D E D B 909-S, 1137-P,S, (1120-P),
                      1119-P&S
    B D D D E D D C B 1136-P
7b G B D D E D E D C 909-S, 1137-P,S, (1120-P),
                    1119-P&S, 1136-P
    7a,b *not clear* 1132-P
8a Et 1119-P
    D ED
    (Ut) tecum 1137-P
    D E
    (Ut cum) *and 8b* 909-S, 1137-S, (1120-P), 887-P,S,
    1119-P&S, 1136-P, 1084-P; 8a,b *not clear* 1132-P
    D E
8b (Compti) 1137-P
    E D D C E D D B
    (incorrupta nosmet tua) 1137-P
    (subsequamur mox vestigi-a)
      C D E C D BC A G 1137-P,S 1132-P,
                      (1120-P)
         "   C   " 909-S, 1119-P&S

Other manuscripts
Paris, B.N.lat.903, fol. 180
Paris, Arsenal 1169, fol. 49 (text only)
Paris, B.N.lat. 9449, fol. 1v
Paris, B.N.n.a.lat.1235, fol. 178
Paris, B.N.lat.10508, fol. 44
Oxford, Bodleian 775, fol. 167v
Cambridge, Corpus Christi College 473, fol. 122
London, B.M. Cotton Caligula A XIV, fol. 43
London, B.M. Royal 2 B IV, fol. 56
Paris, Arsenal 135, fol. 236
Oxford, Bodleian Douce 222, fol. 82

Published versions
Anal.hymn. 53, p. 3

VENIET REX

Manuscripts
Paris B.N.lat.1118, fol. 144: Prose
Paris B.N.lat.1118, fol. 132: Sequence
Paris B.N.lat.1084, fol. 221: Prose
Paris B.N.lat. 1084, fol. 197v: Sequence
Paris B.N.lat.1338, fol. 70v: Prose
Paris B.N.lat.887, fol. 87: Sequence
Paris B.N.lat.909, fol. 110v: Sequence

Variants

1   (justi . . . vita) *erased* 1118-S
      A G   B A C DC B AG B GA AG
    (-pectant justi ab origine mundi et vita) *and* 2
    909-S
      G CG AG
    mundi et vita 1084-P
      E D C

4a   (per cuncta) *and 4b* 1084-S
    B

5a   (In) *and 5b* 1118-S, 1084-P,S ?
      C   B
    (caelis quoque) 909-S
      D

6a   (miracula) *erased, and 6b* 1118-S
      C
    (perpetua) 909-S
      C

7a   (Dominator) *and 7b* 1084-P; 1084-S *varies*
      C
    (carmina) 909-S
      ABC

7b   (dicant) 1338-P
    gloria *MS damaged* 1118-P
      C
    (regna) 1118-P,S, 1084-P, 909-S
      B
    (dominator) 1084-S
      A A
    saecula 1084-P
    Amen 1084-P *(no notes)*

Published versions
Anal.hymn. 7, p. 27.

Notker: CLARE SANCTORUM SENATUS

Text
Von den Steinen, *Notker* II, pp. 80, 172; I, pp. 355ff.,
578f.

Melody
Bannister, melody A 90: Bodleian lat.lit. c. 15: transcription fol. 128–128v; 133; tabulation ("Aurea")
fol. 124–124v; 127–127v, collating St. Gall MSS 484,
p. 289; 278, p. 289; 380, p. 236; 381, p. 477; 382, p.
205 (and others).

Published versions
Anal.hymn. 53, p. 369; Schubiger, p. 33; Drinkwelder,
p. 59; de Goede, p. 120; Aix-la-chapelle, p. 90.

EN VIRGINUM AGMINA

Manuscripts
Paris B.N.lat.1118, fol. 147: Prose
Paris B.N.lat.1084, fol. 274v: Prose
Paris B.N.lat.1138, fol. 123v: Prose

Variants

    G GABC ABCC B C B A A F GGE
2a Et inter   ce-ter-os ordines fulsit lucidum 1118-P
    "   1084-P,
                                  G "   1138-P
2b Et ovans de- currit in aera Christo obvi-am
    GGG F   G A F GFG GG F F E
                                           1084-P
    "   G AGA "
                                         1118-P
    G A ABC ABC C B C B A AGF G G E
                                          1138-P
      G AFGG
    (cum claro lumine) 1118-P
        E E   E E
4a (respuat . . . consortes) 1138-P
    AC
    Has *for* Eas 1084-P
          C D EFF E
    (invenerit requi-escentes) *and 4b* 1138-P
          E E
    (requiescentes) 1084-P
        AC D
4b (Quid digni-us) 1118-P, 1084-P
        E E   E E
    (dignius . . . semper) 1138-P
    -scriptam *for* vitam 1084-P, 1138-P
      F G F E
    (teneamus) 1118-P
        C D EF
    (teneamus parsimoniam) 1138-P
6   Ut nos tartarea 1084-P
    Et nos tartarea 1138-P
    rem facilato 1084-P
    E G G A B B B C D B A B G A F G A B G A E
    (Et . . .)
                                        F E F D 1138-P
      F G A G A G E F G F E
    (simul . . .)   1138-P
      B C D C B C A B G, F G   F F
    (cunctis . . .)   simul . . . laeti-ti-a
                                     1084-P
  DE E
  Amen 1084-P
  Amen *no notes* 1118-P, 1138-P

The transmission is very uncertain about the pitch
location of phrases 4b and 6; 4b might be a fifth
higher, and 6 is sometimes written as though it began
a fifth lower. In 1084-P the pitches throughout 6 are
dubious.

Published versions
Anal.hymn. 7, p. 240; A. Hughes, *Anglo-French Sequelae*,
p. 80.

JUBILEMUS OMNES

  There are two versions, one represented by MSS

1118, 1138, and 1084, another by the remaining sources. The transcription gives the first version, as found in MS 1118, 146; even though represented by only this one witness (both MSS 1084 and 1138 hesitate between the two versions), this one seems intrinsically credible, and certainly not whimsical. The melismatic sources are not decisive, nor is MS 1120, with only the text. The main variants are in the incipit, and the conclusion. In addition, the pitch level of 4b is difficult to determine, and the MS witness seems contradictory; this phrase might lie a fifth higher.

Manuscripts
Paris B.N.lat.1118, fol. 146: Prose
Paris B.N.lat.1118, fol. 132v: Sequence
Paris B.N.lat.1084, fol. 225: Prose
Paris B.N.lat.1084, fol. 198: Sequence
Paris B.N.lat.1138, fol. 42: Prose

Variants
1   E E F E D 1084-S
        BC BC
2b   (qui cre-) 1084-P
        G   A C AC BA G A GG
     Per quem cuncta condita sunt saecula *added* 1084-P
3b   *added* 1118-P
        E E, E E
4a   (solum, ampla) 1118-P, 1084-S (?), 1138-P
4b   (per saecla) *om.* 1084-S
     4b higher? 1118-S
        B B
6   (trinitas) 1084-S, 1138-P
        A B C G A E   F E F D E F A G A
     (et corda regas et protegas et donis nobis pec-
        G E F   G F E
     catorum veniam) 1084-P,S, 1138-P
        F G A G A G E F G F E
     (et dones . . .)   1118-S

Another version
Paris B.N.lat.1240, fol. 87: Prose (added to the MS)
Paris B.N.lat.1119, fol. 144: Prose & Sequence
Paris B.N.lat.1137, fol. 53v: Prose
Paris B.N.lat.1137, fol. 39v: Sequence
(Paris B.N.lat.1120, fol. 107v: Prose (text only)
(Paris B.N.lat.1121, fol. 58: Sequence
(Paris B.N.lat.909, fol. 111: Sequence
(Paris B.N.lat.1138, fol. 10v: Prose (not collated)
     The incipit in these sources—for example, MS 1119—reads:
EEFD G GB G ABC C D G
Jubilemus omnes mo- do una
G A C C AC CB C B AG
Deo nostro qui creavit omnia
G   A   C CAC CB C   B AG
Per quem cuncta condita sunt saecula

In addition, MSS 1119, 1137, 1120 omit 3, Caelum quo plurima.
The ending typically reads
     F G AB A GEF GFE
     et des nobis peccatorum veniam

Published versions
Anal.hymn. 53, p. 9; A. Hughes, *Anglo-French Sequelae*, p. 99.

Notker: STIRPE MARIA REGIA
Text
Von den Steinen, *Notker* II, pp. 68, 171; I, pp. 306ff., 568f.
Melody
Bannister, melody A 49; Bodleian lat.lit. c. 14: transcription fol. 8–10v; tabulation ("Adducentur") fol. 5–6v, collating St. Gall MSS 484, p. 283; 378 (?); 380, p. 209; 381, p. 446; 382, p. 161 (and others).
Published versions
Anal.hymn. 53, p. 162; Schubiger, p. 28; Drinkwelder, p. 49; de Goede, p. 80; Aix-la-chapelle, p. 86; A. Hughes, *Anglo-French Sequelae*, p. 122.

REGNANTEM SEMPITERNA
Manuscripts
Paris B.N.lat.1084, fol. 221v: Prose
Paris B.N.lat.1138, fol. 40: Prose
Paris B.N.lat.1138, fol. 8: Prose (not collated)
Paris B.N.lat.887, fol. 96: Prose
Paris B.N.lat.887, fol. 87: Sequence
Paris B.N.lat.1120, fol. 106v: Prose
Paris B.N.lat.1119, fol. 142: Prose & Sequence
Paris B.N.lat.1137, fol. 52: Prose
Paris B.N.lat.1137, fol. 39: Sequence
Paris B.N.lat.1132, fol. 114: Prose
Paris B.N.lat.1121, fol. 58: Sequence
Paris B.N.lat.909, fol. 111: Sequence

Variants
        F
2   (devote) 1121-S, 909-S, 887-S
     concrepat 1132-P
     divino sono *added manu altera* 887-P
        A A G G F
     (divino sono) 1084-P, 1138 fol. 40
        E D
3a   (vultu) *and 3b* 1138 fol. 40
        C
4a   (Dist-) 1138 fol. 40 *and 4b*; 1119-P&S, (1120-P)
        B C
5a   (Christe) 1137-P *and 5b*
     per omnia *for* clemencia 1137-P
5b   clara *replaced with* astra 887-P
        B C DE
6a   (salus vera) *and 6b* 887-P,S, 1119-P&S, 1121-S,
        909-S, 1132-P, 1137-P,S, (1120-P ?)

```
       E   D E C
7a  (Ut hic tua) 887-P,S and 7b
       EDC
    (tua) 1137-S
8   Qua (regnas) in (saecu-la per infinita). A-men
    G   G  F  E   DEFD G G F E D  EE D
                               1084-P, 1138 fol 40.
    C   D  E      F E D C D E E D  887-P
```

Other manuscripts

Paris, B.N.lat.10508, fol. 44v
Paris, B.N.n.a.lat.1235, fol. 178v
Paris, Arsenal 135, fol. 236
London, B.M. Cotton Caligula A XIV, fol. 43v
Oxford, Bodleian 775, fol. 168
Oxford, Bodleian Douce 222, fol. 82v
Cambridge, Corpus Christi College 473, fol. 122v

Published versions

Anal.hymn. 53, p. 5 (includes a discussion of the melody for phrase 2). *Processionale monasticum ad usum congregationis gallicae . . .* (Solesmis 1893), p. 21; H. Besseler, *Die Musik des Mittelalters und der Renaissance* (Potsdam 1931), p. 84; E. Jammers, *Mittelalterliche Choral* (Mainz 1954), p. 90.

PANGAT LAUDES

Manuscripts

Paris B.N.lat.1118, fol. 145v: Prose
Paris B.N.lat.1118, fol. 132: Sequence
Paris B.N.lat.1084, fol. 224v: Prose
Paris B.N.lat.1084, fol. 198: Sequence
Paris B.N.lat.1138, fol. 40v: Prose
(The two sequences in MS 1118 and MS 1084 seem to hesitate between REGNANTEM SEMPITERNA and PANGAT LAUDES.)

Variants

```
1   compossit 1138-P
    quo possit 1084-P
2a  Sic 1138-P
       D
3a  (Mittendo) 1084-P
       D
3b  (Hac) 1084-P, 1118-P
4b  que redemptor vere constat 1138-P
6b  gloria added, no notes 1084-P
    G  FE DCD  F  D
    (scandere polorum alma) 1138-P ?
```

Published versions
Anal.hymn. 7, p. 29.

Notker: PSALLAT ECCLESIA

Text

Von den Steinen, *Notker* II, pp. 74, 172; I, pp. 172ff., 536ff.

Melody

Bannister, melody A 82: Bodleian lat.lit. c. 15: transcription fol. 16–16v, 21–21v; tabulation ("Laetatus sum") fol. 19–20v, collating St. Gall MSS 484, p. 284; 378, p. 271; 380, p. 220; 381, p. 460; 382, p. 173 (and others).

Published versions

Anal.hymn. 53, p. 398; Schubiger, p. 31; Drinkwelder, p. 61; Moberg, no. 57; de Goede, p. 114; Aix-la-chapelle, p. 39.

Notker: CHRISTUS HUNC DIEM

Text

Von den Steinen, *Notker* II, pp. 52, 168; I, pp. 243ff., 554f.

Melody

Bannister, melody A 20: Bodleian lat.lit. c. 11: transcription fol. 282–282v; 289–291; tabulation ("Dominus is sina") fol. 286–286v; 288–288v, collating St. Gall MSS 484(?); 378, p. 223; 380, p. 186; 381, p. 417; 382, p. 144.

Variants

```
              C
1   (amatoribus)
         B C  B       B C
2   (naturae, divinae, aeternus)
         CB
3   (dedisti)
```

Published versions
Anal.hymn. 53, p. 116; Schubiger, p. 21.

Notker: AGONE TRIUMPHALI

Text

Von den Steinen, *Notker* II, pp. 82, 173; I, pp. 395ff., 591f.

Melody

Bannister, melody A 73: Bodleian lat.lit. c. 14: transcription fol. 279–280v, 283–283v; tabulation ("Vox exultationis") fol. 284–285v, collating St. Gall MSS 484, p. 285; 378, p. 291; 380, p. 237; 381, p. 480; 382, p. 210 (and others).

Published versions

Anal.hymn. 53, p. 370; de Goede, p. 122; Aix-la-chapelle, p. 90.

Notker: OMNES SANCTI SERAPHIM

Text

Von den Steinen, *Notker* II, pp. 78, 192; I, pp. 328ff., 573f.

Melody

Bannister, see AGONE TRIUMPHALI; St. Gall MSS 378, p. 275; 380, p. 225; 381, p. 463; 382, p. 176.

Published versions

Anal.hymn. 53, p. 196; Schubiger, p. 31; Drinkwelder, p. 53; de Goede, p. 97; Aix-la-chapelle, p. 87.

Bibliography

Amalarii Episcopi opera liturgica omnia, ed. J. M. Hanssens. II: *Liber officialis*. 1948

Analecta hymnica medii aevi, ed. G. M. Dreves and C. Blume. 55 vols. 1886–1922. 53: *Liturgische Prosen erster Epoche*, ed. C. Blume und H. M. Bannister. Leipzig, 1911.

Anglès, H. "Die Sequenzen und die Verbeta im mittelalterlichen Spanien," *Svensk Tidskrift för Musikforskning* 43 (1961), 37–47.

Apel, W. *Gregorian Chant*. Bloomington, 1958.

Bannister, H. "The Earliest French Troper and its Date," *Journal of Theological Studies* II (1901), 420–29.

———. "Epiphaniam," *Rassegna Gregoriana* IV (1905).

Bedae venerabilis opera. Corpus Christianorum series latina. Pars IV: *Opera rhythmica*, ed. J. Fraipont. Turnhout, 1955.

Benoit-Castelli, G., and M. Huglo. "L'Origine bretonne du gradual No. 47 de la Bibliothèque de Chartres," *Études grégoriennes* I (1954), 173–78.

Blume, C. "Vom Alleluia zur Sequenz," *Kirchenmusikalisches Jahrbuch* 24 (1911), 1–20.

Bosse, D. *Untersuchung einstimmiger mittelalterlicher Melodien zum "Gloria in excelsis."* Erlangen, 1954.

Brou, L. "Séquences et tropes dans la liturgie mozarabe," *Hispania sacra* IV (1951), 27–41.

Brinkmann, H. "Voraussetzungen und Struktur religiöser Lyrik im Mittelalter," *Mittellateinisches Jahrbuch* 3 (1966), 37–54.

Cardine, E. "Sémiologie grégorienne," *Etudes grégoriennes* XI (1970), 1–158.

Chailley, J., "Les anciens tropaires et séquentiaires de l'Ecole de Saint-Martial de Limoges (Xᵉ–XIᵉ siecles)," *Etudes grégoriennes* II (1957), 163–88.

———. *L'Ecole musicale de Saint-Martial de Limoges jusqu'à la fin du XIᵉ siecle.* Paris, 1960.

Chambers, E. *The Medieval Stage*. Oxford, 1903.

Crocker, R. L. "Hermann's Major Sixth," *Journal of the American Musicological Society* XXV (1972), 19–37.

———. *A History of Musical Style*. New York, 1966.

———. "The Repertory of Proses at Saint Martial de Limoges in the 10th Century," *Journal of the American Musicological Society* XI (1958), 149–64.

———. "The Sequence," *Gattungen der Musik in Einzeldarstellungen: Gedenkschrift Leo Schrade* I (Bern 1973), 269–322.

———. "Some Ninth-Century Sequences," *Journal of the American Musicological Society* XX (1967), 367–402.

———. "The Troping Hypothesis," *Musical Quarterly* LII (1966), 183–203.

Damilano, P. "Sequenze bobbiesi," *Rivista Italiana di Musicologia* 2 (1967), 3–35.

Dix, G. *The Shape of the Liturgy*. Glasgow, 1945.

Dodwell, C., and D. Turner. *Reichenau Reconsidered: A Re-assessment of the Place of Reichenau in Ottonian Art*. Warburg Institute Surveys II, 1965.

Drinkwelder, O. *Ein deutsches Sequentiar aus dem Ende des 12. Jahrhunderts*. Graz. 1914.

Dronke, P. "The Beginnings of the Sequence," *Beiträge zur Geschichte der deutschen Sprache und Literatur* (Tübinger Ausgabe) LXXXVII (1965), 43–73.

Duckett, E. *Carolingian Portraits: A Study of the Ninth Century*. Michigan, 1962.

Duft. J. "Wie Notker zu den Sequenz kam," *Zeitschrift für Schweizerische Kirchengeschichte* 56 (1962), 201–14.

———. "Le Presbyter de Gimedia apporte son antiphonaire à Saint-Gall," *Jumièges. Congrès scientifique du XIIIᵉ Centenaire* (1955), 925–36.

Elfving, L. *Etude lexicographique sur les séquences limousines*. Uppsala, 1962.

Ellard, G. *Master Alcuin, Liturgist*. Chicago, 1956.

Evans, P. *The Early Trope Repertory of Saint Martial de Limoges*. Princeton, 1970.

Ferretti, P. *Esthétique grégorienne* I. Paris, 1938.

——. "Etude sur la notation aquitaine," *Le codex 903 de la Bibliothèque Nationale de Paris, Gradual de Yrieix (XIe siècle)*, ed. A. Mocquereau. *Paléographie musicale* XIII (1930).

Frere, W. *The Winchester Troper, from MSS of the Xth and XIth Centuries.* Henry Bradshaw Society VIII, 1894.

Gajard, J. "Les récitations modales des 3e et 4e modes," *Etudes grégoriennes* I (1954).

Gautier, L. *Histoire de la poésie liturgique au moyen âge: les tropes.* Paris, 1886.

Gerbert, M. *Scriptores Ecclesiastici de musica sacra,* I. San Blasian, 1784).

de Ghellnick, J. *Littérature latine au moyen âge.* 1939.

de Goede, N. *The Utrecht Prosarium.* Cod. Utraiect. Univ. Bibl. 417. *Monumenta musica Neerlandica.* Amsterdam, 1965.

Graduale romanum: Graduale sacrosanctae romanae ecclesiae de tempore et de sanctis . . . restitutum et editum . . . et rhythmicis signis a solesmensibus monachis diligenter ornatum. Paris, Tournai, 1924.

Gregory. *Moralium libri, sive Expositio in librum B. Job,* ed. J. Migne. *Patrologiae cursus completus. Series latina.* 76. 1844–1902.

Handschin, J. "Two Winchester Tropers," *The Journal of Theological Studies* 37 (1936), 34–49.

——. "Über Estampie und Sequenz," *Zeitschrift für Musikwissenschaft* XII (1929/30), 1–20; XIII (1930/31), 113–32.

——. "Über einige Sequenzen-Zitate," *Acta Musicologica* XV (1943), 15–23.

——. "Trope, Sequence, and Conductus," *New Oxford History of Music* II: *Early Music up to 1300,* ed. A. Hughes. Oxford, 1954.

Hefele, C. *Histoire des Conciles,* trans. and ed. H. Leclercq. Vol. IV. 1924.

Hesbert, R. J. *Antiphonale missarum sextuplex.* Brussels, 1935.

——. *Corpus Antiphonalium Officii. Rerum Ecclesiasticarum Documenta.* Series maior. Fontes VII–IX. I—"Cursus romanus"; II—"Cursus monasticus"; III—Editio critica. Rome, 1963–68.

——. ed. *Le prosaire d'Aix-la-Chapelle. Monumenta Musicae Sacrae* III. Rouen, 1961.

——, ed. *Le prosaire de la Sainte-Chapelle. Monumenta Musicae Sacrae* I. Macon, 1952.

Holschneider, A. *Die Organa von Winchester.* Hildesheim, 1968.

Hughes, A. *Anglo-French Sequelae, Edited from the Papers of the late Dr. Henry Mariott Bannister.* The Plainsong & Mediaeval Music Society. Nashdom Abbey, 1934.

Hughes, D. "Further Notes on the Grouping of the Aquitanian Tropers," *Journal of the American Musicological Society* XIX (1966), 3–12.

Huglo, M. "Les listes alléluiatiques dans les témoins du Graduel grégorien." In *Speculum musicae artis: Festgabe für Heinrich Husmann zum 60. Geburtstag.* Munich, 1970, pp. 219–27.

——. "La mélodie grecque du 'Gloria in excelsis,' et son utilisation dans le Gloria XIV," *Révue grégorienne* XXIX (1950), 30–40.

——. "Un nouveau prosaire nivernais," *Ephemerides liturgicae* 71 (1957), 3–30.

——. "Origine de la mélodie du Credo 'authentique' de la Vaticane," *Révue grégorienne* XXX (1951), 68.

——. *Les tonaires—inventaire, analyse, comparaison.* Paris, 1971.

——. Review of E. Wellesz, *A History of Byzantine Music and Hymnography.* In *Révue grégorienne* XXX (1951), 35–42.

Husmann, H. "Das Alleluia Multifarie und die vorgregorianischen Stufe des Sequenzengesangs," *Festschrift Max Schneider* (1955), 17–23.

——. "Die Alleluia und Sequenzen der Mater-Gruppe." In *Kongress-Bericht Wien.* 1956, pp. 276–84.

——. "Alleluia, Sequenz und Prosa im altspanischen Choral." In *Miscelánea en homenaje a Mons. H. Anglés.* Barcelona, 1958–1961, pp. 407–15.

——. "Alleluia, Vers und Sequenz," *Annales musicologiques* IV (1956), 19–53.

——. "Ecce puerpera genuit. Zur Geschichte der teillextierten Sequenzen." In *Festschrift Heinrich Besseler.* Leipzig, 1961, pp. 59–65.

——. "Zum Grossaufbau der Ambrosianischen Alleluia," *Annuario Musical* XII (1957), 17–33.

——. "Justus ut palma. Alleluia und Sequenzen in St. Gallen und St. Martial," *Revue belge de musicologie* X (1956), 112–28.

——. "Die St. Galler Sequenzentradition bei Notker und Ekkehard," *Acta Musicologica* 26 (1954), 6–18.

——. "Die Sequenz Duo tres. Zur Frühgeschichte der Sequenzen in St. Gallen und in St. Martial." In *In memoriam Jacques Handschin.* Strasbourg, 1962, pp. 66–72.

——. "Sequenz und Prosa," *Annales musicologiques* II (1954), 61–91.

——. *Tropen- und Sequenzenhandschriften.* Repertoire Internationale des Sources Musicales Bv[1]. 1964.

Hymns Ancient and Modern. London, 1909.

James, M. *The Apocryphal New Testament*. Oxford, 1924.

Jammers, E. *Der mittelalterliche Choral. Art und Herkunft*. Mainz, 1954.

————. "Rhythmische und tonale Studien zur alteren Sequenz," *Acta Musicologica* 23 (1951), 1–40.

Kendrick, T. *A History of the Vikings*. London, 1930.

Kunz, L. "Rhythmik und formaler Aufbau der frühen Sequenz," *Zeitschrift für deutsches Altertum und deutsche Literatur* 79 (1942), 1–20.

————. "Die Textgestalt der Sequenz, Congaudent angelorum chori," *Deutsche Vierteljahrschrift für Literaturgeschichte* 28 (1954), 273–86.

Lauer, P., ed. *Flodoard, Historia Remensis ecclesiae: Les annales de Flodoard*. Paris, 1905.

————, ed. *Nithard, Historiarum libri quatuor: Histoire des fils de Louis le Pieux*. Paris, 1926.

Lesne, E. *Histoire de la propriété ecclésiastique en France, IV: Les Livres, "Scriptoria" et Bibliothèques du commencement du VIIIᵉ à la fin du XIᵉ siècle*. 1937.

Liber usualis, with introduction and rubrics in English, ed. Benedictines of Solesmes. Tournai, 1934.

Lowe, E. *Codices Latini Antiquiores* V. Oxford, 1950.

Lord, A., "Oral Poetry," *Encyclopedia of Poetry and Poetics*, ed. Alex Preminger. Princeton, 1965.

Meersseman, G. *Der hymnos Akathistos im Abendland. Spicilegium Friburgense 2, 3*. 1958–60. I—Akathistos Akoluthie; II—Gruss Psalter, Gaude Andachten.

Melnicki, M. *Das einstimmige Kyrie des lateinischen Mittelalters*. Regensburg, 1955.

Mesnard, G. "Vers la restauration du dimanche des rameaux," *Etudes grégoriennes* I (1954), 69–81.

Messenger, R. "Sources of the Sequence *Scalam ad Caelos*," *Folia* II (1947), 55–63.

Meyer, W. "Anfang und Ursprung der lateinischen und griechischen rhythmischen Dichtung," and "Die rhythmische lateinische Prosa." In *Gesammelte Abhandlungen zur Mittellateinischen Rhythmik* II. 1905.

Moberg, C. *Über die schwedischen Sequenzen*. Uppsala, 1927.

Mohlberg, L. *Liber Sacramentorum Romanae ecclesiae. Rerum ecclesiasticarum documenta*. Series maior, Fontes. IV. 1959.

Monumenta Germaniae Historica:
   Poetae latini aevi carolini. Vol. 1–2, ed. E. Dummler; vol. 3, ed. L. Traube; vol. 4:1, ed. P. von Winterfeld; vol. 4:2–3, ed. K. Strecker.

Scriptores rerum germanicarum in usum scholarum separatim editi. Vol. 5: *Annales Bertiniani*; vol. 7: *Annales Fuldenses*; vol. 28: *Gesta abbatum Fontanellensium*.

Nicolau, M. *L'Origine du cursus rhythmique et les débuts de l'accent d'intensité en latin*. Paris, 1930.

Norberg, D. *Introduction à l'étude de la versification latine médiévale*. Uppsala, 1958.

Norden, E. *Die antike Kunstprosa vom VI. Jahrhundert vor Christus bis in die Zeit der Renaissance*. 1898.

Oesch, H. *Berno und Hermann von Reichenau als Musiktheoretiker*. Publikationen der Schweizerischen Musikforschenden Gesellschaft. Ser. II, vol. ix. 1961.

Oury, G. "Psalmum dicere cum alleluia," *Epheremides liturgicae* LXXIX (1965).

Paleographie musicale. Les principaux manuscrits de chant grégorien, ambrosien, mozarabe, gallican, publiés en fac-similes phototypiques. Société de Saint Jean l'Evangéliste.
   X. *Le Codex 239 de la Bibliothèque de Laon*, ed. A. Mocquereau. Tournai, 1909.
   XI. *Le Codex 47 de la Bibliothèque de Chartres*, ed. A. Mocquereau. Tournai, 1912.
   XII. *Le Codex F 160 de la Bibliothèque de la Cathédrale de Worcester*, ed. A. Mocquereau. Tournai, 1922.
   Series 2: II. *Cantatorium de Saint-Gall*, ed. A. Mocquereau. Tournai, 1924.

Pignot, J. *Histoire de l'ordre de Cluny*. Paris, 1868.

Polheim, K. *Die lateinische Reimprosa*. 1925

Rand, E. "Sermo de Confusione Diaboli," *Modern Philology* II (1904), 266–67.

Reichert, G. "Strukturprobleme der älteren Sequenz," *Deutsche Vierteljahrschrift für Literaturgeschichte* 23 (1949), 227–51.

Robert, M. "Les adieux à l'alleluia," *Etudes grégoriennes* VII (1967), 41–51.

Ronnau, K. *Die Tropen zum Gloria in excelsis*. Wiesbaden, 1967.

Sackur, E. *Die Cluniacenser*. Halle, 1892–94.

Schlager, K. *Alleluia-Melodien* I. Monumenta monodica medii aevi VII. 1968.

————. *Thematischer Katalog der altesten Alleluia-Melodien*. Erlanger Arbeiten zur Musikwissenschaft, Bd. 2. Munich, 1965.

Schubiger, A. *Die Sängerschule St. Gallens vom achten bis zwölften Jahrhundert*. Einsiedeln, 1858.

Spanke, H. *Deutsche und französische Dichtung des Mittelalters.* Stuttgart, 1943.

————. "Fortschritte in der Geschichte mittelalterlicher Musik. Zur Geschichte der Sequenz und ihrer Neben-formen," *Historisches Vierteljahrschrift* 27 (1932), 374–89.

————. "Aus der Vorgeschichte und Frühgeschichte der Sequenz," *Zeitschrift für deutsches Altertum und deutsche Literatur* 71 (1934), 1–39.

Stäblein, B. "Zur Frühgeschichte der Sequenz," *Archiv für Musikwissenschaft* XVIII (1961), 1–33.

————. "Notkeriana," *Archiv für Musikwissenschaft* XIX/XX (1962/63), 84–99.

————. "Sequenz," *Die Musik in Geschichte und Gegenwart* XII (1965), 522–49.

————. "Die Sequenzmelodie 'Concordia' und ihr geschichtlicher Hintergrund." In *Festschrift Hans Engel.* Kassel, 1964, pp. 364–92.

————. "Das sogenannte aquitanische 'Alleluia Dies sanctificatus' und seine Sequenz." In *Hans Albrecht In Memoriam.* Kassel, 1962, pp. 22–26.

————. "Die Unterlegung von Texten unter Melismen. Tropus, Sequenz und andere Formen," *Kongress-Bericht New York* I (1961), 12–29.

von den Steinen, W. "Die Anfänge der Sequenzendichtung," *Zeitschrift für Schweizerische Kirchengeschichte* 40 (1946) 190–212, 241–68; 41 (1947) 19–48, 122–62.

————. *Notker der Dichter.* Bern, 1948.

Suñol, G. *Introduction à la paléographie musicale grégorienne.* Paris, 1935.

von Tischendrof, C. *Evangelia Apocrypha.* 1876.

de Valour, G. *Le monachisme clunisien des origins au XVᵉ siècle.* II—*L'ordre de Cluny.* Paris, 1970.

Vecchi, G. *Troparium Sequentiarium Nonantolanum. Cod. Casanat. 1741. Pars prior. Monumenta Lyrica Medii Aevi Italica.* I. *Latina.* Modena, 1955.

Vogt, H. *Die Sequenzen des Graduale Abdinghof aus Paderborn.* Münster, Westf., 1972.

Van der Vyver. "Hucbald de Saint-Amand, écolâtre, et l'invention du Nombre d'Or." In *Université de Louvain Recueil de travaux d'histoire et de philologie*, 3ᵐᵉ série, 26ᵐᵉ fasc., pp. 61–79. Louvain, 1947.

Smits van Waesberghe, J. *Musikerziehung: Lehre und Theorie der Musik im Mittelalter. Musikgeschichte in Bildern*, ed. H. Besseler und W. Bachmann. Vol. III, 3. Leipzig, 1969.

————. "Neue Kompositionen der Johannes von Metz (um 975), Hucbalds von St. Armand und Sigeberts von Gemblont." In *Speculum musicae artis: Festgabe für Heinrich Husmann zum 60. Geburtstag.* Munich, 1970, pp. 285–303.

————. "Studien über das Lesen (pronuntiare), das Zitieren, und über die Herausgabe lateinischer musiktheoretischer Traktate (9.–16. Jh.)," *Archiv für Musikwissenschaft* 29 (1972), 66–86.

Wagner, P. *Einführung in die Gregorianischen Melodien.* I: *Ursprung und Entwicklung der liturgischen Gesangsformen.* Leipzig, 1911. III: *Gregorianische Formenlehre.* Leipzig, 1921.

Weakland, R. "The Compositions of Hucbald," *Etudes grégoriennes* III (1959), 153–62.

————. "Hucbald as Musician and Theorist," *Musical Quarterly* XLII (1956), 66–84.

Weiss, G. *Introitus-Tropen. Monumenta monodica medii aevi*, Bd. 3 (1970).

————. "Zum Problem der Gruppierung südfranzösischer Tropare," *Archiv für Musikwissenschaft* XXI (1964), 163–71.

Wellesz, E. *Eastern Elements in Western Chant.* Copenhagen, 1967.

von Winterfeld, P. "Rhythmen- und Sequenzenstudien," *Zeitschrift für deutsches Altertum und deutsche Literatur* 45 (1901), 133–49; 47 (1904), 73–100, 321–99.

Young, K. "The Harrowing of Hell in Liturgical Drama," *Transactions of the Wisconsin Academy of Sciences, Arts, and Letters* XVI (1909) Pt. II, no. 1, 889–947.

Plates

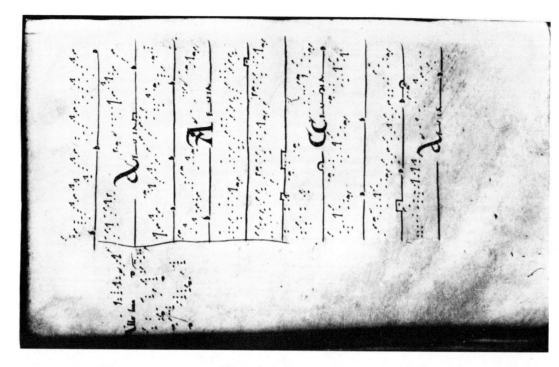

PLATE I. PARIS B.N. LAT. 1118; FOL. 136–136v.

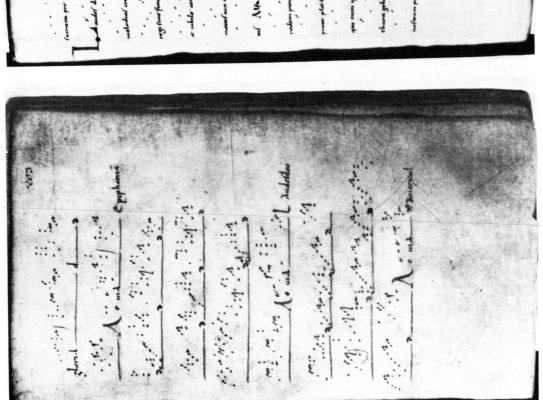

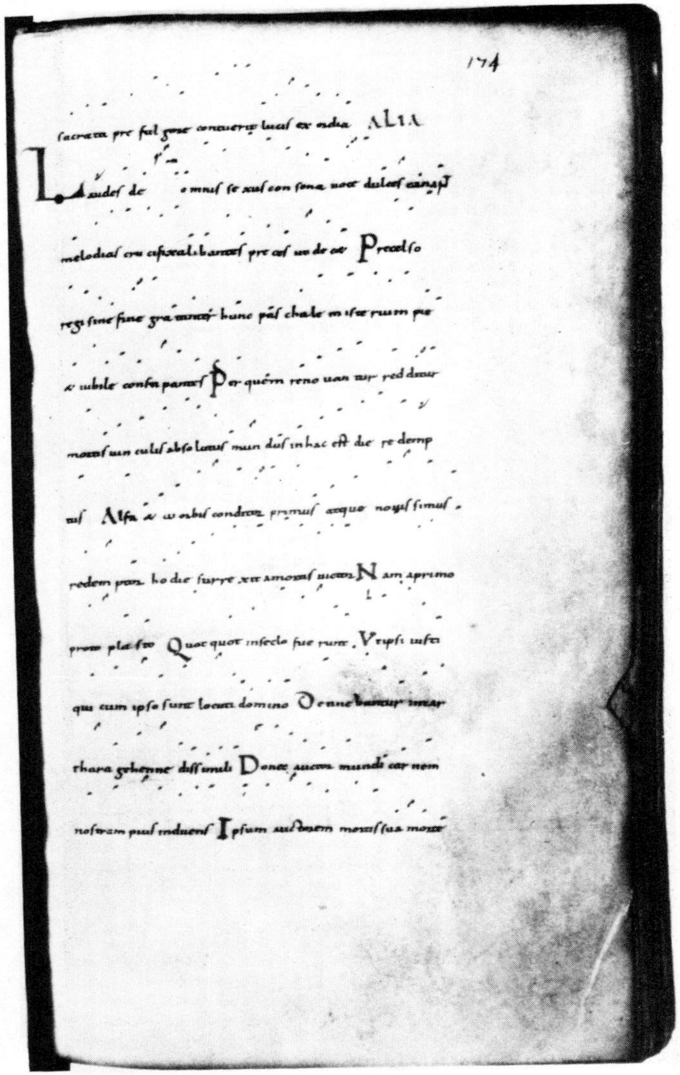

PLATE III. PARIS B.N. LAT. 1118; FOL. 174.

PLATE II. PARIS B.N. LAT. 1084; FOL. 203.

PLATE IV. PARIS B.N. LAT. 1084; FOL. 248v–249.

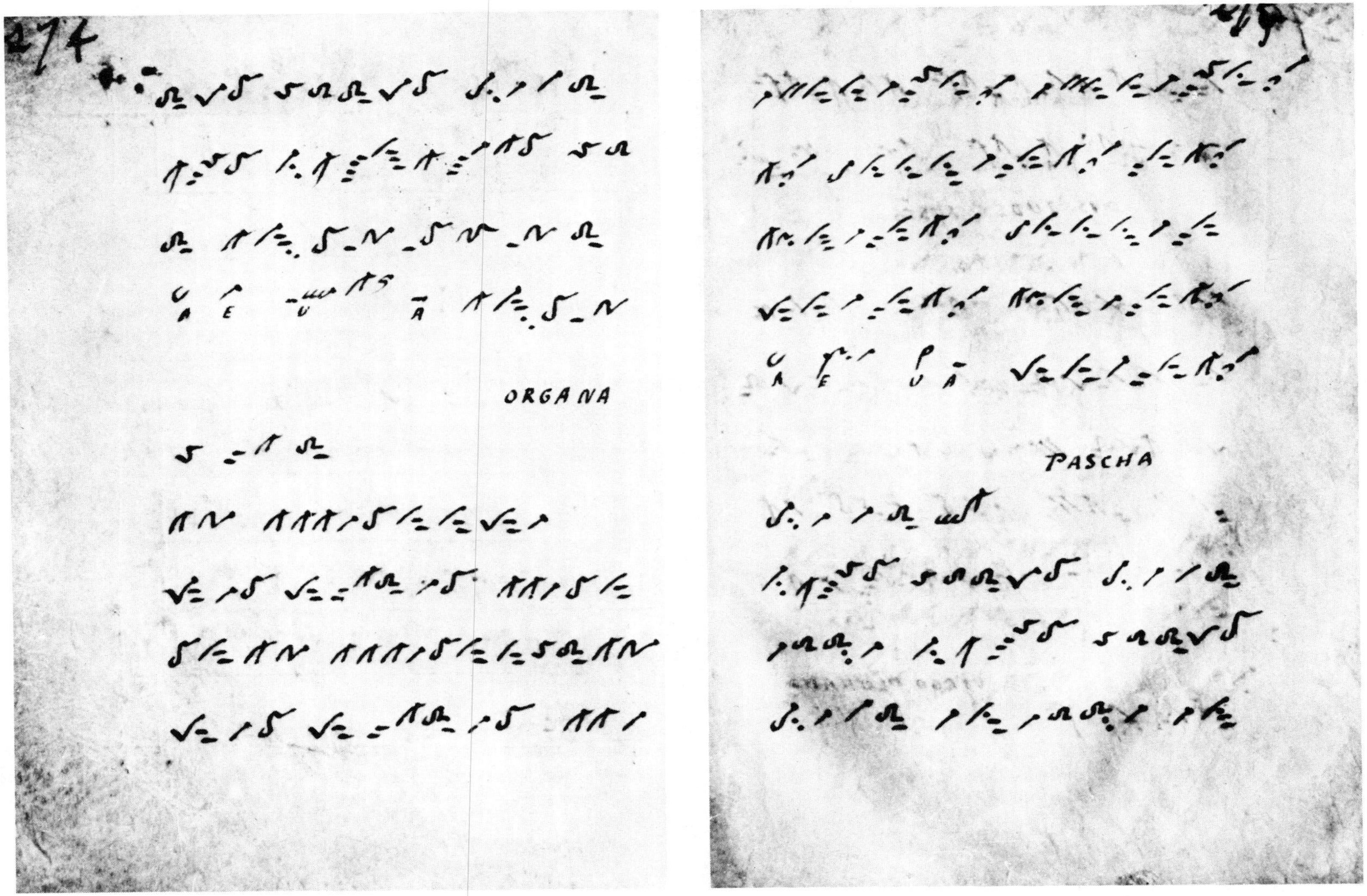

PLATE V. ST. GALL MS 484; PP. 274–275.

Index

referred to, 75, 84, 105, 379

Paris B.N. lat. 1338, 5, 293, 426, 431

   collated, 435, 444

Paris B.N. lat. 9427, 138

Paris B.N. lat. 9448, 5, 159, 425, 436

Paris B.N. lat. 9449, 167, 439, 445

Paris B.N. lat. 10508, 439, 445, 448

Paris B.N. lat. 10510, 5, 425

Paris B.N. lat. 10587, 5, 426

Paris B.N. lat. 12584, 255

Paris B.N. lat. 13252, 88

Paris B.N. lat. 17436, 5, 88, 396, 425, 432

Paris B.N. n.a. lat. 495, 433, 436, 438–439, 444

Paris B.N. n.a. lat. 1177, 439

Paris B.N. n.a. lat. 1871, 258, 397, 426, 431, 434, 436, 439, 441–442

Paris B.N. n.a. lat. 1235, 432, 436, 439, 444–445, 448

Paris B.N. n.a. lat. 2243, 138

Reims B.M. 695, 88

Rome Bibl. Casanatense 1741, 432, 436, 439

Rome Bibl. Vatican lat. 5319, 399

St. Gall Stiftsbibl. 376, 5, 431–448

St. Gall Stiftsbibl. 380, 5, 426, 431–448

St. Gall Stiftsbibl. 378, 5, 426, 431–448

St. Gall Stiftsbibl. 381, 5, 426, 431–448

St. Gall Stiftsbibl. 382, 5, 426, 431–448

St. Gall Stiftsbibl. 476, 426, 431–448

St. Gall Stiftsbibl. 484, 5, 26–27, 60, 230, 282, 426, 431–448

Utrecht Univ. Lib. 417, 16, 26–27, 211

Verona Bibl. Cap. XC(85), 5, 117, 309, 425, 434, 442

Verona Bibl. Cap. CVII, 433–434, 436, 438, 439, 444

Vercelli Bibl. Cap. 146, 439

Vercelli Bibl. Cap. 161, 439

Vercelli Bibl. Cap. 162, 432, 436

Malachi 3, 139

Marcellus, 1

Mark 12, 80

  16, 100, 198

Martyrs, 133, 362, 395

Mary, Blessed Virgin, 405

  in BEATA TU VIRGO, 258–260

  in CONCENTU PARILI, 229, 232

  in CONGAUDENT ANGELORUM, 174–176

  in GAUDE EJA, 89, 407

  in GAUDE MARIA, 255–256, 407

  in REX NOSTRAS, 178–181

  in SANCTA TU VIRGO, 260

  in STIRPE MARIA, 335–337, 395

"Mater" (melody title), 12, 160, 396

  in Notker's Preface, 1

Matthew 2, 167

  10, 145

  11, 272

  18, 359

  25, 197, 337

  27–28, 37, 100, 198

  Matthew, St., 319

Melisma, style of, 147, 317, 333

  triple, for *Descendit*, 399

  See also Alleluia, jubilus-replacement

Melismatic notation, 16, 22, 26, 239, 275, 329, 396–397

  for SALUS AETERNA, 328–329

  for "Justus ut palma minor," 269

Melodie formulae, 388–390

  and modes, 25–26

Melody titles, 12–13, 60, 132, 240, 248, 252, 262, 279, 313

Messenger, R., 224

Meyer, W., 371, 376

Michael, St., 178

Milo, 414

Misset, E., 382

Moberg, C., 3, 430

Modes, 25, 121–122, 173. *See also* Finals

Molinier, A., 411

Monasteries, 411–416

  and development of sequence, 422

  and Norman raids, 413–414

Mont-Blandin, Antiphonary of, 393–396, 399

Motives, use of, in AGONE TRIUMPHALI, 362, 364–366

  in CHRISTUS HUNC DIEM, 359–361

  in CONCENTU PARILI, 231

  in ECCE VICIT, 84

  in EN VIRGINUM, 333–337

  in FORTIS ATQUE AMARA, 140–141

  as Frankish technique, 334, 400, 422–423

  in HÆC DIES QUAM EXCELSUS, 55, 59–60, 69

  in "Justus ut palma major," 283–285, 291, 295, 298

  in NUNC EXULTET, 95

  in OMNIPOTENS DEUS, 305, 311, 313

  in REGNANTEM SEMPITERNA, 348–351

  in REX OMNIPOTENS, 191–193, 198

  in SALUS AETERNA, 317, 327

  in SUMMI TRIUMPHUM, 213, 216–217

Mozart, W. A., 389

Narrative style, in CHRISTI HODIERNA, 183

  in ECCE JAM VENIT, 181

  in LAUDES DEO, 34, 38

  in NUNC EXULTET, 100, 108

  in REX OMNIPOTENS, 189, 195–198

  in SUMMI TRIUMPHUM, 217

Nativity, 181–182, 238, 287, 359. *See also* Christmas

NATUS ANTE SAECULA, 12, 239, 290, 377–378

  discussed, 235–238

  notes, 441

  transcription, 234–235

Neale, J. M., 219

Neuma triplex, 399

Neumatic style, in BEATA TU VIRGO, 260

  in closing, FORTIS ATQUE AMARA, 141

  in HÆC EST SANCTA, 120

  in NUNC EXULTET, 98, 100

  in REX OMNIPOTENS, 193

  in incipits, 377

  in EN VIRGINUM, 331

  in HÆC DIES QUAM EXCELSUS, 54

  in HÆC EST SANCTA, 123

  in LAUDES DEO, 17, 20, 51

Neumes. *See* Notation